THE INSTITUTE FOR POLISH–JEWISH STUDIES

The Institute for Polish–Jewish Studies in Oxford and its sister organization, the American Association for Polish–Jewish Studies, who are responsible for the publication of *Polin*, are learned societies, established following the International Conference on Polish–Jewish Studies held in Oxford in 1984. The Institute is an associate institute of the Oxford Centre for Hebrew and Jewish Studies, and the American Association is linked with the Department of Near Eastern and Judaic Studies at Brandeis University.

Both the Institute and the American Association aim to promote understanding of the Polish Jewish past. They have no building or library of their own and no paid staff; they achieve their aims by encouraging scholarly research and facilitating its publication, and by creating forums for people with a scholarly interest in Polish Jewish topics, both past and present.

Each year since 1986 the Institute has published a volume of scholarly papers in the series *Polin: Studies in Polish Jewry* under the general editorship of Professor Antony Polonsky joined, in 2015, by Professor François Guesnet of University College London. Since 1994 the series has been published on the Institute's behalf by the Littman Library of Jewish Civilization. In March 2000 the entire series was honoured with a National Jewish Book Award from the Jewish Book Council in the United States. More than twenty other works on Polish Jewish topics have also been published with the Institute's assistance.

The editors welcome submission of articles for inclusion in future volumes. In particular, we are always grateful for assistance in extending the geographical range of our journal to Ukraine, Belarus, and Lithuania, both in the period in which these countries were part of the Polish–Lithuanian Commonwealth and subsequently. We also welcome submission of reviews, which are published on the website of the American Association. We are happy to translate articles or reviews submitted in Polish, Russian, Ukrainian, Lithuanian, Hebrew, or German into English. Submissions should be sent to one of the following: Dr Władysław T. Bartoszewski (email: wt@wtbartoszewski. pl); Professor Antony Polonsky (email: polonsky@ brandeis. edu); Professor François Guesnet (f.guesnet @ucl.ac.uk); Professor Joshua Zimmerman (email: zimmerm@ yu.edu).

Further information on the Institute for Polish–Jewish Studies can be found on its website, <www.polishjewishstudies.co.uk>. For the website of the American Association for Polish–Jewish Studies, see <www.aapjstudies.org>.

D1636955

THE LITTMAN LIBRARY OF
JEWISH CIVILIZATION

Dedicated to the memory of
LOUIS THOMAS SIDNEY LITTMAN
*who founded the Littman Library for the love of God
and as an act of charity in memory of his father*
JOSEPH AARON LITTMAN
and to the memory of
ROBERT JOSEPH LITTMAN
who continued what his father Louis had begun

יהא זכרם ברוך

'*Get wisdom, get understanding:
Forsake her not and she shall preserve thee*'
PROV. 4:5

The Littman Library of Jewish Civilization is a registered UK charity
Registered charity no. 1000784

POLIN
STUDIES IN POLISH JEWRY

VOLUME THIRTY-FOUR

Jewish Self-Government in Eastern Europe

Edited by

FRANÇOIS GUESNET

and

ANTONY POLONSKY

Published for
The Institute for Polish–Jewish Studies
and
The American Association for Polish–Jewish Studies

London
The Littman Library of Jewish Civilization
in association with Liverpool University Press
2022

The Littman Library of Jewish Civilization
Registered office: 4th floor, 7–10 Chandos Street, London W1G 9DQ

in association with Liverpool University Press
4 Cambridge Street, Liverpool L69 7ZU, UK
www.liverpooluniversitypress.co.uk/littman

Managing Editor: Connie Webber

Distributed in North America by
Oxford University Press Inc., 198 Madison Avenue
New York, NY 10016, USA

Catalogue records for this book are available from the
British Library and the Library of Congress

ISBN 978–1–800348–23–3 (cloth)
ISBN 978–1–800348–24–0 (pbk)

Publishing co-ordinator: Janet Moth
Copy-editing: Mark Newby
Proof-reading: Andrew Kirk
Index: Bonnie Blackburn
Production, design, and typesetting by
Pete Russell, Faringdon, Oxon.

Printed and bound in Great Britain by
TJ Books Limited, Padstow, Cornwall

Articles appearing in this publication are abstracted and indexed in
Historical Abstracts and America: History and Life

*This volume is dedicated to the memory of two pioneers of
the study of Jewish self-government in eastern Europe*

MAJER BAŁABAN

1877–1942

*Co-founder in 1928 of the Warsaw Institute for Jewish Studies and professor
at Warsaw University, who died in the Warsaw ghetto*

and

MOJŻESZ SCHORR

1874–1941

*Professor at the universities of Lwów and Warsaw and appointee to the
Polish Senate 1935–38, who died in a Soviet prison camp in Uzbekistan*

Editors and Advisers

Contents

Contributors

CORNELIA AUST teaches early modern Jewish history at Bielefeld University. The author of *The Jewish Economic Elite: Making Modern Europe* (2018), she has published widely on Jewish commercial and familial networks. She is currently working on Jewish dress and outward appearance, and co-edited *Dress and Cultural Difference in Early Modern Europe,* a special issue of *European History Yearbook* (2019).

RAINER JOSEF BARZEN is a research and teaching fellow at the Institute for Jewish Studies, Westfälische Wilhelms-Universität, Münster, and explores Jewish social history and Jewish–Christian relations in medieval Germany. Most recently, he published *Taqqanot Qehillot Šum: Die Rechtssatzungen der jüdischen Gemeinden Mainz, Worms und Speyer im hohen und späten Mittelalter,* 2 vols. (2019).

MARTIN BORÝSEK is a postdoctoral research fellow at the University of Potsdam and specializes in early modern Jewish intellectual history and political thought. Among his published papers are 'The Jews of Venetian Candia: The Challenges of External Influences and Internal Diversity as Reflected in *Takkanot Kandiyah*' (2014) and 'Between the Torah, Local Tradition and Secular Government' (in *Dvarim Meatim,* 2016).

PAUL BRYKCZYŃSKI is an independent historian who lives in Ontario. He received his doctorate in European history from the University of Michigan and is the author of *Primed for Violence: Murder, Antisemitism, and Democratic Politics in Interwar Poland* (2016), which is currently being translated into Polish.

MARC CAPLAN earned his doctorate in comparative literature from New York University in 2003. He is currently Brownstone Visiting Professor of Jewish Studies at Dartmouth College. His most recent book is *Yiddish Writers in Weimar Berlin: A Fugitive Modernism* (2021).

MARIA CIEŚLA is an assistant professor at the Tadeusz Manteuffel Institute of History at the Polish Academy of Sciences. She explores the social history of Jews and Jewish–Christian relations in the early modern period in the Polish–Lithuanian Commonwealth. Her most recent book examines Jewish economic activity in the Grand Duchy of Lithuania, *Kupcy, arendarze i rzemieślnicy. Różnorodność zawodowa Żydów w Wielkim Księstwie Litewskim w XVII i XVIII w.* (2018).

FRANÇOIS GUESNET is Professor of Modern Jewish History at University College London. He specializes in the early modern and nineteenth-century history of Polish and east European Jews. Among his publications are *Polnische Juden im 19. Jahrhundert: Lebensbedingungen, Rechtsnormen und Organisation im Wandel* (1998), and, as co-editor with Glenn Dynner, *Warsaw: The Jewish Metropolis. Studies in Honor of the 70th Birthday of Professor Antony Polonsky* (2015).

JÜRGEN HEYDE is a research associate at the Leibniz Institute for the History and Culture of Eastern Europe (GWZO) at Leipzig University and teaches east European and Jewish history at Halle-Wittenberg University. Among his contributions to Polish–Jewish history are *Transkulturelle Kommunikation und Verflechtung. Die jüdischen Wirtschaftseliten in Polen* *vom 14. bis zum 16. Jahrhundert* (2014) and *'Das neue Ghetto'? Raum, Wissen und jüdische Identität im langen 19. Jahrhundert* (2019).

JUDITH KALIK teaches east European and Jewish history at the Hebrew University of Jerusalem and is a research associate at Tel Aviv University. Among her publications are *The Polish Nobility and the Jews in the Dietine Legislation of the Polish–Lithuanian Commonwealth* (Heb. 1997), *Scepter of Judah: Jewish Autonomy in the Eighteenth-Century Crown Poland* (2009), and *Movable Inn: The Rural Jewish Population of Minsk Guberniya in 1793–1914* (2018).

ADAM KAŹMIERCZYK is Professor of Early Modern History at the Jagiellonian University, Kraków. His research focuses on the legal status of Jews and on Jewish–Christian relations in the Polish–Lithuanian Commonwealth. Among his publications are *Żydzi w dobrach prywatnych* (2002) and *Rodziłem się Żydem . . . Konwersje Żydów w Rzeczypospolitej XVII–XVIII wieku* (2015). With Jacob Goldberg, he edited *Sejm Czterech Ziem* (2011), and with Przemysław Zarubin *Żydowski samorząd ziemski. Źródła* (2019).

HANNA KOZIŃSKA-WITT is a freelance historian. Her research focuses on Jewish cultural and urban history in Habsburg Galicia. She is the author of *Die Krakauer Jüdische Reformgemeinde 1864–1874* (1999), *Krakau in Warschaus langem Schatten: Konkurrenzkämpfe in der polnischen Städtelandschaft 1900–1939* (2008), and *Politycy czy klakierzy? Żydzi w krakowskiej radzie miejskiej w XIX wieku* (2019).

VLADIMIR LEVIN is director of the Center for Jewish Art at Hebrew University of Jerusalem. His field of study is the modern social, political, religious, and cultural history of the Jews in eastern Europe. He is the author of *From Revolution to War: Jewish Politics in Russia, 1907–1914* (Heb. 2016), and co-author, with Sergey Kravtsov, of *Synagogues in Ukraine: Volhynia* (2017). He also initiated the Bezalel Narkiss Index of Jewish Art, a digital repository of the Jewish visual heritage.

ARTUR MARKOWSKI is head of the nineteenth-century section of the Faculty of History at Warsaw University and senior historian at the Polin Museum of the History of Polish Jews in Warsaw. He specializes in the history of the Jews in the Russian empire in the nineteenth century. He is the author of *Przemoc antyżydowska i wyobrażenie społeczne: Pogrom białystocki 1906 roku* (2018) and, most recently, co-editor of volumes ii and iii of *Przemoc antyżydowska na ziemiach polskich w XIX i XX w.* (2019).

ANNA MICHAŁOWSKA-MYCIELSKA is an associate professor at the University of Warsaw (Faculty of History), where she heads the Mordechai Anielewicz Center. Her field of study is the history and culture of Jews in the Polish–Lithuanian Commonwealth in the sixteenth to eighteenth centuries, especially Jewish self-government and Jewish–Christian relations. She is the author of *The Jewish Community: Authority and Social Control in Poznań and Swarzędz, 1650–1793* (2008) and *The Council of Lithuanian Jews, 1623–1764* (2016), and has edited two community minute books: *Pinkas kahału swarzędzkiego (1734–1830)* (2005) and *Pinkas kahału boćkowskiego (1714–1817)* (2015).

ANTONY POLONSKY is Professor Emeritus of Holocaust Studies at Brandeis University and Chief Historian of the Global Outreach Educational Program at the Polin Museum of the History of Polish Jews in Warsaw. He is the author of the three-volume *Jews in Poland and Russia* (2010–12), also published in an abridged version, *The Jews in Poland and Russia: A Short History* (2013), all published by the Littman Library.

SZYMON RUDNICKI is Professor Emeritus of Polish Contemporary History at Warsaw University, specializing in the history of Poland. He is the author of several monographs about Polish nationalist and right-wing political movements and Polish–Jewish relations. Among his most important books are *Obóz Narodowo-Radykalny: Geneza i działalność* (1985), *Żydzi w parlamencie II Rzeczypospolitej* (Warsaw, 2004), *Równi, ale niezupełnie* (2008), and *Falanga: Ruch Narodowo-Radykalny* (2018).

MARCOS SILBER is an associate professor at the Department of Jewish History, University of Haifa. Among his areas of expertise are Jewish diaspora nationalism, popular culture in interwar Poland, and Polish–Israeli relations. His publications include *Different Nationality, Equal Citizenship! The Efforts to Achieve Autonomy for Polish Jewry during the First World War* (Heb. 2014) and, with Szymon Rudnicki, *Stosunki polsko-izraelskie (1945–1967): Wybór dokumentów* (2009).

ŁUKASZ SROKA is Professor of History at the Pedagogical University in Kraków. His fields of research are Jewish history and culture in the nineteenth and twentieth centuries, with a focus on Galicia and the history of Israel. He is the author of *In the Light of Vienna: Jews in Lviv, between Tradition and Modernisation (1867–1914)* (2018) and co-author, with Mateusz Sroka, of *Polskie korzenie Izraela* (2015) and, with Krzysztof Chaczko, of *Demokracja izraelska* (2018). Most recently, he published *Człowiek sukcesu w państwie sukcesów: Biografia Marcela Goldmana, krakowianina w Tel Awiwie* (2019).

ADAM TELLER is Professor of History and Judaic Studies at Brown University and a member of the Academic Advisory Board of Polin Museum for the History of Polish Jews, Warsaw. Among his publications on the economic, social, and cultural history of the Jews in early modern Poland–Lithuania are *Living Together: The Jewish Quarter in Poznań during the Seventeenth Century* (Heb. 2003), *Money, Power, and Influence in Eighteenth Century Lithuania: The Jews on the Radziwiłł Estates* (2016), and, most recently, *Surviving Souls: The Great Jewish Refugee Crisis of the Seventeenth Century* (2020).

HANNA WĘGRZYNEK is a historian and deputy director of the Warsaw Ghetto Museum. Her research focuses on Jewish–Christian relations, the history of Jews in Warsaw, and Holocaust education in Polish schools. Most recently, she authored *Regestr osób żydowskich spisany w miesiącu styczniu roku 1778 w Warszawie* (2016), and co-authored, with Konrad Zieliński, *The Bersohn and Bauman Hospital in Warsaw* (2019). She edited *Żydzi i Polacy w okresie walk o niepodległość 1914–1920* (2015) and co-edited, with Antony Polonsky and Andrzej Żbikowski, *New Directions in the History of the Jews in the Polish Lands* (2018).

ANDREI ZAMOISKI is currently a post-doctoral research fellow for a project sponsored by the German War Graves Commission, the German–Russian Museum Berlin-Karlshorst, and the German Historical Institute in Moscow on Soviet and German prisoners of war and internees. His principal field of interest is Jewish history in eastern Europe, with a focus on self-governance, anti-Jewish violence, and Jewish self-defence. He is the author of *Transformatsiya mestechek Sovetskoy Belarusi, 1918–1939* (2013).

Note on Editorial Conventions

Place Names

Political connotations accrue to words, names, and spellings with an alacrity unfortunate for those who would like to maintain neutrality. It seems reasonable to honour the choices of a population on the name of its city or town, but what is one to do when the people have no consensus on their name, or when the town changes its name, and the name its spelling, again and again over time? The politician may always opt for the latest version, but the hapless historian must reckon with them all. This note, then, will be our brief reckoning

There is no problem with places that have accepted English names, such as Warsaw. But every other place name in east-central Europe raises serious problems. A good example is Wilno, Vilna, Vilnius. There are clear objections to all of these. Until 1944 the majority of the population was Polish. The city is today in Lithuania. 'Vilna', though raising the fewest problems, is an artificial construct. In this volume we have adopted the following guidelines, although we are aware that they are not wholly consistent.

1. Towns that have a form which is acceptable in English are given in that form. Some examples are Warsaw, Kiev, Moscow, St Petersburg, Munich.

2. Towns that until 1939 were clearly part of a particular state and shared the majority nationality of that state are given in a form which reflects that situation. Some examples are Breslau, Danzig, Rzeszów, Przemyśl. In Polish, Kraków has always been spelled as such. In English it has more often appeared as Cracow, but the current trend of English follows the local language as much as possible. In keeping with this trend to local determination, then, we shall maintain the Polish spelling.

3. Towns that are in mixed areas take the form in which they are known today and which reflects their present situation. Examples are Poznań, Toruń, and Kaunas. This applies also to bibliographical references. We have made one major exception to this rule, using the common English form for Vilna until its first incorporation into Lithuania in October 1939 and using Vilnius thereafter. Galicia's most diversely named city, and one of its most important, boasts four variants: the Polish Lwów, the German Lemberg, the Russian Lvov, and the Ukrainian Lviv. As this city currently lives under Ukrainian rule, and most of its current residents speak Ukrainian, we use the Ukrainian spelling unless another form is required by the context.

4. Some place names have different forms in Yiddish. Occasionally the subject matter dictates that the Yiddish place name should be the prime form, in which case the corresponding Polish (Ukrainian, Belarusian, Lithuanian) name is given in parentheses at first mention.

Transliteration

Hebrew

An attempt has been made to achieve consistency in the transliteration of Hebrew words. The following are the key distinguishing features of the system that has been adopted:

1. No distinction is made between the *alef* and *ayin*; both are represented by an apostrophe, and only when they appear in an intervocalic position.

2. *Veit* is written *v*; *ḥet* is written *ḥ*; *yod* is written *y* when it functions as a consonant and i when it occurs as a vowel; *khaf* is written *kh*; *tsadi* is written *ts*; *kof* is written *k*.

3. The *dagesh hazak*, represented in some transliteration systems by doubling the letter, is not represented, except in words that have more or less acquired normative English spellings that include doublings, such as Hallel, kabbalah, Kaddish, rabbi, Sukkot, and Yom Kippur.

4. The *sheva na* is represented by an *e*.

5. Hebrew prefixes, prepositions, and conjunctions are not followed by a hyphen when they are transliterated; thus *betoledot ha'am hayehudi*.

6. In the transliteration of the titles of works published in Hebrew, only the first word is capitalized; other than in the titles of works, names of people, places, and institutions are capitalized following the conventions of the English language.

7. The names of individuals are transliterated following the above rules unless the individual concerned followed a different usage.

Yiddish

Transliteration follows the YIVO system except for the names of people, where the spellings they themselves used have been retained.

Russian and Ukrainian

The system used is that of British Standard 2979:1958, without diacritics. Except in bibliographical and other strictly rendered matter, soft and hard signs are indicated by *y* before a vowel (e.g. Ilyich) but are otherwise omitted, and word-final -й, -ий, -ый, -ій in names are simplified to -*y*.

Introduction

FRANÇOIS GUESNET AND **ANTONY POLONSKY**

O ḥevruta o metuta
(Without community, there is death)
Babylonian Talmud, *Ta'anit 23a*

SINCE THEIR EXILE in Babylon in the sixth century BCE, Jews have sought to create institutions to organize community life and the practice of Judaism in the diaspora. This volume investigates the nature and functioning of the system of Jewish self-government created in the medieval Kingdom of Poland and Grand Duchy of Lithuania and in the Polish–Lithuanian Commonwealth. It then examines how this system was partially abolished and transformed under Stanisław August (r. 1764–95), the last king of Poland–Lithuania, and subsequently by the governments of Prussia, Austria, and Russia which partitioned Poland at the end of the eighteenth century. Under the influence of the principles of the Enlightenment, all these rulers sought to drastically limit the operation of Jewish self-government, which was held to prevent the desired transformation of the Jews from an autonomous community into citizens or, where the concept of citizenship did not exist, into useful subjects of their respective rulers. The volume reflects on the successes and failures of Jewish communities to safeguard religious, charitable, and other institutions from state interference in the nineteenth century and their participation in organs of municipal self-government which developed first in the partitioning powers and then in independent Poland. Finally, it explores how, with the emergence at the end of the nineteenth century of new political ideas of Jewish autonomy, attempts were made to create a modernized system of self-government. While useful attempts have been made to understand forms of Jewish local organization under conditions of extreme duress, persecution, and mass murder during the German occupation of Poland and eastern Europe in the Second World War and the Holocaust, this volume does not look beyond the fateful year of 1939.[1]

■

Few other features have shaped the trajectory of east European Jewish history as much as the extent and continuity of Jewish self-government. Among its most important features is the role it played in implementing the constantly changing interpretation of Jewish legal traditions and how its institutions reflected the embeddedness of the Jewish community in the administrative, political, and economic fabric of early modern states, most notably Poland–Lithuania. The differentiated and complex structure of responsibilities in the individual community—most prominently in the form of the board of governors or *kahal*—and the sophistication this showed in shaping relations with the Crown, nobility, the Roman Catholic Church, and the Jews' neighbours, had a long-lasting impact on Jewish political culture. So too did the supra-community structures of regional councils and the two most prominent national councils, the Council of Lithuania and the Council of Four Lands.

The existence of institutions allowing the Jews to govern themselves in western Christendom was partly the result of the fact that medieval and early modern states lacked the resources to administer all aspects of society. Furthermore, Jews were both a pariah group, tolerated in an inferior position, and a corporation with the legal right to govern themselves as did all medieval corporations, whether those of an estate, like the nobility, or of a specific group, like the burghers of a particular town. In this context it should be stressed that freedom in the Middle Ages had a 'local rather than a universal character'.[2] The words 'liberty' and 'freedom' generally appeared in the plural form as in the 'rights and liberties' of a town, province, or estate which were granted by the sovereign and carefully recorded in charters. The rights and obligations of an individual were derived from participation in a given com-munity—the abstract idea of 'human rights' was alien to medieval thinking and only emerged in the eighteenth century.

The Jews could thus be seen, despite their pariah status, as being in the same position as other groups in society, possessing rights which were guaranteed by charters, whether general or limited to a specific region or town or to the institutions through which Jewish self-government was exercised. In this respect, the Jews clearly emulated the 'institutional and legal patterns developed by the non-Jewish nations'.[3] As Rainer Barzen shows in his chapter, the halakhic community regulations—*takanot*—in the Kingdom of Poland, which formed the basis for the functioning of Jewish *kehilot* (autonomous communities), were derived from the Rhineland com-munities of Speyer, Wurms, and Mainz, whose members brought them with them when they migrated from the German to the Polish lands between the twelfth and fourteenth centuries, transforming the character of a community initially derived from the east (Kiev and also perhaps the Khazar kingdom and Byzantium).

In addition, Jewish rights, like those of other medieval corporations, were defined by charter. Since throughout the Middle Ages Jews had no uniform legal status in Christendom, negotiating legal rights when settling in a new area was their normal practice. Beginning in eleventh-century Germany, Jews sought written commitments from national, regional, and local powers to define their rights and obligations with respect to the authorities. The first such charter granted to Jews in Poland was issued in 1264 in Kalisz by Bolesław the Pious, Duke of Wielkopolska (r. 1239–79), to the Jews of his province. Subsequent charters are of several types, general charters applying to the whole country, regional charters, charters regulating the position of the Jews in individual towns, and charters which gave rights to specific individuals.[4] Since they are prescriptive, it is not always clear how they worked in practice.

Initially most of the charters guaranteeing Jewish rights were issued by the king or the grand duke. However, with the growing strength of the nobility and the weakness of the central government in Poland–Lithuania, charters were also granted by great nobles. These were of different types, both general and specific. Of the general charters the most important was that granted by Bolesław the Pious, to which we have already alluded. It was modelled on the Austrian charter of 1240 and formed the basis for many subsequent enumerations of Jewish rights.[5] The charter of Kalisz was obviously prepared for the duke by the Jewish leaders and reflected their desire to protect their position in five principal areas: exemption from the jurisdiction of the municipal authorities, economic rights, security, religious rights, and the character of the 'Jewish oath' which Jews had to take in court proceedings with non-Jews. The Jews were also given the right to choose a rabbi, who was empowered in accordance with Jewish law to issue judgements and enforce them with a ban of excommunication (ḥerem). This charter was confirmed in a slightly altered form by Kazimierz the Great (r. 1333–70) and extended to cover the whole of Poland. As Jürgen Heyde shows in his chapter, this dependence on German models was usual. The charter also formed the basis for that issued in 1388 to the Jews of the Grand Duchy of Lithuania by Grand Duke Vytautas, which was confirmed in 1507, in his capacity of grand duke, by Zygmunt (r. 1506–48).[6]

In addition to these general and specific charters, rights were frequently conceded to Jewish communities in individual towns: royal towns, which were subject to the king and the royal voivode; and private towns, which were subject to their noble owners. In the case of royal towns, these rights were granted by the king. The situation was, however, complicated by the fact that the Christian burghers frequently negotiated special agreements with the Jews, often based on models taken from the German lands. These agreements form the subject of the chapter by Hanna Węgrzynek. As she shows, the increasing dominance of the nobility in the political and social life of the Polish–Lithuanian Commonwealth led to a situation where Jews were divided into two categories: 'royal—remaining under the jurisdiction of royal administrators—and private—subordinated, like other subjects, to the authority of landowners, both secular and clerical. This state of affairs . . . diminished the importance of general royal prerogatives and led a growing number of Jewish communities to seek to obtain individual local privileges.' The first of these was concluded in Kraków in 1469, followed by similar agreements in Poznań, Lublin, and elsewhere, which were given the approval of the sejm. As Węgrzynek shows, these reveal the principal areas of conflict between Christian and Jewish communities.

The position in the private towns of the nobility was usually more favourable to the Jews because of the weaker position of the Christian burghers. As a result, their social status was higher and they did not have to contend with the economic competition they faced in larger centres or the hostility of burgher-controlled municipalities. Maria Cieśla illustrates this triangle of power between the town owner, the Jewish community, and an increasingly assertive representation of Christian burghers with the example of Słuck, located in the north-east of the former Grand Duchy of Lithuania. In 1654 Bogusław Radziwiłł established the sesja miejska (town session). This body, representing the Christian burghers, emerged as a new centre of power requesting control over Jewish contributions to the municipal budget. On the one hand, the *sesja miejska* restricted the autonomy of the local *kahal*—established in 1602 on the basis of a privilege—on the other, new ways to negotiate contributions and responsibilities emerged, with delegates of the Jewish community attending meetings of the *sesja miejska*.

Kings also sometimes supported Jews who were useful to them. Rights were conceded by the Crown to individual merchants, including some Jews. Individuals who were given the titles of *faktor* (agent), *serwitor* (servant), and less frequently *sekretarz* (secretary) were exempt from community authority and subject only to the king. As Jürgen Heyde shows in his chapter, Kazimierz the Great went out of his way to support Lewko the son of Jordan, the most prominent Jew in late fourteenth-century Kraków, although he does not seem to have held any function within the community, with whom on occasion he appears to have been at odds. In Heyde's view, this leaves 'the impression that at the beginning of the fifteenth century the structures and functioning of Jewish self-government, though accepted in general, were barely visible and of little interest to the non-Jewish authorities'. This situation was to change significantly in the following century, as the authorities came to see Jewish community organizations as central to their dealings with the Jewish community. In Heyde's analysis, 'instead of being the principal partners of the non-Jewish authorities, as they had been at the end of the fourteenth century, [the Jewish economic elites] now became part of a triangular relationship, maintaining their own position while dealing with the community leadership as well as with the non-Jewish authorities'. In his chapter, he illustrates this triangular relationship with an analysis of the long and complex history of the relationship of the Fischel family to the king and the Kraków community in the late fifteenth and early sixteenth centuries. Węgrzynek's comparison of the way the king acted as mediator in a dispute between the Jewish and Christian townspeople in Brześć (Brest) in 1538 and how the two communities in Kazimierz reached a legal agreement in 1553 also illustrates the growing importance of Jewish community organizations.

At the centre of the rights which the Jews enjoyed was the right to administer their communities themselves. In Poland–Lithuania there was a three-tier system of Jewish self-government. The key unit in this structure was the local community—the *kehilah* and its administrative organ, the *kahal*. Individual *kehilot* sent representatives to regional councils in the different parts of Poland and Lithuania. Above the regional councils were two national councils, the Council of Four Lands in the Kingdom of Poland and the Council of Lithuania in the grand duchy. A great deal is known about the functioning of these bodies because of the survival of their *pinkasim*, the ledgers in which they recorded their activities. Adam Teller, in his chapter, describes the nature of the *pinkasim* kept by *kahals* and the community scribe's role in managing them. As Judith Kalik points out in her chapter, scribes were also important in the functioning of the Council of Four Lands and the Council of Lithuania. Teller also discusses how, from the end of the eighteenth century, community administration 'particularly in the larger centres, began to move away from the *pinkas* towards the creation and filing of individual documents written in the language of the country and using the archival system known today'. Cornelia Aust in her chapter on the *ḥevrah kadisha* in the Warsaw suburb of Praga discusses how this society's *pinkas* reflects its ongoing activities, despite the attempts of the authorities to close it down, and how valuable these records can be in writing their history.

Jewish self-government had both a secular and a religious character. According to the regulations of the Kraków *kehilah*, enacted in 1595, those who exercised authority on its behalf had been chosen 'according to the prescriptions of our Torah and the statutes we have received from kings and other princes and rulers'.[7] The *kehilah* was administered by the *kahal*, a body of between ten and twenty members, whose members were elected annually. This was headed by a *parnas* (president), a revolving office which changed hands every month or, in smaller *kehilot*, every quarter. The *kahal*'s responsibilities were very wide: it dealt with all matters relating to religious observance; the physical welfare of the community including the relief of the poor and care of the sick, orphans, and the aged; and education. It was also responsible for taxation; control of the economic life of the community; recording marriages, births, and deaths; and the maintenance of community property. The *kahal* also had powers to levy taxes for special purposes, such as ransoming prisoners of war or defraying the expenses of a *shtadlan* (advocate), who represented the community before the king, nobles, sejm, or courts. It also regularly made gifts to prominent officials and churchmen, as described in the chapter by Anna Michałowska-Mycielska.

Kahal elections were not democratic in the modern sense. The candidates for office were required to possess appropriate qualifications, above all financial ones. As a result, community self-government was everywhere in the hands of the Jewish elite, and the proportion of those entitled to vote rarely exceeded 10 to 15 per cent of the adult male population and was frequently much lower. Regulations which sought to prevent the acceptance of office by relatives of existing office-holders and the election of relatives of the rabbi were often ineffective, and oligarchic rule became widespread. There were frequent and bitter struggles for community offices, particularly in the eighteenth century.

Acting as a control on the activity of the *kahal* was a broader, more numerous group referred to as the 'leaders of the community', 'outstanding people', 'those who belong to the assembly', or 'householders who pay taxes'. In Polish documents this group was referred to as *pospólstwo* (the populace). It was made up of those taxpayers (sometimes only a part of them) who did not hold office, and it also dealt with matters of broad concern to the community, such as the appointment of a rabbi or the passage of general legislation.[8]

The *kehilah* leadership was very conscious of the vulnerable position of the community. In all its actions, it took as a basic principle the need to prevent actions by individual Jews which could provoke anti-Jewish hostility. This need governed the economic regulations of the *kahal* and also its sumptuary legislation through which it sought to 'avoid envy' by 'costly display'.

The *kahal* was further buttressed by the existence of *ḥevrot* (associations) created for specific purposes. The most important of these was the *ḥevrah kadisha*, responsible for caring for the dying, burying the dead, and maintaining the ceme-tery.[9] Its origin and evolution until the second half of the nineteenth century, by which time it had lost some of its prestige, particularly in large towns, is the sub-ject of Cornelia Aust's chapter. It was usually the first association to be created in a community, and sometimes even preceded the community's formal establishment. Membership was seen as a great honour and a religious duty and was largely the province of the elite.

Ḥevrot were also established to provide religious education for the young, espe-cially poor children and orphans, and to look after the sick, particularly those who could not afford to pay for such care. This was the province of the ḥevrat bikur holim (society for visiting the sick) which maintained a shelter for the sick, the infirm, and those unable to maintain themselves. Artisans were generally excluded from the principal ḥevrot because of their low status. They were also usually barred from the membership of Christian artisan guilds, although they were on occasion required to pay fees to these guilds and to obey their regulations. Consequently they created their own ḥevrot to regulate their trade, provide mutual support for their members, train apprentices, and perform religious functions which would gain prestige for their members.

The prominent position of the kahal became a concern of the state authorities in the period of the partitions of Poland, leading to its abolition in the Free City of Kraków (1817), the Kingdom of Poland (1822), and finally the Russian empire (1844). Its alleged influence beyond the Jewish community became a trope of anti-Jewish arguments, not in the least due to the translation and publication of excerpts from the pinkasim of the Minsk Jewish community by the convert to Russian Orthodoxy, Iacov Brafman, a major source for antisemitic conspiracy theorists in eastern Europe and beyond.[10]

Two other important elements in the community structure were the rabbinate and the beit din (judicial court). The rabbi was the religious head of the community and was referred to as rav or av beit din (head of the court), denoting his primary official function of chief jurist and head of the judicial apparatus of the community.[11] Where there was a yeshiva, this was usually under his control. He had great authority, not only religious but also secular. He took part in the meetings of the kahal, although he was not a member, and no decision of any importance could be taken without his approval.[12]

The implementation of Jewish law was the responsibility of the beit din comprising twelve judges, who were elected every year and sat in panels of three. They acted with the authority of the kahal and were concerned with all aspects of financial and business life, while the kahal dealt with cases of breaches of the peace. Both the kahal and the beit din did their utmost to prevent Jewish litigants from going to a Christian court, and if any Jew resorted to such a court without the permission of the kahal he was liable to excommunication and other penalties. As the beit din often sided with the leading families who controlled the kahal, Jews frequently did seek recourse to Christian courts.

The core of the autonomous system was the local *kehilah*. Above them were the regional and national councils which were initially established to apportion tax among different *kehilot*: other functions were subsequently added. A good idea of how the regional assemblies functioned can be gathered from the history of the Council of Wielkopolska.[13] It had at its disposal a clerk, tax assessors, and tax collectors. It is first mentioned in 1597 and there are records of its meeting throughout the seventeenth century and up to 1733 in different towns of the province, including Poznań, Gniezno, Kalisz, Nowe Miasto nad Wartą, Jarocin, and Kobylin. Its functions included the election of the chief rabbi of Wielkopolska, who had extensive powers over the Jews of the area, the adoption of measures of protection against common dangers (above all accusations of ritual murder), the collection of the poll tax and levies needed for the common welfare, the negotiation of loans for communal purposes, and the approval and subsidization of book publishing.

A similar council, the Council of Ruthenia, existed for the communities in the 'land of Rus'—the Mogilev, Mtsislavl, and Vitebsk districts of the Grand Duchy of Lithuania. Like that in Wielkopolska, its principal function was apportioning taxes among the local *kehilot* and collecting them. In addition it functioned as the highest legislative and judicial body for the Jews of the region, regulating economic activity, including the purchase and orderly transfer of leases, and adjudicating in disputes between *kehalim* or between individuals and *kehalim*.[14]

The national councils emerged in the late sixteenth century, the first recorded meeting occurring in 1580. Originally there was one national council for the whole of the commonwealth and it is described as the Council of Three Lands—Poland, Ruthenia, and Lithuania—or, more rarely, the Council of Five Lands—Wielkopolska, Małopolska, Ruthenia, Lithuania, and Volhynia. In 1613 Zygmunt III Vasa established separate tax assessments for the Jews of the Kingdom of Poland and those of the Grand Duchy of Lithuania, which led in 1623 to the establishment of a separate Council of Lithuania (Va'ad Medinat Lite).[15]

After the establishment of the Council of Lithuania, the designation Council of Four Lands (Va'ad Arba Aratsot)—Wielkopolska, Małopolska, Ruthenia, and Volhynia—became established for that in the Kingdom of Poland and figures exclusively in the documents of the seventeenth century. The term was still employed in the eighteenth century in spite of the fact that many more regions were now represented. The Council of Four Lands usually met biannually at the great fair in Lublin, which began on the Catholic holiday of Candlemas in February and lasted about a month, and from the beginning of the seventeenth century at that held in Jarosław towards the end of the summer. The Council of Lithuania, for its part, met biannually or triannually at Brest, Zabłudow, Seltsy, and also in some other places. Judith Kalik in her chapter provides an account of who was represented in the Council of Four Lands, a striking prosopographic study of the Jewish elite of Poland.

The principal responsibility of the councils was to apportion the poll tax among the individual communities, and it was for this reason that they were given the recognition and support of the state authorities, who described them in official documents as the 'Jewish council' (*congressus Judaeicus, congressus Judaeorum*) or the 'Jewish sejm' (*sejm żydowski*). The Council of Four Lands apportioned the poll tax among its four constituent provinces, while the detailed apportionment of taxes within each province and each community was the task of the regional councils and the *kehilot*. From 1580 this tax was calculated on a flat rate and levied as a lump sum on the whole Jewish community. By the eighteenth century, representatives of the Crown treasury attended meetings of the council and exercised a supervisory role over their activities. They appointed Jewish trustees to report to them on the council's activities, in effect subordinating them to the control of the Crown. These developments are described in Adam Kaźmierczyk's chapter. Judith Kalik shows the divergent interests of the Jewish delegates to the council and the extent to which its leading members were dependent for their position on their noble patrons, as was the case with Doctor Abraham Isaac Fortis, who was appointed president in 1724. The chapter by Anna Michałowska-Mycielska investigates how the sejm and local *sejmiki* saw the system of Jewish self-government and, in particular, its fiscal obligations and how the Jews sought to influence these assemblies.

Like other parliamentary bodies which were originally convened to ratify taxation, the councils soon acquired additional functions. One of the most important was in the judicial sphere. Even before the formal constitution of the national councils, rabbis from the principal *kehilot* seem to have convened to deal with disputed questions of Jewish law. The principal function of the court of the Council of Four Lands, which seems to have been made up exclusively of rabbis, was to settle disputes between *kehilot* over their respective boundaries, which had important implications for their tax burden and their income. It also dealt with conflicts over where a case should be tried and acted as a court of appeal from the courts of the *kehilot* and regional councils. In 1594 the Council of Four Lands passed an edict requiring rabbinic sanction for books published in Hebrew, and the court attached to it sometimes decided whether such sanction should be granted.

As bodies which were in some senses organs of the state, the councils felt obliged to support state policy. Thus in 1580 the Council of Three Lands confirmed the law forbidding Jews to engage in farming state taxes and customs duties in Wielkopolska, Małopolska, and Mazovia adopted in 1538 by the Polish Sejm in Piotrków, on the grounds that Jewish tax farmers and leaseholders in their pursuit of gain had given rise to accusations against Jews in general and had excited the Christian populace against them. The council also gave its support to edicts forbidding Jewish settlement in specified areas (the privilege 'De non tolerandis Judaeis'), reminding its coreligionists in 1669 of the prohibition on Jews settling in Warsaw. Such edicts were read publicly in all synagogues with the threat of excommunication for those who failed to observe them.

At the same time the councils saw themselves as representing the Jewish community and attempted to put their case to the authorities, sending advocates to Warsaw during the sessions of the sejm in order to alleviate the tax burden on Jews and to ensure the maintenance of the rights they enjoyed. The action of such advocates is extensively discussed in the chapter by Anna Michałowska-Mycielska. Lobbying was particularly important at 'coronation sejms', those held after the election of a new king, since the new monarch was expected to confirm the rights and privileges granted to the Jews by his predecessors. The councils also attempted to combat anti-Jewish activity and in particular blood-libel and accusations of desecrating the host. Such activities were expensive and were financed by special levies on the *kehilot*.

The councils attempted to moderate tensions in the Jewish communities because of the danger of malcontents appealing over the heads of the community leadership to the king, nobles, or churchmen. For the same reason, many of the decrees of the councils call for the prosecution of those who, by their activity, brought the wrath of the government or the Christian populace upon the Jews. Decrees in 1671, 1677, and subsequently prohibited Jews from leasing estates or other enterprises from Poles without the knowledge of the *kehilot* of which they were members. Merchants were enjoined to deal honestly with Christians and not to engage in unlawful practices which could lead to harm to the Jewish community. Attempts were also made to control population movement: in 1673 a regulation of the Council of Four Lands attempted to regulate migration from one Jewish community to another.

The councils also concerned themselves with Jewish religious traditions, issuing regulations on Jewish schools, on the observance of *kashrut*, on Jewish–non-Jewish relations, and on dress. The councils took action against the Shabatean and Frankist heresies in the seventeenth and eighteenth centuries. An indication of the importance of the Council of Four Lands in the Jewish world beyond Poland–Lithuania is that it was consulted when Rabbi Jacob Emden of Altona accused Rabbi Jonathan Eybeschuetz, the chief rabbi of Hamburg, Altona, and Wandsbeck, of being a secret Shabatean.

Polish Jews were very proud of their national councils. Nathan Nata Hanover has given a description of the functioning of the Council of Four Lands which is impressive, even taking into account that he wrote in the aftermath of the Khmelnytsky uprising of 1648 in a work in which, as an exile, he idealized a lost world:

The representatives of the Four Lands had sessions twice in the year . . . at the fair in Lublin, between Purim and Passover, and at the fair in Jarosław in the month of Av or Elul. The representatives of the Four Lands resembled the Sanhedrin in the session chamber in the Temple of Jerusalem. They had jurisdiction over all the Jews of the kingdom of Poland with power to issue injunctions and binding decisions [*takanot*] and to impose penalties at their discretion. Every difficult case was submitted to them for trial. To make the task easier for themselves, the representatives of the Four Lands would select special judges from each land, who were called 'land-judges' [*dayanei medinah*] and who tried civil suits; while criminal cases, disputes over priority of possession [*ḥazakah*] and other difficult cases were tried by the representatives themselves [in full session].[16]

This description is obviously exaggerated. The institutions of Jewish self-government were adversely affected by the decline in the authority of the central government and the growth of the power of the nobility which followed the Khmelnytsky uprising. Thus, the national councils found it increasingly difficult to collect the taxes they were required to pay the government and often had to borrow to fulfil their obligations. This crisis is graphically described in the chapter by Adam Kaźmierczyk. In 1717, as part of the general financial settlement enacted by the Silent Sejm, the Jews were required to pay lump sums of 220,000 zlotys for Poland and 60,000 for Lithuania, but this reorganization failed to resolve the problems of the indirect method of tax collection. The regional councils and local *kehilot* also faced growing difficulties, exacerbated by the interference of royal officials and the noble owners of towns. It would, however, be wrong to deduce a crisis of Jewish community institutions, as inferred by Israel Dinur and Raphael Mahler, for example.[17]

Martin Borýsek's account of the emergence of supra-community Jewish government in Moravia describes a fascinating parallel to the Polish Jewish national councils. Dispersed in a large number of comparatively small communities, the Jews of Moravia in the mid-seventeenth century agreed on the *Shai takanot* (the 311 ordinances), a legal and administrative framework for all communities, their mutual relations, and a collective leadership, known as the 'heads of the land', the same title as delegates to the national councils of Poland–Lithuania. These by-laws also established regular meetings of community delegates. In contrast to the Polish–Lithuanian Commonwealth, these ordinances for supra-community organization were formally recognized by the state, as Borýsek shows. Known until then also as *Takanot medinat mehren*, the ordinances became an integral part of the Habsburg legislation for the Jews of Moravia in 1754.

Attempts to Reform or Abolish Jewish Self-Government

The middle of the eighteenth century was a major turning point for the Jews of Europe. Under the influence of the Enlightenment, many rulers now initiated attempts, carried still further by their constitutional successors in the nineteenth century, to end the persecution of the Jews on religious grounds and transform them into 'useful' subjects, or, where a civil society had been established, into citizens. At this time, the position of the Jews in the Polish–Lithuanian Commonwealth was roughly similar to that elsewhere in Europe. On the one hand, they were, as mentioned above, a corporation, like any of the other corporations into which medieval and early modern society was divided, and administered their own communities. On the other, they were a despised minority, tolerated in an inferior position to attest to the truth of Christianity. Economically, they were everywhere limited to intermediary occupations, the most important of which were money-lending and banking, trading, and leasing. In Poland–Lithuania there were also Jewish artisans and administrators of estates, mills, breweries, distilleries, and inns.

The various European governments sought the political integration of the Jews, their economic and social transformation through the abandonment of 'unproductive' occupations and the purification of their religion from 'medieval', 'barbaric', and 'anti-Christian' elements. The goal of political integration went along with demands for the abolition of Jewish self-government, which was regarded as backward and as perpetuating Jewish 'separatism'. Medieval forms of corporatism were anathema both to governments inspired by the principles of the Enlightenment and to their liberal and constitutional successors.

These issues were first approached during the reign of Stanisław August, which saw an ultimately unsuccessful attempt to reform the political system of Poland–Lithuania and also a somewhat half-hearted effort to transform the position of the Jews and integrate them more fully into the wider society. Those who sought to restructure Jewish life often saw the system of Jewish self-government as a major obstacle to the fulfilment of this goal. Thus Father Hugo Kołłątaj (1750–1812), a key figure in the reform movement, called for the restriction of the scope of Jewish autonomy, which 'turns [Jews] into a state within a state'. In his view, the kahals should lose their powers and the rabbinate should have no jurisdiction except in religious matters. Jews should lose their separate legal status, and all civil and criminal cases should be tried by municipal or noble courts. They should also be placed under the jurisdiction of the towns, whose self-government was one of his basic demands, and removed from the jurisdiction of the royal voivodes.[18]

The opposition of the burghers and the intervention of Prussia, Russia, and Austria to frustrate the reformist plans of the Four Year Sejm meant that no measures were taken to transform the situation of the Jews. The only major reform was in the sphere of taxation. As the chapter by Adam Kaźmierczyk shows, the eighteenth century had seen an increasing indebtedness on the part of the kehilot and a growing failure of the Council of Four Lands and the Council of Lithuania to raise taxes effectively. There was considerable discontent in the sejm with the level of Jewish taxation, and some parliamentary deputies claimed that the Jews held back some of the money they collected. It was also widely believed that the number of Jews was significantly higher than the official figures, which lowered the yield of the poll tax.[19]

Dissatisfaction with the way the Council of Four Lands and the Council of Lithuania administered the poll tax, along with Enlightenment hostility to particularist jurisdictions, led the sejm to dissolve them as part of a reform of the system of financial administration in 1764.[20] The liquidation commission appointed by the sejm to investigate the financial situation of the community showed how high the Jewish level of indebtedness was. As a result, kehilah liquidation commissions were set up to assess the debts of the kehilot and to decide how they could be paid. The poll tax was now collected by the kahals in co-operation with the government and was raised in 1775 to three zlotys per household. (Previously a lump sum had been paid, based on an approximate estimate of one zloty per household.)

These policies were continued by the partitioning powers with varying results. In general, where some modernized form of Jewish self-government was retained, the transformation of the Jews into citizens or subjects was most successful. For this to take place, it was also necessary for there to emerge a significant group of acculturated Jews willing to participate in the transformation of their communities. These conditions could be found most noticeably in Prussia. As a result of the second and third partitions, Prussia acquired extensive Polish territories, the control of which was, for the most part, confirmed at the Treaty of Vienna in 1815. The Prussian bureaucracy was convinced that the Jews could play an important role in strengthening Prussian rule in the area. Their position was first regulated on 11 April 1797 by the General Statute for the Jews of South and New East Prussia. This maintained a reformed system of Jewish corporate self-government—the Jews were to be treated as a separate estate since, in the view of the Prussian bureaucracy, they were not yet ready to avail themselves of the municipal and state rights of citizens. Jewish autonomy was restricted to matters of religion, rabbinic jurisdiction was abolished, and rabbis were henceforth only to be admitted to court proceedings as experts when religious issues were raised. The *kahal* was abolished, and the municipal magistrates were to appoint Jewish officials to administer their communities under the control of the magistrates.

These drastic measures aroused significant Jewish opposition and led to a meeting of the regional Jewish council in Kleczew which petitioned the king to make them less stringent.[21] This intervention was successful, and the *kahals* were allowed to continue to function as under Polish rule. The Prussian state did not yet have the ability to organize the taxation of the Jews in the new territories efficiently and found itself compelled to retain for a period the Polish practice whereby the Jews were assessed for special taxes which they administered themselves.

The Prussian authorities refused to accede to Jewish requests that in legal matters Jews should not be subject to the civil courts. They made one exception to this in the city of Poznań, where the community was granted its own court, organized as a royal tribunal with a government-appointed non-Jewish judge and a non-Jewish clerk, who had to be paid from the community's funds. The impartiality of this court so impressed the local Jewish community that in 1802 the *kahal* asked the authorities to abolish the separate Jewish court, a request which the authorities refused.[22]

There was an inherent contradiction in the Prussian government's policies towards the Jews after 1815. It intervened actively in Jewish life in order to transform the Jewish community, but the reactionary principles which dominated the early post-Napoleonic years meant that the integration of the Jews into the larger population was regarded as undesirable. Accordingly, local authorities were instructed to avoid involvement in internal Jewish affairs as far as possible, intervening only when public order was threatened. This meant that the *kehilot*, which were legally voluntary organizations, could not count on the state to support them in compelling their members to pay community taxes, causing a further deterioration in their financial situation.[23]

The increasingly liberal political climate and the growing financial crisis of the *kehilot* led the Prussian authorities to adopt a more integrationist policy towards the Jews of the regions annexed from Poland. This took the form of the Provisional Regulation on the Status of the Jews in the Grand Duchy of Posen issued on 1 June 1833.[24] As in the earlier legislation of Frederick the Great (r. 1740–86) in his Revised

General Code of 1750, Jews were divided into two categories, a more privileged group of 'naturalized' Jews with essentially equal rights with burghers and the remainder of the community, who were merely 'tolerated'. The legislation of 1833 regulated the pathway to 'naturalization', and within a decade a quarter of Jewish households in the duchy had applied and qualified for this superior status, while a large majority of the Jews of the province fell into the category of 'tolerated' and enjoyed legal protection only as members of a religious community which had corporate rights and was under the control of the state. They were still subject to restrictions on where they could settle, could not acquire real estate, employ Christian servants, journeymen or apprentices, sell alcohol, engage in peddling, or undertake unregulated artisan work.

The scope of Jewish autonomy was also made more specific in this legislation, which declared that 'tolerated' Jewish communities (*Gemeinden*) were to be organized in the towns where the Jews lived. Membership was obligatory, and, although these bodies carried out religious functions, further restrictions were imposed on the role of the rabbi. The Prussian authorities sought to take advantage of the high indebtedness of the *kehilot* and the inability of the community organizations to deal with it to reform them in a way that would make possible the transformation of the Jewish communities of the province.[25] They now became corporations under public law, which allowed them to use the power of the state to collect contributions owed to them by their members.[26] They were to be administered by a board responsible to a representative body, whose election was to be subject to government supervision. Their authority was explicitly restricted to the 'internal affairs' of the community, and in all other respects Jews were subject to the local municipality. This new structure imposed important new obligations on the Jewish communities to which both the acculturated minority and the more conservative majority responded enthusiastically.

The first task with which the *kehilot* were confronted was the settlement of the communities' debts. This took several decades and was slowed by high Jewish emigration from the province which reduced the tax base. By the mid-nineteenth century, however, the finances of almost all the *Gemeinden* had been placed on a healthy footing, which was crucial given the large number of functions, both old and new, with which they were entrusted. They also established a German-language school system which all Jewish children from the ages of 7 to 14 were obliged to attend and which proved a great success. By the 1840s the bulk of Jewish children of elementary school age being educated in a Jewish (if modernized) environment.[27] The *Gemeinden* also retained responsibility for poverty relief, though traditional Jewish *ḥevrot* continued to operate, sometimes in a modernized and reformed manner.

It has often been argued that the integrationist solution to the Jewish problem, the transformation of the Jews into citizens, did not succeed in the Polish lands. The experience of the Jews of the Grand Duchy of Posen is the exception, although the Jews were transformed not into Poles but rather Germans of the Jewish faith.

Certainly, although it fell short of granting the Jews complete legal equality, the 1833 reform of Jewish self-government greatly facilitated the adaptation of the Jews of the province to modern conditions. Its success can be seen in the fact that it was extended to all Jewish communities in Prussia in 1847 and served as the legal foundation for the Jewish *Gemeinden* until their dissolution in 1939.

In Galicia, which the Austrians had acquired somewhat reluctantly from Poland in the first partition in 1772, Emperor Joseph II (who was co-regent with Maria Theresa from 1765 and ruled on his own from 1780 to 1790) attempted to introduce a local variant of his radical and ultimately unsuccessful attempt to transform the Habsburg monarchy into a modernized and enlightened state. One aspect of his policies was the 'reform' of the Jewish population of his different lands. In 1785 the 212,000 Jews of Galicia made up nearly 60 per cent of those in the Habsburg monarchy, and Joseph was determined to transform their position in accordance with his attempt to introduce the principles of the 'well-ordered police-state' which governed his policy elsewhere in the monarchy.[28] In return for a guarantee of the right to practise their religion and to dwell securely in the empire, Joseph expected Jews to end their 'separateness' and to transform their educational system and occupational structure so that they would become 'useful and productive' subjects.[29] In March 1785 he promulgated a law for the Jews of Galicia, supplemented in May 1789 by a Jewish Ordinance, similar to those which he had already issued to the Jews in Lower Austria, the Czech lands, and Hungary.[30] According to its preamble, 'Galician Jews will ... from now on be treated like all other subjects as regards their rights and duties'.[31]

As a result, most, though not all, restrictions on Jews were abolished. They were granted restricted civic (municipal) rights, which were, however, dependent on the willingness of the burghers of the different towns to agree to them. The scope of municipal self-government was, moreover, somewhat limited. Jews were also given restricted freedom to settle in towns and were permitted to employ Christian servants.

Joseph was determined to 'productivize' the Jews, in accordance with physiocratic principles. He promoted Jewish settlement on the land, while, at the same time, seeking to exclude Jews from non-agricultural occupations in the countryside, such as inn-keeping, brewing, and distilling. Jews were, however, to be given unrestricted access to handicrafts, allowed to be apprenticed for a trade with a Christian master, and could open factories. A series of measures were introduced to foster their 'integration', the most important of which was compulsory school attendance. Jews were also obliged to take surnames and to keep their official records in German.

The scope of Jewish autonomy was severely restricted. In 1776 Maria Theresa attempted to create a supra-*kehilah* organization in the form of a General Direktion der Judenschaft, which was composed of representatives from the six regions into which Galicia was divided. This did not fulfil the expectations of the authorities and was abolished in 1789. The powers of individual *kehilot* were significantly reduced. They were responsible for supervising the religious institutions, dispensing charity, and administering the special taxes imposed on the Jews. The poll tax was abolished and replaced by a number of new taxes: a kosher meat tax, a candle tax, a marriage tax, and a residence tax to be levied on Jews from outside the province. Rabbis were deprived of their judicial power and the right to excommunicate members of the community.[32]

In the preamble to his Edict of Toleration for the Jews of Galicia, Joseph had proclaimed their equality in 'rights and duties'. One of the duties he now imposed on them was service in his army, the first time this had been required in modern Europe. Responsibility for supervising the draft lay with the individual *kehilot*.

Joseph's successors, Leopold II (r. 1790–92), Franz II (r. 1792–1835), and Ferdinand II (r. 1835–48), maintained the restrictive and punitive aspects of his policies, while playing down their positive and integrative elements. Franz II limited the participation of Jews in local self-government and, in 1806, yielding to pressure from both Jews and Catholics, abolished the Jewish school system created by Joseph II, a move which was followed by the collapse of most of its schools. During his reign, there were some half-hearted attempts at 'reforming' the Jews. Efforts were made to restrict the circulation of hasidic books and to limit the wearing of traditional Jewish dress. By the middle of the nineteenth century state Jewish schools, both primary and secondary, based on Haskalah principles and generally using German as the language of instruction, had been established in fourteen towns, with a total of some 3,000 students.[33] At the same time, the special Jewish taxes introduced by Maria Theresa and Joseph were maintained, as were restrictions on where Jews could live and the occupations they could pursue.

Kraków was made into a free city under the protection of the partitioning powers until it was incorporated into Galicia after the failure of a revolution there in February 1846. In 1817 a Statute for the Followers of the Law of the Old Testament was enacted. It abolished the *kahal*, replacing it with a Committee for Jewish Affairs, whose authority extended only to religious and charitable matters and which was composed of the rabbi, two other Jews, and a civil servant. The Jews were subordinated to the local administration and judiciary. Rabbis were still elected by the community but had to demonstrate to the civil authorities their knowledge of Polish and German. Jews were not eligible to be elected to the House of Representatives which governed the Free City of Kraków, and the restrictions on their place of residence, which had been in operation before the partitions and which meant they could not own property in Kraków itself, were maintained.[34]

The re-establishment of the Austrian government's authority after the revolution of 1848 was followed by nearly two decades of autocratic rule. The situation changed radically after its defeat at Prussian hands in 1866. The new system established in 1867 granted far-reaching autonomy to Hungary within the borders of the Crown lands of King Stephen and created a constitutional system in cisleithanian Austrian, the area north and west of the River Leitha. In 1868 Galicia was granted wide-ranging autonomy under Polish aristocratic control.

The establishment of a constitutional government in Austria and the granting of Galician autonomy brought to the fore the question of granting full legal equality to the Jews of the province. After some debate, and in the face of considerable opposition, the governor of Galicia, Count Agenor Gołuchowski, was able to secure the passage on 8 October 1868 of a non-discriminatory law on municipal self-government in the Galician sejm which removed 'all the former provisions concerning the special position of the Jews'.[35]

This meant that Jews could now participate on an equal footing in local councils. As Hanna Kozińska-Witt explains, 'Jews served on the councils of two hundred and sixty-one cities in Galicia and lacked representation only on forty-five. They constituted 36 per cent of councillors and had an overall majority on twenty-eight councils. In addition, in the second half of the nineteenth century, they served as mayors in ten cities.' She and Łukasz Sroka explore, for Kraków and Lwów respectively, how Jewish councillors negotiated the often delicate equilibrium between looking after the well-being of the local Jewish population while also assuming responsibility for the wider community. In Kraków, as elsewhere in Galicia, the municipal franchise was highly restrictive. The political division was initially between the conservative majority and the liberal minority, and Jews were to be found on both sides. Within the Jewish community, the Orthodox and the 'progressives' generally co-operated, and from 1905 the position of deputy mayor was held by Józef Sare, a Jewish architect who was also a high official in the municipal administration. Modern political antisemitism also now made an impact on the political scene in Kraków, as described by Kozińska-Witt. In Lwów, the establishment of the city council itself was contested, with local Polish politicians insisting on limiting the number of Jewish councillors. Despite sustained objections from the imperial and provincial authorities, in 1870 Christians were guaranteed 80 of the 100 seats on the city council, thus disenfranchising part of the Jewish electorate.

Under the legislation introducing Jewish legal equality, reformed Jewish community councils were established throughout the province of Galicia. In them a balance was established between the integrationist minority and the more conservative and religious majority. The Jews were now legally a religious community with the guaranteed right to form institutions to serve its needs. All Jews who did not declare themselves *konfessionslos* (without religious affiliation) were required to belong to a *Gemeinde*. Each *Gemeinde* was required to organize its activity in accordance with a set of regulations which it created and which, in the case of Galicia, had to be approved by the governor. One of their obligations was to supervise the education of the young in accordance with the School Ordinance of 25 May 1868. Anticipating the constitutional changes, the governor of Galicia issued, in accordance with a ministerial circular of 4 January 1867, guidelines for the legal organization of Jewish community councils and this was followed by general Austrian legislation laying down that there could be only one community council in each town. The guidelines for community legislation also held that a person could only be a member of one *Gemeinde*, where he was required to pay the community tax. In addition, the statutes of each *Gemeinde* were to specify how the authorities were to be elected, how they were to operate, and what contribution they were required to make to the local municipality. In addition the community council was to regulate the functioning of a system of arbitration, the selection of community functionaries, and the provision of religious education. Community councils retained their monopoly over kosher slaughtering, which provided them with a large part of their income, either from directly administering slaughterhouses or leasing out the right to provide kosher meat. Much of the remainder of their income came from a tax on those eligible to participate in community elections. A newly reformed statute for *ḥevrot kadisha* was also introduced.[36]

The Kingdom of Poland was an autonomous, semi-constitutional state created at the Congress of Vienna to satisfy, at least in part, the national aspirations of the Poles, while taking into account the *raison d'état* of the Romanovs with whom it was in dynastic union. Its autonomous status was severely restricted after the unsuccessful Polish uprising of 1830–1 and almost entirely done away with in the aftermath of that of 1863–4. It did, however, possess a constitution and a concept of citizenship, which meant that, in theory at least, there was a basis for the transformation of the Jews into citizens.

When, in 1818, the ten-year limit set on the decision not to grant Jews civil rights in the Napoleonic Duchy of Warsaw came to an end, the Council of State under the leadership of the viceroy, General Józef Zajączek, a former Jacobin now turned arch-conservative, induced Tsar Alexander, in his capacity as king of Poland, to maintain the existing restrictions.[37] Jews, with a small number of exceptions, were still barred from living on the main streets of central Warsaw. Jewish quarters were also maintained in fifty-five other towns, and an additional ninety towns still possessed the right to totally exclude Jews. The levy imposed on Jews visiting Warsaw, which had been abolished in 1811, was reintroduced in 1826, and Jews were also barred from living within twenty versts (thirty miles) of the frontier.[38] A tax on kosher meat was introduced, and further efforts were made to limit the involvement of Jews in the sale of alcohol. Although initially Jews were expected to serve in the military in the same way as other citizens, it was now decided to exempt them 'until such time as they be given the rights of political life'. In compensation for this exemption the Jews of the kingdom outside Warsaw paid an annual 'recruit' tax of 600,000 florins, while those of Warsaw paid 700,000 florins.[39]

On 1 January 1822 the *kahal*, which had been the subject of several hostile government investigations and a significant degree of criticism by Jews themselves, as described by Artur Markowski in his chapter, was abolished. Its functions were taken over by synagogue supervisory boards, also called community boards, which had been established on 20 March 1821. They were meant to play the role of supervisory bodies in relation to Jewish activity and were headed by the community rabbi and his assistant and three elected 'supervisors' supported by a secretary and two assistants. Their competence was restricted to religious matters, the administration of synagogues, *mikva'ot*, and *kashrut*; the dispensing of charity; and control of the tax on kosher meat and the recruit tax. These boards were ultimately responsible to the commissions which ran each of the ten provinces of the kingdom. In the course of the nineteenth century the number of supervisors was significantly increased in larger towns like Warsaw and Łódź. By 1856 there were 346 such synagogue supervisory boards in the kingdom. The reasons for the abolition of the *kahal* and the way in which these boards functioned are fully discussed by Artur Markowski.

In order to strengthen the supervisory boards and to diminish Jewish 'separateness', on 28 March 1822 the most important of the *ḥevrot*, the *ḥevrah kadisha*, was declared illegal. However, as Cornelia Aust and François Guesnet clearly show, such bodies continued to exist everywhere in the kingdom. In Warsaw, the Jewish community reacted by creating the Burial Administration, which, as Cornelia Aust demonstrates, regulated the sale of flour for Passover and kosher butchering. The funds produced in this way, which constituted the largest source of income for the synagogue board, were administered independently of it, thus effectively undermining the purpose of the 1822 legislation.[40] Well into the 1840s the official budget submitted by the board to the authorities did not include any details of income and expenses connected with burials.[41] Like the traditional *ḥevrot kadisha*, the Burial Administration in Warsaw took action against what it saw as religious dissidence through discriminatory burial practices.[42] Accordingly, it retained control of a wide range of community responsibilities.

The Jewish response to the creation of the supervisory boards was largely negative. As Markowski observes, 'the old and the new structures somehow intermingled. Individuals serving as *kahal* elders often became board members and all that changed was their title and their area of responsibility.' As a result the old *kehilah* establishment initially remained in control. A study from the interwar period comes to the conclusion that 'the abolition of the *kahal* should not be seen as a major turning-point in the life of the Jews of the Kingdom of Poland and of their communal self-government. The synagogue supervisory board was in fact the continuation of the *kahal* but with diminished powers.'[43] In fact, these boards were soon faced with new responsibilities resulting from the social problems caused by industrialization and urbanization. This can clearly be seen in Warsaw, the capital and largest town in the kingdom, where a structure of co-existing centres of community power and influence emerged. This was the result of a number of factors—the dismantling of the traditional community institutions; competing claims to leadership by traditional rabbinic elites, the hasidic movement, and new, Western-oriented integrationists; the abolition of the chief rabbinate in 1874; and the willingness of an integrationist intelligentsia to take up central functions in the newly created community administration, now renamed the Board of the Jewish Community of Warsaw. The board, elected by a much broader group than the boards elsewhere in the kingdom, developed a number of institutions and agencies of its own. Alongside these there emerged independent schools, *ḥevrot*, charities, and places of worship, which developed without any significant input or supervision from the community administration.

The emerging industrial centre of Łódź also saw the development of a full range of community bodies, charities, and institutions, a variegated structure that would remain essentially unchallenged until the late nineteenth century, as François Guesnet shows in his chapter. In the last third of the nineteenth century progressives were also able to establish themselves in a strong position on such bodies in Częstochowa, Radom, Zawiercie, and other towns.

As was the case elsewhere in the Polish lands, government attempts to transform Jewish life divided the Jewish community, with the majority of Orthodox, whether rabbinic or hasidic, hostile to the changes. The nineteenth century did, however, see the emergence in the kingdom of a significant group of acculturated and Polonized Jews. This circle of relatively acculturated Jews included financiers (among them the leaseholders of the kosher meat monopoly, until 1862 the principal source of income of the synagogue supervisory boards), bankers, and army suppliers, most of whom were closely associated with the rulers of the kingdom. The conflict between the hasidim and the maskilim was much less bitter in the Kingdom of Poland than it was in Galicia or in the western provinces of the tsarist empire. After the government reforms of 1821 the hasidim were soon represented in significant numbers on the boards in many areas, including Warsaw, but were obliged to work together with the more secularized members of the community so as to present a united front to the authorities.

One important organization which fostered a significant group of Polonized Jews was the Warsaw Rabbinic School established in 1826. Ultimately it did not produce rabbis but educated and acculturated Jews who sought the reform of the community. The inability to establish a successfully functioning rabbinic school which could produce a modern rabbinate constituted a failure both of policy and of implementation. The goal should have been to create a university-level institution similar to those which appeared somewhat later in Germany, an aim not envisaged either by those committed to the radical transformation of Polish Jewry, like Antoni Eisenbaum, or by those more rooted in traditional Jewish values, like Abraham Stern. The Polish educational bureaucracy had very little understanding of, or sympathy for, these issues, and the political upheavals which marked the period between 1815 and 1864 made the consistent implementation of policy impossible.

Polish–Jewish relations began to improve in the first years of the reign of Tsar Alexander II. The Jews were now the beneficiaries of a three-way struggle for their support. While the Polish opposition aimed to enlist them for the anti-tsarist insurrection they were planning, Alexander Wielopolski, nominated by Alexander II as viceroy, hoped they would form a significant part of the middle class of the healthier Polish society he was intending to foster, in which rural society would also be transformed on the English or Prussian model. The Russian government, alarmed by the situation in the Congress Kingdom, was willing to acquiesce in Wielopolski's desire to grant full legal equality to the Jews. As a consequence, by a decree on 4 June 1862 (NS), the viceroy abolished all the main restrictions on Jewish activity, in effect establishing the Jews as equal citizens. Jews were granted the right to own farmland and urban properties. All special Jewish taxes, including the tax on kosher meat, were abolished, and the synagogue supervisory boards were authorized to levy a community tax. The outbreak of the 1863 uprising prevented Wielopolski from introducing radical reforms of the Jewish community, which would have established a version of the French consistorial system and, he believed, foster further Jewish reform.[44]

The 1863 uprising, ill-conceived and poorly planned, never had a chance of success and its crushing by the Russians was followed by two generations in which all aspects of Polish national individuality were suppressed. However, the legal equality granted to the Jews was not rescinded after the uprising was suppressed. The dominant intellectual tone was set by the 'positivists', the Polish counterpart of west European liberals, and among their cardinal political tenets was the view that the uprisings of 1830–1 and 1863 had failed because they had appealed to too narrow a circle of Polish society. One of their main aims was to incorporate into the nation those groups which had lain outside this circle or which had been at best marginal: peasants, women, Jews. They saw education, and self-education, as fundamental to achieving this goal, which they also hoped would foster the emergence of a middle class, now seen as the main repository of liberal values.

The positivists' belief that the Jewish elite could undertake a fundamental transformation of Jewish society was also misplaced. The Jewish elite embraced positivist views, but understood their social isolation and relative weakness well, even if they had been able to obtain a disproportionate influence by gaining control of the synagogue supervisory boards in Warsaw, Łódź, and elsewhere in the Kingdom of Poland after an initial struggle with more Orthodox elements, above all the hasidim. These boards still retained control over many aspects of Jewish life, including education. By this stage, as Artur Markowski clearly demonstrates, 'the structures of Jewish self-government, first the supervisory boards and then somewhat later the Board of the Jewish Community of Warsaw into which the local supervisory board was transformed, evolved from a subordinate, almost passive position to one of activity and significant authority'.

The situation developed very differently in the tsarist empire itself. The bulk of the Jews there, some 1.2 million in 1820, lived in the areas annexed as a result of the partitions of Poland–Lithuania. Before this, only a very small number of Jews, who had kept their identities hidden, had lived within its borders. The dominant Russian Orthodox Church, like the western Christian Church, had a strong tradition of anti-Judaism and supersessionism, and hostility to the Jews persisted into the eighteenth century.

In spite of this unfavourable background, the Russian tsars from the time of Catherine the Great (r. 1762–96) did attempt to 'transform' their Jewish population into 'useful subjects'. However, the process in Russia had some specific features which made it different from what occurred elsewhere in Europe and in the remaining Polish lands. In the first place, Russia was not an estate society, like the countries which had been part of Western Christendom, but an autocracy, which derived its political ideas and institutions from Byzantium and from the two centuries of Tatar rule to which the Grand Duchy of Muscovy had been subjected.

Under Peter the Great (r. 1682–1725), and later Empress Catherine, attempts had been made to transform Russia into an estate society along Western lines, with four main estates: nobles, merchants, townspeople, and peasants. Of these estates only the nobility was granted rights, albeit limited, by Catherine's Charter of the Nobility in 1786 and even these did not seriously compromise the autocratic nature of the government. However, the ineffectiveness of the tsarist bureaucracy meant that these estates were self-administered. It has often been argued that the attempt to impose an estate society on Russia, where the patrimonial model was so firmly established, met with very little success. Yet the division into estates did correspond to some Russian social realities. The problem of where to place the Jews in this hierarchy constantly perplexed tsarist administrators. The Russian bureaucracy was constantly looking for an element within Jewish society which they could use to reform the Jews in the Russian interest.

There was considerable continuity in the policies pursued by the tsarist government towards the Jews from the first incorporation of significant numbers of Jews into the empire in 1772 until 1881. These policies were part of an attempt to transform the empire into a 'properly governed state' on the model of eighteenth-century Austria and Prussia. Two main principles underpinned the actions of the government. In the first place there was the belief that Jews were a harmful element. By their oppressive behaviour, they disrupted relations between landlords and peasants in the sensitive western provinces of the empire and action needed to be taken in order to limit their deleterious influence. Secondly, the leading tsarist officials, for the most part men of the Enlightenment, shared the general European view that the faults of the Jews were not innate but the consequence of their unfortunate history. Although the negative behaviour of the Jews had to be curbed, Jewish society could be made over by 'rational' reforms, which in the autocratic tsarist empire would transform them, not into citizens, but into useful subjects.

Between 1772 and the death of Tsar Alexander I in 1825, the tsarist government attempted only intermittently to implement these principles. Catherine II was a convinced believer in the principles of the Enlightenment, which she sought to apply in the reorganization of her empire, whose extent had increased enormously during the eighteenth century. In May 1786 Catherine induced the senate to issue an edict Concerning the Protection of the Rights of Jews in Russia in Respect of their Legal Responsibility, which affirmed unequivocally that, since Jews had already been 'accorded a status equal to that of others', all 'Jews must be able to enjoy the privileges and rights appropriate to their calling and fortune, without distinction of origin and religion'.[45] This high-flown declaration remained largely a dead letter. Its limitations were clear when, in December 1791, a government decree rejected a claim by some Jewish traders that they should be allowed to establish themselves as merchants in Smolensk and Moscow, in effect creating what came to be known as the 'Pale of Permanent Jewish Settlement' to which all Jews were restricted.

Alexander (r. 1801–25) was strongly influenced by liberal views in the early years of his reign before the war with Napoleon, and was also much better informed about Jewish matters, partly because of his close relationship with Adam Czartoryski, a Polish nobleman and reformer, who held the post of Russian foreign minister between 1804 and 1806. The legal situation of the Jews needed clarification, and it was for this purpose that in November 1802 Alexander created the Committee for the Organization of Jewish Life, the first of many such bodies in the tsarist empire. The committee, after some discussion, came up with a general programme for 'Jewish reform'.

The Statute on the Jews which it established combined Enlightenment-derived ideas for the transformation of the Jews with the now traditional Russian preoccupation with the need to limit their 'harmful impact' on the peasantry of the areas acquired from Poland–Lithuania, claiming that it was motivated by 'solicitude for the true welfare of the Jews' as well as by 'the advantage of the native population in those provinces in which these people are permitted to reside'.[46] It allowed Jewish children free access to state schools and universities and granted Jews the right to open their own secular schools in which the language of instruction could be German, Polish, or Russian. After a period of six years all Jewish public and commercial documents would have to use one of these languages. Jews who were elected to municipal councils or served as *kahal* members or rabbis were to demonstrate after a similar period their written and spoken knowledge of one of these languages. Jewish members of municipal councils were required to wear European-style clothes.

The statute attempted to delineate the respective spheres of competence of the civic authorities and the Jewish autonomous institutions. Jews were now to be subject to the authority of the towns, the police, and the common law courts. At the same time, in spite of the attacks on the system of Jewish self-government, the government did not abolish the *kehilah*. Rabbis were responsible for 'all ceremonies of the Jewish faith and the deciding of all disputes of a religious character' but were expressly forbidden to excommunicate members of the community.[47] A 'dissident' sect had the right to establish its own synagogue and elect its own rabbi in any community, giving legal sanction to the expansion of hasidism. The implications of this for the structure of Jewish self-government are clearly spelled out in the chapter by Vladimir Levin. As he shows, 'the autonomous community was identical with the worshippers of the great synagogue' (the main and often only synagogue established in a particular town). The predominance of the great synagogue was now effectively ended, 'severing the link between the town's whole community and a particular synagogue'. In his chapter he discusses how this worked itself out in different ways in Lithuania and Volhynia.

Jewish economic life was to be radically transformed, and all Jews were to be placed in one of four categories: merchants, townspeople, manufacturers and artisans, and farmers. Accordingly, inn-keeping and all types of leasing linked with agriculture were to be barred to Jews. The limitations on Jewish residence imposed by the Pale of Settlement, whose boundaries were now fixed, were retained, although there were exemptions for merchants, artisans, and manufacturers. This reform was only sporadically implemented and its results were largely negative. After his victory in the Napoleonic wars, Alexander again took up the Jewish issue. His growing mystical inclinations manifested themselves in his hope that he would become the instrument of divine providence and accomplish the conversion of the Jews, something which he had also discussed with Czartoryski. These years also saw the enactment of a number of restrictive anti-Jewish measures.

Alexander was succeeded by his brother Nicholas I (r. 1825–55), who was in many ways the last of the enlightened despots. He undertook a radical reform of Jewish life as part of his attempt to establish effective methods of state administration and control which would unify his multi-confessional and ethnically diverse empire. His goal was to turn the Jews into loyal subjects by establishing direct state supervision of the life and religious activity of the Jewish community and eliminating the traditional mediators between the state and the Jews.

The first major measure he promulgated, the imposition of conscription on the Jews, reflected his own militarism. The induction of Jews into the army elsewhere in Europe was part of the process of transforming them into citizens. This was not the case in Russia, where military service was not a general obligation but was imposed selectively on different estates and social and religious groups. Jews had initially been exempt from military service, because they were generally felt to be unsuitable as recruits. This was not the view of Nicholas. He was a convinced believer in the value of the army as a school for virtue which could play a major role in the transformation of his Jewish subjects. His imposition of conscription on the Jews was punitive and the cause of great suffering and major disruption to Jewish life. The involvement of the community leadership in enforcing the draft caused enormous shock, undermining deep-rooted traditions of social solidarity. It precipitated a breakdown of community bonds which manifested itself in a number of ways, including violent protests against the *kahal* and those it employed to organize the recruitment, denunciations to the government, and attempts to leave the community.

During the first decade of his rule Nicholas introduced few other changes to the policies towards the Jews which had been laid down by his predecessors. It was only on 13 April 1835 that the attempt of the Committee for the Organization of Jewish Life to systematize the legislation on the Jews led to the promulgation of a statute on the Jews. It formally established the borders of the Pale of Settlement, which were to remain until the First World War. Jews could reside outside the Pale if they inherited property outside it, if they were involved in court proceedings outside it for a prolonged period of time, by studying at academic institutions, and through involvement in some commercial enterprises. The statute also established the self-government of each synagogue and prayer house in a town in the form of synagogue boards, later called spiritual boards. These only gradually came to function effectively, but as Vladimir Levin shows, they were to become the basis for a new form of Jewish self-government, particularly in Moscow, St Petersburg, and Novorossia (southern Russia/Ukraine), above all when Crown rabbis were elected by their congregations.

The need to consolidate the government's hold over the former Polish provinces in the aftermath of the uprising of 1830–1, and the recurrence of famine there in the late 1830s, led Nicholas to undertake a further initiative in relation to the Jews. He requested Pavel Kiselev, one of his leading officials, to review what had been done in the area and to report whether changes were necessary. The first major initiative to be put into practice was the establishment of a network of state-sponsored Jewish schools. The second, embodied in a law of 19 December 1844, abolished the *kahal*. Its place was to be taken by the local municipal authority, which would also exercise jurisdiction over Jews living in the surrounding countryside. In fact, the responsibilities of the *kahal* were taken over by the Jewish community officials responsible for collecting taxes, conducting censuses, and ensuring that conscription quotas were met. The Jews still did not pay tax directly to the government, and local Jewish communities continued to participate in the apportionment of the tax burden, both nationally and locally. The community officials were responsible for the collection of money to support philanthropic and other community services and had the same legal responsibilities as the elders of communities established by artisans or townspeople. They were to be aided in their duties by elected assistants. Together with the officers elected under the 1827 conscription statute, they would be directly subordinate to the local authorities. How this worked in practice is described in the chapter by Vladimir Levin.

This measure did not integrate the Jews into the larger administrative system, abolish all aspects of Jewish community organization, or abrogate the status of rabbinic courts, since Russia lacked the administrative resources to fully subordinate Jews to the estate structure established by Catherine. Moreover, to do so would have meant writing off the substantial arrears in taxes which were owed by the *kehilot*. In the conflict between the government's desire to reform the Jews and its interest in taxation and recruitment, it was the latter which took precedence.

However, although the structures of Jewish self-government did continue to exist, the new legislation contributed to further undermining their legitimacy within the Jewish community. In the 1830s there had been many protests against the unfairness of the recruitment and taxation policies. Now a new phenomenon emerged: Jews began to take the drastic step of petitioning the authorities to be allowed to secede from the community.

At the local level, the Rabbinic Commission established in 1848 sought to consolidate the institution of officially recognized 'state rabbis'. It was partly in order to create a cadre of state rabbis that in 1847 the government had established two state rabbinical seminaries on the model of that in Warsaw, one in Vilna and the other in Zhitomir, as mandated by the law of November 1844. In addition to training rabbis, these schools were to produce the educated laymen who would transform Russian Jewish life. The rabbinical schools provided employment for the cream of the Russian Haskalah. However, like that in Warsaw, they did not achieve what was expected of them.

The accession of Alexander II (r. 1855–81) was greeted with high hopes. After the stagnation and repression of the last years of Nicholas II's reign, it was expected that his successor would introduce the radical reforms whose necessity had been made obvious by Russia's poor performance in the ongoing Crimean War. The Jewish elite placed similar hopes in the 'reforming tsar'. On 31 March 1856 Alexander called on Pavel Kiselev, as chairman of the Committee for the Organization of Jewish Life, to conduct a comprehensive review of Russian legislation dealing with the Jews so as to facilitate 'the merger of this people with the native population insofar as the moral status of the Jews makes this possible'.[48]

The first issue which it discussed was how far the existing restrictions on Jewish residence and choice of occupation should be relaxed. The policy adopted was one of 'selective integration', the rewarding of those sections of Jewish society which had succeeded in transforming themselves along the lines advocated by the authorities and could be incorporated relatively easily into the Russian social structure. These relaxations on the restrictions on Jewish settlement only affected a small minority of Jews. Nevertheless, one of their consequences was the development of the Jewish community of St Petersburg. Jewish notables such as Shemuel Poliakov and Evzel Guenzburg established themselves there and became effective advocates for the Jewish cause.

Jews also benefited from the reform of local government in 1864 which saw the establishment of district and provincial assemblies with executive committees in all except the nine formerly Polish provinces and some provinces in the north and far east. They were given the right to levy taxes and to spend the proceeds on schools, public health, roads, and other social services, although they were also required to carry out tasks deputed to them by the authorities. Jews who satisfied the requirements of the property-qualified franchise were able to vote and be elected to these assemblies. In Ukraine, in particular, Jews began to participate in rural assemblies and were also sometimes appointed to rural offices.

Calls for the reform of Jewish self-government persisted. In the aftermath of the Russian revolution of 1904–7, the idea gained ground that it was necessary, given that there were only two Jewish duma deputies, to create a body which would represent Jewish interests and advise the deputies. The proposal in the duma in late 1909 of a bill which would legalize denominational societies and other bodies made up of adherents of non-Christian faiths led to the convening of a conference in Kovno in November 1909, whose importance is described by Vladimir Levin. At this conference, Genrikh Sliozberg, a leading Russian Jewish liberal, explained that 'we have neither a community structure nor a community organization'.[49] The conference saw as its goal the laying down of guidelines for the establishment of Jewish community bodies and reached a surprising degree of consensus. The future local Jewish community body was to be governed by a council elected by direct vote. This would, in turn, elect an executive of seven to ten members which would be the governing body of the community. All Jews over the age of 18, whether or not they were affiliated with a synagogue, who had not converted to another religion, would be eligible to vote. Once the new community structure had been established, the kosher meat tax would be replaced by a progressive income tax which all members of the community except those whose income was below a certain level would be obliged to pay. The administration of this tax would be controlled by a committee responsible to the community council. However, there was no chance of implementing these changes in the reactionary climate in the tsarist empire after the suppression of the revolution of 1904–7.

Jewish Struggles for Autonomy before the Second World War

The wave of pogroms of 1881–2 ushered in a new period in the history of the Jews of the former Polish–Lithuanian Commonwealth. From the 1870s there had been growing scepticism about the commitment of the Jewish elite to the processes of 'merger' and 'reconciliation', while Judeophobia was increasingly widespread in conservative circles. The tsarist authorities reacted to the pogroms by claiming that the Jews themselves were responsible for the violence to which they had been subjected because of their 'exploitation' of the surrounding population. Their consequent rejection of the policy of transforming their Jews into useful subjects led to a crisis among the supporters of integrationist principles within the Jewish elite, as integrating and transforming the community through education and Russification no longer seemed to offer a secure future in the tsarist empire. Instead of religion, ethnicity was now seen by many as the main marker of Jewish identity, while others came to perceive socialism, with its promise of a new and equal world, as the solution to the Jewish problem. From the tsarist empire, this 'new Jewish politics' spread to the Kingdom of Poland and Galicia, where integrationist policies, though more successful than in the tsarist empire, had also encountered considerable resistance and were now increasingly discredited in both Jewish and non-Jewish eyes. It even had an impact in Prussian Poland, the one area of former Poland–Lithuania where integration had seemed successful.

One of the goals of this new Jewish politics from the 1880s onwards was to establish Jewish national autonomy in the diaspora. Different aspects of this issue are discussed in the chapters by Marcos Silber and Szymon Rudnicki. Szymon Rudnicki investigates the reason for the failure to establish Jewish national autonomy in interwar Poland.

The Council of Four Lands and the Council of Lithuania were now seen as models to be emulated. Israel Halperin, who was responsible for a monumental edition of the *pinkas* of the Council of Four Lands, to which he devoted eighteen years of his life, wrote in his introduction that it was begun after the First World War 'in the days of struggle for Jewish autonomy in Poland, when it seemed that there was a prospect of domestic Jewish government in the diaspora'.[50] The history of the *kahal* was now also seen, as Adam Teller demonstrates, in a highly romanticized manner.

'National autonomism', the movement which sought to establish a non-territorial form of autonomy, did so in rejection of what it saw as Zionism's 'Palestinocentrism' and lack of interest in the diaspora. It drew on the concept of national–personal autonomy developed by the Austro-Marxists Karl Renner, in his pamphlet *State and Nation*, and Otto Bauer, in his book *The Nationalities Question and Social Democracy*.[51] Renner and Bauer saw national–personal autonomy as a way to organize geographically divided members of different nations 'not in territorial bodies but in simple association of persons', thus divorcing the concept of nationality from territory.[52] The principal ideas of Jewish autonomism were set out with admirable clarity by its principal ideologist Simon Dubnow. He argued that the Jewish diaspora had always made up a single unit and that its local components had sought and achieved far-reaching autonomy. The concept of national autonomy was based on the assumption that

all sections of the Jewish people, though divided in their political allegiance, form one spiritual or historico-cultural nation, which like all national minority groups in countries with a mixed population, are in duty bound to fight in their several lands at one and the same time, not only for their civil equality but also for their national rights—the autonomy of the Jewish community, school and language . . . The fate of universal Jewry ought not to be bound up with one single centre. We should take into account the historic fact of a multiplicity of centres of which those that have the largest numbers and can boast of the most genuine development of a national Jewish life are entitled to the hegemony of the Jewish people.[53]

Dubnow, who had set up the Jewish People's Party (Folkists) before the war, described his goals in a series of 'letters' on 'the old and new Judaism'.[54] In them, confronted with the rise of intolerant ethno-nationalism in Europe, he argued that the Jews should not establish a rival Jewish 'national egoism'[55] but should cultivate a 'national individualism', which did not aim to deprive other nations of political freedom or cultural autonomy.[56] In a multi-national state, the government was bound to set limits to the autonomy it could concede to individual nationalities, which should not go beyond the point at which such autonomy conflicted with that granted to others.[57] In the Kingdom of Poland, his principal supporter was Noyekh Prilutski who, in 1909, founded the Yiddish daily Der moment to support these views.

Autonomism had more success in independent Lithuania. The first years of Lithuanian independence were marked by a far-reaching experiment in Jewish autonomy which was adopted as official policy for large Jewish communities by the Twelfth Zionist Congress in Karlsbad in September 1921. The experiment attracted wide attention across the Jewish world and was taken as a model by some Jewish politicians in Poland, most notably Yitzhak Grünbaum, leader of the Zionists in the Congress Kingdom and Kresy. Lithuania seemed fertile soil on which to establish a system of Jewish self-government, particularly if the new Lithuania included the major Litvak centres of Vilna and Minsk, as many hoped would be the case.

Jewish autonomy also seemed to be in the interests of the Lithuanians. The bulk of the Lithuanian lands had remained largely agricultural until the First World War. Relations between Jews, who were the principal intermediaries between the town and manor and the countryside, and the mainly peasant Lithuanians took the form of an ambivalent symbiosis. This relationship was largely peaceful and anti-Jewish violence was rare, although, as elsewhere, the relationship was marked by mutual contempt.

During and after the war Lithuanian statesmen had hoped that the Jews would support their claims to Vilna, and, given the multi-ethnic character of the area they wished to incorporate into their emerging state, they believed that Jewish national autonomy would also make it more attractive to their potential Belarusian and German citizens. What the Jews understood by autonomy was clearly set out in the memorandum submitted to the Paris Peace Conference by the Committee of Jewish Delegations. It called for Jewish minorities everywhere to be recognized as autonomous and independent bodies with the right to direct their own religious, cultural, philanthropic, and social institutions. In relation to Lithuania, Jews should be granted full rights in the spheres of politics, economics, and language and should enjoy representation in parliament, courts, and administrative bodies in accordance with their proportion of the population. Jewish autonomy should be based on three sets of institutions: re-established local *kahals*, a Jewish national council, and a ministry for Jewish affairs.

The Lithuanians responded positively to these demands, although they were committed to an ethnic Lithuanian state, because the area they wished to incorporate included substantial numbers of other nationalities. Seeking to gain Jewish support, on 5 August 1919, Augustinas Voldemaras, the Lithuanian foreign minister, presented a memorandum to the Committee of Jewish Delegations at the Paris Peace Conference, drafted by Doctor Simon Rosenbaum, a General Zionist who was the Lithuanian deputy foreign minister. It had four main points: it conceded proportional representation in parliament, the administration, and the judiciary; it established a ministry to deal with Jewish affairs; it granted Jews full rights as citizens and the right to use Yiddish in public life and in governmental institutions; and it gave Jews autonomy in all internal matters including religion, social services, education, and cultural affairs. The *kehilot* and a Jewish national council elected by Jews were to constitute the operating agencies of Jewish autonomy. They were to be governmental bodies, organized on a territorial basis, with the right to issue ordinances that would be binding both on Jews and on the agencies of the Lithuanian government.

It soon became apparent that within Lithuanian Jewry there were very different views about the nature of the autonomy being sought. The Zionists and Folkists saw this as a national project, a means of achieving a form of sovereignty in the diaspora. The Orthodox, organized in Lithuania in the Akhdes party, were above all concerned with religious matters and were uncomfortable with the secular and often anti-religious agenda of the Zionists and Folkists. The Lithuanian parties were also divided. Most supported the autonomous project in the hope that it would assist the country in regaining control of Vilna. While the parties of the left also favoured it on ideological grounds, many on the right, above all the Christian Democrats, were concerned with the extent to which it would dilute the Lithuanian character of the state.

The structures of the autonomist system were put in place in the early 1920s. However, in May 1923 a new government had emerged in Lithuania, effectively controlled by the Christian Democrats, which was determined, in co-operation with the Akhdes party, to bring the system to an end. In March 1924 the government introduced a new law, On Jewish National Communities, which allowed Jews to organize *kehilot* in their places of residence but laid down that 'Lithuanian citizens of Jewish nationality' were not obliged to be members of these bodies. More than one *kehilah* could be established in a locality, and their functions were to be primarily religious. The law rescinded the provisional law giving the *kehilot* the right to tax Jews. *Kehilah* taxes were now not to exceed the amount of state taxes paid in any year. The *kehilot* retained the right to organize intercommunity congresses, which could elect their central councils, but no provision was made for a legally recognized Jewish national council. New *kehilah* elections were scheduled for 1 February 1926.

This law clearly undermined the Jewish autonomous system and was seen by the Zionists and Folkists as the product of collusion between the government and Akhdes. The Jewish National Council convened a Conference of Jewish Communities in September 1925, which proposed a boycott of elections to the new *kehilot*. This boycott proved quite successful, and the minister of the interior was compelled to intervene and compel the *kehilot* to go into liquidation. In order to prevent the property of the *kehilot* from falling into the hands of Akhdes (who were also now becoming known as Agudat Yisrael, as in Poland), the Zionists and Folkists set up two foundations: Ezrah, to which non-religious property was to be transferred, and Adat Yisrael, for religious property. The transfer of property was carried out slowly in the hope that the new parliamentary elections, scheduled for May 1926, would bring a more sympathetic government to power.

The new Populist–Social Democratic coalition government that emerged after these elections was more sympathetic to Jewish interests, but any attempt to re-establish the autonomous system was forestalled by the growing political crisis. Opposition to any concessions to minorities and the left by the government and general dissatisfaction with the functioning of the democratic system led in December 1926 to its overthrow in the coup that brought Antanas Smetona to power. The political system became increasingly autocratic and no longer had any place for Jewish or indeed any sort of autonomy, though the highly developed Jewish private school system and the Jewish co-operative banking system survived. The coup was welcomed by the Orthodox, who now called for the return to their control of Jewish hospitals, homes for the elderly, *mikva'ot*, and cemeteries, which had been handed over to the Adat Yisrael foundation.

The reasons for the collapse of the autonomous experiment in Lithuania are clear. The two sides had unrealistic expectations of each other. The Lithuanians believed that the Jews would aid them in acquiring Vilna and Klaipėda, in attracting Belarusians to a multinational Lithuania, and in reconciling Germans to Lithuanian rule. They had much less need of the Jews in the fairly homogeneous Lithuania that actually emerged, while it soon became clear that Jewish support would not be a significant factor in acquiring Vilna. Also, the more far-reaching goals of the secular Zionist and autonomist parties were seen as suspect by Orthodox political groupings. It may be, too, that there is an inherent contradiction between the basic principles of the liberal state and the guaranteeing of group rights.

Andrei Zamoiski's chapter investigates the extent to which the Jewish soviets set up in Soviet Belarus in the interwar period can be seen as a form of Jewish self-government. Although the Bolsheviks held that the Jews were not a nation and that their long-term fate was clearly to be integrated into the nations in which they lived, they recognized that they possessed some proto-national characteristics. In order to facilitate their integration into the new socialist world, they were prepared for a period to tolerate a specific socialist Jewish identity, expressed through a secularized version of Yiddish and organized on a non-territorial basis. In this respect, the Jews were classed with other non-territorial nations in the Soviet Union, such as Latvians, Poles, Germans, and Estonians.

The central role in running the autonomous Jewish structures and representing the Party to the Jews was entrusted to the prepared Jewish Section of the Communist Party (Evsektsiya) established in 1918. The Evsektsiya's policies had two aspects. It was responsible for the suppression of those aspects of Jewish life which were regarded as anti-Soviet: religion, Zionism, and rival socialist organizations; and for establishing and administering the institutional structure which was to underlie the creation of a socialist Jewish identity. One important part of this was a network of Yiddish schools.

Most shtetl Jews during the civil war had regarded the Bolsheviks as a lesser evil than the Whites, Ukrainian nationalists, and peasant anarchists who had been responsible for the overwhelming majority of the pogroms. However, their support for the new regime was greatly undermined by its anti-religious policies and by the abolition of private trade and the requisitions which were a feature of war communism. In addition, Jews in the shtetl were also very adversely affected by the actions taken against those of 'harmful' social background, who were classed as *lishentsy* and deprived of civil rights, as described by Zamoiski.

Nominally, the shtetls in Belarus and Ukraine were governed by a local soviet, which was often, as Zamoiski points out, seen as a form of Jewish self-government. In line with Soviet encouragement of minority languages, it conducted its affairs in Yiddish and was elected, although many Jews were deprived of the right to vote. By 1930 there were 160 such Jewish national soviets in Ukraine—which included 12 per cent of the Jewish population—and three Jewish oblasts. There were fewer in Belarus, twenty-four Jewish councils in 1932 and four Jewish rural councils.

Zamoiski describes a conflict in 1927 in the shtetl of Kapatkevichy in Polesie over the rebuilding of the *mikveh* between the more conservative older generation of the town and the younger one, committed to building socialism. Such attempts to use religious buildings for secular purposes were typical of the way the younger activists sought to transform the shtetl. Zamoiski also describes the functions of the Jewish soviets and the way new institutions were created to take over the tasks previously carried out by the *kahal*. Thus, for example, non-governmental charity organizations were seen by local and central authorities as 'clerical', and an attempt was made to replace them by 'socialist' mutual aid associations.

By the 1930s it had become clear that the Jewish soviets were not fulfilling the role expected of them by the Soviet authorities. With the intensification of Russification and centralization, the Soviet regime no longer had a need for such 'national' institutions, which had also in many cases aroused the hostility of the local district leadership. As a result, in 1937, the role of soviets in small towns was reorganized and the national soviets abolished.

Zamoiski's conclusion is clear:

Jewish soviets had nothing in common with earlier forms of Jewish self-government. The old and new Jewish elites did operate on the same 'Jewish street' but in competition. Traditional Jewish self-government did not have any possibility of survival under such unfavourable political conditions.

In the early years of Polish independence, the main supporter of autonomist ideas were the Folkists, a Polish version of the party established by Simon Dubnow, headed in Warsaw by the redoubtable Noyekh Prilutski, whose activity during the war is described in Marcos Silber's chapter. Though not opposed to settlement in Palestine, the Folkists held that the Jewish problem in the diaspora would be solved by granting autonomy to Jewish communities: they should have the right to tax themselves, establish their own welfare organizations, and run a network of Jewish schools financed by the government. The party was not hostile to the revival of Hebrew, but argued that Yiddish was the national language of Polish Jews. It was strong, particularly in larger towns, although its support declined in the interwar period from a peak in the two years following the war, partly because the charismatic Prilutski lacked the skills of a practical politician and partly because his group had little support outside the Polish capital.[58]

Autonomism also had support from the Zionists of the Kingdom of Poland and Kresy, organized in the Jewish National Council and led by Yitzhak Grünbaum, as described in the chapters by Marcos Silber and Szymon Rudnicki. Influenced by the acute national conflicts in these areas, Grünbaum demanded full cultural autonomy for the Jews with the right to run their own independent network of schools, established and financed by the state, and called for the transformation of Poland from a 'national state' to a 'state of nationalities'.[59] His position was strongly opposed by the Zionists of Galicia, headed by Leon Reich, who, coming from an area where ethnic conflict was less acute, demanded only full civil rights for Jews in Poland, which they believed could be secured by a direct approach to the Polish government.

Grünbaum constantly stressed the need for a vigorous and uncompromising defence of Jewish national rights—characteristically, the published collection of his articles bears the title *The Wars of Polish Jews*. This led him to advocate the creation of a Bloc of National Minorities before the parliamentary elections of 1922, and he induced a number of non-Zionist Jewish parties, mostly from the former Kingdom of Poland and Kresy, to stand on this platform, in particular the Orthodox Agudat Yisrael and the non-political Union of Merchants. Altogether seventeen deputies were elected from the Jewish parties in the Bloc of National Minorities list in the elections of November 1922.[60]

The east Galician Zionists opposed the creation of the Bloc of National Minorities, both because it would excessively antagonize the Poles and because, in their view, the Jews had no real common interests with the other national minorities. The Ukrainians and Belarusians wanted national independence or territorial autonomy, while the Germans wanted a revision of the Versailles Treaty. The Jews, however, could accept the existing boundaries of Poland: what they needed was the implementation of the rights granted them, especially as they had been guaranteed by both the constitution and the National Minorities Treaty. In addition, the Ukrainians and Belarusians were largely rural, and their economic interests in matters such as taxation were at odds with those of the largely urban Jews.

The situation of the Jews was significantly improved under the non-party government of Władysław Grabski, which took power in December 1923 and which managed to reach an agreement with the Jewish caucus in the sejm. The dispute between Reich and Grünbaum over the correct tactics to use in parliament had, by early 1925, given way to an increasing acceptance of Reich's moderate position. On 5 July 1925 an agreement was reached between him and his deputy Rabbi Ozjasz Thon, on the one hand, and Foreign Minister Aleksander Skrzyński and the minister for education and religious affairs, the Endek, Stanisław Grabski (brother of Władysław), on the other.[61] The Jewish caucus issued a statement in which it 'firmly [upheld] the principle of the integrity of Poland, and its interests as a Great Power',[62] in return for which the government promised to introduce a number of measures to alleviate the position of the Jews. Primary schools with Yiddish as the language of instruction were to be established; Jews in schools and in the army would not be placed in a position which would compel them to violate their religious beliefs; Yiddish and Hebrew could be employed at public meetings; and the local Jewish system of community organization (the *kahal*) was to be extended over the whole country and democratized.[63] In addition, Skrzyński wrote a letter to Nahum Sokolow of the World Zionist Congress expressing support for the creation of a Jewish national centre in Palestine.[64]

The agreement aroused much opposition in the Jewish caucus, but was finally accepted. However, when it was published after some delay the government stated that it intended to implement only those issues relating to cultural and religious matters and not those dealing with the political and economic grievances of the Jews. The government's apparent bad faith led Reich to resign as leader of the Jewish caucus, to be succeeded by the more radical Apolinary Hartglas, who was close to Grünbaum.

The situation changed considerably with the coup that brought Piłsudski back to power in May 1926. The post-coup government sought now to improve relations with all the national minorities and, regarding the Jews, to oppose economic antisemitism and ensure adequate credits for Jewish trade. The law on compulsory Sunday rest would be modified and all still-existing laws which discriminated against Jews would be abrogated. Zionism would be supported, and Jewish community structures reorganized. State primary Yiddish-language schools were to be created and government aid would be provided to Jewish private schools. Finally, pressure would be exerted on the universities to do away with the unofficial *numerus clausus* (the restriction on the number of Jews admitted).

Some attempts were made to implement this new policy, and the Jewish political leadership responded favourably to the government's initiatives. However, as so often happens, good intentions were not enough. The government could do little against economic antisemitism; it did not provide funds for Jewish private schools; and the *numerus clausus* was still applied in practice. Nevertheless, the different Jewish factions in parliament were generally satisfied with government behaviour in the 1920s, regarding the Piłsudski regime as far better than the alternatives, whether of the right or of the left.[65] Under these circumstances support for radical confrontational policies and for national–personal autonomy waned considerably.

National–personal autonomy was always a somewhat utopian project. It aroused strong opposition from Orthodox religious groupings who rejected its emphasis on diaspora nationalism, highlighting the secular/religious divide in the community. It was also anathema to large sections of Polish, Ukrainian, and Lithuanian society, as it raised fears of diluting the national character of their states. Ultimately, with its commitment to imposing a national identity on all Jews except those who opted out and to conferring on the local *kehilot* the right to tax those Jews, it was probably incompatible with the principles of liberalism and of a civil society.

Under these circumstances, the actions of local *kehilot* and Jewish involvement in municipal affairs in the towns where they lived became more fruitful expressions of Jewish self-government. Polish independence made possible the creation of a single uniform system of Jewish self-government for the nearly 900 *kehilot* in the country. In his chapter, Antony Polonsky examines how they functioned in the interwar years. He also investigates the role of Jewish councillors in the various municipalities of independent Poland and the role of Jewish members of the sejm, a topic also discussed by Szymon Rudnicki.

Conclusion

The pre-partition system of Jewish self-government has been variously evaluated. According to Shmuel Ettinger, it is 'no wonder, therefore, that the Council of the Lands was regarded as the greatest expression of Jewish aspirations towards self-rule since the institution of the Gaonate came to an end'.[66] This view was not always shared. According to Emanuel Ringelblum, a supporter of the revolutionary Po'alei Tsiyon Left group:

Our historians like to portray Jewish autonomy in old Poland as the finest jewel [in the crown] of [Polish Jewry]. In fact, however, there were many [terrible] aspects . . . of the Jewish autonomous organs. Everywhere power lay in the hands of a clique of despots who treated communal assets as if they were their own private property . . . The abuses and the robbery of the *kehilah* barons who ruled over the Jewish masses for hundreds of years, was a sad chapter in the history of the Jewish collective.[67]

The long history of Jewish autonomous organizations in pre-partition Poland–Lithuania accustomed Jews to working in representative bodies. Government attempts to reform or even to abolish Jewish self-government in the nineteenth century led to the emergence of very different systems in the different partitions, some more and some less effective. Everywhere Jewish self-government persisted and from the late nineteenth century was seen as the basis for a system of Jewish national autonomy. Although it proved incapable of implementation both in Poland and in Lithuania, *kehilot* continued to function and acquired new responsibilities. Jews were also represented both in parliament and on municipal councils. It is clear that the long tradition of Jewish self-government had a significant impact on the Jewish commitment to representative government elsewhere, above all in Israel. It does also seem, paradoxically, that participation in Polish and Lithuanian parliamentary life and, even more, engagement in local government in both countries, even for those parties committed to a national understanding of the Jewish identity, was more fruitful and brought greater results.

Notes

1   Y. Gutman and C. J. Haft (eds.), *Patterns of Jewish Leadership in Nazi Europe, 1933–45: Proceedings of the Third Yad Vashem International Historical Conference, Jerusalem, April 4–7, 1977* (Jerusalem, 1977); J. Trunk, *Judenrat: The Jewish Councils in Eastern Europe under Nazi Occupation* (New York, 1972); S. Kassow, *Who Will Write Our History? Emanuel Ringelblum, the Warsaw Ghetto, and the Oyneg Shabbes Archive* (Bloomington, Ind., 2007).

2   M. Janowski, *Polish Liberal Thought before 1918* (Budapest, 2004), 1.

3   S. W. Baron, *The Jewish Community: Its History and Structure to the American Revolution*, 3 vols. (New York, 1942), i. 22.

4   See *Jewish Privileges in the Polish Commonwealth: Charters of Rights Granted to Jewish Communities in Poland–Lithuania in the Sixteenth to Eighteenth Centuries*, ed. J. Goldberg, 3 vols. (Jerusalem, 1985–2001).

5   The charter of 1264 has not been preserved, but the introduction to the privilege granted by Kazimierz the Great in 1334 states that it is a confirmation of the earlier document (B. D. Weinryb, *A Social and Economic History of the Jewish Community in Poland* (Philadelphia, 1976), 339 n. 1). The privileges were collected by the Polish Chancellor Jan Łaski in 1506. For the general charters, see M. Schorr, 'Krakovskii svod statutov i privilegii', *Evreiskaya starina*, 1909, no. 1, pp. 247–64; no. 3, pp. 76–100; no. 4, pp. 223–45; id., 'Zasadnicze prawa Żydów w Polsce przedrozbiorowej', in I. Schiper, A. Tartakower, and A. Hafftka (eds.), *Żydzi w Polsce Odrodzonej: Działalność społeczna, gospodarcza, oświatowa i kulturalna*, 2 vols. (Warsaw, 1932–3), i. 191–9; M. Bałaban, 'Pravovoi stroi evreev v Pol'she v srednie i novye veka', *Evreiskaya starina*, 1910, no. 2, pp. 38–69, 161–91; L. Gumplowicz, *Prawodawstwo polskie względem Żydów* (Kraków, 1867); P. Bloch, *Die General Privilegien der Polnischen Judenschaft* (Poznań, 1892). For a full English translation of the charter as ratified by Kazimierz IV Jagiellończyk in 1453, see F. Guesnet and J. Tomaszewski (eds.), *Sources on Jewish Self-Government in the Polish Lands from Its Inception to the Present: A Source Reader* (Boston, Mass., forthcoming).

6   See S. Lazutka and E. Gudavicius, *Privilege to Jews Granted by Vytautas the Great in 1388* (Moscow, 1993).

7   M. Bałaban, 'Die Krakauer Judengemeinde-Ordnung von 1595 und ihre Nachträge', *Jahrbuch der Jüdisch-Literarischen Gesellschaft*, 10 (1913), 296–360; 11 (1916), 88–114: 309.

8   See G. D. Hundert, *Jews in Poland–Lithuania in the Eighteenth Century: A Genealogy of Modernity* (Berkeley, Calif., 2004), 83.

9   On the *ḥevrah kadisha* in Vilna, see I. Cohen, *Vilna* (Philadelphia, 1943), 124–9.

10 J. D. Klier, *Imperial Russia's Jewish Question, 1855–1881* (Cambridge, 2005), 263–83.

11 On the functions of the rabbi, see M. Rosman, *The Lords' Jews: Magnate–Jewish Relations in the Polish–Lithuanian Commonwealth during the Eighteenth Century* (Cambridge, Mass., 1990), 198–9; A. Teller, 'The Laicization of Early Modern Jewish Society: The Development of the Polish Communal Rabbinate in the 16th Century', in M. Graetz (ed.), *Schöpferische Momente des europäischen Judentums in der frühen Neuzeit* (Heidelberg, 2000), 333–49.

12 For the position of the rabbinate, see Hundert, *Jews in Poland–Lithuania in the Eighteenth Century*, 84–6.

13 See *The Jewish Encyclopedia*, 12 vols. (New York, 1904–10), x. 141.

14 See D. Fishman, *Russia's First Modern Jews: The Jews of Shklov* (New York, 1995), 2–3; I. Trunk, 'Der va'ad medinas rusiya (raysn)', *YIVO bleter*, 40 (1956), 63–85; S. Mstislavski [S. Dubnow], 'Oblastnye kagal'nye seimy v voevodstve Volynskim i v Belorussii (1666–1764), *Voskhod*, 14/4 (1894), 24–42; *Pinkas hamedinah, o pinkas va'ad hakehilot harashiyot bimedinat lita*, ed. S. Dubnow (Berlin, 1925), no. 949; P. Marek, 'Beloruskaya synagoga i ee territoriya', *Voskhod*, 23/5 (1903), 71–82.

15 For the minutes of the Council of Four Lands, see *Pinkas va'ad arba aratsot: likutei takanot ketavim ureshumot*, ed. I. Halperin (Jerusalem, 1945); 2nd rev. edn., ed. I. Bartal (Jerusalem, 1990); for those of the Council of Lithuania, see *Pinkas hamedinah*; see also M. Rosman, 'A Minority Views the Majority: Jewish Attitudes towards the Polish–Lithuanian Commonwealth and Interaction with Poles', *Polin*, 4 (1989), 31–41; J. Goldberg, 'The Jewish Sejm: Its Origins and Functions', in A. Polonsky, J. Basista, and A. Link-Lenczowski (eds.), *The Jews in Old Poland, 1000–1795* (London, 1993), 147–64.

16 N. Hanover, *Abyss of Despair*, trans. A. Mesch (New Brunswick, NJ, 1950), 119–20.

17 See B. Dinur, *Bemifneh hadorot* (Jerusalem, 1972), 100, 104; R. Mahler, *Toledot hayehudim bepolin: kalkalah, ḥevrah, hamatsav hamishpati* (Merhavia, 1946).

18 See H. Kołłątaj, *Listy Anonima i Prawo polityczne narodu polskiego*, ed. B. Leśnodorski and H. Wereszycka, 2 vols. (Kraków, 1954).

19 'O zniesienie Sejmu żydowskiego instabat', *Diarjusze sejmowe z wieku XVIII*, 3 vols. (Warsaw, 1911–37), ii. 76, 78, 127, 160, 175–7, 180, 251; iii. 69–70, 8.

20 *Pinkas va'ad arba aratsot*, p. xli, no. 43.

21 L. Lewin, 'Ein Judentag aus Süd- und Neuostpreußen', *Monatsschrift für die Geschichte und Wissenschaft des Judentums*, 59 (1915), 180–92, 278–300.

22 P. Bloch, 'Judenwesen', in R. Prümers (ed.), *Das Jahr 1793: Urkunde und Aktenstücke zur Geschichte der Organisation Südpreußen* (Poznań, 1895), 591–605: 600–1 n. 3.

23 Geheimes Staatsarchiv, Berlin, I. HA, Rep. 90, no. 33, fos. 168–71: Oberpräsident Flottwell, letter to Secretary of the Interior Brenn, 5 Oct. 1832.

24 'Vorläufigen Verordnung wegen des Judenwesens im Großherzogtum Posen', in L. von Rönne and H. Simon, *Die früheren und gegenwärtige Verhältnisse der Juden in den sämmtlichen Landestheilen des preussischen Staates* (Breslau, 1843), 305–9; repr. in S. Kemlein, *Die*

Posener Juden, 1815–1848: Entwicklungsprozesse einer polnischen Judenheit unter preussischer Herrschaft (Hamburg, 1997), 331–7.

25 For the origins of this regulation, see Kemlein, *Die Posener Juden*, 96–9.

26 Oberpräsident Flottwell, instruction to the royal government of Poznań and Bydgoszcz to ensure the implementation of the decree of 1 June (14 Jan. 1834), in Rönne and Simon, *Die Verhältnisse der Juden*, 309–14.

27 M. Laubert, 'Zur Entwicklung des jüdischen Schulwesens in der Provinz Posen', *Zeitschrift für die Geschichte der Juden in Deutschland*, 2/4 (1930), 304–21: 313.

28 See M. Raeff, 'The Well-Ordered Police State and the Development of Modernity in Seventeenth and Eighteenth Century Europe: An Attempt at a Comparative Approach', *American Historical Review*, 80 (1975), 1221–43; id., *The Well-Ordered Police State: Social and Institutional Change through Law in the Germanies and Russia, 1600–1800* (New Haven, Conn., 1983).

29 See esp. W. McCagg, *A History of Habsburg Jews, 1670–1918* (Bloomington, Ind., 1989); J. Karniel, 'Das Toleranzpatent Josephs II. für Juden Galiziens und Lodomeriens', *Jahrbuch des Instituts für Deutsche Geschichte*, 11 (1982), 55–89.

30 On its origins, see J. Karniel, 'Fürst Kaunitz und die Juden', *Jahrbuch des Instituts für Deutsche Geschichte*, 12 (1983), 15–27: 22–3.

31 Quoted in M. Bałaban, *Dzieje Żydów w Galicyi i w Rzeczypospolitej Krakowskiej 1772–1868* (Lwów, 1914), 47.

32 Ibid. 35–55.

33 Ibid. 32–4, 150.

34 See Bałaban, *Dzieje Żydów w Galicji*, 110; W. Bartel, *Ustrój i prawo Wolnego Miasta Krakowa 1815–1846* (Kraków, 1976).

35 F. Friedmann, 'Die Judenfrage im galizischen Landtag', in *Monatschrift für Geschichte des Judentums* 72 (1927), 457–77: 473.

36 See A. Żbikowski, *Żydzi krakowscy i ich gmina w latach 1869–1919* (Warsaw, 1994), 109–34.

37 A. Eisenbach, *Kwestia równouprawnienia Żydów w Królestwie Polskim* (Warsaw, 1972), 30; Yu. Gessen, *Istoriya evreiskogo naroda v Rossii*, 2 vols. (Leningrad, 1925–7), i. 222–3.

38 For the restrictions on the Jews, see Eisenbach, *Kwestia równouprawnienia Żydów w Królestwie Polskim*, ch. 1; id., 'Mobilność terytorialna ludności żydowskiej w Królestwie Polskim', in W. Kula and J. Leskiewiczowa (eds.), *Społeczeństwo Królestwa Polskiego*, iii (Warsaw, 1966), 177–316.

39 Gessen, *Istoriya evreiskogo naroda v Rossii*, i. 231; Eisenbach, *Kwestia równouprawnienia Żydów w Królestwie Polskim*, 36.

40 In 1824, of an income of approximately 23,000 zlotys, the Burial Administration provided 17,000 (F. Guesnet, *Polnische Juden im 19. Jahrhundert: Lebensbedingungen, Rechtsnormen und Organisation im Wandel* (Cologne, 1998), 370).

41 Ibid. 371.

42 I. Schiper, *Żydzi Królestwa Polskiego w dobie powstania listopadowego* (Warsaw, 1932), 43.

43 D. Szterenkac, 'Zniesienia kahałów i utworzenie dozorów bóżniczych (w pierwszych latach Królestwa Polskiego)', MA thesis (University of Warsaw, n.d.), 71.

44 On the terms of the emancipation, see Guesnet, *Polnische Juden*, 52; Eisenbach, *Kwestia równouprawnienia Żydów w Królestwie Polskim*, 510–13.

45 V. O. Levanda, *Polnyi khronologicheskii sbornik zakonov i polozhenii, kasayushchikhsya evreev* (St Petersburg, 1874), 391, no. 16.

46 For the statute, see *Polnoe sobranie zakonov Rossiiskoi imperii*, 1/xxviii, no. 21547 (9 Dec. 1804).

47 Ibid.

48 Quoted in Klier, *Imperial Russia's Jewish Question, 1885–1881*, 15.

49 G. Sliozberg, *Dela minuvshikh dnei: Zapiski russkogo evreya*, 3 vols. (Paris, 1933–4), iii. 188.

50 I. Halperin, 'Hakdamah', in *Pinkas va'ad arba aratsot*, 8.

51 K. Renner, *Staat und Nation* (Vienna, 1899); O. Bauer, *Die Nationalitätenfrage und die Sozialdemokratie* (Vienna, 1907).

52 Bauer, *Die Nationalitätenfrage und die Sozialdemokratie*, pp. i–ii.

53 S. Dubnow, *A History of the Jews in Russia and Poland*, 3 vols. (Philadelphia, 1920), iii. 54–5.

54 S. Dubnow, *Pis'ma o starom i novom evreistve (1897–1907)* (St Petersburg, 1907); Eng. trans.: *Nationalism and History: Essays on Old and New Judaism*, ed. K. S. Pinson (Philadelphia, 1958).

55 See J. Veidlinger, 'Simon Dubnow Recontextualized: The Sociological Conception of Jewish History and the Russian Intellectual Legacy', *Jahrbuch des Simon-Dubnow-Instituts*, 3 (2004), 411–27: 425.

56 S. Dubnow, 'Pis'mo tret'e: Etika natsionalizma', in id., *Pis'ma o starom i novom evreistve*, 53–73: 61; id., 'Third Letter: The Ethics of Nationalism', in id. *Nationalism and History*, 116–30: 121.

57 Dubnow, 'Pis'mo tret'e', 62; id., 'Third Letter', 122.

58 See K. Weiser, *Jewish People, Yiddish Nation. Noyekh Prilutski and the Folkists in Poland* (Toronto, 2011); M. Silber, *Le'umiyut shonah, ezraḥut shavah! hama'avak lehasagat otonomyah liyehudei polin bemilḥemet ha'olam harishonah* (Tel Aviv, 2014); A. Hafftka, 'Żydowskie stronnictwa polityczne w Polsce Odrodzonej', in Schiper, Tartakower, and Hafftka (eds.), *Żydzi w Polsce Odrodzonej*, ii. 268–9.

59 Hafftka, 'Żydowskie stronnictwa polityczne w Polsce Odrodzonej', For Grünbaum's views, see I. Grünbaum, *Milḥamot yehudei polanyah* (Jerusalem, 1946); R. Frister, *Lelo pesharah* (Tel Aviv, 1987).

60 Hafftka, 'Życie parlamentarne Żydów w Polsce Odrodzonej', 293; see also Grünbaum, *Milḥamot yehudei polanyah*.

61 Wolf's account of his mission is to be found in the Archives of the Board of Deputies of British Jews, London Metropolitan Archives; Reich's account of the negotiations is in the Reich papers in the Central Zionist Archives, Jerusalem. There is an extensive literature on the agreement (see M. Landau, 'Mekomah shel ha'ugoda (mishenat 1925) bemasekhet hayaḥasim haḥadadiyim polanim-yehudim', *Zion*, 37 (1972), 66–110; P. Korzec, 'Das Abkommen zwischen der Regierung Grabski und der jüdischen Parlamentsvertretung', *Jahrbücher für Geschichte Osteuropas*, 20/3 (1972), 331–66; E. Mendelsohn, 'Reflections on the Ugoda', in S. Yeivin (ed.), *Sefer rafa'el mahler: kovets meḥkarim betoledot yisra'el, mugash lo bimelot lo shivim veḥamesh shanah* (Merhavia, 1974), 87–102; J. Tomaszewski, 'Władysław Grabski wobec kwestii żydowskiej', *Biuletyn Żydowskiego Instytutu Historycznego*, 161 (1992), 35–51). The best account of their course is to be found in S. Rudnicki, *Żydzi w parlamencie II Rzeczypospolitej* (Warsaw, 2004), 175–88.

62 *Nasz Przegląd*, 1 July 1925.

63 For the terms of the agreement, as published by the government, see *Robotnik*, 12 July 1925.

64 *Nasz Przegląd*, 2 July 1925.

65 On the disputes among Jewish sejm deputies, see Rudnicki, *Żydzi w parlamencie II Rzeczypospolitej*, 261–75.

66 S. Ettinger, 'The Council of Four Lands', in Polonsky, Basista, and Link-Lenczowski (eds.), *The Jews in Old Poland*, 93–109: 94.

67 Quoted in S. Kassow, *Who Will Write Our History?*, 75.

The Transfer of Tradition from West to East

The Takanot Shum between the Rhineland and Poland in the Late Middle Ages and the Early Modern Period

RAINER JOSEF BARZEN

THE PRESENCE of Jews in Poland has been documented since the eleventh century. The first Jewish migrants probably entered what became the Kingdom of Poland mainly from south-eastern Europe. Between the twelfth and fourteenth centuries they were joined by Jews from the Holy Roman Empire. This Ashkenazi immigration into Poland has been frequently discussed. Its consequence was the establishment of a community with an Ashkenazi character, which, over time, became a part of the Ashkenazi cultural sphere. These processes can be observed in the migration of *takanot* (halakhic community ordinances) from the French and German lands to the Polish lands. From the late Middle Ages these ordinances were known as the Takanot Shum, the ordinances of the 'Shum' communities—Speyer, Worms, and Mainz—in the Rhineland. Their migration from west to east is a particularly fruitful field of investigation because it covers two different areas of Jewish culture. On the one hand, *takanot* are halakhic texts with a legal character, the creation of which requires one or more scholars. On the other hand, they also have a constitutional and political character since their implementation requires the support of the leadership of the Jewish community. The theory and practice of formulating social rules, as well as their introduction and transmission, are thus a key element of the cultural transfer from the Jews of the west to the Jews in Poland.

The Beginnings of Ashkenazi Immigration

The significance of the transfer of such ordinances and the changes that can be observed because of it derive from the fact that the earliest Jewish communities in Poland were not of Ashkenazi origin. Israel Ta-Shma and others have shown that, at the latest, from the twelfth century small Jewish centres were established in the south of the newly established Kingdom of Poland, in Kraków and Wrocław.[1] Their origin is to be sought in the east (Kiev and also perhaps the Khazar kingdom and Byzantium).[2] Contacts with individual members of these communities during the twelfth century[3] and with their representatives and sages during the thirteenth century[4] are documented by the responsa of western Jewish sages, who in turn were active in communities along the transitional zone between the German-speaking and Slavonic worlds.[5]

This border area was also significant for the Jewish settlement of eastern Europe. Thus, the Hebrew versions of Slavonic women's names on the thirteenth-century tombstones in the Jewish cemetery in Spandau show that the Jewish communities of the new settlement area in the east of the Holy Roman Empire were still part of a Slavonic environment.[6] Culturally they were not yet part of the Ashkenazi world, the communities in the western part of the Holy Roman Empire. Yet a reshaping of these communities through the influence of Ashkenazi intellectuals and their students was in full force, as is shown in the works of sages from the communities of 'Germania Slavica' (or 'Erets Kena'an').[7] This reshaping was not solely an intellectual phenomenon but was accompanied by a population movement from west to east. This Jewish settlement took place as part of a general German migration eastwards and brought new Jewish communities to locations with existing Jewish populations as well as those without.[8]

The Transformation of Jewish Society in Poland

Jewish settlement continued in the fourteenth century and did not stop at the Polish border, even though the numbers who settled in the Kingdom of Poland were not as great as those in the east German lands. Certainly, after the thirteenth century, the immigration of Ashkenazi Jews to Poland could not be attributed solely to the persecutions in the first half of the fourteenth century. These may have increased the number of Jewish immigrants, but they actually only strengthened a general trend. The new immigrants first settled in existing Jewish communities such as Kraków,[9] Płock,[10] and Kalisz,[11] and subsequently in newly founded communities, such as Lublin,[12] Lwów (Lviv),[13] and Poznań.[14] They took with them their ideas of community organization and halakhic understanding which were in various ways at odds with those of the already existing Jewish communities. Elchanan Reiner has provided a wealth of information about the co-existence of the established Jewish community and the new Jewish migrants in Kraków and Kazimierz. Jewish immigration from the west, especially from Prague and Bohemia, led to the establishment of a second, 'Bohemian' community in Kraków and Kazimierz in the fifteenth century alongside the already long-existing Polish Jewish community. This new community had its own rabbi, Rabbi Perets, and its own independent organization, customs, and judicial authorities, which the migrants brought with them from the west. In the course of the fifteenth century these differences led to bitter conflicts between the two Jewish communities over who should hold the leading positions, which culminated in a battle for the control of the main synagogue, the Altschul in Kazimierz. For a brief time the Polish king was called in to mediate.[15] These conflicts can be traced back to changes in the social composition of immigrants in the fifteenth century. In the thirteenth and fourteenth centuries Jewish immigrants were still mainly from the lower social classes of their original communities in the German lands and were willing to adapt to the existing customs in Poland. In the fifteenth century the increasingly difficult conditions,[16] which led to expulsions from most parts of the German lands by the end of the century, affected the leading social classes of the large urban communities. These people increasingly sought refuge in Poland, first in Poznań and subsequently in Kraków.[17] Their economic power and thus, from their perspective, their intellectual and cultural superiority, would in a few generations lead to the original Jewish communities coming under the control of the Ashkenazi immigrants.[18] This process gradually transformed the existing Polish Jewish traditions so that Polish Jewry became more and more part of the Ashkenazi world.

The situation in Kraków, in which a second community developed parallel to the original community as a result of immigration, also occurred elsewhere. For example, in the thirteenth century in Prague Ashkenazi immigrants encountered Czech-speaking local Jewish residents.[19] In Strassburg (Strasbourg), the expulsion of Jews from the Kingdom of France into the Holy Roman Empire in 1306 led to a differentiation between 'Welschen' (French-speaking) and 'Tutschen' (German-speaking) Jews.[20] There is good reason to postulate the parallel existence of an old 'Ruthenian' Jewish community and a new community of Ashkenazi immigrants in fourteenth-century Lwów (Lviv).[21] It can be also assumed that in other locations, such as Magdeburg, Meissen, and Vienna, local, non-Ashkenazi Jews were faced with Ashkenazi immigrants as part of the thirteenth- and fourteenth-century Jewish population movements. This area requires further investigation.

The Takanot Shum as an Example

The migration of halakhic traditions to the new areas of Ashkenazi settlement in Italy and Poland was strongly connected to the mobility of scholars.[22] Hebrew manuscripts played a decisive role in this migration. These included 'manuals' of halakhic works compiled for personal use, often containing *takanot*, which were then used in the new communities as a prototype for the community administration that was now necessary. The migration of *takanot* from the communities of Speyer, Worms, and Mainz to Italy can be documented through manuscripts that reached northern Italy along with their owner, Hayim Rapp Zoten (Teufel), in the fifteenth century from Mainz.[23]

Jewish immigrants in the late fourteenth and fifteenth centuries must have taken Hebrew manuscripts to their new homes in the Kingdom of Poland. The Takanot Shum were probably transported to Poland by Moses Minz, a highly prominent bearer of Ashkenazi tradition. He was the former rabbi of Mainz,[24] who went to Landau and then Bamberg (1468) after the expulsion of his community in 1462 and finally settled in Poznań in 1474.[25] His published responsa contain two different sets of *takanot* from the Shum communities. These two sets of *takanot* have a specific transmission history in Poland and other east European countries. In this respect, the form that the cultural transfer from Germany to Poland took was different from comparable phenomena of cultural transfer, such as the migration of French *takanot* to the Rhineland in the twelfth and thirteenth centuries, since it took place after the development of printing.[26] The *editio princeps* of Moses Minz's responsa appeared in Kraków in 1517.[27] It remains to be clarified whether the dissemination of the two sets of *takanot* goes back to this edition alone, or if other manuscripts from the German lands could have played a role. Moses Minz integrated the two sets of *takanot* at different places in his responsa. The first set is a revision or adaptation of early thirteenth-century *takanot* concerning *yibum vehalitsah*, the ritual removal of a shoe when a levirate marriage is not possible (Deut. 25: 5–10).[28] The original text was from the early thirteenth century and goes back to David ben Kalonymos of Münzenberg. It had been passed down since then along with other collections of *takanot* as part of the *takanot* of Speyer, Worms, and Mainz.[29] In 1381 a revised version of these *takanot* was enacted again for these communities and beyond.[30] The second set of *takanot* from the Shum communities occurs almost at the end of Minz's responsa. This is the complete set of Takanot Shum as they must have existed since the fourteenth century.[31]

Solomon Luria and the Takanot Shum on Levirate Marriage

The Takanot Shum of 1381 have a complex reception history in Poland. Solomon Luria (c.1510–73), in his halakhic work *Yam shel shelomoh*,[32] quotes the *takanot* on levirate marriage almost completely, but based his quotations not on the printed version of Moses Minz but on one or more manuscripts.[33] A closer look at his family background may give a few hints as to how such manuscripts could have been available to him. Luria,[34] along with Moses Isserles (c.1520–72),[35] a student of the great 'Polish' Jewish scholar Shalom Shakhna (c.1495–1558),[36] came from an old Ashkenazi family, which can be traced back to the fourteenth century.[37] Solomon was the fourth generation of the Luria family to have settled in Poland–Lithuania. His great-grandfather Yehiel Luria moved from southern Germany to Brest (Brisk): he is the first rabbi of Brest to be known by name.[38] His great-grandfather's brother, Yohanan Luria (c.1440–c.1514), who stayed in Germany, had moved to Alsace and was a rabbi and head of a yeshiva.[39] Yehiel's father, Aaron Luria,[40] stayed in Germany with his father-in-law, Solomon Shapira, in Landau near Speyer, and was also a rabbi.[41] He maintained a correspondence with Moses Minz, which Minz continued with Aaron's son and Yehiel's brother, Yohanan Luria.[42] Thus Solomon Luria's great-grandfather Yehiel Luria and Moses Minz were of the same generation, that which finally turned its back on Germany and settled in Poland. Yehiel's son, Abraham Luria,[43] was the head of the rabbinical court in Brest. Abraham's son, Yehiel Luria,[44] who was Solomon Luria's father, also lived in Brest before he became the head of the rabbinical court in Słuck (Slutsk).[45] His early death may have been the reason why Solomon Luria lived with his maternal grandfather, Isaac Klauber (Kloiber),[46] in Poznań. Isaac himself had moved to Poznań from the Rhineland, probably from Worms.[47] So Solomon Luria was descended from German immigrants on both sides of his family, families that had lived in Worms, Speyer, or at least very close to one of the Shum communities. Therefore it is quite possible that Luria had access to manuscripts of the *takanot* of 1381.

Comparison of the *takanot* on levirate marriage in Minz's and Luria's texts shows that the two authors had different reasons for including them. The text in Minz's responsa can be subdivided into seven sections that follow the redaction process from the thirteenth century to the version included in the Takanot Shum and includes the signatures of the witnesses of their renewal in 1381. This text was probably not compiled by Minz, as it is known in this form in several manuscripts.[48] So Minz has presented a source text in the best sense.

The *takanot* on levirate marriage in Solomon Luria's *Yam shel shelomoh* are also divided into seven sections. However, Luria's interest lay in whether or not the *takanot* were applicable to his own time, and the divisions are dictated by the other writers he engaged with. In the first two sections he quotes Meir ben Barukh of Rothenburg[49] and Israel Isserlein[50] on their understanding of these *takanot*.[51] In the third section, he presents the text of the *takanot*. This section can be divided into three subsections: the thirteenth-century *takanot* on levirate marriage and a list of signatures;[52] a commentary by Meir of Rothenburg in which Luria refers to the ordinances as *takanot shel shum*, 'ordinances of Shum';[53] and the 1381 revision of the *takanot* on levirate marriage with the list of signatures from that version.[54]

The texts from the three subsections correspond to the versions of the *takanot* on levirate marriage as they are known from the comprehensive and final edition of the Takanot Shum and the separate transmissions of the *takanot* on levirate marriage; however, Luria's versions are shorter. Up to five lines of subsection 3: 1 are missing, and the subsequent sentences lead to the assumption that the text was shortened deliberately. The list of signatures following the *takanot* text was shortened, and Meir of Rothenburg's addendum, which follows the list and comprises subsection 3: 2, is known from the 1381 versions,[55] but not from the complete version of the Takanot Shum. Luria follows Meir of Rothenburg's addendum with a short remark of his own about where the text was found.[56] The text in subsection 3: 3 is almost half its original length and the signature list is also shorter.[57] The three subsections correspond in their sequence to the *takanot* of 1381; nevertheless, it cannot be ruled out that Luria added the third subsection to his text on the basis of another manuscript.[58] What is certain is that Luria did not use any version of the complete Takanot Shum, whether in manuscript or in print, in Moses Minz's responsa, since Meir of Rothenburg's addendum is not present in any of these versions. Textual variants between Minz's printed version and the manuscripts of the 1381 text also show that in the case discussed here the printed version was not used as a reference by Solomon Luria.

Solomon Luria's work was not distributed widely during his lifetime, and *Yam shel shelomoh* was first published only in the eighteenth century. Whether or not the *takanot* were applied in a community in Poland requires further investigation. However, the reception of the *takanot* on levirate marriage by Solomon Luria remains a scholarly reception in a legal context, not a community one.

Moses Minz and the Takanot Shum on the 'Return of the Dowry'

The reception of the second set of *takanot* transmitted by Moses Minz was different. Until now it has been impossible to trace the direct transmission of the text, completely or partially, as part of the *takanot* of a specific Polish community—from late sixteenth-century Kraków, for example—as this text of the Takanot Shum followed its own linguistic conventions without any earlier model.[59] Maybe this lack of documented history is the result of manuscripts not surviving and needs further investigation. That it was not uncommon to pass on legal texts of this sort can be seen from the history of the privileges granted to the Jewish communities by the Polish king[60] or from legal agreements between Polish cities and their Jewish communities:[61] both were based on models from the German lands.

However, a section of the Takanot Shum included in Minz's responsa was accepted in Poland, and not only in limited scholarly circles but in a practical community context. These were the *takanot* on the return of the dowry, which had been authorized by Rabbenu Tam (*c.*1100–71) and integrated into the Takanot Shum in the early thirteenth century. They regulate the return of the dowry to the bride's father if his daughter dies within two years of marriage without any descendants.[62]

Moses Isserles (*c.*1520–72) of Kraków decided to include the *takanot* on the return of the dowry in his *Mapah*, a commentary on the *Shulḥan arukh*. In chapter 53 of the section 'Even ha'ezer', he added two paragraphs to Joseph Karo's text as part of his commentary, which he expressly attributed to Rabbenu Tam.[63] The contents of the second paragraph correspond to the known *takanot* on the return of the dowry. The first sentence of this section is as follows:

The father's or the heir's [claim] that half of the dowry must be repaid can even be confirmed in the second year of marriage ...

This is the custom in the lands that act according to the *Takanot kehilot shum*.[64]

Isserles' text corresponds to the content of the *takanot* but not to their literal wording as preserved in two traditions of the Takanot Shum that also include the Rhenish modification of Rabbenu Tam's original ruling.[65] However, it is possible that Isserles used another manuscript. Only two such manuscripts have been preserved,[66] and it seems more plausible that Isserles knew the fuller version of the Takanot Shum, including Rabbenu Tam's ruling and its Rhenish modification, from Minz's responsa.[67] Thus, the version in Isserles' *Mapah* goes back to a printed book.

In order to understand the significance of the integration of the French–Rhenish *takanot* into the *Mapah*, it needs to be interpreted in light of the literary work of Moses Isserles. It may seem that there is little difference between Moses Isserles' and Solomon Luria's origins and education. Isserles also came from a German immigrant family,[68] and studied with Solomon Luria under Shalom Shakhna in Lublin. However, his attitude to his own writings was completely different from that of the scholars of the previous generation. Neither Shakhna nor his teacher, Jacob Pollak (c.1460–after 1532),[69] the first known great scholar of early modern Polish Jewry, left any writings. Luria and Isserles' contemporaries interpreted this reticence to formulate and disseminate their own personal opinions, especially regarding the Ashkenazi tradition, as a sign of modesty and respect for their predecessors.[70] While Solomon Luria did produce his own writings, they were only printed and disseminated on a large scale after his death,[71] Moses Isserles did not feel bound by this convention. He wrote legal works within the Ashkenazi tradition, such as *Torat hahatat*, which were intended to replace standard works such as *Sha'arei dura* by Isaac ben Meir of Düren (fourteenth century).[72] He addressed his contemporary Jewish society in Poland and even discussed local Jewish legislation—for which another German Jewish scholar, Hayim ben Bezalel of Friedberg (1520–88), later criticized him.[73] Isserles' inclusion of local precedents in his legal thinking required his works to be published as soon as possible. This accelerated the transition from an oral tradition based on the authority of venerable teachers to a written tradition based on books, which made knowledge accessible to a broader readership.[74] It also facilitated a distancing from the old Ashkenazi world of the German lands. The here and now of his Polish present was closer to him. Thus he wrote: 'A piece of dry bread in peace is better, in these areas [Poland] … where their hatred does not swallow us up like it did in the German lands.'[75]

The Takanot Shum, the *Mapah*, and the *Shulhan Arukh*

Moses Isserles displayed a creative approach to Ashkenazi traditions. It was not just a matter of preserving the text with its layers of later glosses;[76] rather, he selected those he deemed relevant for his purposes, rearranged them, and summarized them in order to make his interpretation of them clear to his readers.[77] This was also the process he used in composing the *Mapah*. Along with many other traditions and regulations, he found a place in it for the French–Rhenish *takanot* on the return of the dowry.

When Joseph Karo's (1488–1575) *Shulhan arukh*, published in 1564/5 in Venice, reached the Ashkenazi communities in Germany and Poland, it was a purely Sephardi work.[78] Its emphasis on Sephardi judicial traditions and its structure as a compendium of laws fit Karo's halakhic world but not that of the Ashkenazim.[79] Only a few years later, the *Shulhan arukh* was published in Kraków with the *Mapah* commentary. Isserles himself was responsible for the whole text: the original *Shulhan arukh* and his own comments, which he inserted as glosses, allowing the two texts to flow into one another.[80] According to contemporary sources, it was published from his handwritten copy after his death in 1572.[81] This form of the *Shulhan arukh* is ultimately what made it the normative code of the Ashkenazi world.[82] It was Isserles' decision to transfer the French–Rhenish *takanot* on the return of the dowry into the *Shulhan arukh* and the authority provided by a printed book which preserved them and increased their acceptance in other parts of the Ashkenazi world.[83] What was involved was the transformation of the old traditions of France and Germany to a new Polish Ashkenazi tradition. In the introduction to his *Mapah* and in his summary of the *takanot* on the return of the dowry, Isserles emphasized the French roots of many Ashkenazi traditions and transmissions.[84]

The history of the French–Rhenish *takanot* on the return of the dowry in the east European diaspora of early modern times did not end with their integration into the *Mapah*. They were also independently accepted in Bohemia and Moravia[85] and in Hungary.[86]

The *takanot* on the return of the dowry included by Isserles in his *Mapah* were also in use in the Polish–Lithuanian Commonwealth in the eighteenth century, where their authority derived from the fact that they were held to be from the Shum communities. In the last meeting of the Jewish Council of Lithuania in 1761 they were formally declared to be valid.[87] In the Jewish communities of Vilna, Grodno, and Pińsk they were also accepted as Takanot Shum, but in other communities, like Brest (Brisk) and Slutsk (Słuck), they were subjected to stronger criticism.[88] As late as the nineteenth century the influential Rabbi Abraham Zvi Hirsch Eisenstadt (1813–68) of Białystok confirmed the long-standing validity of Takanot Shum in Poland: 'for in Poland the Takanat Shum were adopted in the whole realm'.[89]

Conclusion

At present, the transfer of the Rhenish Takanot Shum can only serve as a single case of what may have been a larger phenomenon. It cannot be ruled out that *takanot* from other communities in the German lands also developed their own history of intellectual migration, like the *takanot* of Bamberg,[90] which were also used by Moses Minz, or the *takanot* of Franconia,[91] which were perhaps known to him. This issue needs to the subject of future research.

The migration of the French–Rhenish *takanot* to the new, prosperous Jewish communities of the Kingdom of Poland and later the Polish–Lithuanian Commonwealth must be understood in the context of the eastern migration of Ashkenazi Jews. The authority of the *takanot* was increased by the Ashkenazi elite who from the fourteenth century on emigrated increasingly from the German lands. In the fourteenth and fifteenth century, this elite had already begun to influence the existing Jewish communities in the Kingdom of Poland. However, this process of Ashkenization had an earlier precedent.[92] The local Jewish communities in the former Slavonic regions between the Elbe, Saale, and Oder rivers in the eastern part of the Holy Roman Empire had already experienced this transformation. This taking over of an existing Jewish community by an immigrant group can be compared to the phenomenon of Sephardi immigration into the Jewish communities of North Africa and the eastern Mediterranean region, which took place at about the same time. In both regions the newly arrived immigrants maintained a new diaspora consciousness towards the old homeland of their ancestors,[93] and named themselves after their countries of origin, 'Spanish' and 'German', 'Sephardim' and 'Ashkenazim'.

At the same time, this Ashkenization created something new in the Jewish world. Based on late medieval German halakhic traditions which were brought to the small, non-Ashkenazi Jewish communities in Poland, a new Jewish civilization was formed outside the German lands, which could also spread eastwards with the expansion of Polish-ruled territory: early modern Ashkenazi Judaism.[94]

Notes

1 I. M. Ta-Shma, 'On the History of the Jews in Twelfth- and Thirteenth-Century Poland', *Polin*, 10 (1997), 287–317; J. Wijaczka, 'Die Einwanderung der Juden und antijüdische Exzesse in Polen im späten Mittelalter', in F. Burgard, A. Haverkamp, and G. Mentgen (eds.), *Judenvertreibungen in Mittelalter und früher Neuzeit* (Hanover, 1999), 241–56: 241–2; J. Heyde, 'Jüdische Siedlung und Gemeindebildung im mittelalterlichen Polen', in C. Cluse, A. Haverkamp, and I. J. Yuval (eds.), *Jüdische Gemeinden und ihr christlicher Kontext in kulturräumlich vergleichender Betrachtung von der Spätantike bis zum 18. Jahrhundert* (Hanover, 2003), 249–66; H. Zaremska, *Juden im mittelalterlichen Polen und die Krakauer Judengemeinde* (Osnabrück, 2013), 240–3; S. Stampfer, 'Settling Down in Eastern Europe', in T. Grill (ed.), *Jews and Germans in Eastern Europe: Shared and Comparative Histories* (Berlin, 2018), 1–20.

2 Ta-Shma, 'On the History of the Jews in Twelfth- and Thirteenth-Century Poland', 292–3 nn. 15–17, 306; O. Pritsak, 'The Pre-Ashkenazic Jews of Eastern Europe in relation to the Khazars, the Rus' and the Lithuanians', in P. J. Potichnyj and H. Aster (eds.), *Ukrainian–Jewish Relations in Historical Perspective* (Edmonton, Alberta, 1988), 3–21; W. Moskovich, M. Chlenov, and A. Torpusman (eds.), *The Knaanites: Jews in the Medieval Slavic World* (Jerusalem, 2014).

3 Ta-Shma, 'On the History of the Jews in Twelfth- and Thirteenth-Century Poland', 288–98.

4 Jacob Svara of Kraków, Moses Poler, Mordekhai of Poland, Isaac of Poland, Simeon Polner, Pinchas of Poland, Isaac of Wrocław, Eleazar of Lublin (see ibid. 301–7, 309–13). On the role of Yehudah Hehasid in these connections to the Polish communities, see ibid. 308, 310, 314–17.

5 R. J. Barzen, 'West and East in Ashkenaz in the Time of Judah he-Ḥasid', *Jewish History*, 34 (2021), 1–25. On the so-called 'Germania Slavica', see F. Backhaus, 'Das größte Siedel-werk des deutschen Volkes: Zur Erforschung der Germania Slavica in Deutschland', in C. Lübke (ed.), *Struktur und Wandel im Früh- und Hochmittelalter: Eine Bestandsaufnahme aktueller Forschungen zur Germania Slavica* (Stuttgart, 1998), 17–29.

6 M. Brocke, 'Die mittelalterlichen jüdischen Grabmale in Spandau (1244–1474)', *Ausgrabungen in Berlin*, 9 (1994), 8–116.

7 See E. E. Urbach, 'Yitshak or zarua (meisen, vien)', in id., *Ba'alei hatosafot: toledoteihem, ḥibureihem, shitatam*, 2 vols. (Jerusalem, 1996), i. 436–47; id., 'Hizkiyah ben ya'akov ben meir (magdeburg)', in id. (ed.), *Ba'alei hatosafot*, i. 564–6; Avraham ben Azriel, *Arugat habosem*, ed. E. E. Urbach (Jerusalem, 1939–63), vi. 113–27. On the term *kena'an* for the Slavonic lands, that is, from a western perspective, see M. Weinreich, 'Yiddish, Knaanic, Slavic: The Basic Relationships', in M. Halle (ed.), *For Roman Jakobson: Essays on the Occasion of His Sixtieth Birthday* (The Hague, 1956), 622–32: 623.

8 S. Netzer, 'Wanderungen der Juden und Neusiedlung in Osteuropa', in M. Brocke (ed.), *Beter und Rebellen: Aus 1000 Jahren Judentum in Polen* (Frankfurt am Main, 1983), 33–49: 37–40, 39 n. 14; A. Haverkamp, 'Germany', in R. Chazan (ed.), *The Cambridge History of Judaism*, vi: *The Middle Ages: The Christian World* (Cambridge, 2018), 239–81: 252; A. Teller, 'Telling the Difference: Some Comparative Perspectives on the Jews' Legal Status in the

Polish–Lithuanian Commonwealth and the Holy Roman Empire', *Polin*, 22 (2009), 109–41: 113–14, 120; Barzen, 'West and East in Ashkenaz', 16–20.

9   On a Jewish presence before 1050, see Ta-Shma, 'On the History of the Jews in Twelfth-and Thirteenth-Century Poland', 287; see also Heyde, 'Jüdische Siedlung und Gemeindebildung im mittelalterlichen Polen', 252, 261–6; S. A. Cygielman, *Yehudei polin velita ad shenat tav/ḥet (1648): mevo'ot umeḥkarim mevo'arim* (Jerusalem, 1991), 33 n. 9a; L. Zygner, 'Die multikonfessionelle Gesellschaft in den polnischen Städten des Spätmittelalters und der Frühen Neuzeit', *Documenta Pragensia*, 33 (2014), 299–313: 309 n. 26; see H. Petersen, 'Kraków', in G. D. Hundert (ed.), *Yivo Encyclopedia of Jews of Eastern Europe* (New Haven, Conn., 2008).

10   A Jewish community existed in 1237 (Heyde, 'Jüdische Siedlung und Gemeindebildung im mittelalterlichen Polen', 252).

11   A Jewish community existed in 1287 (ibid.).

12   A Jewish community existed before 1350 (Cygielman, *Yehudei polin*, 118 n. 6d; A. Michałowska-Mycielska, 'Lublin', in Hundert (ed.), *Yivo Encyclopedia of Jews of Eastern Europe*; H. Petersen, *Judengemeinde und Stadtgemeinde in Polen: Lemberg 1356–1581* (Wiesbaden, 2003).

13   A Jewish community existed in 1357 (Heyde, 'Jüdische Siedlung und Gemeindebildung im mittelalterlichen Polen', 256–7, esp. 259 n. 41; Zygner, 'Die multikonfessionelle Gesellschaft', 312).

14   A Jewish community existed at least by 1379 (Cygielman, *Yehudei polin*, 34 n. 11a; A. Michałowska-Mycielska, 'Poznań', in Hundert (ed.), *Yivo Encyclopedia of Jews of Eastern Europe*; Zygner, 'Die multikonfessionelle Gesellschaft', 309–10 n. 26; J. Perles, *Geschichte der Juden in Posen* (Breslau, 1865)).

15   E. Reiner, '"Asher kol gedolei ha'arets hazot talmidav". r. ya'akov polak: rishon verosh leḥakhmei krakov', in id. (ed.), *Kroke — kazimierz — krakow: meḥkarim betoledot yehudei krakow* (Tel Aviv, 2001), 51–3.

16   Teller, 'Telling the Difference', 115.

17   Y. J. Yuval, *Ḥakhamim bedoram: hamanhigut haruḥanit shel yehudei germanyah beshalhei yemei habeinayim* (Jerusalem, 1988), 377–84; Reiner, '"Asher kol gedolei ha'arets hazot talmidav"', 50–1. On the migration of Jacob Pollak to Kraków and his role in the ongoing conflict between the two communities, his chief rabbinate in Małopolska, and his stay in the land of Israel, see ibid. 53–60; on the development of the Jewish settlements in Poland during the fifteenth century, see Zygner, 'Die multikonfessionelle Gesellschaft', 306, 310 n. 34.

18   Reiner, '"Asher kol gedolei ha'arets hazot talmidav"', 53.

19   On Czech as the mother tongue of the Jews in Prague and Bohemia during the thirteenth century, see R. Jakobson and M. Halle, 'The Term Canaan in Medieval Hebrew', in M. Altbauer (ed.), *For Max Weinreich on His Seventieth Birthday: Studies in Jewish Language, Literature and Society* (The Hague, 1964), 147–72: 166; see also D. Katz, 'Knaanic in the Medieval and Modern Scholarly Imagination', in O. Bláha, R. Dittmann, and L. Uličná (eds.), *Knaanic Language: Structure and Historical Background* (Prague, 2013), 159–90: 173. On the existence of an early synagogue (Altschul) and a Jewish settlement in the twelfth century beside the later Ashkenazi Jewish quarter and its new synagogue (Altneuschul) from the thirteenth century, see S. Paulus, *Die Architektur der Synagoge im Mittelalter: Überlieferung und Bestand* (Petersberg, Hesse, 2007), 438, 441.

20   A. Haverkamp, 'Ebrei in Italia e in Germania nel tardo medioevo: Spunti per un confronto',

in U. Israel and R. C. Mueller (eds.), 'Interstizi': Culture ebraico-cristiane a Venezia e nei suoi domini dal Medioevo all'età moderna (Rome, 2010), 47–100: 91; A. Haverkamp, 'Juden zwischen Romania und Germania: Zur Kulturgeschichte Europas im Mittelalter', in R. Bohlen, Begegnung mit dem Judentum (Trier, 2007), 39–67: 60; repr. in C. Cluse and J. R. Müller (eds.), Alfred Haverkamp: Neue Forschungen zur mittelalterlichen Geschichte 2000–2011. Festgabe zum 75. Geburtstag des Verfassers (Hanover, 2012), 41–57; G. Mentgen, Studien zur Geschichte der Juden im mittelalterlichen Elsaß (Hanover, 1995), 83–4, 131–2; 'Quellen zur Geschichte der Juden im Elsass (1273–1347)', EL01, no. 226, Medieval Ashkenaz: Corpus der Quellen zur Geschichte der Juden im spätmittelalterlichen Reich website, visited 30 July 2019.

21 There were two Jewish communities in Lwów up to the eighteenth century, one 'outside the city', where the original Ruthenian city was located, and one 'inside the city', within the city founded in the fourteenth century according to German law (V. Melamed, Evrei vo L'vove: XIII – pervaya polovina XX veka (Lviv, 1994), 32; see also Petersen, Judengemeinde und Stadtgemeinde in Polen, 40–1 n. 17).

22 S. Netzer, 'Wanderungen der Juden', 37–40; Cygielman, Yehudei polin, 28.

23 Mantua Comunita Israelitica, MS ebr. 8 (15th cent.); see R. J. Barzen, Taqqanot Qehillot Šum: Die Rechtssatzungen der jüdischen Gemeinden Mainz, Worms und Speyer im hohen und späten Mittelalter, 2 vols. (Wiesbaden, 2019), ii. 219; A. Möschter, Juden im venezianischen Treviso (1389–1509) (Hanover, 2008), 73–5; 88–90.

24 M. Breuer, 'R. Moses Minz', in F. Schütz, 'Mainz', in A. Maimon, M. Breuer, and Y. Guggenheim (eds.), Germania Judaica, iii: 1350–1519, pt. 2 (Ortschaftsartikel Mährisch-Budwitz — Zwolle) (Tübingen, 1995), 786–813: 801–2.

25 Y. S. Domb, 'Mavo', in Moses Minz, She'elot uteshuvot, 2 vols. (Jerusalem, 1991), i. 13–15; Yuval, Ḥakhamim bedoram, 206.

26 L. Finkelstein, Self-Government in the Middle Ages (Philadelphia, 1924), 152–5, 192–3; Barzen, Taqqanot Qehillot Šum, i. 239–47, 250; R. J. Barzen, 'Die Schum-Gemeinden und ihre Rechtssatzungen: Geschichte und Wirkungsgeschichte', in P. Heberer and U. Reuter (eds.), Die Schum-Gemeinden Speyer-Worms-Mainz: Auf dem Weg zum Welterbe (Regensburg, 2013), 23–35: 33. On the influence of this media revolution on the self-perception of Jewish sages in Germany and Poland, see E. Reiner, 'The Ashkenazi Elite at the Beginning of the Modern Era: Manuscript versus Printed Book', Polin, 10 (1997), 85–97: 87–8, 91, 93, 96.

27 Domb, 'Mavo', 24.

28 Minz, She'elot uteshuvot, i, no. 10 (pp. 37–41); Barzen, Taqqanot Qehillot Šum, i. 229–31.

29 See Barzen, Taqqanot Qehillot Šum, i. 173, 226; for the original text, see ibid., ii. 380–92.

30 Barzen, Taqqanot Qehillot Šum, i. 75–9, 227–32; for the text and an English translation, see Finkelstein, Self-Government, 251–6.

31 Minz, She'elot uteshuvot, ii, no. 102 (pp. 499–507); Barzen, Taqqanot Qehillot Šum, ii. 488–500. This version was also published in Meir of Rothenburg's responsa in 1608 (Meir of Rothenburg, She'elot uteshuvot, i: Defus prag, ed. Y. Farbstein (Jerusalem, 2014), no. 119). Seven earlier versions from the thirteenth and fourteenth centuries have been preserved in manuscripts from the thirteenth to seventeenth centuries. The earliest version was introduced as a shared legal text for all three Shum communities in the year 1220. For a synoptic edition of all nine versions with additional material, see Barzen, Taqqanot Qehillot Šum, ii. 274–645. On the transmission of the various manuscripts and early print versions, see ibid., i. 168–258; on the final version, see ibid., i. 186–7, 202–9.

32 Solomon ben Yehiel Luria, *Yam shel shelomoh* (Jerusalem, 1996), 4: 18; see Barzen, *Taqqanot Qehillot Šum*, i. 230; see also M. Raffeld, *Hamaharshal veha 'yam shel shelomoh'* (Ramat Gan, 1991); id., 'Hamaharshal vesamkhutam shel sifrei kitsur hilkhatiyim', *Shenaton hamishpat ha'ivri*, 18–19 (1992–4), 427–37; id., 'Al me'at sheki'in kebalim bemishnato hahilkhatit shel hamaharshal', *Da'at*, 36 (1996), 15–33; S. Assaf, 'Mashehu letoledot maharshal', in *Sefer hayovel likhvod levi gintsberg / Louis Ginzberg Jubilee Volume on the Occasion of His Seventieth Birthday*, 2 vols. (Philadelphia, 1946), ii. 45–64: 47.

33 Finkelstein, *Self-Government*, 251–6; Barzen, *Taqqanot Qehillot Šum*, i. 229–31; Bodleian Library, Oxford, MS 820 (15th cent.), fos. 45ᵛ–47ᵛ; MS 693 (16th cent.), fo. 121ᵛ; MS 864 (16th cent.), fo. 330ᵛ.

34 On his life, see Reiner, 'The Ashkenazi Elite', 93 n. 22; Assaf, 'Mashehu letoledot maharshal', 45–63; M. Raffeld, 'Luria, Shelomoh ben Yehiel', in Hundert (ed.), *The Yivo Encyclopedia of Jews in Eastern Europe*; E. Reiner, 'Temurot biyeshivot polin ve'ashkenaz bame'ot ha-16– ha-17 vehavikuaḥ al hapilpul', in I. Bartal, C. Turniansky, and E. Mendelson (eds.), *Keminhag ashkenaz vepolin. sefer yovel lechone shmeruk: kovets meḥkarim betarbut yehudit* (Jerusalem, 1993), 1–80, esp. 55–60.

35 On his life, see Reiner, 'The Ashkenazi Elite', 93 n. 22; S. M. Chones, *Sefer toledot haposkim* (New York, 1946), 174–85; M. Raffeld, 'Isserles, Mosheh ben Yisrael', in Hundert (ed.), *Yivo Encyclopedia of Jews of Eastern Europe*; A. Ziv, *Rabenu mosheh iserlis (rema): ḥayav, yetsirotav vede'otav, ḥaverav, talmidav vetse'etsa'av* (New York, 1972).

36 Reiner, 'The Ashkenazi Elite', 89 n. 12; Assaf, 'Mashehu letoledot maharshal', 47; M. Raffeld, 'Hazikah shebein harema lerabi shalom shakhna', *Sinai*, 107 (1991), 239–41; id., 'Hilkhatah kebatrei etsel ḥakhmei ashkenaz upolin bame'ot ha-15–16: mekorot usefiḥin', *Sidra*, 8 (1996), 119–40; Reiner, '"Asher kol gedolei ha'arets hazot talmidav"', 43–68, esp. 43–5; id., 'Temurot biyeshivot polin', 51; id., 'Shakhnah, Shalom', in Hundert (ed.), *Yivo Encyclopedia of Jews of Eastern Europe*.

37 On the family in Germany, see Yuval, *Ḥakhamim bedoram*, 249–53. Miriam Shapira, the wife of Aaron Luria, was considered to be the matriarch of the Luria family (R. Reuter, 'Worms', in Maimon, Breuer, and Guggenheim (eds.), *Germania Judaica*, iii, pt. 2, 1671–97: 1679). She was the daughter of Solomon Shapira, the rabbi of Heilbronn and Landau (P. Sauer, 'Heilbronn', in Maimon, Breuer, and Guggenheim (eds.), *Germania Judaica*, iii, pt. 1 (*Ortschaftsartikel Aach – Lychen*) (Tübingen, 1987), 531–40: 535; Y. Yuval, 'R. Salomo Shapira', in K. H. Debus, 'Landau in der Pfalz', in Maimon, Breuer, and Guggenheim (eds.), *Germania Judaica*, iii, pt. 1, 703–11: 705–6). She taught at a yeshiva in Alsace (M. Breuer and Y. Guggenheim, 'Die Jüdische Gemeinde', in Maimon, Breuer, and Guggenheim (eds.), *Germania Judaica*, iii, pt. 3 (*Gebietsartikel, Einleitungsartikel und Indices*) (Tübingen, 2003), 2079–138: 2109; S. Epstein, *Mishpaḥat luria* (Vienna, 1901), 11; S. Ashkenazi, *Nashim lamdaniyot: sekirah historit* (Tel Aviv, 1982), 25–7; ead., *Dor uminhagav: oreḥot zemanim ve'iyunim beyisra'el* (Tel Aviv, 1987), 204–5). Solomon Luria recorded his family genealogy down to the sixteenth century (Solomon ben Yehiel Luria, *Sefer she'elot uteshuvot rashal* (Fürth, 1768), n.p.; see also Epstein, *Mishpaḥat luria*, 13–14, 17).

38 According to a letter from Moses Luria, rabbi and head of the rabbinical court in Worms, to Solomon Luria (see Epstein, *Mishpaḥat luria*, 13).

39 Epstein, *Mishpaḥat luria*, 13; Mentgen, *Studien zur Geschichte der Juden im mittelalterlichen Elsaß*, 60, 64, 183, 312, 537; F. Rapp and G. Fournier, 'Hagenau, Reichslandvogtei', in Maimon, Breuer, and Guggenheim (eds.), *Germania Judaica*, iii, pt. 3, 1859–62: 1860. He was in Heilbronn and Worms in 1510/11 (Reuter, 'Worms', 1680–1 n. 13; A. Chavatzelet, 'Rabenu

yoḥanan luria', in J. Hoffman (ed.), *Yoḥanan luria: meshivat nefesh* (Jerusalem, 1992), 13–22).

40 Epstein, *Mishpaḥat luria*, 13.

41 Reuter, 'Worms', 1679–80, 1682, 1693, 1695.

42 Minz, *She'elot uteshuvot*, i, nos. 19 (p. 87), 72 (p. 291).

43 Epstein, *Mishpaḥat luria*, 13.

45 Assaf, 'Mashehu letoledot maharshal', 45.

46 Ibid.; Epstein, *Mishpaḥat luria*, 14.

47 Assaf, 'Mashehu letoledot maharshal', 45; M. Raffeld, 'R. yitsḥak kloiber: hanhagotav, morashato umisaviv lahen', in D. Sperber, *Minhagei yisra'el: mekorot vetoledot*, viii (Jerusalem, 2007), 174–5; Reiner, 'Temurot biyshivot polin', 53.

48 On the transmission of the signatures in the various manuscripts, see Minz, *She'elot uteshuvot*, i, no. 10 (p. 40); Barzen, *Taqqanot Qehillot Šum*, i. 78 n. 474; 79 n. 477.

49 Meir of Rothenburg, *She'elot uteshuvot*, i, no. 563; Barzen, *Taqqanot Qehillot Šum*, ii. 380 n. 276.

50 Israel Isserlein, *Sefer terumat hadeshen*, i: *Responsa*, ed. S. Avitan (Jerusalem, 1990), no. 220.

51 It is interesting that in Luria's version both authors call the ordinances *takanot hakehilot*, 'ordinances of the communities'. So, here, the Shum communities are simply 'the communities' (Luria, *Yam shel shelomoh*, 4: 18, §§1, 2).

52 Luria, *Yam shel shelomoh*, 4: 18, §3: 1; see Barzen, *Taqqanot Qehillot Šum*, i. 230. On the transmission history of this version, see ibid., i. 226; for the synoptic edition, see ibid., ii. 381–93, 465–71.

53 Luria, *Yam shel shelomoh*, 4: 18, §3: 2; see Barzen, *Taqqanot Qehillot Šum*, i. 230; cf. Minz, *She'elot uteshuvot*, i, no. 10 (p. 38).

54 Luria, *Yam shel shelomoh*, 4: 18 §3: 3; see Barzen, *Taqqanot Qehillot Šum*, i. 230; see Minz, *She'elot uteshuvot*, i, no. 10 (pp. 39–40).

55 On the signatures and their contexts in the manuscripts, see Barzen, *Taqqanot Qehillot Šum*, i. 78 n. 474; 79 n. 477; 229–31.

56 'I found in an old book . . .' (Luria, *Yam shel shelomoh*, 4: 18 §3: 3).

57 Five of nine names are missing (ibid.; cf. Minz, *She'elot uteshuvot*, i, no. 10 (p. 40)).

58 'And I also found an ordinance from the younger sages . . .' (Luria, *Yam shel shelomoh*, 4: 18 §3: 3).

59 H. Petersen, 'Selbstverständnis einer polnischen Judengemeinde des 16. Jahrhunderts: Die Taqanot Qraqa aus dem Jahre 1595', in Cluse, Haverkamp, and Yuval (eds.), *Jüdische Gemeinden und ihr christlicher Kontext*, 507–11; M. Bałaban, 'Die Krakauer Judengemeinde-Ordnung von 1595 und ihre Nachträge', *Jahrbuch der Jüdisch-Literarischen Gesellschaft*, 10 (1913), 296–360; 11 (1916), 88–114.

60 Z. Kowalska, 'Die großpolnischen und schlesischen Judenschutzbriefe des 13. Jahrhunderts im Verhältnis zu den Privilegien Kaiser Friedrichs II. (1238) und Herzog Friedrichs II. von Österreich (1244)', *Zeitschrift für Ostmitteleuropa-Forschung*, 47 (1998), 1–20; Teller, 'Telling the Difference', 113, 116, 120, 140.

61 On the possible transfer of texts of legal agreements from Germany to Poland, especially from the Jewish communities of Regensburg and Cologne, see F. Guesnet, 'Agreements between Neighbours: The "Ugody" as a Source on Jewish–Christian Relations in Early Modern Poland', *Jewish History*, 24 (2010), 257–70: 264–5.

62 See Finkelstein, *Self-Government*, 163–5; Barzen, *Taqqanot Qehillot Šum*, i. 239–47; ii. 488–98.

63 Moses Isserles, *Mapah*, 'Even ha'ezer', 53: 3 §§9, 16. Moses Isserles' method of organizing the overwhelming amount of knowledge of his time is comparable to that of Joseph Karo. On Karo's method, see T. Kelman, '"Efsok halakhah ve'akhria bein hasevarot ki zehu hatakhlit": meimad pesikat hahalakhah besefer beit yosef lerabi yosef karo', Ph.D. thesis (Ben-Gurion University of the Negev, 2018), 94–7; see also id., '"All of the differing opinions of the *poskim*, no one fails to appear": The Use of Ashkenazic Works in R. Joseph Karo's *Beit Yosef*', in S. Rauschenberg (ed.), *Sephardim and Ashkenazim: Jewish–Jewish Encounters in History and Literature* (Berlin, 2020), 89–101.

64 Moses Isserles, *Mapah*, 'Even ha'ezer', 53: 3 §§16–17; see Barzen, *Taqqanot Qehillot Šum*, i. 110–11; see also id., 'Schum-Gemeinden', 34.

65 See Barzen, *Taqqanot Qehillot Šum*, ii. 488–501; see also Isserles, *Mapah*, 'Even ha'ezer', 53: 3 §§16–18.

66 Biblioteka Wydziału Orientalistycznego Uniwersytetu Warszawskiego, MS 258 (14th/15th cent.), fos. 126ʳ–127ᵛ; London School of Jewish Studies (Montefiore Collection), MS 146 (15th cent.), fos. 50ʳ–51ᵛ; see Barzen, *Taqqanot Qehillot Šum*, i. 212–19; ii. 488–500.

67 Minz, *She'elot uteshuvot*, ii, no. 102 §48 (p. 504); see Barzen, *Taqqanot Qehillot Šum*, ii. 488–500.

68 B. E. Klein, 'Raumkonzeptionen jüdischer Gelehrter in Mittelalter und Früher Neuzeit und ihre kulturellen Implikationen', in H. Busche and S. Heßbrüggen-Walter (eds.), *Departure for Modern Europe: A Handbook of Early Modern Philosophy (1400–1700)* (Hamburg, 2011), 840–50: 847; I. Twersky, 'The Shulhan 'Aruk: Enduring Code of Jewish Law', *Judaism*, 16 (1967), 141–58: 145 n. 15. Isserles' mother was a member of the Luria family (J. Davis, 'The Reception of the Shulhan 'Arukh and the Formation of Ashkenazic Jewish Identity', *AJS Review*, 26 (2002), 251–76: 261). On Isserles' parents' migration from Germany to Kraków in 1490, see Stampfer, 'Settling Down', 4; B. Weinryb, *The Jews of Poland: A Social and Economic History of the Jewish Community in Poland from 1100 to 1800* (Philadelphia, 1972), 30.

69 See Reiner, 'The Ashkenazi Elite', 89 n. 13; F. Seibt and M. Tischler, 'Prag', in Maimon, Breuer, and Guggenheim (eds.), *Germania Judaica*, iii, pt. 2, 1116–51: 1129 n. 288; Reiner, '"Asher kol gedolei ha'arets hazot talmidav"', 45–50; Reiner, 'Pollak, Ya'akov Ben Yosef', in Hundert (ed.), *Yivo Encyclopedia of Jews of Eastern Europe*.

70 Reiner, 'The Ashkenazi Elite', 87 n. 8, 89–90 n. 15; I. J. Yuval, 'Rishonim ve'aḥaronim, *antiqui et moderni*', *Zion*, 57 (1992), 369–94.

71 E. Fram, 'Timing May Not Be Everything . . . But It Helps: Some Historical Factors that Contributed to the Success of Shulhan Arukh', *Report of the Oxford Centre for Hebrew and Jewish Studies* (2008–9), 103–15: 112.

72 Reiner, '"Asher kol gedolei ha'arets hazot talmidav"', 44; id., 'The Ashkenazi Elite', 86 n. 6, 94.

73 Reiner, 'The Ashkenazi Elite', 85–9; Klein, 'Raumkonzeptionen', 848–9; Davis, 'The Reception of the Shulhan Arukh', 264.

74 Reiner, 'The Ashkenazi Elite', 93–5.

75 Moses Isserles, *She'elot uteshuvot harema*, ed. A. Ziv (Jerusalem, 1971), no. 95; Netzer, 'Wanderungen der Juden', 44; Klein, 'Raumkonzeptionen', 847–8; Davis, 'The Reception of the Shulhan 'Arukh', 265; Teller, 'Telling the Difference', 128.

76 Reiner, 'The Ashkenazi Elite', 94.

77 Ibid. 93–4, 97; Twersky, 'The Shulhan 'Aruk', 150 n. 29.

78 See Twersky, 'The Shulhan 'Aruk'; E. Shochetman, ''Al hasetirot bashulḥan arukh ve'al

mahuto shel haḥibur umaterotav', *Asufot*, 3 (1989), 323–9; Davis, 'The Reception of the Shulhan 'Arukh', 254–5; Reiner, '"Asher kol gedolei ha'arets hazot talmidav"', 44; id., 'The Ashkenazi Elite', 96 n. 28.

79 Reiner, 'The Ashkenazi Elite', 96 n. 26; Klein, 'Raumkonzeptionen', 845.

80 Reiner, 'The Ashkenazi Elite', 97; Klein, 'Raumkonzeptionen', 847.

81 Actually, Isserles published small sections of his commentary in 1569 and began publishing his comments on the entire *Shulḥan arukh* in 1570. The first complete edition of the *Shulḥan arukh* with the *Mapah* was published from 1578 to 1580 (Reiner, '"Asher kol gedolei ha'arets hazot talmidav"', 44; id., 'The Ashkenazi Elite', 97; Fram, 'Timing May Not Be Everything', 111–12; Davis, 'The Reception of the Shulhan 'Arukh', 263–4).

82 Twersky, 'The Shulhan 'Aruk', 149 . On the acceptance of the *Shulḥan arukh* with Isserles' *Mapah* as the normative code, see Davis, 'The Reception of the Shulhan 'Arukh', 253, 272–4, 276.

83 Reiner, 'The Ashkenazi Elite', 97; Twersky, 'The Shulhan 'Aruk', 150–1, 156–7.

84 Davis, 'The Reception of the Shulhan 'Arukh', 259–60.

85 S. Assaf, 'Hatakanot vehaminhagim hashonot biyrushat haba'al et ishto', *Mada'ei ha-yahadut*, 1 (1926), 79–96: 93.

86 Barzen, *Taqqanot Qehillot Šum*, i. 111; Barzen, 'Schum-Gemeinden', 34.

87 *Pinkas hamedinah o pinkas va'ad hakehilot harashiyot bimdinat lita*, ed. S. Dubnow (Berlin, 1925), no. 981; see also Assaf, 'Hatakanot vehaminhagim hashonot', 93, n. 2; Barzen, *Taqqanot Qehillot Šum*, i. 111; id., 'Schum-Gemeinden', 32.

88 Assaf, 'Hatakanot vehaminhagim hashonot', 93.

89 Abraham Zvi Hirsch Eisenstadt, *Piṯhei teshuvah* (Vilna, 1862), 'Even ha'ezer', 53: 13; Assaf, 'Hatakanot vehaminhagim hashonot', 92 n. 11; Barzen, *Taqqanot Qehillot Šum*, i. 111; id., 'Schum-Gemeinden', 32.

90 *Takanot medinat franken*. Minz, *She'elot uteshuvot*, i, nos. 60 (pp. 244–5), 67 (pp. 281–6); ii, nos. 80–1 (pp. 383–97).

91 *Takanot medinat bamberg*. Israel Bruna, *Responsa*, ed. M. Hershler (Jerusalem, 1960), 174, no. 257; R. J. Barzen, 'Ländliche Jüdische Siedlungen und Niederlassungen im Hoch- und Spätmittelalter in Aschkenas. Typologie, Struktur und Vernetzung', *Aschkenas*, 21 (2013), 5–35: 26.

92 Barzen, 'West and East in Ashkenaz', 1, 16–20. One of the first to use the term 'Ashkenization' was Michael Stanislawski (see M. Stanislawski, 'The Yiddish Shevet Yehudah: A Study in the "Ashkenization" of a Spanish-Jewish Classic', in E. Carlebach, J. M. Efron, and D. N. Myers (eds.), *Jewish History and Jewish Memory: Essays in Honour of Yosef Hayim Yerushalmi* (Hanover, NH, 1998), 134–52).

93 D. A. Wacks, *Double Diaspora in Sephardic Literature: Jewish Cultural Production before and after 1492* (Bloomington, Ind., 2015); A. Mirski, A. Grossman, and Y. Kaplan (eds.), *Galut aḥar golah: meḥkarim betoledot am yisra'el mugashim leprofesor ḥayim beinart limlot lo shivim shanah* (Jerusalem, 1988); Eng. trans.: *Exile and Diaspora: Studies in the History of the Jewish People Presented to Professor Haim Beinart* (Jerusalem, 1991).

94 Max Weinreich distinguished between 'Ashkenaz I', the Jews of the medieval German-speaking lands, and 'Ashkenaz II', the Jews of the later centres in eastern Europe, mostly early modern Poland (M. Weinreich, *History of the Yiddish Language*, ed. P. Glasser, trans. S. Noble and J. A. Fishman, 2 vols. (New Haven, Conn., 2008), i. 3–4).

The Beginnings of
Jewish Self-Government in Poland
A Tangled History

JÜRGEN HEYDE

THIS CHAPTER examines the contribution of the Jewish economic elite to the development of Jewish self-government in the Kingdom of Poland up to the sixteenth century. Beginning with the earliest cases of Jewish community and court organization, it discusses self-government as a tangled process of communication between Jewish and non-Jewish actors and analyses the role of the Jewish economic elite as an element of the community leadership, through the lens of non-Jewish documents, the largest part of the available source material for this period.

Jewish self-government in medieval Poland has been for the most part discussed in the context of the legal and institutional ramifications of the 'general privileges' granted to Jews from the thirteenth to the fifteenth centuries. To illustrate the institutional history of Jewish communities, Majer Bałaban and, more recently, Hanna Zaremska have drawn on the well-documented and researched examples of the high-medieval Rhineland *takanot*, comparing them to the oldest statutes of the Kraków community dating from the end of the sixteenth century.[1]

The impact of the Jewish economic elite on Jewish self-government in Poland–Lithuania has been extensively studied in works on the seventeenth and eighteenth centuries. In his classic monograph *Tradition and Crisis*, Jacob Katz underlined the ambiguity of the situation of the elite: on the one hand, their close contacts with the non-Jewish elite (nobles and royal officials) helped safeguard the economic livelihood of the Jewish population in general, but, on the other, their economic power could also be used to assert their own interests against those of the community.[2] Gershon Hundert,[3] Moshe Rosman,[4] Adam Teller,[5] and Maria Cieśla[6] all discussed examples of this ambiguity. At the same time they emphasized that the role of the Jewish economic elite within the system of Jewish self-government cannot be analysed as a dichotomous, inner-Jewish relationship but needs to be understood as part of (at least) a triangle, in which the representatives of the Jewish communities interacted just as actively with the non-Jewish authorities as with the members of the Jewish economic elite. On the non-Jewish side there is also no clear-cut political agenda. In his study of the Jews on the estates of the Sieniawski and Czartoryski families, Moshe Rosman pointed out that the nobles, in contrast to the royal administration, had no interest in strengthening Jewish self-government, as they strove for a maximum of control over their latifundia. Against this, Adam Teller has shown that on the Radziwiłł estates the landlords did support the autonomy of the

Jewish institutions, as long as there were no direct conflicts of interest. In her work on trans-religious relations in Rzeszów (owned by the Lubomirski family), Yvonne Kleinmann came to similar conclusions.[7]

This chapter traces the evolution of this complex relationship in three sections. The first deals with the earliest examples of self-government up to the late fourteenth century. The second discusses changes in the fifteenth century, especially the growing visibility of community institutions and the *kahal* leadership to the non-Jewish authorities and its impact on the relations between the economic elite and the community. The third section discusses a particular case, that of the Fischel family of Kraków, who, despite having to fight against being banned from the community in the 1470s, quickly rose into the ranks of the *kahal* elders and dominated Jewish community life in Kraków well into the sixteenth century. Their story highlights various aspects of this tangled history: the struggle for domination in the community and beyond, resistance to these efforts, the use of non-Jewish authorities in inner-Jewish conflicts, and the significance and limitations of non-Jewish agendas to Jewish self-government in the early sixteenth century.

Early Traces

In a compilation of rabbinic writings from the early eleventh century, the *Sefer hadinim* by Rabbi Judah ben Meir (Judah Hakohen) of Mainz, a rabbinic court in Kraków is mentioned disputing the case of two merchants active on the trade route to Ruthenia.[8] At this time Kraków was a major trading hub within Polish territory but not yet a political centre—it became the seat of a duke only after the reinstitution of the monarchy under Kazimierz the Restorer in the second half of the century. Thus the Kraków rabbinic court did not derive its authority from a non-Jewish source but from the acceptance of the halakhic authority of the judges by the litigating parties.

From the thirteenth century on there is evidence of Jewish settlements in several towns, usually political centres. There was a Jewish cemetery in Wrocław before 1203,[9] and a 'Jewish well' is mentioned in a privilege for Płock in 1237.[10] In both cases, it seems likely that non-Jewish authorities had been involved in granting these permissions, but direct documentation is lacking. This changes for the second half of the century: in 1287 Duke Przemysł II of Wielkopolska confirmed the acquisition of land for a cemetery by 'the Jewish elders of Kalisz and their community'.[11] This is the first Polish document where the elders as representatives of the community can be found negotiating with non-Jewish authorities.

In Kalisz, the initiative clearly came from the community, but the rulers of the Piast dynasty were also actively pursuing a policy towards Jews. Przemysł's uncle and predecessor as duke of Wielkopolska, Bolesław the Pious, issued a privilege to the Jews of his territory in 1264, the first of the general privileges in late medieval Poland. This privilege, and its confirmation by Kazimierz the Great in the fourteenth century, mention Jewish community institutions, such as the synagogue and the cemetery, and emphasize the monarch's protection of them. Jewish self-government is only touched on indirectly when the privilege acknowledges an inner-Jewish mechanism for settling conflicts whose functioning should not be interfered with by the judge appointed by the monarch or the voivode unless a complaint is explicitly made to him. Another indication of the independence of the Jewish court is the fact that it was usually held in the synagogue.[12]

However, there is no mention of Jewish elders or the rabbi as the head of the court. The only person mentioned by name (apart from the monarch) is Falk of Kalisz, to whom the confirmation of 1364 was given.[13] The document's wording—that the privilege was issued 'into the hands of Falk, Jew of Kalisz'[14]—gives no indication as to his function within the community. As the oldest records of the court of Kalisz date from the end of the fourteenth century, there are no other sources available that might provide a clearer image. A few years later, however, two documents from neighbouring regions provide considerable detail on the individual actors, the community, and the non-Jewish authorities. Both were issued in 1370, the first in Kraków, the other in the Silesian Duchy of Świdnica.

The Kraków document was issued to Lewko, son of Jordan, by far the most prominent Jew in late fourteenth-century Kraków, whose influence also extended well beyond the city. In response to a request by King Kazimierz and because of the extraordinary services Lewko and his father Jordan had rendered to the city over a long period, the Kraków city council extended its special protection to Lewko, his wife and descendants, and the 'bishop of the Jews' (*episcopus Judaeorum*), Casym or any other Jew whom Lewko and his family chose as bishop in the course of time. Lewko and his family appear as the central recipients of the document. The *episcopus Judaeorum* is named as well; not by virtue of his own position in the community, however, but because of the fact that Lewko and his family chose him for the position. The city council issued the document and provided its own justification for it, but it did so on the incentive of the king himself. Thus neither the issuer nor the recipient of the privilege were independent actors. Instead, there is a web of interrelations that warrants a closer look.

Although Jews had been present in the records of the Kraków town court from the very beginning of the fourteenth century, the first record of a credit transaction between a Jew and a burgher dates from 1365, when the Kraków burgher Heincz Keczerer and his sister Katherina pledged to repay a loan of 7 marks in Polish currency to Lewko by the following Passover.[15] This was the first in a series of transactions between Lewko and the burghers of Kraków in the following decades—for several years he was the only Jew to conduct this kind of business.

Lewko's activities were not limited to Kraków. He maintained far-reaching relations with the king and the aristocracy: in 1368 King Kazimierz appointed him head of the royal mint and leased to him—together with a consortium of Kraków burghers—a salt mine in Wieliczka.[16] On behalf of the king, Lewko paid money to the royal steward and collected payments from the city of Kraków for the royal vicegerent.[17] King Louis of Hungary and Poland took loans from Lewko for over 33,000 florins altogether, and Louis's daughter Jadwiga paid back credits to Duke

Siemowit of Mazovia at the beginning of her reign.[18] Lewko acted as creditor to various members of the high nobility and to members of the Kraków city council. He was a towering figure in the economic life of the late fourteenth century, but there is no record of him holding any office within the Jewish community.

At the beginning of the fifteenth century a second Jewish family, represented by Jossman and his son Cussiel, gained importance in the moneylending business with burghers and noblemen. In 1407 the Kraków city council acknowledged the position of Lewko's heirs (Lewko died in 1395) and of Jossman's family by issuing an almost identical document to that of 1370. Again, the king's incentive was mentioned, as well as the extension of protection to the *episcopus Judaeorum*—while the name of the incumbent of this office was not even mentioned anymore.

In neighbouring Silesia in 1370, Duchess Agnes of Świdnica issued a privilege to the Jews on the occasion of the reopening of the synagogue after the persecutions of 1348. The Jews were represented by the elders, a group of four people who were to be elected by the Jews of Świdnica every year. These elders would appoint a 'bishop', a 'proficient man' who should be 'obedient' to the community, and, if he proved unsuitable, then the elders could replace him after a year or two. If they could not find another, the elders themselves would have the authority to judge all breaches of Jewish law; if they were not able to do so, they should turn to a proficient man and get advice from him.[19]

In this privilege the duchess communicates with an elected body of representatives, but again the 'bishop' as the head of the Jewish court is described as being in a subaltern position, appointed and dismissed by the elders. The elders used the non-Jewish authority to assert their dominance over the rabbi/'bishop'. This situation bears more than a passing resemblance to what Eleazar ben Nathan of Mainz wrote to Judah Hehasid in the middle of the twelfth century: 'In most places in Poland, Russia, and Hungary, where, owing to poverty, there are no Torah scholars, they hire an intelligent man wherever they can and he serves them as leader in prayer and as a religious mentor and teacher of their children, and they assure his livelihood in return.'[20] This opinion is backed by the few available non-Jewish documents. In the Kraków city records, two people are described as 'Jewish bishops': Casym, who is mentioned only once, in the privilege for Lewko of 1370, and Smoyl, who is recorded as 'bishop' in 1373 in three different transactions where he acted as a creditor to burghers.[21] In the following year and again in 1376 there are additional records of Smoyl but without the title of 'bishop'.[22]

What do the documents of Świdnica and Kraków reveal about Jewish self-government in the late fourteenth century? It seems that the non-Jewish authorities were only beginning to show interest in the functioning and social hierarchies of Jewish communities. In particular, the privilege issued by Agnes of Świdnica reflects their dependence on information given by their partners in communication. The elders approached the duchess, who was willing to reinstitute a Jewish community in the town. With regard to how this community was organized, she relied on what the elders presented to her—effectively confirming a form of Jewish self-government led by the community elders.

In Kraków, the situation was different: the reason why the documents of 1370 and 1407 were issued had nothing to do with the community as a whole but with the relationship between the city council, the king, and Lewko's family. In 1369 the Kraków city council sent a letter to the king, arguing that the city had not fulfilled its obligations to strengthen its defences, because it had been ruined by 'Jewish dominion'. Jews were accused of having committed various outrageous crimes and acts of violence. Lewko and his family were at the centre of the attacks: he was said to have taken the property of many burghers and forced them to leave town. The council's own records, however, only note credit transactions that had been repaid in full. One of the burghers Lewko allegedly forced out of town is mentioned in the records in the years 1370 to 1372; most of the other accusations were so vague that there was no way of proving or disproving them.[23]

In the light of the privilege from 1370, the accusations appear to be an attempt to divert the king's attention from the shortcomings of the council and get rid of an up-and-coming but already well-connected competitor (Lewko's first credit transaction with a burgher had been only four years earlier). The timing of the privilege may then be explained as making amends to Lewko and his family and the king. Neither King Kazimierz nor the city council, however, had any motivation to include the *episcopus Judaeorum* in the privilege. This must have been Lewko's incentive, reflecting his standing within the community and sending a signal to the non-Jewish authorities that the attack on him had concerned not only himself and his family but the functioning of the Jewish community as a whole.

The issuing of the renewed privilege of 1407 reflected a similar constellation of forces. According to the Polish chronicler Jan Długosz, around Easter that year there had been an outbreak of anti-Jewish violence.[24] In the following years the city council undertook a long series of court cases (lasting until 1412) against the suspected perpetrators among the burghers of Kraków.[25] Again, there were anti-Jewish narratives: a contemporary one connected with the monastery of Mogiła near Kraków[26] and another which Długosz included decades later in his chronicle.[27] In August 1407 the city council issued a renewed privilege to the members of the two leading Jewish families. This time, the whole incentive seems to have come from the non-Jewish authorities, so that even though the fragment about the *episcopus Judaeorum* was maintained, the name of the actual person was omitted.

Taken together, these episodes leave the impression that at the beginning of the fifteenth century the structures and functioning of Jewish self-government, though accepted in general, were barely visible and of little interest to the non-Jewish authorities. The community as a representative body did not regularly figure in communications with the non-Jewish authorities. As a result, great caution must be exercised in ascribing to Lewko an overwhelming influence in the community because of his relationship with the non-Jewish elite or in stating that Lewko and his family chose the *episcopus Judaeorum*. At no time does Lewko identify himself as holding an office in the community; however, it is remarkable that the privilege speaks about the *episcopus Judaeorum* but not about the community elders.

Visibility and Interaction

The structures of the community became more visible to the non-Jewish authorities during the fifteenth century. In the middle years of the century there were no longer such towering figures within Kraków Jewry as Lewko, the group of persons interacting with non-Jews increased, and more Jews identified themselves through their position within the community.[28] Most significant is the change in terminology concerning the rabbi as head of the internal Jewish court. The old term *episcopus Judaeorum* vanished shortly after 1400, replaced by *doctor Judaeorum* (1431) or *senior scholae* (1453).[29] From the 1430s the titles of *senior* or *schkolnyk* are mentioned in non-Jewish sources,[30] and from the 1460s the elders begin to appear as a group in various transactions.[31]

In the mid-fifteenth century these mentions followed a specific pattern: they were used to legitimize a person by accentuating his position within the community but appeared only the first time such a person was introduced to the court. After this the titles were usually omitted, just like references to kinship or the place of origin once they were no longer necessary for purposes of identification.[32]

When King Kazimierz Jagiellończyk confirmed the privileges of the Jews of Wielkopolska and Mazovia in 1453, the original document was said to be lost and so an updated version of the privilege was issued: the updates later found their way into in the ordinance of Voivode Andrzej Tęczyński for the Jews of Małopolska of 1527.[33] The king emphasized much more strongly than in the older documents the adherence (not servitude) of the Jews to the royal chamber, thus underlining his exclusive position as overlord against the aspirations of voivodes and other dignitaries.[34]

More important, however, is the prominent role assigned to the community elders and the rabbinate.[35] According to the privilege, the elders had full authority over all members of the community; resistance or showing disrespect to the elders became a punishable offence, and a fine had to be paid not only to the community but also to the voivode.[36] The internal Jewish court also received more attention. The document stated expressly that conflicts among Jews had to be tried first before the elders of the community. If no agreement could be reached within the community, the parties could appeal to the voivode.[37] The *judex Judaeorum*, a nobleman selected by the voivode to judge cases between Jews and non-Jews, could now be appointed only with the consent of the community. In the paragraphs concerning how litigants had to be summoned to court, the *shamash* (*scolny, servitor scholae*) and his role were defined. Another part referred to the rabbi—as *senior scholae*—and his authority to impose a ban in cases where a Jew was accused of theft or receiving stolen goods.

These provisions show the growing self-esteem of the community elders, whose authority was now given legitimacy by the non-Jewish authorities. Community structures and offices were presented to the non-Jewish public, thus strengthening the position of the elders as representatives of the local Jewish population. The secular power now acknowledged the authority of the rabbi and also, to a certain extent, integrated his court into the non-Jewish court system. On a more general level, the increasing awareness of Jewish community structures mirrors an overall trend towards representative bodies becoming political and social actors in the fifteenth century, which can be seen, for example, in the growing role of regional diets, culminating in the establishment of the Polish sejm at the end of the century.

While the community leadership now came to the attention of the non-Jewish public, the Jewish economic elite did not vanish from the political scene. However, instead of being the principal partners of the non-Jewish authorities, as they had been at the end of the fourteenth century, they now became part of a triangular relationship, maintaining their own position while dealing with the community leadership as well as with the non-Jewish authorities.

An example of close co-operation between a member of the economic elite, the community, and the non-Jewish authorities can be found in Poznań in the years 1457 and 1458. Sloma, a Jewish merchant mainly active in Wielkopolska and Silesia, found himself in a conflict with Ionas, a Jew from Sambor in Red Ruthenia; he brought this before the city council after having also involved the community authorities and the Jewish court. The town scribe noted in 1457 that Ionas had confessed to insulting 'certain Christians and Jews (namely Sloma's sons-in-law as well as his sons and daughters) in an unspeakable manner', and had committed other crimes and violations of honour for which he deserved to be punished. At the request of 'certain people' and with the consent of the Jews he was punished with banishment from the city: if he ever returned, he would be punished by death.[38] When Ionas did return the next year his case had not been forgotten: he was arrested by the Jews and held to be deserving of the death penalty. He was again freed after solemnly promising never to approach within forty miles of Poznań. He also denied having caused any injury to Sloma and his sons-in-law. He was then handed over to the magistrate, who confirmed the verdict of banishment.[39]

The Poznań magistrate implemented a sentence that had been passed without his involvement. The verdict of the Jewish court was neither verified nor subjected to a separate investigation. Furthermore, in the sentence of 1457, the town court tried to claim some responsibility for the trial by stating that Christians had also been affected by Ionas's insults. In fact, despite the involvement of Sloma in the trial, all the alleged victims remained anonymous: the same situation recurred in the second trial. The phrase 'certain Christians and Jews' only provided the magistrate with a formal lever to act against Ionas. However, the legal dimension is the least important part of this case: what is important is what it reveals about the communications between Sloma, the Jewish community, and the magistrate of Poznań. Sloma was held in such high regard in his community that the alleged insults to members of his family justified a draconian sentence. The sentence itself reveals more about Sloma's position in the community than about Ionas and his alleged crime, because neither in the first trial nor after his return and subsequent arrest had the imposition of the death penalty ever been intended. The Polish court merely approved the verdict in the first trial and in the second executed a sentence imposed by an internal Jewish court. In order to defend the honour of Sloma's family, both the community and the magistrate were content to act together.

A second case in mid-fifteenth-century Kraków was more complicated, since it involved a conflict between members of the Jewish economic elite and the community. This time, on the side of the non-Jewish authorities, it was not the magistrate who was involved, but the king's court. The petitioners were from a wealthy Jewish family whose principal members were named Izrael and Miriama, who had been active in business since at least 1456 and had created a network of almost exclusively female clients. In 1465 Izrael and Miriama, together with their relatives, turned to the king asking for a ruling that would forbid the community to threaten or exclude them. The king's secretary imposed a pledge of 4,000 marks to guarantee that both parties adhered to the ruling. Nineteen members of the community leadership were listed by name, and the whole of the community agreed not to take any steps against Miriama and Izrael before the return of the Jewish envoys who were sent—at the king's request—to the royal court to hear and report back the verdict.

There is no record of the outcome of this conflict, but Miriama remained active in Kraków until 1483. She had succeeded in engaging the highest non-Jewish authorities in what appeared to be an inner-community conflict. The record suggests that she had been threatened with expulsion from the community or some other form of ban: the long list of community elders underlined the severity of the issue. One interesting aspect of the case is that the king requested that Jewish envoys come to his court to report the case and deliver the verdict.

The trials of Miriama and Ionas show how non-Jewish authorities could be used in inner-Jewish conflicts. In both cases the non-Jewish authorities did not try to override the Jewish verdict but, rather, emphasized the need for Jewish involvement in the process, whether by executing a Jewish sentence or by requesting that the case be presented by Jewish envoys. They illustrate that the Jewish court was perceived as part of the general judicial system while at the same time the ability of the Jewish authorities to act independently was maintained.

The Economic Elite and Community Leadership: The Fischel Family of Kraków

Non-Jewish sources from the end of the fifteenth century contain even more evidence about Jewish community structures and the functioning of Jewish communities. Time and again, community leaders and the economic elite relied on non-Jewish authorities to advance their interests, whereas non-Jewish actors used the increasing contact to assert their influence over the Jewish population.

The Fischel family were leading actors in Jewish life in Kraków from the late fifteenth to well into the sixteenth century. They developed close contacts with the royal court and had great influence in the community, which makes them a uniquely suitable subject to study the complex relationships analysed in this chapter. The Fischels were present in Kraków at least from the 1460s, having moved there possibly from Prague or Germany.[40] Ephraim Fischel, the first known member of the family in the city, and his sons Jacob, Moses, and Joseph (Joshua) were soon numbered among the leading personalities of the Jewish community. Together with twenty-five other Kraków Jews, Moses signed a guarantee for a Jewish merchant from Bochnia:[41] Hanna Zaremska regards these signatories as the members of the extended community leadership.[42]

A few years later, in 1477, Moses and his brother Jacob found themselves in sharp conflict with the community, which issued a sentence expelling them from the city. The elders went to the *judex Judaeorum*, Nicolai Chamiecz, and had the sentence confirmed. Subsequently Moses himself appealed to Chamiecz, also acting on behalf of his now deceased brother. He provided evidence in the form of letters to disprove the accusations against them and succeeded in having the verdict overturned. The argument did not end there, but went to the voivode's court, where the scribe noted that, after multiple controversies and insults, the elders of the community and Fischel came together in the presence of the voivode and consented to an agreement: all the accusatory letters which inculpated any of the parties would be withdrawn and regarded as null and void, and nobody would make any mention of the conflict again. The settlement was guaranteed by a pledge of 400 marks; in case of violation the party who had fulfilled the agreement should receive half of this sum, the other half going to the *starosta* (sheriff) of Kraków. To this the parties agreed of their own free will, abjuring any law or evidence that might undermine the compromise.[43]

The conflict between the Fischel brothers and the community elders is one of the few occasions where the appeal procedures mentioned in the Jewish privileges can be seen to have been of practical use. Soon after the original verdict, the community turned to the non-Jewish authorities to have the sentence confirmed, and also in order to make sure it could be enforced. When Fischel appealed, the elders did not back down, so a compromise had to be negotiated at the next level. Through all these instances the non-Jewish judges respected the Jewish arguments and formulated their verdicts on that basis, just as both parties turned to the non-Jewish authorities of their own free will.

Just a few years later, in 1485, Moses Fischel was listed among the community elders who signed away the trading rights of the Jews in Kraków (with very minor exceptions) and acknowledged the magistrate's unrestricted control over the marketplace, effectively receiving nothing in return.[44] He probably died soon afterwards, because in 1489 his wife Rachela was described as a widow.[45] Rachela originally came from Prague and had married Moses Fischel after his family had settled in Kraków.[46] From 1483 she frequently appears in the Kraków records as a merchant, lending to and borrowing from a broad range of non-Jewish business partners.[47]

One of her sons, Moses, had close ties to King Jan Olbracht and King Alexander. From as early as 1499 he leased the Jewish taxes of the whole kingdom and acted in this role as a banker to the king, paying out sums to royal dignitaries.[48] He was involved in a conflict with the Jewish community of Gniezno. The elders there accused him of abuse and extortionate demands and turned to Archbishop Frederic, the king's youngest brother, for help.[49] After his intercession Moses Fischel lost the lease of the Jewish taxes in Gniezno, and the community there thenceforth paid taxes to a royal official.[50]

Soon afterwards, in 1503, King Alexander issued a privilege to another member of the Fischel family, Moses' brother-in-law, Jakub Polak, who was already well known as a rabbi in Prague. Recognizing Polak's proficiency in Hebrew and in Jewish law, the king appointed him *doctor Judaeorum*, with the authority to judge legal disputes. He was also required to uphold moral standards and fulfil all the obligations of a Jewish legal scholar. The king further instructed the Jews to accept him as an expert in Jewish law and to obey him in everything regarding his office.[51]

This document exemplifies the king's aim of strengthening his authority over the Jews. Later scholarship often interpreted it as a far-reaching claim by the king to ordain rabbis. Yet the privilege for Jakub Polak gives him no right to interfere directly in community affairs but rather sends a symbolic message: there was no definition of the geographical extent of the rabbi's power nor any reference to the rabbinical ban as there had been in previous documents issued to rabbis or community elders.[52]

At the beginning of the sixteenth century Rachela Fischel was still considered the head of the family. A few years after King Alexander's privilege, Jakub Polak had been forced to leave Kraków.[53] He came back only in 1509 to settle some private affairs, for which King Zygmunt issued him a letter of safe conduct in which he was identified additionally as Rachela Fischel's son-in-law.[54] When, ten years later, a conflict among the leading families led to the division of the Jewish community into a Polish synagogue (headed by the Fischel family) and a Bohemian synagogue (headed by the Bohemus family) each side presented its candidate for the community rabbinate. The candidate from the Polish community, Rabbi Asher Leml, was also identified by his relationship to Rachela.[55]

The incidents leading to the division of the community may serve as an example, on the one hand, of how the Fischel family was able to make use of non-Jewish authorities and, on the other, of how the king acted as patron, moderating the interests of factions and exerting his own influence in favour of his clients. Thus, King Zygmunt at first confirmed both candidates, referring to the fact that in former times there had been two rabbis in the community. In questions of marriage and divorce, the community could turn to either of them and treat them according to the old custom, on pain of a fine of 100 silver marks if they failed to do so.

The king's effort to settle the conflict and keep the community undivided failed. Before long the Fischels acquired another privilege that was meant to guarantee priority to their rabbi, Asher Leml, over the other candidate, Rabbi Perecz. The rift in the community could no longer be ignored. King Zygmunt declared, in accordance with the wishes of the Fischels, that Rabbi Perecz and his followers could use the synagogue only with the consent of Asher Leml, but simultaneously he confirmed the existence of a second, 'Bohemian', community under Rabbi Perecz's leadership. The community elders were also divided. The privilege decreed that Asher Leml and his supporters should nominate two elders and one *shamash*. It was not mentioned whether the other two elders should come from the Bohemian side or if there would be a different mechanism to fill these positions.[56]

In the second and third decades of the sixteenth century another of Rachela Fischel's sons—referred to as Franczek in the sources—established close links with the royal court. In 1512 King Zygmunt appointed him 'general collector' of Jewish taxes in Małopolska and Ruthenia. To enable him to collect these taxes, the king granted him the right to visit any town or place where Jews lived, either in person or by proxy. Every Jew was ordered to support him in his work and to guarantee his safety. Furthermore, as long as he was in office Franczek Fischel was not under the jurisdiction of any voivode or dignitary in the kingdom: only the king had the power to judge him in his court.[57] However, the communities in Kraków and, a little later, Lwów (Lviv) were not included in his mission.[58]

There was resistance to Franczek Fischel's new position, and not only in Kraków and Lwów. He was unable to deliver the expected sums, and in 1514 King Zygmunt appointed another Jew from Kraków, Abraham Bohemus, who had been the general tax collector for the Jews in Wielkopolska and Mazovia in 1512.[59] He also encountered resistance. Finally, in 1517, he reached a settlement with the community of Lwów, leaving the collection of the Jewish taxes mostly to the elders.[60] In 1519 he resigned as general tax collector, but continued to lease Jewish taxes at least until 1525, though now without special prerogatives.[61]

The Jewish communities in Poland had treated the appointment of general tax collectors by King Zygmunt as an attempt to extend his power into a central part of Jewish self-government—the allocation of taxes among the members of the community. This view was confirmed by a royal mandate of 1514 ordering all rabbis, under threat of punishment, to impose a ban on anybody resisting the general tax collector, in order to ensure more rapid delivery of taxes.[62] After multiple complaints from communities over abuse and infringements by the general tax collectors, King Zygmunt decided to put the collection of taxes into the hands of the community elders, and in 1519 he issued the first privilege in this matter to the community of Poznań.[63]

Conclusion

In the sixteenth century, Jewish self-government was a tangled system of institutional and personal relationships between Jewish communities, the Jewish economic elite, and non-Jewish authorities; this differed substantially from that of earlier centuries. The oldest available sources provide sporadic information about a Jewish court system functioning independently of the non-Jewish authorities and hint at community organization and a community leadership communicating with those authorities only when necessary. Only in the late fourteenth century does the Jewish economic elite become visible in the historical records, being perceived as individual actors, whose ties to the community remain mostly invisible. Apparently, the communities did not use members of the Jewish economic elite as representatives in their contacts with the non-Jewish authorities, while members of the economic elite did not seek leadership positions within the community.

Non-Jewish authorities had little knowledge of the structure of the Jewish community. The privileges granted to the Jews of Świdnica and to Lewko of Kraków relied solely on the information provided by their Jewish interlocutors—both mention the rabbi as head of the Jewish court as an apparently essential part of Jewish society, but both describe him as a subaltern figure, dependent on either the Świdnica elders or Lewko's family.

This situation changed in the course of the fifteenth century. Increasingly, non-Jewish records mention the positions Jews held in their community: inner-Jewish affairs were taken to non-Jewish authorities not only by members of the economic elite but by the communities as well. Thus, communication between Jews and non-Jews became less ad hoc and more of an integrated factor in negotiating Jewish interests. At the beginning of the sixteenth century, non-Jewish authorities also started using these lines of communication to exert influence within the Jewish population. Again, this was not just about conflict or control: King Zygmunt's involvement in the balancing of power between the Jewish economic elite and the community shows clearly that non-Jewish authorities needed to be understood not as a form of superstructure controlling the Jewish population but as an integral part of a general set of governmental institutions, which comprised the Jewish community and supra-community bodies as well. Jewish self-government functioned within this general framework on the basis of what might be called, a little anachronistically, 'subsidiarity'. It was not 'autonomous' in the sense that it functioned apart from its non-Jewish surroundings. Non-Jewish authorities played a part in this system: they pursued their own agenda but could also be used by Jewish actors and accepted inner-Jewish regulations.

The Jewish economic elite acted as a conduit that not only involved non-Jewish actors in inner-Jewish affairs but also induced the community leadership to take a more active approach in their relations with non-Jewish authorities. While in the late fourteenth century the mention of the head of the Jewish court in the Kraków privilege appears as an inconsequential gesture, during the fifteenth century communities actively used their ties to non-Jewish authorities—in co-operation with the economic elite as well as in situations of conflict. The sixteenth century witnessed further intensification of contacts: mechanisms of negotiation had developed that allowed the communities to defend their interests even against the combined agency of the king and the Jewish economic elite. They proved to be a decisive factor in making Jewish self-government a stable factor in the political and social system of early modern Poland.

Notes

1 M. Bałaban, *Historja Żydów w Krakowie i na Kazimierzu, 1304–1868*, 2 vols. (Kraków, 1931–6), i. 75–7, 323–58; H. Zaremska, *Żydzi w średniowiecznej Polsce: Gmina krakowska* (Warsaw, 2011), 367–409. For a critical evaluation of the historiography of Jewish autonomy in the German lands, see A. Gotzmann, *Jüdische Autonomie in der Frühen Neuzeit: Recht und Gemeinschaft im deutschen Judentum* (Göttingen, 2008), 7–23.

2 J. Katz, *Masoret umashber: hahevrah hayehudit bemotsa'ei yemei-habeinayim*, 4th edn. (Jerusalem, 1985), 232–3; abridged Eng. trans.: *Tradition and Crisis: Jewish Society at the End of the Middle Ages* (New York, 1961); Eng. trans.: *Tradition and Crisis: Jewish Society at the End of the Middle Ages*, trans. B. D. Cooperman (New York, 1993; repr. 2000), 171–2.

3 G. D. Hundert, *The Jews in a Polish Private Town: The Case of Opatów in the Eighteenth Century* (Baltimore, 1992), 118–28.

4 M. Rosman, *The Lords' Jews: Magnate–Jewish Relations in the Polish–Lithuanian Commonwealth during the Eighteenth Century* (Cambridge, Mass., 1990), 144–84.

5 A. Teller, *Money, Power, and Influence in Eighteenth-Century Lithuania: The Jews on the Radziwiłł Estates* (Stanford, Calif., 2016), 73–105.

6 M. Cieśla, 'Mojżeszowicz, Gordon, Ickowicz: The Jewish Economic Elites in the Grand Duchy of Lithuania (Seventeenth and Eighteenth Century)', *Acta Poloniae Historica*, 107 (2013), 101–27.

7 Y. Kleinmann, 'Städtische Gemeinschaft: Christen und Juden im frühneuzeitlichen Rzeszów', *Osteuropa*, 62/10 (2012), 3–24; ead., 'Rechtsinstrumente in einer ethnisch-religiös gemischten Stadtgesellschaft des frühneuzeitlichen Polen: Der Fall Rzeszów', in J. Gleixner et al. (eds.), *Konkurrierende Ordnungen: Verschränkungen von Religion, Staat und Nation in Ostmitteleuropa vom 16. bis zum 20. Jahrhundert* (Munich, 2015), 159–99.

8 See I. A. Agus, *Urban Civilization in Pre-Crusade Europe: A Study of Organized Town-Life in Northwestern Europe during the Tenth and Eleventh Centuries Based on the Responsa Literature*, 2 vols. (Leiden, 1968), i, no. 21; Zaremska, *Żydzi w średniowiecznej Polsce*, 331–3; I. M. Ta-Shma, 'On the History of the Jews in Twelfth- and Thirteenth-Century Poland', *Polin*, 10 (1997), 287–317: 287–8. On Judah ben Meir and *Sefer hadinim*, see Agus, *Urban Civilization*, i. 43–5.

9 *Hebrajskie inskrypcje na Śląsku XIII–XVIII wieku*, ed. M. Wodziński (Wrocław, 1996), no. 1.

10 *Zbiór dokumentów i listów miasta Płocka*, ed. S. M. Szacherska, 2 vols. (Warsaw, 1975–87), i, no. 9.

11 *Kodeks dyplomatyczny Wielkopolski/Codex diplomaticus Maioris Poloniae*, i, ed. I. Zakrzewski (Poznań, 1877), no. 574.

12 *Kodeks dyplomatyczny Wielkopolski*, i, no. 605 §§22, 30.

13 *Russko-evreiskii arkhiv: Dokumenty i materialy dlya istorii evreev v Rossii*, ed. S. A. Bershadsky, 3 vols. (St Petersburg, 1882–1903), iii, no. 1.

14 Ibid.

15 *Żydzi w średniowiecznym Krakowie: Wypisy źródłowe z ksiąg miejskich krakowskich/The Jews in Medieval Kraków: Selected Records from Kraków Municipal Books*, ed. B. Wyrozumska (Kraków, 1995), no. 32.

16 *Starodawne prawa polskiego pomniki*, ed. A. Z. Helcel, 12 vols. (Kraków, 1856–1921), i. 217–18; Bałaban, *Historja Żydów w Krakowie i na Kazimierzu*, i. 18–21; I. Schipper, *Studya nad stosunkami gospodarczymi Żydów w Polsce podczas średniowiecza* (Lwów, 1911), 119–21; E. Müller, *Żydzi w Krakowie w drugiej połowie XIV stulecia* (Kraków, 1906), 33–5.

17 *Żydzi w średniowiecznym Krakowie*, no. 57; Schipper, *Studya nad stosunkami gospodarczymi Żydów*, 118.

18 *Codex diplomaticus Poloniae*, ed. L. Rzyszczewski and A. Muczkowski, ii/2 (Warsaw, 1852), nos. 532, 552; J. Wyrozumski, 'Żydzi w średniowiecznym Krakowie', *Krzysztofory*, 15 (1988), 8–13: 11; Bałaban, *Historja Żydów w Krakowie i na Kazimierzu*, i. 19; Schipper, *Studya nad stosunkami gospodarczymi Żydów*, 121.

19 L. Oelsner, *Schlesische Urkunden zur Geschichte der Juden im Mittelalter* (Vienna, 1864), no. 32.

20 Cited in Ta-Shma, 'On the History of the Jews in Twelfth- and Thirteenth-Century Poland', 288–9; *Źródła hebrajskie do dziejów Słowian i niektórych innych ludów środkowej i wschodniej Europy: Wyjątki z pism religijnych i prawniczych XI–XIII w.*, ed. F. Kupfer and T. Lewicki (Wrocław, 1956), 159.

21 *Żydzi w średniowiecznym Krakowie*, nos. 66, 67, 68.

22 Ibid., nos. 73, 78.

23 Ibid., no. 48; see J. Heyde, *Transkulturelle Kommunikation und Verflechtung. Die jüdischen Wirtschaftseliten in Polen vom 14. bis zum 16. Jahrhundert* (Wiesbaden, 2014), 88–92.

24 J. Długosz, *Annales seu Cronicae incliti Regni Poloniae*, 12 vols. (Warsaw, 1964–2005), x/xi. 15–17.

25 See J. Wyrozumski, *Dzieje Krakowa*, i: *Kraków do schyłku wieków średnich* (Kraków, 1992), 326–8; *Żydzi w średniowiecznym Krakowie*, nos. 165–235 passim.

26 H. Zaremska, 'Jan Długosz o tumulcie krakowskim w 1407 roku', in C. Kuklo (ed.), *Między polityką a kulturą* (Warsaw, 1999), 155–66: 163.

27 Ibid.; for a reconstruction of the events, see Zaremska, *Żydzi w średniowiecznej Polsce*, 456–77; for the narrative strategies of the chronicler, see J. Heyde, 'Images and Narratives: Germans and Jews in the "Annales seu Cronicae incliti Regni Poloniae" of Jan Długosz', in T. Grill (ed.), *Jews and Germans in Eastern Europe: Shared and Comparative Histories* (Berlin, 2018), 21–45: 36–45.

28 Heyde, *Transkulturelle Kommunikation*, 114–19.

29 *Starodawne prawa polskiego pomniki*, ii, no. 2353; 'Jura Judaeis', art. 7, in *Jus Polonicum: Codicibus veteribus manuscriptis et editionibus quibusque collatis*, ed. J. V. Bandtkie (Warsaw, 1831), 1–21.

30 *Żydzi w średniowiecznym Krakowie*, nos. 302, 328.

31 Zaremska, *Żydzi w średniowiecznej Polsce*, 374–5.

32 J. Heyde, 'Samorząd żydowski a władze nieżydowskie w średniowieczu', in A. Pobóg-Lenartowicz, R. Trawka, and L. Poniewozik (eds.), *Obcy w mieście, obcy w klasztorze: Ciągłość i zmiana w życiu wspólnot lokalnych na ziemiach polskich w średniowieczu* (Rzeszów, 2019), 95–108: 100–2.

33 Heyde, *Transkulturelle Kommunikation*, 82–6.

34 For an analysis of the changes, see ibid. 31–3.

35 S. A. Cygielman, 'The Basic Privileges of the Jews of Great Poland as Reflected in Polish Historiography', *Polin*, 2 (1987), 117–47: 119.

36 'Jura Judaeis', art. 11.

37 Ibid., art. 10.

38 *Akta radzieckie poznańskie / Acta consularia Posnaniensia*, ed. K. Kaczmarczyk, 3 vols. (Poznań, 1925–48), i, no. 719 (11 May 1457).

39 Ibid. i, no. 778 (21 Sept. 1458).

40 M. Bałaban, 'Jakob Pollack, der Baal Chillukim in Krakau und seine Zeit', *Monatsschrift für Geschichte und Wissenschaft des Judentums*, 57 (1913), 59–72, 197–210: 72; H. Zaremska, 'Rachela Fiszel: Żydowska wdowa w średniowiecznym Krakowie', *Kwartalnik Historii Żydów*, 207 (2003), 381–90: 384.

41 *Starodawne prawa polskiego pomniki*, ii, no. 3934.

42 Zaremska, 'Rachela Fiszel', 384 n. 26.

43 *Starodawne prawa polskiego pomniki*, ii, no. 4192.

44 This was a unilateral declaration in Hebrew. A Latin translation was confirmed by the voivode in the same year. In 1492 a German translation followed, which was also inscribed into the city records. Bałaban commented on the document bitterly, viewing it as a precursor of the forthcoming catastrophe—the expulsion of the Jews from Kraków to Kazimierz in 1495 (Bałaban, *Historja Żydów w Krakowie i na Kazimierzu*, i. 59–61). For the Latin version, see *Codicis diplomatici civitatis Cracoviensis/Kodeks dyplomatyczny miasta Krakowa 1257–1506*, ed. F. Piekosiński, 2 vols. (Kraków, 1879), i, no. 193; *Żydzi w średniowiecznym Krakowie*, no. 708; for the Hebrew version, see F. H. Wettstein, 'Mipinkasei hakahal bekraka lekorot yisra'el veḥakhamav, rabanav uminhagav bepolanyah bikhlal uvekraka bifrat', in M. Brann and F. Rosenthal (eds.), *Gedenkbukh zur Erinnerung an David Kaufmann* (Breslau, 1900; repr. New York, 1980), 69–84: 69–70 (the original is lost; a facsimile is printed in Bałaban, *Historja Żydów w Krakowie i na Kazimierzu*, i, after p. 114).

45 *Starodawne prawa polskiego pomniki*, ii, no. 4351; see Zaremska, 'Rachela Fiszel', 384.

46 Zaremska, 'Rachela Fiszel', 382–3; on the Fischel family, see Schipper, *Studya nad stosunkami gospodarczymi Żydów*, 209–11, 216, 241, 245, 272–6; Bałaban, *Historja Żydów w Krakowie i na Kazimierzu*, i. 68–70.

47 Zaremska, 'Rachela Fiszel', 385–8.

48 *Liber quitantiarum Alexandri regis ab a. 1502 ad 1506 (Księga skarbowa króla Aleksandra Jag.)*, ed. A. Pawiński (Warsaw, 1897), 53, 55, 61, 101, 103, 105; Heyde, *Transkulturelle Kommunikation*, 193–5. Moses converted in 1503 and took the name Stefan (K. Miaskowski, 'Z dziejów rodziny Łaskich: Prymas Łaski a Stefan Fiszel-Powidzki', *Roczniki Historyczne*, 5 (1929), 83–9). Zaremska points out that the conversion did not lead to a break in the family. Stefan continued to live in the Jewish part of Kazimierz close to his mother and brother-in-law, Jakub Polak (Zaremska, 'Rachela Fiszel', 388).

49 Biblioteka Raczyńskich, Poznań, Codex 85: 'Zbiór przywilejów miast wielkopolskich', odpis nowoczesny rękopisu z r. 1564', fo. 81v [162–3]: *Inhibitio exigendi Contributionis pro Judaeum Fischel Cracoviensem ab Judaeis Gnesnae agentibus Fredericus Miseratione Divina Cardinalis Archiepiscopus Gnesnensis et Primas episcopusque Cracoviensis* (22 June 1499); cf. J. Heyde, 'Jüdische Eliten in Polen zu Beginn der Frühen Neuzeit', *Aschkenas*, 13 (2003), 117–65: 138–9 n. 71. The document only refers to 'Judeus Fischel' without giving a first name, but the genealogy of the Fischel family strongly suggests that it was Stefan (M. Horn, 'Żydzi i mieszczanie na służbie królów polskich i wielkich książąt litewskich w latach 1386–1506. Część 1: Uwagi wstępne. Bankierzy i celnicy', *Biuletyn Żydowskiego Instytutu Historycznego*, 135–6 (1985), 3–19: 9).

50 Heyde, *Transkulturelle Kommunikation*, 139.

51 Bałaban, *Historja Żydów w Krakowie i na Kazimierzu*, i. 107–8 n. 4.

52 Elchanan Reiner emphasizes that this privilege could not be considered as the foundation of a community rabbinate (E. Reiner, '"Asher kol gedolei ha'arets hazot talmidav": r. ya'akov polak, rishon verosh leḥakhmei krakov', in id. (ed.), *Kroke – kazimierz – krakov: meḥkarim betoledot yehudei krakov* (Tel Aviv, 2001), 55); on other documents mentioning the rabbinical ban, see Heyde, 'Jüdische Eliten in Polen', 119–27.

53 Bałaban, *Historja Żydów w Krakowie i na Kazimierzu*, i. 108–10.

54 *Russko-evreiskii arkhiv*, iii, no. 63.

55 *Dyplomatariusz dotyczący Żydów w dawnej Polsce na źródłach archiwalnych osnuty (1388–1782)*, ed. M. Bersohn (Warsaw, 1910), no. 20; *Russko-evreiskii arkhiv*, iii, no. 121.

56 *Dyplomatariusz dotyczący Żydów*, no. 21a; *Russko-evreiskii arkhiv*, iii, no. 122; Heyde, 'Jüdische Eliten in Polen', 136–8; A. Teller, 'The Laicization of Early Modern Jewish Society: The Development of the Polish Communal Rabbinate in the Sixteenth Century', in M. Graetz (ed.), *Schöpferische Momente des europäischen Judentums in der frühen Neuzeit* (Heidelberg, 2000), 333–49: 342.

57 *Russko-evreiskii arkhiv*, iii, no. 82; on general tax collectors, see Heyde, 'Jüdische Eliten in Polen', 138–43.

58 M. Horn, 'Żydzi i mieszczanie w służbie celnej Zygmunta Starego i Zygmunta Augusta', *Biuletyn Żydowskiego Instytutu Historycznego*, 141 (1987), 3–20: 12.

59 *Acta Tomiciana per Stanislaum Gorski Canonicum*, iii: *1514–1515* (Poznań, 1853), no. 252.

60 Schipper, *Studya nad stosunkami gospodarczymi Żydów w Polsce podczas średniowiecza* (Lwów, 1911), 349.

61 Bałaban, *Historja Żydów w Krakowie i na Kazimierzu*, i. 105; Horn, 'Żydzi i mieszczanie w służbie celnej Zygmunta Starego i Zygmunta Augusta', 10–11.

62 *Acta Tomiciana*, iii, no. 313.

63 *Russko-evreiskii arkhiv*, iii, no. 114.

The Emergence of Medinat Mehren
Establishing Jewish Supra-Community Government in Early Modern Moravia and Its Central European Contexts

MARTIN BORÝSEK

Introduction

Gaya (Kyjov), a small provincial town in southern Moravia, lying some 40 kilometres south-east of the capital Brünn (Brno) in close proximity to the Austrian and Hungarian (nowadays Slovakian) borders, was not one of the major centres of Moravian Jewry in the mid-seventeenth century. The town did have an organized Jewish community, established in 1603, and its members did show some initiative since they were able to obtain a protective decree from Emperor Matthias[1] when, in 1613, the town's Christians tried to ban Jewish merchants from selling their goods in the marketplace. However, in comparison with other Moravian Jewish communities, such as Nikolsburg (Mikulov), Proßnitz (Prostějov), Boskowitz (Boskovice), and Trebitsch (Třebíč), the community of Gaya was modest in both numbers[2] and significance. Yet it was here that, in 1650, Moravian Jewry can be understood to have been established as an institutional unit, when the town hosted delegates from the Jewish communities of the province who formulated an extensive and detailed set of statutes and administrative ordinances binding on all the Jews of the area. The resulting group of texts, put together during the month of Tamuz of the Jewish year 5410 (30 June–28 July 1650), were to become known as *Shai takanot* (the 311 ordinances) and had many attributes of a comprehensive community constitution. They define in a systematic way the organization, territorial divisions, and administrative offices of Moravian Jewry, the mutual relations of the respective communities and districts, and the competence and responsibilities of its various officers. Other issues also figure prominently. A lengthy set of ordinances regulated the proceedings of community courts and, in more general terms, provided rules for settling legal matters within the limited autonomy granted to Moravian Jewish communities.

The 311 ordinances, which were approved by the leading officials of Moravian Jewry in February 1651 in Nikolsburg, stand at the beginning of a remarkable sequence of Jewish legislative texts, periodically approved and amended in the course of the next century, with the last set of ordinances being issued in 1748.[3] The resulting corpus presents a fascinating testimony to the existence of a specific quasi-political entity, the Moravian *Landesjudenschaft*[4] or, to use the language of *Shai takanot*, Medinat Mehren (the Land of Moravia).[5] In this chapter, I shall explore the emergence of this concept and set it in its political and historical context.

First, I will describe the Moravian community of the mid-seventeenth century in its historical, political, and cultural context and the relation of the *takanot* to the General Ordinance Regarding Moravian Jewry of 1754, the Habsburg government's replacement for Jewish internal legislation. I will then comment in more detail on the collection of texts now known as *Takanot medinat mehren* and assess their textual history and the role of Israel Halperin in preparing the critical edition. After a detailed overview of the collection's contents and language, I will analyse how the original *Shai takanot* regulated one specific issue, namely the authority of community offices and office-holders and, more specifically, how it established a balance of power between the respective communities and districts into which the Jewry of the land was divided. I have chosen this particular topic for two main reasons. The first is of a more practical nature, namely the great number of *takanot* addressing the issue and the richness of the information they contain. The second, more fundamental, reason is the material's potential to illuminate the emerging pan-Moravian network of Jewish communities, Medinat Mehren, as a coherent quasi-political organization[6] functioning according to a binding set of rules and administered by elected officials whose authority was recognized both by the members of the Jewish communities themselves and by the state's bureaucratic apparatus, which for a period of time was prepared to accept the Jewry of Moravia and its leaders as its official partners. This will enable me to evaluate the position of the *kahal* (community council) as the immediate executive power with jurisdiction over individual Jewish communities. Furthermore, it sheds light on the relations between the different communities and their *kahal*s and on the vertical hierarchy within the administration of the various institutional bodies of Moravian Jewry. This case study will thus show in concrete terms how a newly established large-scale network of Jewish communities worked, and illuminate the place of seventeenth-century Medinat Mehren in the context of Jewish autonomy in early modern central Europe and more widely in the landscape of newly established supra-community networks, of which the Council of Four Lands in Poland is the best known. This will help to resolve the question of whether the national organizations of Jews in smaller state-like units such as Moravia were autonomous phenomena that developed independently but in a similar socio-historical context to the Polish council or whether the example of Poland was a direct inspiration and moving force behind their establishment.

Historical Context

A Jewish presence in the area of the modern-day Czech Republic can be attested from the tenth century, with the earliest material and textual evidence relating to the Jewish community in Prague, the capital city of the Duchy of Bohemia and, from the early thirteenth century, of the Kingdom of Bohemia. In Bohemia, Prague remained the economic and cultural hegemon of the country's Jewry and in time also developed into a significant religious centre.[7] Jews were present also in the secondary Crown lands that belonged to the medieval and early modern Czech state:[8] the Margravate of Moravia, lying immediately to the east of Bohemia and roughly half its size, being the most ancient and most thoroughly integrated of them. In contrast to that of Bohemia, the Moravian Jewish population remained distinctly decentralized, lacking anywhere that could claim hegemony similar to that enjoyed by Prague. This state of affairs was furthered by the royal decree of 1454 which forbade Jews to reside or trade in the royal towns of Moravia (that is, those subject directly to the Crown and not owing allegiance and tax obligations to any aristocratic or ecclesiastical liege lord) in perpetuity. This ended the Jewish presence in the ancient Moravian capital Olmütz (Olomouc) and other major centres of the province, including Brünn, which became the capital in 1641.[9] Unlike many other decrees of expulsion issued in the Habsburg Crown lands during the later Middle Ages and the early modern era, this proved long-lasting and effective, and it was not until the nineteenth century that Jewish communities were re-established in the largest and economically most important cities of Moravia. Instead, a network of lively Jewish communities developed in the area's small and medium-sized towns. The communities of Boskowitz, Trebitsch, Proßnitz, and especially Nikolsburg gradually became important centres of Jewish economic, religious, and cultural activities, known and respected far beyond the borders of the land. These provincial centres were complemented by a large number of Jewish communities in smaller towns, which, although not as prominent, nevertheless managed to support vibrant Jewish populations. The significance of these less populous communities is demonstrated, among other things, by the fact that many of the general assemblies of early modern Medinat Mehren took place in Moravia's smaller Jewish settlements.[10]

The representatives of Moravian Jewry who formulated the oldest extant set of Moravian *takanot* convened in Gaya in the middle of a century of deep and long-lasting changes for the whole of the Bohemian Crown lands and for wider central Europe. The Thirty Years War that had barely ended left in its wake widespread material and economic devastation accompanied by a deep sense of moral crisis, which prompted among the social elite an urgent need to create a new, functioning social order.[11] In the Bohemian Crown lands, which since 1526 had belonged to the Habsburg monarchy, the war was intimately connected with the long-lasting tensions between Catholics and non-Catholics. The 1648 peace settlement confirmed the Habsburgs' hold on the land and constituted a step forward in their effort to re-Catholicize its entire Christian population. This project, which gradually proved largely successful, went hand in hand with a systematic effort to increase central control over the internal affairs of Bohemia, Moravia, and Silesia and to make these provinces *de jure* as well as *de facto* hereditary possessions of the Habsburg dynasty. Even though this process was in its early stages in 1650, the social and political pressures were palpable, and the Jews, ever vulnerable at times of popular unrest and tension, tried to ensure a functioning modus vivendi with the state and their Christian neighbours. They were particularly conscious of the atrocities that had devastated the Jewish communities of Poland–Lithuania during the Khmelnytsky uprising that broke out in 1648. In this context, it is perhaps surprising that the 'administrative sections' of *Shai takanot* contain very few direct references to the government of the realm and the state's executive powers as the source and guarantor of the Jews' institutional autonomy.[12] However, the consequent development, as documented in the subsequent collections of *Takanot medinat mehren*, and the fact that these *takanot* were eventually to be adapted by the state as the basis for its official regulation of Jewish community life in the mid-eighteenth century, demonstrate clearly that the administrative ordinances of the incipient supra-community organization had the state's recognition. In addition, the Jewish officials elected on the basis of *Shai takanot* and its later amendments were accepted by the secular authorities as recognized representatives of their people. It is therefore appropriate to see the initial formulation of the Moravian supra-community legislation as a step towards creating an organized autonomous polity that could speak for Moravian Jewry as a whole. The existing *Takanot medinat mehren* were not the first community ordinances enacted in Jewish Moravia, but, as well as being the oldest such texts to survive, they document the emergence of what can be called a political entity, albeit one whose authority was inevitably limited and whose recognition by the state was precarious.

Takanot were certainly produced by Moravian Jewish communities before the mid-seventeenth century.[13] This can be presumed both from the text of *Shai takanot*, which alludes to already existing community institutions and even older *takanot*, and from the state's Jewish legislation, which contains references to Jewish elders and community *takanot* and councils. However, such older community legislation has not survived apart from a few fragments appended to *Shai takanot* by its authors. Its text is therefore the oldest extant evidence of the internal administration of Moravian Jewish communities. It is also apparent from the text that it documents an ongoing process of individual Jewish communities merging into one, diverse, but basically coherent, organization. This organization developed into the highest representative of Moravian Jewry and was acknowledged by the state as the quasi-official body responsible for Jewish affairs in the province and the proper conduct of the Jews.

During the eighteenth century, and especially after the ascent of Empress Maria Theresa (r. 1740–80), the Habsburg monarchy became increasingly centralized and the state's bureaucratic apparatus gained ever greater influence over public life. One consequence of this was that the Jewish communities in Habsburg Crown lands were subjected to ever greater limitation and stricter control. The existence of a partially independent legislative, executive, and judicial system peculiar to one confessional community came to be seen as both an anachronism and an obstacle to the smooth functioning of the state. From the middle of the eighteenth century, in accordance with the programme of enlightened absolutism, it became the state's objective to impose on Jewish communities an effective supervision that would facilitate more control over their affairs and eventually eliminate their special status, insofar as this was seen to hinder the effective exploitation of the Jews for the state's (mainly economic) purposes. To achieve this goal, in 1754 the Habsburg government issued the General-Polizei-Prozess- und Kommerzialordnung für Maehrische Judenschaft (General Ordinance Regarding Moravian Jewry), which, on the one hand, guaranteed the Jews' right to exercise their religion and to maintain the relevant religious institutions in their communities and, on the other, clearly set out their tax and other obligations towards the state.[14] This marked the effective end of Jewish self-government in the province.

The Text of *Shai Takanot*

The critical edition of *Takanot medinat mehren*, published by Israel Halperin in 1951, was based on the various manuscripts available to him when he compiled it shortly after the Second World War. As he mentions in the preface, his main source was a manuscript located in Frankfurt am Main until the First World War.[15] Unfortunately, he does not specify which manuscript it was, nor does he elaborate on its post-war location. He also mentions that the same manuscript was the basis for Gerson Wolf's German translation.[16] Halperin mentions other manuscripts of the initial collection of *takanot* and some of the subsequent collections of Moravian *takanot* that he used. Only a few of them are identified by signature numbers, the most important being MS Opp. 616 and MS 149 in the Bodleian Library in Oxford.[17] Other manuscripts mentioned are held by the Jewish Theological Seminary in New York,[18] Hebrew Union College in Cincinnati, and the Budapest University of Jewish Studies.[19] Halperin's critical edition of *Takanot medinat mehren* is therefore an eclectic text, which does not seek to reproduce any one manuscript but rather to take the best readings from all the manuscripts he identified as belonging to the project of Moravian supra-community legislation prior to Maria Theresa's General Ordinance of 1754. In this respect, it closely resembles his edition of the *pinkas* (ledger) of the Council of Four Lands.[20]

Ktiv, the digital database of Hebrew manuscripts held by the National Library of Israel in Jerusalem, lists a total of nine manuscripts under the heading *Takanot medinat mehren*, including the manuscripts Halperin explicitly mentions. Most of them do not bear a precise date, unlike the *takanot* they record, and are believed to be later copies, made mainly in the eighteenth century after Medinat Mehren ceased to have any legal authority over its member communities. They vary greatly in length, MS 10748 from the Jewish Theological Seminary being 23 folios long and MS Opp. 616 from Oxford 225 folios. The descriptions of several of these manuscripts in the library catalogue explicitly state that they differ from Halperin's edition.[21] However, his version is considered to be in general agreement with those manuscripts which do contain parts of the original *Shai takanot*. Another manuscript, not included in the Jerusalem database, is held by the Jewish Museum of Prague. In her recent study of its linguistic profile, Lenka Uličná argued that it is a Hebrew retranslation of those passages of Maria Theresa's General Ordinance of 1754 based on the original *Shai takanot* made probably shortly after its issue.[22] At any rate, Halperin's remains the most extensive and most carefully prepared edition of the original Moravian *takanot* and can be considered as the appropriate basis for an assessment of the institutional emergence of Medinat Mehren as the representative body of Moravian Jewry.

Content and Composition of *Shai Takanot*

The corpus of 311 ordinances formulated in July 1650 in Gaya may, with justification, be considered an ambitious attempt to provide Moravian Jewry with something akin to a constitution, in practice if not in name. It is a comprehensive, very detailed, code of regulations whose basic goal was to create a set of community and supra-community institutions, rules for appointing men to hold offices within these institutions, and a legal framework for settling potential disputes within and among Moravian Jewish communities. Perhaps somewhat surprisingly, little attention is paid to the relation with the state authorities and no mention is made of the privileges given to the Jewish communities by the state. It would seem therefore that *Shai takanot* was intentionally formulated chiefly for the purposes of internal debate, taking advantage of the sovereign's protection which was officially extended to the Jews of the Habsburg Crown lands, creating a 'legal niche' within which they felt free to articulate their own rules without restriction. This sense of freedom is also suggested by the absence of the conventional eulogies that would usually accompany references to the government.[23] Such formulae, expressing the obligatory respect for the state's authority, do appear in a small number of *takanot* that explicitly define eligibility for certain offices held by Jewish leaders in the state's name and in the text of the prescribed oath taken upon assuming those offices.[24] On the whole therefore, it is plausible that the *takanot*, regulating the widest variety of religious, social, and administrative issues, were proposed as an ideal model, an example to be followed as far as circumstances allowed (and as far as the Moravian Jews themselves were ready to observe the regulations dictated by their elected leaders).

Given the status of *Shai takanot* as the first set of regulations binding for the whole of Moravia, it may also be surprising that it does not contain a preamble in which the authors attribute their activity to divine inspiration or validate it through proof-texts from the Bible or other canonical texts. Nor is there a 'technical' preface, explaining the *raison d'être* of the *takanot* or summarizing their context.[25] In fact, *Shai takanot* begins seemingly *in mediis rebus*, listing the conditions under which elementary schools should be established in individual Jewish communities. The opening of the first *takanah* can serve as a starting point for several observations regarding its place within *Shai takanot* and the collection's concept and organization:

'The Fear of the Lord is the Beginning of Wisdom' [Ps. 111: 10], the Pillar of the Torah
Each and every community wherein dwell thirty landlords (this being the total population, the entirety of said community), is obliged to maintain one respectable teacher [qualified to be a] judge of a rabbinic court, who shall run a religious school there, where no fewer than six boys and six young men shall study.[26]

Thus, the code of community and supra-community legislation that was to be the foundation of Jewish autonomy in Moravia does not start with a clear definition of its purpose, its jurisdiction, or the very terms it is going to use in relation to Jewish communities and their officials (although such definitions appear later as needed). Rather, it clearly speaks to an audience familiar with the context and living within an established system of community institutions. To see how *Shai takanot* proceeded to create within this context a new, rigorous system of legislative rule requires an examination of the headings of the *takanot* to see what areas they regulate and what—if indeed any—logical sequence they follow.

From a formal point of view, *Shai takanot* is divided into five sections of greatly uneven length, each introduced by a heading. As mentioned above, the first item is the institution of schools and religious education in larger communities (*takanot* 1–17), introduced by the biblical verse evoking wisdom and fear of God. The second section (*takanot* 18–23), under the heading 'If I Forget You, Jerusalem, May My Right Hand Forget Its Skill' (Ps 137:5), is likewise devoted to a particular practical topic, the collection of charitable donations to support Jewish settlements in the Land of Israel, including specific arrangements regarding foreign messengers arriving to collect money and instructions on how to check their credentials. Only then is attention devoted to the central topic of *Shai takanot*: the organization of Jewish communities throughout Moravia, their division into districts, the definition of executive offices, the mechanisms for elections, and so on.

The central section of *Shai takanot* is headed 'Rules for Elections of Their Excellencies the Highly Honoured Heads of the Land, May Their Rock Protect Them'. Despite this rather specific heading, the 152 *takanot* (24–175) in fact regulate a wide range of issues relating to Jewish administration throughout Moravia. Only the first twenty-two (24–45) deal directly with electing the officers and leaders of the Jews of the land, including the frequency of the elections and duration of the various terms of office. Subsequent *takanot* regulate relations between the executive officers of the districts, the members of the national council, and other important personages, such as the chief rabbi, and seek to protect the independence of their respective offices and jurisdictions. Fourteen *takanot* (46–59) regulate relationships between the district councils, their jurisdictions, and the proper conduct of elections. The subsequent nineteen *takanot* are devoted to the judicial powers of the national council and its relation to religious courts of justice, the chief rabbi, and the rabbis of the communities[27] and to disciplinary regulations dealing with misconduct in judicial matters (60–78). The rest of this central section (79–175) can be less easily divided into subsections, because the progression of topics is unclear (some issues dealt with in earlier paragraphs re-emerge, seemingly out of context)[28] and a great variety of subjects is addressed. Many of these *takanot* concern financial matters, community accounts,[29] and the taxes collected by the Jewish authorities,[30] whilst others revisit disciplinary[31] or judicial matters.[32] One topic touched upon only briefly, but which had great significance for Jewish coexistence with the majority society, is the issue of advocates (*shtadlanim*), individuals officially appointed by the community (or, in this case, by Medinat Mehren) to represent its interests vis-à-vis the state.[33]

Even in this miscellaneous section, more substantial blocks of *takanot* on a single topic do appear, as is the case with *takanot* 137–57, which regulate rabbinical ordinations, the rabbis' obligation to co-operate with lay councils in disciplinary and other judicial matters, and other rabbinical responsibilities. Towards the end of the section, the *takanot* turn away from constitutional policy to family law, including particularities of divorce procedures and match-making.[34] The very last issue to be addressed by 'Rules for Elections' is once again the administration of charitable activities, namely the provision of dowries for the poor.[35] Despite the title, therefore, the unifying principle that binds the *takanot* in this section is not their relation to elections, but their concern with matters that are in the competence of the elected national authorities or that directly regulated their exercise of office.

The fourth section, comprising the next 121 *takanot* (176–296), is headed 'Rules Regarding the Communities'. As the name suggests, it is essentially a counterpart of 'Rules for Elections' concerning arrangements within individual Jewish communities. Given the lack of earlier source material, it is impossible to make any definite statements but it is reasonable to assume that these *takanot* were to a great extent inspired by existing practice and its written codification. The early chapters of the section define the qualifications required of the head of a Jewish community, including the state's consent (*takanot* 177–83).[36] Subsequent *takanot* specify the size of community councils (depending on the size of the communities), the taxes which individual communities were entitled to raise for their own needs (as opposed to the taxes due to Medinat Mehren), and the communities' authority to pronounce judgements in disputes between individual Jews and the community representatives. 'Rules Regarding the Communities' also contains a number of *takanot* dealing with relationships between individual Jewish communities and the central Jewish administration of Moravia. This is true in judicial matters, as can be seen in *takanot* 213–19, where details on how to appeal against decisions by Jewish courts are provided, and also in legislative matters.

The last fifteen *takanot* (297–311) follow under the heading: 'We have Copied These Items Letter for Letter and Word for Word from the *Takanot* of Old and This is Their Content'. This content is quite random in relation to previous sections, including sumptuary legislation,[37] the decision to insert a prayer for the emperor in the sabbath synagogue service,[38] and the assertion of the individual communities' duty to accept Medinat Mehren's legislation.[39] The real importance of this section is that it provides textual proof from a Jewish source that there was a functioning Jewish autonomous organization prior to 1650, including a supra-community network called the *medinah*.[40]

In my view *Shai takanot* should be seen as an effective constitution for the emerging Medinat Mehren or at least a first step towards one. A superficial overview of its contents, however, seemingly challenges this argument because of the demonstrably patchy character of the collection: what can be seen as a serious attempt to order the administrative and legislative matters of Moravian Jewry as a whole and of its respective communities comes only after two shorter sets of practical *takanot* addressing the particular issues of local schools and charitable donations for Jews in the Land of Israel that were apparently the pressing business of the day. What is more, even the two larger sections, on community and supra-community administration, read rather more like the minutes of a lively, sometimes perhaps heated, debate, recording the views and principles of the disputants. There was presumably some sense of order, but it was in constant competition with the need to put in writing new ideas as they emerged and address matters of immediate importance, as witnessed by *takanot* regulating match-making or the provision of dowries to poor brides interspersed with the more obviously constitutional questions of the judicial auth-ority of rabbis. If *Shai takanot* can be seen as a constitution *sui generis*, it is thanks to its practical character and its potential to provide the framework for sound and long-lasting community and supra-community order. The gradual adjustment of this framework to the changing conditions of life in the Baroque-era Habsburg state for over a century testifies to its flexibility but also to its essential strength as a legal document and source of a functioning legislative system.

The Language of *Shai Takanot*

Although it is broadly correct that *Shai takanot* is a collection of Hebrew texts, there is an important caveat: whilst Hebrew is indeed the main linguistic medium of the *takanot,* many of them are written in a mixture of Hebrew and Yiddish:[41] sometimes there is as much Yiddish as Hebrew. As an example, I shall cite once more the opening of the very first *takanah,* this time translating only the Hebrew component:

Each and every community *doz da hot* thirty landlords (*di da in* total *zeynen,* the entirety of said community), *iz* obliged *tzu haltn eyn* respectable teacher [qualified to be a] judge of a rabbinic court, *der da zol* run a religious school there, where *nit veniger az* six boys and six young men shall study.[42]

Even this short sample shows that Yiddish played a prominent role in the linguistic make-up of the text, far beyond providing occasional loanwords reflecting specific cultural and social elements of its users' lives. Instead, Yiddish, the everyday language of seventeenth-century Moravian Jews, spontaneously penetrates the higher-register Hebrew discourse, so that both languages are used within one sentence and even within one short phrase, effectively creating a mixed language whose syntax is neither Semitic nor Germanic.[43] What is also remarkable, however, is that not all of the 311 *takanot* have this hybrid character: roughly 55 per cent of them are written more or less entirely in Hebrew. This Hebrew is of varying stylistic quality, showing the various levels of the authors' linguistic mastery, but is generally simple and easy to understand.[44] However, *Shai takanot* cannot be neatly separated into 'Hebrew' and 'mixed' sections: the two linguistic types are interspersed freely across the collection. This second level of code-mixing is yet another proof that *Shai takanot* is the work of many authors who differed in their level of education and linguistic expertise but who were capable of producing a body of legal literature in a shared linguistic medium. Since this is not a philological study, I cannot explore other questions related to the linguistic profile of *Shai takanot* and later Moravian *takanot*, but even this brief overview suggests that Hebrew played a prominent role in Jewish public life in the mid-seventeenth century and that it was, to a certain degree, accessible even to Jews—or at the very least the more affluent and prominent of them—outside the narrowly defined religious or liturgical discourse.

Shai Takanot and the Foundations of Medinat Mehren

The importance and interest of *Shai takanot* lie in the depth and extent of the information it provides about the institutional structure of Moravian Jewry and its desire to organize itself and to take advantage of the limited legal autonomy granted by the Habsburg state. In the following I examine closely several *takanot* from 'Rules for Elections' which define the basic principles of the emerging Medinat Mehren. Particular points of interest are the definition of the leading offices, the officials' legislative and executive authority, the division of Moravia into three districts which were guaranteed representation in the national council, and the mechanisms that regulated their mutual relations.

Although the section of *Shai takanot* devoted to national administration is titled 'Rules for Elections', its scope is much wider and it addresses more fundamental issues. The very first *takanah* of this section introduces one of the key institutions of Medinat Mehren, which is constantly referred to in subsequent *takanot*, reflecting its power and influence. To cite the *takanah* itself:

We reached a unanimous agreement that we shall choose six perfect and intelligent men, men of vigour and fear of God, to be 'heads of the land', namely two from each district. They shall have the power to excommunicate and punish sinners and rebels and those who disrupt the law and they shall perform their exalted role with grace.[45]

'Heads of the land' (*rashei hamedinah*) also figured in the title of Jewish leaders in Poland–Lithuania. The six heads of the land, the collective leadership of Jewish Moravia, are here introduced as an executive body whose key power is the authority to punish transgressors through excommunication (*herem*). The power to excommunicate is not to be underestimated. On the one hand, it may rightly be said that the penalty demonstrates how limited the executive power of the Jewish representatives was—any more serious penalties were reserved to the judicial powers of the state and thus were outside the Jews' influence. On the other hand, it had another very palpable consequence: excommunicating offenders from the collective of Medinat Mehren, the heir of the medieval *universitas Judaeorum*, deprived them of the fundamental protection enjoyed by individuals in pre-modern society—membership of a wider corporation, recognized by the state and designated by it to be their representative and protector. Such an arrangement was doubly important and the threat doubly severe for the Jewish community whose position was always precarious. It may therefore not be an exaggeration to read this first *takanah* of 'Rules for Elections' as a reflection of the power granted to the heads of the land by the Jewish 'law-givers' of Moravia, the basis of their importance. The *takanah* further calls for the election of six additional members of the executive, called *mevorarim* (the elected), to assist the heads of the land. Again, two were appointed from each district.[46]

The next *takanah* lays out the rules for electoral assemblies, *va'adei hahithadshut*: 'All communities in the land shall send delegates to that town where they are to convene in order to re-elect Their Excellencies the Heads of the Land and the new *mevorarim*.'[47] The rest of the *takanah* then specifies which communities are entitled to send delegates, linking their eligibility to how much tax they pay to the central institutions: one delegate from a community that paid at least half a gulden a year and two from one that paid at least one gulden. It is also explicitly stated that any community that paid less than half a gulden was not entitled to be represented at the assembly.[48] The six heads of the land and the *mevorarim* constituted the full council (*va'ad shalem*), which had executive authority in matters concerning all of Moravian Jewry. There were also three pairs of *rashei hagalil* (heads of districts), who sat in a separate small council (*va'ad katan*) twice a year to decide matters of regional importance.[49] The delegates of individual communities also chose the Council of the Land (*va'ad hamedinah*) at the electoral assemblies. This council was composed of fifteen members, five from each district, and was to advise the heads of the land. The specifics of the election to this body are laid out in *takanah* 27:

The said delegates of the communities, when they come to the assembly, shall meet in the synagogue or another prominent building, and there the delegates from the upper district shall sit together, as well as the delegates from the central and lower districts. Each district shall elect five intelligent and wise men, who must be acceptable one to another, as well as to Their Excellencies the Heads of the Land, may their Rock protect them.[50]

The first *takanah* that specifies the actual election rules thus establishes the separate selection of legislators from the districts, but only under the condition of their acceptability to the heads of the land, who therefore implicitly assume the role of arbitrators. The role the fifteen councillors are to fulfil is outlined in the following *takanah* in an eloquent manner:

These fifteen men shall sit in council and argue about public affairs, all the issues they deem necessary [to discuss]. They should inform Their Excellencies the Heads of the Land and Their Excellencies the *Mevorarim* [about their decisions] and take into consideration the needs of the hour.[51]

Later in the *takanah*, it is specified that the full council should serve as the arbitrator of any conflicts and divisions within the Council of the Land.[52] In practice, therefore there is a decidedly blurred line between the executive and legislative branch of the national administration. This becomes more apparent in *takanah* 30, which specifies that the fifteen members of the Council of the Land actually include the six heads of the land and that therefore only nine of them are elected solely for the purpose of legislative deliberations. In this *takanah*, it is specified that three names were to be taken by the chief scribe from each of three urns, into which the delegates from each district placed the names of their candidates.[53] There is no more precise information regarding the number of candidates or the conditions of their selection, but it seems that an element of chance was intentionally introduced into the election procedure to avoid any bias. However, this is counterbalanced by the repeated assertion that the candidates must be acceptable to each other, which implies the possibility of subsequent changes if the group found itself unable to work together in a constructive manner.

These *takanot* distribute the posts of the heads of the land, the *mevorarim*, and the members of the Council of the Land equally among the three districts of Jewish Moravia. There is no description in this *takanah* or in any of the others in 'Rules for Elections' of the districts. However, the latest set of *takanot* included in Halperin's edition of *Takanot medinat mehren*, which was accepted in Butschowitz in late summer of 1748, does include a list of signatories according to their respective communities and districts.[54] Even taking into account that the list is not exhaustive and that the borders may have changed between 1650 and 1748, it does provide a general geographical outline of the three districts: the upper district was represented by signatories from sixteen communities in northern and central Moravia, from Hotzenplotz (Osoblaha) on the Silesian border to Austerlitz (Slavkov u Brna) in the vicinity of Brünn; the central district by delegates from sixteen communities south and south-west of Brünn, towards the Austrian border in the south and the Bohemian border in the west; the representatives of the lower district came from nine communities in the south-eastern corner of the land, along the Austrian and Hungarian borders. This distribution shows somewhat sparser Jewish settlement in the northern half of the land, which nevertheless contained three of the largest and most prosperous Jewish communities, Proßnitz, Boskowitz, and Holleschau (Holešov). The central district contained two important communities, Trebitsch and Nikolsburg. The lower district, however, was represented chiefly by smaller communities in less significant provincial towns, including Gaya. These districts are also mentioned in the older *takanot* of *Shai takanot*, which indicates that they were known to the representatives of Moravian Jewry who met in Gaya in 1650. In any case, *takanah* 24 establishes regionalism and decentralization as a leading principle of the administration of the land, in keeping with the generally decentralized character of Jewish settlement in Moravia.

This emphasis on regionalism is reflected also by the large amount of space given to the internal affairs of individual communities. However, this decentralization has clear limits, as is apparent from the great care that is given to defining the several Moravian-wide Jewish institutions and to balancing power between them. One *takanah* addresses this matter in no uncertain terms:

Each head of a community shall have a duty to keep the *takanot* of the land in the archive of his community, may its Rock protect it, so that they know how they should proceed, lest they ever miss the target.[55]

Apart from the factual content, confirming the strong emphasis on the supra-community dimension of Moravian Jewish autonomy, two points are worthy of attention. Firstly, this brief *takanah* is one of the few older *takanot* that have been kept and copied into *Shai takanot*, making clear the importance assigned to the *takanot* of the land and to the idea of Medinat Mehren itself both by the law-givers at the Gaya assembly of 1650 and by their anonymous predecessors. Secondly, in this short text there is a literary device otherwise extremely rare in the Moravian *takanot*, an allusion to a biblical text. The words 'lest they ever miss the target' echo Judges 20: 16, thus invoking divine inspiration for the community legislators. The whole verse reads 'Among all these soldiers there were seven hundred select troops who were left-handed, each of whom could sling a stone at a hair and not miss.' While the insertion of these few words may seem a modest way of building such a connection, the very rareness of such invocation in the wider textual context makes it stand out and confirms the great importance ascribed to the community and supra-community law-making not only as a practical arrangement but as a spiritual virtue.

Conclusion

In this short introduction to *Shai takanot* it has not been possible to cover all the important aspects of this remarkable collection. I have presented it as a foundation document, building upon a pre-existing tradition that was able to establish a viable way of public life for the Jewish community of early modern Moravia. In so doing, the authors of the *takanot* displayed remarkable diplomatic ability. Firstly, the *takanot* deftly reconcile the ambitions of individual Jewish communities to keep control over their internal affairs with the need for a more rigorous control on a Moravia-wide level. Secondly, and perhaps most remarkably, the *takanot* included in 'Rules for Elections' show a deep understanding of practical politics and the need to balance power and authority between the various legislative and executive officers and between the districts. Lastly, the *takanot* show the ability of the Moravian Jewish leaders to use the opportunity to build up their supra-community network at the same time as the general rebuilding of central European society at a crucial period of the seventeenth century, the end of the Thirty Years War. Although 'great history' is never directly commented on in the text, it is apparent that the renewed peace and the slow process of stabilization and economic renewal provided the Jews with an opportunity to administer their affairs in a climate of limited tolerance and even create a quasi-constitutional system. This system, remarkably embodied in *Shai takanot* and its later amendments, was to remain the foundation of Jewish life in Moravia during the next century, a period when the wider society, while still essentially pre-modern, was characterized by the increasing rationalization of public affairs and an ever greater openness to the ideas of religious tolerance and civic values. *Shai takanot* accordingly bears witness to the emergence of Medinat Mehren and to the Jews' successful response to the challenges and opportunities presented by life in early modern Habsburg-ruled central Europe. The next phase of the history of the

Jews of Moravia, inaugurated by Maria Theresa's General Ordinance of 1754, was a first step towards the modern period when religion was ever more obviously confined to the private sphere and the path for a new way of organizing Jewish life in central Europe was opening.

Notes

1 The Habsburg emperor, younger brother of the recently deposed and deceased Rudolph II, was simultaneously the King of Bohemia and thus *ex officio* also Margrave of Moravia. For the history of the community of Gaya, see A. Ehrlich and E. Hayek, 'Geschichte der Juden in Gaya', in H. Gold (ed.), *Die Juden und Judengemeinden Mährens in Vergangenheit und Gegenwart*, i: *Einzelbeiträge zur Geschichte der Juden in Mähren* (Brünn, 1929), 199–205.

2 There were eleven Jewish families in Gaya in 1650 (ibid. 202). In comparison, Boskowitz had thirty-one Jewish houses in 1657, and Nikolsburg, the largest Moravian community at that time, had 146 families living in ninety-eight houses in the same year (see H. Gold, 'Geschichte der Juden in Boskowitz', in id. (ed.), *Juden und Judengemeinden*, i. 123–36: 124; B. M. Trapp, 'Die Geschichte der Juden in Nikolsburg', in Gold (ed.), *Juden und Judengemeinden*, i. 417–50: 422).

3 The critical edition of *Takanot medinat mehren*, prepared by Israel Halperin, contains 655 individual *takanot*, the last of which were issued on 5 September 1748, by the assembly of Jewish communities held in Butschowitz (Bučovice) (see *Seder hameshulaḥim mikol hakehilot hamedinah hameshulaḥim bava'ad hagadol k"k budeshpitz beḥodesh elul shenat tk"ḥ lp"k*, in *Takanot medinat mehren* ([5]410–508)/*Constitutiones congressus generalis Iudaeorum Moraviensium 1650–1748*, ed. I. Halperin (Jerusalem, 1951), 235–7).

4 For the development of the notion of *Landesjudenschaft*, see B. Nosek, 'Soziale Differenzierungen und Streitigkeiten in jüdischen Kultusgemeinden der böhmischen Ländern im 17. Jahrhundert und Entstehung der *Landesjudenschaft*', *Judaica Bohemiae*, 12/2 (1976), 59–92.

5 The consistent use of 'Medinat Mehren' to denote the central Jewish administration of the land without an explicit mention of its Jewish identity seems to correspond to the practice of some other early modern Jewish communities: for example, the use of the term 'Portuguese nation' by Jews of Portuguese descent in sixteenth-century Amsterdam (see I. Elbogen, 'Die Bezeichnung "jüdische Nation": Eine Untersuchung', *Monatsschrift für Geschichte und Wissenschaft des Judentums*, 63/4 (1919), 200–8: 203).

6 For the implications of a Jewish community's status as a political unit in the early modern Holy Roman Empire, see A. Gotzmann, *Jüdische Autonomie in der frühen Neuzeit: Recht und Gemeinschaft im deutschen Judentum* (Göttingen, 2008), 112–26.

7 For the early history of the Prague Jewish community and the Jews of Bohemia, see T. Pěkný, *Historie Židů v Čechách a na Moravě* (Prague, 2001), 11–18; for the intellectual activities of the Prague community in the High Middle Ages, see L. Uličná, 'Hlavní proudy středověkého (pre)aškenázského myšlení a tzv. pražská komentátorská škola: Hledání identity v podmínkách izolace a integrace', in J. Šedinová et al. (eds.), *Dialog myšlenkových proudů středověkého judaismu: Mezi integrací a izolací* (Prague, 2011), 268–331, esp. 268–75, 292–302.

8 In the mid-fourteenth century the composite state ruled from Prague was formally united into the Lands of the Bohemian Crown, with the secondary provinces becoming dependencies of the Kingdom of Bohemia by law as well as by tradition. For a recent summary of

the fourteenth-century state formation of the Bohemian Crown, see F. Šmahel and M. Nodl, 'Čechy a české země ve 14. a 15. století', in J. Klápště and I. Šedivý (eds.), *Dějiny Česka* (Prague, 2019), 70–99, esp. 72–5.

9 For the process of resettlement of the expelled Jews in the smaller townships held by nobles and the Church in the context of the establishment of larger Jewish craftsmen's networks in the later Middle Ages and early modern times, see M. Wischnitzer, 'Origins of the Jewish Artisan Class in Bohemia and Moravia, 1500–1648', *Jewish Social Studies*, 16/4 (1954), 335–50: 335–6.

10 For example, the assemblies held on 22 August 1686 in Kanitz (Dolní Kounice) and on 19 August 1697 in Lundenburg (Břeclav).

11 For the sense of moral crisis at the end of the Thirty Years War, see M. Greengrass, *Christendom Destroyed: Europe 1517–1648* (London, 2014), 675–80.

12 This contrasts with some other preserved collections of early modern Jewish *takanot*. For example, *Takanot kandiyah*, from the Jewish community of Chania, the capital of Crete when the island was under Venetian dominance, includes a selection of Venetian state legislation concerning the Jews in Hebrew translation (see *Statuta Iudaeorum Candiae eorumque memorabilia*, ed. E. S. Artom and U. Cassuto (Jerusalem, 1943)).

13 See Halperin, 'Hakdamah', in *Takanot medinat mehren*, pp. ix–xvi: ix.

14 For the circumstances under which the General Ordinance was issued, see M. Marada, 'Kodifikace právního postavení židovského obyvatelstva na Moravě v Generálním řádu Marie Terezie z roku 1754', *Časopis Matice moravské*, 106 (1987), 94–107.

15 Halperin, 'Hakdamah', p. xv.

16 G. Wolf, *Die alten Statuten der jüdischen Gemeinden in Mähren (311 Takkanot), samt den nachfolgenden Synodalbeschlüssen* (Vienna, 1880). This is the first known scholarly edition of the text.

17 A. Neubauer, *Catalogue of the Hebrew Manuscripts in the Bodleian Library and in the College Libraries of Oxford* (Oxford, 1886), §§2216, 2217.

18 This seems to be either Jewish Theological Seminary, New York, MS 10748 or MS 8881. MS 8881 contains a record of the *takanot*, issued between 1653 and 1728.

19 Probably Országos Rabbiképző – Zsidó Egyetem, Budapest, MS K 13, a later copy made in 1764. Bibliographic information on these manuscripts is available at the National Library of Israel website, Ktiv digital database (visited 24 Sept. 2019).

20 *Pinkas va'ad arba aratsot: likutei takanot ketavim vereshumot*, ed. I. Halperin (Jerusalem, 1945); 2nd revd. edn., ed. I. Bartal (Jerusalem, 1990); see I. Bartal, 'The *Pinkas* of the Council of the Four Lands', in A. Polonsky, J. Basista, and A. Link-Lenczowski (eds.), *The Jews in Old Poland, 1000–1795* (London, 1993), 110–18, esp. 113–16.

21 L. Uličná, 'Policejní řád pro moravské židovstvo: K pojmu jazyková apropriace', in D. Boušek, M. Křížová, and P. Sládek (eds.), *Dvarim meatim: Studie pro Jiřinu Šedinovou* (Prague, 2016), 156–62: 159.

22 Židovské muzeum v Praze, ŽMP 11.659 / MS 203. According to Uličná, the manuscript has two different signatures since it was considered to be a record of a Jewish assembly by one of the editors of the museum's two library catalogues and a translation of the General Ordinance by the other (Uličná, 'Policejní řád pro moravské židovstvo', 156–8).

23 In comparison, the Cretan *takanot* abound with phrases like 'the most exalted realm of Venice', 'Their Excellencies our lords and governors, may Their Majesty ever increase', and similar.

24 See *Takanot medinat mehren*, nos. 177–9.

25 It is probable that Israel Halperin, too, considered the possibility that his sources were incomplete, since in a footnote to *takanah* 1 he mentions that the 'manuscripts available to us lack any introduction, preamble, signatures or dates' (*Takanot medinat mehren*, 1 n. 1).

26 *Takanot medinat mehren*, no. 1: 1–4. Appropriately the quote from Psalm 111 alludes to the topic of education and its religious dimension. It is one of the very few direct biblical quotations in the whole corpus.

27 From these ordinances, it is apparent that there was no place for any 'separation of Church and state' in the modern sense, as will be described in more detail in the next section.

28 For example, dividing the three districts into smaller administrative units (*Takanot medinat mehren*, no. 102) or the circumstances under which a rabbi may not sit in judgement on his own (ibid., no. 157).

29 See esp. *Takanot medinat mehren*, nos. 70–102.

30 See ibid., no. 113.

31 For example, slander against community officials (ibid., no. 79).

32 For example, the chief rabbi's authority to supervise courts' verdicts and report miscarriages of justice (ibid., no. 84).

33 See ibid., nos. 100–1.

34 See ibid., nos. 159–61, 170–1.

35 Ibid., nos. 174–5.

36 *Takanah* 178 contains the text of the oath that a newly appointed head of the community was obliged to take, one of the few passage in which *Shai takanot* directly addresses the relations between the Moravian Jewish representatives and the secular authorities.

37 See *Takanot medinat mehren*, no 297.

38 See ibid., no. 300. In 1650 the emperor was Ferdinand III (r. 1637–57).

39 See ibid., no. 308.

40 This term is used in, for example, *takanot* 301: 1; 305: 2; 311: 7.

41 I briefly discussed the language of *Shai takanot* in M. Borýsek, 'Mezi Tórou, místními zvyky a světskou mocí: Legislativní texty židovských obcí raně novověké Evropy na příkladě moravských *311 takanot* a krétských *Takanot Kandi'a'*, in Boušek, Křížová, and Sládek (eds.), *Dvarim meatim*, 141–55: 144.

42 *Takanot medinat mehren*, no. 1: 2–4.

43 On the issues of 'code-switching' and 'code-mixing' in spoken and written multilingual discourse, see e.g. P. Muysken, *Bilingual Speech: A Typology of Code-Mixing* (Cambridge, 2000).

44 There are in total 141 *takanot* written solely or partially in the mixed language, the remaining 170 being decisively Hebrew (including a small number of *takanot* in which an occasional Yiddish word or phrase appears sporadically). In the critical edition, the bilingual *takanot* are accompanied by Halperin's Hebrew translation, which respects the style and linguistic register of the Hebrew element in the original *takanot*.

45 *Takanot medinat mehren*, no. 24: 1–4.

46 See ibid., no. 24: 4–6.

47 Ibid., no. 25: 1–2.

48 Ibid., no. 25: 2–3.

49 Ibid., no. 74.

50 Ibid., no. 27: 1–6.

51 Ibid., no. 28: 1–3

52 Ibid., no. 28: 4–6.

53 Ibid., no. 30: 1–7.

54 See *Seder hameshulaḥim mikol hakehilot hamedinah*.

55 *Takanot medinat mehren*, no. 308: 1–2.

The East European *Pinkas Kahal*

Form and Function

ADAM TELLER

THE *pinkasei kahal* discussed here were the record books kept by the executive councils of most European Jewish communities in the early modern period. As such, they have proved one of the most important sources for the study of early modern Jewish history, and, on their basis, many studies have been written dealing with the social, economic, administrative, religious, and cultural lives of European Jewry of the period.[1] A characteristic of this research, however, is that it focuses closely on the texts themselves, while largely ignoring the significance of their physical context. Yet without understanding the nature and function of the *pinkas kahal* in which the texts were written and the significance of their inscription there, any reading of them must lack a crucial dimension.

This chapter will try to help fill that gap and so enrich our understanding of this key source for the history of the Jews in early modern eastern Europe. To do so, it will embrace some of the insights provided by research on the history of the book, most particularly the material history of the book or the study of the book as artefact. Its focus will therefore be on the physical form, structure, and organization of the *pinkas*.[2]

In fact, the very name of the *pinkas kahal* suggests that it should first and foremost be viewed as an object rather than a text. This is because it was called a *pinkas* and not a *sefer*, the Hebrew word for book.[3] The term *pinkas* actually means 'notebook', and these were widely used in pre-modern Jewish society. It was not just community organizations that kept them—individuals kept them too. *Mohalim* would keep *pinkasim* to note the circumcisions they did; businessmen would keep *pinkasim* to note the various deals they made; students would keep *pinkasim* into which they copied the texts they were studying; and mystics would keep *pinkasim* in which they noted their sins (and sometimes their dreams too).[4] Thus the *pinkas* was distinguished from the *sefer* in both its physical form and the way texts were entered into it. The *pinkas* was a notebook or register, initially of blank pages, in which its owner wrote, from time to time, various texts or entries of interest.

This format was, of course, very useful for institutions—and not only Jewish ones —that wanted to keep a running record of their activity.[5] Early modern Polish–Lithuanian Jewish society was a complex web of institutions—from small, local guilds to the great transregional councils, such as the Council of Lithuania and the Polish Council of Four Lands.[6] *Pinkasim*, or fragments of them, from all of these different kinds of institution have survived, giving the distinct impression that managing a *pinkas* of some sort was an integral part of early modern Jewish organizational life.

The focus of this chapter is on what might be termed 'mid-range' *pinkasim*, those of individual communities, particularly the *pinkasei kahal*—the registers of the community councils. However, the fact that community administration was also made up of many other bodies, each of which kept its own *pinkas*, should not be ignored. Thus, for example, the *gaba'im* (synagogue treasurers) would keep a *pinkas* noting aspects of the synagogue's organization, particularly financial and charitable disbursements and the different decisions they made to regulate their work.[7] The judges in the *beit din* (rabbinical court) would keep a *pinkas* recording the cases they heard, and the tax assessors would keep a *pinkas* with a record of the taxes assessed for and paid by each community member.[8] Taken together, these various notebooks make up what might be called a set of *pinkasei kehilah* (all the *pinkasim* of the community) which together reflect the rich and multifaceted sweep of community life. Thus, the *pinkas kahal* was only part of the complex of *pinkasim*, although, since the *kahal* was the community's supreme governing body, it might be viewed as the most important of them. This chapter will, therefore, try to characterize that particular kind of *pinkas*, analyse how it functioned, and understand its role in the life of both the *kahal* and the community as a whole.

Since *pinkasim* were kept by communities in many different political, cultural, and social settings, the discussion here will be limited to those of the Jewish communities in the Polish–Lithuanian Commonwealth, which in the early modern period was the largest concentration of Jews in Europe, if not the world.[9] It will therefore provide only a partial picture of the early modern *pinkas kahal*, but one which can be complemented by studies of community *pinkasim* from other regions, such as the work of Stefan Litt on the *pinkasim* of the Ashkenazi communities in the Netherlands.[10]

Research in this field is particularly complex because there are many layers of misconceptions about the early modern *pinkas kahal* which developed in the various cultural and political milieux of east European Jews in the nineteenth and twentieth centuries and have continued to be repeated, often uncritically, by generations of scholars.

A key change in attitude towards the *pinkas* seems to have taken place at the turn of the nineteenth century, when a romantic rather than a utilitarian view of it began to develop. This can be seen on the title page of the *pinkas kahal* from the Lithuanian community of Wyłkowyszki (Vilkaviškis), where the copyist (himself the son of a former community scribe) wrote a panegyric to the *pinkas* itself. The text, composed in the late 1790s or early 1800s, is a mosaic of truncated quotations from the Bible and prayer book and so is extremely difficult to translate accurately. This is the opening sentence:

[Jews of my] generation behold [Jer. 2: 31] the Temple [Zech. 11: 13],[11] a building of precious cornerstones, exceedingly firm [Isa. 28: 16], [that can be seen] from this *pinkas*, open to the learned. It displays its splendid glory [Esther 1: 4] as it memorializes the past, recalling many deeds and enumerating all the characters.[12] All the flocks are gathered there [Gen. 29: 3] as if in an enclosure humming with people [Mic. 2: 12].[13]

As Israel Bartal has shown, the maskilim of the nineteenth century adopted this view of the *pinkas kahal* as somehow embodying the entire history of the early modern Jewish community, but turned it on its head so that they could excoriate both the institution and its past, which they despised.[14] In his novel *An Ass's Burial*, Peretz Smolenskin was scathing:

A *pinkas* can be found in every town where Jews live, and in it they and everything that happened in the town will be written as an everlasting memory. There is mention of girls who lost their virginity by accident and through rape, of denouncers and those who caused Jews to lose money to non-Jews, of those who rebelled against community authority and those who ate non-kosher meat, of those who stole the silver from synagogues and those who carried a kerchief on the sabbath. [It tells of] the house that was destroyed by demons and ghosts, and of sinners whose sins or mockery of the burial society caused the outbreak of plague. In this text will be inscribed all those who transgressed the law of Israel and in their death they will pay for their sins, for they will be given an ass's burial.[15]

Following the maskilim, in the twentieth century, Jewish nationalists of many different stripes took an equally romantic—though now highly positive—view of the *pinkas*. Many of them viewed it as the ultimate expression of the Jewish autonomous bodies of the early modern period—bodies the nationalists saw as foreshadowing the Jewish national institutions they wanted to create.[16] Others took the *pinkas* as somehow embodying the spirit of the nation. Avrom Rechtman, who participated in An-sky's great ethnographic expedition of 1912, expressed this in lyrical terms:

The *pinkas* is the mirror of the people's life [*folkslebn*] in past generations. The *pinkas* reflects the people's feelings, its joys and its sorrows, how it expressed its concerns and what made up its demands. Through the *pinkas* we can assess the life of the individual and the *kahal* in all its breadth and all its depth. We can learn from them about the way of life as it was, as well as relations within society, between one society and another, between one community and another, and also of the Jews' attitude towards the outside, non-Jewish world which surrounded them.[17]

What was common to both approaches, of course, was a highly romanticized view of the *pinkas* as somehow embodying the Jews' history and spirit, though the values each imparted to it were quite different.

In the face of these products of the overheated Jewish imagination, a rather more sober discussion of the *pinkas kahal* is called for, which would do well to start by determining what it was not. First, the *pinkas kahal* was not a record of *kahal* meetings or any kind of minutes of their discussions. In usual circumstances, the *kahal* would meet once a week (often on a Sunday morning) to discuss matters of importance to the community they were running.[18] As far as can be determined, no verbatim record has survived of any of those hundreds of thousands of meetings held in the Jewish communities of the Polish–Lithuanian Commonwealth in the early modern period.

The *pinkas* was also not a systematic recording of the decisions taken and regulations issued at the weekly *kahal* meetings. There are *pinkasim* of that sort, containing systematic sets of regulations chronologically arranged: the *pinkas* of the electoral college of the Poznań community, the *pinkas hakesherim*, is one such, the *pinkas* of the Council of Lithuania another.[19] *Pinkasei kahal* did not take that form: their records were much more sporadic and disorganized. Only a few decisions and regulations from any given year were recorded, suggesting that the vast majority were simply not written into the register.[20]

Finally, despite the deepest desires of both maskilim and Jewish nationalists, the *pinkas* was not a kind of 'community memory'. The vast majority of entries dealt with highly technical matters, such as taxation and other economic issues that fell within the purview of the *kahal*.[21] Major events in the community's life were recorded only in so far as the *kahal* had to make decisions or issue regulations to deal with them.[22] In addition, the *pinkas* was not available for the community to consult but was jealously guarded by the leadership. The Kraków community constitution of 1595 specified that the *pinkas kahal* should be in the hands of the two community scribes (*edei demata*) locked away in a chest that only they could open.[23]

The community scribe (also called *safra demata*) was therefore the key figure in the management of the *pinkas*. According to the 1595 constitution, only the scribes were allowed to actually write in the *pinkas* (although they needed instructions from the *kahal* before they could do so).[24] In fact, then, the *pinkas* as a physical object was actually the territory of the scribe who was also responsible for locating various decisions recorded in it when the *kahal* or the people with whom they dealt needed copies made.[25]

The *pinkas kahal* in the Polish–Lithuanian Commonwealth was very much, therefore, a technical document. Only matters dealt with by the *kahal* were included in it. These could, of course, be of enormous significance for running the community, although not in the romantic way assumed by previous generations. The question of population control through the granting or retraction of residence rights was one such crucial topic.[26] The management of the annual elections to the *kahal* was another: many *pinkasim* contain the lists of those elected each year.

An exception to this was the Poznań community, where the members of the electoral college did not disband after the elections but remained as a kind of supervisory body, focused on the ways the *kahal* did its work. The *pinkas hakesherim* contained not only the annual election lists but also the regulations issued regarding the functioning of the *kahal*.[27] No other community, however, seems to have had this arrangement.

Other issues dealt with by the Polish–Lithuanian *pinkasei kahal* include the management of community charity (most often done by means of regulations concerning the *gaba'im*), the employment of the rabbi and other community officials (cantors, slaughterers, doctors, midwives, teachers, and so on), sumptuary regulations, the formation of special committees to deal with pressing issues, and relations with the non-Jewish authorities.

Despite this, it was rare for the east European *kahal* to use the *pinkas* as the place for an all-embracing community constitution. In some communities, this was simply not necessary: in Kraków a complete and very extensive constitution was drawn up in 1595 quite separate from the *pinkas kahal*, while in Poznań constitutional matters fell within the purview of the electoral college, which, as mentioned above, had its own *pinkas*.[28] The *pinkasei kahal* of other communities such as Tykocin did contain some quite limited sets of constitutional regulations, but the only more comprehensive example known is in the *pinkas* of the Ukrainian community of Dubno.[29]

All this suggests that the *pinkas kahal* was never meant to be any kind of systematic record. This conclusion is supported by two other aspects of the *pinkas* itself. First of all, as already mentioned, only a very limited number of regulations were recorded from any given year. In the Tykocin *pinkas*, for example, the average number of regulations registered each year was about seven. In the busiest years, such as 1690 or 1718, the number could reach somewhere between twenty-five and thirty, but there are only two entries each for 1676, 1679, 1733, and 1744. The whole decade of the 1750s is represented by a mere twenty-eight entries. It is simply inconceivable that these reflected the sum total of the *kahal*'s activities in those years.[30]

The other aspect of the Polish–Lithuanian *pinkas kahal* that bears witness to its unsystematic nature is the way in which the regulations were entered into it. There seems to be no real logic to the *pinkasei kahal* as we have them. Strict chronological order is not kept, with documents from different years (even different decades) sometimes appearing on the same page. It seems to have been commonplace for scribes to leave empty pages as they worked, presumably to allow for the insertion of material from a later date into an earlier section.

On the basis of the *pinkas kahal* from Frankfurt am Main, Debra Kaplan has suggested that it may be possible to identify places in the *pinkas* that have thematic clusters of material, an insight that the east European materials seem to bear out.[31] It might be possible to extend this idea and argue that there were, in fact, two types of clustering at work simultaneously in the *pinkasim*, thematic and chronological. Even on this level, however, the registration was very far from systematic.

How then can these two phenomena, the small number of regulations entered into the *pinkas* and the unsystematic way in which this was done, be explained? Some light may be shed on the first of these by the 1595 constitution of the Kraków community. In the section dealing with the scribes, it gives a schedule of payments they could charge for their services. Among other things, it states: 'For the drawing up of a contract or when someone wants to have a document entered in the *pinkas kahal*, whether it is a ruling of the court [*beit din*] or of the *kahal* itself: 2 grosze. For making a copy of one of the above: 1 grosz.'[32] This seems to reflect a situation in which an entry in the *pinkas kahal* was only one of three forms an official document might take: the first was as a free-standing document before it was entered into the *pinkas*; the second was the entry in the *pinkas* itself; and the third was a copy of the *pinkas* entry, for the use of the interested parties.[33] Of all these, however, it was the registration in the *pinkas* that gave the document its official standing in community affairs.[34]

This was important not just for the regulations issued by the *kahal* itself. Decisions taken by other community bodies, such as the *beit din*, that were of particular significance for the whole Jewish population of the town also had to be copied into the *pinkas kahal* to give them the authority they needed.[35] On a broader scale, it would seem that regulations issued by the regional Jewish councils and the transregional Council of Four Lands were only binding in any given community once they were copied into the *pinkas kahal*.[36] Since the original *pinkas* of the Council of the Lands is now lost, much of its content can be discovered by checking various *pinkasei kahal*, such as those of Lwów (Lviv), Poznań, Tykocin, and Kraków, into which copies were made.[37]

As far as individuals were concerned, the regulation from the 1595 constitution of the Kraków community quoted above also seems to show that having rulings copied into the *pinkas* was a choice that had to paid for. Clearly, then, not every ruling was expected to be entered into the *pinkas*. Sadly, however, beyond the financial issue, we have no way of understanding on what basis documents were copied into it or not. But it does not seem unreasonable to suggest that the *kahal* itself might have done most of its work on paper in the form of individual documents, each of which was delivered to the party or parties involved and only in exceptional circumstances entered into the *pinkas*. In the nature of things, most of these individual paper documents have been lost and only those few copied into the *pinkas* remain.

There is even less evidence to explain the highly unsystematic way in which regulations and documents were copied into the *pinkas*. It has been argued that the poor organization of the *pinkas* is characteristic of communities whose own internal organization was not highly sophisticated.[38] The case of Poznań renders this unlikely. Its *pinkas kahal* was indeed haphazardly organized, with many entries out of chronological order and a very poor thematic arrangement. However, the Poznań community was one of the most sophisticated and best organized of the Jewish communities in Europe as a whole in the late sixteenth and early seventeenth centuries. Each year, a hundred or so officials were elected to a wide range of posts, all of which seem to have functioned together reasonably well. In addition, there was the well-organized and systematic *pinkas hakesherim*. In this case, at least, the haphazard organization of the *pinkas kahal* in no way reflected the organization of the community.[39]

In looking for a better explanation, the 1595 constitution of the Kraków community is again suggestive: 'The scribes shall not make a copy of a document for anyone other than the parties concerned, whether it comes from the *pinkas kahal* or the *pinkas beit din*. They will also not open these books for anyone except the parties involved.'[40] As noted above, this text demonstrates that it was the scribes who controlled the *pinkasim*, with all the material therein. It was their job to know their way around the *pinkas* and to be able to find the relevant documents for the interested parties. More important than that, however, the scribe's control of the *pinkas* was also a source of authority within the community, since it was his signature attesting to the copy's accuracy that gave such documents their validity.[41]

The scribes of the Jewish communities in the Polish–Lithuanian Commonwealth remain quite shadowy characters. There is very little documentation relating to individual scribes, their training, or their career paths. A rare description can be found in an introductory page to a manuscript copy of the halakhic text *Hazeh hatenufah*, made for David Oppenheim, the famous rabbi of Prague and an avid book collector.[42] The scribe who copied the book (he did not give his name) wrote a brief personal introduction, which he began with an apology for any mistakes that might have crept into the text. He then went on to give a brief description of his career.

As a boy of 6 or 7, he learned not just how to read but how to write too. So talented was he that he was given the honour of writing in individual letters during the making of a Torah scroll. By the time he was 11, he was studying in a yeshiva in Przemyśl, moving on to Lisko (Lesko) a couple of years later. In both places, he wrote, he was told by the rabbis to copy various texts, whose numbers, he said, reached the hundreds. The last stage of his education seems to have been the yeshiva in Pińczów, where the rabbi, Leib Zunz, made him his personal scribe and had him copy 'bundles of texts, some extremely long'. By the age of 22 he was living in Volodymyr-Volynsky (Włodzimierz), where he acted—or was employed—as scribe to the Jewish regional council of Volhynia. After that, at some undetermined time in the early eighteenth century, he got the very prestigious job of scribe to Oppenheim, perhaps the leading rabbi of the day.[43]

If the text is to be believed, it would seem that training to be a scribe was a process that took many years. Even if we assume that the author's experiences as a 6- or 7-year-old had no real bearing on his future career, by the age of 11 he seems to have been well on the path to it. His training was less in calligraphy and writing skills than in gaining experience with the various different texts he would be called upon to copy.[44] He clearly had a good education and, to judge from his opening comment to *Hazeh hatenufah*, knew the book he was copying.

Another conclusion to be drawn from the text is that the scribe, though clearly highly respectable, was not a member of the elite of Jewish society, socio-economic or rabbinic. In general, there is no evidence of community scribes going on to become community rabbis or to hold high offices in the community administration, though the best educated of them might sometimes serve on the *beit din*, assuming the title *dayana vesafra* (judge and scribe).[45] For the most part, then, scribes would seem to have been individuals who were quite well off and had an advanced Jewish education but who lacked the great wealth, social connections or family background that would have allowed them to take their place at the top table of Jewish leaders.[46]

Another sign of this lower status is that they were not called upon to deal with documents in non-Jewish languages, a *sine qua non* for a community leader. Having said that, some did know Polish to quite a high level: the scribe of the Wyłkowyszki community actually copied into the *pinkas kahal* a Hebrew transcription of the Polish-language privilege granted to the community by the king in 1792.[47] On the whole, however, scribes had to be well educated and literate in Hebrew, with the ability to compose and copy complex documents in that language—a fact that would have placed them in what is today sometimes called the 'secondary elite' of Jewish intellectuals.[48]

For such a person, the post of community scribe must have been highly attractive. Though not a member of the *kahal*, the scribe controlled the drafting of the materials that came out of its meetings. Community members—and even the community leadership—had to come to the scribe when they needed their documents authenticated. In addition, he assumed responsibility (and was paid) for drawing up all legal documents needed by community members.[49] As a result, he was a figure treated with great respect: in Vilna, for example, the community provided its scribe with an apartment of his own just as it did the rabbi.[50]

Since the standing and authority that his post brought was based to a very great extent on his control of the *pinkas*, it was in the scribe's best interest to manage its use in such a way that it would not be easy for anyone else to access and read it. For lack of a better explanation, then, perhaps the way he kept the *pinkas* was a subtle (or not so subtle) means of ensuring that he, more than anyone else, would be the person best able to extract the relevant information from it, thus buttressing his position in community life. Though this remains just a hypothesis, it does point to the very real need to have a much better grasp of the figure of the scribe and his role and position in Jewish society for a deeper understanding of the *pinkas kahal* and how it functioned.

Developments in the later eighteenth century, and particularly the encroachment of enlightened absolutist regimes on *kahal* administration, seem to have posed a particular threat for both the *pinkas* and the community scribe. First of all, Polish began to find its way into the *pinkasim* as a way of allowing the non-Jewish authorities to supervise and control Jewish community life. These texts sometimes took the form of bilingual regulations, as can be seen in documents from Zabłudów and Zasław (Izyaslav).[51] Completely Polish documents could also be written into the *pinkas*, as can be seen in a number of surviving *pinkasim*, such as those from Włodawa, Boćki, Tykocin, and Swarzędz.[52] Although it is hard to determine definitively who actually wrote the Polish documents into the *pinkasim*, it does not seem to have been the community scribe himself.[53]

As the eighteenth century came to an end, the idea of using Jewish languages for community administration fell out of favour with the non-Jewish authorities,[54] and, with their ever greater intrusion into Jewish community life over the course of the nineteenth century, community administration, particularly in the larger centres, began to move away from the *pinkas* towards the creation and filing of individual documents written in the language of the country and using the archival system known today.[55]

This may not have affected community administration very significantly. The Jewish socioeconomic elite, who had always known non-Jewish languages at a reasonably high level in order to do business, were after all used to using individual documents in their administrative work. In the end, it was only the use of the *pinkas* as artefact—

that is, as the register into which to copy whatever texts the *kahal* wanted—that was affected.

For the community scribes, on the other hand, the replacement of the *pinkas* with individual documents in the local language posed a very serious threat. The skills they possessed—the ability to write Hebrew and to navigate the *pinkas* with ease—were now of little use. Scribes could still make a living by working privately, but their central place in community life disappeared. They were, therefore, among the hardest hit by the administrative changes of the nineteenth century and the consequent abandonment of the *pinkas kahal.*

Notes

I prepared this chapter as part of the Pinkassim Project: Recovering the Records of European Jewry, which was undertaken in conjunction with the National Library of Israel (NLI) and with the generous support of the Rothschild Foundation (Hanadiv) Europe. As a result of the project, some 200 early modern *pinkasei kahal*, many of them from eastern Europe, are now scanned and openly available on the NLI website, 'Pinkasim Collection: The International Repository of Communal Ledgers', visited 3 Mar. 2020.

1 For a bibliography of such studies, see NLI website, Pinkasim Collection, 'Bibliography', visited 3 Mar. 2020.

2 Studying the material history of the book in order to grasp the importance of its physicality and structure, including the very shape of the page, for the early modern communications revolution has a long pedigree and underlies the discussion here. For a brief but illuminating survey, see D. Pearson, *Books as History: The Importance of Books Beyond Their Texts* (London, 2008), 27–75; see also A. Johns, 'The Coming of Print to Europe', in L. Howsam (ed.), *The Cambridge Companion to the History of the Book* (Cambridge, 2015), 107–24. Of particular importance for this chapter is Gérard Genette's work on 'paratext'. This is less because it deals with paratexts as such than because it borrows from Genette's method of analysis. He examines the texts with which he is concerned through their 'spatial, temporal, substantial, pragmatic, and functional characteristics' in order to come to a deeper understanding of their content from the nature of their production and their physicality. That is the goal here. See G. Genette, *Paratexts: Thresholds of Interpretation*, trans. J. E. Lewin (Cambridge, 1997), 1–15, esp. 4.

3 One of the few examples of calling the *pinkas kahal* a *sefer* was in the community of Poznań, which referred to its *pinkas* as *sefer hazikhronot*, 'the book of memories'. This was clearly an exception. In one or two other cases, the word *sefer* was used even when the object itself was regularly called a *pinkas*, but this was done simply to recall the biblical phrase, 'write this as *a memorial in the book*' (Exod. 17: 14). In the vast majority of cases, however, the Hebrew term *pinkas* was the only one used.

4 J. H. Chajes, 'Accounting for the Self: Preliminary Generic-Historical Reflections on Early Modern Jewish Egodocuments', *Jewish Quarterly Review*, 95 (2005), 1–15.

5 Many early modern Polish institutions kept similar sorts of record books. They did not have a special name but were simply called books, *księgi*. Thus, there are court records of various kinds, such as *księgi grodzkie*; records of town councils, *księgi miejskie*; and even of guilds, *księgi cechowe*.

6 The best survey of Jewish institutional life in early modern Poland–Lithuania remains

M. Bałaban, 'Ha'otonomiyah hayehudit', in I. Halperin (ed.), *Beit yisra'el bepolin*, 2 vols. (Jerusalem, 1948–54), i. 44–65.

7   One of the richest and most complete *pinkasim* of this kind from Poland–Lithuania to survive is that of the Poznań community (Central Archives for the History of the Jewish People, Jerusalem (hereafter CAHJP), PL-Po-9: *Pinkas gaba'ei beit hakneset*).

8   The *pinkas beit din* of the Kraków community for the years 1764 to 1805 can be found in Archiwum Państwowe Kraków, Akta żydowskie III/11/1: Wyroki sądu rabinackiego na Kazimierzu, 1764–1805.

9   G. D. Hundert, *Jews in Poland–Lithuania in the Eighteenth Century: A Genealogy of Modernity* (Berkeley, Calif., 2004), 21–31.

10   S. Litt, *Pinkas, Kahal, and the Mediene: The Records of Dutch Ashkenazi Communities in the Eighteenth Century as Historical Sources* (Leiden, 2008).

11   The meaning of the original Hebrew is unclear; the translation follows Rashi's explanation. It refers, presumably, to the Wyłkowyszki community.

12   This follows the 'zikhronot' prayers from the Rosh Hashanah prayer book.

13   CAHJP, LI-27: *Pinkas k"k vilkovishky*.

14   I. Bartal, 'The *Pinkas*: From Communal Archive to Total History', *Polin*, 29 (2017), 19–40.

15   P. Smolenskin, *Kevurat ḥamor* (Warsaw, 1904/5), 47; see also Bartal, 'The *Pinkas*', 23.

16   S. Dubnow, 'Mavo', in *Pinkas hamedinah, o pinkas va'ad hakehilot harashiyot bimedinat lita* (Berlin, 1925), p. xi.

17   A. Rekhtman, *Yidishe etnografye un folklor: zikhroynes vegn der etnografisher ekspeditsye, ongefirt fun sh. an-sky* (Buenos Aires, 1958), 195; cf. Litt, *Pinkas, Kahal, and the Mediene*, 7.

18   M. Bałaban, *Historja Żydów w Krakowie i na Kazimierzu, 1304–1868*, 2 vols. (Kraków, 1931–6), i. 333–5.

19   *Pinkas hakesherim shel kehilat pozna (5381–5595)*, ed. D. Evron (Jerusalem, 1967); *Pinkas hamedinah*.

20   In Poznań, the *kesherim* did not approve of this state of affairs, ordering in 1627: 'The monthly chair of the *kahal* must order the scribe to inscribe in the *pinkas* everything agreed on by the *kahal* whether by majority vote or unanimously' (*Pinkas hakesherim* (ed. Evron), no. 23).

21   For example, just under a quarter of the early modern entries in the *pinkas kahal* from Horki consist simply of taxpayer registers, and, as if to emphasize the technical aspect of the *pinkas*, the number of annual election lists is even larger (NLI, Ms. Heb. 4°920: *Pinkas kehilat horki*).

22   Thus, for example, the fire that ravaged the Dubno community on 22 August 1752 is mentioned in the *pinkas* only in connection with donations the *kahal* received from other communities in order to help with the relief efforts (H. Z. Margolis, *Dubna rabati* (Warsaw, 1910), 63–4).

23   M. Bałaban, 'Die Krakauer Judengemeinde-Ordnung von 1595 und ihre Nachträge', *Jahrbuch der Jüdisch-Literarischen Gesellschaft*, 10 (1913), 296–360; 11 (1916), 88–114: no. 66; for the whole text of the constitution with a Polish translation, see *Statut krakowskiej gminy żydowskiej z roku 1595 i jego uzupełnienia*, ed. A. Jakimyszyn (Kraków, 2005).

24   This fact was often noted by scribes in other communities, such as, for example, Włodawa, where Shemuel ben Avraham Halevi wrote: 'I have signed this on the orders of the communal leadership' (B. Weinryb, 'Texts and Studies in the Communal History of Polish Jewry/Te'udot letoledot hakehilot hayehudiyot bepolin', *Proceedings of the American Academy for Jewish Research*, 19 (1950), 1–264 (Heb. section): no. 5). For other examples, see

ibid., no. 3; *Pinkas kahal tiktin, 1621–1806*, ed. M. Nadav, 2 vols. (Jerusalem, 1997–2000), i, no. 105; *Pinkas hakesherim* (ed. Evron), no. 20.

25 See *Pinkas va'ad arba aratsot: likutei takanot ketavim vereshumot*, ed. I. Halperin (Jerusalem, 1945); 2nd revd. edn., ed. I. Bartal (Jerusalem, 1990), no. 393.

26 For texts from the Poznań *pinkas*, see Weinryb 'Texts and Studies', nos. 1–36; see also M. Siemiaticki, 'Ḥezkat hakehilah bepolin', *Hamishpat ha'ivri*, 5 (1936–7), 45–92.

27 CAHJP, PL-Po-1: *Pinkas hakesherim*.

28 Bałaban, 'Die Krakauer Judengemeinde-Ordnung'; *Pinkas hakesherim* (ed. Evron).

29 For Tykocin, see *Pinkas kahal tiktin*, i, nos. 171–4, 453–6; for Dubno, see *Jüdische Gemeindestatuten aus dem aschkenasischen Kulturraum, 1650–1850*, ed. S. Litt (Göttingen, 2014), 399–426.

30 Nadav, 'Hate'udot lefi seder khronologi', in *Pinkas kahal tiktin*, ii. 25–82.

31 D. Kaplan, *Give and Take: Jewish Public Charity in Early Modern Germany* (Philadelphia, 2020), 123–55; see NLI, Ms. Heb. 24°662: *Pinkas kehilat frankfurt demayn*.

32 Bałaban, 'Die Krakauer Judengemeinde-Ordnung', no. 64.

33 In Polish society, the *księgi grodzkie* seem to have functioned in a similar way. As well as recording the cases heard by the court, the *księga grodzka* was where people could have important documents (e.g. wills, business contracts, and even royal privileges) copied and from which authenticated copies could later be taken (S. Grodziski, *Z dziejów staropolskiej kultury prawnej* (Kraków, 2004), 171).

34 *Pinkas va'ad arba aratsot*, no. 527; *Pinkas kahału swarzędzkiego (1734–1830)*, ed. A. Michałowska-Mycielska (Warsaw, 2005), no. 17; Margolis, *Dubna rabati*, 72. In very rare cases, a document might be given the authority of the *pinkas kahal* not by being copied into it but by being physically glued into it (see *Pinkas kahal tiktin*, i, nos. 92, 386).

35 See e.g. a ruling by the *beit din* of Lwów copied into the *pinkas kahal* (S. Buber, *Anshei shem* (Kraków, 1895), no. 13).

36 For examples of regulations issued by regional and transregional councils that were copied into *pinkasei kahal*, see e.g. Buber, *Anshei shem*, nos. 2, 4, 6, 7, 8, 9; L. Lewin, *Neue Materialen zur Geschichte der Vierländersynode*, 3 vols. (Frankfurt am Main, 1905–16); id., *Die Landessynode der grospolnischen Judenschaft* (Frankfurt am Main, 1926).

37 I. Bartal, 'The Pinkas of the Council of the Four Lands', in A. Polonsky, J. Basista, and A. Link-Lenczowski (eds.), *The Jews in Old Poland, 1000–1795* (London, 1993), 110–18.

38 Litt, *Pinkas, Kahal, and the Mediene*, 93.

39 On the structure of the Poznań community institutions in the seventeenth century, see A. Teller, *Ḥayim betsavta: harova hayehudi shel poznan bamaḥatsit harishonah shel hame'ah ha-17* (Jerusalem, 2003).

40 Bałaban, 'Die Krakauer Judengemeinde-Ordnung', no. 66.

41 *Pinkas hamedinah*, no. 1001; Weinryb, 'Texts and Studies', nos. 26–7; *Pinkas kahal tiktin*, i, no. 164. It should be stressed that it was the scribe's rather than the rabbi's signature that authenticated the text of the community regulations in the *pinkas*. If the rabbi wanted to participate in a particularly important decision, he would join the elders in signing the original document which the scribe would then copy into the *pinkas*.

42 J. Teplitsky, *Prince of the Press: How One Collector Built History's Most Enduring and Remarkable Jewish Library* (New Haven, Conn., 2019), 49–50.

43 Bodleian Library, Oxford, MS Opp. 289: Moses of Brussels, *Hazeh hatenufah*, Vienna 1716, 2r.

44 It is possible that it was the precocious calligraphic skills he demonstrated aged 6 or 7 that first put him on the road to becoming a scribe.

45 See e.g. *Pinkas kahału boćkowskiego (1714–1817)*, ed. A. Michałowska-Mycielska (Warsaw, 2015), nos. 44–5.

46 An exception to this was the wealthy community leader Judah ben Eliezer from Vilna, who, in return for a particularly large donation to the community, was granted the title of *safra vedayana* in perpetuity, presumably so that he would be able to recoup his expenses from the salary and various payments the scribe received for drawing up documents. This case is exceptional in at least two ways: Judah was a prominent community leader before he was appointed scribe, and the position of scribe in Vilna was up for sale (Y. Kloizner, 'Yehudah safra vedayana (hayesod): lidemutam shel hayaḥasim vehanimusim hatsiburiyim bevilna bame'ah ha-18', *Zion*, 2 (1937), 137–52).

47 For the text in both Hebrew letters and re-transcribed back into Polish, see *Jewish Privileges in the Polish Commonwealth: Charters of Rights Granted to Jewish Communities in Poland–Lithuania in the Sixteenth to Eighteenth Centuries*, ed. J. Goldberg, 3 vols. (Jerusalem, 1985–2001), i. 360–6.

48 E. Reiner, 'A Biography of an Agent of Culture: Eleazar Altschul of Prague and His Literary Activity', in M. Graetz (ed.), *Schöpferische Momente des europäischen Judentums, 16.–18. Jh* (Heidelberg, 2000), 243–7.

49 *Pinkas hakesherim* (ed. Evron), no. 1543. For a (fragmentary) price list of the scribe's services to the wider community, see *Pinkas kahal tiktin*, i, no. 858.

50 Kloizner, 'Yehudah safra vedayana', 145. This was an exceptional case. Much more common was granting tax breaks to scribes (see e.g. Margolis, *Dubna rabati*, 57–8; *Pinkas kahal tiktin*, i, no. 39).

51 NLI, Ms. Heb. 4°103: *Pinkas kehilat zabludove*, 265–6. On the Zasław material and bilingual sets of regulations in general, see J. Goldberg, 'Hamishar hakimona'i hayehudi bepolin bame'ah ha-18: takanot laḥenvanim bezaslav uvebrody ushe'elat hamekorot ha'ivriyim-hapolaniyim letoledot hamishar vehaḥevrah hayehudiyim', in E. Mendelsohn and C. Shmeruk (eds.), *Kovets meḥkarim al yehudei polin: sefer lezikhro shel paul glikson* (Jerusalem, 1987), 11–28.

52 For Włodawa, see Weinryb, 'Texts and Studies', no. 51; for Boćki, see *Pinkas kahału boćkowskiego*, nos. 178–81; for Tykocin, see *Pinkas kahal tiktin*, i, nos. 1008–10; for Swarzędz, see *Pinkas kahału swarzędzkiego*, nos. 73, 114 (includes a document in Latin). In addition, since Swarzędz came under Prussian control after the third partition of Poland in 1795, its *pinkas* also contains some documents in German (ibid., nos. 61–2).

53 A. Michałowska-Mycielska, *The Jewish Community: Authority and Social Control in Poznań and Swarzędz, 1650–1793*, trans. A. Adamowicz (Wrocław, 2008), 55–6.

54 For a detailed treatment of this process, see I. Bartal, '"Mavo": hapinkas kemashal', in id., *Letaken am: ne'orut ule'umiyut bemizraḥ eiropah* (Jerusalem, 2013), 1–33.

55 That was not always the case in the smaller, rural communities where rates of change were considerably slower. Thus, for example, the *pinkas kahal* of the Horki community contains records from throughout the nineteenth century and some even from the twentieth.

The Role of Legal Agreements in Developing Christian–Jewish Relations in Polish Towns and Cities

HANNA WĘGRZYNEK

IN HIS MONOGRAPH on the Jews of Kraków and Kazimierz, Majer Bałaban wrote:

At the same time, negotiations continued between the elders of the Jewish local community and the municipal government of Kazimierz. The negotiations were slow and difficult, since they had to cover a series of private and public issues, including the purchase or expropriation of municipal, ecclesiastical, and private land; the question of a new cemetery; the gates between the Jewish and Christian towns; the walls or fences meant to surround the new ghetto; and numerous issues concerned with trade which the municipality wanted to settle.[1]

This brief statement and Bałaban's discussion of the decisions taken do not do full justice to the scope and significance of the legal agreement reached in 1553 between the municipality of Kazimierz and the Jews residing there. The importance of this document, and of others signed at the same time, stems not only from the multifaceted nature of the agreement, which covered a great many issues central to the operation of the city and its Jewish community, but also from its role in shaping the Jews' legal status and its effect on local Jewish self-government and Christian–Jewish relations.

The document to which Bałaban refers has up to now not been adequately studied, which is also the case with other similar agreements between Jews and cities in the sixteenth century, a time of significant social and economic changes associated with the increasing political role of the nobility and the development of the grain trade. The circumstances of these documents' creation and the scope of decisions taken require a more detailed analysis.

In the sixteenth century the Polish–Lithuanian Commonwealth saw profound social change leading to the establishment of a polity in which one social group—the nobility—achieved a dominant position. These changes affected the legal status of other social groups, the middle classes and the peasantry, as well as the Jews. On the basis of laws passed in 1539, landowners assumed jurisdiction over the Jews residing on their lands.[2] Simplifying greatly, this meant that the Jews were divided into two categories: royal—remaining under the jurisdiction of royal administrators—and private—subordinated, like other subjects, to the authority of landowners, both secular and clerical. This state of affairs led to further changes. It diminished the importance of general royal prerogatives and led a growing number of Jewish communities to seek to obtain individual local privileges. Admittedly, many of these charters were modelled on general legislation, but having individual privileges gave a greater guarantee of respect, rights, and freedoms. Not only Jews in private towns but also those living in royal towns tried to obtain such charters. As Jacob Goldberg has shown, local privileges of this type had a significant effect on the Jews' legal status.[3] Henceforth, they were no longer under the jurisdiction of a unified legal system. Just like towns, individual local Jewish communities had differing laws and duties, although based on similar principles and models.

Jewish privileges, especially those granted by towns, caused much controversy. From the point of view of the townspeople, they infringed on their rights in the areas of commerce and crafts: the Jews became another social group, alongside the clergy and the nobility, living and working in the town but outside the local municipal laws which regulated competition. This was significant, especially given the increase in numbers of local Jewish communities at the beginning of the sixteenth century, and it led to a growing number of conflicts. Such clashes were common in large cities, which were the most attractive from an economic standpoint and where the largest Jewish communities were located. These issues have been discussed by many historians, most recently Jürgen Heyde, Hanna Zaremska, and Rex Rexheuser, reaching new and interesting conclusions.[4] Smaller localities doubtless experienced similar conflicts, but a lack of sources has not up to now permitted a detailed examination of this phenomenon.

Royal privileges guaranteed Jews the freedom to settle and to do business in Poland. As a result, urban centres had to come to terms with their presence while seeking to have as much influence as possible over the conditions under which Jewish economic activity took place. This led to the emergence of legal agreements. The first legal agreements between Jews and towns were made in the second half of the fifteenth century, the best-known being those in Kraków associated with the Jewish community's move from Żydowska Street (Św. Anny Street) to Szpiglarska Street (Św. Tomasza Street) in 1469 and then to Kazimierz in 1495 and with issues of trade in 1484 and 1502. Majer Bałaban, Ignacy Schiper, and, more recently, Hanna Zaremska and Bożena Wyrozumska, have examined these issues.[5] Similar arrangements, dealing with both the extent of Jewish settlement and their activities, were made at the start of the sixteenth century in Poznań and subsequently in other urban centres.[6]

During the first half of the sixteenth century the practice of concluding legal agreements between city authorities and local Jewish communities became the recommended way of regulating the conditions under which their residence was allowed and was given legal sanction. One of the clauses of the law 'De Judeis', adopted at the Sejm of 1538 in Piotrków, reads:

It is our desire that the Jews not be permitted to trade freely in all things. In transactions involving the purchase and sale of food they are throughout our kingdom to abide by the practices established by us and to obey them. Let them also follow in their entirety the pacts and agreements in place in some of the largest cities in our kingdom.[7]

Such agreements are mentioned three times in the 1560s in the deliberations of the Polish sejm. The Sejm of 1562/3 resolved that, 'since deputies complain that all trade and supply of food is being monopolized by the Jews at the expense of our townspeople and subjects, we demand that the statute of 1538 be respected'.[8] The issue of legal agreement was again taken up at the Sejm of 1565, where the following resolution was adopted:

Given that [the Jews] could not at present reveal the pacts that the towns have with them and they with the towns, and taking nothing away from the urban pacts and leaving them in place, let us postpone them to the next sejm of Crown Poland, so that there towns-people and Jews can make pacts and agreements with the towns on the subject of trade in food.[9]

At the next sejm, two years later, it was affirmed that 'the Jews, notwithstanding the pacts that they have with the towns, are not to take business away from townspeople nor to engage in it'.[10]

From the middle of the sixteenth century several legal agreements were reached between urban centres and local Jewish communities which were clearly the result of these resolutions. Among them is the agreement reached in Kazimierz in 1553 described by Bałaban.[11] This document is exceptionally interesting because of the character and detailed nature of the resolutions adopted. Its contents illuminate a number of key issues, such as the topography of the city and the organization of the areas settled by Jews, the role of Jewish self-government, details of the daily func-tioning of the city's inhabitants, and how community relations were normalized.

Negotiations were conducted between, on the Kraków side, the mayors and coun-cillors of Kazimierz and Stradom and the *pospólstwo* (townspeople), represented by the chairman and jurors of the people's court; and, on the Jewish side, by six elders and a rabbi and four representatives of the 'Jewish *pospólstwo*', including two more rabbis. It is unclear what role the representatives of the Jewish *pospólstwo* played in the community. They may have been minor officials, but it is surprising that two rabbis were included. It is possible that the composition of the Jewish negotiating team was intended to mirror that of the Christian one. There can be no doubt that the townspeople demanded that their representatives participate in important de-cisions affecting the city. Such a trend can be seen in many cities and towns in the commonwealth in the mid-sixteenth century.[12]

The significance of the agreement was such that it was signed in the castle court in the presence not only of the mayor, the councillors, and the chairman and jurors of the people's court but also of the voivode and sheriff (*starosta*) of Kraków. In addi-tion, within two months it was to be entered into the court records in Kazimierz and the 'Jewish records of Kazimierz'. The Jews undertook 'at their own expense to seek approval, for this legal agreement and privilege at the general sejm from His Majesty and would, according to their obligations under the partnership, observe these decisions'.[13] The king approved the agreement on 15 September 1553, guaranteeing its inviolability. It was intended to put an end to all existing disagreements and disputes. As in other such documents, the agreement's collegial and permanent character were emphasized, stating that its drafters 'were drawing up a legal agreement that would last forever'.[14]

The circumstances surrounding the creation of this document are rooted in local conditions. On the one hand, Jews were moving to Kazimierz from other towns and countries, including the Kingdom of Bohemia, leading to rapid demographic growth and contributing to growing economic antagonisms due to increased competition in the local market. These issues alarmed the Catholic Church. Among the resolutions of the 1542 provincial synod of Piotrków was a reference to the rapidly growing Jewish population in the Kingdom of Poland, especially in Kraków.[15] On the other hand, in the mid-sixteenth century, Kraków and its neighbouring towns were frequently stricken by plague—the most severe was in 1546, which led to the deaths of nearly half the population, followed by a second outbreak a few years later. This led to depopulation, with negative economic consequences.[16] Kazimierz was unable to meet its obligations to the treasury, since many houses and plots of land remained empty and were not producing the necessary taxes for the local coffers. Thus, the city fell behind in its payments, including those for a military expedition approved by the sejm. Furthermore, maintaining order and security, especially the upkeep of the city walls, caused substantial problems. It was precisely these financial issues and the expenses of running the town that the Kazimierz magistrate referred to when permitting the expansion of the area occupied by the Jewish population. According to the agreement:

Because of . . . the inadequate number of citizens, payments from these places to the commonwealth's treasury have fallen. Hence the aforementioned mayor and councillors, as well as the whole *pospólstwo* of the town of Kazimierz, in order to safeguard the interests of the treasury, sell, gift, and give all the previously mentioned lots, houses with gardens, and the aforementioned corner plots to the Jews of Kazimierz by means of the laws of inheritance and freehold, renouncing all rights and giving up all title to everything, leaving nothing for themselves or their heirs.[17]

It appears then that, in this case, not only the desire to put an end to the earlier disputes, which are mentioned several times in the document, but also concrete financial needs led to the legal agreement.

On the strength of the agreement, the area inhabited by Jews was expanded significantly. At the same time, however, access to the city proper was very restricted. There were to be only three large gates and one small gate, and 'no one was allowed to construct their own paths and gates to the city'.[18] An agreement was also reached about several houses inhabited by Catholics which backed onto Jewish properties and gardens. The isolation of the Jewish quarter was emphasized by the resolutions on sewage. It was made clear that this should not flow in the direction of the city. On pain of relatively high fines, dumping refuse over the fences of Jewish houses and on the city ramparts was forbidden. These resolutions committed the Jews to maintaining the cleanliness of the district but can also be seen as handing over full control to them, especially as they also had to 'ensure that the city walls surrounding their streets be intact, not in poor condition, and without defects'.[19] Jews were also able to take advantage of some city privileges. They could use the municipal meadows on the same terms as the other inhabitants of the city, 'having paid the requisite fees according to the custom of Christians'.[20] This issue was covered in the legal agreement of June 1533, whose details are not known.[21]

A key element of the agreement was the issue of trade in meat and beverages, especially alcohol. The Jews undertook not to sell liquor to Christians or to take alcoholic beverages imported from abroad, Kraków beer, or Kazimierz mead out of their district. This ban did not cover beer brewed in Kazimierz. It was also agreed that the Jews would be free to run eight slaughterhouses and 'should have their own licensed butchers' but were not permitted 'to sell kosher meat to Catholics'.[22] A high fine of up to 5 grzywnas was imposed on those who failed to observe these provisions. The Jewish elders were to hand over half of this fee to the Kazimierz municipality, the other half to the voivode. This compelled the Jewish elders to ensure that the members of their community abided by the agreement.

Two years after the legal agreement in Kazimierz was signed, a similar agreement was reached in Lublin.[23] Like the Jews of Kraków, the Jews of Lublin lived in a separate district—called Podzamcze—which received Magdeburg rights and became a town in 1595. Both Kraków and Lublin were among the commonwealth's principal commercial centres, where Jews were significant competitors of the local burghers, who had succeeded in moving them outside the city walls but had not stopped their economic activity. In the sixteenth century both Kazimierz and Podzamcze played an exceptional part in the life of the Jewish community of Poland, as the seats of local, regional, and national self-government and lively centres of Jewish religious and cultural life, with famous yeshivas and printing houses. It is hardly surprising then that the agreements reached here had an effect on the regulations adopted by other Jewish communities.

Both legal agreements were very extensive, which makes it possible to compare them and to ascertain the attitudes of the townspeople towards the Jews. Unlike the Kazimierz agreement, that agreed in Lublin in 1555 avoided the issue of Jewish settlement and focused instead on trade and, to a lesser extent, crafts. As mentioned above, in the middle of the sixteenth century Jews lived in Podzamcze, between the castle erected by King Kazimierz and the city walls near the Brama Grodzka (the town gate) and in the suburbs of Czwartek and Lwowskie (later known as Kalinowszczyzna and Słomiany Rynek).[24] This area came under the jurisdiction of the king, but the *starosta* (sheriff) of Lublin was responsible for its day-to-day administration. The Jewish community in Podzamcze was one of the largest in the commonwealth, as shown by the tax rolls of 1507 and the census of 1564, according to which sixty-six of the houses there belonged to Jews.[25] For the Jews of Podzamcze, as for those of Kazimierz in relation to Kraków, Lublin, within whose walls they could neither live nor purchase property, was a far more attractive area in which to pursue their activities.

During the first half of the sixteenth century the local Jewish community in Podzamcze was involved in a considerable amount of legislative activity. It now received a privilege granting it extensive freedoms but was also affected by the adoption of several royal decisions limiting Jewish economic activity.[26] Decrees issued by the *starosta* and confirmed by the king of Poland permitted them to engage in trades and commerce, set up slaughterhouses, erect a synagogue, and maintain their own cemetery.[27] However, the growing number of Jews and the privileges they enjoyed, including relief from customs duties, did not please the townspeople.[28] The area of Jewish settlement also caused dispute. It has not been possible to ascertain if Lublin had the law 'De non tolerandis Judaeis' (the right to exclude Jews), which it possibly adopted in 1535.[29] However, there is no doubt that, apart from certain exceptions, Jews did not reside within the city walls, even though they were very active there, especially in the area of commerce.[30]

The contradictory nature of the legislation affecting the Podzamcze community, with its privileges and restrictions, was undoubtedly the result of growing conflict. On the one hand, Jews wished to acquire the broadest possible freedoms, especially economic ones; while, on the other, the townspeople wanted to limit their activities.

The 1555 legal agreement focused on commercial issues, especially retail trade, which had aroused the greatest controversy. It dealt, in the first instance, with the most expensive goods. On market days, Mondays and Fridays, Jews were permitted to sell cloth measured by the ell but nothing smaller. All manner of goods, including expensive spices such as pepper and saffron, could be sold by the dram and the pound. A great deal of attention was paid to purchasing food. Livestock and fowl had to be bought—as was the case with the townspeople—within the confines of the city or nearby: that is, on the market square or in Krakowskie Przedmieście or Podzamcze. Purchasing goods on the roads leading into the city was prohibited in order to prevent the purchase of products at lower prices. Similar restrictions were adopted in other urban centres. In this case they were intensified by the stipulation that intermediaries were not to be hired from among the townspeople of Lublin for this purpose. Goods purchased inappropriately or in the wrong place were liable to confiscation.

There were extensive regulations covering the meat trade. Jews were permitted to sell meat in their own slaughterhouses. Councillors could issue a ban on buying meat from Jews, with the exception of the hindquarters of a carcass. Co-operation between Jewish and Christian butchers was prohibited, as was setting up partnerships with 'Christians engaged in this trade and [or] running . . . joint businesses with them.'[31]

The legal agreement laid down not only which goods Jews could trade in but how they were to do this. They were banned from selling in public places, on squares and streets, and from booths, temporary tables, or door to door. However, on market days they were permitted to trade in retail goods indoors, through open windows, in entrance halls, and in basements: 'they can also open their windows, they can sell all manner of food in ground-floor shops, lower basements, or in their storerooms.'[32] These permissions did not apply during fairs, when space was assigned for them to erect stalls to sell food and prepared meals. It was in a rather isolated location near the cemetery and the Tatar mosque, a long way from Grodzka Street, which was the principal artery of Lublin. This was ostensibly to prevent traders or soup kitchens blocking the road. Jews were also given the right to rent shops in the town, with the reservation that they could not be used to store wine.

The most extensive part of the legal agreement dealt with the production and sale of alcohol. Jews were allowed to sell wine, beer, and mead, but only for the needs of the Jewish community, both local and transient. The amount involved was specified in detail as fifteen barrels of wine a day, which first had to be inspected by the appropriate city officials. This limit could only be raised with the permission of the council. The beer and mead for sale had to be produced by Christians. A minor exception permitted Jews to produce their own mead for Passover. The ban on production also included so-called 'wild spirits', undoubtedly of high alcoholic content. Jews, however, could sell this, but only in designated locations.

Among the disputed crafts was the making of candles, which in those days were one of the basic articles of daily life. The city called for Jews to be banned completely from the trade, but an agreement was reached that Lublin city council would set a limit to the number of candles produced and sold by Jews.

For the right to trade and sell alcohol, the Jews were meant to pay specific fees to the city. However, they were exempted from paying tolls if they carried goods on their own carts. The *starosta* was to decide in the case of the other fees that Christian inhabitants paid, such as market fees, the fee to use the town weight, and *strygielt*, a fee on the retail sale of cloth. In this last case the townspeople drew attention to the arrangements included in the royal privilege, probably the document issued by King Zygmunt I in 1531.[33]

One of the provisions relating directly to Christian–Jewish relations was the ban on employing Christian servants. The appropriate regulations in this matter were to be issued by the *starosta* of Lublin or the bishop of Kraków. The issue of Christian servants, especially wet nurses, had been raised many times since the thirteenth century in general Church legislation, including that in Poland.[34] However, this problem rarely appeared in secular legislation, and only in the seventeenth century in provincial *sejmiki*.[35]

Jews were entitled to bring any case against Christians to the town court in accordance with Magdeburg law 'like other local people [burghers]'.[36] However, disputes concerning the legal agreement were to be resolved by the *starosta* of Lublin or by other mediators selected by both parties, Christians and Jews.

The equal status granted to Jews in the agreement was underlined by the statement that, apart from matters explicitly dealt with, Jews 'enjoy the same freedom and rights as are enjoyed by the Christian citizens of the town of Lublin'.[37] The agreement was signed at Lublin Castle in the presence of the deputy *starosta* and, as was emphasized, of numerous other people, including a great many representatives of the nobility. The city was represented by the mayor, the councillors, and the chairman and jurors of the people's court. The Podzamcze Jews were represented by five elders, including three rabbis, and five *minores* (junior elders) representing the Jewish *pospólstwo*. It can be assumed that the initiative for signing a legal agreement came from the *starosta*. This is explicitly mentioned in the renewals of the agreement in 1560 and 1570.[38]

The agreement was to last five years, with the possibility of renewal, which in fact happened several times. It was described as a 'legal and amicable' arrangement whose intention was that 'concord and permanent peace be maintained between us'.[39] Its importance is attested by the statement in it that it had primacy over the laws and privileges conferred earlier on both parties and that, 'while this legal agreement is in force and is binding, both parties are to live peacefully with one another, having recourse to no other laws'.[40]

Analysis of the contents of the legal agreements signed in Kazimierz and at Lublin Castle reveals several fundamental issues that appear in both, and which were later to feature in similar agreements made in other towns. These items indicate the principal areas of conflict between the Christian and Jewish communities. In addition to general issues, considerable stress was placed on regulations of a local nature, highlighting the specifics of relations in the area.

The principal problem in most agreements was the issue of Jews acquiring property and the areas where they could reside. The townspeople usually wanted to restrict access to the most economically attractive and prestigious areas in the centre of town, such as the market square. These issues were handled in a somewhat different way in the agreements in Kazimierz and Lublin. In Kazimierz, the townspeople, because of pressing economic concerns, were prepared to extend the area of Jewish settlement, with the proviso that it be kept separate from the Christian part of the town. The Lublin legal agreement ignored this issue. This was because in the middle of the sixteenth century Podzamcze came under the jurisdiction of the king and his officials, and theoretically the townspeople of Lublin had no say in the matter, as is evident from regulations adopted at the time.[41] Several months before the signing of the Lublin agreement the Jews were given three large squares in Podzamcze, on both sides of the river Czechówka, where they were also permitted to set up slaughterhouses. The decision in this matter was made by Stanisław Gabriel Tęczyński, voivode of Lublin, and confirmed by King Zygmunt August.[42] This does not alter the fact that Lublin was interested in the new regulations introduced in Podzamcze, which was the cause of numerous disputes with royal officials, especially *starostas*. The situation became even more complicated when the inhabitants of Podzamcze succeeded in gaining their independence and establishing themselves as their own town. In 1595 they received Magdeburg rights, allowing them to establish their own council, court, and craft guilds.[43] Despite the legal changes, the Lublin authorities took the view that Podzamcze was a private jurisdiction and tried to control its economic activity.[44] Podzamcze's independent development represented serious competition for Lublin, as did its growing Jewish town and the other private jurisdictions. In the 1555 legal agreement the townspeople of Lublin had shown great restraint in the matter of Jewish settlement. This would change after Podzamcze acquired the status of a town, which made possible more far-reaching action on its part. Now, as in Kazimierz, the Jewish district was surrounded by a wall with access through three gates.

A central issue in practically every legal agreement was the freedom for Jews to undertake economic activity, especially trade. Towns and cities usually sought to limit Jewish involvement in retail trade, both in expensive products, such as spices and cloth, and in commodities in daily use, especially alcohol and meat. These issues are to be found in the agreements in Kazimierz and Lublin, where restrictions on Jewish trade are intended, above all, to eliminate competition. The greatest number of disputes was caused by the sale of meat. Jewish butchers dealt in a considerable amount of non-kosher meat, since Jews did not consume the hindquarters of cattle, and they willingly sold such meat for a low price, thus taking away custom from Christian butchers. This was doubtless the reason for the inclusion in the Lublin legal agreement of a ban on the retail sale of meat.

Restrictions were also imposed on where meat could be sold in both Lublin and Kraków. Their aim was to remove Jewish traders from locations with the heaviest traffic and the greatest number of customers: the market square and the most popular streets.

The delimitation of the area of Jewish settlement and attempts to reduce competition in trade were central to the legal agreements between towns and local Jewish communities. These issues reflect the towns' and cities' desire to protect the interests of their Christian citizens. In the struggle against Jewish competition, the townspeople found an ally in the Roman Catholic Church. This is to be seen at the 1542 synod of Piotrków, barely a dozen or so years before the legal agreements in Kazimierz and Lublin. Two of the resolutions adopted there were the most detailed regulations dealing with Jews adopted by the Church in pre-partition Poland–Lithuania.[45] On trade, it was resolved that Jews be prohibited from selling goods on market squares and bridges and in shops and only be permitted to do so in their own homes. These regulations recall the clauses of the Lublin legal agreement.

The synod also resolved that employing Christian servants be forbidden and that servants already in Jewish service be dismissed. The Church's preoccupation was not so much with Christians working for Jews as with their working in Jewish homes and thus in enclosed spaces that were harder to control. The king was called on to forbid the employment of Christian wet nurses on pain of a stiff fine. This prohibition has its origins in the thirteenth-century papal law on the Eucharist. The Church held that the feeding of Jewish children by Christian girls who had taken Holy Communion could constitute desecration of the host, since their milk contained the body and blood of Christ.[46] A provision forbidding the employment of wet nurses can be found in the Lublin agreement. It had no great significance from the point of view of the economic interests of the Christian townspeople and reflected rather the view of the Catholic Church. The ban on employing Christian servants, which could be seen more broadly as a ban on working and co-operating with Jews, should be understood differently. This prohibition is similar to the provision in the Lublin agreement prohibiting co-operation between Jewish and Christian butchers, which was the product of guild regulations limiting the number of master craftsmen and journeymen in any given trade. However, there were also cases when townspeople, to advance their own interests rather than those of the town or the Church, sought co-operation with Jewish craftsmen.

As has already been mentioned, the synod of Piotrków also dealt with the subject of Jewish settlement, especially in Kraków. One of the resolutions adopted was to petition the king to intervene over the influx of large numbers of Jews into the Kingdom of Poland from neighbouring countries, which was, in the opinion of the clergy, harmful to Christians and could have grave consequences. Their number should be limited, so that they could be accommodated in the area previously assigned to them, they were not to buy houses from Christians, and those they had already purchased were to be sold back by a specific date or be confiscated.

The principal provisions of the Kazimierz legal agreement of 1553 were clearly at odds with the resolutions of the synod of Piotrków. The city decided not only to expand the area of the Jewish district but also to allow the sale of houses. In this instance the driving force was the financial crisis caused by the plague and the need to refill the municipal coffers. Practical considerations dominated: the expansion of the area of Jewish settlement was meant to increase revenue and to make it possible to honour the obligations of the town, above all regarding its defences. Thirty years later the decision was taken to expand the Jewish district again.[47] It did, however, remain cut off from the Christian town, which was in accordance with the desires of the clergy. The Kazimierz legal agreement included specific recommendations on how to separate the area of the city where Jews lived with a precisely established number of large and small gates leading into the Christian town, which clearly limited day-to-day contact and contributed not only to economic but also to cultural isolation.

The segregationist aspirations of Church statutes went considerably further. The synod of Piotrków called for Jews to wear distinguishing clothing, forbade the building of new synagogues—and even called for the demolition of a new, brick synagogue in Kraków—recommending instead the renovation of existing ones. These resolutions were typical of ecclesiastical legislation regarding Jews, accepted both in Poland and in other countries and also issued by popes and synods. Their main aim was to keep Christians and Jews separated, although their complete expulsion was not demanded. Their presence of Jews was tolerated by the Church on the grounds that, in the words of the synod of Piotrków, 'it is right that, in memory of the Passion of Christ our Saviour, the Jews be tolerated by the Church, but they should multiply as little as possible'.[48] The policies of towns that agreed to the presence of Jews but limited their economic activities can be seen in a similar light, although the justification was economic rather than theological. The burghers understood and accepted, at least partially, religious and cultural diversity, which was not regarded as exceptional in the multi-ethnic commonwealth.

This is evident in the clauses in the legal agreements of both Kazimierz and Lublin, which contain guarantees for preparing and selling food in accordance with Jewish religious requirements. The Kazimierz agreement states that 'they should have their own certified butchers in order to that they may have meat acceptable according to the Jewish religion'.[49] In the Lublin agreement, provision was made for the sale in the market of 'cooked and raw food according to the Jewish custom'.[50] Permission was likewise given for restrictions on alcohol to be lifted and mead distilled for the holiday of Passover, 'in order that their need for these products during the festival should be satisfied'.[51]

The significance of these legal agreements rested not only on the fact that they were intended to regulate relations and especially commercial activity in the towns involved. It was equally important that bilateral agreements be reached to which both parties were committed. Furthermore, although Christians and Jews were not treated in equal fashion in all clauses, failure to adhere to the terms of the agreement was upheld with stiff fines identical for both parties:

The breach of this agreement, which has been accepted by both parties, namely the mayor, councilmen, and the whole *pospólstwo* of the town of Kazimierz, as well as the elders of the Kazimierz synagogue and the *pospólstwo* of this synagogue, will be punished by a fine of 2,000 grzywnas, to be paid by the party breaking the legal agreement accepted by both parties, half to be paid to the royal treasury, the other to the party behaving peacefully and not violating this legal agreement.[52]

The issue of who represented the two sides should be noted. During the sixteenth century the system of bilateral legal agreements was just beginning to emerge. The legal agreement reached in Kazimierz in 1553 can be compared to a document from Brześć (Brest) dated 1538, barely fifteen years earlier.[53] The subject matter and circumstances surrounding the creation of both were similar: they dealt with the Jewish settlement and its expansion which had caused conflict in both towns. Although the term *concordia* (agreement) appears in the Brześć document, this was not a legal agreement between two parties, but an arrangement ending a dispute. The Jews and the townspeople were not represented by their representatives, and the names of councillors and Jewish elders are not even mentioned. The king not only approved the agreement but was also its mediator. In contrast, in the Kazimierz legal agreement the representatives of the two sides are clearly described: 'the mayor, councilmen, and *pospólstwo* of the town of Kazimierz, as well as the elders of the Kazimierz synagogue and the *pospólstwo* of this synagogue'. It was emphasized that a legal agreement had been reached between the two communities.[54] Royal assent was granted only to a confirmed agreement. The only thing the two documents have in common is that they resolved conflicts.

The similarity of the composition of the Christian and Jewish negotiating teams in the legal agreements of Kazimierz and Lublin is striking. The possibility that the structure and functions of Jewish self-government changed under the influence of the legal agreements and the associated need for a trustworthy negotiating team cannot be ruled out. This seems to confirm the view, which has become increasingly accepted in recent years, that Jewish self-government in Poland developed over a long period and benefited from local models, so that its institutions changed a great deal from those of the German Rhineland from which they were originally derived.[55] The setting up of Jewish guilds in the commonwealth is another example of a response to specific local conditions.[56]

The selection of negotiating teams for legal agreements reflected similarities in the structures of Polish and Jewish self-government and represents yet another example of how the two sides responded to local conditions. On the Christian side, the composition of the negotiating team replicated established city institutions in both Kazimierz and Lublin. Initially, as Heyde has noted, local Jewish communities were represented by one person, and only towards the end of the fifteenth century did larger delegations, reflecting the organization of Jewish self-government, become the norm.[57] This is clearly the case, although qualifications should be made. Until the end of the Polish–Lithuanian Commonwealth, alongside the local Jewish elders, the position of *shtadlan* (advocate) as a one-man negotiator was retained. However, the extent of his duties and responsibilities appears to be smaller than that of the representatives of the community body. It should be noted too that, in the case of the Lublin legal agreement, it is clear that the elders were meant to ensure that its resolutions were respected. In Kazimierz, this was understood rather more broadly. In this case, responsibility for executing the terms of the agreement fell not only on the representatives but on all the members of the local community: 'the elders and the whole Kazimierz synagogue'. This phrase duplicates formulas that are typical for city documents, and reflects contemporary attitudes among townspeople, who wished to have an influence on the running of the town. In their understanding, such a permanent legal agreement involved obligations not only on the part of their representatives but also on the part of the whole population of the town.

These documents were accorded a high status. The composition of the negotiating teams, the presence of royal officials, and the place where the legal agreement was signed are proof of this. In the case of Lublin, the agreement was signed in the castle, one of the king's residences and the place where his officials were located. In addition, the monarch's approval was sought. As a result, such legal agreements acquired the status of royal documents and became binding law. The document signed in Kazimierz was described as 'a legal agreement and privilege'.[58] In Lublin, it was stated that the decisions taken had greater force than the rights acquired earlier by both parties. This makes it clear that special significance was given to these agreements. This had a significant impact on shaping further relations and on the conviction that joint action was effective.

As a way of normalizing life in towns, legal agreements acquired a rather permanent character. The document signed in Kazimierz was meant to be permanent; that in Lublin was to last for only five years, but in 1560 it was renewed for another two years.[59] Subsequent legal agreements, similar to that of 1555, were signed in 1570 and 1581.[60] This means that in the sixteenth century at least four agreements were reached between the city of Lublin and the local Jewish community. These were later renewed several more times.[61] The effectiveness of this sort of arrangement meant that these agreements were used to try and resolve a growing number of problems. As has already been mentioned, the area of Jewish settlement in Kazimierz was expanded several times by legal agreements, including those of 1583 and 1608.[62] In Lublin, and then in Podzamcze, legal agreements were a widely applied mechanism, and over a dozen of them were reached, not only with the city but also with guilds and even religious institutions.[63] Furthermore, attempts were made in Lublin to normalize relations not only with the Jews but also with other religious and ethnic groups.[64] It is worth emphasizing, too, that the Lublin legal agreement became a template for other cities. Its wording was adopted in 1581 in Lwów (Lviv), one of the most important economic centres of the commonwealth.[65]

Despite the significant differences on specific issues, the thrust of the regulations adopted in Kazimierz and Lublin was similar. One key aim was to isolate the Jewish population not only in terms of the area where Jews lived but also in terms of daily interactions. The ban on selling goods, especially meat, to Christians cannot be seen solely within the context of trade rivalry: it also reflected religious differences. The wording of the legal agreements echoed the contemporary social and religious situation associated with the crisis in the Church and the spread of the Reformation. The similarity of the regulations adopted by the townspeople to Church legislation, which represented an example of co-operation by various social groups, is thus not surprising. The various resolutions adopted by the nobility in the sejm, most notably the law 'De Judeis', which strengthened the position of the Christian middle classes, should be seen in a similar light.

The spread of legal agreements during the sixteenth century was connected to the growing activity of towns, resulting from their strengthening economic position and the country's political transformation. The burgher estate wanted to protect its interests and to be able to take decisions for itself that were far broader in scope. While admittedly support in towns and cities for the Reformation was somewhat limited, they did not remain indifferent to the political and social changes that were occurring and they were able to take advantage of them. It should be recalled that the beginning of the sixteenth century saw a wave of public disturbances—between 1517 and 1525 alone there were close to thirty riots, the result of conflicts between municipal councils and ordinary inhabitants aiming to strengthen their position. In some cities, Lublin for example, these disturbances led to changes in the functioning of the municipal government.[66]

At the same time there was a desire to solve other problems, such as the presence in towns and cities of growing numbers of people, including Jews, who were not subject to municipal law. From the 1480s conflict over the retail sale of cloth and meat grew in the largest centres, such as Kraków, Lwów, Sandomierz, and Poznań.[67] It flared up again in the 1520s. It was then that, for the first time, cities, including Warsaw, adopted the 'De non tolerandis Judaeis' law.[68] These events preceded parliamentary legislation regarding legal agreements, including the 'De Judaeis' law, as a result of which towns and cities, at least in theory, could have an influence on the expansion of Jewish settlement and activity.

It is worth noting that towns regulated relations with other religious and ethnic groups, just as they did with the Jews. The similarity of arguments used against both Jews and foreigners shows how sixteenth-century legislation was an element in a consistent municipal policy whose objective was to eliminate competition. It resulted in resolutions of the sejm limiting the rights of different groups defined in ethnic and religious term: Scots, Italians, Jews, Ruthenians, and Protestants.[69] Various solutions were adopted, but they were similar for all those who were seen as different or foreign. Among the most restrictive was the ban on settlement. In terms of Jews this was 'De non tolerandis Judaeis', which from the first quarter of the sixteenth century became more widespread.[70] Similar regulations also applied to Protestants, who were banned from residing in Warsaw, Poznań, and elsewhere.[71] Resolutions limiting economic activity—trade and crafts—were less restrictive. In this instance, too, different religious and ethnic groups were treated similarly. The statutes of the Lublin guild of surgeons adopted identical bans on Jews and Protestants.[72]

The legal agreements were much milder in tone. It is hard to maintain that both parties had equal status, but they did have the opportunity to state their case and take a position. The negotiations brought those who lived in a particular town closer together, regardless of religious or ethnic differences. One clear objective was not co-operation but isolation and the imposition of legal restrictions on one of the parties. The legal agreements between towns and Jewish communities were in reality one-sided and for the most part laid down what was permissible and what was not for one of the parties—the Jews. It was rare to find in them injunctions affecting Christians, telling them what and what not to do. Jews were treated as outsiders and had to follow rules laid down by the townspeople, despite the fact that most of the agreements emphasized mutual friendship and the desire to maintain good rela-tions. Of course, this was not true of every agreement, especially those made in private towns, where the owner's wishes played a decisive part. In the large royal towns and cities, the townspeople enjoyed greater independence and had more power to protect their position. As a result, they were not always willing to bend to the will of officials. This does not mean that legal agreements in royal towns and cities did nothing but limit the rights of Jews. They also conferred on Jews similar rights to the townspeople, such as use of the public meadows in Kazimierz. The rights granted to Jews in the Lublin agreements were even broader: in the areas not specifically dealt with, they were to enjoy the same freedoms as burghers. In this case, the dec-larations of friendship and partnership took a concrete form.

The sejm's endorsement of legal agreements as putting the Jews' legal status in towns and cities on an equal footing with their privileges made them part of the regulations governing the various social, religious, and ethnic groups in the towns. These agreements had been preceded by conflicts as one party sought to impose its will on the other. However, these conflicts did not lead to satisfactory outcomes.

As a result, mutually acceptable agreements were sought, although they were hedged in by restrictive safeguards in the form of monetary fines. This is testimony to the development of a legal culture, and represents an attempt to find a way for various religious and ethnic groups to coexist peacefully.

Translated from the Polish by Jarosław Garliński

Notes

1 M. Bałaban, *Historja Żydów w Krakowie i na Kazimierzu 1304–1868*, 2 vols. (Kraków, 1931–6; repr. 1991), i. 190.

2 *Sejmy i sejmiki koronne wobec Żydów: Wybór tekstów źródłowych*, ed. A. Michałowska-Mycielska (Warsaw, 2006), 33.

3 *Jewish Privileges in the Polish Commonwealth: Charters of Rights Granted to Jewish Communities in Poland–Lithuania in the Sixteenth to Eighteenth Centuries*, ed. J. Goldberg, 3 vols. (Jerusalem, 1985–2001), i. 11.

4 J. Heyde, 'Polityka Rady miejskiej Lwowa wobec Żydów i Ormian w XV/XVI wieku: Heterogeniczność etniczno-religijna w mieście jako wyzwanie ustrojowe', *Kwartalnik Historii Kultury Materialnej*, 63 (2015), 283–92; H. Zaremska, *Żydzi w średniowiecznej Polsce: Gmina krakowska* (Warsaw, 2011); R. Rexheuser, *Kulturen und Gedächtnis: Studien und Reflexionen zur Geschichte des östlichen Europas* (Wiesbaden, 2008), 13–38.

5 Bałaban, *Historja Żydów w Krakowie i na Kazimierzu*, i. 57; I. Schipper, *Studya nad stosunkami gospodarczymi Żydów w Polsce podczas średniowiecza* (Lwów, 1911), 338; Zaremska, *Żydzi w średniowiecznej Polsce*, 493; B. Wyrozumska, *The Jews in Mediaeval Cracow: Selected Records from Cracow Municipal Books* (Kraków, 1995), 186; ead., 'Czy Jan Olbracht wygnał Żydów z Krakowa?', *Rocznik Krakowski*, 59 (1993), 5–11.

6 L. Koczy, 'Studja nad dziejami gospodarczymi Żydów poznańskich przed połową wieku XVII', *Kronika Miasta Poznania*, 12 (1934), 334; Rexheuser, *Kulturen und Gedächtnis*, 13; H. Węgrzynek, 'Agreements between Towns and Kahals and Their Impact on the Legal Status of Polish Jews', in A. Polonsky, H. Węgrzynek, and A. Żbikowski (eds.), *New Directions in the History of the Jews in the Polish Lands* (Brighton, Mass., 2018), 219–31.

7 *Volumina legum: Leges, statuta, constitutiones et privilegia Regni Poloniae, Magni Ducatus Lithuaniae*, 10 vols. (St Petersburg, 1859–60), i. 259; *Sejmy i sejmiki koronne wobec Żydów*, 32.

8 *Volumina legum*, ii. 20; *Volumina constitutionum*, ed. S. Grodziski et al., 4 vols. (Warsaw, 2005), ii. 114; *Sejmy i sejmiki koronne wobec Żydów*, 36.

9 *Volumina legum*, ii. 51; *Volumina constitutionum*, ii. 172; *Sejmy i sejmiki koronne wobec Żydów*, 36.

10 *Volumina legum*, ii. 68; *Volumina constitutionum*, ii. 200; *Sejmy i sejmiki koronne wobec Żydów*, 36.

11 Central Archives for the History of the Jewish People, Jerusalem, PL-183: 'Ugoda między Magistratem Miasta a Synagogą Kazimierską powagą Najaśniejszego Zygmunta Augusta Króla Polski aprobowana: Roku Pańskiego 1553'. This is a copy of the original document probably made in the eighteenth century. The original is lost. For the Latin version, see *Dyplomatariusz dotyczący Żydów w dawnej Polsce na źródłch archiwalnych osnuty (1388–1782)*, ed. M. Bersohn (Warsaw, 1910), no. 62.

12 R. Szczygieł, *Konflikty społeczne w Lublinie w pierwszej połowie XVI wieku* (Warsaw, 1977),

98; J. Wyrozumski, *Dzieje Krakowa*, i: *Kraków do schyłku wieków średnich* (Kraków, 1992), 518; J. Bieniarzówna and J. M. Małecki, *Dzieje Krakowa*, ii: *Kraków w wiekach XVI–XVIII* (Kraków, 1984), 13, 51.

13   'Ugoda między Magistratem Miasta a Synagogą Kazimierską', 6.

14   Ibid. 2.

15   *Materyjały do historyi ustawodawstwa synodalnego w Polsce w w. XVI*, ed. B. Ulanowski (Kraków, 1895), 67–8.

16   Bieniarzówna and Małecki, *Dzieje Krakowa*, ii. 43.

17   'Ugoda między Magistratem Miasta a Synagogą Kazimierską', 3.

18   Ibid.

19   Ibid. 5.

20   Ibid. 4.

21   Archiwum Narodowe, Kraków, 29/34 Archiwum miasta Kazimierza pod Krakowem, K176: spisy treści do ksiąg inskrypcji, , 1530–1603, 25.

22   'Ugoda między Magistratem Miasta a Synagogą Kazimierską', 5.

23   Tsentral'nyi derzhavnyi istorychnyi arkhiv Ukrayiny, Lviv, f. 52, op. 1, spr. 138, fos. 12–18: 'Copia transactionis inter Communitatem Lublinen' et Iudeos Lublin' Anno Dni' 1555'.

24   J. Mazurkiewicz, *Jurydyki lubelskie* (Wrocł., 1956), 27.

25   *Lustracja województwa lubelskiego 1565*, ed. A. Wyczański (Wrocłw, 1959), 6; M. Horn, 'Najstarszy rejestr osiedli żydowskich w Polsce z 1507 r.', *Biuletyn Żydowskiego Instytutu Historycznego*, 91 (1974), 11–15.

26   Biblioteka im. Hieronima Łopacińskiego, Lublin, MS 116: 'Sumaryusz dokumentów przeciw żydom 1530–1700'; *Materiały do historii Lublina, 1317–1792*, ed. J. Riabinin (Lublin, 1938), no. 369; *Dyplomatariusz dotyczący Żydów*, nos. 25, 49, 56, 482.

27   Archiwum Państwowe, Lublin (hereafter APL), Akta Luźne Miasta Lublina 87: 'Akta dotyczące stosunków miasta z Żydami i spraw ludności żydowskiej w Lublinie XVI–XVII', 1501–1700; 145: 'Kopiariusz przywilejów miejskich', 1501–1700; 313: Lustratio Capitaneatus Lublinensis, 1614; *Lustracja województwa lubelskiego 1661*, ed. H. Oprawko and K. Schuster (Warsaw 1962), 110–11; *Materiały do historii*, nos. 118, 126, 131, 187, 205, 209; *Russko-evreiskii arkhiv: Dokumenty i materialy dlya istorii evreev v Rossii*, ed. S. Bershadsky, 3 vols. (St Petersburg, 1882–1903), iii. nos. 157, 158, 169, 172; *Dyplomatariusz dotyczący Żydów*, nos. 64, 66, 76, 102, 106.

28   'Akta dotyczące stosunków miasta z Żydami i spraw ludności żydowskiej w Lublinie XVI–VII'; 'Sumaryusz dokumentów przeciw żydom 1530–1700'; Biblioteka im. Hieronima Łopacińskiego, MS 1387: 'Odpisy dokumentów dotyczących Żydów lubelskich 1535–1792'; Szczygieł, *Konflikty społeczne*, 130; J. Riabinin, *Z dziejów Żydów lubelskich* (Lublin, 1936), 5.

29   A. Kuwałek and R. Kuwałek, 'Żydzi i chrześcijanie w Lublinie w XVI i XVII wieku: Przyczynek do dziejów Żydów w Lublinie w okresie staropolskim', in T. Radzik (ed.), *Żydzi w Lublinie: Materiały do dziejów społeczności żydowskiej Lublina*, 2 vols. (Lublin, 1995–8), ii. 9–31: 10; J. Goldberg, 'De non tolerandis Iudaeis: On the Introduction of the Anti-Jewish Laws into Polish Towns and the Struggle against Them', in S. Yeivin (ed.), *Studies in Jewish History Presented to Professor Raphael Mahler on His Seventy-Fifth Birthday* (Merhavia, 1974), 39–52.

30   'Akta dotyczące stosunków miasta z Żydami i spraw ludności żydowskiej w Lublinie XVI–VII'; 'Sumaryusz dokumentów przeciw żydom 1530–1700'; *Materiały do historii*, nos. 115, 116, 142, 149; Szczygieł, *Konflikty społeczne*, 134; Riabinin, *Z dziejów Żydów*, 6; M. Bałaban, *Żydowskie miasto w Lublinie* (Lublin, 1991), 13.

31 'Copia transactionis inter Communitatem Lublinen' et Iudeos Lublin'', fo. 15v.

32 Ibid., fo. 15r.

33 APL, Dokumenty miasta Lublina, 49; Zygmunt król Polski postanawia, że Żydzi z przedmieścia lubelskiego obowiązani są do opłaty podatku od mierzenia sukna (strygielt), 1531.

34 *Kodeks dyplomatyczny Wielkopolski/Codex diplomaticus Maioris Poloniae*, i, ed. I. Zakrzewski (Poznań, 1877), 370; *Materyjały do historyi ustawodawstwa synodalnego w Polsce*, 67; A. Kaźmierczyk, 'The Problem of Christian Servants as Reflected in the Legal Codes of the Polish Lithuanian Commonwealth during the Second Half of the Seventeenth Century and in the Saxon Period', *Gal-ed*, 15–16 (1997), 23–40; H. Węgrzynek, 'Kościół katolicki a Żydzi w Małopolsce w XVI wieku', in W. Kowalski and J. Muszyńska (eds.), *Kościół katolicki w Małopolsce w średniowieczu i we wczesnym okresie nowożytnym* (Kielce, 2001), 225–36; ead., '*Czarna legenda' Żydów: Procesy o rzekome mordy rytualne w dawnej Polsce* (Warsaw, 1995), 28.

35 A. Kaźmierczyk, *Sejmy i sejmiki szlacheckie wobec Żydów w drugiej połowie XVII wieku* (Warsaw, 1994), 88.

36 'Copia transactionis inter Communitatem Lublinen' et Iudeos Lublin'', fo. 16v.

37 Ibid., fo. 17r.

38 M. Trojanowska, *Dokument miejski lubelski od XIV do XVIII wieku: Studium dyplomatyczne* (Warsaw, 1977), no. 5; 'Akta dotyczące stosunków miasta z Żydami i spraw ludności żydowskiej w Lublinie XVI–VII'.

39 'Copia transactionis inter Communitatem Lublinen' et Iudeos Lublin'', fo. 17r.

40 Ibid.

41 *Materiały do historii*, no. 275.

42 *Dyplomatariusz dotyczący Żydów*, no. 64.

43 APL, Księgi grodzkie i ziemskie lubelskie (Relacje, manifestacje, oblaty), 36; *Materiały do historii*, nos. 257, 258, 290, 360, 369; Mazurkiewicz, *Jurydyki lubelskie*, 36, 87, 93.

44 Mazurkiewicz, *Jurydyki lubelskie*, 103.

45 *Materyjały do historyi ustawodawstwa synodalnego w Polsce*, 67–8.

46 Węgrzynek, '*Czarna legenda' Żydów*, 28.

47 Bałaban, *Historja Żydów w Krakowie i na Kazimierzu*, i. 190, 196, 208.

48 *Materyjały do historyi ustawodawstwa synodalnego w Polsce*, 67–8.

49 'Ugoda między Magistratem Miasta a Synagogą Kazimierską', 5.

50 'Copia transactionis inter Communitatem Lublinen' et Iudeos Lublin'', fo. 16v.

51 Ibid., fo. 14r.

52 'Ugoda między Magistratem Miasta a Synagogą Kazimierską', 5.

53 *Dyplomatariusz dotyczący Żydów*, no. 44.

54 'Ugoda między Magistratem Miasta a Synagogą Kazimierską', 6.

55 Zaremska, *Żydzi w średniowiecznej Polsce*, 367; F. Guesnet, 'Agreements between Neighbours: The "Ugody" as a Source on Jewish–Christian Relations in Early Modern Poland', *Jewish History*, 24 (2010), 257–70; J. Heyde, *Transkulturelle Kommunikation und Verflechtung: Die jüdischen Wirtschaftseliten in Polen vom 14. bis zum 16. Jahrhundert* (Wiesbaden, 2014); id., 'Samorząd żydowski a włdze nieżydowskie w średniowieczu', in A. Pobóg-Lenartowicz, R. Trawka, and L. Poniewozik (eds.), *Materiały V Kongresu Mediewistów Polskich*, ix: *Obcy w mieście, obcy w klasztorze: Ciągłość i zmiana wspólnot lokalnych na ziemiach polskich w średniowieczu* (Rzeszów, 2019), 95–108; id., 'Relations between Jews and Non-Jews in the Polish–Lithuanian Commonwealth: Perceptions and Practices', in Polon-

sky, Węgrzynek, and Żbikowski (eds.), *New Directions in the History of the Jews in the Polish Lands*, 198–218.

56 A. Michałowska, *Między demokracją a oligarchią: Władze gmin żydowskich w Poznaniu i Swarzędzu (od połowy XVII do końca XVIII wieku)* (Warsaw, 2000), 144.

57 Heyde, 'Samorząd żydowski a władze nieżydowskie w średniowieczu', 95.

58 'Ugoda między Magistratem Miasta a Synagogą Kazimierską', 6.

59 Trojanowska, *Dokument miejski lubelski*, no. 5.

60 'Akta dotyczące stosunków miasta z Żydami i spraw ludności żydowskiej w Lublinie XVI–VII'.

61 *Lauda miejskie lubelskie XVII wieku*, ed. J. Riabinin (Lublin, 1935), no. 143.

62 *Dyplomatariusz dotyczący Żydów*, no. 211; J. Morgensztern, 'Regesty z Metryki Koronnej do historii Żydów w Polsce (1588–1632)', *Biuletyn Żydowskiego Instytutu Historycznego*, 51 (1964), 59–78: no. 16; Bałaban, *Historja Żydów w Krakowie i na Kazimierzu*, i. 190, 196, 208.

63 *Dyplomatariusz dotyczący Żydów*, no. 243; J. Morgensztern, 'Regesty z Metryki Koronnej do historii Żydów w Polsce (1633–1660)', *Biuletyn Żydowskiego Instytutu Historycznego*, 58 (1966), 107–48: no. 73; H. Gmiterek, 'Z dziejów Żydów lubelskich: Ugoda na Podzamczu z 1642 roku', in J. Kłpeć et al. (eds.), *W służbie Klio…: Księga poświęcona pamięci Profesora Tadeusza Radzika* (Lublin, 2012), 59–69; H. Węgrzynek, 'Der Vergleich als Mittel der Kommunikation und Konfliktlösung. Lubliner Franziskaner und Judengemeinde im 17. Jahrhundert', in Y. Kleinmann (ed.), *Kommunikation durch symbolische Akte: Religiöse Heterogenität und politische Herrschaft in Polen–Litauen* (Stuttgart, 2010), 209–27.

64 Trojanowska, *Dokument miejski lubelski*, no. 5.

65 H. Gmiterek, 'Żydzi lwowscy i ich związki z Lublinem w XVII wieku', in P. Jusiak and A. Sochacka (eds.), *Scientia nihil est quam veritas imago: Studia ofiarowane Profesorowi Ryszardowi Szczygłowi w siedemdziesięciolecie urodzin* (Lublin, 2014), 562–70.

66 Szczygieł, *Konflikty społeczne*, 98.

67 M. Bałaban, *Żydzi lwowscy na przełomie XVI i XVII wieku* (Lwów, 1906), 395; Zaremska, *Żydzi w średniowiecznej Polsce*, 211.

68 Archiwum Główne Akt Dawnych, Warsaw, Zbiór dokumentów pergaminowych, 1557: 'Zygmunt I Król Polski zabrania Żydom mieszkać w Starej jak w Nowej Warszawie i na ich przedmieściach, wyjątek stanowią poborca ceł Moise z rodziną', 1527; T. Wierzbowski, *Przywileje królewskiego miasta stołecznego Starej Warszawy 1376–1772* (Warsaw, 1913), 35.

69 *Volumina legum*, ii. 20.

70 Goldberg, 'De non tolerandis Iudaeis'.

71 Archiwum Główne Akt Dawnych, Archiwum Zamoyskich, 3004: 'Iura et privilegia Civitatis Antiquae Varsoviae contra Hereticos et Iudeos 1483–1730', 1–3; T. Stegner, *Ewangelicy warszawscy 1815–1918* (Warsaw, 1993), 7; M. Bogucka and H. Samsonowicz, *Dzieje miast i mieszczaństwa w Polsce przedrozbiorowej* (Wrocłw, 1986), 536.

72 *Lauda miejskie lubelskie*, no. 175.

Between the Castle and the Town Hall
The *Kahal* of Słuck in the Seventeenth Century

MARIA CIEŚLA

THERE HAS BEEN MUCH study of the functioning of autonomous Jewish community bodies, *kahals*, in the private towns of the Polish–Lithuanian Commonwealth during the eighteenth century.[1] Scholars have investigated their structure, how their members were selected, and the manner in which the noble owners of such towns interfered in their activities. There are many case studies of different towns, most often describing how *kahals* were made dependent on the owners of the town and their representatives[2] and of the significance of *kahals* within the administrative structure of noble estates.[3] Many comparative studies have demonstrated the similarity in structure between the *kahals* and municipal councils, pointing out that both, at least in theory, had the same degree of legal autonomy and were chosen in the same way. The obligations of town and *kahal* functionaries have also been compared.[4] Earlier studies have pointed out that *kahals* were similar to municipal councils not only in structure but also in their day-to-day functioning, and were obliged to find some way of co-operating with each other. Pre-war Polish Jewish historiography has stressed conflicts in royal towns between the town authorities and the Jewish community bodies, motivated mostly by economic competition and often taking a violent form.[5] Much less is known about the contacts between the *kahals* and the local authorities in private towns and the extent to which they were subordinate to the municipality. Attention has focused exclusively on their legal subordination to the town's owner. Most studies have stressed this dependence and concluded that, in private towns, the burghers were deprived of any real legal autonomy or genuine power.[6] Polish historians have alluded to the right of Jews to participate in the selection of town councils, although this issue has never been examined in detail.[7]

In this chapter I examine the functioning of the *kahal* from the perspective of municipal politics, analysing the division of power between the nobility, the municipality, and the Jewish community. I am primarily interested in the dependence of the *kahal* on the local municipal authorities and the way the contacts between these bodies worked in practice, how power and obligations were divided in the context of the government of the town, and how conflicts between the *kahal* and the town authorities were resolved. I take Słuck (Slutsk) as a case study. This town, located in the Grand Duchy of Lithuania, was the home of a large Jewish community, which played a significant role in Jewish community life in the Polish–Lithuanian Commonwealth. Above all, I examine the actions of the Jewish community from the perspective of Christians—the municipality and the owner of the town. This is inevitable given the available material. A rich collection of documents of all types relating to the town has survived, but among them there are virtually no Jewish sources. The one exception is the incomplete *pinkas* (ledger) of the *ḥevrah kadisha*, which is merely a list of those who died and sheds no light on the functioning of the *kahal*.

In 1601 Janusz Radziwiłł, the town's owner, granted a charter to the Jews wanting to settle in Słuck. This was typical of those issued to the Jewish communities in most private towns in the Polish–Lithuanian Commonwealth, giving them the freedom to choose their places of residence, placing them under the jurisdiction of the owner's representative in the town, and making them independent of the jurisdiction of the municipal council. The Jews were exempted from all financial obligations to the municipality—they were required only to pay rent to the town's owner, who also granted them the right to trade freely and to undertake all artisan trades.[8]

This privilege led, in the first half of the seventeenth century, to the rapid growth of the local Jewish community, which by 1689 had reached around 3,500, constituting between 38 and 40 per cent of the population of the town.[9] In less than a century Słuck had become one of the five most important Jewish communities in the Grand Duchy of Lithuania, and in 1691 the Jewish Council of Lithuania recognized the independent status of its *kehilah*. The elders of the council, granting it extensive rights, stressed that it had become a major centre for Torah study.[10]

A number of factors had contributed to the rapid development of Słuck, which at this time was one of the largest private towns in Lithuania, with a total population of around 7,000. Jews were now eagerly settling in private towns which offered them favourable conditions under noble protection.[11] Słuck was particularly attractive because it was a major centre of trade and artisanry.[12] Its rapid development was facilitated by its geographical position and the policy of the Radziwiłłs. Situated at the intersection of trading routes linking eastern, western, and southern markets, it was a place where merchants from beyond the eastern and southern borders of the Grand Duchy of Lithuania congregated. The town's merchants, principally Jews, were particularly active in northern markets (above all in Königsberg).

Research has shown how the Radziwiłłs, from their castle at Birże (Biržai), actively encouraged the economic development of their estates in a way that was modern for the period. They attempted to develop their infrastructure and provide assistance to their subjects, both Jews and Christians, particularly if it was a question of increasing the profitability of their estates.[13] Paradoxically, the military character of Słuck was also of considerable significance in the development of the local Jewish community. The local garrison played an important role in the defensive system of the Grand Duchy of Lithuania, as was evident during the wars with Muscovy in the mid-seventeenth century, during which the armies of Tsar Aleksey Mikhailovich (r. 1645–76) unsuccessfully besieged the town for several days.[14] The local fortress, rebuilt at the same time, gave shelter to many Jewish fugitives fleeing the Khmelnytsky uprising as well as the wars, a large number of whom remained in the town after military operations ceased.[15]

According to the 1601 privilege, the Jews were 'free to build a Jewish synagogue according to their preference and to use it freely and for all time'. In addition, Janusz Radziwiłł's representative was 'to ensure that they are given a place to bury their dead outside the town'.[16] Thus were established the necessary preconditions for the creation of an autonomous Jewish community. From the perspective of the owner of the town, the executive of this community, the *kahal*, was to fulfil two basic functions—to ensure the establishment of functioning religious institutions and to represent the Jewish community to the outside world. The *kahal* was also an administrative body, subordinate to the administration of the landowner's estate and following its instructions.[17] As in other towns in the Polish–Lithuanian Commonwealth, the *kahal* was responsible for organizing Jewish religious life and creating a system of jurisdiction over it. The court of the *kahal*, whose activity was legitimated by the owner of the town, sat in a building near the synagogue, where it adjudicated internal disputes among Jews. Alongside the synagogue there was also a hospital and sanctuary for the sick and aged. The local *ḥevrah kadisha* administered the cemetery, and a system of schools—*ḥeders*—was established.[18] The *kahal* was also a fiscal institution collecting internal Jewish levies and state taxes.[19]

The local Christian administrative bodies had a decisive influence over the functioning of the *kahal*. Although in the sixteenth century Słuck was one of the largest towns in Lithuania, it did not possess the right of municipal autonomy. In 1441 its owners had granted it a charter based on Magdeburg law, but this does not seem to have significantly altered the way the town was administered.[20] The documents which have been preserved suggest that until the mid-seventeenth century no autonomous institutions based on Magdeburg law functioned in the town. The situation now began to change. As a result of the threat posed by Tsar Aleksey's advancing armies, Bogusław Radziwiłł reorganized the local government in the town.[21] In 1652 he granted it a new privilege in accordance with Magdeburg law, which initiated an extended process of transforming how authority and municipal jurisdiction were exercised.

In December 1654 Radziwiłł set up the *sesja miejska* (town session), an advisory body made up of eleven burghers, the mayor, and the commander of the fortress. Its members, who were recruited from the richest merchant families, were nominated by the owner. Its principal obligation was 'to provide what is necessary for the strengthening of the fortifications of the town'.[22] Above all, in the view of the town's owner it was to assist in the organization and financing of the local garrison.

The creation of the *sesja miejska* fundamentally altered the balance of power in the town. Until the middle of the seventeenth century all local matters had been decided by the owner. By conceding a representative role to the burghers, he relinquished some of his power. The burghers eagerly took possession of their new rights, gradually taking over various aspects of the administration of the town. In the first years of its activity, the *sesja miejska* had very limited power: at its weekly meeting it discussed various issues, above all the maintenance of order and financial questions linked with the levying of taxes and the economic life of the town. All major decisions were still taken by the town's owner or his representative.[23] If matters not directly linked with defence or how taxes were levied were discussed, they were dealt with at the end of the meeting in the form of proposals which were put forward to be accepted or rejected by the owner or his deputy.[24]

The power of the *sesja miejska* began to grow. In its first years, it took over the levying of various taxes connected with economic life. Subsequently, it acquired the right to control the sale of real estate.[25] At the beginning of the eighteenth century the burghers established their judicial independence from the town's owner.[26] The inhabitants of the town were also now obliged, at the behest of the *sesja miejska*, to take part in its defence, an obligation which also fell upon local Jews.[27] These developments meant that in some areas Jews were no longer directly dependent on the town's owner and were required to follow the instructions of the town authorities.

The biggest change in the way the *kahal* functioned was caused by the *sesja miejska* taking over a part of the municipal finances. From the 1650s the municipality began to collect rents from Christians. In order to ensure that the town's finances were in a satisfactory state, it became concerned that real estate should not fall into Jewish hands. From its point of view the purchase of a house or a plot of land by a Jew meant the loss of some of its income, since rent from such properties was paid directly into the treasury of the noble. For this reason efforts were now made to slow the growth of the Jewish quarter. Among the most common documents preserved in the Słuck archive are petitions to the town's owner and notes in the minutes of the *sesja miejska* complaining about the increase in the number of Jews and the new areas of the town they were occupying. In most of these, the burghers demanded that Jews purchasing new houses or plots should agree to renounce the right to pay their rent to the town's owner and instead should bear the same fiscal obligations as Christians.

These arguments seem to have convinced the town's owner, who allowed the municipality to take control of the sale and purchase of real estate in the town. In December 1658 Kazimierz Kłokocki and Władysław Huryn, the local representatives of the Radziwiłłs, issued an ordinance forbidding Jews to buy or sell real estate 'through Jewish books'. The sale and purchase of plots of land were now to be registered by the administration of the estate, a significant restriction on the autonomy of the *kahal*. Until this time, transactions between Jews had been recorded in Hebrew in the appropriate *pinkasim*. The aim of the ordinance seems to have been the limitation of the purchase and sale of real estate by Jews.[28] A year later, in 1659, these same representatives ordered that 'the mayor's office should make sure that Jews do not buy any more houses'.[29] In 1661 the town's owner conceded to the town authorities the right to issue privileges for the purchase of real estate. Thus, from the 1660s, a Jew wishing to purchase a house, plot, or stall in the town had to appear before the *sesja miejska* to request permission. In most cases the sale of a house was postponed to a subsequent meeting in the hope that a Christian buyer could be found. If this was not the case, permission was often refused.[30]

The minutes of the *sesja miejska* make clear the hostile attitude of the town authorities to the Jews. The negative aspects of Jewish activity in the town were frequently discussed in meetings of the *sesja miejska*, often in the context of concrete decisions on taxation or military obligations. These discussions were often accompanied by stereotypical and hostile observations on Jews. Their dishonesty was frequently stressed, as was the claim that 'in buying foodstuffs they should not be allowed to harm Christians by pre-empting them or running between the wagons [bringing food to the town]'.[31] They were accused of ill will and consciously acting to the detriment of Christians, of dealing in stolen goods, of trading on Christian holidays, and of making burghers drunk. The further growth of Jewish trade would, it was argued, lead to the downfall of the town.[32] Accusations of this type confirm the hostility of the town authorities to Jews but do not seem to have significantly affected the actual conditions in which they lived in the town.

Despite the obvious distaste for Jews and the conflicts to which this led, in a number of areas it turned out to be possible to create successfully functioning systems of mutual co-operation. The members of the *sesja miejska* treated the *kahal* as the official representative of the Jews living in the town and imposed administrative responsibilities on it, including, among others, the collection of taxes and the organization of the defences. The representatives of the *kahal* attempted, above all, to preserve the independence and autonomy of the local Jewish community.

Co-operation between the *sesja miejska* and the *kahal* was organized through the mediation of officials of both bodies. The official link between the *kahal* and the Christian authorities was the sexton (*shamash*; *szkolnik*). Among his responsibilities were the representation of the *kahal* at the *sesja miejska* and in the courts. In Słuck, as in some other autonomous Jewish communities, the sexton also served as advocate (*shtadlan*).[33] The *kahal* employed several sextons—in 1697 there were seven. There was a hierarchy among them: a small number represented the community to the outside world, while others were concerned to keep order in the synagogue or to supervise the running of such institutions as the cemetery or the refuge for the sick.[34] Little is known about the social origins of sextons. Almost all appear in the Christian sources exclusively as official representatives of the Jewish community structure. They were paid officials of the *kahal*: in 1733, 175 zlotys were set aside annually for their salaries.[35] In 1689 most of them lived on Żydowska Street, where the majority of residents were not well-off. Some rented rooms from richer neighbours rather than owning their own homes.[36] Nevertheless, the work of a sexton required some well-defined skills, particularly knowledge of Polish, and possibly of Ruthenian. The sources also show that the majority had a broad knowledge of the law, and in trials were able to refer not only to privileges granted to the *kahal* but also to the Third Lithuanian Statute.[37]

In some situations, the *kahal* was represented by the 'kahal elders'. It is not clear who they were: presumably the *parnas* (president of the *kahal*) and the senior members. In Słuck, as in the majority of towns in the Polish–Lithuanian Commonwealth, elections to the *kahal* were conducted during the intermediate days of Passover. Active and passive voting rights were possessed by those who paid the required level of tax. Thirteen individuals were chosen. The offices of president and senior councillor were honorary and were not reimbursed by the *kahal*.[38] Most frequently, rich merchants or leasers of noble properties were selected as presidents. Community offices were often *de facto* hereditary, as was the case in many other Jewish communities in the Polish–Lithuanian Commonwealth. An excellent example is the family of Hercyk Szlomowicz. Szlomowicz and, after him, his son-in-law Michał Ickowicz were for many years members of the *kahal* power structure. Szlomowicz was a merchant and leaseholder. He traded widely, frequently visiting Breslau and Königsberg. For many years he held the lease of the town's taxes.[39] Michał Ickowicz was a trusted factor of the Radziwiłłs, maintaining close relations with Stanisław Niezabitowski, the Radziwiłłs' steward, who used him as a courier in his contacts with Ludwika Karolina Radziwiłł, daughter of Bogusław Radziwiłł. Like his father-in-law he traded extensively and, making use of the protection of the Radziwiłłs, leased taxes and worked as a goldsmith. Both Hercyk and Michał belonged to a small group of Słuck Jews who for the most part moved in Christian circles. The family owned an impressive mansion located on the market square, where their neighbours were Christian. So too were many of their business partners. Both Hercyk and Michał used their close contacts with Christians, especially the Radziwiłłs, to lobby on behalf of the *kahal*.

Co-operation between the town authorities and the *kahal* was based, above all, on the participation of representatives of the *kahal* in the meetings of the *sesja miejska*. Usually the sexton, sometimes together with a *kahal* elder, was summoned several times a month to such meetings, where he would be given detailed instructions on the level of taxation, the organization of the list of taxpayers, and so on. The sexton was only a messenger communicating information; the ultimate decisions were taken by the *kahal* elders. Representatives of the *kahal*, the elder Abram Łazarewicz and the sexton Nohim, appeared before the *sesja miejska* for the first time in February 1655, barely two months after the body had been called into existence. Its members instructed the *kahal* to stockpile provisions for the Jews in case of a siege.[40] In March 1666 the sexton was summoned because the Jews' taxes were overdue.[41] In 1673 information was provided on how the state taxes were to be divided, with particular attention being devoted to the hearth tax.[42] Representatives of the *kahal* also took part in the ceremonial meetings of the *sesja miejska*. Thus in June 1660 'the letter of the prince . . . was read in the presence of the assembled burghers and the Jewish elders'.[43]

In giving instructions to the *kahal*, the *sesja miejska* did not interfere in the manner of their execution. For the municipal authorities, it was important only that the tax quotas assigned to the Jews (which were usually high) should be fulfilled and that the Jews should contribute to the defence of the town. By not interfering and showing no interest in the way its instructions were implemented, the *sesja miejska* recognized the autonomous status of the *kahal* and the right of its leaders to make decisions on behalf of the members of their community. In this way it legitimized the role of the *kahal* as one of the administrative organs of the Radziwiłł estate. At the same time, in the hierarchy of power, the position of the Jewish community was very weak and the *kahal* was in effect a subordinate body whose function was to implement the decisions of the municipal authorities and the owner of the town.

However, the activity of the representatives of the *kahal* at the meetings of the *sesja miejska* was not limited to listening passively to instructions. From the beginning, *kahal* elders were aware of the new division of power in the town, and attempted to obtain formal recognition of the right to influence the decisions of the municipality. Their main interests were economic policy and taxation. In these areas the *kahal* representatives were very active and tried to negotiate the best conditions for the Jews. In particular, they sought to maintain the independent status of the *kahal*.

Only a few months after the creation of the *sesja miejska*, the Jews obtained the right to participate in the division of the excise tax. In January 1656 it was decided that:

The excise duties on mead and spirits should be placed in good order. And since local Słuck Jews are also affected by these duties, it is right that one Jew should be chosen to consider how these are to be regulated and how much should be contributed to the town treasury. The placing of these excise duties should be properly levied.[44]

Given the rather hostile attitude of the *sesja miejska* to the Jews, this decision is somewhat surprising, and it is not known what induced the burghers to take it. At the same time, the representatives of the *kahal* obtained the right to participate in the commission which organized the quartering of the soldiers of the Słuck garrison. In this case, the Jews obtained the privilege as a result of the personal decision of Bogusław Radziwiłł. Replying to the petition of the *kahal* he ordained that Dawid Romanowski, who held the general lease on the town revenues, should be a member of the commission allocating responsibility for the town's military obligations. He was chosen because of his links with Radziwiłł, and it is not known whether he fulfilled any official function in the *kahal*.[45] It was only after the privilege granted to the Jews by the owner was presented to the *sesja miejska* that it was resolved that 'Dawid Jakubowicz, the Jew designated by the Jewish synagogue as their representative, is to appear every Thursday at our meetings in connection with Jewish issues related to the stationing of soldiers in Jewish homes and is to meet once a week with the representatives of the town.'[46]

Representatives of the *kahal* were also present at meetings of the *sesja miejska* dealing with financial matters. Most frequently, the sexton placed the requests of the *kahal* before the *sesja miejska*. The matters raised by the Jews were discussed, and they were given the right of responding and presenting documents for examination. Thus, in July 1667, the representatives of the *kahal* 'made a complaint and request' that the division of the hearth tax be revised. As a result, a commission was established to produce a revised allocation of liabilities under this tax.[47] The sexton also appeared before meetings of the *sesja miejska* when the Jews sought a postponement in the payment of their taxes.[48] The details of such decisions were discussed with the Jewish delegation, although agreement could not always be reached. For instance, in January 1672 an obligatory price for beer was set in the town. The price proposed by the members of the *sesja miejska* was significantly lower than that sought by the Jews, and at the request of the representatives of the *kahal* the matter was assigned to the general steward for decision.[49]

There was often conflict between the *kahal* and the *sesja miejska*. The Jews accused the burghers of failing to respect their rights and of imposing excessively high taxes. The burghers accused the Jews of a lack of interest in the running of the town and of not participating in the meetings of the *sesja miejska*. On key issues, the *kahal* authorities sought to obtain written confirmation of their rights. In the second half of the seventeenth century they usually approached the town's owner directly.

This was the method used to attempt to resolve the long-drawn-out conflict on Jewish participation in the division of the town's revenues. The representatives of the *kahal* appealed on several occasions to Bogusław Radziwiłł to confirm their right to participate. The first such document was issued in 1657, a year after the representatives of the *kahal* were given the right to participate in the assignment of taxes, a right which was renewed in 1661.[50]

The intervention of the town's owner in a conflict between the Jewish community and the municipality should not come as a surprise. In the second half of the seventeenth century the *kahal* did not seek to establish an amicable relationship with the town authorities in Słuck. When conflicts broke out, it sought the support of the Radziwiłłs. It seems that Jewish merchants—especially those engaged in international trade who frequently went to Königsberg, where Bogusław Radziwiłł lived —were able to approach him quite easily.[51] Characteristically, it was they, rather than the office-holders of the *kahal*, who represented the community in such cases. 'Economic inducements' also contributed to the effectiveness of Jewish lobbying. In other towns of the Polish–Lithuanian Commonwealth petitions were often supported by gifts, and *kahals* budgeted for such expenses.[52] Christian burghers used a different tactic. Representatives of the *sesja miejska* usually collaborated closely with the officials of the Radziwiłł estate. Their principal ally in conflicts with the Jewish community was the town governor. Only if he was unable to assist did they have recourse directly to the town's owner.

The support of Bogusław Radziwiłł did not bring an end to the conflict over Jewish involvement in the division of the tax revenues, which broke out again at the beginning of the eighteenth century. On this occasion, an attempt was made to resolve it by recourse to the courts. This change of tactics was the result both of a new owner and of a change in the way the Słuck properties were administered.[53] In the first half of the eighteenth century the stewards of the estate seem to have had more influence in the town than the owner, who now lived permanently in the Holy Roman Empire. In 1712 the local *kahal*—represented by the sexton—summoned the town authorities to the court of the governor, accusing them of not respecting the earlier princely privileges by not allowing the Jews to participate in the division of the tax revenues. The *kahal* was very well prepared for the trial. The sexton presented the privilege granted by Bogusław Radziwiłł, setting out clearly its main points. During the trial, at the *kahal*'s request, Trochim Hersiejowicz, a member of the *sesja miejska*, testified on its behalf. As a result of the trial, taxes collected from Jews were assigned to the *kahal* and were not placed in the 'Christian' town coffers.[54] This division demonstrated the autonomy and independence of the *kahal*.

The case of Słuck shows that *kahals*, in carrying out their administrative functions, played an active role in local politics. The Jewish elders responded effectively to the change in the structure of its government and were able to ensure for themselves the right to participate in decision-making in certain areas. It is worth underlining the competence of Jewish officials, their ability, and practical knowledge, which allowed them to function effectively in relation to other bodies dealing with the government of the town.

In the hierarchy of municipal power, the *kahal* was at the bottom: it was subordinate both to the owner of the town and to the municipality. However, for many Jews, it was the only body they encountered which enjoyed any measure of power. The majority of the Jewish inhabitants of Słuck never attended meetings of the *sesja miejska* and did not have any contact with the town's owner. The *kahal* was for them the only institution which exercised both internal religious authority and secular power. Accordingly, the *kahal*, which stockpiled supplies in case of a siege, collected taxes and levies, provided information on what was happening in the town, and participated in its defence, should be seen, in practice, as the 'Jewish town hall'.

Notes

1 J. Goldberg, 'Gminy żydowskie (kahały) w systemie władztwa dominalnego szlacheckiej Rzeczypospolitej', in id., *Żydzi w społeczeństwie, gospodarce i kulturze Rzeczypospolitej szlacheckiej* (Kraków, 2012), 1–18.

2 A. Teller, 'Radziwiłł, Rabinowicz, and the Rabbi of Świerz: The Magnates' Attitude to Jewish Regional Autonomy in the Eighteenth Century', in id. (ed.), *Studies in the History of the Jews in Old Poland in Honor of Jacob Goldberg* (Jerusalem, 1998), 246–76; M. Rosman, 'An Exploitative Regime and the Opposition to It in Międzybóż, ca. 1730', in S. Almog et al. (eds.), *Transition and Change in Modern Jewish History: Essays Presented in Honor of Shmuel Ettinger* (Jerusalem, 1987), pp. xi–xxx; A. Kaźmierczyk, 'Żydzi w miastach prywatnych: Wybrane aspekty', *Roczniki Dziejów Społecznych i Gospodarczych*, 77 (2016), 357–78.

3 M. Rosman, *The Lords' Jews: Magnate–Jewish Relations in the Polish–Lithuanian Commonwealth during the Eighteenth Century* (Cambridge, Mass., 1990); A. Teller, *Money, Power, and Influence in Eighteenth-Century Lithuania: The Jews on the Radziwiłł Estates* (Stanford, Calif., 2016).

4 Pre-war Polish Jewish historians used this comparative methodology in analysing the functioning of autonomous Jewish communities in royal towns (see M. Bałaban, *Żydzi lwowscy na przełomie XVI i XVII w.* (Warsaw, 1909), 239–332; see also G. D. Hundert, 'Kahał i samorząd miejski w miastach prywatnych w XVII i XVIII w.', in A. Link-Lenczowski, A. Polonsky, and J. Basista (eds.), *Żydzi w dawnej Rzeczypospolitej: Materiały z konferencji 'Autonomia Żydów w Rzeczypospolitej szlacheckiej', Międzywydziałowy Zakład Historii i kultury Żydów w Polsce, Uniwersytet Jagielloński 22–26.IX.1986* (Wrocław, 1991), 66–75; id., *The Jews in a Polish Private Town: The Case of Opatów in the Eighteenth Century* (Baltimore, 1992), 85–134).

5 M. Bałaban, *Historja Żydów w Krakowie i na Kazimierzu, 1304–1868*, 2 vols. (Kraków, 1931–6), ii. 67–79.

6 Hundert, *The Jews in a Polish Private Town*, 136.

7 A. Kaźmierczyk, *Żydzi w dobrach prywatnych w świetle sądowniczej i administracyjnej praktyki dóbr magnackich w wiekach XVI–XVIII* (Kraków, 2002), 183.

8 *Jewish Privileges in the Polish Commonwealth: Charters of Rights Granted to Jewish Communities in Poland–Lithuania in the Sixteenth to Eighteenth Centuries*, ed. J. Goldberg, 3 vols. (Jerusalem, 1985–2001), i. 301–2. On the legal situation of the Jews in the Polish–Lithuanian Commonwealth, see A. Teller, 'Telling the Difference: Some Comparative Perspectives on the Jews' Legal Status in Poland and in the Holy Roman Empire', *Polin*, 22 (2010), 109–41.

9 Archiwum Główne Akt Dawnych, Warsaw (hereafter AGAD), Archiwum Radziwiłłowskie (hereafter AR), 25/3835/1: inventory of Słuck, 1689.

10 *Pinkas hamedinah, o pinkas va'ad hakehilot harashiyot bimedinat lita*, ed. S. Dubnow (Berlin, 1925), no. 829. On how the *kehilah* of Słuck achieved this status, see Teller, 'Radziwiłł, Rabinowicz, and the Rabbi of Świerz'.

11 Teller, *Money, Power, and Influence in Eighteenth-Century Lithuania*, 25–43.

12 On the history of the town, see A. Gritskevich [Hrytskevich], *Drevnii gorod na Sluchi* (Minsk, 1985); R. Degiel, *Protestanci i prawosławni: Patronat wyznaniowy Radziwiłłów birżańskich nad Cerkwią prawosławną w księstwie słuckim w XVII w.* (Warsaw, 2000); M. Volkaw, *Slutsk na starykh planakh* (Minsk, 2017).

13 U. Augustyniak, *Dwór i klientela Krzysztofa Radziwiłła (1585–1640): Mechanizmy patronatu* (Warsaw, 2001); A. Czapak, 'Gospodarka w dobrach radziwiłłowskich w XVII wieku w świetle instruktarzy ekonomicznych', in J. Urwanowicz, E. Dubas-Urwanowicz, and P. Guzowski (eds.), *Władza i prestiż: Magnateria Rzeczypospolitej w XVI–XVII w* (Białystok, 2003), 405–10; M. Miłuński, 'Zarząd dóbr Bogusława Radziwiłła w latach 1639–1669', in U. Augustyniak (ed.), *Administracja i życie codzienne w dobrach Radziwiłłów XVI–XVIII wieku* (Warsaw, 2009), 195–283; Teller, *Money, Power, and Influence in Eighteenth-Century Lithuania*.

14 A. P. Hryckiewicz [Hrytskevich], 'Warowne miasta magnackie na Białorusi i Litwie', *Przegląd Historyczny*, 61/3 (1970), 432–4; M. Volkaw, 'Slutskaya tsytadel' XVII–XVIII st.', *Belaruski histarychny ahlyad*, 19/1–2 (2012), 31–66.

15 Between 1642 and 1661 the number of Jewish homes rose by eighty-seven (see M. Cieśla, 'Communities and Their Temples: Orthodox, Jewish, Protestant and Catholic. Religious Delimitations in the Historical Topography of Słuck', *Acta Poloniae Historica*, 116 (2017), 7–33: 20; A. Teller, *Rescue the Surviving Souls: The Great Jewish Refugee Crisis of the 17th Century* (Princeton, NJ, 2020), 23–88).

16 *Jewish Privileges in the Polish Commonwealth*, i. 301–2.

17 Goldberg, 'Gminy żydowskie (kahały) w systemie władztwa dominalnego', 4–5. In my analysis I deal only with the administrative functions of the *kahal* and ignore the religious aspect of its activity. On how religious issues were treated in the modern period, see J. Katz, *Masoret umashber: haḥevrah hayehudit bemotsa'ei yemei-habeinayim*, 4th edn. (Jerusalem, 1985); abridged Eng. trans.: *Tradition and Crisis: Jewish Society at the End of the Middle Ages* (New York, 1961); Eng. trans.: *Tradition and Crisis: Jewish Society at the End of the Middle Ages*, trans. B. D. Cooperman (New York, 1993; repr. 2000); J. Woolf, 'Communal and Religious Organisation', in *The Cambridge History of Judaism*, 8 vols. (Cambridge, 2018), vi. 380–92; G. D. Hundert, *Jews in Poland–Lithuania in the Eighteenth*

Century: A Genealogy of Modernity (Berkeley, Calif., 2004); Pol. trans.: *Żydzi w Rzeczy-pospolitej Obojga Narodów w XVIII wieku: Genealogia nowoczesności* (Warsaw, 2007); A. Michałowska-Mycielska, *The Jewish Community: Authority and Social Control in Poznań and Swarzędz, 1650–1793*, trans. A. Adamowicz (Wrocław, 2008).

18 Inwentarz Słucka, 1689; AGAD, AR 23/137/4, ss. 50–2: Bogusław Radziwiłł, reply to a petition of the Jews, 2 Feb. 1661.

19 Hundert, *Jews in Poland–Lithuania in the Eighteenth Century*, 79–98; *Żydzi w Rzeczypospolitej Obojga Narodów w XVIII wieku*, 111–36.

20 J. Bardach, 'Ustrój miast na prawie magdeburskim w Wielkim Księstwie Litewskim do połowy XVII wieku', in id., *O dawnej i niedawnej Litwie* (Poznań, 1988), 72–119: 90.

21 On the military situation in the town, see K. Kossarzecki, 'Słuck wobec zagrożenia moskiewskiego i kozackiego podczas wojny z Moskwą w latach 1654–1667', *Materiały do historii wojskowości*, 2 (2004), 94–105.

22 AGAD, AR 23/132/1, s. 4: copies of privileges and letters given to the Słuck *sesja miejska*.

23 Because Bogusław Radziwiłł and his daughter, Ludwika Karolina, the owners of the town, mostly lived abroad, Słuck was administered by local officials. On the administration of the town, see Miłuński, 'Zarząd dóbr Bogusława Radziwiłła w latach 1639–1669'.

24 The minutes of the Słuck *sesja miejska* are held by the Archiwum Główne Akt Dawnych (AR 23/134/2; 23/154/5) and the Natsyyanal'ny historychny arkhiw Belarusi, Minsk (henceforth NHAB) (f. 1825, op. 1, dd. 8, 14). The only complete copy of the minutes from the seventeenth century is to be found in Lietuvos mokslų akademijos Vrublevskių biblioteka, Vilnius (ff. 40–889).

25 Cieśla, 'Communities and Their Temples'.

26 It is not clear when the town court began to function. The first verdict I have found is from the early eighteenth century (NHAB, f. 146, op. 3, d. 21).

27 AGAD, AR 23/132/1, s. 18: 'A copy of the privileges, letters and replies to petitions of His Highness Prince Bogusław Radziwiłł, our merciful hereditary lord given to the Słuck *sesja miejska*', 24 Nov. 1655.

28 AGAD, AR 23/134/2, s. 123: privilege of the Radziwiłł representatives, 15 Dec. 1658.

29 AGAD, AR 23/154/5, ss. 160–2: memorandum of the Słuck *sesja miejska*, 16 Sept. 1659.

30 The issue of the purchase of real estate by Jews appears frequently in the minutes of the Słuck *sesja miejska*. For instance, on 11 Mar. 1669 (NHAB, f. 1825, op. 1, d. 14, s. 48v); 24 Oct. 1680; 4, 10 June 1681; 15, 22 June 1682 (AGAD, AR 23/154/5, s. 94–5).

31 AGAD, AR 23/134/2, s. 49: minutes of Słuck *sesja miejska*, 2 May 1656. This same issue was raised at the meetings of 5 Feb. and 24 May 1657.

32 Minutes of Słuck *sesja miejska*, 2 May 1656; AGAD, AR 23/154/5, s. 2: minutes of Słuck *sesja miejska*, 17 Feb. 1667; AR 23/134/, ss. 323–424: Słuck *sesja miejska*, petitions to the Radziwiłł administrators, 1671.

33 In most autonomous Jewish communities, the advocate represented the community to the non-Jewish world (see Bałaban, *Żydzi lwowscy na przełomie XVI i XVII w.*, 234–6; A. Michałowska, *Między demokracją a oligarchią: Władze gmin żydowskich w Poznaniu i Swarzędzu (od połowy XVII do końca XVIII wieku)* (Warsaw, 2000), 56). The case of Słuck was not unique. In Tykocin, the offices of sexton and advocate were combined (see F. Guesnet, 'Politik der Vormoderne: "Shtadlanuth" am Vorabend der polnischen Teilungen', *Jahrbuch des Simon-Dubnow-Instituts*, 1 (2002), 240); on advocates in general, see S. Ury, 'The *Shtadlan* of the Polish–Lithuanian Commonwealth: Noble Advocate or Unbridled Opportunist?', *Polin*, 15 (2002), 267–99.

34 Inwentarz Słucka, 1689. On the responsibilities of sextons, see Hundert, *The Jews in a Polish Private Town*, 89–91.

35 AGAD, AR 23/137/4, ss. 146–9: 'Expenses of the Słuck synagogue for the year 1733, from Passover to Rosh Hashana, set out in a table according to the customs of this synagogue as a *kahal*'.

36 Inwentarz Słucka, 1689.

37 Lietuvos valstybės istorijos archyvas, Vilnius, f. 1280, ap. 1, b. 121: economic agreement between Ajzyk the Jew, representing the Słuck *kahal*, and the monks of the monastery of St Heliasz and other Słuck burghers, 11 Nov. 1704; b. 21: agreement on the issue of the masters and other artisans of the guild of shoemakers with Dawid Józef Bachmant, glazier, 5 Dec. 1695.

38 On these elections, see A. Michałowska-Mycielska, 'Władza dominialna a konflikt w gminie: Wybory władz gminnych i rabina w Słucku 1709–1711', in M. Wodziński and A. Michałowska-Mycielska (eds.), *Małżeństwo z rozsądku? Żydzi w społeczeństwie dawnej Rzeczypospolitej* (Wrocław, 2007), 59–73.

39 AGAD, AR 5/17469: Krzysztof Winkler to Bogusław Radziwiłł, 16 Nov. 1669; Lietuvos valstybės istorijos archyvas, Metryka Litewska 375, no. 30: 'Accusation of the honourable Eudoklia Ihnatowiczowa, mayor of Mohylew, against the unbelieving Jew, Hercyk Szlomowicz of Słuck', 1 Feb. 1683; AGAD, AR 23/136/8, ss. 80–9: 'Verifications of Hercyk Szmlomowicz's allegations against the leaseholder of the town taxes of Słuck', 9 May 1682. Hercyk Szlomowicz was involved in a long-lasting dispute with the archimandrite, Teodozy Wasilewicz, who accused him of apostasy (see AR 7/541, ss. 80–5: Hercyka Szlomowicza, protestation, 17 Nov 1674).

40 AGAD, AR 23/134/2, s. 7: minutes of Słuck *sesja miejska*, 20 June 1656.

41 NHAB, f. 1825, d. 14: minutes of Słuck *sesja miejska*, 2, 9 Mar. 1666.

42 AGAD, AR 23/154/5, ss. 45–6: minutes of Słuck *sesja miejska*, 19 May; 6 June; 1, 8 Sept; 5 Oct. 1673.

43 AGAD, AR 23/154/5, s. 32: minutes of Słuck *sesja miejska*, 22 June 1660.

44 AGAD, AR 23/134/2, s. 56: minutes of Słuck *sesja miejska*, 10 Jan. 1656.

45 AGAD, AR 23/137/1, s. 401: petition from the Jews of Słuck, 17 June 1650.

46 AGAD, AR 23/134/2, s. 2: minutes of Słuck *sesja miejska*, 13 Oct. 1661.

47 AGAD, AR 23/154/5, s. 39: minutes of Słuck *sesja miejska*, 12 June 1667.

48 AGAD, AR 23/154/5, s. 42: minutes of Słuck *sesja miejska*, 13 Mar. 1669.

49 AGAD, AR 23/154/5, s. 44: minutes of Słuck *sesja miejska*, 14 Jan. 1672.

50 AGAD, AR 23/135/1, s. 46: 'Economic trial between the burghers and members of the Słuck *sesja miejska*', 29 Jan. 1712.

51 M. Cieśla, *Kupcy, arendarze i rzemieślnicy: Różnorodność zawodowa Żydów w Wielkim Księstwie Litewskim w XVII i XVIII w.* (Warsaw, 2018), 148–211.

52 Hundert, *The Jews in a Polish Private Town*, 101.

53 After the death of Ludwika Karolina, part of the Radziwiłł estate, the 'dobra neuburskie' which included Słuck, became the property of her daughter Ludwika Augusta. This property became the subject of a long-lasting conflict and as a result practical power in the town was exercised by Radziwiłł officials. See J. Lesiński, 'Spory o dobra neuburskie', *Miscellanea Historico-Archivistica*, 6 (1996), 95–113.

54 'Economic trial between the burghers and members of the Słuck *sesja miejska*', 29 Jan. 1712.

Office Holders of the Council of Four Lands, 1595–1764

JUDITH KALIK

THE COUNCIL OF FOUR LANDS consisted of representatives of the Jewish communities of Crown Poland. It was not a truly autonomous body, as its members more often represented their noble patrons than their constituencies. The formula governing the representation of local constituencies is known only from a 1753 ordinance of the commissioner of the treasury, Kazimierz Granowski.[1] According to this document, the Council of Four Lands consisted of two equal groups of twenty-five members, the 'seniors' (*starszyzna*) and 'juniors' (*symplarze*). The first formed a permanent committee, which conducted business between plenary sessions of the council, where the members of the second group were also in attendance. However, a comparison of Granowski's ordinance with other documents of the council shows that this formula was valid for a single year only.[2] At its plenary sessions the council also elected a kind of Jewish 'government' consisting of officials of four ranks: the president, who served as leader of the council,[3] advocates, who were responsible for relations with non-Jewish authorities (political and ecclesiastical institutions and powerful individuals),[4] and treasurers[5] and scribes[6] (the same person held both positions), who acted as secretaries of the treasury, being responsible for the assessment of the Jewish poll tax and other dues.

Since the actual *pinkas* (ledger) of the Council of Four Lands has not survived, the names of the office holders can be only partially reconstructed. Four groups of documents are available, two published and two unpublished. The published ones are the surviving Hebrew and Yiddish documents of the council edited by Israel Halperin[7] and the Polish, Latin, German, and Ruthenian documents related to the council edited by Jacob Goldberg and Adam Kaźmierczyk.[8] The unpublished documents are the Jewish poll-tax assignments for the second half of the seventeenth century held in the Crown Treasury Archives[9] and the Jewish poll-tax assessment lists for 1717 to 1764 in the Military Treasury Archives,[10] both groups held in the Central Archives of Historical Records in Warsaw. Many important documents relating to the Council of Four Lands can also be found in the Princes Czartoryski Library, among them the systematic records of the Jewish poll tax for the last decades of the seventeenth century and the first decade of the eighteenth century, which are missing from the Central Archives,[11] and some sporadic assessment lists from 1717 to 1764 similar to those found in the Central Archives. However, the most important documents related to the Council of Four Lands in this library are various letters of Polish officials, Jewish communities, and individuals, such as Adam Komorowski, the archbishop of Gniezno and the primate of Poland and Lithuania, from 1752[12] and the report about the intervention of the Council of Four Lands in an outbreak of violence in the Jewish community of Granów in 1724.[13] Finally, there is a document dealing with the debts of the Council of Four Lands to the Dominican convent from 1697 in the Central State Historical Archives of Ukraine in Lviv.[14]

The names of members and officials of the council appear in the first group of documents as signatures. In the seventeenth-century tax assignments, these names also appear as signatures but also in numerous Hebrew remarks concerning other community expenses written in the margins of the documents. In the eighteenth-century poll-tax assessment lists, the names of Jewish elders and officials appear in a different context. In those cases when no poll-tax assessments were made of individual taxpayers (usually leaseholders), large amounts of money are designated as 'for assessment by the elders', whose names, titles, and places of residence are recorded. Since the elders appear to be responsible for assessing the poll tax in their communities independently of the Council of Four Lands, they were not necessarily members of the council. Therefore only the names of those listed as officials of the council have been included.

Correlating the names of the office holders and councillors mentioned in these different sources is often difficult because of the discrepancy between Polish and Hebrew appellations. Often the same individual appears under a Polish nickname in the Polish sources but under his official Hebrew name in the Jewish sources. Thus, the personal physician of the Polish king, Jan III Sobieski, who served as president of the Council of Four Lands in 1697, was called in Hebrew Simhah Menahem, son of Yohanan Barukh, but was known in the Polish sources as Emanuel de Jona. Hebrew nicknames were also in use, some of them quite picturesque—Ephraim Zalman Shor Velo Adam (Bull and not a Man), which is a talmudic expression referring to a reduced responsibility for damages (*BK* 28*b*). The titles of books were also used, such as Rabbi Shabtai Ba'al Siftei Kohen (Author of the *Siftei kohen*, an important early modern commentary on the *Shulḥan arukh*), whose son Moses was a member of the council. Most of these nicknames were in Yiddish, but some were Slavic, especially, in the late sixteenth century: Wolk (Wolf), Slonik (Little Elephant, both Ruthenian), Jeleń (Deer, Polish).

All the available information about names, places of residence, and years in office of all known council officials and representatives of its constituent bodies is presented in a series of six tables in the appendix to this chapter. Hebrew names are given in their conventional English forms, rather than their Hebrew or Polish transliterations (for example, Moses, rather than Mosheh or Moszko). In cases of serious discrepancies the Polish nicknames are added in parentheses. I begin by outlining the content of these tables.

Presidents (Table 1)

The president of the Council of Four Lands was the highest-ranking Jew in Crown Poland. He was seen by Jews and non-Jews alike as the main spokesman of Polish

Jewry before the Polish civil authorities. Holding this office was usually the peak of a personal career for those who had previously distinguished themselves in various public roles. It was reserved for rich Jews with personal connections with powerful Polish patrons. In Polish, the title was the same as that of the marshal of the sejm.

The earliest known president of the Jews of Poland was Pinhas Halevi, son of Israel, of the influential family of Horowitz, which came originally from Gerona and had been settled in Bohemia since the fourteenth century.[15] Pinhas Halevi was born in Prague and moved to Kraków when he married Miriam Beilah, sister of Rabbi Moses Isserles (the Rema). He was never explicitly described as president in the sources, but Yom Tov Lipmann Heller (1579–1654) in his *Megilat eivah* called him 'yoshev rosh of all the leaders of the Four Lands of Crown Poland'.[16]

Israel, son of Samuel of Tarnopol, served originally as a chairman of the rabbinical court at Włodzimierz (Volodymyr) in Volhynia, but also represented the major community of Tarnopol in the regional council of Ruthenia and in the Council of Four Lands from 1671 to 1683. Moses Judah Zelig Halperin, son of Eliezer Lipman of Poznań, was the great-grandson of Zevulon Eliezer, the founder of the Polish branch of the Heilprin family of Franconian origin. He served as a representative of Poznań in the Council of Four Lands from 1669 to 1693.

Doctor Simhah Menahem, son of Yohanan Barukh, also known as Emanuel de Jona, came from a prominent medical family: his father, two of his brothers, Eliezer and Jacob, and his maternal grandfather, Menahem Zunsdorf, were all physicians. Like his father and brother Jacob, Simhah Menahem studied in Padua, where he graduated as a doctor of medicine in 1664. In the late 1680s or early 1690s he was invited to the royal court at Żółkiew (Zhovkva), where he became a personal physician to the king, Jan III Sobieski (1674–96).[17] After the king's death, he was accused of poisoning him, but the case never came to court.[18]

It is unknown whether this accusation affected the political career of Simhah Menahem, but in 1699 Zacharias Mendel Kantorowicz of Kraków replaced him as president of the Council of Four Lands.[19] He was a rich merchant and moneylender, and dominated the Jewish community of Kraków–Kazimierz for twenty-five years, being the son-in-law of Shalom Shakhna, the former president of the community, who died in 1688. The tyrannical rule of Kantorowicz aroused strong opposition in Kazimierz which came to a head in 1715 when Kantorowicz fled to Pińczów, where he bought a rabbinical position.[20]

The next crisis of leadership in the Council of Four Lands occurred in 1724, when President Abraham Isserles, who had represented the Lublin community in the council since 1699, was dismissed and Doctor Abraham Isaac Fortis appointed in his place. Fortis was the second Jewish physician to hold the office of president. He was an Italian Jew who had studied medicine at Padua and Mantua and settled in Poland in the late seventeenth century together with his brother Doctor Lebrman Levy Ostilla, initially in Lwów (Lviv) and, from 1706, in Rzeszów, where he became a court physician to Prince Lubomirski of Rzeszów and Count Potocki of Leżajsk.[21]

The position of Isserles had seemed strong. During the council's session in

Jarosław in August 1724 all twenty members of the upper house signed a letter of support for him.[22] In addition, Tomasz Orzechowski, deputy voivode of Przemyśl, accused Fortis in the court of the Ruthenian voivodeship of responsibility for riots during the session of the council which had caused harm to his estate near Jarosław.[23] In December of that year the king himself, August II, granted Isserles a protective letter guaranteeing no harm should be done to him after his return to Lublin.[24] None of this helped. Fortis wrote powerful letters in perfect Latin, describing himself as *excellens*, and his rival Isserles as *infidelis*[25] and did not hesitate even to attack Orzechowski.[26] What was the secret of his power—a foreigner without any family connections in Poland? Most likely, as in the case of Simhah Menahem, the previous physician who held the office of president of the council, a decisive role was played by powerful patients.

Joshua Heshel, son of Samuel of Chełm, president between 1732 and 1739, was a veteran Jewish politician who had an exemplary personal career in the council. He represented the Chełm community from 1719[27] and served as a treasurer and scribe of the Council of Four Lands from 1726.[28] His successor, Abraham, son of Joseph of Leszno, served as president for fourteen years from 1739 to 1753. He also represented his community in the council from 1730, but in May 1753 Karol Sedlnicki, Grand Treasurer of the Crown, dismissed him and appointed Abraham, son of Hayim Halperin of Lublin, as president.[29] This was a consequence of the internal Jewish conflict between the supporters and opponents of Jacob Emden and his 'crusade' against real and imaginary Shabateans. Abraham, son of Joseph of Leszno, whose son, Zacharias Mendel, married Emden's daughter, supported Emden, while Abraham, son of Hayim Halperin of Lublin, whose son, Jacob Hayim, signed an order of excommunication against Emden, sided with Jonathan Eibeschütz, Emden's enemy.[30] However, in September of the same year Kazimierz Granowski dismissed all the treasurers and scribes of the council who had served since 1739 and appointed new ones including Abraham, son of Joseph,[31] who had served as a treasurer from 1751. Since the crisis of 1753 concerned mostly the treasurers and scribes of the council, it will be discussed in the next section.

The new president, Abraham, son of Hayim, was the second member of the Halperin family to hold the office. He was well connected to the Jewish political elite through his family ties: his father, Hayim, was a stepson of Abraham Isserles; and his son, Jacob Hayim, married Hayah, daughter of Abraham Isaac Fortis.[32] Abraham himself had represented Lublin in the council since 1724.[33]

Abraham's son, Moses Pinhas Halperin, the rabbi of Świerz, succeeded his father as president in 1760.[34] This was the only time the office of president passed from father to son and the only time a rabbi took the secular position of president. This unusual nomination was probably the result of the intervention of Moses' patron, Prince Michał Kazimierz Radziwiłł, lord of Żółkiew.[35] The last president of the council was Meir, son of Joel of Dubno—the only three surviving pages from the *pinkas* of the Council of Four Lands were found in his personal archive in Dubno.[36]

Treasurers and Scribes (Table 2)

Since the treasurers and scribes were responsible for the finances of the Council of Four Lands, they were the most important and powerful positions in the Jewish community of Poland. As a result, competition for them led to many tensions within the Jewish elite.

The tendency to make the office hereditary was halted in 1726 when David Jacob Tevel, son of Ephraim Fishel of Włodzimierz, tried to inherit the office from his father, one of the most influential and long-serving treasurers and scribes of the council, who had held the office from 1679 to 1724. Jan Jerzy Przebendowski, the grand treasurer of the Crown, rejected his candidacy.[37] This ruling had only a temporary effect—in 1750 King August III issued a special privilege for Leib, son of Samuel of Krzemieniec, a general scribe of the Council of Four Lands and the Council of Volhynia, stipulating that both of his offices could be inherited by his son.[38]

Another controversial matter was the appointment of rabbis as treasurers and scribes. In 1739 the Council of Four Lands asked Treasury Commissioner Jakub Działyński to exclude rabbis from administrative positions in the council.[39] It is not clear to what extent this petition was implemented, but tension between the secular and religious elites of Polish Jewry is clearly visible. As Adam Teller has observed, based on an examination of rabbinical titles in the signatures on the documents of the Council of Four Lands, the growing presence of rabbis among the treasurers and scribes during the first decades of the eighteenth century triggered tensions.[40] The difficulty in analysing this problem lies in the usual absence of the title 'rabbi' in many of the Hebrew documents of the Council of Four Lands. Since the Polish, Latin, and German documents, and poll tax lists do regularly indicate the rabbinical titles of the Jewish officials, this information can significantly clarify the picture. About 40 per cent of the treasurers and scribes appointed after 1739 were also rabbis (nine out of twenty-one). It is clear from this evidence that the council's petition to Działyński was never implemented, and it is therefore premature to speak about a decline in the power of the Polish rabbinate during the eighteenth century. It seems that, like Polish bishops, rabbis also often occupied influential secular offices.

Some individuals held the office of rabbi outside of their community of residence and constituted a third group in the council: Wulf, son of Nahum of Lelów, for example, was rabbi of Nowemiasto Korczyn (Nowy Korczyn) but represented Opatów as scribe of the council from 1742 to 1744. Moses Pinhas, son of Abraham Halperin, was rabbi of Świerz but represented Żółkiew as treasurer of the council in 1755.

The major crisis concerning the treasurers and scribes was Granowski's dismissal of all those who had served for over fourteen years in 1753. Those dismissed included Leib, son of Samuel, rabbi of Krzemieniec; Saul, son of Jacob, rabbi of Włodzimierz; Issaschar, son of Joshua (Berek Oszujowicz), rabbi of Ciechanowiec; and David, son of Moses of Zamość.[41] Granowski appointed new treasurers and scribes in their place: Abraham, son of Haim Halperin of Lublin, the new president of the council;

Abraham, son of Joseph of Leszno, the former president and treasurer of Wielko-polska; Nahum of Wodzisław, president of Kraków and treasurer of Małopolska; and Moses Pinhas, son of Abraham Halperin of Żółkiew, treasurer of Ruthenia.[42] One month later, Barukh, son of David, the trade agent of Karol Sedlnicki, complained on behalf of the other members of the council that the dismissed treasurers had secretly obtained new nominations from Sedlnicki and remained in office.[43] Thus, it seems that the crisis of 1753 reflected the conflict between Granowski and Sedlnicki, his direct superior. Furthermore, in May 1753 Sedlnicki dismissed Abraham, son of Joseph, from the office of president of the council, but in September of the same year Granowski appointed him as a treasurer.

Advocates (Table 3)

Relatively little information is available about the advocates of the Council of Four Lands, since they usually did not sign council documents. Only a few people are designated as advocates of the council; however, some of those designated as local advocates certainly also served as advocates of the council. For example, Leib, son of Israel (Lewek Israelowicz) of Lublin, signed (in Polish) numerous poll-tax assign-ments for Rzeszów,[44] Wielkopolska,[45] Małopolska,[46] Chełm–Bełz,[47] Ruthenia,[48] and Poznań.[49]

Knowledge of Polish was an essential requirement of an advocate. Thus, in 1726 Nisan, son of Judah of Ciechanowiec, appointed as an advocate of the council in 1730, translated a verdict of the arbitration court in a dispute between the communities of Ciechanowiec and Węgrów.[50] Personal ties with the highest Polish dignitaries were also necessary for success. For instance, Judah Leib Mordecai Nikiel, who served as an advocate from 1638 to 1658, was a personal trade agent of Jan II Kazimierz Waza (1648–68).[51] Sometimes such ties could be dangerous, as when loyalty to the noble patron clashed with the interests of the Jewish community. Barukh Segal of Poznań was an advocate in 1699 but was dismissed in 1700 in dishonour and expelled from his community. He was accused of being an informer on behalf of Polish authorities during a fair of Toruń.[52] For some Jewish politicians, the office of advocate served as a starting point in their career. Ephraim Fishel of Włodzimierz, for example, served as an advocate in 1671 and 1672, and in 1679 he became a scribe of the Council of Four Lands.

Representatives of the Constituencies (Tables 4–6)

The original 'four lands' of the council were Wielkopolska, Małopolska, Volhynia, and Lithuania. However, the earliest known composition of the council in 1595 con-sisted of seven constituencies: Małopolska (Kraków), Wielkopolska (Poznań), Lublin, Chełm–Bełz (Bełz and Luboml), Ruthenia (Lwów), Volhynia (Krzemieniec and Włodzimierz), and Lithuania.[53] In 1623 the Jews of Lithuania gained indepen-dence from the Council of Four Lands and formed their own Council of Lithuania,[54] but representatives of some of the major communities of the Grand Duchy of Lithuania continued, until the mid-seventeenth century, to take a seat on the Council of Four Lands, probably because of the unsettled financial problems of some communities (see Table 6c). The fragmentation of the remaining constituencies continued also in the seventeenth and eighteenth centuries. Thus, at the beginning of the seventeenth century, the regional councils of Wielkopolska and Małopolska became independent of the urban communities of Kraków and Poznań, and the community of Przemyśl was separated from the regional council of Ruthenia. However, some residents of Kraków and Poznań continued to represent their respective regional councils and not their urban communities. In the late seventeenth century the major community of Rzeszów separated from Małopolska and the regional council of Przemyśl became independent from the urban community of Przemyśl. In 1718 the regional council of the Zamoyski Entail (major communities of Zamość, Szczebrzeszyn, Tarnogród, and Turobin) separated from the regional council of Chełm–Bełz;[55] in 1720 the regional council of Podolia separated from the regional council of Ruthenia;[56] and later, in the eighteenth century, the regional council of Lublin became independent of the urban community of Lublin.

As a result of this fragmentation, the Council of Four Lands came to be composed of representatives of three kinds of constituencies. There were urban communities that were independent of the regional councils (Kraków, Poznań, Lublin, Przemyśl, and Ciechanowiec), major communities (Rzeszów, Tykocin, and Węgrów) comprising several urban communities, and regional councils (Chełm–Bełz, Wielkopolska, Małopolska, Lublin, the Zamoyski Entail, Przemyśl, Ruthenia, and Volhynia) comprising several major communities.

These constituencies were represented in the council very disproportionately. Large urban communities and regional councils sent several representatives to the council annually, while other constituencies were badly under-represented. Podolia had no representation on the council at all. This had serious repercussions for the level of taxation assessed by the council for different communities. Communities regularly represented in the council could effectively lobby for tax reductions, and exemptions, while those under-represented or not represented at all were usually over-taxed. Thus, for example, the Jewish community of Kalisz, a member of the regional council of Wielkopolska, which was regularly represented in the council, paid no poll tax between 1717 and 1764. However, the Jews of Podolia and Bracław voivodeship (administratively belonging to the regional council of Ruthenia), which had no representation in the council, paid their poll tax regularly without any exemptions during the same period.[57]

For this reason, many communities tried to increase their representation on the council. Thus, the Council of Opatów in 1745 petitioned the town's owner, Paweł Karol Sanguszko, to increase their representation from one to two or three delegates.[58] However, the only delegate of Opatów on the council, Ezekiel, son of Tsevi Hirsh Landau (Hazkiel Jeleniowicz), opposed this proposal, being eager to preserve his monopoly of representation of his community in the council.[59] In his reply, Paweł

Sanguszko backed Ezekiel Landau and refused to increase Opatów's representation in the council.[60] It seems that Opatów's delegate served the interests of his Polish lord more than the interests of his community.

The hereditary principle, which was abolished with various degrees of success in the nomination of officials of the council, was much more prevalent in the selection of the members of the council itself. As mentioned above, David Jacob Tevel, son of Ephraim Fishel, was unsuccessful in his attempt to inherit the office of his father in 1726, but descendants of Ephraim Fishel represented the community of Włodzimierz in Volhynia for three generations. These were David Jacob Tevel himself between 1713 and 1718, his brother Samuel Hakatan in 1718, and his son Saul between 1742 and 1751. Several other powerful family groups also succeeded in gaining control of the representation of their communities in the council for several generations. The Landau clan practically monopolized the representation of Małopolska between 1718 and 1758. Simon Ze'ev Wulf, son of Ezekiel, represented Tarnów between 1718 and 1724; his nephews, Judah Isaac and Ezekiel (Hazkiel Jeleniowicz), the sons of Tsevi Hirsh, represented Opatów between 1723 and 1749; Benjamin Wulf, son of Ezekiel, and his son Ezekiel (Hazkiel Wulfowicz) represented Tarnów between 1730 and 1758 (see Table 6d). Other members of this family were also very active in Ruthenia, Lublin, and Wielkopolska.[61] The Auerbach, Halperin, Horowitz, and Katzenellenbogen families were no less prominent in their own communities. Although the hereditary principle was never formalized in the council, the hereditary membership of magnate families in the Polish senate probably influenced the personal composition of the upper house of the Council of Four Lands.

Representatives to the council were theoretically elected by their local community councils, but in practice the voice of the local Polish magnate was usually decisive. Thus, in 1725, Paweł Sanguszko simply ordered the Jewish community of Wiśnicz to send his court jeweller, Giec, son of Solomon, as their delegate to the session of the Council of Four Lands.[62]

Conclusion

The bicameral structure of the Council of Four Lands not only imitated the bicameral Polish sejm, it was a reflection of the political structure of the Polish–Lithuanian Commonwealth. Far from being democratic, the 'republic of nobles' was highly competitive. All rival factions of the Polish magnates were represented in the senate (the upper house of the sejm) and controlled the lower house through their clients among the middle and lesser nobility. The Jewish Council of Four Lands served as a kind of a chessboard for the Polish magnates, with their Jewish clients playing the role of pawns. Of course, the Jewish politicians knew how to use the rivalry between different magnate factions, as well other forces in Polish politics (the king, the Church, the sejm) to their own advantage. However, the patron–client relations between Polish magnates and Jewish politicians played a decisive role in the latter group's fortunes and political careers. The competition inside the Jewish political elite for positions of power in the council had its own logic, but all the rival factions had to ensure for themselves the protection of influential noble patrons, who were also linked with the rival factions within the Polish nobility. Both Jews and Poles saw each other merely as tools to be used for achieving their own objectives. However, there is little doubt that the Jewish clients depended on their noble Polish patrons, not vice versa.

APPENDIX

Table 1 Presidents of the Council of Four Lands

Name	Place of residence	Pinkas va'ad arba aratsot	Sejm Czterech Ziem	Central Archives, Warsaw
Pinhas Halevi, son of Israel Horovitz	Kraków	1595, 1597		
Elias	Poznań	1649		
David	Leszno	1671		
Israel, son of Samuel	Tarnopol		1678	
Moses Judah Zelig (Seelde) Halperin, son of Eliezer Lipman	Poznań		1680	
Abraham, son of Hirsh	Lublin		1681	
Simhah Menahem, son of Yohanan Baruch (Emanuel de Jona)	Lwów	1697		
Zacharias Mendel Kantorowicz	Kraków	1700	1699, 1702	
Jacob Abraham, son of Isaac	Żółkiew Brody	1718	1717, 1718	
Abraham Isserlis, son of Israel	Lublin	1719, 1720, 1724	1719, 1720, 1721, 1723, 1724	
Abraham Isaac Fortis, son of Samuel	Rzeszów	1730	1724, 1726, 1730	
Abel, son of Iser			1732	
Joshua Heshel, son of Samuel of Kraków	Chełm	1739	1739	
Abraham, son of Joseph	Leszno	1740, 1742, 1743, 1751, 1752	1739, 1744, 1748, 1750, 1751, 1753	1741, 1742, 1743, 1747
Abraham, son of Hayim Halperin	Lublin	1753, 1754, 1755, 1756, 1757	1753, 1754, 1755	1754
Moses Pinhas, son of Abraham Halperin	Żółkiew		1760	
Meir, son of Joel	Dubno	1760, 1762, 1763		

Table 2 Treasurers and scribes of the Council of Four Lands

Name	Place of residence	Title	*Pinkas va'ad arba aratsot*	*Sejm Czterech Ziem*	Central Archives, Warsaw; Central Archives, Lviv
Benjamin, son of Abraham	Lublin	scribe	1614		
Joseph	Kraków	scribe		1659	
Abraham, son of Solomon	Włodzimierz	scribe treasurer	1672, 1673, 1676	1662, 1666, 1676	1669[a] 1670[b] 1679[c] 1680[d] 1683[e] 1684[f]
Solomon, son of Joseph	Lublin	scribe	1668, 1677, 1681, 1687, 1688		
Tsevi Hirsh, son of Samson	Zamość	treasurer scribe	1690, 1694		1690[g] 1692[h] 1697[i]
Jacob Becal		scribe			1693[j]
Hayim		treasurer			1693[k]
Eliezer Lipman, son of Abraham		treasurer			1696[l]
Issaschar Ber		treasurer			1696[m]
Ephraim Fishel, son of Aryeh Leib	Włodzimierz	treasurer scribe	1679, 1717	1699, 1703, 1705, 1710, 1717, 1718, 1719, 1721, 1724	1690[n] 1692,[o] 1722
Neta Hoshea of Kraków	Satanów	rabbi treasurer		1723	
Mordecai, son of Isaac (Marek Rabinowicz)	Brody	treasurer scribe	1724, 1725, 1728, 1729, 1737, 1739, 1742, 1744, 1748	1723, 1728, 1732, 1739, 1744	1739, 1741, 1742, 1744, 1746, 1747
Isaac	Lelów	treasurer	1728, 1737	1723	
Shalom, son of Hanokh	Lublin	scribe	1725		

[a] AGAD, ASK, dz. VI, syg. 14, p. 150.
[b] Ibid., p. 158.
[c] AGAD, ASK, dz. VI, syg. 22, pp. 102, 123, 144.
[d] AGAD, ASK, dz. VI, syg. 23, p. 6.
[e] Ibid., p. 410.
[f] Ibid., pp. 873, 900.
[g] AGAD, ASK, dz. III, syg. 7, p. 982.
[h] Ibid., p. 997.
[i] TsDIAL, f. 418, op. 1, spr. 5, pp. 70–1.
[j] AGAD, ASK, dz. VI, syg. 24, p. 713.
[k] Ibid., p. 674.
[l] AGAD, ASK, dz. VI, syg. 25, p. 244.
[m] Ibid.
[n] Ibid., dz. III, syg. 7, p. 982.
[o] Ibid., p. 997.

Table 2 Treasurers and scribes of the Council of Four Lands (*cont.*)

Name	Place of residence	Title	*Pinkas va'ad arba aratsot*	*Sejm Czterech Ziem*	Central Archives, Warsaw; Central Archives, Lviv
Joshua Heshel Halevi, son of Samuel	Ciechanowiec	rabbi scribe treasurer	1726, 1728, 1729, 1732, 1739	1732, 1733	
Joshua Heshel, son of Samuel	Chełm	treasurer scribe	1726, 1728, 1731, 1737, 1739, 1742	1732, 1739, 1743, 1744	1739, 1742, 1743, 1747
Hoshea, son of Solomon	Poznań	treasurer scribe			1739
Wulf, son of Nahum of Lelów	Nowemiasto Korczyn, Opatów	rabbi scribe		1743, 1753	1742, 1743, 1744
Leib, son of Samuel	Krzemieniec	rabbi scribe treasurer	1750, 1751, 1752, 1753	1743, 1744, 1753	1743
Heshel, son of Meir	Chełm	scribe treasurer		1744, 1748	
Saul, son of Jacob	Włodzimierz	rabbi treasurer	1752, 1753	1744, 1753	1742, 1744
Issaschar, son of Joshua (Beresz Oszujowicz)	Ciechanowiec	rabbi scribe treasurer	1752, 1753, 1754, 1755, 1762	1744, 1753, 1762	1744, 1754
Isaac, son of Abraham	Opatów	treasurer scribe	1751		1747, 1755, 1762
Mordecai, son of Shalom		treasurer	1748		1750
Abraham, son of Isaac of Tarłów	Zamość	rabbi scribe treasurer	1751, 1752, 1753, 1754, 1755, 1758	1750, 1754	1753
Abraham, son of Joseph	Leszno	treasurer	1751, 1752, 1753	1753, 1754	
Solomon	Lublin	scribe	1751	1751	
Isaac Issaschar, son of Moses Wolf (Berek Rabinowicz)	Brody	treasurer scribe	1751, 1754, 1755	1763	1759, 1761
Isaac, son of Jacob		scribe		1752	
David, son of Moses	Zamość	treasurer		1753	1754
Nahum	Wodzisław	treasurer	1753		
Moses Pinhas, son of Abraham Halperin of Lublin	Żółkiew Świerz	rabbi treasurer scribe	1754, 1756, 1757, 1761, 1763	1753, 1754, 1758, 1759, 1763	1755

Table 2 Treasurers and scribes of the Council of Four Lands (*cont.*)

Name	Place of residence	Title	Pinkas va'ad arba aratsot	Sejm Czterech Ziem	Central Archives, Warsaw; Central Archives, Lviv
Isaac, son of Herz	Opoczno	scribe		1754	
Benjamin Wulf of Witków	Hrubieszów	rabbi treasurer scribe	1755		1754, 1755
Hayim	Połonne	rabbi treasurer	1755		1762
Leib, son of Samuel of Brody	Tarnogród	treasurer scribe	1755	1763	1755, 1757, 1759, 1761
Israel	Krzemieniec	treasurer	1755		
Isaac, son of Samuel of Wodzisław	Chełm	rabbi scribe			1755
Tsevi Hirsh, son of Isaac (Herszko Berkowicz)	Brody	scribe			1761

Table 3 Advocates of the Council of Four Lands

Name	Place of residence	Pinkas va'ad arba aratsot	Sejm Czterech Ziem	Central Archives, Warsaw
Judah Leib Mordecai		1649, 1658	1637, 1638	
Nikiel		1659	1646, 1647	
Samuel Mendel	Lublin		1638	
Simon	Brześć Litewski, Lwów(?)	1661		
Israel Liberman			1662	
Solomon, son of Jacob	Poznań	1666		
Moses, son of Mordecai		1667, 1669, 1671, 1672, 1674, 1676	1665, 1666	
Ephraim Fishel, son of Aryeh Leib	Włodzimierz	1671, 1672		
Eli, son of Mordecai		1673		
Leib, son of Israel	Lublin			1678[a] 1682[b] 1683[c]

[a] AGAD, ASK, dz. VI, syg. 23, p. 98.   [b] Ibid., pp. 266, 267, 270, 271, 311, 333, 383.   [c] Ibid., pp. 445, 472, 699.

Table 3 Advocates of the Council of Four Lands (*cont.*)

Name	Place of residence	*Pinkas va'ad arba aratsot*	*Sejm Czterech Ziem*	Central Archives, Warsaw
Barukh Segal	Poznań	1699		
Hayim, son of Emanuel	Uściług		1721	
Nisan, son of Judah	Ciechanowiec	1730		
Isaac		1753		
Simon	Lublin		1756	

Table 4 Representatives of independent urban communities

Name	*Pinkas va'ad arba aratsot*	*Sejm Czterech Ziem*	Central Archives, Lviv
(a) Kraków			
Moses Mordecai, son of Samuel Margaliyot	1595		
Abraham, son of Isaac Reizlish	1595		
Yekutiel, son of Moses Halevi Landau	1595		
Moses, son of Judah	1607		
Isaac, son of Jacob		1617	
Isaac, son of Pinhas Halevi Horovitz	1621, 1622, 1627		
Judah, son of Aaron Moses	1628, 1642		
Mordecai Sholis	1644		
Simon Ze'ev Wulf, son of Caleb Abraham	1644		
Judah Abraham, son of Israel Hendlish	1653, 1655		
Moses, son of Isaac Bunmish	1654, 1668, 1670		
Samuel Eliezer, son of Ephraim	1655		
Naphtali Avigdor		1662	
Jonas, son of Hayim		1662	
Saul, son of Moses Katzenellenbogen	1664, 1671, 1673, 1677, 1678		
Ari Judah, son of Mordecai	1664		

Table 4 Representatives of independent urban communities (*cont.*)

Name	Pinkas va'ad arba aratsot	Sejm Czterech Ziem	Central Archives, Lviv
(a) Kraków (*cont.*)			
Abraham, son of Nathan Halevi (Abram Doktorowicz)	1667, 1672, 1673, 1683, 1684, 1687, 1688, 1689, 1690, 1691	1672	
Hayim, son of Theodor	1667		
Jacob Abraham, son of Samuel	1669		
Issaschar Ber, son of Joshua Heshel (Ber Doktorowicz)	1669, 1671, 1673, 1678, 1683, 1684, 1689, 1690	1678	
Aryeh Leib, son of Zacharias	1670		
Moses, son of Joshua	1671		
Tsevi Hirsh, son of Solomon Shapira	1671, 1672, 1677		
Hayim, son of Ari Leib	1671		
Samuel, son of Tsevi Hirsh	1671		
Hayim, son of Judah Leib Ashkenazi	1673		
Isaac Zelig, son of Abraham Joel Ashkenazi (Felix Joelowicz)	1678	1678, 1680	
Samuel Isaiah		1680	
Jacob	1681		
Joseph, son of Isaac Candt	1692		1697[a]
Hayim, son of Or Shraga Faibush Bloch	1693		
Ephraim, son of Israel			1697[b]
Aryeh Judah Leib, son of Judah Tsevi Hirsh	1698, 1700	1699	
Zacharias Mendel, son of Jacob Kantorowicz	1699, 1700, 1713		
Hayim, son of David (Joachim David)		1702	
Simon, son of Judah Leib Yolish (Szymon Joles)	1718, 1721	1718, 1724, 1726	
Moses, son of Shalom Halevi (Nauchowicz)	1718	1718	
Meir, son of Isaac		1724	

[a] TsDIAL, f. 418, op. 1, spr. 5, pp. 70–1.   [b] Ibid.

Table 4   Representatives of independent urban communities (*cont.*)

Name	Pinkas va'ad arba aratsot	Sejm Czterech Ziem	Central Archives, Lviv
(a) Kraków (*cont.*)			
Leib		1724	
Joshua, son of Shalom Shakhna Kantorowicz	1730		
Hayim of Lublin		1730	
Yehiel Michael, son of Solomon	1730	1739, 1743	
Abraham Kahana	1731		
Judah Leib Kahana of Tykocin	1754	1750	
Michael		1750	
(b) Poznań			
Saul (Samuel) Hilmensh	1595		
Tevel	1595		
Mordecai Upler	1595		
Joseph, son of Abraham Shapira	1603, 1609		
Samuel Eliezer, son of Judah Halevi	1603, 1607, 1609, 1614, 1617, 1618, 1623		
Mordecai Yafe, son of Abraham	1607, 1609, 1612		
Abraham, son of Solomon		1616	
Isaac Aizik, son of Nathan (Yonathan) Shapira	1618		
Isaac, son of Moses	1621, 1622		
Moses Levi, son of Levi Hakohen Ashkenazi	1627		
Aaron, son of Israel Nathan	1642, 1644		
Joseph Judah, son of Jacob	1644		
Joseph Mendel	1669, 1678	1662	
Isaac, son of Abraham Ashkenazi		1662	
Mordecai (Marek)	1664		
Jacob, son of Ezekiel of Węgrów	1664		
Jacob Benjamin, son of Solomon Auerbach		1666	
Solomon, son of Jacob	1666, 1667		
Yekutiel Zalman, son of Jacob Kletschiller	1667		

Table 4 Representatives of independent urban communities (*cont.*)

Name	Pinkas va'ad arba aratsot	Sejm Czterech Ziem	Central Archives, Lviv
(*b*) **Poznań** (*cont.*)			
Samuel, son of Hayim Menahem	1669, 1671, 1673, 1677, 1678, 1683, 1690, 1693	1678	
Moses Judah Zelig Halperin, son of Eliezer Lipman	1671, 1672, 1673, 1689	1672	
Jacob, son of Joel	1672		
Tsevi Hirsh, son of Joel	1678, 1683, 1687	1678	
Yehiel Michael, son of Naphtali Herz (Michael Mostalowicz)	1681		
Kalonymos, son of Moses	1684		
Eliezer, son of Abraham Ezekiel		1685	
Samuel, son of Leib	1687, 1691		
Judah Leib, son of Abraham	1687, 1688, 1691		1697[c]
Isaiah Kohen Shapira	1689		
Samuel Zanwil, son of Moses	1690	1693, 1699, 1717, 1719	
Uri Faibush Joseph, son of Hayim (Hilowicz) Kohen Ashkenazi		1691	
Moses, son of Leib		1699	
Abraham		1702	
Simon, son of Leib	1718	1717, 1718	
Isaac, son of Jacob Rabinowicz	1718, 1719		
Or Shraga, son of Yehiel Lifshits		1724	
Berek Neumark		1724	
Meir		1724	
Dov Ber		1730, 1739	
Judah Leib, son of Isaac (Aizekowicz) of Rzeszów		1739	
Moses Joshua Halevi of Kraków	1730		
Jacob Moses, son of Benjamin	1730		
Meir Hazak of Ustrzyki	1754		

[c] TsDIAL, f. 418, op. 1, spr. 5, pp. 70–1.

Table 4 Representatives of independent urban communities (*cont.*)

Name	Pinkas va'ad arba aratsot	Sejm Czterech Ziem	Central Archives, Lviv
(c) Lublin			
Isaac, son of Neta Hakohen Shapira	1595		
Moses Kats	1595		
Tsevi Hirsh (Jeleń)		1616	
Ephraim, son of Naphtali called Zalman Shor Velo Adam (Bull and not Man)	1618		
Moses, son of Meir Kats	1627		
Solomon Rofe (Physician) Luria	1628		
Jacob, son of Ephraim Naphtali Hirsh	1642		
Leib Manlish, son of Samuel	1644		
Joshua Heshel, son of Jacob	1654		
Joseph, son of David	1654		
Moses, son of Isaac Bunmish	1663, 1664, 1671		
Jacob of Prague, son of Aaron Reuven Ashkenazi	1661, 1671, 1672, 1673	1672	
Aaron, son of Joseph Auerbach	1661, 1669, 1672, 1673, 1678, 1689	1672, 1678	
Jacob Kopel		1662	
Joseph, son of Eliezer Ashkenazi		1662, 1666	
Isaac, son of Leib Temerlish (Rabinowicz)	1683	1666	
Jacob		1666	
Mordecai, son of Shemaryah Shmerl	1671, 1678	1678, 1680	
Benjamin Wulf, son of Abraham Halperin	1673, 1687, 1693	1686	
Joseph Ashkenazi, son of Jacob Bachrach	1677, 1687, 1689	1678	
Isaac, son of Judah	1683, 1684, 1687		
Leib Temerlish	1687, 1690		
Judah Leib	1690		
Meir Rofe (Physician), son of Judah Leib Rofe	1693, 1700	1699	
Mordecai Ziskind, son of Moses Rotenberg (Aleksander Rotenberg)	1698, 1713		

Table 4 Representatives of independent urban communities (*cont.*)

Name	Pinkas va'ad arba aratsot	Sejm Czterech Ziem	Central Archives, Lviv
(c) Lublin (*cont.*)			
Mendel, son of Saul			1697[d]
Mordecai, son of Tsevi Hirsh	1699, 1713, 1718, 1724	1699	
Abraham, son of Israel Isserlish (Doktorowicz)		1702	
Michael, son of Abraham	1713, 1718, 1725, 1730	1718, 1721	
Simon, son of Joseph Nahush		1717, 1718, 1719	
Abraham, son of Iser Raska	1718, 1721, 1724	1724	
Joshua Heshel, son of Meir		1718	
Meir		1719, 1730	
Faibush, son of Isaac		1719	
Hirsh Pakiej		1721	
Zelig, son of Abraham Szmuklarz (Shpiglezish)		1724	
Abraham, son of Hayim	1724, 1725, 1730, 1739, 1743, 1744, 1748, 1750, 1751		
Isaac (Aizik), son of Ari Judah Leib Segal	1724, 1727, 1731	1724, 1730	
Idel, son of Kapol	1725		
Aaron, son of Azriel	1725		
Moses, son of Wulf		1730	
Moses, son of Meir	1742		
Leib		1748	
David Ber, son of Abraham Landau	1754		
(d) Przemyśl			
Moses, son of Abraham	1603		
Samuel, son of Joshua Segal Horowitz	1621, 1622		
Samuel, son of Meshulam	1623		

[d] TsDIAL, f. 418, op. 1, spr. 5, pp. 70–1.

Table 4 Representatives of independent urban communities (*cont.*)

Name	Pinkas va'ad arba aratsot	Sejm Czterech Ziem	Central Archives, Lviv
(*d*) Przemyśl (*cont.*)			
Menahem Mendel, son of Joel Faibush	1644		
Hirsh, son of Solomon (Jeleń Salomonowicz)	1644		
Aryeh Leib, son of Zacharias	1654		
Naphtali Hirsh		1662	
Joseph, son of Yekutiel Lozil Halevi Horowitz	1663, 1670, 1671, 1677, 1678, 1680, 1681		
Benjamin Bunim, son of Theodor	1678	1666	
Simon Ginzburg		1666	
Aaron, son of Meir	1669, 1673, 1687, 1688		
Judah Leib, son of Naphtali Isaac	1671, 1677, 1678		
Moses, son of Issaschar Ashkenazi	1677, 1687		
Leib, son of Barukh		1678	
Moses, son of Isaac		1680, 1699	
Leib, son of Nathan		1680	
Eliezer	1681		
Isaac Kahana	1681		
Jonas, son of Moses	1690		
Asher Ashkenazi	1690		
Joseph Segal, son of Moses of Lwów	1695, 1696, 1698, 1700		
Joseph, son of Isaac	1713		
Moses Kahana Zeira, son of Joseph	1699	1717, 1718	
Michael		1717, 1718	
Ezekiel Feibel Teomim	1718	1724	
Joseph		1726	
Meir, son of Isaac Fortis of Komarno	1730		
Eliezer, son of Michael of Stryj	1730, 1742		
Noah Rabinowicz		1739, 1748	
Isaac of Sieniawa	1754		

Table 4 Representatives of independent urban communities (*cont.*)

Name	Pinkas va'ad arba aratsot	Sejm Czterech Ziem	Central Archives, Lviv
(e) Ciechanowiec			
Abraham, son of Eliezer		1753	
Issaschar, son Beresh, son of Joshua Segal	1755		

Table 5 Representatives of the major communities

Name	Pinkas va'ad arba aratsot	Sejm Czterech Ziem
(a) Rzeszów		
Azriel	1687	
Leib, son of Samuel	1692	
Israel Krakower	1699	
Solomon, son of Moses Rabinowicz	1718, 1721, 1724	1717, 1718, 1723, 1724
Lipmann Kahana		1724
Ari Leib, son of Saul	1724	
Joseph of Tyśmenica		1739
Wulf, son of Zalman		1744
(b) Tykocin		
Jacob, son of Samuel	1673, 1677, 1687	
Meir, son of Solomon	1677	1678
Hayim Meizlish	1687	
Aryeh Judah Leib, son of Samuel Tsevi Hirsh	1689	
Mordecai, son of Leib	1692	
Isaac, son of Benjamin Wulf of Opatów	1718	
Isaac, son of Nehemiah	1721	
Nathan Neta, son of Hirsh	1724	1724
Samuel Bachrach, son of Solomon	1724, 1730	1724, 1739
Simhah Bunim, son of Judah Leib Kahana	1754	
Judah Leib Kahana	1754	
(c) Węgrów		
Moses, son of Moses Mordechai	1685, 1688	
Ber Segal of Kraków	1726, 1740	1739

Table 6 Representatives of the regional councils

Name	Place of residence	*Pinkas va'ad arba aratsot*	*Sejm Czterech Ziem*	Central Archives, Lviv
(a) Chełm–Bełz (Tesha Kehilot)				
Judah Leib, son of Eliezer	Luboml	1595, 1597		
Leib	Bełz	1595		
David, son of Jacob	Szczebrzeszyn	1603		
Joseph, son of Mattathias Delacourt	Szczebrzeszyn	1617		
Jacob, son of Abraham	Szczebrzeszyn	1621, 1622, 1642		
Pinhas Zelig, son of Asher Nahush	Chełm	1661, 1677		
Moses, son of Mendel	Tarnogród		1662	
Zelig, son of Joseph	Chełm		1662, 1677	
Nahum, son of Meir Rapaport	Bełz	1671		
Mordecai, son of Benjamin	Chełm	1663, 1668, 1670		
Wulf Ginzburg		1681		
Judah	Szczebrzeszyn	1664		
Uberlo (Eberla), son of Isaac	Tarnogród		1666	
Tsevi Hirsh, son of Samson Maizlish	Bełz	1667, 1678, 1689, 1690, 1691	1678	
Jacob, son of Jonas	Luboml	1669, 1672		
Isaac, son of Or Shraga Faibush of Kraków	Turobin	1670		
Joseph, son of David Kahana Shapira	Szczebrzeszyn	1671		
Yekutiel, son of Joshua Aharon of Lublin	Chełm	1671		
Moses Halevi Landau, son of Moses Joshua	Chełm	1672, 1673		
David Tevel, son of Eliezer	Turobin	1673	1680	
Meshulam Faibush, son of Menahem Ashkenazi Ginzburg	Hrubieszów	1677		
Asher, son of Isaac	Chęciny, Bełz	1677, 1685, 1688		
Meir, son of Joseph	Turobin	1678, 1687	1678	
Jacob, son of Mordecai	Luboml	1680		
Hilel, son of Jonas	Chełm	1687		
Tsevi Hirsh, son of Shemesh	Zamość	1687, 1688		
Joel, son of Gad	Szczebrzeszyn	1688		
Zacharias Mendel, son of Ari Leib	Turobin	1688, 1689, 1691		
Meir, son of Eli	Turobin	1689		

Table 6   Representatives of the regional councils (*cont.*)

Name	Place of residence	*Pinkas va'ad arba aratsot*	*Sejm Czterech Ziem*	Central Archives, Lviv
(a) Chełm–Bełz (Tesha Kehilot) (*cont.*)				
Aryeh Judah Leib, son of Samuel Tsevi Hirsh	Zamość	1689		
Nathan Neta, son of Jacob	Tarnogród	1691		
Aaron, son of Jacob	Zamość	1692		
Moses, son of Tsevi Hirsh Segal	Turobin	1698, 1700		
Zacharias Mendel	Bełz	1700	1699	
Moses, son of Mordecai	Sokal	1699	1699	
Aaron Samuel, son of Azriel Lemel Kahana Shapira	Szczebrzeszyn	1713		
Samuel, son of Mordecai Margaliyot of Kraków	Hrubieszów	1718	1718	
Moses, son of Zelig	Chełm		1718	
Tsevi Hirsh, son of Pinhas Zelig of Krzemieniec	Hrubieszów, Chełm	1718, 1719, 1721, 1730, 1731	1719	
Joshua Heshel	Chełm		1719, 1724	
Dr Joseph Heshel			1724	
Issaschar Ber, son of Meir of Lublin	Luboml	1724	1724	
Abraham, son of Joel Margaliyot of Łęczyca	Hrubieszów		1724, 1730	
Israel Moses, son of Berish Rabinowicz of Lublin	Chełm	1730	1730	
Samuel Zanwil, son of Simon	Chełm		1730	
Pinhas Zelig, son of Naphtali	Chełm	1730		
Joseph, son of Israel	Luboml	1751, 1755	1750	
Solomon, son of Moses	Chełm	1751		
(b) Wielkopolska				
Solomon Ephraim, son of Aaron	Łęczyca	1603, 1609, 1617		
Samuel, son of Jacob	Kalisz	1644		
Leib	Szydłów	1644		
Issaschar, son of Faibel	Rzeszów[a]		1662	
Israel, son of Nathan Shapira	Kalisz	1663, 1670		
Shemayah, son of Issaschar Ber Shalit	Inowrocław	1664		
Naphtali, son of Or Shraga Bloch	Łęczyca	1664		

[a] 'Issaschar, son of Faibel, who is the rabbi of Rzeszów, but was elected from the Jews of the voivodeship of Poznań' (*Sejm Czterech Ziem*, 187).

Table 6   Representatives of the regional councils (*cont.*)

Name	Place of residence	*Pinkas va'ad arba aratsot*	*Sejm Czterech Ziem*	Central Archives, Lviv
(b) Wielkopolska (*cont.*)				
Moses, son of Hayim			1666	
Judah, son of Hirsh	Pińczów[b]		1666	
Shabtai, son of David		1666		
Samuel, son of Hayim Menahem	Poznań[c]	1667, 1684		
Samuel, son of Yohanan	Wronki	1669	1673	
Moses, son of Moses Mordecai	Piła	1671		
Avigdor (Victor), son of Abraham	Krotoszyn	1671, 1678, 1683	1678, 1680, 1683	
David	Leszno	1673		
Moses, son of Shabtai Ba'al Siftei Kohen		1677		
Meir, son of David Joseph	Kalisz	1677, 1684, 1687		
Joseph, son of Elias Chęciner	Kalisz	1678	1678, 1683	
Mordecai, son of Joseph	Kalisz	1680		
Meir, son of Moser Brisker	Leszno	1683		
Ari Leib, son of Jonas	Leszno	1683	1685	
Aaron, son of Isaac	Leszno		1685, 1686	
Benjamin, son of Moses Katzenellenbogen		1687		
Joseph, son of Naphtali Herz of Lwów	Szydłów, Poznań	1687		
Gabriel, son of Judah Leib of Kraków	Poznań[d]	1688, 1693		
Jacob Moses, son of Abraham	Leszno	1689, 1691, 1692		
Naphtali, son of Isaac	Poznań[e]	1691, 1693, 1698		
Leib Mordecai	Krotoszyn	1700	1691	
Jacob Zelig	Kalisz	1692	1691	
Leib, son of Faibush	Kalisz	1692		
Aaron, son of Moses	Leszno	1692		
Samuel Hellman, son of Israel Halperin	Krotoszyn	1692, 1693	1693	
Isaac Leib	Krotoszyn		1702	
Leib Isaac	Leszno		1702	

[b] 'Judah, son of Hirsh, from Pińczow, from the Kalisz voivodeship' (ibid. 191).
[c] 'From the regional council of Poznań' (*Pinkas va'ad arba aratsot*, 194).
[d] 'From Kraków, elected from Poznań and the regional council' (ibid. 210).
[e] 'Resident of the holy community of Poznań and the regional council' (ibid. 240).

Table 6 Representatives of the regional councils (*cont.*)

Name	Place of residence	*Pinkas va'ad arba aratsot*	*Sejm Czterech Ziem*	Central Archives, Lviv
(*b*) **Wielkopolska** (*cont.*)				
Leib Barukh	Krotoszyn		1702	
Menahem Mendel, son of Moses	Krotoszyn	1713		
Jacob	Poznań[f]		1717, 1718, 1724	
Isaac, son of Azriel Zelig	Kalisz	1718, 1724, 1727	1718	
Herzl	Leszno	1718	1718	
Moses, son of Menahem Mendel Auerbach (Rabinowicz)	Krotoszyn	1730	1718	
Simon, son of Menahem Mendel Auerbach	Krotoszyn	1718		
Joseph, son of Aryeh Judah	Kalisz		1724	
Leib Halevi		1724		
Ari Judah Leib, son of Isaac	Krotoszyn		1724, 1739	
Leib, son of Moses	Krotoszyn	1724, 1739		
Abraham, son of Joseph (Rabinowicz)	Leszno	1730, 1742		
Eliezer Leib	Krotoszyn		1739	
Samuel, son of Leib	Krotoszyn	1739		
Aryeh Judah Leib, son of Mordecai	Krotoszyn	1740		
Joseph Segal Landau	Opatów[g]		1748, 1750	
(*c*) **Lithuania**				
Hayim		1595		
Wulf		1595		
Judah, son of Ovadyah Eilenberg	Brześć Litewski	1607		
Meir, son of Saul Katzenellenbogen	Brześć Litewski	1623		
Solomon Zalman, son of Jeremiah Jacob	Brześć Litewski	1644		
Naphtali, son of Isaac	Pińsk	1644		
Moses, son of Nathan Shapira	Pińsk	1654		
Jonas, son of Isaiah Teumim of Prague	Grodno	1654		
Judah, son of Benjamin Wulf	Grodno	1654		
(*d*) **Małopolska**				
Or Shraga, son of Samuel Bloch Faibel		1628, 1642, 1661		

[f] 'Jacob, rabbi in Poznań and in the same voivodeship' (*Sejm Czterech Ziem*, 238).

[g] 'Joseph Landau of Opatów' (ibid. 277); 'Joseph Segal Landau delegated from the voivodeship of Poznań' (ibid.

Table 6 Representatives of the regional councils (*cont.*)

Name	Place of residence	*Pinkas va'ad arba aratsot*	*Sejm Czterech Ziem*	Central Archives, Lviv
(*d*) **Małopolska** (*cont.*)				
Abraham Heshel	Kraków[h]		1662	
Judah Leib	Szydłów		1662	
Jacob, son of Joseph	Kraków[i]		1666	
David Marperk			1666	
Abraham, son of Nathan Halevi			1666	
Avigdor Judah Leib, son of Hanokh Hena of Prague	Pińczów	1667, 1669, 1673, 1677, 1678, 1683, 1684, 1689	1666, 1678, 1680	
Menahem, son of Benjamin	Sandomierz	1667, 1671		
Isaac Leib, son of Benjamin Ze'ev Wulf	Opatów	1668, 1671, 1678, 1680	1680	
Moses Jacob Judah Leib, son of Meir	Szydłów	1671, 1673		
Jacob Joseph, son of Aaron	Olkusz		1672, 1678	
Isaac, son of Or Shraga	Szydłów		1685	
Leib, son of Israel	Opatów	1677		
David Tevel, son of Eliezer		1683		
Mordecai, son of Nathan Neta Kahana		1685		
Saul, son of Moses Katzenellenbogen	Pińczów	1688, 1691, 1692	1699	
Judah Leib	Chęciny	1690		
Simon, son of Jacob	Wodzisław		1691	
Mordecai Leib	Wodzisław	1692		
Mordecai Mannel	Olkusz	1692		
Aaron, son of Leib	Pińczów	1692		
Jacob, son of Eliezer	Pińczów		1693	
Aaron Menahem Mendel	Opatów	1693		
Saul, son of Abraham Joshua Heshel Shakhna		1698, 1700	1699	
Tsevi Hirsh, son of Ezekiel Segal Landau	Opatów	1699		
Eliezer, son of Judah	Pińczów		1702, 1723	
Meir, son of Benjamin Wulf Halperin of Lublin	Opatów	1713, 1718		
Judah Leib, son of Isaac Aizik	Szydłów	1713		

[h] 'Abraham Heshel, the rabbi of the Jews of Kraków, delegated by the Kraków voivodeship' (ibid. 187).
[i] 'Jacob, son of Joseph, the Jewish elder of the voivodeship of Kraków' (ibid. 189); 'Jacob, son of Joseph of Kraków' (ibid. 190).

Table 6 Representatives of the regional councils (*cont.*)

Name	Place of residence	Pinkas va'ad arba aratsot	Sejm Czterech Ziem	Central Archives, Lviv
(*d*) **Małopolska** (*cont.*)				
Benjamin Ze'ev Segal Horowitz (Wulf Syrkish)		1713		
Abraham Isaac Hazak Fortis			1717, 1718, 1724	
Ari Judah Leib	Krakówᴶ	1718, 1724, 1727	1718, 1724	
Simon Ze'ev Wulf Segal Levi Landau	Tarnów	1718	1724	
Judah, son of Tsevi Hirsh Segal Levi Landau	Opatów	1719, 1721, 1724, 1730	1723, 1724, 1726	
Isaac, son of Tsevi Hirsh Landau	Opatów	1724		
Giez, son of Solomon	Wiśnicz		1725	
Benjamin Wulf, son of Ezekiel Landau	Tarnów	1730	1750	
Pinhas, son of Isaac Meir Teumim	Wiśnicz	1731	1730	
Avigdor	Chęciny		1730	
Ezekiel, son of Tsevi Hirsh Segal Landau (Hazkiel Jeleniowicz)	Opatów	1739, 1742	1739, 1743, 1744, 1745	
Ezekiel, son of Benjamin	Tarnów		1739, 1744	
Wulf Segal Landau (Hazkiel Wulfowicz)			1754, 1758	
Joseph Saul	Nowemiasto Korczyn	1751, 1754	1750, 1753	
Joseph, son of Avigdor	Chęciny	1751, 1754	1753	
Abraham, son of Joseph	Opatów		1753	
Israel, son of Saul	Pińczów	1754		
Nahum			1753	
Tsevi Hirsh	Opoczno	1755		
Ezekiel, son of Avigdor	Ostrowiec	1755		
(*e*) **Lublin**				
David Beresh, son of Aryeh Leib of Zamość	Kraśnik	1754		
Naphtali Hirsh, son of Avigdor	Żelichów	1754, 1755		
Jacob Hakatan Landau	Lubartów	1755		
(*f*) **Zamoyski Entail**				
Solomon	Tarnogród	1718	1718	
Isaac, son of Judah Leib	Tarnogród	1718, 1731	1718	
Jan	Tarnogród		1718	

ᴶ 'Leib, rabbi of Kraków, delegated from the district of Kraków' (ibid. 221).

Table 6 Representatives of the regional councils (*cont.*)

Name	Place of residence	*Pinkas va'ad arba aratsot*	*Sejm Czterech Ziem*	Central Archives, Lviv
(f) Zamoyski Entail (*cont.*)				
Pinhas Zelig, son of Naphtali Hirsh	Szczebrzeszyn	1719		
Israel Plaszowicz			1724	
Ari Leib, son of Barukh of Lublin	Zamość	1724, 1731, 1754		
Joseph	Zamość		1726	
Ari Leib, son of Samuel	Tarnogród	1751, 1754	1743, 1750, 1753	
Jacob Isaac, son of Moses Hayim (Icyk Rabinowicz)	Zamość	1754		
Abraham Hakohen, son of Isaac of Tarłów	Zamość	1755		
(g) Przemyśl				
Naphtali Hirsh, son of Benjamin Wulf	Jarosław	1681		
Isaiah, son of Nathan Neta of Kraków	Jarosław	1697		
Joshua, son of Samuel of Kraków	Dobromil	1713		
Abraham Frankel Teumim	Jarosław	1724	1724	
Benjamin Bunim	Przemyśl[k]	1730		
Abraham Aaron Slaszowicz			1739	
Eliezer, son of Isaac	Dobromil		1743, 1744	
Moses Hoshea Leib	Jarosław		1744	
Noah, son of Yehiel Michael	Przeworsk	1751, 1754, 1755	1744	
Nathan, son of Jacob Joshua	Przeworsk	1752, 1754		
Samuel, son of Leib	Dobromil		1753	
Zacharias Mendel	Drohobycz	1754		
Tsevi Hirsh, son of Joseph Horowitz	Jarosław	1754		
(h) Ruthenia				
Abraham, son of Shabtai Horowitz	Lwów	1595		
Barukh	Lwów	1595		
Moses, son of Jacob Israel Tsiporish	Lwów	1595, 1597		
Benjamin Aaron, son of Abraham Slonik	Podhajce	1603		
Joshua, son of Alexander Wolk	Lwów	1603, 1607		
Moses Mordecai, son of Nathan Hakohen	Lwów	1607		

k 'From Przemyśl, from the regional council' (Pinkas va'ad arba aratsot, 316).

Table 6 Representatives of the regional councils (*cont.*)

Name	Place of residence	*Pinkas va'ad arba aratsot*	*Sejm Czterech Ziem*	Central Archives, Lviv
(*h*) Ruthenia (*cont.*)				
Alexander Wulf, son of Moses Hakohen Ashkenazi	Lwów	1607, 1617, 1618		
Ziskind			1616	
Samson, son of Isaac Bochner	Lwów	1618, 1623, 1628		
Ephraim Gompricht Osserów	Lwów	1627		
Abraham, son of Moses Halperin	Lwów	1627, 1628		
Abraham, son of Israel Yehiel Rapaport Shrenzel	Lwów	1642, 1644		
Aryeh Leib, son of Zacharias	Przemyśl[I]		1662	
David, son of Samuel Levy of Włodzimierz	Lwów	1654, 1663, 1664		
Yekutiel Zalman, son of Aaron	Lwów	1661		
Naphtali, son of Abraham	Satanów	1661		
Hirsh, son of Fishel	Lwów		1662	
Samuel, son of Jacob	Lwów		1666	
Moses, son of Aaron	Żółkiew		1666	
Isaac Aizik, son of Eliezer Aronish	Lwów	1667, 1671, 1677		
Tsevi Hirsh, son of Zacharias Mendel	Lwów	1670, 1671, 1677, 1678, 1680, 1681, 1685		
Asher, son of David Halevi	Lwów	1671, 1678	1678	
Hayim, son of Joshua of Kraków	Kołomyja	1671		
Israel, son of Samuel	Tarnopol	1671, 1673, 1677, 1678, 1680, 1681, 1683		
Moses, son of Israel Harif	Lwów	1673, 1685, 1687		
Hayim, son of Leib	Jaworów	1673, 1683, 1687, 1688, 1689, 1690		
Judah Leib Segal, son of Jacob	Lwów	1677		
Abraham Aronish, son of Shemaryah	Lwów	1677		

[I] 'Leib, son of Zacharias, who is now rabbi of Przemyśl, elected from the voivodeship of Ruś, from the Jews of Lwów' (*Sejm Czterech Ziem*, 187).

Table 6 Representatives of the regional councils (*cont.*)

Name	Place of residence	Pinkas va'ad arba aratsot	Sejm Czterech Ziem	Central Archives, Lviv
(h) Ruthenia (*cont.*)				
David Zelig, son of Isaac of Prague	Buczacz	1677, 1683, 1687, 1689, 1690	1680	
Ari Judah Leib, son of Moses of Włodzimierz	Lwów	1677, 1681, 1685, 1687, 1688, 1691, 1692		
Menahem Mendel, son of Yehiel Michael (Mendel Michelowicz)	Lwów	1683, 1684, 1687, 1688, 1689, 1690, 1700	1678	
Joshua Heshel, son of Tsevi Hirsh (Herszel Doktorowicz)	Lwów	1678	1678	
Menahem Mendel, son of Nathan	Brody	1678	1678	
Solomon, son of Jacob	Lwów		1680	
Judah Abraham, son of Isaac Levi	Lwów	1681		
Mordecai Gimpel, son of Jacob of Lublin	Lwów	1683, 1687		
Ze'ev, son of Haikish	Lwów	1687, 1690		
Isaiah, son of Menahem Mendel Katzenellenbogen	Lwów	1687		
Moses Meshel	Lwów	1687, 1688	1699	
Hayim Mach, son of David (Joachim Dawidowicz)	Lwów	1688, 1689, 1693	1693, 1699	
Pinhas Moses, son of Israel Harif	Lwów	1691, 1692, 1693, 1698, 1700		
Ze'ev Wulf, son of Pinhas	Lwów	1693		
Leib, son of Solomon	Lwów			1697[m]
Jacob of Buczacz	Żółkiew			1697[n]
Mordecai, son of Abraham	Lwów	1699	1699	
Gershon Nathan, son of Betsalel	Żółkiew	1699		
Jacob, son of Moses	Lwów	1699		
Moses, son of Mordecai	Lwów	1713	1702, 1718	
Hayim	Lwów		1717	
Elias, son of Abraham	Lwów	1718	1717	
Abraham Kahana of Kraków	Lwów	1718	1717	
Naphtali Herzl	Lwów		1717, 1718	

[m] TsDIAL, f. 418, op. 1, spr. 5, pp. 70–1.   [n] Ibid.

Table 6 Representatives of the regional councils (*cont.*)

Name	Place of residence	Pinkas va'ad arba aratsot	Sejm Czterech Ziem	Central Archives, Lviv
(*h*) **Ruthenia** (*cont.*)				
Abraham of Brody	Lwów		1718	
Yekutiel Eliezer Margaliyot	Lwów	1718		
Abraham	Żółkiew		1718	
Meir	Lwów		1719, 1724	
Shemesh (Szamsia)	Żółkiew		1719	
Neta, son of Moses	Lwów		1719	
Jacob, son of Eliezer of Szczebrzeszyn	Lwów		1723, 1724	
Moses Rabinowicz	Pińczów°		1724	
Joseph	Lwów		1724	
Hayim	Lwów		1724	
Zacharias Mendel	Lwów		1724	
Jacob Aaron, son of Mordecai of Stryj	Lwów	1724	1724	
Ari Judah Leib Landau	Lwów, Brody	1730, 1742		
Yekutiel Zalman, son of Segal Epstein	Lwów	1730		
Jacob Joseph, son of Isaac Krakower	Brody	1730, 1739, 1742		
Aryeh Leib Hakohen Rapaport	Lwów	1730, 1742		
Isaac Segal Landau of Żółkiew	Lwów	1731	1730	
Joshua Heshel, son of Isaac (Szyja Esiel)	Tarnopol	1731	1730	
Eliezer Litman	Brody, Lwów	1739	1730, 1739	
Saul, son of Mordecai	Żółkiew		1739	
Jacob Rabinowicz	Brody		1739	
Jacob	Tarnopol	1742		
Israel, son of Mordecai	Żółkiew	1742		
Leib, son of Daniel	Brody		1744	
Moses Pinhas, son of Hayim			1750	
Isaac Issaschar Beresh, son of Moses Wulf (Berek Rabinowicz)	Brody	1754	1753, 1754	
David Beresh of Kowel	Stanisławów	1755		
Tsevi Hirsh, son of Isaac Issaschar Beresh (Hershko Berkowicz)	Brody, Żółkiew	1755		
Hayim Kohen Rapaport	Lwów	1755		
(*i*) **Volhynia**				
Zanwil	Włodzimierz	1595		

° 'Moses Rabinowicz of Pińczów in Ruthenia' (*Sejm Czterech Ziem*, 236).

Table 6 Representatives of the regional councils (*cont.*)

Name	Place of residence	*Pinkas va'ad arba aratsot*	*Sejm Czterech Ziem*	Central Archives, Lviv
(*i*) **Volhynia** (*cont.*)				
Abraham	Krzemieniec	1595		
Yekutiel, son of Elyakim Ashkenazi		1627		
Gedalyah, son of Israel	Ostróg	1644		
Jacob	Krzemieniec	1644		
Azaryah Benjamin Wulf, son of Abraham	Włodzimierz	1653		
Samuel Zanwil, son of Zacharias Mendel Shapira	Włodzimierz	1655, 1673	1662	
Isaac, son of Ozer	Krzemieniec	1655, 1661	1662, 1666	
Ze'ev Wulf, son of Nathan		1661		
Issaschar, son of Abraham	Łuck		1662	
Nahman, son of Meir Rapaport	Dubno	1663		
Nahman, son of Solomon Naphtali	Włodzimierz	1664		
David, son of Yehiel	Łuck		1666	
Israel, son of Samuel	Kowel		1666	
Judah, son of Noah	Łuck		1666	
Aaron Zelig, son of Judah Leib Hakohen	Ostróg	1672, 1673, 1683	1666, 1672	
Samuel Barkai, son of Meir	Ostróg	1670, 1678		
Joseph, son of Moses	Włodzimierz	1671		
Meir, son of Joseph	Włodzimierz	1672	1672	
Abraham, son of Judah Leib	Łuck	1673, 1678	1678	
Moses, son of Mordecai	Włodzimierz	1677		
Joseph, son of David	Ostróg	1678	1678	
Eliezer, son of Leib	Łuck		1680	
Ephraim Fishel, son of Aryeh Leib	Włodzimierz	1683, 1684, 1687, 1688		
Hayim, son of Moses Meshulam	Kowel	1687		
Yekutiel, son of Joshua Aaron of Lublin	Włodzimierz	1687, 1688, 1700		
Israel, son of Isaac Aizik	Ołyka	1689		
Judah Idel, son of Hirsh of Lublin	Kowel	1689		
Joel, son of Isaac Aizik Halperin	Łuck, Ostróg	1689, 1691, 1693, 1700, 1713	1699	
Joshua Heshel, son of Tsevi Hirsh	Krzemieniec	1689	1699	
Joshua Segal	Kowel	1690		

Table 6 Representatives of the regional councils (*cont.*)

Name	Place of residence	Pinkas va'ad arba aratsot	Sejm Czterech Ziem	Central Archives, Lviv
(*i*) **Volhynia** (*cont.*)				
Barukh, son of Isaiah	Kowel	1692		
Samuel, son of Shakhna of Kraków	Dubno	1693		
Isaiah, son of Moses Meshulam	Łuck	1697		
Mordecai, son of Tsevi Hirsh	Łuck	1699, 1700	1699	
Naphtali Hirsh, son of Israel	Kowel	1700		
David Jacob Tevel, son of Ephraim Fishel (Fiszlowicz)	Włodzimierz	1713, 1718	1717, 1718	
Abraham, son of Tsevi Hirsh	Kowel	1713		
Abraham, son of Meir	Ostróg	1718	1717	
Samuel Hakatan, son of Ephraim Fishel of Włodzimierz	Krzemieniec	1718	1718	
Naphtali of Frankfurt	Ostróg		1718	
Joseph, son of Perets	Ostróg	1721		
Joshua Heshel, son of Eliezer	Dubno	1724, 1727	1724	
David, son of Abraham	Dubno	1724	1724	
Eliezer (Lajzeł)			1724	
Ari Leib, son of Samuel	Krzemieniec	1739, 1742	1724, 1739, 1750	
Israel, son of Eliezer Lipman Halperin		1727		
Moses, son of Menahem Mendel Margaliyot	Zasław	1730		
Joseph, son of Pesah	Krzemieniec	1730	1750	
Abraham, son of Joshua Levy of Kraków	Dubno	1739	1739	
Saul, son of Jacob, son of Ephraim Fishel	Włodzimierz	1742, 1751	1748	
Jacob, son of Aryeh Leib	Łuck	1754, 1755		
Saul, son of Aryeh Leib of Amsterdam	Dubno	1754		

Notes

1 See J. Goldberg and A. Wein, 'Ordynacja dla sejmu żydowskiego ziem koronnych z 1753 r.', *Biuletyn Żydowskiego Instytutu Historycznego*, 52 (1964), 17–34; A. Leszczyński, 'Dyspozycja komisarza Skarbu Koronnego wydana 22 października 1753 r. Sejmowi Żydów Korony w Jarosławiu', *Biuletyn Żydowskiego Instytutu Historycznego*, 114–15 (1980), 113–27; *Sejm Czterech Ziem: Źródła*, ed. J. Goldberg and A. Kaźmierczyk (Warsaw, 2011), 138–50.

2 I. Halperin, 'Live'ayat herkevo shel va'ad arba ha'aratsot', in id., *Yehudim veyahadut bemizraḥ-eiropah: meḥkarim betoledoteihem* (Jerusalem, 1969), 46–7; J. Kalik, *Scepter of Judah: The Jewish Autonomy in the Eighteenth-Century Crown Poland* (Leiden, 2009), 109–10.

3 Referred to in the sources as *parnas* (Heb.), *marszałek* (Pol.), and *oberster Aufseer* (Germ.).

4 Referred to in the sources as *shtadlan* (Heb.), *syndyk* (Pol.), and *syndicus* (Lat.).

5 Referred to in the sources as *ne'eman* (Heb.), *wiernik* (Pol.), *fidelis* (Lat.), and *Beglaubigter* (Germ.).

6 Referred to in the sources as *sofer* (Heb.), *safra* (Aram.), *pisarz* (Pol.), *notarius*, and *scriba* (Lat.).

7 *Pinkas va'ad arba aratsot: likutei takanot ketavim vereshumot*, ed. I. Halperin (Jerusalem, 1945); 2nd revd. edn., ed. I. Bartal (Jerusalem, 1990).

8 *Sejm Czterech Ziem*.

9 Archiwum Główne Akt Dawnych, Warsaw (henceforth AGAD), 1/7/0 Archiwum Skarbu Koronnego (hereafter ASK), III, syg. 7; VI, syg. 14, 22, 23, 24, 25. I wish to thank the Israeli Academy of Sciences, which sponsored my research on these documents in 2015 in the framework of Israel Bartal's research project 'The Council of Four Lands'.

10 AGAD, Archiwum Skarbu Wojskowego, 84; see Kalik, *Scepter of Judah*, 111–29.

11 Biblioteka Książąt Czartoryskich, Kraków (hereafter BC) 2572 IV: 'Akta skarbowo-wojskowe z początku XVIII wieku'.

12 BC 1693 IV: '"Ciekawości 1753–1768 ks. I": Kopie akt, listów, mów, wotów oraz pism ulotnych z lat 1750–1768, zwłaszcza z r. 1767 oraz druki dotyczące spraw różnowierców w latach 1766–1767'.

13 BC 3822 IV: 'Zbiór akt grodzkich i prywatnych ułożonych wg miejscowości M: Międzybóż II -sądowych, majątkowych z lat 1663–1744 dotyczacych dóbr Sieniawskich, Czartoryskich', 61–334.

14 Tsentral'nyi derzhavnyi istorychnyi arkhiv Ukrainy, Lviv (hereafter TsDIAL), f. 418, op. 1, spr. 5, fos. 70–1: Council of Four Lands, debts to Dominican convent, 1697.

15 See H. D. Friedberg, *Toledot mishpaḥat horowits* (Antwerp, 1928); T. H. Horowits, *Toledot mishpaḥat horowits* (Kraków, 1935).

16 Yom Tov Lipmann Heller, *Megilat eivah* (Breslau, 1837), 14.

17 See M. Bałaban, 'Dr. Emanuel de Jona, lekarz nadworny Jana III', in id., *Z historji Żydów w Polsce: Szkice i studja* (Warsaw, 1920), 49–58; id., 'Lekarze żydowscy w dawnej Rzeczypospolitej', in I. Schiper, A. Tartakower, and A. Hafftka (eds.), *Żydzi w Polsce Odrodzonej: Działalność społeczna, gospodarcza, oświatowa i kulturalna*, 2 vols. (Warsaw, 1932–3), i. 298–9.

18 See I. N. Gath, 'Gilgulah shel alilah, anatomyah shel kavanat zadon: moto shel melekh polin, yan hasheishi sobieski', *Gal-ed*, 25 (2017), 67–82.

19 *Sejm Czterech Ziem*, 206.

20 See M. Bałaban, *Historja Żydów w Krakowie i na Kazimierzu, 1304–1868*, 2 vols. (Kraków, 1931–6), ii. 231–50; Heb. trans.: *Toledot hayehudim bekrakov uvekazimierz, 1304–1868*, ed. J. Goldberg, trans. D. Weinfeld et al., 2 vols. (Jerusalem, 2002), ii. 608–22.

21 See Bałaban, 'Lekarze żydowscy w dawnej Rzeczypospolitej', 299–300.

22 *Sejm Czterech Ziem*, 237–8.

23 Ibid. 244–5.

24 Ibid. 112.

25 Ibid. 243.

26 Ibid. 244–5.

27 Ibid. 223.

28 *Pinkas va'ad arba aratsot*, 303.

29 *Sejm Czterech Ziem*, 127–8.

30 See Y. Trunk, 'Leveirur emdato shel avraham ben yoske, parnas va'ad arba aratsot, bemaḥloket bein yonatan eybeshuts veya'akov emden', *Zion*, 38 (1973), 174–9; J. Goldberg, 'Va'ad arba aratsot bamishtar hamedini vehaḥevrati shel mamlekhet polin-lita', in id., *Haḥevrah hayehudit bemamlekhet polin-lita* (Jerusalem, 1999), 127–8.

31 *Sejm Czterech Ziem*, 133.

32 *Pinkas va'ad arba aratsot*, 293–4.

33 Ibid. 299; *Sejm Czterech Ziem*, 236, 239.

34 *Sejm Czterech Ziem*, 392.

35 On this connection, see A. Teller, 'Radziwiłł, Rabinowicz, and the Rabbi of Świerz: The Magnates' Attitude to Jewish Regional Autonomy in the Eighteenth Century', in id. (ed.), *Studies in the History of the Jews in Old Poland in Honor of Jacob Goldberg* (Jerusalem, 1998), 246–76.

36 Halperin, 'Hakdamah', in *Pinkas va'ad arba aratsot*, p. vii.

37 *Sejm Czterech Ziem*, 113.

38 Ibid. 124–5.

39 Ibid. 116–20.

40 See A. Teller, 'Rabbis without a Function? The Polish Rabbinate and the Council of Four Lands in the Sixteenth to Eighteenth Centuries', in J. Wertheimer (ed.), *Jewish Religious Leadership: Image and Reality*, 2 vols. (New York, 2004), i. 371–400.

41 *Sejm Czterech Ziem*, 148, 150.

42 Ibid. 133.

43 Ibid. 278–9.

44 AGAD, ASK, dz. VI, syg. 23, pp. 266, 270, 271: poll tax assessments, 1682.

45 Ibid. 267.

46 Ibid. 311, 333.

47 Ibid. 271, 472.

48 Ibid. 383.

49 Ibid. 699.

50 Halperin, notes to *Pinkas va'ad arba aratsot*, 312 n. 1.

51 Ibid. 61 n. 1.

52 *Pinkas va'ad arba aratsot*, 254–5.

53 Ibid. 9–10.

54 See A. Michałowska-Mycielska, *Sejm Żydów litewskich (1623–1764)* (Warsaw, 2014).

55 *Sejm Czterech Ziem*, 223–5.

56 Ibid. 106–7.

57 See Kalik, *Scepter of Judah*, 132.

58 *Sejm Czterech Ziem*, 343–7.

59 Ibid. 348–52.

60 Ibid. 352–3. On the conflict between Ezekiel Landau and the community of Opatów, see G. D. Hundert, *The Jews in a Polish Private Town: The Case of Opatów in the Eighteenth Century* (Baltimore, 1992), 127–32.

61 See B. Freiberg, *Benei landa lemishpeḥotam* (Frankfurt am Main, 1905).

62 *Sejm Czterech Ziem*, 326.

Jewish Delegates at the Noble Sejm and *Sejmiki* between the Sixteenth and Eighteenth Centuries

ANNA MICHAŁOWSKA-MYCIELSKA

THE SYSTEM of 'noble democracy' which prevailed in the Polish–Lithuanian Commonwealth between the sixteenth and eighteenth centuries meant that the most important issues of internal and foreign policy were decided by parliaments (sejms) and local assemblies of the nobility (*sejmiki*). These also had an enormous influence on the situation of Jews in the commonwealth, deciding, above all, policy on Jewish settlement and economic activity and establishing the level of taxation to be paid by the Jewish population.

It is worth emphasizing that resolutions proposed by the sejm and the *sejmiki* had both a normative and an aspirational character and thus illustrate both the Jews' true position in the commonwealth and the nobility's attitude towards Jewish issues. Resolutions often dealt simultaneously with a large range of topics, and, in them, legal provisions, arguments both rational and religious, and stereotypical views of Jews were randomly intermingled.

Among the issues affecting Jews, fiscal matters, especially the assessment and collection of the Jewish poll tax, were most discussed by the nobility in the sejm and *sejmiki*.[1] The poll tax, introduced in the middle of the sixteenth century, was initially assessed—as its name suggests—on individuals, but in 1581, because of the difficulty of collecting it in this way, it was resolved to collect it as a lump sum. The lump sum was periodically increased, but its level was frequently criticized by the nobility in *sejmiki*. From the first half of the seventeenth century there were demands for it to be paid by all Jews, that is by every individual taxpayer, because it was believed that the lump sum did not reflect the appropriate level of taxation for the large and continually growing Jewish population. Resolutions passed in the *sejmiki* on the poll tax also included demands that it be paid in specie: silver or even gold. The nobility was, in addition, interested in the uses to which the tax would be put. A custom had developed that it should be used to give 'gifts to the Tatars', a tribute paid to the Crimean khanate, although no resolutions of the sejm had earmarked it for that purpose. The *sejmiki* called for this to be formalized especially in the second half of the seventeenth century when the Tatar threat was extremely serious. It was also proposed that the money raised from the Jewish poll tax be used to meet various short-term needs, such as paying the army or strengthening the forts in the commonwealth's eastern marches.

In addition to the poll tax, the sejm and *sejmiki* also imposed other taxes on Jews.

Among these were extraordinary military taxes (often called supplementary poll taxes), *szos* (a tax on houses in royal towns), *podymne* (a hearth tax), *szelężne* (a tax on the sale of alcohol), *czopowe* (a tax on the production and sale of alcohol), and various types of customs duties. Resolutions of the sejm and *sejmiki* were inconsistent here: in one instance Jews were relieved of all taxation except the poll tax; on another occasion it was emphasized that they were obliged to bear the same fiscal obligations as other citizens. Sometimes Jews were required to raise a certain number of soldiers for a military campaign or to provide a specific amount of gunpowder and lead, but these obligations could also be met by a sum of money.

A second group of resolutions dealt with Jewish economic activity. Jews were prohibited from farming state revenues, duties, and tolls and leasing salt mines and landed estates.[2] These resolutions were often accompanied by arguments of a religious nature: since these duties involved Christians taking an oath, for this to be administered by a Jew would be sacrilegious. Restrictions were proposed on Jewish commercial activity (including a prohibition on trading in skins, tallow, lead, and gunpowder), artisanry and, especially, the selling of alcohol. These restrictions were justified on the grounds that Jews were depriving poor Christians of an income.

A third group of resolutions dealt with religious matters and contact between Jews and Christians. Above all, Jews were forbidden to hire Christian servants, male or female.[3] The location of synagogues near Christian churches was sometimes banned, as was the construction of new synagogues and the repair of old ones. It can be assumed that the nobility often proposed such resolutions at sejms and *sejmiki* at the behest of the Church, usually to support decisions taken at episcopal synods.[4] However, the sejm and *sejmiki* rarely called for Jews to be punished as a result of religiously biased accusations, such as profanation of the host, ritual murder, or blasphemy.

Sometimes *sejmiki* called for Jews to be expelled from a voivodeship or land.[5] Such resolutions were most frequently adopted by the *sejmiki* of the Duchy of Mazovia, especially in the instructions to delegates to the sejm from this area. Here the local nobility invoked privileges dating from the time of the Piast princes which forbade Jews from settling in the duchy. However, there were also resolutions protecting Jews from anti-Jewish riots and attacks by townspeople and students.

The resolutions of the sejm and *sejmiki* reveal that noble opinion was in no way consistent and that the nobles were primarily motivated by economic considerations. The major landowners on whose lands Jews played an important role were inclined to protect them, while the poorer nobles, for whom Jewish tenants and managers represented competition, were interested in limiting their rights or burdening them with obligations. In addition, it is evident that opinions on Jewish issues differed greatly in the different areas of the commonwealth, and changed over time.

The *sejmiki*, made up of nobles from specific voivodeships, lands, and *powiats*, had real power in the areas where they were located, and in practice the implementation of the decisions of the sejm depended on them.[6] As a result, the organs of Jewish self-government closely followed the course of debates and the resolutions passed.[7]

They paid particular attention to the *sejmiki*, which met before sessions of the sejm and elected its members. Efforts were made to block harmful resolutions and ensure the passage of those seen as helpful. This often meant forestalling proposals put forward by townspeople, who also followed proceedings in the *sejmiki* and the sejm and attempted to influence their decisions.[8] Efforts were made to ensure the election of members of the sejm who were favourably disposed towards Jews, to gain the goodwill of those elected, and to insert provisions favourable to the Jews in the *sejmiki*'s directions to those elected to the sejm. Not only did individual communities seek to have their local interests taken into account in these directions, but efforts were also made to ensure that any resolutions passed were beneficial to the Jewish population as a whole.

The Jewish Council of Lithuania took action even before the *sejmiki* assembled. Three or four weeks before they met, the Jewish elders urged communities in the area where they were to be convened to take action to prevent resolutions unfavourable to the Jews being proposed. They were advised to shower those elected with gifts and to encourage them to show goodwill towards the Jews.[9] In places where pre-sejm *sejmiki* were to be held, the elders of all the local communities were instructed to observe whether new motions harmful to Jews were being proposed, or whether people willing to vote for them in the sejm were being elected. A local community that failed to take appropriate action to influence the local *sejmik* was liable to a fine of 100 red zlotys.[10]

Advocates (*shtadlonim, syndyki*) had the role of representing the Jewish community and interceding in all matters on its behalf with the non-Jewish authorities.[11] The Council of Four Lands and the Council of Lithuania also had their own advocates, whose activities are described below. Advocates were employed on short-term contracts and received a regular salary. They were expected to have knowledge of non-Jewish languages (Polish and Latin), skill in public speaking, an understanding of how non-Jewish courts and offices worked, and contacts among the local non-Jewish elite.

Contracts were concluded with advocates, defining their obligations and privileges (salary and additional benefits, such as accommodation, refunds for expenses incurred while performing duties outside the local area, tax exemptions, and so on). As Scott Ury has pointed out, the similarities between these contracts reveal the common nature of advocates' responsibilities throughout the commonwealth, in terms of both duties and expectations.[12] In addition to those who held the office full-time, advocates were sometimes appointed for specific tasks. Advocates' spheres of responsibility differed in scale and extent: community advocates took care for the most part of their own community and worked locally, whereas the advocates of the Council of Four Lands and the Council of Lithuania dealt with issues affecting the Jews in general and worked with the central government—the king, the sejm, central officials, and the great landowners. Local advocates, especially those representing large local communities, were also sent to the court or to sessions of the sejm to represent their local community rather than the Jews at large. When it sent its advocate, Boruch, to Warsaw in 1699 (the date suggests that it was to the sejm), the Poznań community made him swear an oath to represent, above all, the interests of the Poznań community and not to waste time on general issues or those of other communities.[13] The activity of local advocates at the sejm was sometimes intended to secure the confirmation of local rights from the monarch, as discussed below.

Obtaining the goodwill of the nobility at *sejmiki* required funding: these expenses were described in the Hebrew sources as *hotsa'ot seymiks* (sejm outgoings). The surviving accounts of the Opatów community kept during the pre-sejm *sejmik* of Sandomierz voivodeship in 1752 contain details of the recipients of gifts (sometimes coerced) and also describe their nature and value. Noble officials (including the voivode, deputy voivode, the castellan of Sandomierz, and the castellan of Radom) and individual nobles were given cash, sugar, coffee, lemons, oranges, meat, and cloth. Their servants and soldiers were given less expensive items: bread, tobacco, snuff, and handkerchiefs. Among the expenses were payments to guards and to a *shamash* (sexton) for 'his work during an assembly' and losses incurred in financial transactions conducted on preferential terms for certain great landowners.[14] Similar gifts were offered during *sejmiki* at which deputies were chosen for the Crown Tribunal and those which dealt with administrative and treasury matters.[15]

The expenses incurred at *sejmiki* were often considerable. In 1646 the *pinkas* (ledger) of the Poznań *kahal* recorded expenses at the sejm and *sejmiki* of 1,500 zlotys. Even greater sums were required to block an increase in the poll tax at a *sejmik* in Środa in 1688, where efforts by the advocates of the Poznań community and the whole district proved successful. However, it was impossible to repeat this success in the case of the hearth tax, where 'no inducements worked'. Information on the amounts involved are provided by notes dating from 1715 regarding a dispute between the Poznań community and its dependent community of Swarzędz. The latter was obliged to pay for 10 per cent of this kind of expenditure, and its unpaid charge for expenses during the 1688 *sejmik* in Środa was 800 Polish zlotys. This means the total sum expended amounted to 8,000 zlotys.[16]

Gifts were meant not only to gain the goodwill of those who participated in *sejmiki*, but also to prevent theft and violence during the sessions, mainly by the servants of the nobility and soldiers. A complaint from the Jews of Brześć Litewski (Brest) made to the office of the *starosta* (high sheriff) in 1759 shows how serious this could be. In this case, the initiators of the disturbances were Jan Zaborowski, speaker of the *sejmik*, and his deputy, Michał Jackiewicz, who, together with a mob, drove out the Jews who had gathered in the synagogue, looted Jewish homes and market stalls, chased Jews through the streets with sabres extorting money and luxury items such as snuffboxes, and injured the *shamash*. The *starosta*'s office condemned Zaborowski to two weeks' imprisonment and guaranteed the Brześć Jews' safety during gatherings of the nobility.[17]

The Council of Lithuania decided who was to pay for the expenses incurred during *sejmiki*. Initially, in the resolutions of 1623, the council required the principal communities and the communities under their jurisdiction to cover the costs.[18] A few years later it was specified that the expenses were to be shared between the principal communities and the local ones in the same proportion as the land tax.[19] In 1634, no doubt owing to the large sums being disbursed, the Council of Lithuania resolved that expenses for *sejmiki* were a common expense and should be borne by the whole country.[20] In 1670 a reminder was issued of the need to cover expenses during *sejmiki*, when 'the nobility greedily eyes Jewish money'. At the same time, given what a burden this was on the council, a limit was set on how much communities could be refunded from the central funds. For the principal communities this was 150 zlotys; for the local ones 30 kopa of Lithuanian grosz (75 zlotys).[21] Three years later the council resolved that places that did not have a full-time *minyan* (quorum of ten adult males) would be refunded a maximum of 20 zlotys.[22]

The expenses connected with meetings of *sejmiki* were frequently the subject of controversy and dispute. When they were included in the general accounts in 1627, the elders from Volhynia refused to accept them, and the matter had to be resolved by the court of the Council of Four Lands. Similarly, when the elders from Poznań wanted to include the 130 Polish zlotys spent during the previous two *sejmiki* in the general accounts, the issue was left to be decided by the next meeting of the Council of Four Lands in 1628.[23]

The division of funds to provide gifts for noble members of the sejm was also the subject of disputes between Jews in the Kingdom of Poland and in the Grand Duchy of Lithuania, with mutual accusations of unfair division of the expenses. In 1623, a few months before the establishment of the Council of Lithuania as a separate body, the court of the Council of Four Lands decided that the Lithuanian Jews were not obliged to contribute to the expenditure on gifts for members of the sejm, since they were already giving gifts to sejm deputies from the Grand Duchy of Lithuania.[24]

The institutions of Jewish self-government followed sessions of the sejm of the Polish–Lithuanian Commonwealth and their resolutions with particular attention. The awareness that to a great extent the circumstances of the Jewish population depended on what they decided was reflected in the formula added to the notes on forthcoming meetings of the sejm in the *pinkas* of the Council of Lithuania: 'May this be for the good of all Israel!'

The sejm set the level of poll tax to be paid by Jews, and the council's major anxiety was that it would be raised. Several notes in the *pinkas* of the Council of Lithuania express the hope that a resolution on the Jewish poll tax would not be passed and that the current level of taxation would be maintained.[25] Rumours of plans to raise the poll tax were sedulously noted.[26]

To a great extent the meetings of the sejm determined when the Council of Four Lands and the Council of Lithuania convened. Because of the need to set and collect the poll tax, the dates of the sessions of the Council of Lithuania were established after the sejm had met, by which stage the amount of the lump sum was known. In 1628 the Council of Lithuania decided that, like the sejm, its sessions would be held every two years.[27] This pattern was followed between 1637 and 1661. However, later, between 1664 and 1691, a practice was established of holding sessions every three years, which was probably associated with the widely accepted three-year economic cycle, as evinced in the prevalence of three-year leases. From the end of the seventeenth century the Council of Lithuania met less regularly. A similar phenomenon can also be observed with the Council of Four Lands.[28] This is often explained in the historiography as a result of the crisis in Jewish self-government in the eighteenth century,[29] but it is more likely that the decisive cause was the introduction by the Silent Sejm of 1717 of a fixed rate for the Jewish poll tax.

The Council of Four Lands and the Council of Lithuania met after the sejm and, as Jacob Goldberg argues, played the same role from the fiscal point of view as the *sejmiki*.[30] This led to meetings of the councils being postponed if the sejm did not meet. In 1694, when the sejm called for the end of the previous year did not meet because of the illness of King Jan III Sobieski, the king allowed the meeting of the Council of Four Lands to be postponed. In his words, this was 'in spite of the fact that, according to their customs, the Jews of Poland hold their national assembly every two years during the fair in Jarosław'. He also ordered that the rate of Jewish poll tax adopted at the previous council should stand.[31]

Sometimes the activities of the Council of Four Lands and the Council of Lithuania were linked with sessions of the sejm for other reasons. In 1664 the minutes of the Council of Lithuania noted that two individuals, contrary to instructions and without the agreement of the principal communities, had attempted to obtain the lease of the Lithuanian customs. However, it was noted that 'for hidden reasons' the case against them had been postponed until the end of the sejm taking place in Warsaw.[32] It is probable that there was no desire to publicize Jewish leasing of state revenues—to which the nobility had long objected—while the sejm was in session.

Advocates of the Council of Four Lands and the Council of Lithuania regularly attended meetings of the sejm in Warsaw and Grodno, where they were responsible for defending the interests of all Jews, which often required extensive travel.[33] Such an advocate might also deal with matters affecting local communities. Thus the contract drawn up in 1761 at the hiring of Hayim ben Joseph as advocate for the Council of Lithuania makes it clear that every community, including the principal ones, that used his services for its own needs was obliged to remunerate him.[34]

As was the case with those employed by *kahals*, an advocate employed by the Council of Four Lands or the Council of Lithuania was expected to possess linguistic and oratorical skills, and especially to have contacts among the great landowners and the most important officials of the commonwealth. Efforts were made to appoint people who had the right to reside at the royal court or at the mansions of nobles, because they worked there as agents, suppliers, or bankers. A great many advocates, as well as elders, scribes, and treasurers of the Council of Four Lands, were royal servitors.[35] Being a royal servitor conferred a special status: inclusion in the circle of officials who were subject only to the royal judiciary and therefore exempt from the jurisdiction of other courts and from some taxes and fees. It also conferred the right to reside at the royal court[36] and, in the case of landowners' agents, in their mansions.

Candidates for the position of council advocate tried to gain the protection of the king or of a landowner. As Jacob Goldberg notes, in the eighteenth century Jewish leaders living on private estates and supported by 'their' landowners played a growing role in the Council of Four Lands. Hieronim Florian Radziwiłł, the owner of the town of Slutsk (Słuck), in a 1755 letter to his brother Michał Kazimierz, voivode of Vilna and Grand Hetman of Lithuania, asked a favour for 'his' Jew, Zelig, who was applying for the post of advocate of the Council of Lithuania. He also recommended the rejection of another candidate, a Brześć Jew, Israel, who had 'impudently' failed to seek his patronage.[37] Such connections with the royal court and great landowners gave advocates and other representatives of the Jewish councils the ability to function effectively during the sejm.

In addition to advocates, the elders, scribes, treasurers, and specially elected delegates of the Council of Four Lands attended meetings of the sejm. Like advocates, scribes and treasurers received regular salaries and, in the event of having to travel, additional stipends and payment of their expenses. The Council of Lithuania also imposed on each principal community the obligation to send one delegate to the sejm, and the regulations most frequently refer to such leaders.[38] Their expenses and salary were paid from funds provided by the council. In 1632 permission was also granted to the Mińsk community to send its own representative, although only half of his expenses would be covered by the council.[39] It was emphasized that these representatives were to arrive punctually for the start of the sejm.[40] There was a reminder in 1670 that two community leaders had to be present at each session of the sejm, and that the leader of the Brest community should always be present at the opening session of the sejm.[41] Delegates sometimes experienced problems reaching sessions of the sejm as, for instance, in 1720, when representatives of the Council of Four Lands did not make it to Warsaw on account of the plague.[42]

The Council of Lithuania expressly forbade individuals who had not received written permission from the principal communities to attend the sejm. A subsequent resolution required the appropriate papers to be shown to the Jewish leaders attending the sejm in Warsaw. Those who defied this resolution were threatened with severe punishment, and community leaders were instructed to use all means to prevent them going. A warning was given that, in the event of any problems, such individuals could not count on any assistance, and they were also to be informed of this by the council's advocates in Warsaw.[43] However, in 1661 it was noted that this ban was being widely ignored, and that many individuals were attending the sejm on their own initiative, which had led to considerable conflict. As a result, the ban was reiterated and the principal communities were to announce it in their synagogues thirty days before a sejm was to meet. Those who disobeyed were threatened with excommunication.[44]

During sessions of the sejm, Jewish leaders from Poland and Lithuania had the opportunity to meet each other. The presence of representatives of the Council of Four Lands and of the Council of Lithuania at such sessions meant that they could confer and take decisions on matters other than those related to contacts with the non-Jewish authorities. A note in the *pinkas* of the Council of Lithuania for 1676 describes a decision on merchants travelling from Lithuania to Poland which was taken jointly by leaders of Jewish communities from Poland and Lithuania during their stay in Kraków, thus documenting their presence at the Coronation Sejm in Kraków between 2 February and 13 March 1676.[45] Other matters were also settled on these occasions. A 1662 decree by the Council of Four Lands dealing with a dispute between the elders of Kazimierz and Mendel from Poznań noted that the two sides had reached an agreement 'during the last sejm in Warsaw'.[46] Contact was also possible when they were returning from a meeting of the sejm.[47]

Jewish delegates at the sejm also undertook to intercede on behalf of the Jews. They included efforts to block resolutions that were hostile to Jews, above all those increasing the poll tax or introducing additional burdens, and adding favourable clauses to resolutions. As in the case of the *sejmiki*, this was often linked to thwarting efforts by the representatives of the towns, who, like the Jewish delegates, settled all manner of business in the corridors, and tried to influence the wording of the resolutions of the sejm.

These actions by Jewish representatives often led to accusations of disrupting the sejm.[48] In 1744 instructions from the *sejmik* of the land of Liw to deputies to the sejm called attention to the fact that the very large number of Jews in the commonwealth 'have their own parliaments and destroy ours'.[49] In 1750 the French and Prussian envoys, aiming to halt the session, suggested to Stanisław Wincenty Jabłonowski, voivode of Rawa, that he should warn the representatives of the Council of Four Lands of alleged plans to raise Jewish taxes. It is not clear, however, how effective this was.[50]

Jewish representatives also attended sejms at which the monarch was crowned (coronation sejms). There they would try to obtain privileges for Jews or to secure the ratification of those that had been granted by previous rulers. They were concerned with all types of privilege—general, provincial, and local. The ratification of the privileges of the Jews of Lithuania by Jan Kazimierz three days after the end of the Coronation Sejm in Warsaw on 17 February 1649 alluded to previous such confirmations at their coronation sejms by Zygmunt III, on 1 February 1588, and Władysław IV, on 15 February 1633. The document issued by Zygmunt III in 1588 contains the information that Jews from Brześć, Troki, Grodno, and Pińsk, and other towns belonging to the king, nobles, and the church, made a humble request to the monarch to ratify their privileges, both general and local, demonstrating co-operation not only between different Jewish communities but also between Jews and Karaites.[51]

Individual communities also attempted to have their privileges ratified during coronation sejms.[52] Monarchs confirmed privileges during ordinary and, more rarely, extraordinary sessions of the sejm and shortly afterwards.[53] Jacob Goldberg's collection of Jewish privileges includes the texts of those privileges that have survived. There were undoubtedly many more communities who sought to have their privileges confirmed, but the documents are lost. Confirmation of the privileges of local communities was also sometimes recorded in the resolutions of the sejm.[54]

It is hard to assess the effectiveness of Jewish delegates at sessions of the sejm, especially since their instructions were usually expressed in rather general terms, such as to take action on behalf of all Jews, and attempts to forestall unfavourable resolutions, for example, could have failed for a variety of reasons. Sometimes positive results can be perceived. Thus in 1651 it was noted in the *pinkas* of the Council of Lithuania that, during the previous sejm in Warsaw, its leaders had made strenuous efforts to ensure that the hearth tax, introduced two years earlier and meant to be paid by each individual Jew, could be paid as a lump sum.[55] These efforts were clearly successful, since, in the resolutions of the extraordinary session of the Sejm of 1652 in Warsaw, the hearth tax on the Jews of Lithuania is expressed as a lump sum (20,000 zlotys).[56] The next sejm, in 1653, also expressed the obligations under this tax as a lump sum.[57] In 1655 the Council of Lithuania advised its advocates to make efforts to use the help of non-Jews in collecting taxes from Jews. Interestingly, a clause was sought in the resolution on this tax that each great landowner and administrator was to help collecting taxes, including arrears, from communities, in line with the decisions of their principal community.[58] A clause was added to one of the resolutions of the Extraordinary Sejm of 1655 that in the Grand Duchy of Lithuania, the collection of the Jewish poll tax was to be enforced 'on all those reluctant to pay by all offices'.[59]

The presence and activities of Jewish delegates at the sejm involved very large expenditures. Senators and members of the sejm heading for a session were given gifts (we can speculate on the extent to which this constituted their main source of income). The Council of Lithuania recognized that the gifts given to the great landowners as they passed through the principal communities on their way to the sejm were a common expense to be borne by the entire country. It was stipulated, however, that this referred only to gifts to nobles accompanying the king, whose help would be necessary in advancing the interests of Lithuanian Jews.[60] The intercession of such people was necessary to obtain favourable decisions from the monarch. Royal proclamations often contained the information that they had been issued at the request of Jews assisted by 'distinguished members of the council and officials at Our side'.[61]

Sebastian Śleszkowski (*c.*1576–1648), known for his anti-Jewish polemics, described the arrival in Warsaw of Jewish delegates from various towns in Poland a week or two before a sejm. These delegates did nothing before the beginning of the session apart from 'rolling up various roots in tubes' (packaging spices in paper cones), which they later distributed to the senators and members of the sejm arriving in Warsaw, 'greeting them and congratulating them on their happy arrival'. The writer warns his readers of the fatal consequences of accepting such gifts which, with the help of spells and curses, were meant to bewitch Christians.[62] In spite of its anti-Jewish character, the accuracy of this description of handing out gifts at the start of a sejm and thereby obtaining goodwill seems beyond doubt.

The king and members of the royal family were also honoured. During the king's passage through the country to Grodno for the sejm, he was greeted and showered with gifts in the towns through which he passed.[63] The Council of Lithuania divided up the expenses incurred. In the case of the three principal local communities

(Brześć, Grodno, and Pińsk), all expenses were to be covered from the council's general fund, or, if this was not done, half from the general fund and half from the resources of the specific community.[64] In 1647 it was specified that this referred only to presents for the king and queen, stipulating that the council was not responsible for gifts to nobles or their servants.[65]

Like the expenses incurred during *sejmiki*, the outgoings during sejms were enormous. In the accounts of the Council of Four Lands drawn up in 1739, it was recorded that 50,874 zlotys had been spent.[66] Such outgoings were seen as communal and to be covered from the funds of the council. This required the accumulation of considerable sums in cash. The Council of Lithuania ordered that a portion of the land tax collected by Jews be sent to the town where the sejm was being held. In 1647 it was decided that thirty days before a session of the sejm each district should send its principal community a specified amount of its tax revenues and that the community would send this, together with its own contribution, so that the sum would be available on the first day of the session. Districts that did not send their money on time were threatened with a loan to be taken out to cover the sum, and with being liable for both the principal and the interest accrued.[67] Three years later yet another means of raising funds was agreed on: Jewish leaders arriving in Warsaw were authorized to seize the assets of individuals from local communities that were in arrears. Such communities were obliged to refund these individuals' losses with interest.[68] The community leaders were to note down those places that had not sent money, and the *dayanim* (rabbinical judges) at the fairs of Kopyl and Stołowicze, which were held after the sejm met, were to curse the leaders of such *kahal*s. They were also to requisition their assets to cover the expenses and damages incurred.[69] The resolutions of the Council of Lithuania reveal a continual increase in expenditure, the result both of inflation and of the rising costs incurred by Jewish delegates at the sejm.

Delegates to the sejm received money to cover their living expenses. In 1679 the Council of Lithuania decided that each delegate, whether at the sejm in Warsaw or in Grodno, was to receive 20 zlotys, as well as travel expenses. It was forbidden to request additional expenses for a cook or servant.[70] Other sums were specified in a subsequent resolution by the council in the same year: leaders of the four principal local communities attending a sejm in Warsaw or in Grodno were to receive 50 zlotys for their efforts and 30 kopa of Lithuanian grosz for expenses during the sejm.[71]

The Council of Lithuania ordered delegates to Warsaw to meet and settle their expenses before their departure. An expense that had not been documented as having been incurred in Warsaw would not be eligible for subsequent reimbursement from communal funds.[72] A regulation dating from 1661 calls for noting expenses in 'the Warsaw *pinkas*',[73] suggesting that a special ledger existed for this purpose.

The division of expenses incurred during a sejm was often the subject of dispute between the Council of Four Lands and the Council of Lithuania. In 1633 a court of the Council of Four Lands in Lublin decided that Polish Jews were to give gifts to members of the sejm from Polish lands, and Lithuanian Jews to those from the territory of the Grand Duchy of Lithuania. Jews from Lithuania were to bear one-seventh of the expenses for 'violence in Warsaw', which seems to have meant the costs of ensuring the safety of Jews travelling to Warsaw for the sejm.[74] This judgement did not put an end to disputes. In 1670 the financial claims of the two councils for expenses incurred in attending the sejm were again the subject of a court case. The judgement noted that the claims related to large expenditures incurred by leaders of Jewish communities from Poland during a coronation sejm in Kraków and they were intended to counteract the efforts of 'a certain bad individual' who sought to expel all the Jews from the country. The leaders of Jewish communities in Lithuania in turn claimed that they themselves had incurred considerable expenses in connection with the same matter. The judgement ordered the Council of Lithuania to pay the Council of Four Lands the sum of 2,500 zlotys, which was meant to satisfy both parties. It was also stipulated that if in future the Jews faced the threat of expulsion and if expenditure was required to prevent it, then the Council of Lithuania was not obliged to render the Council of Four Lands assistance until 6,000 zlotys had been spent. If the sum involved rose to 15,000 zlotys the matter would be adjudicated by Polish and Lithuanian rabbis.[75]

In 1678 Łęczna was the site of yet another court case regarding expenses incurred by the Council of Four Lands in blocking a rise in the poll tax during a coronation sejm and a sejm in Warsaw. The leaders of Jewish communities in Lithuania were warned that if they did not attend, a judgement would be issued *in absentia* and the assets of individual Lithuanian Jews, currently in Poland, would be seized.[76]

Three years later, in 1681, a court of Polish and Lithuanian rabbis again gathered in Łęczna to take up the same issue. The Polish Jews' claims revolved around expenses incurred during sejms in Warsaw, including payments to the advocate of the Council of Four Lands and gifts for the king and nobles. The Lithuanian Jews argued that the sejm also met in Grodno and that they had incurred expenses there. The judgement gave the Council of Four Lands two options: demand from the Council of Lithuania either one-fourteenth of all expenses or a lump sum of 9,000 zlotys. It was decided that henceforth at each sejm the two sides were to bear all the costs separately: the Jews of Poland for presents for the king and the great Polish landowners and the Lithuanian Jews for presents for the king and the great Lithuanian landowners. This principle of dividing costs was to be followed even in times of great danger, such as when there was a threat of expulsion. It was stipulated that it was possible to render each other assistance, but only by interceding with 'one's own' dignitaries: in other words, that Polish Jews should intercede with Polish dignitaries on behalf of Lithuanian Jews and vice versa.[77]

After the dissolution of the Council of Four Lands and the Council of Lithuania in 1764, Jewish intercession took a new form with the establishment of Jewish plenipotentiaries during the Four Year Sejm (1788–92), when one of the subjects of debate was a reform of the status of Jews in the commonwealth. As Jacob Goldberg points out, these plenipotentiaries differed greatly from advocates, who acted on their own or in small groups, interceding in an ad hoc manner on behalf of all Jews, specific communities, or individuals. Plenipotentiaries were, by contrast, a large group of around 120 with instructions from their local communities.[78] From among them a group of fifteen was chosen, who were to stay in direct touch with the king and his secretary, Scipione Piattoli, who dealt with issues of reform. The same criteria operated as when hiring advocates: they were meant to be men of intelligence, who knew Polish and who understood the political situation, allowing them to operate at the royal court. Plenipotentiaries dealt with the most important issues affecting the whole Jewish community—they drew up and presented to the authorities and parliamentary committees memoranda on matters such as Jewish economic activity and the judicial machinery affecting Jews. Their efforts certainly had an impact on the deliberations of the sejm.[79]

Jewish activities at sessions of the sejm and *sejmiki* were a very visible element of political life at the time. This was reflected in the work of many Polish writers, especially those expressing hostility to Jews. Such writers emphasized Jewish solidarity and their widespread corruption of the nobility, often exaggerating Jewish influence and power. For example, Szymon Starowolski (1588–1656) wrote: 'Who receives the most support for his affairs at *sejmiki* and sejms? The Jew.'[80]

Those who supported Jewish activities, especially if they accepted money and gifts, were also subject to criticism. Jan Stanisław Jabłonowski (1669–1731) quotes the proverb: 'He who speaks for the Jews has already been bribed, and he who speaks against them wants to be bribed.'[81] However, Jędrzej Kitowicz (1728–1804), writing about efforts to expel the Jews from Warsaw, remarked that in particular the Ruthenian and Lithuanian members of the sejm took the side of the Jews:

It is no easy task to expel the Jews from places to which they have taken a liking, especially when they have as many defenders as persecutors. As often as the Estates gather in parliamentary sessions to chase the Jews out of Warsaw, so do the Ruthenian and Lithuanian members, brought up among the Jews, knowing no other citizens in their towns apart from Jews, brought up to obtain their goods and all their other requirements from Jews, and even fed from their schooldays on Jewish plum-cakes and bagels, served Jewish spirits, some even indulging in unworthy friendships with and related to Jewish girls, even those who in Warsaw sell their bodies; others under the influence of gifts from the Israelites—support the Jews wholeheartedly.[82]

It should be emphasized that seeking to obtain goodwill by means of 'presents' was a widespread practice in the Polish–Lithuanian Commonwealth, and not only employed by Jews. What today would be seen as corruption was accepted according to the standards of a time in which the dividing line between the public and private spheres was fluid. An informal system of connections, the client system, was based on the reciprocal exchange of both tangible and intangible benefits. The Jews' activities within the framework of the client system, involving above all the nobility, and to some extent the clergy, is a subject which requires further study.

In summary, an analysis of Jewish sources reveals that the Jewish presence and activities at *sejmiki* and sejms were neither accidental nor transitory. They constituted a permanent element of the activities of the organizations of Jewish self-government, at both the local and the central level, regulated by a series of ordinances. Income sources were also established for them, and expenditure—depending on the importance of the issue—was met from the funds of the Council of Four Lands and the Council of Lithuania. The rhythm of meetings of *sejmiki* and sejms to a great extent shaped the rhythm of the operation of Jewish organizations, above all the national councils. Sejms were also a time when Jewish representatives from the various regions of the commonwealth could meet, providing an opportunity for joint discussion and settling disputes and claims.

This subject requires further study. In order fully to understand the activities undertaken by the Jews, the strategies employed, the correlation of forces, and the specific situation at each sejm and *sejmik*, and to recreate the network of connections between Jewish representatives and non-Jewish politicians, it is essential to investigate the non-Jewish sources, above all the minutes of the sejms and *sejmiki* and the correspondence of the nobility. Such a study, given the vast range of the sources and the extended period which needs to be investigated, presents the researcher with a considerable challenge.

Translated from the Polish by Jarosław Garliński

Notes

1 See *Sejmy i sejmiki koronne wobec Żydów: Wybór tekstów źródłowych*, ed. A. Michałowska-Mycielska (Warsaw, 2006); A. Kaźmierczyk, *Sejmy i sejmiki szlacheckie wobec Żydów w drugiej połowie XVII wieku* (Warsaw, 1994).

2 For the attitudes of the nobility to Jewish leaseholding, see J. Kalik, 'Szlachta Attitudes towards Jewish Arenda in the Seventeenth and Eighteenth Centuries', *Gal-ed*, 14 (1995), 15–25.

3 See J. Kalik, 'Christian Servants Employed by Jews in the Polish–Lithuanian Commonwealth in the Seventeenth and Eighteenth Centuries', *Polin*, 14 (2001), 259–70; A. Kaźmierczyk, 'The Problem of Christian Servants as Reflected in the Legal Codes of the Polish–Lithuanian Commonwealth during the Second Half of the Seventeenth Century and in the Saxon Period', *Gal-ed*, 15–16 (1997), 23–40; J. Krupa, 'Sejmiki Rzeczypospolitej szlacheckiej za panowania Augusta II wobec problemów zatrudniania przez Żydów czeladzi chrześcijańskiej (1697–1733)', *Studia Judaica* (Kraków), 2 (1999), 11–23.

4 For ecclesiastical legislation affecting Jews, see J. Kalik, 'Jews in Catholic Ecclesiastical Legislation in the Polish–Lithuanian Commonwealth', *Kwartalnik Historii Żydów*, 209 (2004), 26–39.

5 See A. Kaźmierczyk, 'Problem ekspulsji Żydów w uchwałach sejmikowych w 2. połowie XVII wieku', in K. Matwijowski (ed.), *Z historii ludności żydowskiej w Polsce i na Śląsku* (Wrocław, 1994), 63–70.

6 The Silent Sejm of 1717 did indeed reduce the power of the *sejmiki*, but, because of the weakness of the central government, this was never implemented. The real reduction of the powers of the *sejmiki* began only in the reign of Stanisław August Poniatowski. See A. B. Zakrzewski, *Sejmiki Wielkiego Księstwa Litewskiego XVI–XVIII w. Ustrój i funkcjonowanie: Sejmik trocki* (Warsaw, 2000), 209.

7 A drawing by Jan Piotr Norblin, entitled 'Sejmik w małym miasteczku' ('Sejmik in a Small Town') currently in the Kórnik Library of the Polish Academy of Sciences (MK 3380),

shows Jewish interest in the debates at a *sejmik*. It depicts four Jews sitting on a roof gazing at the assembled nobility. See also A. Kępińska, *Sejmiki w rysunkach J. P. Norblina* (Warsaw, 1958), ills. IV, XXXII.

8 On the activity of the representatives of the city of Lwów (Lviv) at sejms and *sejmiki*, see J. Goldberg, 'Posłowie miasta Lwowa na sejmy wobec Żydów lwowskich w XVII–XVIII wieku', in id., *Żydzi w społeczeństwie, gospodarce i kulturze Rzeczypospolitej szlacheckiej* (Kraków, 2012), 47–57. Goldberg writes that representatives from Lwów were active both in the local *sejmik* and the general *sejmik* at Sądowa Wisznia. They attempted to obtain decisions favourable to the citizens of Lwów, above all in cases of conflict with Jews over economic matters. In 1696 such regulations were also embodied in resolutions of the general *sejmik* (despite the efforts of advocates from the local Jewish community, who were present in Sądowa Wisznia); however, they were not passed by the sejm thanks to effective action on the part of representatives of the Council of Four Lands and the Council of Lithuania.

9 *Pinkas hamedinah, o pinkas va'ad hakehilot harashiyot bimedinat lita*, ed. S. Dubnow (Berlin, 1925), no. 147 (1628).

10 Ibid., no. 10 (1623).

11 For a discussion of the office of advocate based on printed *pinkasim* from the Poznań Jewish community and the *pinkasim* of the Polish and Lithuanian councils, see S. Ury, 'The *Shtadlan* of the Polish–Lithuanian Commonwealth: Noble Advocate or Unbridled Opportunist?', *Polin*, 15 (2002), 267–99; on advocates in the Jewish community, see A. Michałowska-Mycielska, *The Jewish Community: Authority and Social Control in Poznań and Swarzędz, 1650–1793*, trans. A. Adamowicz (Wrocław, 2008), 54–5.

12 Ury, 'The *Shtadlan* of the Polish–Lithuanian Commonwealth', 272. Ury quotes two contracts: one with Nisan, son of Judah, of the Council of Four Lands from 1730 and one with Hayim, son of Joseph, of the Council of Lithuania from 1761 (Ury dates it incorrectly to 1781).

13 *Pinkas va'ad arba aratsot: likutei takanot ketavim ureshumot*, ed. I. Halperin (Jerusalem, 1945); 2nd revd. edn., ed. I. Bartal (Jerusalem 1990), no. 519 (1699). The ordinary sejm sat in Warsaw between 16 June and 30 July 1699. Dates of sejms are from W. Konopczyński, *Chronologia sejmów polskich 1493–1793* (Kraków, 1948).

14 A. Leszczyński, 'Ekspensy kahału opatowskiego na sejmiki szlacheckie województwa sandomierskiego w 1752 r.', *Czasopismo Prawno-Historyczne*, 38 (1986), 193–5.

15 Ibid. 195.

16 I. Lewin, 'Udział Żydów w wyborach sejmowych w dawnej Polsce', in id., *Z historii i tradycji: Szkice z dziejów kultury żydowskiej* (Warsaw, 1983), 44–5.

17 *Akty izdavaemye Vilenskoyu arkheograficheskoyu komissieyu dlya razbora drevnikh aktov* v: *Akty Brestskogo i Gorodnyanskogo gorodskikh sudov)* (Vilna, 1871), no. 462.

18 *Pinkas hamedinah*, no. 10 (1623).

19 Ibid., no. 111 (1627).

20 Ibid., no. 296 (1634); repeated in 1639 (ibid., no. 369).

21 Ibid., no. 654 (1670). The precept that each principal community was owed 150 zlotys for each *sejmik* was restated in 1761. This was connected to the requests of the Vilna community, which was demanding a refund of the expenses that it had incurred at the *sejmik* of the Starodub, Smoleńsk, and Vilna *powiats*, which was held in Vilna (I. Halpern (ed.), 'Tosafot umiluim lepinkas medinat lita', *Ḥorev*, 2 (1934–5), 67–86, 123–200: no. 92 (1761).

22 *Pinkas hamedinah*, no. 691 (1673).

23 *Pinkas va'ad arba aratsot*, no. 153 (1627).

24 *Pinkas hamedinah*, supplement 1, no. 1 (1623). Dubnow amends this date to 1633, which appears to be incorrect; see A. Michałowska-Mycielska, *Sejm Żydów litewskich (1623–1764)* (Warsaw, 2014), 34 n. 28.

25 e.g. *Pinkas hamedinah*, nos. 108 (1626), 253 (1631). The Council of Lithuania hoped that the poll tax would not be raised, which would allow taxes to be collected to pay off the council's debts.

26 Ibid., no. 504 (1655).

27 Ibid., no. 192 (1628).

28 J. Goldberg and A. Kaźmierczyk, 'Introduction', in *Sejm Czterech Ziem: Źródła*, ed. J. Goldberg and A. Kaźmierczyk (Warsaw, 2011), 23–43: 33.

29 In the historiography—for instance, the works of Majer Bałaban or Simon Dubnow—the view is expressed that there was a crisis in Jewish autonomy caused by wartime destruction in the middle of the seventeenth century and the beginning of the eighteenth. This theory is undermined by Mordechai Nadav who describes the 'normal' operation of local and district organizations in Podlasie (M. Nadav, 'Iyun behitraḥashuyot beshalosh kehilot bepolin-lita biymei milḥemet hatsafon ule'aḥareiha (beshalish harishon shel hame'ah ha-18)', in *Proceedings of the Eighth World Congress of Jewish Studies, Jerusalem, August 16–21, 1981*, Division B: *The History of the Jewish People* (Jerusalem 1982), 89–96 (Heb. section); id., 'Kahał tykociński a osadnictwo żydowskie na wsi w XVII i XVIII wieku', *Studia Podlaskie*, 2 (1989), 39–47: 40–1).

30 Goldberg and Kaźmierczyk, 'Introduction', 33.

31 *Sejm Czterech Ziem*, 95–6.

32 *Pinkas hamedinah*, no. 585 (1664).

33 On the mobility of advocates, see J. Goldberg, 'Żydzi polscy na gościńcach krajowych i obcych w XVII–XVIII wieku', in id., *Żydzi w społeczeństwie, gospodarce i kulturze Rzeczypospolitej szlacheckiej*, 77–92: 78.

34 *Pinkas hamedinah*, supplement 2, no. 6 (1761).

35 A safe-conduct issued in 1646 to Marek, the advocate-general of the Council of Four Lands, who was also a royal factor of King Władysław IV, affirmed that his wife and sons were not to be harmed by the townspeople and were to be allowed to reside peacefully at their inn in Warsaw (*Sejm Czterech Ziem*, 69). In turn, in a decree of Władysław IV forbidding Jews to reside or trade in Warsaw, it was made clear that this did not apply to 'Markus Nekel' (the Marek mentioned above) (Archiwum Główne Akt Dawnych, Warsaw, Zbiór dokumentów pergaminowych, 1651: Władysław IV, decree regarding the residence of Jews in Warsaw, 1 Feb. 1648). Likewise, in 1760 August III included Pejsak Chaimowicz of Opatów among the royal agents and named him as an advocate (M. Horn, *Regesty dokumentów i ekscerpty z Metryki Koronnej do historii Żydów w Polsce 1697–1795*, 2 vols. (Wrocław 1984), i. 17 (no. 92)). Holding two positions was clearly quite common.

36 A debenture bond issued by the elders of the Council of Four Lands at the Jarosław Fair in 1666 mentions 'Moses Markowicz, advocate of the Jews of the council in residence at His Majesty's Court' (*Sejm Czterech Ziem*, 190). Jan III Sobieski, when including Fiszel Lewkowicz, the scribe of the Council of Four Lands, in the retinue of royal servitors, guaranteed that he would be 'free to reside permanently at Our Court and wherever We should be, as well as to live wherever he pleases' (*Sejm Czterech Ziem*, 98).

37 Archiwum Główne Akt Dawnych, Archiwum Radziwiłłów IV, koperta 144, str. 22: Hieronim Florian Radziwiłł, letter to his brother, Michał Kazimierz Radziwiłł, Nov. 1755.

38 *Pinkas hamedinah*, nos. 269 (1632), 688 (1673), 761 (1679).

39 Ibid., no. 269 (1632).

40 The sejm minutes show that noble senators and members often arrived late for sessions, hoping in this way to reduce costs. It can be assumed that Jewish representatives may well have delayed their arrival on similar grounds.

41 *Pinkas hamedinah*, no. 636 (1670).

42 *Sejm Czterech Ziem*, 227.

43 *Pinkas hamedinah*, no. 39 (1623).

44 Ibid., no. 534 (1661).

45 Ibid., no. 731 (1676).

46 *Sejm Czterech Ziem*, 186. The sejm was held in Warsaw in 1661.

47 In the 1720 agreement between the elders of the Chełm and Bełz districts and the elders of the Zamoyski Entail, the possibility was mooted of turning to arbitration by the Jewish elders of Poland who were returning from the sejm in Warsaw (*Sejm Czterech Ziem*, 224).

48 A sejm could be halted by the *liberum veto*. The opposition of a single member nullified all legislation passed, thus causing the sejm to be abandoned without passing any resolutions. This was a frequent occurrence in the eighteenth century.

49 *Sejmy i sejmiki koronne wobec Żydów*, 359. An article by Ludwik Glatman is devoted to this question. However, its clearly antisemitic character and use of unattributed and thus hard-to-verify material make it difficult to take it seriously as an academic text (see L. Glatman, 'Jak żydzi zrywali Sejmy. Szkic historyczny z XVIII wieku', in id., *Szkice historyczne* (Kraków, 1906), 103–17).

50 Goldberg and Kaźmierczyk, 'Introduction', 36; Z. Zielińska, *Walka 'Familii' o reformę Rzeczypospolitej 1743–1752* (Warsaw, 1983), 309.

51 *Akty izdavaemye Vilenskoyu arkheograficheskoyu komissieyu*, v, no. 71; *Jewish Privileges in the Polish Commonwealth: Charters of Rights Granted to Jewish Communities in Poland–Lithuania in the Sixteenth to Eighteenth Centuries*, ed. J. Goldberg, 3 vols. (Jerusalem, 1985–2001), i. 352.

52 The communities of Kalisz, Lelów, Poznań, Przemyśl, Szydłów, Wronki, Fordon, Kołomyja, and Kozienice had their privileges ratified by Władysław IV in 1633; Przemyśl, Pyzdry, and Warta had theirs ratified by Jan Kazimierz in 1649; Chęciny, Kalisz, Kałusz, Lelów, Poznań, and Kołomyja by Michał Korybut Wiśniowiecki in 1669; and Łęczyca and Poznań by Jan Sobieski in 1676. Other communities had their privileges ratified shortly after a coronation sejm: Rohatyn by Władysław IV; Kalisz, Lelów, and Sokal by Jan Kazimierz; Będzin, Lublin, Przedbórz, Przemyśl, and Rohatyn by Michał Korybut Wiśniowiecki; Chęciny, Kałusz, Lwów, Płock, Sokal, and Szydłów by Jan Sobieski; and Poznań by August III in 1697 (*Jewish Privileges in the Polish Commonwealth*).

53 The privileges of Wronki (1528), Ratno (1557, 1578, 1589, 1661, 1791–2), Poznań (1559, 1564, 1661), Międzybóż (1567), Kowal (1569), Pyzdry (1576), Kołomyja (1576), Przemyśl (1578, 1638), Kamionka (1589), Stobnica (1589), Dębno (1593), Kowel (1611, 1635, 1679, 1699, 1791–2), Leżajsk (1635), Wojnia (Wohyń) (1643, 1683), Stryj (1650, 1677), Połaniec (1652), Krzyczew (1667), Inowrocław (1681), Frydlandek (1766), and Łuków (1791–2) were confirmed during ordinary sessions of the sejm. The privileges of Poznań (1576), Kowal (1578), Warta (1641), Łuków (1659), Lwów (1670), Nowy Korczyn (1670), Wyłkowyszki (1679), Łuków (1699), Chęciny (1720), Inowrocław (1722), and Szydłów (1722) were confirmed shortly after the meeting of the sejm. Privileges were more rarely confirmed during extraordinary sessions of the sejm (Przedbórz (1634), Lwów, Sandomierz (1658), Wojnia (1670), Warta (1673), Nowy Korczyn (1736), and Kozienice (1767)), or shortly after their end (Szydłów (1672), Lublin (1736)) (*Jewish Privileges in the Polish Commonwealth*). The

confirmation of the privilege of the Warka community in 1673 is interesting, because the Sejm of 1673 was a continuation of an assembly called by the Gołąb Confederation and was not preceded by a proclamation and meetings of the *sejmiki*. This shows that efforts to advance Jewish interests were made even in atypical situations and the Jews paid constant attention to the political situation in the commonwealth.

54 Ratification of the privileges of the Jews of Parcz, issued in the royal chancellery, was noted in the resolutions of the Sejm of 1678/9 in Grodno (*Sejmy i sejmiki koronne wobec Żydów*, no. CXVI). At the same sejm, the rights of the Jews of Mohylew to reside in Mohylew itself were ratified and made permanent. It was confirmed too that the Jews of Mohylew had recently contributed greatly to the upkeep of the fortress (*Sejmy i sejmiki koronne wobec Żydów*, no. CXVII). The rights of the city of Przemyśl were noted in the resolutions of the Ordinary Sejm of 1667 in Warsaw, including 'preserving the Jews their rights' (*Sejmy i sejmiki koronne wobec Żydów*, no. CII).

55 *Pinkas hamedinah*, no. 487 (1651).

56 *Sejmy i sejmiki koronne wobec Żydów*, no. XC.

57 Ibid., no. XCI

58 *Pinkas hamedinah*, no. 518 (1655).

59 *Sejmy i sejmiki koronne wobec Żydów*, no. XCIV

60 *Pinkas hamedinah*, no. 162 (1628).

61 In the ratification of the privileges of the Jews of Kraków issued by King Zygmunt August on 4 January 1557, during the sejm in Warsaw, it stated that the issue was presented to the king by some members of the royal council on behalf of the Jews of Kraków (*Sejmy i sejmiki koronne wobec Żydów*, no. XIX). In the ratification of privileges for Lithuanian Jews, issued by King August III on 28 November 1746, it was noted that it had been issued at the request of senators and officials residing alongside the king, interceding on behalf of the Jews of Vilna, Grodno, Brześć, Pińsk, and other Lithuanian towns (Central Archives for the History of the Jewish People, Jerusalem, PL 238: confirmation of the privilege for Lithuanian Jews issued by King August III, 28 Nov. 1746).

62 S. Śleszkowski, *Odkrycie zdrad, złośliwych ceremonii, tajemnych rad, praktyk szkodliwych Rzeczypospolitej i straszliwych zamysłów żydowskich* (Braniewo, 1621), fos. 54ᵛ–55.

63 Adam Stanisław Naruszewicz describes in his diary the gifts Jews presented to the king on his way to the Sejm of 1784. In Nieśwież there was a table decorated with various figures and a pyramid topped with a crown, coats of arms, and the king's initials; in Duboja, a great Toruń honey cake decorated with the king's intertwined initials in silver and gold made by Abraham Konstantynowski, a Białystok goldsmith, with an inscription on the bottom in Hebrew: 'Long live the King!' and the text of a speech of welcome on richly decorated parchment (A. S. Naruszewicz, *Dyjaryjusz podróży Jego Królewskiej Mości na sejm grodzieński*, ed. M. Bober-Jankowska (Warsaw, 2008), 64–5, 291). For the texts of such speeches welcoming the king in Polish, Hebrew, French, and English, see ibid. 284–5, 291–2, 294–5, 326–8, 33–3.

64 *Pinkas hamedinah*, no. 398 (1639).

65 Ibid., no. 437 (1647).

66 *Pinkas va'ad arba aratsot*, no. 640 (1739). As the editor, Israel Halpern, explains, it was proposed at the Sejm of 1738 in Warsaw that an additional tax of 450,000 zlotys, called a 'merchants' donation', be levied on the Jews. It can thus be surmised that the above expenditure was connected to efforts aimed at forestalling this proposal.

67 *Pinkas hamedinah*, no. 441 (1647). However, in 1649, everyone was reminded of the duty to collect three units of land tax for each day of the sejm. Thus, at the end of the first three

days of the Coronation Sejm in Kraków an instruction was given to collect nine units of land tax and an additional one (ibid., no. 455).

68 Ibid., no. 486 (1650).

69 Ibid., no. 543 (1661).

70 Ibid., no. 760 (1679).

71 Ibid., no. 761 (1679).

72 Ibid., no. 380 (1639).

73 Ibid., no. 551 (1661).

74 Ibid., supplement 1, no. 1 (1633).

75 Ibid., supplement 1, no. 5 (1670); *Pinkas va'ad arba aratsot* no. 277 (1670).

76 *Pinkas hamedinah*, supplement 1, no. 7 (1678); *Pinkas va'ad arba aratsot*, no. 368 (1678).

77 *Pinkas hamedinah*, supplement 1, no. 7 (1681).

78 On the plenipotentiaries' authority, see *Materiały do dziejów Sejmu Czteroletniego*, ed. A. Eisenbach et al., 6 vols. (Wrocław, 1955–69), vi. 376–8, 384–6.

79 See J. Goldberg, 'Pierwszy ruch polityczny wśród Żydów polskich: Plenipotenci żydowscy w dobie Sejmu Czteroletniego', in id., *Żydzi w społeczeństwie, gospodarce i kulturze Rzeczypospolitej szlacheckiej*, 19–34.

80 S. Starowolski, *Wady staropolskie: Przedruk dzieła Robak sumnienia złego, człowieka niebogobojnego i o zbawienie swoje niedbałego* (Kraków, 1853), 87.

81 [J. S. Jabłonowski], *Skrupuł bez skrupułu w Polsce, albo Oświecenie grzechów narodowi naszemu polskiemu zwyczajniejszych, a za grzechy nie mianych*, ed. J. Turowski (Kraków, 1858), 21.

82 J. Kitowicz, *Pamiętniki, czyli Historia polska*, ed. P. Matuszewska, 2nd edn. (Warsaw, 2005), 442.

Permanent Crisis

The Decline of Jewish Self-Government in Poland in the Seventeenth and Eighteenth Centuries

ADAM KAŹMIERCZYK

THIS CHAPTER seeks to show how Jewish self-government functioned during a period of profound crisis for the Polish–Lithuanian state and to demonstrate the ways in which political and structural conditions influenced its form and functions. Jews in the commonwealth constituted a unique confessional group with regard to their number and, above all, their religion, but the subject of this chapter is their obligations to the state as taxpayers. I analyse Jewish self-government in the light of the non-Jewish sources which highlight this issue. I will not examine the enormous significance of Jewish self-government for the religious and social life of Polish Jews, topics which are better represented in the Jewish sources.

Jewish autonomy, as it developed in the Polish–Lithuanian state, has been treated by some historians as a unique phenomenon both in the history of the Jews of Europe and within the commonwealth itself. This is particularly the case with the *va'adim*, or Jewish councils.[1] One of the fathers of the historiography of Polish Jews, Mojżesz Schorr, described the *va'adim* in elevated language as 'the highest form of autonomy—they were a legislative body and acted as such in relation to the state authorities, met regularly according to established norms and carried out charitable work.'[2] The demographic expansion of the Jewish population, and particularly its growing influence on the economy of the state, did indeed mean that Jewish self-government, compared with similar institutions of other ethnic or religious groups (Scots, Armenians, Italians), was far more developed and had a much greater influence not only on the lives of the Jews themselves but also on the financial position and general functioning of the state. Jewish self-government developed in response to the deficiencies of the republic's treasury administration, which was unable to collect taxes effectively; as a result of this, according to historians of the Polish fiscal system, a general tendency emerged at the end of the sixteenth and beginning of the seventeenth centuries to introduce a flat rate of tax based on the allocation to different groups of a fixed sum to be paid.[3] In the case of the Jews, who were more mobile than other taxpayers, a system of collection without the participation of the Jewish elders was simply unworkable.[4] From the end of the sixteenth century to 1764, when radical reforms were instituted, the system of Jewish self-government responded to political events and social and economic changes, but the changes in its functioning were closely bound up with the collection of the Jewish poll tax, the main task imposed on the Jewish elders by the state.

Until 1648 the Jewish communities of the main royal cities in each province of Poland—Kraków in Małopolska, Poznań in Wielkopolska, and Lwów in Red Ruthenia —exerted overwhelming influence on the structure of Jewish self-government. The elders of these cities, their governance extending throughout the province, decided on the level of taxation of the smaller towns and exercised judicial authority over their Jewish inhabitants. Their chief obligation towards the state was the administration of the Jewish poll tax which, despite its name, was replaced from the end of the sixteenth century with a fixed sum imposed on the whole Jewish community and which from the reign of Zygmunt III (r. 1587–1632) was generally farmed out for collection to the Jews themselves, either for a prearranged sum or by negotiation with the Crown treasurer.[5] Leasing the poll tax to the Jewish elders ensured punctual payment of the tax, which was designated, among other things, for the costs of the military, and relieved the administration of the cost of collecting it, since these costs were borne by the Jews themselves.[6]

The Khmelnytsky uprising in 1648 and subsequent wars with Russia, Sweden, and Turkey led to a permanent crisis in the Polish–Lithuanian state. Although the claims of enormous losses, both demographic and material, among the Jews have been shown, in the light of recent research, to be exaggerated,[7] there were nevertheless dramatic consequences for the functioning of Jewish self-government.

In the first decade after 1648 it became clear that the Jewish elders of the principal towns were unable to cope with the obligations imposed by the state. Precise data is lacking, but it seems that the main *kahals* bore the heaviest financial burden, since they were answerable for the arrears of the entire province. In addition, they were often faced with the refusal of smaller *kahals*, which were shielded by their noble owners or leaseholders, to fulfil their fiscal obligations. Given the difficulties of the times, this protection from taxation and the more favourable conditions offered to new settlers encouraged Jews (including the Jewish elite) to move to private towns. Jews from smaller localities, taking advantage of their noble patronage, refused to pay the taxes imposed by the elders of the main towns or the debts incurred for the needs of Jewry throughout the province. Towards the end of the 1650s King Jan Kazimierz (r. 1648–68), in response to a petition from the elders of the Council of Four Lands, issued a proclamation according to which protecting one's 'own' Jews from paying taxes was forbidden. According to the proclamation, this referred, above all, to Jewish war refugees who, as is clear from the sources, were settling in new localities.[8]

The difficulties inherent in collecting the poll tax meant that the Jewish elders were often unable to deliver the required sums to the locations specified by the treasury. Gradually, settlement was made through *asygnacje*: documents issued by the treasury to provincial councils and *kahals*, specifying the amount they were obliged to pay to the holder of the document, the *asygnatariusz*. The poll-tax accounts for 1662 reveal that the Jews paid their taxes only partly in the form of cash; the rest was paid through *asygnacje*, which slowed the process of collection. Some provincial councils and *kahals* had not paid a single zloty by September 1663 and still owed somewhat more than half the amount due. In addition, the provincial elders did not deposit the poll tax they had collected (approximately 46 per cent of the total due) until the meeting of the Council of Four Lands in Jarosław.[9] Initially, as in 1667, the *asygnatariusze* would go to Jarosław to collect the taxes;[10] subsequently, they demanded the tax directly from the provincial elders.

These changes were the result of the unwillingness of the *kahal* elders to levy the required tax and the inefficiency of the Jewish collectors. Towards the end of his reign, Jan Kazimierz was compelled to issue a proclamation in response to a petition from the elders of the Council of Four Lands, in which he guaranteed their safety and ordered that their collectors be given all necessary assistance. As he stated, the reason for the proclamation was that 'there are to be found among the faithless Jews those living on noble or Church estates and holding leases who hide behind their masters' patronage and not only do not wish to issue or pay the appointed taxes, but the above-named faithless Jews have also begun to insult the collectors'.[11] Ten years later, the elders of Kowel (a royal city) protested that the collector they had sent to Kamień Koszyrski had barely escaped with his life. The chief culprits in Kamień Koszyrski were the landowner and his officials, but it is hard to believe that the difficulties of the Jewish collector from Kowel occurred without the complicity of the local Jews. This was only one small town, but according to the protestors, for six years they had suffered losses of as much as 10,000 zlotys on its account.[12]

Faced with the recalcitrance of the *kahals* subject to them, the Jewish provincial elders were forced to fall back on the courts of the commonwealth. In 1674 Irsz Samsonowicz, a Jew from Bełz and a provincial elder from Chełm, summoned the *kahal* in Tomaszów Lubelski to an extraordinary court of the Bełz voivodeship because of its failure to pay in full the tax levied by the provincial elders. Irsz, who had been sent to collect the tax, demanded the return of 1,500 zlotys, which he had paid into the public treasury on behalf of the Jews of Tomaszów.[13]

The proclamation of Jan Kazimierz of 1667, issued as a response to the Jews' petition, confirms the changes taking place among the Jewish social elite.[14] This broad and exceptionally detailed document allows for a partial reconstruction of the complaints of the elders of the Council of Four Lands. The problem was the widespread recalcitrance of the principal *kahals* of Poland. This was not exclusively a question of refusing to pay taxes but also, as the king noted, of failing to appear before the elders' courts and ignoring their rulings. The second accusation was that Jews in smaller localities were beginning to form separate districts. Although the king did not articulate this precisely, it is, in my opinion, how the following phrase should be interpreted: 'breaking free of direction and government they wish to be their own directors *contra usum et consuetudinem, quae de iure vim legis obtinet* [contrary to custom and what rights the law enforces] and want no dependency on the elders of the principal towns'.[15] Furthermore, the accusation was made that these new elites were not chosen in accordance with custom, but were appointed 'with the support of various nobles and their functionaries'.[16] Apparently, the king had in mind here the custom of making agreements or issuing proclamations in which the choice of a specific person for office was dictated.[17] In any case, the king warned that every Jew who took up the office of elder not through election but through the patronage of the powerful would be excluded from society. Furthermore, he upheld the judgement of the Council of Four Lands in 1667 in which the elders of the council unanimously removed from their body one Zelek Józefowicz and his son, who were found guilty of such actions.[18]

The proclamation of Jan Kazimierz also indicates other changes affecting Jewish self-government and the system of collecting the Jewish poll tax. One of these was the growing role of *asygnatariusze*, mainly military personnel, in the collection of taxes. The sovereign ordered:

Asygnatariusze are to collect taxes not only from the Jews of the commonwealth's principal towns but also from other smaller regional towns, villages, and estates—royal, ecclesiastical, and noble—as indicated and apportioned by the Jewish elders of the principal towns—going there to collect *sub executione fisci* [under the authority of the treasury] the tax and quota as apportioned *ex propositione* [by the proposal] of the Jewish elders.[19]

During the reign of Jan III Sobieski (r. 1674–96) the burden of collecting the Jewish poll tax was gradually taken over by military deputies. In 1684 Piotr Opaliński, the governor of Wielkopolska, attempting to facilitate the collection of the Jewish poll tax, issued a proclamation in which he called for the provision of assistance to those 'who, to enforce [the tax], accompany the Jewish deputies of the provincial elders'.[20] This could refer to the holders of the *asygnacje*, who were accompanied by a Jewish guide, or to the Jewish collectors (assigned by the provincial elders), who were accompanied by assigned or hired Christians (from the nobility, usually military). Both types of action are to be found in the sources. In 1698, the treasurer Hieronim Augustyn Lubomirski recommended to the *asygnatariusze* that 'they travel with the Jew assigned by the elders'.[21] Walenty Molderf's protest of 1692 shows that the provincial elders of Chełm and Bełz hired nobles to protect collectors while levying taxes, in all probability from the owners of property and their officials. Molderf was to receive 600 zlotys per quarter, plus repayment of costs incurred, for accompanying the provincial scribe Moszek Lewkowicz.[22] There was some justification for hiring a noble for protection or even to collect the money from rural lessees (Jews living in smaller, particularly noble towns and localities),[23] since the provincial elders encountered difficulties not only in collecting the poll tax but also in repaying interest on the community's debts, court fees, gifts, and so on.

In the 1690s Lubomirski, probably to facilitate tax collection, sent out courtiers, cavalry officers, and officers from his regiment with *asygnacje* to assist the provincial elders.[24] Certainly the growing role of the military in tax collecting had deleterious consequences for Jews, sometimes leading to the use of force, beatings, and the desecration of synagogues.[25] In 1696 the collector sent by the Łuck *kahal*, assisted by his servants, extracted money due from the Jews of Kaszówka at the Żydyczyn fair by force.[26]

The new system for collecting poll tax can be observed in Wielkopolska, where the practice emerged of the *asygnatariusz* appearing in Kalisz (a key *kahal* in the province) and presenting the *asygnacja* to the provincial elders. He would then collect a small part in cash, while the elders[27] or the voivode[28] would convoke a council, where the division of taxes between particular *kahals* would be established. In an emergency, such apportioning could be performed by a clerk, who issued *asygnacje* for provincial *kahals* to military deputies, who were then to present them to the *kahal* elders and collect the tax due.[29] In this way, the costs of levying the tax were transferred to the deputies and did not directly affect the provincial elders. Understandably, the *asygnatariusze* attempted to shift the growing costs of collection onto the Jewish taxpayers, which is why regulations appeared during the reign of Jan III capping the costs demanded by the deputies (the first known Crown treasury ordinance dates from 1690).[30]

The difficulty of collecting the Jewish poll tax was only one of the phenomena accompanying the crisis of Jewish self-government after 1648. Another was the division of the existing large provinces. It is difficult to ascertain whether it was the action of elders from new centres which led to the break-up of the established provincial divisions in Wielkopolska and Małopolska or whether the Kraków and Poznań *kehilot* themselves wished to shed the burden of responsibility for the taxes of the whole province. Majer Bałaban took the first view, arguing that it was the aspirations of the smaller *kahals* in Małopolska and their elites which led to their independence of Kraków and to the exclusion of the Kraków *kahal* from Kraków–Sandomierz province.[31] He argued that Kraków's loss of authority was gradual: first the northern *kahals* became independent, and then, in 1692, the Kazimierz *kahal* also lost hegemony over the southern *kahals*, and, finally the Kraków–Sandomierz province was established.[32] In fact, the *kahals* which Bałaban termed 'northern' belonged to the Sandomierz voivodeship, in which the most important were the noble towns of Opatów and Pińczów.[33] Presumably, the emancipation of these *kahals* from Kraków's jurisdiction was supported by the Sandomierz voivode, as well, of course, as the towns' owners. Bałaban assumed that the absence of delegates from Kraków at the Council of Four Lands in 1666 was caused by their reluctance to sit down with representatives of other *kahals* of Małopolska: apparently the representatives of the Kraków *kahal* adopted this form of obstruction in order to avoid being compelled to accept unfavourable decisions.[34] As a consequence of this, at the beginning of the eighteenth century Mendel Kantorowicz, the last influential provincial elder from Kraków and a former president of the Council of Four Lands, moved (or rather escaped) to Pińczów where he took up the office of rabbi.[35] Even the provincial rabbi of Kraków resided outside the town for a long period.[36]

In Wielkopolska, the most important *kahal*, that of Poznań, also lost its preeminence. The problem of precedence there was even more complicated than in Małopolska. Whereas the Kraków *kahal* had in fact earlier exercised jurisdiction over the *kahals* of only two voivodeships, Poznań had originally exercised jurisdiction over *kahals* from twelve. Here, Kalisz, also a royal town, at first took precedence as Poznań lost its pre-eminence. It was only in 1732 that the bankrupt Kalisz Jews passed the leadership of the *kahals* to the private towns of Leszno and Krotoszyn.[37]

In Wielkopolska and Małopolska, the main towns lost their leading role, but both provinces preserved their territorial integrity, albeit gradually becoming dominated by smaller centres in the hands of the nobility. It was a different matter in Ruthenia, where not only was the primacy of Lwów called into question but a division occurred into separate provinces, districts, or even independent *kahals*. The Rzeszów *kahal* was listed independently of Ruthenia for the first time in the *asygnacje* of 1674,[38] and its independence was confirmed by the Council of Four Lands. The sejm of 1678/9 in Grodno agreed a settlement with the 'synagogue' (the Council of Four Lands) accepting the Rzeszów *kahal*'s secession from Ruthenia, undoubtedly as a result of the activity of Lubomirski.[39]

The situation of Podole and Bracław was more complicated. Attempts to establish the separate status of Podole began after the renewal of Jewish settlement following the Polish–Turkish war of 1683–99 (it is difficult to ascertain what the situation had been previously). August II (r. 1697–1733) issued a proclamation ending the subordination of the Jews of Podole to Ruthenia.[40] The Podole voivode, Stefan Humiecki, was understandably a supporter of the separation of Podole and most probably worked with Adam Mikołaj Sieniawski, the owner of the biggest latifundium in the area, who, immediately after the king's decision, ordered 'his' Jews to obey the voivode.[41] It is also possible that this initiative was supported by the local Jewish elite, prompted not only by ambition and the hope of lowering taxes but also by religious motives—in Podole, many Jews were followers of the Shabatean heresy.[42] Thanks to Humiecki, in 1718 the Council of Four Lands in Łęczna accepted the creation of a separate region in Podole, five years after the royal proclamation.[43] The subsequent efforts of the voivode of Ruthenia, Jan Stanisław Jabłonowski, to restore the authority of Ruthenian Jews over Podole were unsuccessful, and independent Podole province survived until 1764, although eastern Podole (Bracław province) was returned to Ruthenia.[44]

In the 1670s the process began of separating the Jewish communities of the Zamoyski Entail from those of Chełm–Bełz province which was at the time administered by Gryzelda Wiśniowiecka, the mother of King Michał Korybut Wiśniowiecki (r. 1669–73).[45] The king, who, theoretically, should have been interested in maintaining the integrity of Chełm–Bełz, acted instead in his mother's interests (and potentially those of his heirs) and precipitated the process of decentralization. However, it was only in 1721 that the Jewish communities of the Zamoyski Entail became completely separate, when attempts to conclude an agreement with Chełm–Bełz failed.[46] Certain common obligations remained, and the Jews of the Zamoyski Entail shared a common clerk with Chełm–Bełz.[47] The reasons for the separation of the Zamoyski Entail are not clear, but it was, above all, the result of the fears of the elders of Chełm–Bełz that they would be dominated by the Zamoyski Entail, despite their greater numbers (over forty *kahals* as against nine). This was because the elders of the Zamoyski Entail were subordinate to the will of a single noble, whereas those in the rest of the province, where ownership was dispersed between the Crown and the nobility, were not in a position to take a unified stance.[48]

Further conflict between the elders of Bełz–Chełm nearly led to a further division of the area.[49] The agreement of 1725 which maintained the area's unity did not mean that subsequent co-operation between the elders was without conflict. For example, in 1743 a Bełz Jew, Abram Pietruszka, as president of the council convened in Kryłów to approve the funds to pay the province's debts, protested that the elders of Chełm had independently and illegally collected dues from the *kahals* of their land and, instead of paying off at least a portion of their debt, had used the funds for their own purposes.[50]

The division of provinces and the new independence of smaller *kahals* were not only the consequences of 1648 but also of the dramatic growth of the indebtedness of the organs of Jewish self-government. The Council of Four Lands and the provincial *kahals* only managed to fulfil their fiscal obligations by borrowing from the nobility and various ecclesiastical institutions, sometimes with the agreement of the king or the voivodes but even more frequently without such permission. In 1665 King Jan Kazimierz permitted the Jews of Ruthenia, including both Lwów *kahals*, to borrow money, since their poverty meant they were not in a position to pay the tax for the maintenance of the army.[51] In 1678 the provincial elders of Łuck, faced with the necessity of paying two *asygnacje*, hastily borrowed 23,000 zlotys from the nobility, no doubt on very unfavourable terms, to pay one of them: 'We the elders of the Łuck *kehilah* had to bow before the esteemed citizens of the Volhynia voivodeship who have favour and credit with His Highness, in order to obtain the sum of 23,000 zlotys.'[52] It was not until the *asygnacja* was paid that they established the obligations of each *kahal*, but only for the amount specified in the loan. Repayment of the total debt of the province, amounting to 43,000 zlotys, was deferred to a later meeting.[53]

The debts of Jewish provincial councils are quite well documented in Wielkopolska, since in the reign of Jan III Sobieski (r. 1674–96) the province was bankrupt and not in a position either to pay its tax obligations or to settle its debts. In 1694 the king was obliged to summon a special commission of local officials in Kalisz to liquidate the debts of the province[54] (a similar commission was set up a little later to liquidate the debts of the Kalisz *kahal*).[55] The commission established that, even after its reduction, the debts amounted to 440,000 zlotys (previously it had been 481,000), at least twice the annual poll tax paid by the entire Jewish population of the kingdom.[56] It is worth noting that the commissioners acquitted Wulf Jakub, who was essentially fulfilling the role of president, and the provincial elders of embezzlement and confirmed that the debts incurred had been allocated for the needs of the province.[57] The commission recognized that the best way of satisfying the creditors would be to divide the debt between the principal *kahals* of the province. Doubtless, this decision was taken in agreement with the provincial rabbi and elders, who decided on the division of the debt at their meeting in Zduny (they approved a tariff on the basis of which the commission issued *asygnacje* to particular *kahals*).[58]

In this way, the debts of the organs of Jewish provincial self-government were transferred to the *kahals*.[59] The commissioners hoped that, by issuing *asygnacje* to one or more specific *kahals* instead of to the whole province, the creditors and *asygnatariusze* would not hinder each other and that procedures for collecting taxes would be improved. As soon became apparent, some of the *kahals* failed to fulfil their obligations, and creditors once again began claiming their debts from the provinces by both legal and illegal means.[60] From the creditors' point of view, the exercise had ended in disaster, but this was in part the result of subsequent political developments—the interregnum after the death of Jan III Sobieski, and the Great Northern War (1700–21).

Another result of the crisis affecting Jewish self-government after 1648 was conflicts and struggles for power between Jewish elders. In order to strengthen their own position, many elders sought the protection of noble patrons. Attempts to limit such dealings, such as the decree of the Council of Four Lands drawing on the proclamation of Jan III,[61] could not succeed given the weakening of central authority and of the authority of the voivodes. Sometimes these conflicts ended in upheaval and the more or less legal deposition of older elites. In January 1687 two provincial elders from Kalisz lodged a protest with the castle court against a group of Jews from Kalisz and Leszno, accusing them of rebelling against the *kahal* and provincial elders and defying the Kalisz voivode, whose ruling they had ignored.[62] They claimed that, 'acting *per fas et nefas* [by any means, legal or illegal], [they had] initiated a protest and incited other towns to follow, without waiting for the appointed time or for the *asygnacje* to be checked, and gathered in a certain town and appointed elders from among themselves, leaders of all kinds of rebellions'.[63] The revolt in the province was preceded by elections to the *kahal* in Kalisz, which were intended to provide new leadership. The rebels, according to the protestors, also adopted a range of actions against the provincial authorities and the local Jews. They appealed to the nobility not to grant them any more loans; they hindered trading by ordinary Jews; they refused to pay state taxes; and they exposed the provincial elders to legal costs. One injured party, Marek Józefowicz, a clerk of Wielkopolska, was forced to resign his office.[64] The case, brought to the Kalisz voivode's court by the protestors, evidently failed, since Wulf Jakub, one of the defendants, continued in office until 1695.[65] The new elders were no more successful in coping with the province's problems, and seven years later it proved necessary to establish a Crown commission.

At the end of the seventeenth century, with the Crown treasury and Jewish self-government in a state of permanent crisis and the latter unable to ensure collection of the Jewish poll tax, an attempt was made—apparently on the initiative of Hieronim Augustyn Lubomirski—to organize and rationalize the implementation of taxes by the Jewish elders. The paucity of sources makes it difficult to evaluate if the situation throughout the kingdom was as dramatic as that in Wielkopolska, where, in 1697, deputies of the royal artillery claimed that in the course of three months they had managed with difficulty to collect barely a third of the quota of 18,948 zlotys owed them on the basis of the treasury's assessment.[66] The reason for this fiasco was partly because the provincial clerk had issued *asygnacje* for localities where there were no Jews or to *kahals* which had already paid the tax, but most frequently it was the result of a refusal to pay tax on the orders of the landowner or leaseholder of a given locality.

An almost identical situation occurred in Volhynia, where one of the *asygnatariusze* complained that not only were the Jews of the town and province of Łuck unwilling to pay the poll tax but stated publicly that '*asygnatariusze*, Your Graces' predecessors, remained here among us in Volhynia for a year and more in order to collect the requisite taxes and even so have left without the full amount, and yet Your Graces wish to be seen as the best and collect the money without any labour'.[67] Unlike the initiative of 1694, it was Lubomirski who attempted to resolve the crisis of Wielkopolska, working with the elders of the Council of Four Lands, whose task was to set the affairs of the province in order, to determine the scope of territorial jurisdiction of particular *kahals*, and to set the level of taxation at the provincial council in Toruń.[68] The decisions undertaken by the Toruń council revealed a new trend. A tariff was set for a number of years in which it was clearly outlined how much each *kahal* (together with its subordinate *kahals*) should pay to the Crown treasury, or, alternatively, to the province's creditors.[69] Thus the practice of calling ad hoc local councils which then approved the division of obligations each time was modified.[70] From then on local councils had at most to modify a general tariff (for example to provide relief to a *kahal* suffering some natural disaster). Similar decisions were apparently taken with regard to other provinces. In this period Lubomirski appointed Commissioner Kazimierz Michał Mierzwiński to supervise the Council of Volhynia and ensure the approval of a new tariff.[71]

These actions did not have positive results, mainly because of the Great Northern War, which exacerbated all the ills affecting Jewish self-government.[72] The councils convoked did not materialize because of boycotts by smaller *kahals*. In 1702 the provincial elders of Kalisz, Leszno, and Krotoszyn protested against the *kahals* of Wielkopolska, because, despite proclamations being issued three times summoning them to Osieczna, they had waited in vain for them for five weeks, together with the provincial rabbi of Poznań.[73] The elders would sometimes gather beyond the country's borders[74] or in secret. In 1706 the Crown treasury commissioner, convening a provincial Jewish council, declared that he had secretly informed the elders of Kalisz and Krotoszyn of its location, precautions undoubtedly taken for fear of the *asygnatariusze* attempting to collect the poll tax by force.[75] Again, it seems the negative consequences of the Great Northern War affected the principal *kahals* to a greater degree than the rest.[76]

The appalling condition of the state finances and particularly the enormous arrears with respect to the army led the nobility, during the negotiations preceding the Silent Sejm of 1717, to seek a more effective way of financing the army at the same time as they were considering the Jewish poll tax. A reform was then enacted which preserved many existing elements of Jewish self-government and did not question the general principle of the Jewish elders setting the level of the Jewish poll tax which fell to each province and *kahal*. At the same time it introduced tighter control over the Jews and their financial obligations to the state.

The statute of 1717 shaped Jewish self-government until 1764 and therefore requires detailed discussion.[77] The poll tax now became a permanent tax paid by the

Jews of the commonwealth to the treasuries of both parts of the state, the Kingdom of Poland and the Grand Duchy of Lithuania. In the case of Poland, the sum of 220,000 zlotys a year was to be paid as an addition to the billeting of troops during the winter.[78] From the point of view of Jewish self-government, one important change was that the Crown treasurer now administered the tax, and though, admittedly, he lost the power to freely organize its levying, he gained the right to name three general clerks from among the Jews, one each for Małopolska, Wielkopolska, and Ruthenia. He was also responsible for approving and probably appointing the president of the Council of Four Lands.[79] The office of clerk had existed for much longer, and Treasurer Jan Jerzy Przebendowski apparently only confirmed those in the office who had held it earlier,[80] but their position and role was now strengthened. The statute laid down 'which of the Jews are to come with the provincial elders to the treasury *pro die 14 Februarii 1717 anni* [on 14 February 1717] and present written annual *sympla* [tariffs] that the smaller towns and *kahals* of each province are rightly to pay *absque praeaggravatione* [without excessive burden]'.[81] In reality, after 1717 the elders of the Council of Four Lands together with the creditors decided the distribution schedule, the 'assessment' of the Jewish poll tax for particular provinces, districts, and *kahals* under the laws of the province, in order to raise the required amount of 220,000 zlotys, plus additional sums to cover the stipends of the scribes and treasurer.[82] On the basis of the general assessment, the creditors of particular provinces and districts established local assessments, containing a list of localities and individuals along with the rate of poll tax. After these were ratified, the Crown treasury issued *asygnacje* to individuals in the army. In this way, the existing practice of collecting poll tax through military deputies was formally ratified. All court cases from 1717 were passed on to the treasury tribunal in Radom (previously, particularly where debts were concerned, the provincial elders had been summoned to the Crown tribunal).

From the resolutions of this tribunal, it seems that, at least in the first years after 1717, attempts were made to treat the *generalność* (the president, clerks, and certain elders of the Council of Four Lands) as a body responsible for all the Jews in Poland. Hence in 1723, the treasury tribunal imposed a fine on the *generalność*, which the latter was to pass on to *kahals* and individuals engaged in illicit trade.[83] That and similar decisions of the tribunal were challenged by the nobles and seen as an illegal way of raising taxes (only the sejm could impose or raise taxes).[84]

Despite the fact that the Silent Sejm made the Council of Four Lands subordinate to the Crown treasurer, the elders contested his authority on more than one occasion. Jan Ansgary Czapski, in a letter to his aunt, Teresa Potocka, complained:

You yourself may see, My Lady and Benefactress, how in Poland Jewry takes precedence over us—they heed and apprehend neither the decree of Radom nor the orders of the treasury, but having the law on their side allowing them to order their own accounts at their conferences, as being better aware and conscious of their own situation, they tax themselves according to the judgement of their elders, and if the treasury should wish to query their assessments, giving relief to the injured, then do the Jews quickly find protectors and defenders.[85]

One point of contention concerned the nominations to the key positions of president and clerks. Any attempt to replace the nominee approved by the Crown treasurer was treated as an infringement of his prerogatives. In 1726, in its declaration, the treasury tribunal resisted attempts by the Jews to replace the provincial scribe and confirmed Dawid Mankiewicz, scribe of Wielkopolska, in the office.[86] Mankiewicz, son of Abraham of Inowrocław, was one of the parties in the ongoing conflict in Wielkopolska. In 1729, together with other Krotoszyn elders, he initiated a lawsuit in the treasury tribunal against Józef Lewkowicz and the provincial elders of Kalisz and Leszno, claiming that for nine years Lewkowicz had occupied the office of president against law and custom, blocking other candidates and, in addition, exposing the Krotoszyn *kahal* to considerable expense and loss.[87]

The tribunal seems to have referred the case to the Council of Four Lands, which considered the claims of the Krotoszyn *kahal* at its meeting in 1730. It conceded they were justified and recognized that from 1731 the president of the provincial council should come from Krotoszyn. However, the finding also went against Mankiewicz. The council decided that the office of president should be filled by Moszek Rabinowicz of Krotoszyn, while Mankiewicz, as the perpetrator of acts 'impossible to describe or record that almost ruined the entire province of Wielkopolska', was to be removed from all offices.[88] The council further forbade the remaining elders of the province to serve with him, and should the Krotoszyn community attempt to appoint him president it would lose its right to elect the president from among the members of its community.[89] His opponents clearly won, since on 28 August 1731 Mankiewicz declared before the castle court in Kalisz that he would not reside in Krotoszyn or any town within several miles of it and would make no claims on anyone living in the lands of Wielkopolska.[90] His spectacular downfall was surely brought about by the loss of his most powerful patrons—the deaths of Przebendowski in February 1729 and Maciej Radomicki in 1728.

The authority of the Crown treasurers over Jewish self-government was also questioned by the voivodes, no doubt appealing to their 'ancient' rights.[91] Much depended on the position of the treasurer and voivodes in the hierarchy of the kingdom. The case of the provincial rabbi of Kraków demonstrates that the respected and influential Sandomierz voivode, Jan Tarło, was able, at least in part, to control the provincial elders.[92] The activities of his successor, Jan Wielopolski, provoked protest on the part of Crown Treasurer Karol Sedlnicki, who sued the voivode at a treasury tribunal.[93] It is worth noting, however, that Wielopolski managed, with the support of some of the provincial elders, to convene a congress at Stobnica at which his commissioners approved a law for the province and determined a tariff.[94] Since he had infringed the interests of Barbara Sanguszkowa and her Jewish client Haszkiel Wulfowicz Landau, an elder from Tarnów and president of the provincial council, they summoned the voivode and the provincial elders (including the general scribes of the province) before a tribunal. Among other things, Haszkiel accused the voivode of calling a 'private' congress without informing him.[95]

The biggest threat to the authority of the Crown treasurer over the Jewish system of self-government came from the great nobles. Noble patronage, which had long plagued Jewish self-government, not only failed to disappear but after 1717 became a universal phenomenon. In the majority of provinces, the *kahals* in royal cities completely lost their significance in favour of those in private towns. Chełm–Bełz remained an exception because of its large number of noble landowners, and the *kahals* in the royal cities of Chełm–Bełz were able to maintain their primacy. In neighbouring Ruthenia, the position of Lwów was so weakened, despite the efforts of the voivodes, that towards the end of the 1750s there was not a single Lwów Jew among the provincial elders.[86]

The most powerful nobles attempted to control the Jewish provincial councils in a number of ways, including intervening with the treasurer on behalf of the elders from their estates. Barbara Sanguszkowa in a letter to Sedlnicki in 1758, interceded on behalf of Lejba Szmujlowicz, rabbi of Krzemieniec and a clerk of the Council of Four Lands, when he was under arrest, and also on behalf of Haszkiel Wulfowicz Landau.[87] Others resorted to threats, advancing the representatives of their 'own' *kahals* in the council's structures. Seweryn Józef Rzewuski, the Grand Crown Referendary, under threat of legal action, advised the Chełm provincial elders that, in accordance with the principle of rotating service, they should permit the elders of the Luboml *kahal* to hold office (president, elders, clerks, tax assessors), and to participate in the Council of Four Lands on an equal footing with the Chełm *kahal*.[98] In addition, Rzewuski demanded a lowering of the level of the poll tax. Similarly in 1721 Janusz Wiśniowiecki threatened Fiszel Lewkowicz, a clerk of the Council of Four Lands, with serious consequences should he raise the poll tax for the Jews of Zamość.[99]

The provincial elders were overseen, in turn, by a system of *konsensy* and *instrumenty*, written instructions with which they were bound to comply. The president of the Council of Four Lands, Abraham Chaimowicz, in a letter to Eustachy Potocki, undertook to protect the Jews of the Potocki estates from excessive taxes and, in return, requested protection for himself and his sons, particularly the rabbi of Kurów and Radzyń.[100]

Apart from lowering taxes, the nobles' policies aimed to strengthen the position of the *kahals* on their own estates and ultimately to defend the status of the principal *kahal* in a particular area. As Adam Teller has noted, the defence of economic interests sometimes meant that nobles clashed over the protection of 'their' Jews.[101] Ruthenia, where Żółkiew had played a dominant role from the reign of Jan III, saw a clash between the Czartoryski, Potocki, and Radziwiłł families. Sobieski, who during his reign tended to promote Jews from his estates rather than Jews from royal towns, including Lwów, issued a privilege stating that the president of the provisional council should be chosen from the Jews of Żółkiew. After his death, his sons enjoyed neither the authority nor the prestige to maintain the precedence of Jews from Żółkiew, and the elders of Brody, thanks to the patronage of the Potockis, gained ever stronger influence. After the death of Iser Markowicz the pre-eminence of Żółkiew was further eroded, and, despite the efforts of the new owner, Michał Kazimierz Radziwiłł, the office of president was no longer held exclusively by Jews from

Żółkiew. In 1752 Radziwiłł was obliged to accept a settlement which ensured that this office went to Iser's son-in-law, Pinchas Abramowicz, along with two Jews from Brody. Radziwiłł was also forced to abandon the privilege granted by Jan III.[102]

The division of the office among two or, as in this case, three persons after 1717 also occurred in other provinces and was a way of satisfying the ambitions of disputing parties. In Ruthenia, even the office of provincial rabbi was shared.[103] The office of clerk was the one most frequently shared. In Małopolska, there were two clerks from the 1740s onwards, and this division went even further in Ruthenia: alongside the clerks from Ruthenia there were two from Volhynia, also described as clerks of the Council of Four Lands.[104]

Noble patronage clearly had its negative aspects. Elders who, in the opinion of the Crown treasurer, voivodes, or nobles, jeopardized their interests, risked imprisonment or fines. This is quite well exemplified by the case of Pinchas Abramowicz, rabbi of Świrz and, at the time, one of the presidents of the Ruthenian provincial council. Radziwiłł issued an *instrument* confirming his office, of which the contents are unknown, but they included several conditions according to which the office should be exercised. One of these was undoubtedly the duty to provide protection for Jews from the towns and villages belonging to Radziwiłł. The provincial elders, however, including Pinchas, incurred a sizeable debt for the needs of the province to another noble without Radziwiłł's agreement, which the latter saw as breaking the conditions of the *instrument*.[105] On Radziwiłł's orders, Pinchas was arrested, clapped in irons, and brought before him. An investigation confirmed the majority of the accusations, and Radziwiłł pronounced a humiliating sentence.[106] Pinchas was sentenced to a hefty fine and a public flogging: 100 strokes immediately after sentencing and another 200 in his home town, after being taken there in shackles. Most interesting, however, is that after carrying out the sentence, Radziwiłł immediately ordered him to be returned to office. It seems that Radziwiłł was aware that he could not replace Pinchas, a member of the Jewish elite,[107] with another Jew from his own estate against the will of the Jews of the Ruthenian lands. If he wished to maintain influence over the obligations placed on his Jews, he had to tolerate Pinchas. Otherwise, in the struggle for pre-eminence in Ruthenia, Brody (and particularly the second president of the provisional council, Berek Rabinowicz) would have eliminated the influence of Żółkiew.

This incident illustrates the complexity of the situation and the limitations on how far those in power could influence Jewish self-government. The decentralized state structure and multitude of jurisdictions forced both sides to accept various compromises, forge alliances, and seek patrons, but led also to situations in which elders' abilities to take independent action was limited (and not only in the case of taxes but also over internal Jewish matters)[108] and exposed them to persecution from various quarters. In any case, a high position in Jewish society did not protect them from aggression, particularly on the part of the debtors or disgruntled deputies.[109]

The arrest or persecution of a representative of the Jewish elders by a noble would immediately provoke the reaction of his patron. When Eustachy Potocki imprisoned

Berek Rabinowicz, president of the Ruthenian provincial council, in Radzyń, Stanis-ław Potocki, a landowner from Brody, and Karol Sedlnicki intervened. The whole affair should probably be interpreted as a battle between two groups within the Jewish elite. Eustachy Potocki, while making efforts to improve the situation of the Jews of his estates, oppressed the opponents of his Jewish partner, Abraham Chaimowicz, president of the Council of Four Lands, whose son Pinhas had been humiliated in the same year, probably as a result of the intrigues among the Jewish elders. A direct cause was the debts incurred by Pinhas's rival Berek Rabinowicz and his allies among the elders (and the concessions favouring the creditor and the Jews of Lesko).

Other nobles did not possess the power or prestige to influence Jewish self-government directly. This does not mean that they did not try. Some attempted to bring cases against the elders before the treasury tribunal in order to lower the tax obligations of the kahals in their towns. These cases were often drawn out, expensive, and usually unsuccessful. The owner of Beresteczko, together with the kahal in the town, were for decades involved in a legal struggle with the provincial elders of Volhynia.[110] Sometimes, to avoid further trials, agreements were reached, although these were not always upheld by the provincial elders.[111] Another practice was for the landowner to lend money to the Jewish elders as representatives of the province.[112] The goal was to ensure that the tax on the noble's kahal should remain relatively low, providing guarantees that the amount would not be raised higher, and, above all, that the interest on the loan would be paid by his own Jews. In this way, the kahal avoided the burdensome and expensive payment of poll tax to the military deputies (and, as it were, disappeared from the poll-tax assessments). Occasionally, additional benefits also accrued: for example, further localities were added to the kahal's juris-diction or its representatives were accepted into the circle of provincial elders.[113]

Pressured in this way, it was difficult for the Jewish elders to fulfil the duties imposed by the state. The poll-tax assessments they prepared were sometimes late and, the deputies claimed, often inaccurate.[114] Above all, the modifications intro-duced in 1717 failed to eliminate the universal phenomenon of the refusal of smaller kahals to accept the control of the Jewish provincial councils or larger kahals. In the regions where the authority of kahals was weak and where there were many noble landowners each with Jewish leaseholders, the kahal elders were unable to extract the taxes from the leaseholders. It therefore transferred its problem to the army by including the names of the leaseholders in the asygnacje. This practice aroused the objections of the treasury authorities, but its repetition bears witness to the dura-bility of the phenomenon.[115] The names of leaseholders were also included in the asygnacje because of disputes between kahals concerning who had authority over the surrounding villages, making it easer for leaseholders to avoid paying taxes, a matter which was often settled through long and costly legal cases in both Jewish and lay courts.[116] An indicator of the decline of the Jewish judicial system was the recourse to ecclesiastical courts by the provinces of Przemyśl and Turka to settle disputes concerning authority over leaseholders.[117] In turn, rural leaseholders accused the *kahal* and provincial authorities of imposing excessive burdens. In the course of a dispute between leaseholders of the Sandomierz royal estates and the *kahal* in Ulanów, the former argued that they were paying over 800 zlotys in poll tax, whereas according to the assessment of the provincial elders, the whole *kahal* (including the leaseholders) should not pay more than 1,200 zlotys. Given that the poll tax was also paid by leaseholders of noble properties, in their opinion the Jews of Ulanów had passed all the costs on to the rural leaseholders. The arguments of the *kahal* elders, that the *kahal* maintained the synagogue and cemetery and bore the cost of other obligations, were rejected, since the leaseholders maintained that they were forced to pay a fee every time they used them.[118]

The somewhat patchy records bear witness to ongoing conflicts between the provincial elders, the *kahal*s, and ordinary Jews. The relations between the provincial elders and the community bodies which they supposedly represented were not always harmonious. The Polish sources say nothing about how these bodies were elected, but indicate that in the eighteenth century the Jewish provincial councils were in the hands of a very narrow elite which controlled the most important provincial and rabbinical offices, which, in practice, were increasingly inherited. In Kraków–Sandomierz, the Landau family played a dominant role, and the representatives of its Opatów line from the seventeenth century held various offices by inheritance.[119] This was possible thanks to the support of the owners of Opatów, as was the case with Paweł Karol Sanguszko in 1744, who ignored the complaints of the local Jewish population and acted to preserve calm in the town.[120] In other provinces, conflicts broke out because key offices, such as that of president or clerk, were held for many years by a single person whose rule was seen as unjust.[121] Mutual accusations of violating laws and customs, corruption, and of using the taxes and payments collected for private purposes were universal.[122] In 1753 Sedlnicki himself expressed the view that the Jews as a whole collected a million zlotys annually in taxes from the community.[123]

Attempts by Kazimierz Granowski on the recommendation of Karol Sedlnicki to modify the entire system of tax collection and, as a consequence, the system of Jewish self-government during the meeting of the Council of Four Lands in 1753 did not result in any significant improvements.[124] The existing system of poll-tax collection seems to have been generally viewed as inefficient and unfair.[125] It was also undoubtedly very expensive and led to protracted and ruinous lawsuits. The Jewish provincial councils were not in a position to pay debts incurred as far back as the seventeenth century, despite the fact that many of their debts had been transferred to specific *kahal*s. Dissatisfaction was voiced by the military, landowners, creditors, and the Jews themselves, while at the same time, particularly from the 1740s, the idea of 'army auctions' to increase the number of troops was put forward more and more often, something which could not be achieved without raising taxes and rationalizing their collection.

The evolving system of Jewish self-government established in 1717 was finally abolished in 1764. The Convocation Sejm of that year raised the level of taxes, removed the flat-rate system, and ordered a census of the Jewish population. At the same time, Jewish national and provincial councils were abolished, but the institution of the *kahal* was retained. Henceforth, the size of the tax was to depend on the number of Jews. The practice of fixing the level of taxation according to wealth was partially abandoned, although at the level of a *kahal* with rural subordinate bodies, the poor still had their tax obligations met for them. Jewish provincial structures did not disappear entirely; the provincial rabbinate survived, but the provincial elders lost the power to impose taxes, a prerogative they had enjoyed since the end of the Middle Ages, nor could they incur debts.[126] Without the legitimization of the state, their authority had to depend on charisma and the respect they enjoyed among Jews (which was not always forthcoming). With the abolition of the Jewish national and provincial councils, the focus of Jewish self-government shifted from the central and regional level to the *kahals* and the elders who led them.

After 1648, as a result of the loss of the authority of the Jewish elite at a national and provincial level, Jewish self-government, like the Polish–Lithuanian state, became increasingly decentralized and inefficient. The existence of multiple centres of authority meant that it was never dominated by a single group or able to maintain its independence from the non-Jewish world. The specific features of the Kingdom of Poland also meant that Jewish self-government there took a somewhat different form from that in the Grand Duchy of Lithuania. In the duchy, despite shrinking royal authority, the original system of Jewish self-government (similar to that which had existed in Poland before 1648) survived. Local forms of self-government, such as the Council of Belarus, continued to exist;[127] however, until 1764 the elders of the five main communities still had a deciding voice.

Why did Jewish self-government in Poland evolve differently, with the appearance of different territorial units, such as the Jewish provincial councils? There seem to be a number of reasons. Firstly, until the beginning of the eighteenth century, the Grand Duchy of Lithuania was dominated by a single noble family, consecutively by the Radziwiłłs, Pacs, and Sapiehas. Secondly, the voivode was also the town governor of the capital of his voivodeship. Consequently, the vice voivode was one of the judges of the castle court. Thirdly, in 1717 the Silent Sejm allocated the poll tax to pay the salary of the Grand Hetman of Lithuania and the *straż trybunalska*, a special military unit which enforced the law and held the prisoners of the tribunal, which was under his command. As all Jewish litigants had contact with the unit, maintaining the goodwill of the officers and soldiers was in the Jews' best interests. The hetman usually served as voivode of Vilna and was undoubtedly the most important person in the duchy. In Poland, by contrast, the Jewish elders did not have such a stable authority to deal with. As a result of the weakening of the central government, the limited authority of the voivodes and the phenomenon of 'lordly patronage', the Jewish elders had to function in a political system characterized by many different and rival centres of authority and jurisdiction.

As is evident, Jewish self-government was not an institution independent of the outside world, but combined Jewish traditions with those adopted from the commonwealth's political system, as Jacob Goldberg, among others, has shown.[128] In addition, particularly in the eighteenth century, Jewish representative bodies remained under the influence of various institutions and people in the common-wealth. They evolved and adapted to the structural, economic, and social conditions, and it is difficult to treat them as completely autonomous representatives of Jewish society. Accordingly the view of historians of the older generation (Bałaban, Raphael Mahler) that self-government was completely dependent on the whims of the nobil-ity must be seen as exaggerated.[129] The national and provincial councils were abol-ished because they were not in a position to fulfil the basic tasks set them by the state. They were relics of a past epoch, which did attempt to adapt to political and social change in the commonwealth, but the moment the state finally began to modernize, there was no longer room for such an archaic, inefficient body. Jewish territorial self-government survived for as long as it did, despite growing complaints and criticisms, because of the inability of the commonwealth to reform the administration of its treasury.

Translated from the Polish by Anna Zarańko

Notes

This chapter is the outcome of a research project at the Jagiellonian University as part of the Narodowy Program Rozwoju Humanistyki, Żydowski samorząd ziemski w Koronie. Other publications resulting from the project include *Żydowski samorząd ziemski w Koronie (XVII–XVIII wiek): Źródła*, ed. A. Kaźmierczyk and P. Zarubin (Kraków, 2019); A. Kaźmierczyk, 'Czy rzeczywiście niezależni? Samorząd terytorialny Żydów a ustrój Rzeczypospolitej', in W. Bondyra et al. (eds.), *Studia z dziejów Europy Środkowo-Wschod-niej* (Lublin, 2018), 93–107.

1 A. Leszczyński, *Sejm Żydów Korony 1623–1764* (Warsaw, 1994) (Leszczyński also dedicated a significant part of his work to the lower tiers of Jewish self-government); J. Kalik, *Scepter of Judah: The Jewish Autonomy in the Eighteenth-Century Crown Poland* (Leiden, 2009); see also A. Kaźmierczyk, review of Kalik, *Scepter of Judah*, *Kwartalnik Historyczny*, 118 (2011), 577–83; J. Kalik, 'Reassessment of the Jewish Poll Tax Assessment Lists from Eighteenth-Century Crown Poland', in A. Polonsky, H. Węgrzynek, and A. Żbikowski (ed.), *New Directions in the History of the Jews in the Polish Lands* (Boston, 2018), 255–60; A. Polonsky, *The Jews in Poland and Russia*, 3 vols. (Oxford, 2010–12), i. 406–7; P. Zarubin, 'Żydzi ziemstwa lubelskiego w wiekach XVII–XVIII', in Bondyra et al. (eds.), *Studia z dziejów Europy Środkowo-Wschodniej*, 663–82; *Pinkas va'ad arba aratsot: likutei takanot ketavim ureshumot*, ed. I. Halperin (Jerusalem, 1945); 2nd revd. edn., ed. I. Bartal (Jerusalem, 1990); *Sejm Czterech Ziem: Źródła*, ed. J. Goldberg and A. Kaźmierczyk (Warsaw, 2011).

2 M. Schorr, *Organizacya Żydów w Polsce (od najdawniejszych czasów aż do r. 1772* (Lwów, 1899), 52; J. Goldberg and A. Kaźmierczyk, 'Introduction', in *Sejm Czterech Ziem*, 23–43: 24.

3 R. Rybarski, *Skarb i pieniądz za Jana Kazimierza, Michała Korybuta i Jana III* (Warsaw, 1939), 39–42.

4 *Sejm Czterech Ziem*, 28; A. Kaźmierczyk and P. Zarubin, 'Introduction', in *Żydowski samorząd ziemski*, 37–63.

5 Kaźmierczyk and Zarubin, 'Introduction', 40.

6   *Żydowski samorząd ziemski*, 77.

7   S. Stampfer, 'What Actually Happened to the Jews of Ukraine in 1648?', *Jewish History*, 17 (2003), 207–27.

8   *Żydowski samorząd ziemski*, 91.

9   *Sejm Czterech Ziem*, 77. The settlement did not encompass Wielkopolska.

10   Ibid. 81.

11   *Żydowski samorząd ziemski*, 99–100.

12   Ibid. 394.

13   Tsentral'nyi derzhavnyi istorychnyi arkhiv Ukrayiny, Lviv (hereafter TsDIAL), f. 1, op. 1, spr. 264, fos. 379–81: court summons for Tomaszów Jews, 29 Jan. 1674.

14   *Sejm Czterech Ziem*, 87–8.

15   Ibid. 88.

16   Ibid. 89.

17   Ibid. 326. In 1725 Paweł Karol Sanguszko ordered the elders in his towns to elect his jeweller as an elder for Kraków–Sandomierz.

18   Ibid. 89.

19   Ibid. 88. Similarly in 1683, the king ordered the collection of dues not directly from the elders, but from the *kahals* and individual Jews indicated in the *asygnacje* prepared by provincial Jews (see *Żydowski samorząd ziemski*, 122).

20   Ibid. 123–4. The collectors were expected to carry copies of this proclamation.

21   Ibid. 162.

22   Ibid. 417–20. It is worth adding that disputes regarding the unpaid debts of the provincial elders (fixed by the court) to Molderf and his heirs continued at least until the 1740s (TsDIAL, f. 1, op. 1, spr. 339, fos. 246–7: summons for the elders of Bełz–Chełm to appear at the castle court in Bełz, 20 Jan. 1746).

23   TsDIAL, f. 15, op. 1, spr. 217, fos. 8–10: Dydnia leaseholder, declaration against poll tax collectors, 5 Jan. 1723

24   Tsentral'nyi derzhavnyi istorychnyi arkhiv Ukrayiny, Kiev (hereafter TsDIAK), f. 25, op. 1, spr. 425, fo. 606: *asygnacja* issued by the treasury to Volhynian Jews, 2 Nov. 1692. In 1692 Lubomirski authorized his courtier Łukasz Wolski to seal up synagogues, imprison insubordinates, and confiscate goods.

25   *Żydowski samorząd ziemski*, 423.

26   Ibid. 425.

27   Kaźmierczyk and Zarubin, 'Introduction', 43.

28   e.g. Wojciech Breza in 1694 (*Żydowski samorząd ziemski*, 147–8) and Rafał Leszczyński in 1696 (Archiwum Państwowe, Poznań (hereafter APP), Kaliskie grodzkie 306, fo. 73: Rafał Leszczyński, proclamation, 1696).

29   Kaźmierczyk and Zarubin, 'Introduction', 43.

30   *Żydowski samorząd ziemski*, 137, 145, 155–6, 160–1, 175–6, 181–2.

31   M. Bałaban, *Historja Żydów w Krakowie i na Kazimierzu, 1304–1868*, 2 vols. (Kraków, 1931–6), ii. 251–4.

32   M. Bałaban, *Z zagadnień ustrojowych żydostwa polskiego: Lwów a ziemstwo rusko-bracławskie w XVIII w.* (Lwów, 1932), 2.

33   On 1 December 1664 the *kahals* of the Sandomierz voivodeship had concluded a contract for an annuity of 14,000 zlotys with Archdeacon Sebastian Kokwiński acting on behalf of the Sandomierz College of Canons (*Żydowski samorząd ziemski*, 389–92).

34 Bałaban, *Historja Żydów w Krakowie i na Kazimierzu*, ii. 254–5. In 1608, for the first time, a representative of the province and not Kraków appeared in the Council of Four Lands (Leszczyński, *Sejm Żydów Korony*, 89).

35 Bałaban, *Historja Żydów w Krakowie i na Kazimierzu*, ii. 242.

36 Ibid. 263–90; A. Kaźmierczyk, 'Konwersja, *jichus* i walka o władzę w ziemstwie krakowsko-sandomierskim w latach czterdziestych XVIII wieku', in A. Jagodzińska (ed.), *W poszukiwaniu religii doskonałej? Konwersja a Żydzi* (Wrocław, 2012), 31–47.

37 Kaźmierczyk and Zarubin, 'Introduction', 53.

38 J. Krochmal, *Krzyż i menora: Żydzi i chrześcijanie w Przemyślu w latach 1559–1772* (Przemyśl, 1996), 26–32.

39 *Volumina legum: Leges, statuta, constitutiones et privilegia Regni Poloniae, Magni Ducatus Lithuaniae*, 10 vols. (St Petersburg, 1859–60), v. 272 (1678–79).

40 Bałaban, *Z zagadnień ustrojowych*, 4. August II in a proclamation of 1 June 1713, returned authority over the Jews to the Podole voivode 'forsaken during the war' and excluded them from the jurisdiction of the Ruthenian Jews (*Arkhiv Yugo-Zapadnoi Rossii izdavaemyi Komissiei dlya razbora drevnikh aktov*, pt. 5, vol. i: *Akty o gorodakh* (Kiev, 1869), 257–8).

41 *Żydowski samorząd ziemski*, 184, 444.

42 P. Maciejko, *Mixed Multitude: Jacob Frank and the Frankist Movement, 1755–1816* (Philadelphia, 2011), 10.

43 *Sejm Czterech Ziem*, 11, 317–19.

44 Bałaban, *Z zagadnień ustrojowych*, 7; *Żydowski samorząd ziemski*, 195–6.

45 Leszczyński, *Sejm Żydów Korony*, 73.

46 *Żydowski samorząd ziemski*, 192–4, 319–31, 447–54.

47 Ibid. 230–5, 319–31.

48 Ibid. 324.

49 Ibid. 338–41.

50 Ibid. 502.

51 TsDIAL, f. 9, op. 1, spr. 420, fos. 301–2: proclamation, Warsaw, 1 Sept. 1667.

52 *Żydowski samorząd ziemski*, 275.

53 Ibid. 275–9.

54 See ibid. 149–54.

55 APP, Kaliskie grodzkie 305, fos. 528ʳ–530ʳ: mandate of Jan III, Warsaw, 17 Mar. 1695.

56 *Żydowski samorząd ziemski*, 153. It is not clear what the amount of the debt was specified in. The amount of the poll tax was 105,000 'good [i.e. silver] coins', that is 210,000 in *currentis monetae* (i.e. copper).

57 Ibid. 157.

58 Ibid. 289. For example, to Kalisz (56,755 zlotys) (APP, Kaliskie grodzkie 306, fos. 248ʳ–51ᵛ: royal commission, declaration concerning Kalisz community, 28 Sept. 1695) and Krotoszyn (43,000 zlotys) (APP, Poznańskie grodzkie 807, fos. 33ʳ–34ʳ: royal commission, declaration concerning Krotoszyn community, 28 Sept. 1695).

59 From the commission's indemnities, it emerges that the *kahals* paid part of their obligations in cash and for the rest they issued promissory notes, to be paid by themselves not the provincial council.

60 Kaźmierczyk and Zarubin, 'Introduction', 46.

61 See *Sejm Czterech Ziem*, 87–8.

62 See *Żydowski samorząd ziemski*, 127–9.

63 Ibid. 411.

64 Ibid. 403–5. Józefowicz claimed that, among other things, his house had been attacked, his wife and children evicted, his property looted, bills of exchange seized, and he himself forced to sign off on the debts of the (new) provincial elders (see ibid. 406–8).

65 See APP, Kaliskie grodzkie 298, fos. 548ᵛ–549ᵛ: court summons for new provincial elders of Kalisz, 7 Jan. 1687; see also *Żydowski samorząd ziemski*, 130.

66 *Żydowski samorząd ziemski*, 430–3.

67 TsDIAK, f. 28, op. 1, spr. 144, fo. 322ᵛ: deputy of company of *asygnatariusze*, declaration against Jews of Łuck, 29 May 1699.

68 *Sejm Czterech Ziem*, 99, 205–8; *Żydowski samorząd ziemski*, 300, 305–9.

69 *Sejm Czterech Ziem*, 207. As stated 'as such it will continue unchanged for three years nor shall anyone intervene to lower it'.

70 A similar tariff was approved by the Jewish provincial council in Wojsławice for Chełm–Bełz and the Zamoyski Entail in 1697. Each community was allocated its share of every 1,000 zlotys of tax due. The total each community had to pay was adjusted annually depending on how much tax the province had to pay. So if the province had to pay 11,000 zlotys, the amount each *kahal* had to pay was their share multiplied by eleven (Archiwum Państwowe, Lublin, 'Chełm: Relacje, Manifestacje, oblaty', 11 Luźne: register of distribution of Jewish poll tax by towns and cities of Chełm–Bełz, Wojsławice, 1697, fos. 3ʳ–4ᵛ).

71 J. Raba, 'Protokol shel kinus va'ad galil volin bishnat 1700 (ḥalukat mas hagulgolet) (Podział podatku pogłównego)', *Gal-ed*, 6 (1982), 220; Rybarski, *Skarb i pieniądz*, 225; *Żydowski samorząd ziemski*, 173–4.

72 Kaźmierczyk and Zarubin, 'Introduction', 47.

73 *Żydowski Samorząd Ziemski*, 439–40; see also 178.

74 APP, Kaliskie grodzkie 313, fo. 127ʳ: plenipotency of land elders, 2 Apr. 1704.

75 APP, Kaliskie grodzkie 314, fos. 473ʳ, 474: treasury commisioner, proclamations, 20 Dec. 1706.

76 TsDIAL, f. 9, op. 1, spr. 488, fos. 2845–7: A.M. Sieniawski's proclamation protecting the Jews of Lwów, 2 Nov. 1707. The hetman advised the governor to protect the Jews and prevent the levying of the taxes since not only was the poll tax issued a year ahead but they bore the additional cost of the upkeep of the Lwów garrison.

77 *Volumina legum*, vi. 289–90.

78 This was subsequently exchanged for a monetary provision for maintaining the cavalry during the winter. On military finances during the period 1717 to 1764, see T. Ciesielski, *Armia koronna w czasach Augusta III* (Warsaw, 2009), 19–47.

79 *Sejm Czterech Ziem*, 127. At the meeting of the Council of Four Lands in 1753, Karol Sedlnicki declared Abraham Chaimowicz president, as the use of the word *postanawiam* (I decide) suggests. On the other hand, it is known that earlier terms of office and the principle of rotation were in force: that is, the office would be taken up by elders from different provinces or even regions (Kaźmierczyk and Zarubin, 'Introduction', 50). A letter of 1725 from Michał Potocki to Izaak Fortis concerning his efforts to attain the office of president (despite the principle of rotation, since the office should have fallen to a citizen of Chełm–Bełz) confirms the key role of the Crown treasurer (*Sejm Czterech Ziem*, 191).

80 It is clear that in 1687 Fiszel Lewkowicz, chosen to be clerk by the elders for the 'general congress' and confirmed by King Jan III, remained in office until his death in 1726 (*Żydowski samorząd ziemski*, 131–2). In that year, Przebendowski chose three clerks from among the six candidates proposed to him (*Sejm Czterech Ziem*, 113).

81 *Volumina legum*, vi. 289.

82 Kalik, *Scepter of Judah*.

83 *Sejm Czterech Ziem*, 110.

84 Kaźmierczyk, *Czy rzeczywiście niezależni*, 103; *Sejm Czterech Ziem*, 319–20.

85 Archiwum Główne Akt Dawnych, Warsaw, Archiwum Potockich z Łańcuta, 3810 Korespondencja różnych z różnymi, 4–7: Jan Ansgary Czapski, letter to Teresa Potocka, Nowa Wieś, 28 Oct. 1741.

86 *Żydowski samorząd ziemski*, 198–9.

87 Ibid. 454–5, 467–9.

88 Ibid. 347.

89 Ibid. 435–51.

90 APP, Kaliskie grodzkie 347, fo. 260: Dawid Mankiewicz, testimony, 28 Aug. 1731.

91 *Żydowski samorząd ziemski*, 237.

92 Kaźmierczyk, 'Konwersja, *jichus* i walka o władzę w ziemstwie krakowsko-sandomierskim', 31–47; *Sejm Czterech Ziem*, 122–3; *Żydowski samorząd ziemski*, 214–20, 483–96, 498–500.

93 *Żydowski samorząd ziemski*, 567–8, 571–2. Each accused the other of abusing their privileges.

94 *Sejm Czterech Ziem*, 366–71.

95 Ibid. 371, 373–6.

96 Kaźmierczyk and Zarubin, 'Introduction', 53; TsDIAL, f. 9, op. 1, spr. 579, fos. 711–12: advocate of the Jews of Lwów, declaration against Jews of Dolina, Rożniatów, and Drohobycz, 23 May 1758.

97 *Sejm Czterech Ziem*, 384.

98 *Żydowski samorząd ziemski*, 483.

99 Ibid. 452. Among other things, denying his son the office of rabbi.

100 Archiwum Główne Akt Dawnych, Archiwum Publiczne Potockich, 170 Listy różnych osób do Eustachego Potockiego, 105–7: Abraham Chaimowicz, letter to Eustachy Potocki, 13 Aug. 1754.

101 A. Teller, 'Radziwiłł, Rabinowicz, and the Rabbi of Świerz: The Magnates' Attitude to Jewish Regional Autonomy in the Eighteenth Century', *Studies in the History of the Jews in Old Poland in Honor of Jacob Goldberg* (Jerusalem, 1998), 246–76: 261.

102 *Żydzi polscy 1648–1772: Źródła*, ed. A. Kaźmierczyk (Kraków, 2001), 68–9; Teller, 'Radziwiłł, Rabinowicz, and the Rabbi of Świerz', 263, 271–2.

103 Bałaban, *Z zagadnień ustrojowych*, 14–20; *Żydowski samorząd ziemski*, 581–3.

104 In Volhynia, Szowel Jakubowicz, rabbi of Włodzimierz, and Lejba Szmołowicz, rabbi of Krzemieniec, also served as clerks (*Żydowski samorząd ziemski*, 533).

105 Teller, 'Radziwiłł, Rabinowicz, and the Rabbi of Świerz', 258–75; *Sejm Czterech Ziem*, 364–5; Kaźmierczyk and Zarubin, 'Introduction'.

106 *Żydowski samorząd ziemski*, 561–6.

107 He was not only the son-in-law of the previous president of the provincial council but also the son of the current president of the Council of Four Lands, Abraham Chaimowicz.

108 On the activities of Sedlnicki as a broker in the conflict between Jacob Emden and Jonathan Eibeschütz, see P. Maciejko, 'Baruch Yavan and the Frankist Movement: Intercession in an Age of Upheaval', *Jahrbuch des Simon Dubnow Instituts*, 4 (2005), 333–54.

109 In 1743 Skrzetuski, demanding payment of his debt, sent his servants who, among other things, befouled (apparently with dung from the stables) the house of the clerk of the

Council of Four Lands and the Council of Volhynia, Szowel Jakubowicz, rabbi of Włodzimierz (TSDIAK, f. 28, op. 1, spr. 163, fo. 363: advocate of the Jews of Ludmir–Włodzimierz, declaration on behalf of rabbi of Ludmir, 10 May 1743). Seven years later, Szowel was assaulted by Mikołaj Jełowicki. Jełowicki, who was passing through Milatyn by chance, on hearing that Jews were gathered in the town for the *sejmik* of Volhynia, summoned Szowel and demanded the return of the debt. After the rabbi's beating, the alarmed Jews scattered and the *sejmik* did not undertake any resolutions on tax (TsDIAK, f. 28, op. 1, spr. 169, fos. 304–5: Szowel Jakubowicz, rabbi of Ludmir, declaration against Jełowicki, 10 Sept. 1750).

110 TsDIAK, f. 28, op. 1, spr. 152, fo. 393: court summons for elders of Volhynia, 10 July 1729; f. 256, op. 1, spr. 130, fo. 71: decree of treasury tribunal against elders of Volhynia, 27 May 1758.

111 *Żydowski samorząd ziemski*, 586–90, 596–8.

112 Ibid. 546–60.

113 Such a condition appears in the contract with Józef Ossoliński, the owner of Lesko.

114 *Żydowski samorząd ziemski*, 225–6. The treasury tribunal of 1747 demanded 'that the Jewish elders chosen and bearing [office] *per provincias* [in the provinces] should not presume to tender to the treasury from their localities unreliable and completely unbelievable assessments'.

115 *Sejm Czterech Ziem*, 114.

116 Ibid. 271–4.

117 *Żydowski samorząd ziemski*, 575–80.

118 Ibid. 518–19.

119 G. D. Hundert, *The Jews in a Polish Private Town: The Case of Opatów in the Eighteenth Century* (Baltimore, 1992), 118–22.

120 Ibid. 128; *Sejm Czterech Ziem*, 343–53.

121 *Żydowski samorząd ziemski*, 466–9, 474–6, 503, 510–12, 532–7, 584–5, 592–3.

122 Ibid. 254.

123 Ibid. 248; M. Nycz, *Geneza reform skarbowych Sejmu Niemego. Studium z dziejów skarbowo-wojskowych z lat 1697–1717* (Poznań, 1938), 59.

124 *Sejm Czterech Ziem*, 14, 17; for the ordinance, see ibid. 138–50.

125 *Volumina legum*, vii. 44. The legislators justified the change of 1764 as follows: 'As we know very well, beyond the levied *in vim* [as due] Jewish poll tax in the sum of 220,000 Polish zlotys universally established by the constitution *anno* [of the year] 1717, the Jewish elders are accustomed to collect for their own private dispositions and disbursements far greater sums, considerably burdening the whole of Jewry, especially those residing in the royal and noble towns, for their own use and private *expensa* [expenses].'

126 *Volumina legum*, vii. 44–50.

127 I. Trunk, 'The Council of the Province of White Russia', *YIVO Annual of Jewish Social Science*, 11 (1956/7), 188–210.

128 Goldberg and Kaźmierczyk, 'Introduction', 24.

129 G. D. Hundert, *Jews in Poland–Lithuania in the Eighteenth Century: A Genealogy of Modernity* (Berkeley, Calif., 2004), 110.

2. THE LONG NINETEENTH CENTURY

Burying the Dead, Saving the Community
Jewish Burial Societies as Informal Centres of Jewish Self-Government

CORNELIA AUST

KHAYIM BETSALEL GRINBERG'S Yiddish comedy *Di khevre-kedishe sude*, published in Warsaw in 1883, is an amusing account of the chaotic events around the annual banquet of a burial society. Although the author's intention was to poke fun at 'the Jewish upper crust' and, more generally, to depict 'human weaknesses', the setting of his story is noteworthy.[1] At the centre of his story, Grinberg placed a Jewish institution, the *ḥevrah kadisha*, that officially no longer existed but was still apparently part of everyday life among Jews in Warsaw and in eastern Europe more generally. The fact that it was now an object of ridicule also suggests a decline in its authority.

For more than two centuries, the *ḥevrah kadisha* had been part and parcel of Jewish community life in eastern Europe. The early modern period saw a strengthening of institutions of community self-government across Europe, and burial societies were one knot in a densely woven web of local, regional, and national institutions including many different *ḥevrot* which took over a wide variety of charitable tasks in most Jewish communities, including organizing study groups, dressing and feeding the poor, visiting the sick, and last but not least burying the dead. This last and unavoidable part of the life cycle and its related beliefs and the fact that most Jewish communities only had one cemetery gave the burial societies considerable power.[2] The authority of the *ḥevrah kadisha* became especially apparent when it was officially abolished together with the *kahal* and all other institutions of Jewish self-government in the Congress Kingdom of Poland in 1822.[3]

In this chapter I will briefly describe the emergence of the *ḥevrah kadisha* in eastern Europe within the general development of Jewish autonomy in early modern Europe and then show how and why burial societies preserved their autonomy and their key position in the Jewish community far into the nineteenth century. To discuss this development I will examine the case of the burial society in Praga, opposite Warsaw, on the eastern bank of the river Vistula, which unlike many other *ḥevrot kadisha* was only founded in the last quarter of the eighteenth century. Though the original *pinkas* (ledger) of the burial society, which was kept from 1785 to 1870, has not survived, it was copied and provided with a Polish translation by H. Kirszenbaum and A. Fajner in 1911 and is kept today in the Central Archives of the History of the

Jewish People in Jerusalem,[4] together with the much shorter *pinkas* from Warsaw from 1875 to 1905.[5]

The Emergence of Jewish Burial Societies in Eastern Europe

The emergence of the *ḥevrah kadisha*, the 'holy society', goes back to the idea of *gemilut ḥasadim* (lovingkindness), an act of charity that cannot be returned by the recipient. Many burial societies, like the one in Warsaw (Anshei Gomelei Hesed Shel Emet), included this attribute in their name.[6] It remains difficult to trace the emergence of the first *ḥevrot kadisha* in Ashkenazi communities in eastern Europe. Certainly, they were not part of the earliest Jewish community life, as is often believed and has also been argued by early researchers.[7] Jewish historians have debated whether early modern *ḥevrot* were directly related to the *ḥavurot* of antiquity or if they were a new form of community organization that only emerged in the early modern period. Although different societies geared towards charity existed in the Jewish communities of antiquity, they were not directly related to the new phenomenon of the burial society.[8] The first charitable societies in Ashkenazi communities, however, were the *ḥevrat bikur ḥolim*—mostly active in taking care of the sick—and the *hekdesh*, a shelter for the transient poor, the sick, and the elderly who had no other place to go.[9]

The first burial societies emerged among Sephardi Jews on the Iberian Peninsula in the thirteenth century. They were responsible for visiting and taking care of the sick, the burial of the dead, and sometimes supporting the poor and the endowment of orphan brides. A number of burial societies were subsequently founded in Italy, mainly in the sixteenth century. The first *ḥevrah kadisha* in eastern Europe was founded in Prague in 1564.[10] By the early eighteenth century, at the latest, most Jewish communities across eastern Europe had a burial society. It seems most likely that Sephardi influences, which travelled north through Italy, and local necessities contributed to their emergence. The increasing size of communities, migration, the new importance of Lurianic kabbalah and liturgy, and a 'sudden explosion of works codifying the laws that fix ritual and good conduct in all circumstances' furthered this development.[11]

The emergence of Jewish burial societies took place at a time when increasingly sophisticated community structures were developing in European Jewish communities. Thus, the development of *ḥevrot kadisha* was part of community cohesion typical of Jewish communities in the early modern period.[12] Some historians have argued that Jewish burial societies had similar structures and tasks to medieval Christian fraternities and guilds and that they took these institutions as their models. Although similarities certainly existed—including the general mission of administering charity, a similar distribution of tasks among the society's members, and the importance of the communal meal—it remains unclear if there was anything more than a similar structural development. Guilds and fraternities in Christian society, which also existed long before the sixteenth century, were mostly organized along occupational lines. Although Jewish burial societies sometimes included organizational structures for the mutual support of occupational groups, like a fund for grave-diggers or *sandakim* (who hold the child at a circumcision), they always served the entire community.[13]

The burial societies of seventeenth- and eighteenth-century eastern Europe were highly restrictive, usually including only the most wealthy and highly regarded members of the Jewish community. In addition to their relative social exclusivity, considerable time and financial resources were necessary to carry out the society's tasks. Based on the three core pillars of human behaviour according to the Talmud—*torah* (study of the Torah), *avodah* (service to God), and *gemilut ḥasadim*—the *ḥevrah kadisha* was a closely knit web which exerted a great deal of social pressure on its members. In addition to its core tasks of taking care of the sick and the dying, washing the dead body and preparing it for burial, the burial itself, and the maintenance of the cemetery, many burial societies took on additional tasks. The Viennese burial society, for example, provided clothes for the poor and, in particular, for poor brides; contributed financially to the building of a synagogue; and collected money for the poor of Palestine and the ransom of prisoners.[14]

The most important task of all burial societies was to take care of the dead. This included washing the corpse, transporting it to the cemetery (usually on a bier, rarely in a coffin), and the burial itself. The *takanot* (ordinances) of the burial societies usually detailed the procedures and the division of tasks, the number of members who were to accompany the dead, and the burial fees, which usually depended on the member's age, gender, status, reputation, and wealth. Though it was traditionally considered an honour to fulfil these duties, members could buy their way out. In eastern Europe, this occurred increasingly in the second half of the eighteenth century.[15]

It is not clear whether the power of the *ḥevrah kadisha* was a result of its unique position within the community, its control of the (usually only) cemetery, or a wide social consensus over how the dead should be cared for and a proper burial ensured. Although all burial societies listed a, sometimes long, catalogue of punishments for deviant behaviour—including fines, (temporary) exclusion, and more drastic measures, such as withholding burial rites or a 'donkey's burial' (*kevurat ḥamor*), outside or at a corner of the cemetery, usually reserved for those who committed suicide—it remains mostly unclear from the available sources to what extent such sanctions were applied.[16] Towards the end of the eighteenth century an erosion of consensus over the role of the traditional *ḥevrah kadisha* occurred in some European Jewish communities, mostly those strongly influenced by the Haskalah, such as Berlin, Königsberg, and Breslau, which led to fierce disputes and the foundation of alternative burial societies.[17] Despite these conflicts, the burial societies of early modern Ashkenazi communities were part of the community cohesion that David Ruderman sees as a central feature of early modern Jewry. Although community structures obviously existed earlier, the new forms surpassed their medieval predecessors in their size and their longevity.[18] The *ḥevrah kadisha*, although it developed later than basic community structures such as the *kahal*, became a central feature of most Jewish communities and, as will be described in this chapter, retained its importance in the Congress Kingdom of Poland far into the nineteenth century. Though community structures and *pinkasim* have received increasing attention as a source of community history in the last decade, surprisingly little attention has been paid to the burial societies and their *pinkasim* as a source of community cohesion and authority.[19]

A New Community

Community structures and autonomy were particularly highly developed in the territories of the Polish–Lithuanian Commonwealth, from the local *kahal* to the national organs of self-government, the Council of Four Lands and the Council of Lithuania. This extensive web of self-governing institutions saw some weakening in the second half of the eighteenth century, when the last Polish king, Stanisław August Poniatowski, abolished the national councils at the beginning of his reign in 1764 and 1765 in his quest for administrative centralization. Though the abolition of the national councils had no immediate impact on Jewish self-government at the local level, this step towards centralization of the Polish state foreshadowed the further undermining of Jewish autonomy.[20]

In Poland, burial societies had existed since the seventeenth century. In the Lithuanian community of Słuck, a *ḥevrah kadisha* had existed since 1680. The *pinkas* does not disclose much information about elections and society officials but mainly registered burials: an indication that probably another *pinkas* recording the daily business of the *ḥevrah* existed.[21] Zamość had a burial society similar to those further west in 1687. Its tasks included not only taking care of the sick and dying, organizing burials, and taking care of the cemetery, but also taking care of the poor. Its *takanot* instituted a strict separation between *kahal* and burial society, forbidding simultaneous service in the leadership of both institutions. Swarzędz, a Jewish community east of Poznań founded as a branch of the Poznań community on the basis of a privilege issued in 1621 by Zygmunt Grudziński, had a functioning *ḥevrah kadisha* at least from 1732.[22]

In early modern Poland, the extensive system of Jewish self-government was limited mainly by one legal measure, the privilege 'De non tolerandis Judaeis', which allowed (mostly) royal towns to ban Jewish settlement. The Polish capital of Warsaw held this privilege from 1527. Nevertheless, Jews moved to Warsaw in increasing numbers during the second half of the eighteenth century, settling mostly on the private property of Polish nobles or in Praga.[23] In Praga, existing settlement restrictions were not strictly enforced, and in 1765 about seventy families were counted as living permanently in the town. In 1775 these restrictions were abolished, legalizing the existing settlement of Jewish families. Their number rose continuously, and Praga became a stepping stone for migration into Warsaw.[24]

Some rudimentary forms of community organization had probably existed prior to 1775. In 1768 local Jews presented a petition to the magistrate in the 'name of the whole "congregation" of Jews from Praga'. However, initially, although Jews living in Praga belonged administratively to the Jewish community of Węgrów, the deceased were brought to Sochaczew and Grodzisk to be buried, some even until 1794. In 1780 a cemetery was established in Praga,[25] located on land purchased for this purpose by the prominent Jewish merchant and entrepreneur Szmuel Jakubowicz Zbyt-kower.[26] He had previously been active in the establishment of community struc-tures. Jakubowicz was appointed as *parnas* (president) of the Praga community by the authorities in 1788, probably based on the authority that he had gained within the community with the purchase of the cemetery and the foundation of the *ḥevrah kadisha* in 1785.[27] The foundational document of the burial society, dating from 1 May 1785, explicitly mentions him by his Hebrew name, Shemuel ben Avigdor, as its founder.

The foundational document contains the first *takanot* of the burial society. It was not included in the *pinkas* of the *ḥevrah kadisha*, but the *takanot* were written into the *pinkas* in 1787.[28] The *pinkas* itself opens with the first meeting of the elders and the *parnas*, following the first elections in 1785, and then sets out regulations typical of *ḥevrot kadisha*. The annual elections were to take place during the intermediate days of Passover. Five—later six—members of the burial society were chosen by lot to appoint the three—later four—*gaba'im* (assistants) and also sometimes one or two substitutes, two accountants, and two clerks, one for the finances and one for the *pinkas* of the burial society.[29]

The first and relatively short *takanot* stipulated that two members were always obliged to visit the sick and call a *gabai* when an individual's life was approaching its end. In a case of death, the *gabai* of the month together with at least three other members had to initiate the necessary tasks, such as the washing of the corpse and the digging of the grave. The members who were to take on these tasks were drawn by lot. The gravediggers were not to take any action without the advice and knowledge of at least one *gabai*. The *takanot* also threatened members who refused to fulfil their obligations with fines and exclusion from the annual elections, a common fea-ture of early modern community ordinances. Women were responsible for washing female deceased but were not full members of the society. The burial fee was to be set according to the dead person's wealth by one or more of the *gaba'im*.[30] Thus, the *takanot* placed a considerable amount of power in the hands of the *gaba'im*. It is diffi-cult to determine whether Szmuel Jakubowicz Zbytkower or other *gaba'im* abused their powers as has repeatedly been claimed in the scholarship on this topic.[31]

There has been much debate over the social make-up of the burial societies, with some scholars arguing that they were very exclusive and others claiming they were less so. In the case of Praga, exact numbers of members are not known. The *pinkas* lists thirty-eight signatures in 1785; a year later there are forty-two. New members, sometimes up to fifteen, were admitted every year. These new members were allowed to participate in the elections two years later if they were married and had paid their fees for joining the society. Some, however, remained in the status of novice for many years.[32] Nevertheless, the membership remained a relatively small circle. In 1810, when, according to Eisenbach, about 1,300 Jews lived in Praga, the ḥevrah kadisha had about 100 members and was, thus, probably limited to the higher echelons of the Jewish community.[33] Such a structure was common, although it was not apparently a feature of every ḥevrah kadisha. As Anna Michałowska-Mycielska has shown in the case of Swarzędz, about every second male community member may have been a member of the ḥevrah kadisha and the number of annual admissions was quite high.[34] In Zamość, the opposite seems to have been the case. The statutes of 1709 explicitly prohibited accepting more than one new member a year, and a long waiting period was required before a member could be elected an elder.[35] In addition, the burial society made strong efforts to keep poorer Jews out of its ranks.[36] Despite conflicting evidence, these cases and the similar structure of burial societies in eastern Europe point to strong attempts to limit membership to 'worthy'—meaning 'tax-paying'—members of the Jewish community.

From the beginning, the pinkas of the Praga ḥevrah kadisha shows the large range of tasks it performed. In 1802 it decided that all foreign traders of oxen and other goods had to pay the krupka—originally a tax on kosher meat, which was later expanded to include all transactions by Jews—directly to the burial society. This demonstrates its power, since in this way it took over a basic function of the kahal.[37] It was also responsible, according to a takanah of 1809, for the purchase, grinding, and distribution of flour to the poor at Passover.[38] In 1818 the ḥevrah kadisha also assumed control of the ḥevrat sandakut, the society responsible for providing sandakim, after it decided that the role 'had fallen to unsuitable people'.[39] From the same year until 1848, the gaba'im and other functionaries of the ḥevrat bikur ḥolim were listed in the pinkas of the ḥevrah kadisha, which suggests a close connection between the two.[40] Although, as mentioned above, in the seventeenth and eighteenth centuries some burial societies in eastern Europe assumed tasks that were not directly related to caring for the dying and the dead, the scale here seems different. The Praga burial society united in its hands most of the central tasks of the community to the point where there was little left to the kahal.

Strife was not unknown in the burial society and, at least partly, found its way into the pinkas. Initially the Praga society was united with the one in Warsaw, where Jews were only allowed to settle on the property of nobles and where a cemetery was established only in 1806. According to the pinkas, both societies decided in August 1785 to hold joint elections and to observe the same fast days and days for celebratory banquets. By 1795 the ḥevrot had separated, though the reason is not clear from the pinkas itself.[41] Possibly differing religious orientations led to conflict either between hasidim and their opponents or between the more Orthodox and those parts of Warsaw's Jewish population that leaned towards religious reform and acculturation.

Unlike the conflicts in ḥevrot kadisha in Prussia in the second half of the eighteenth century concerning members' behaviour, such as wearing a beard or the time of burial, conflicts in Praga mostly arose from personal friction.[42] In 1812 the electors introduced a takanah according to which 'if a member of the ḥevrah kadisha opens his mouth to slander another member of the ḥevrah and there are two admissible witnesses ... he has committed an eternal transgression, unless he demonstrates great repentance'.[43] Although the *pinkas* usually does not provide many details, it notes a number of fines and exclusions from the *ḥevrah*, although none of the latter seem to have been permanent. A similar example can be found in the *pinkas* of the Zamość burial society, where in 1812 a certain Szlama from Lwów 'raised his voice against the leadership of the burial society'. Warned by the *ḥevrah kadisha* that his name would be entered into the *pinkas* and he would be punished if he did not repent within four weeks, he appeared in front of the *ḥevrah kadisha* with an apology and an 'appropriate gift', seeking to be pardoned.[44]

In addition to slander of individual members or the burial society itself, a repeated reason for punishment was embezzlement. In 1799, for example, a certain Aaron ben Israel Moses from Chęciny, a former *gabai*, was expelled because he had been found in possession of society money and refused to present the accounts to the accountants and, moreover, had slandered the society.[45] In 1817 Tsevi ben Nehemyah, who had become a member of the burial society earlier that year, was said to have slandered the *gaba'im* in front of non-Jews. He was excluded from the elections for five years, and the *pinkas* records that he was allowed to participate in elections again in 1822.[46]

The Praga *ḥevrah kadisha* was founded comparatively late because of settlement restrictions but has all the characteristics of a typical early modern burial society, including regular elections, taking care of the sick and dying, performing burials, and maintaining the cemetery. Its activities were later extended to cover more general charity and control of some community institutions. The annual elections, the fast days, and the annual banquet played a central role in the life of the society and its members. As in many other burial societies, the leadership sought to limit the number of members to maintain its exclusive character, although the tasks the members had to fulfil were often time- and money-consuming.

The Abolition of the *Kahal* and New Powers for the *Ḥevrah Kadisha*

The Praga *ḥevrah kadisha* was founded at a time when Jewish autonomy was already under attack. As part of his attempts to reform the Polish state under severe internal and external pressure, King Stanisław August abolished the two national Jewish councils in 1764 and 1765. Although the 'Jewish question' was a minor issue during the Four Year Sejm (1788–92) in Warsaw, the issue of Jewish community autonomy was intensely debated by those who sought to reorganize the legal and social status of the Jews in Poland.[47] In the light of developments following the French revolution and the emancipation of the Jews of France as individuals, though not as a corporate group, Jewish autonomy became a topic of debate in Poland. Maskilim, such as Zalkind Hourwitz, a Polish Jew living in France, devoted much attention to the reforms of the Jewish community. Although Hourwitz mostly referred to the situation in France, his essay on the subject, 'Apologie des Juifs', was translated into

Polish and read by members of the Four Year Sejm. Regarding Jewish autonomy, he called for the abolition of the rabbinate, which he claimed was expensive and unnecessary, but took a more favourable view of the other institutions of Jewish self-government: 'Although I have said that the Jewish nation and Christians should be reconciled, this does not mean that their *kahals* . . . should be abolished. Let them maintain their synagogues, hospitals, and cemeteries and let those who wish to belong to them continue to pay all the taxes they paid before.'[48]

During the period of the Four Year Sejm, Christian opinions on Jewish autonomy were divided. They included negative voices who rejected any attempts at reform, arguing that Jews could not be integrated into Polish society because of their religious and national distinctiveness. Others like Hugo Kołłątaj, deputy chancellor of Crown Poland, were willing to grant legal rights after a period of 'improvement' but called for the abolition of any separate legal status including that of the *kehilot*.[49] Likewise, Mateusz Butrymowicz, a liberal member of the Four Year Sejm, demanded the abolition of Jewish autonomy which he saw as a 'state within a state'.[50]

Most Jewish community representatives rejected the abolition of autonomy, although some argued for it.[51] While Rabbi Herszel Józefowicz of Chełm presented the arguments of a majority of Polish Jewry, Szymel Wolfowicz from Vilna saw the system of Jewish self-government as flawed and at times corrupt and thus something which should be abolished. However, he drew a distinction between the *kahal* and the *ḥevrot*, noting that it was the *ḥevrot*, and especially the *ḥevrah kadisha*, that ministered to the sick, the poor, and the deceased. He stressed that, although the elders of the *ḥevrah kadisha* set the fees for burials—a practice that was open to abuse—they were elected by the community and most of their funds went to the poor. Moreover, according to him, 'almost all Jews are members of the burial society'. In his eyes, it was only the *kahal* that was corrupt and should be abolished.[52] Thus, at this time, the critics of Jewish self-government mostly attacked the community rabbis and the *kahal* but not the charitable societies. The fact that even Jewish reformers in Poland did not argue for the eradication of the *ḥevrot* might be one of the reasons why the burial societies were able to persist even after their official abolition.

A few years later, Jacques Calmanson (1722–1811), King Stanisław August's physician and a maskil, published a plan for reforming Jewish life in Poland, in French in 1796 and in a Polish translation in 1797. He moved beyond a critique of the *kahal* and included the burial society within the realm of institutions that needed to be reformed. He described in detail the traditional tasks of the burial society but lamented:

As is the way of the world the burial society, in its essence a sacred and beneficial institution, has suffered the same fate as all human undertakings . . . Over time it has become corrupted and has strayed from the purpose set for it by those who took pity on the poor and the destitute . . . However, because of the hard-heartedness of the synagogue's leaders and especially the greed of its supervisors, the sums allocated to relieve the destitution and suffering of the poor are now used only for extravagance and indulgence.[53]

He harshly criticized the elders of the burial society, calling them 'undistinguished men of law who owe their position not to their talent or proven integrity but to the patronage which their machinations have procured'.[54] He thus called for the reorganization of the burial society under the supervision of a reformed *kahal*, which he described elsewhere in his treatise. Though certainly much more critical of the burial society, Calmanson was aware of its importance and wanted to see it reformed. Instead of demanding the abolition of the *kahal*, he rather argued for reform of the institutions of Jewish self-government.

Since the first partition of Poland in 1772 different measures and rules had been applied in different parts of the collapsing Polish–Lithuanian Commonwealth, but all efforts to reform the Jewish communities on Polish lands, whether those of Jewish reformers or of Polish administrators, came to a halt with the second and third partitions in 1793 and 1795. In Prussia, Jewish self-government was officially abolished, though some institutions obviously continued to exist. The *pinkas* of the Swarzędz *ḥevrah kadisha*, for example, ends in 1818, though it is not clear if the burial society was also abolished. The city had become part of Prussia in 1793 and was part of the Duchy of Warsaw from 1807 until it became Prussian again in 1815. It remains unclear when the *ḥevrah kadisha* turned into a voluntary society according to Prussian law, but it continued its tasks throughout the nineteenth century.[55] In Galicia, which had become part of the Habsburg empire, traditional Jewish self-government was abolished in 1789, after various attempts to reform it.[56] In the territories of the Russian partition, the traditional institutions of self-government retained most of their power in the first decades after the partition, as Russian rulers and administrators sought to understand the new Jewish population in its territories. Despite some serious limitation of the *kahal*'s activities in 1797, most *ḥevrot* continued to function until the official abolition of the *kahal* in 1844. In the Pale of Settlement, the regulations of Tsar Paul I and his successors weakened the *kahal* and at the same time increased the power of voluntary societies in general and the burial societies in particular.[57] In the Congress Kingdom of Poland, however, the *kahal* and all other institutions of Jewish self-government were abolished in 1822.

Until the abolition of the *kahal* in 1822 neither official nor internal Jewish criticism threatened the power of the *ḥevrah kadisha*. Its position was based on its official recognition and—what was probably more important—a consensus among at least large parts of the Jewish population about the role and functioning of the burial society within the community. In March 1822 the Government Commission for Religious Denominations and Public Enlightenment demanded that all voivodeship commissions and the magistrate of Warsaw 'regard as illegal . . . all burial societies like all other societies among the people of the Old Covenant, and not tolerate their activity; and if they are in charge of collecting religious fees, to move this [task] to the Synagogue Administration'.[58] Nevertheless there is no mention of any official abolition of the *ḥevrah kadisha* in the *pinkas* of the Praga burial society.

On the contrary, it seems that the Praga *ḥevrah kadisha* was able to strengthen its power in the 1830s. After a first regulation concerning the sale of flour for Passover in

1809, renewed *takanot* were added in 1826, 1830, 1834, and 1837 that regulated the place of sale and the fees to be paid to the *ḥevrah kadisha*. Any merchant who did not register with the *ḥevrah kadisha* ran the risk of having his flour declared unfit. In 1830 the burial society decided 'that all local merchants in flour for Passover have to come to the *gabai* of the month every year on 1 Adar. He will provide them with the permission to grind the wheat for the flour for Passover, but if the *gabai* does not give him permission, the rabbi will not declare the wheat or the millstones to be kosher'.[59] Foreign merchants had to pay a higher fee on their flour for Passover and likewise needed permission from the *ḥevrah kadisha*. In 1837 they were even advised to not sell their flour at the same place as local merchants but only at a specific spot, which they had to rent from the *ḥevrah kadisha*. On the Warsaw side of the Vistula, the *ḥevrah kadisha* likewise regulated the sale of flour for Passover until the mid-nineteenth century.[60] When the merchants in Praga appeared before the *gaba'im* of the burial society in 1830, they were threatened with being noted in the *pinkas* with serious consequences for the future.[61] In addition to flour for Passover, the *ḥevrah kadisha* also took over the regulation of kosher butchering and established *takanot* for ritual slaughterers and meat inspectors in Praga in 1834. This included control of the knives and the sale of the kosher and non-kosher parts of slaughtered animals.[62]

In addition to acquiring in this way important sources of income, the *ḥevrah kadisha* in Praga constantly increased its power over other fields of religious life and other *ḥevrot*. In 1836 the elders of the *ḥevrah kadisha* intervened in a conflict within the *ḥevrat tehilim* (prayer society), demonstrating its power over an important area of religious life. After 1837 the elders and other functionaries of the *ḥevrat talmud torah* (study society) and after 1847 of a soup kitchen were elected by the electors of the *ḥevrah kadisha*, suggesting close links between these *ḥevrot*. In 1859 the *ḥevrah kadisha* also appointed the two inspectors of the chest of the *tsedakah le'erets yisra'el* (the society for the collection of charity for Jews living in the Land of Israel).[63] Similarly, the tasks of the *ḥevrat bikur ḥolim* were taken over by the burial society in 1846. From this year on no separate elders for the society for visiting the sick were elected. One of the few mentions in the *pinkas* of the changing circumstances of Jewish life in mid-nineteenth-century Warsaw was the introduction of a quarterly fee for all members of the burial society in 1838. This fee was to cover the hiring of men to visit the sick and dying, including the night vigil, a task that apparently could not be fulfilled exclusively by the members of the burial society due to the growing numbers of Jewish inhabitants.[64] A similar increase in obligations can also be seen on the Warsaw side of the city. Renamed the Burial Administration, the former *ḥevrah kadisha* not only took care of the sick, the dying, and the dead but was also involved in a number of additional charitable tasks such as providing clothing, financial assistance, firewood, and flour for Passover to the poor; funding for religious schools; and granting small loans.[65]

Despite the official abolition of the *kahal* and the *ḥevrot*, the *ḥevrah kadisha* continued its existence, apparently supported by a wide consensus within the Jewish population. Throughout the Congress Kingdom of Poland the burial societies adopted additional tasks that had originally belonged to the *kahal* in many communities.[66] Mordechai Zalkin has described a similar development in Vilna in the Pale of Settlement. Prior to 1821 different *ḥevrot* including the burial society had assumed a large number of tasks that would have originally belonged to the *kahal*, including providing alms for the poor, paying for wet nurses for orphans, providing burials for the poor, and distributing charity and food before Passover. Likewise, the kosher-meat tax went straight to the *ḥevrah kadisha* and not into the hands of the *kahal*. After the abolition of the *kahal* the burial society continued to exist under the name Hevrat Tsedakah Gedolah and took over larger parts of community administration far into the second half of the nineteenth century.[67]

Unlike the *pinkas* of the Praga *ḥevrah kadisha*, the *pinkas* of the Zamość *ḥevrah kadisha* provides at least a brief glimpse of the changing political conditions after 1822. An entry from 1825 refers to the new situation that developed following the abolition of the *kahal*. The entry hints at a chaotic situation within the burial society, and possibly within the Jewish community more generally, and calls for new elections, which apparently had not taken place for the past two years. The entry then emphasizes that the new members of the official community board, which had replaced the *kahal*, held the same power as the leaders of the *kahal* had. Moreover, the electoral board of the burial society was to consult with the members of the community board when new candidates were to be elected to the leadership of the burial society. As before in the case of the *kahal*, leaders of the community board were prohibited from taking leadership positions in the burial society and vice versa.[68] It is remarkable that the *ḥevrah kadisha*, which was abolished along with the *kahal* in 1822, officially recognized and lent support to the new community leadership, a clear reflection of the burial society's power within the community. However, even before 1822, the Zamość burial society sometimes had to provide financial aid to the *kahal* and had always made sure to maintain its independence.[69] Similarly the *ḥevrot kadisha* in Lublin and Łódź continued to fulfil their traditional tasks, although the new community board was officially responsible for the burials in these two rapidly growing communities.[70]

Although the burial societies seem to have assumed more power within many Jewish communities following the official abolition of the *kahal* and the appointment of state-recognized community boards, some challenges to their power do become visible in the first half of the nineteenth century. A general consensus on the need for a charitable society and the importance of the tasks related to burials that was visible in the debates at the end of the eighteenth century continued well into the nineteenth century. However, one central challenge for the traditional burial societies was the rapid growth of the Jewish communities, which imposed severe strain on voluntary charitable work.

A Crumbling Consensus

Towards the last quarter of the nineteenth century the consensus on the structures of community self-government seemed to crumble, at least in the larger cities of the

Congress Kingdom of Poland. This is especially true for Warsaw, including Praga, by then the largest Jewish settlement in the world. It seems that the end of the burial society in Praga and the general crumbling of central community structures and organizations was directly linked with the rapid growth of the Jewish community in Warsaw. In 1850 somewhat under 40,000 Jewish men and women were registered in Warsaw; this number had more than tripled by 1880 and was probably much higher due to the large number of unregistered Jewish inhabitants.[71] These demographic changes also included an influx of Russian-speaking Jewish immigrants, 'Litvaks', who had sympathy neither for hasidism nor for those mostly acculturated Jews who supported the Polish cause. Thus, they added to the different Jewish denominations within the city, and the 'selective co-operation' between mitnagedim, who dominated the community leadership until around 1850, the growing number of hasidim, and a smaller but influential group of wealthy and reform-oriented Jews became increasingly difficult to maintain.[72]

Nevertheless, these growing conflicts and the challenges of urbanization and population growth are not reflected in the *pinkas* of the Praga burial society.[73] As mentioned, the elders of the burial society succeeded in concentrating more power in their hands after 1822. The *pinkas*, however, does not disclose how the ḥevrah kadisha responded to the new challenges of immigration into Warsaw and the increasing denominational and social diversity of the Jewish community. It is difficult even to say how much the willingness to personally fulfil obligations concerning the dead and burial declined. The number of conflicts within the burial society, as far as they were noted down in the *pinkas*, does not seem to have increased in the second half of the nineteenth century. The elections and the alteration between the elders and other functionaries continued and the numbers of newly accepted members fell only slightly between 1840 and 1870.[74] Even an investigation in 1843, after which the Praga ḥevrah kadisha was officially abolished, its possessions confiscated, and all its tasks assumed by the community board in Warsaw, did not alter the structure of entries in the *pinkas*. Although two elders of the ḥevrah kadisha and one elder of the ḥevrat talmud torah signed the minutes recording this incident,[75] it did not leave any trace in the *pinkas* of the burial society, which continued to note down elections and new members as if nothing had happened.

The same seems to be true for the ḥevrah kadisha in Warsaw, founded around 1790, when the elders for Warsaw were no longer recorded in the *pinkas* of the Praga ḥevrah kadisha. After the abolition of all forms of self-government in 1822, notables of the Jewish community created the Burial Administration, officially dependent on the community board. Despite conflicts between reform-oriented Jews in Warsaw and the Burial Administration in the 1830s and the renewed prohibition of the ḥevrah kadisha in 1843, it continued to exist. Fees for burials remained the largest source of income for the community board and, according to Ignacy Schiper, the burial society also sought to maintain and control the religious observance of Warsaw's Jewish inhabitants by applying or at least threatening discriminatory burial practices.[76]

A surviving *pinkas* for the Warsaw burial society provides some glimpse into its inner life for the years 1865 to 1905.[77] The *takanot* of 1866 list the traditional tasks of a *ḥevrah kadisha*: visiting the sick, charity for the sick, the organization of the funeral procession, and the burial itself. The elders were to name twelve individuals and six replacements, who had to spend one day at the cemetery each every two weeks, supervise the observance of the rules, and in the evening report to the *gabai*. The *pinkas* does not disclose if this task was paid or voluntary.[78] The members of the *ḥevrah kadisha* were instructed to pray before beginning their work and to visit the ritual bath before entering the cemetery. They were told to abstain from profane conversations and arguing while handling the corpse and during the burial procession. In relation to visiting the sick, the *takanot* also provide exact regulations. The *gabai* decided who had to visit the sick and who was to read sections from the Mishnah for the soul of the departed. The visits had to take place at home and in the hospital. The visitor had to assess the condition of the sick person and if necessary prepare him or her for death and at the appropriate time ask the women and children to leave the room. Transgression of these regulations was punished with fines. The *takanot* also prohibited gambling. The annual banquet of the burial society still occupied its traditionally important place: in addition to the members of the *ḥevrah kadisha*, the chief rabbi of Warsaw and members of the community board were invited to attend.[79]

Despite the harmonious image given by the *pinkasim*, burial societies in the Congress Kingdom of Poland were now subject to increased criticism. As François Guesnet has shown in great detail, the criticism that emerged in Poland and Russia from the 1830s onward, voiced primarily by reform-oriented Jews, for example in the Polish Jewish newspaper *Izraelita*, led to investigations and sometimes repeated prohibitions—as in Warsaw in 1843—but usually not to the end of the *ḥevrah kadisha* involved. Often, the critique was directed less against the existence of the burial society as such and more against the form of and rituals accompanying the burial, such as washing the dead body at home or taking it to the cemetery without a proper hearse and without a coffin.[80] In Warsaw, a first attempt in the early 1830s to use a hearse failed, and when hearses were finally introduced in 1848 they were mostly used by the bourgeois and reform-oriented members of the community. In the last quarter of the century, the community did have a simple hearse, which was probably necessary because of the distances in the rapidly growing city. The use of two different hearses went along with repeated arguments over the question of whether the coachman had to walk alongside the hearse as demanded by the Orthodox part of the Jewish population. The use of coffins was only allowed after 1886, while permission to decorate the hearse with flowers had to be retracted immediately after it was granted in 1880. The building of a *taharah* house for washing the dead on the premises of the cemetery had been discussed since the 1860s but the house was only erected in 1878.[81] Similar developments can be traced in other large communities in the Congress Kingdom of Poland. In Łódź a hearse was introduced in 1880, but coffins were not in use even in 1896, although two years later a *taharah* house was erected at the cemetery.[82]

What brought the Praga burial society to an end was, thus, not structural challenges in the system of self-government or criticism of burial practices but the failure to establish a united community leadership in Warsaw. After the death in 1868 of Yeshayah Mushkat, rabbi and supreme judge of the Praga Jewish community with its semi-autonomous status, and that, two years later, of the Warsaw chief rabbi, Dov Ber Meisl, it became impossible for the different forces within the community to find a new chief rabbi. A last attempt with the election of Rabbi Jacob Gesundheit in 1870 failed with his demise in 1873, triggered by the 'unholy alliance' of hasidim and integrationists. Mushkat's death led to the abolition of what remained of Praga's community self-government and to the official incorporation of the Praga *hevrah kadisha* into the Warsaw Burial Administration in 1870.[83] The Praga *pinkas* ends with the election of new elders for the burial society, the society for visiting the sick, the *hevrat talmud torah*, and the poor kitchen, and the request of a certain Natanael Waldberg to be admitted into the *hevrah kadisha* on the intermediate days of Passover in April 1870.[84] The Warsaw *pinkas* equally does not show any trace of the incorporation of its Praga counterpart: no former members of the Praga burial society appear in the *pinkas* from Warsaw in any official function. Certainly, the Warsaw Burial Administration had other challenges to deal with, considering the mostly poor Jewish inhabitants of Warsaw. While the wealthy were usually buried in Warsaw, the old Praga cemetery was used for burying the poor into the last quarter of the nineteenth century.[85] In 1905 the *pinkas* of the Warsaw *hevrah kadisha*, though it functioned officially through the Burial Administration, ends likewise with an entry naming the newly elected elders. The same year, the community board had succeeded in uniting in a single body the ten Warsaw *hevrot* that were involved in taking care of the sick; most likely this included the burial society as well.[86]

Despite some crumbling of the consensus on the form of burial it was mainly the size and diversity of the Warsaw Jewish community that brought the burial societies to an end and led the community board to take over their tasks. Burial societies continued to exist in smaller towns across the Kingdom of Poland, some into the twentieth century. The *hevrah kadisha* in Zamość continued to function until 1885 while in the small town of Mordy a surviving *pinkas* of the burial society covers the years 1893 to 1914.[87] A similar pattern can be discerned in towns in the Pale of Settlement. Here the Russian administration strongly differentiated between the *kahal*, considered a negative force within the community and in relation to the authorities, and the *hevrot*, which were seen in a much more positive light as voluntary societies fulfilling specific tasks within the community. As in the Congress Kingdom of Poland, many *hevrot* took over some of the functions of the *kahal*, as Yohanan Petrovsky-Shtern has shown for Kamenets-Podolsky.[88] In 1938 Shemuel Winter claimed that 'until today' there were 'numerous' *hevrot* in nearly every Polish shtetl. According to him, the *hevrah kadisha* of Brisk (Brest) had a *pinkas* covering the years 1848 to 1931, with a traditional set of *takanot* recorded in 1887.[89] The *hevrah kadisha* in Słuck seems to have existed in some form up to 1924.[90]

Conclusion

From the seventeenth century the *ḥevrah kadisha* was one of the most important elements of Jewish self-government across Europe. Independently of the general degree of autonomy in a given state or region, the Jewish burial society fulfilled crucial tasks with regard to charity, taking care of the sick, the dying, and the dead, and maintaining the community cemetery. Its relationship with the *kahal* might vary, as did the additional charitable functions it assumed. However, the importance of burying the dead and control of the (usually, only) cemetery made the *ḥevrah kadisha* different from other voluntary *ḥevrot*. Though all *ḥevrot* sought to ensure discipline among their members, the power of the burial society extended over the whole Jewish community. While social and political changes including the Haskalah, Jewish emancipation, and acculturation transformed the position of traditional burial societies in the German-speaking lands, they did not cease to function, but continued to exist or were re-established in many Jewish communities as voluntary societies under the supervision of the community board. By contrast, during the nineteenth century in the Congress Kingdom of Poland and eastern Europe in general they were able to assume additional powers.

The debates about Jewish autonomy in the last years of the Polish–Lithuanian Commonwealth have focused strongly on criticism of rabbis and the *kahal* and less so on charitable societies, including the burial societies. Moreover, a broad consensus about the importance of laying the dead to rest in an appropriate manner guaranteed them additional power. The burial societies in Praga and Warsaw had an elevated status in comparison to the *kahal* from their inception, clearly a consequence of the late establishment of the Jewish communities in both towns. With the abolition of Jewish self-government in 1822, the burial societies were able to use their social capital to continue their traditional work within the Jewish community and even take over additional tasks traditionally performed by the *kahal*. Even reform-oriented parts of the Jewish population seem to have been reconciled to the continued existence of such a traditional institution as the *ḥevrah kadisha*.

Only in the second half of the nineteenth century did the increasing critique of certain burial rituals and even more the massive growth of the Jewish population in Warsaw bring an end to the dominant position enjoyed by burial societies. Factional disputes within the more and more diverse Jewish community weakened the power of the *ḥevrah kadisha* and furnished the state authorities with more opportunities for intervention. Moreover, the size of the community made it impossible to retain the exclusive character of the burial society and for it to fulfil its many obligations through voluntary and unpaid work. However, in smaller communities in the former Polish–Lithuanian Commonwealth, burial societies continued to exist in their traditional form, often up until the Second World War.

This chapter has also highlighted the significance of the *pinkas* as a source of Jewish community history. *Pinkasim* are an important source for writing community history as they provide a glimpse into the inner workings of community institutions, including the conflicts within them and with other bodies. However, the case of the Praga *ḥevrah kadisha* can also serve as a warning. While it details internal conflicts in the society—slander against the *gaba'im*, protests by merchants of flour for Passover, and many other such disputes—it remains silent on outside changes. If we only relied on the *pinkas* we would know nothing about the abolition of the *kahal* and the *ḥevrot* in 1822, the wide-ranging police and state attempts to end the activities of *ḥevrot* in 1843–4, or why the *ḥevrah kadisha* in Praga ceased to exist in 1870.

Notes

I wish to thank François Guesnet not only for sparking my interest in matters of Jewish community organization in general and the *ḥevrah kadisha* in particular more than twenty years ago, but also, together with Antony Polonsky, for inviting me to return to this topic by contributing to this volume.

1 On the story, see F. Guesnet, 'A Tuml in the Shtetl: Khayim Betsalel Grinberg's "Di Khevre-Kedishe Sude"', *Polin*, 16 (2003), 93–106: 93–4.

2 On death and burial in early modern Ashkenazi communities, see S.-A. Goldberg, *Crossing the Jabbok: Illness and Death in Ashkenazi Judaism in Sixteenth- through Nineteenth-Century Prague*, trans. C. Cosman (London, 1996); E. Horowitz, 'The Jews of Europe and the Moment of Death in Medieval and Modern Times', *Judaism*, 44 (1995), 271–81.

3 On the abolition of the *kahal* in Poland, see D. Szterenkac, 'Zniesienie kahałów i utworzenie dozorów bóżniczych w pierwszych latach Królestwa Polskiego', MA thesis (University of Warsaw, 1932); F. Guesnet, *Polnische Juden im 19. Jahrhundert: Lebensbedingungen, Rechtsnormen und Organisation im Wandel* (Cologne, 1998), 223–9; on the abolition of the *kahal* in Russia, see A. Shochat, 'Hahanhagah bikehilot rusyah im bitul hakahal', *Zion*, 44 (1977), 143–233; I. Levitats, 'The Jewish Association (Hevrah) in Russia during the First Half of the Nineteenth Century', *Jewish Review*, 1 (1943), 83–112.

4 Central Archives of the History of the Jewish People, Jerusalem (hereafter CAHJP), PL 4: 'Pinkas haḥevrah kadisha depraga / Księga bractwa pogrzebowego na Pradze 1785–1870', copy by H. Kirszenbaum and A. Fajner, 1911.

5 CAHJP, PL 358: 'Pinkas miḥevrat anshei gomelei ḥesed shel emet bevarsha'.

6 See E. Frisch, *An Historical Survey of Jewish Philanthropy: From the Earliest Times to the Nineteenth Century* (New York, 1969), 92–4; J. R. Marcus, *Communal Sick-Care in the German Ghetto* (Cincinnati, 1947), 248–52; see also Goldberg, *Crossing the Jabbok*, 105–6.

7 Avigdor Farine argued that 'a Hevra Qadisha must have existed in all Jewish communities at a very early time' and that east European *ḥevrot* of the nineteenth century simply preserved medieval structures (A. Farine, 'Charity and Study Societies in Europe of the Sixteenth–Eighteenth Centuries', *Jewish Quarterly Review*, 64 (1973/4), 16–47, 164–75: 17).

8 On continuity between the Jewish charitable societies of antiquity and the *ḥevrah kadisha*, see Goldberg, *Crossing the Jabbok*, 18, 82–3; Farine, 'Charity and Study Societies', 17; Frisch, *An Historical Survey of Jewish Philanthropy*, 101, 108–10, 156; on the absence of such continuity, see Marcus, *Communal Sick-Care*, 55–9; F. Baer, 'Der Ursprung der Chewra', *Zeitschrift für jüdische Wohlfahrtspflege*, 1 (1929), 241–7: 246.

9 Marcus, *Communal Sick-Care*, 274–5; A. Reinke, *Judentum und Wohlfahrtspflege in Deutschland: Das jüdische Krankenhaus in Breslau 1726–1944* (Hanover, 1999), 42.

10 Among the early foundations was Huesca (1323) in Spain, followed by Modena (1516) and Ferrara (1552) in Italy. After the one in Prague, burial societies were founded in the Ash-

kenazi communities of Frankfurt am Main (1597), Worms (1609), Amsterdam (1609), and Metz (1621) (Baer, 'Der Ursprung der Chewra', 243; Marcus, *Communal Sick-Care*, 61; Horowitz, 'The Jews of Europe and the Moment of Death', 271; Reinke, *Judentum und Wohlfahrtspflege*, 32; Goldberg, *Crossing the Jabbok*, 85–6, 91).

11 Goldberg, *Crossing the Jabbok*, 75, see also 65–80.

12 D. B. Ruderman, *Early Modern Jewry: A New Cultural History* (Princeton, NJ, 2010), 57–98.

13 Jacob Marcus argues that Christian guilds were important models for the ḥevrah kadisha (Marcus, *Communal Sick-Care*, 67–79), while Sylvie-Anne Goldberg rejects this argument (Goldberg, *Crossing the Jabbok*, 90–9). On medieval Christian guilds in Central Europe, see e.g. O. G. Oexle, 'Die mittelalterlichen Gilden: Ihre Selbstdeutung und ihr Beitrag zur Formung sozialer Strukturen', *Miscellanea Mediaevalia*, 12 (1979), 203–26.

14 B. Wachstein, *Die Gründung der Wiener Chewra Kadischa im Jahre 1763* (Vienna, 1911). On the tasks of the ḥevrah kadisha, see Marcus, *Communal Sick-Care*, 116; id., 'The Triesch Hebra Kaddisha, 1687–1828', *Hebrew Union College Annual*, 19 (1945–6), 169–204: 189–90; L. Lewin, *Geschichte der Israelitischen Kranken-Verpflegungs-Anstalt und Beerdigungs-Gesellschaft zu Breslau 1726–1926 (hevra kadisha)* (Breslau, 1926), 109–10; H. Flesch, 'Zur Geschichte der mähr. "heiligen Vereine" (Chewra Kadischa)', *Jahrbuch der Jüdisch-Literarischen Gesellschaft*, 21 (1930), 217–58: 232; H. Vogelstein (ed.), *Festschrift zum 200jährigen Bestehen des israelitischen Vereins für Krankenpflege und Beerdigung Chewra Kaddischa zu Königsberg i. Pr., 1704–1904* (Königsberg, 1904), p. xi.

15 Vogelstein, *Festschrift zum 200jährigen Bestehen des israelitischen Vereins*, pp. vii, ix–x, xii–xiii, 29–34; Lewin, *Geschichte der Israelitischen Kranken-Verpflegungs-Anstalt und Beerdigungs-Gesellschaft*, 11, 110–11; Wachstein, *Die Gründung der Wiener Chewra Kadischa*, 21; Marcus, 'The Triesch Hebra Kaddisha', 194; on coffins, see Goldberg, *Crossing the Jabbok*, 222; G. Zürn, *Die Altonaer jüdische Gemeinde (1611–1873): Ritus und soziale Institutionen des Todes im Wandel* (Hamburg, 2001), 125. A series of paintings from Prague from 1780 illustrates the tasks of the ḥevrah kadisha (see D. Altshuler (ed.), *The Precious Legacy: Judaic Treasures from the Czechoslovak State Collections* (New York, 1983), 154–8).

16 For examples and related discussions, see Lewin, *Geschichte der Israelitischen Kranken-Verpflegungs-Anstalt und Beerdigungs-Gesellschaft*, 111; Goldberg, *Crossing the Jabbok*, 95, 219–20; Wachstein, *Die Gründung der Wiener Chewra Kadischa*, 21; Flesch, 'Zur Geschichte der mähr. "heiligen Vereine"', 222, 226, 230–2; Vogelstein, *Festschrift zum 200jährigen Bestehen des israelitischen Vereins*, pp. xi, xvi; Marcus, 'The Triesch Hebra Kaddisha', 187–8; id., *Communal Sick-Care*, 102; Zürn, *Die Altonaer jüdische Gemeinde*, 111–13.

17 M. Samet, 'Halanat metim: letoledot hapulmus al kevi'at zeman hamavet', *Asufot*, 4 (1989), 413–65; C. Aust, 'Conflicting Authorities: Rabbis, Physicians, Lay Leaders and the Question of Burial', in D. Shulman (ed.), *Meditations on Authority* (Jerusalem, 2013), 87–100.

18 Ruderman, *Early Modern Jewry*, 57–98, esp. 94–5.

19 I. Bartal, 'The Pinkas: From Communal Archive to Total History', *Polin*, 29 (2017), 21–40. A large project has been instituted, collecting and publishing community *pinkasim* ('Pinkasim Collection: The International Repository of Communal Ledgers', National Library of Israel website, visited 27 June 2019). See also S. Litt (ed.), *Jüdische Gemeindestatuten aus dem aschkenasischen Kulturraum 1650–1850* (Göttingen, 2014). Besides older works from the beginning of the twentieth century, rather few works deal with burial societies in particular, with the exception of Goldberg, *Crossing the Jabbok*; M. Zalkin, 'Who Wields the Power? The Kahal and Chevrot in Vilna at the Beginning of the 19th Century', in I. Lempertas (ed.), *The Gaon of Vilnius and the Annals of Jewish Culture* (Vilnius, 1998),

354–60; Y. Petrovsky-Shtern, 'Russian Legislation and Jewish Self-Governing Institutions: The Case of Kamenets-Podolskii', *Jews in Russia and Eastern Europe*, 56 (2006), 107–30.

20 A. Teller, 'Councils', in G. D. Hundert (ed.), *YIVO Encyclopedia of Jews in Eastern Europe* (New Haven, Conn., 2008), 352–7.

21 H. D. Boonin et al., 'The Pinkas of the Chevra Kadisha of Slutsk', *Avotaynu*, 13 (1997), 28–33.

22 A. Michałowska, 'Charity and the Charity Society (Khevra Kadisha) in the Jewish Community of Swarzędz in the Eighteenth Century', *Acta Poloniae Historica*, 87 (2003), 78–88: 81.

23 A 1792 census that included the properties of nobles and both sides of the Vistula counted 6,750 Jews (A. Eisenbach, 'Żydzi warszawscy i sprawa żydowska w XVIII w.', in J. Kowecki, H. Szwankowska, and A. Zahorski (eds.), *Warszawa XVIII wieku*, 3 vols. (Warsaw, 1972–5), iii. 229–98: 236; B. Grochulska, *Warszawa na mapie Polski stanisławowskiej: Podstawy gospodarcze rozwoju miasta* (Warsaw, 1980), 25–6). On early Jewish migration to Warsaw, see H. Węgrzynek, 'Illegal Immigrants: The Jews of Warsaw, 1527–1792', in G. Dynner and F. Guesnet (eds.), *Warsaw: The Jewish Metropolis. Essays in Honor of the 75th Birthday of Professor Antony Polonsky* (Leiden, 2015), 19–41.

24 A. Eisenbach, 'The Jewish Population in Warsaw at the Turn of the Eighteenth Century', *Polin*, 3 (1988), 46–77: 48; C. Aust, *The Jewish Economic Elite: Making Modern Europe* (Bloomington, Ind., 2018), 112–13.

25 Eisenbach, 'The Jewish Population in Warsaw', 48, 61; H. Kirszenbaum, 'Bractwo pogrzebowe na Pradze', *Kwartalnik Poświęcony Badaniu Przeszłości Żydów w Polsce*, 3 (1913), 133–46: 134.

26 On Zbytkower, see E. Ringelblum, 'Szmul Zbytkower', *Zion*, 3 (1938), 246–66, 337–55; A. Michałowska, 'Szmul Jakubowicz Zbytkower', *Biuletyn Żydowskiego Instytutu Historycznego*, 162–3 (1992), 79–90; Aust, *The Jewish Economic Elite*, 115–18; on his connection to hasidic circles, see G. Dynner, *Men of Silk: The Hasidic Conquest of Polish Jewish Society* (Oxford, 2006), 94–9.

27 Aust, *The Jewish Economic Elite*, 117–18. According to Jacob Shatzky, five *parnasim* were appointed in Warsaw and six in Praga between 1759 and 1794 (J. Shatzky, *Geshikhte fun yidn in varshe*, 3 vols. (New York, 1947–53), i. 123–7).

28 'Z pinkasu Bractwa pogrzebowego praskiego', *Kwartalnik Poświęcony Badaniu Przeszłości Żydów w Polsce*, 1 (1912), 138–44; repr. in P. Fijałkowski, *Warszawska społeczność żydowska w okresie stanisławowskim 1764–1795: Rozwój w dobie wielkich zmian* (Warsaw, 2016), 377–80; 'Pinkas haḥevrah kadisha depraga', 3 (Kirszenbaum and Fajner, 5, 7).

29 'Pinkas haḥevrah kadisha depraga', 1 (Kirszenbaum and Fajner, 1). Only in the years 1790, 1792, and 1807 are no elections mentioned. In Swarzędz, elections were held likewise annually on the intermediate days of Passover (Michałowska, 'Charity and the Charity Society', 81).

30 'Pinkas haḥevrah kadisha depraga', 3, 10, 40 (Kirszenbaum and Fajner, 5, 7, 19, 69). In 1788 four women responsible for washing the dead are listed in the *pinkas* (ibid. 12 (Kirszenbaum and Fajner, 21)).

31 Shatzky, *Geshikhte fun yidn in varshe*, i. 146; E. N. Frenk, *Meshumadim in poyln in 19tn yorhundert* (Warsaw, 1923), 27–8; T. Korzon, *Wewnętrzne dzieje Polski za Stanisława Augusta (1764–1794): Badania historyczne ze stanowiska ekonomicznego i administracyjnego*, 4 vols. (Kraków, 1882–6), i. 224–5.

32 'Pinkas haḥevrah kadisha depraga', 5, 10, 53 (Kirszenbaum and Fajner, 9, 19, 93).

33 Eisenbach, 'The Jewish Population', 61; C. Aust, 'Kontinuität und Wandel in den jüdischen Gemeinden Berlins und Warschaus im Übergang vom 18. zum 19. Jahrhundert. Ein kontrastierender Vergleich am Beispiel der Beerdigungsbruderschaften (Chewrot Kadischa)', MA thesis (Free University of Berlin, 2003), 46, 125.

34 A. Michałowska-Mycielska, *The Jewish Community: Authority and Social Control in Poznań and Swarzędz, 1650–1793*, trans. A. Adamowicz (Wrocław, 2008), 146–7.

35 E. Kupfer, 'Pinkas bractwa pogrzebowego i dobroczynnego w Zamościu', *Biuletyn Żydowskiego Instytutu Historycznego*, 2 (1951), 47–80: 62–3.

36 Ibid.

37 'Pinkas haḥevrah kadisha depraga', 28 (Kirszenbaum and Fajner, 49). On the *kropka*, see A. Teller, *Money, Power, and Influence in Eighteenth-Century Lithuania: The Jews on the Radziwiłł Estates* (Stanford, Calif., 2016), 54, 140.

38 'Pinkas haḥevrah kadisha depraga', 38 (Kirszenbaum and Fajner, 65). Additional *takanot* concerning flour for Passover can also be found in 1830, 1834, and 1837. See also Guesnet, *Polnische Juden*, 378–80.

39 'Pinkas haḥevrah kadisha depraga', 93 (Kirszenbaum and Fajner, 127, 129).

40 Ibid. 96, 98, 101, 106, 112–15, 118, 121–2, 124–5, 127–30, 133 (Kirszenbaum and Fajner, 133, 135, 141, 149, 153, 155, 157, 163, 167, 169, 171, 173, 177, 179, 185, 187).

41 Ibid. 5 (Kirszenbaum and Fajner, 9); Kirszenbaum, 'Bractwo pogrzebowe na Pradze', 135. Praga had officially become a part of the city of Warsaw in 1791.

42 Aust, 'Kontinuität und Wandel', 38–41, 80–2.

43 'Pinkas haḥevrah kadisha depraga', 42 (Kirszenbaum and Fajner, 73); see also ibid. 47 (Kirszenbaum and Fajner, 81).

44 Kupfer, 'Pinkas bractwa pogrzebowego', 75. On slander and the power of the burial society in Russian Jewry, see Y. Petrovsky-Shtern, *The Golden Age Shtetl: A New History of Jewish Life in East Europe* (Princeton, NJ, 2014), 157–60.

45 'Pinkas haḥevrah kadisha depraga', 24 (Kirszenbaum and Fajner, 43). In another case, Yehudah Leib ben David was excluded from prayer and Torah reading for eight weeks in 1811 after he had slandered the accountant Dov ben Mathias (ibid. 86 (Kirszenbaum and Fajner, 119)).

46 Ibid. 38, 47, 57 (Kirszenbaum and Fajner, 65, 81, 101); see also ibid. 23, 30, 50–1 (Kirszenbaum and Fajner, 41, 51, 89, 91).

47 A. Eisenbach, 'Sejm Czteroletni i Żydzi', in A. Link-Lenczowski (ed.), *Żydzi w dawnej Rzeczypospolitej: Materiały z konferencji 'Autonomia Żydów w Rzeczypospolitej szlacheckiej', Uniwersytet Jagielloński 22–26 IX 1986* (Wrocław, 1991), 180–91.

48 *Materiały do dziejów Sejmu Czteroletniego*, ed. A. Eisenbach et al., 6 vols. (Wrocław, 1955–69), vi. 113–18: 118. I would like to thank Anna Podolska for the translation. See also C. Aust, 'The Period of the Partitions of Poland–Lithuania (1772–1815)', in *Sources on Jewish Self-Government in Poland from Its Inception to the Present: A Critical and Annotated Source Reader*, ed. F. Guesnet and J. Tomaszewski (Boston, Mass., forthcoming).

49 A. Polonsky, *The Jews in Poland and Russia*, 3 vols. (Oxford, 2010), i. 201.

50 *Materiały do dziejów Sejmu Czteroletniego*, vi. 120–2.

51 On Jewish community representation in Poland, see F. Guesnet, 'Politik der Vormoderne: *Shtadlanuth* am Vorabend der polnischen Teilungen', *Jahrbuch des Simon-Dubnow-Instituts*, 1 (2002), 235–55; S. Ury, 'The *Shtadlan* of the Polish–Lithuanian Commonwealth: Noble Advocate or Unbridled Opportunist?', *Polin*, 15 (2002), 267–99.

52 *Materiały do dziejów Sejmu Czteroletniego*, vi. 141–5; see also Aust, 'The Period of the Partitions of Poland–Lithuania'.

53 J. Calmanson, *Uwagi nad ninieyszym stanem Żydów polskich y ich wydoskonaleniem* (Warsaw, 1797), 46–7. I would like to thank Anna Podolska for the translation. See also Aust, 'The Period of the Partitions of Poland–Lithuania'.

54 Calmanson, *Uwagi nad ninieyszym stanem Żydów polskich*, 47. I would like to thank Anna Podolska for the translation. See also Aust, 'The Period of the Partitions of Poland–Lithuania'.

55 On changes under Prussian rule, see S. Kemlein, *Die Posener Juden 1815–1848: Entwicklungsprozesse einer polnischen Judenheit unter preußischer Herrschaft* (Hamburg, 1997), 77–8, 126–8. In 1843 sixty-one out of seventy-five Jewish communities in the Grand Duchy of Posen (under Prussian rule) had a burial society; only a few very small communities lacked one.

56 J. Karniel, 'Das Toleranzpatent Kaiser Josephs II. für die Juden Galiziens und Lodomeriens', *Jahrbuch des Instituts für Deutsche Geschichte*, 11 (1982), 35–89.

57 Petrovsky-Shtern, 'Russian Legislation and Jewish Self-Governing Institutions'; see also J. D. Klier, *Russia Gathers Her Jews: The Origins of the 'Jewish Question' in Russia, 1772–1825* (DeKalb, Ill., 1986), 131–6; Petrovsky-Shtern, *The Golden Age Shtetl*, 342; Shochat, 'Hahanhagah bikehilot rusyah im bitul hakahal', 143–233.

58 Archiwum Główne Akt Dawnych, Warsaw, Centralne Władze Wyznaniowe Królestwa Polskiego, 1420: Kommissja Rządowa Wyznań Religijnych i Oświecenia Publicznego, 'Zniesienie Bractw pogrzebowych' (28 Mar. 1822), 8; cited in Guesnet, *Polnische Juden*, 224.

59 'Pinkas haḥevrah kadisha depraga', 68, 97, 108, 115 (Kirszenbaum and Fajner, 115, 133, 149, 157).

60 See Guesnet, *Polnische Juden*, 378–9.

61 'Pinkas haḥevrah kadisha depraga', 68 (Kirszenbaum and Fajner, 117).

62 Ibid. 109 (Kirszenbaum and Fajner, 151); see also Kirszenbaum, 'Bractwo pogrzebowe na Pradze', 141–2.

63 'Pinkas haḥevrah kadisha depraga', 113, 150 (Kirszenbaum and Fajner, 155, 209).

64 Ibid. 57, 66, 118, 137 (Kirszenbaum and Fajner, 101, 113, 115, 161, 189).

65 F. Guesnet, 'From Community to Metropolis: The Jews of Warsaw, 1850–1880', in Dynner and Guesnet (eds.), *Warsaw*, 128–53: 137–8.

66 Levitats, 'The Jewish Association', 87.

67 Zalkin, 'Who Wields the Power?', 355, 359; see also Shochat, 'Hahanhagah bikehilot rusyah im bitul hakahal', 176–8.

68 Kupfer, 'Pinkas bractwa pogrzebowego', 51, 69.

69 Ibid. 53–4.

70 For details on this process, see Guesnet, *Polnische Juden*, 321–2. The community boards in both cases only budgeted for the spending of minimal sums on burials in 1843 that would clearly not have met the needs of the two communities. Thus, it seems likely that the burial societies continued to function with their own budgets.

71 Guesnet, 'From Community to Metropolis', 128.

72 Ibid. 129, 137.

73 In 1810 the burial society signed a contract with Judyta Jakubowiczowa, the widow of the founder of the cemetery and the burial society, Szmuel Jakubowicz Zbytkower. According to the contract, the *ḥevrah kadisha* had to administer the cemetery, received the income from selling burial plots, and had to pay an annual rent of 400 zlotys to Judyta Jakubo-

wiczowa and her descendants. Judyta belonged to the well-off Jewish bourgeoisie living in Warsaw, but was buried in Praga in 1829, despite the establishment of the new Jewish cemetery on Okopowa Street (Aust, *The Jewish Economic Elite*, 163–4).

74 See Aust, 'Kontinuität und Wandel', 93–4.

75 Guesnet, *Polnische Juden*, 374.

76 Ibid. 370–7; see also Shatzky, *Geshikhte fun yidn in varshe*, i. 277–8; Guesnet, 'From Community to Metropolis', 137–8; I. Schiper, *Żydzi Królestwa Polskiego w dobie powstania listopadowego* (Warsaw, 1932), 43.

77 Praga is mentioned in the *pinkas* for the first time in 1875 ('Pinkas miḥevrat anshei gomelei ḥesed shel emet', 1a, 2).

78 Ibid. 4, 9. Shatzky mentions twenty-five paid workers at the cemetery in 1878 (J. Shatzky, 'Institutional Aspects of Jewish Life in Warsaw in the Second Half of the 19th Century', *YIVO Annual*, 10 (1955), 9–44: 26).

79 'Pinkas miḥevrat anshei gomelei ḥesed shel emet', 9–10; see also Guesnet, *Polnische Juden*, 381.

80 Guesnet, *Polnische Juden*, 227, 307–10; see also A. Markowski, 'Did Jewish Self-Government Exist in the Kingdom of Poland between 1815 and 1915?', in this volume.

81 See Guesnet, *Polnische Juden*, 304–5, 310–13; Shatzky, *Geshikhte fun yidn in varshe*, ii. 60; iii. 126; see also H. Nussbaum, *Szkice historyczne z życia Żydów w Warszawie od pierwszych śladów pobytu ich w tem mieście do chwili obecnej* (Warsaw, 1881), 84.

82 Guesnet, *Polnische Juden*, 318, 323–4.

83 Guesnet, 'From Community to Metropolis', 140, 144, 148–9. On the fate of R. Jacob Gesundheit, see S. Stampfer, 'An Unhappy Community and an Even Unhappier Rabbi', in Dynner and Guesnet (eds.), *Warsaw*, 154–79.

84 'Pinkas haḥevrah kadisha depraga', 170–1 (Kirszenbaum and Fajner, 239, 41).

85 Shatzky, *Geshikhte fun yidn in varshe*, iii. 126; Guesnet, *Polnische Juden*, 304 n. 173. Between 1881 and 1883 more than 85 per cent of the Jewish burials in Warsaw were poor burials; the costs of 57 per cent of all burials were completely covered by the Jewish community.

86 'Pinkas miḥevrat anshei gomelei ḥesed shel emet', 2; Guesnet, *Polnische Juden*, 229, 445–6.

87 S. Winter, 'Pinkasim fun ḥevrot', *YIVO bleter*, 13 (1938), 77–94; Kupfer, 'Pinkas bractwa pogrzebowego', 47–80; A. Wein, 'Pinkas bractwa pogrzebowego w Mordach', *Biuletyn Żydowskiego Instytutu Historycznego*, 63 (1967), 57–64; see also Shochat, 'Hahanhagah bikehilot rusyah im bitul hakahal', 203–4.

88 Petrovsky-Shtern, 'Russian Legislation and Jewish Self-Governing Institutions', 108–10.

89 Winter, 'Pinkasim fun ḥevrot'.

90 Boonin et al., 'The Pinkas of the Chevra Kadisha of Slutsk', 29.

Did Jewish Self-Government Exist in the Kingdom of Poland between 1815 and 1915?

ARTUR MARKOWSKI

Introduction

In the hundred years from 1815 to 1915, the Kingdom of Poland saw radical structural, organizational, and political changes in the functioning of Jewish self-government. The traditional *kahal* was officially abolished in 1822 and was superseded by synagogue supervisory boards that had been created slightly earlier, in 1821. One of the key questions is whether these boards were a continuation of the traditional form of Jewish self-government or simply a state agency designed to control and administer the Jewish community. The answer is not simple. It is not enough merely to compare the spheres of activity of these two bodies; the broader context of their operations, their place in the structures of authority, and how they were seen by the Jewish community need to be understood. An additional difficulty arises from the fact that, before 1815, alongside the *kahal*, Jewish self-government also included various voluntary associations (*ḥevrot*), to which the authorities of the Congress Kingdom had been strongly hostile, banning their activities in March 1822. The earlier role of *ḥevrot* cannot be evaluated unambiguously, since it is possible to see them not as an element of Jewish self-government existing alongside the *kahal* but rather as a competing centre of power.

The main sources for evaluating this issue are the petitions and complaints of Jews against the *kahals* and *ḥevrot* dating from the establishment of the Congress Kingdom, and subsequent denunciations of their illegal activity which exist for the whole period down to 1915. What is clear from these documents is that in the course of the nineteenth century the structures of Jewish self-government, first the synagogue supervisory boards and then somewhat later the Board of the Jewish Community of Warsaw into which the local supervisory board was transformed, evolved from a subordinate, almost passive, position to one of activity and significant authority.[1]

The concept of 'self-government' during this period raises a number of issues, as do its various models, which I will describe later in this chapter. A possible working definition could be formulated as follows: Jewish self-government is an administrative institution created to meet the needs of local Jewish communities. The members of this institution are selected by representatives of these communities from among their members.[2]

It is also worth bearing in mind that from the late eighteenth century onwards a number of changes took place in the world of ideas. This period saw the emergence and development of the European Enlightenment, with its universal social message and pragmatic approach to religious difference, and its Jewish counterpart, the Haskalah, which sought a new, progressive path in the social and intellectual development of European Jews.[3]

In order to determine whether Jewish self-government continued to exist in the Kingdom of Poland into the nineteenth century, it is crucial to place the agency supervising and running the Jewish community within the broader context of the problem of the community's autonomy after the partitions of Poland–Lithuania. Under the Polish–Lithuanian Commonwealth, the local *kahal*, the provincial councils, and the Jewish national councils in the Polish kingdom and Lithuania constituted a broad-based system of Jewish legal autonomy. By 1821 all of these had ceased to exist, and it is necessary to determine how the newly established synagogue supervisory boards fitted into the changing political and legal situation and into the new position of the Jewish community.

Artur Eisenbach, in his monumental work on the emancipation of the Jews of the Polish lands in the nineteenth century, demonstrated how Jewish autonomy was significantly limited by the introduction by the partitioning powers of new legislation, first in the Duchy of Warsaw and later in the Kingdom of Poland.[4] In the kingdom, as described by Marcin Wodziński and François Guesnet, a wavering and indecisive policy was pursued regarding the Jews, but one which reflected the Enlightenment belief in the need to centralize the state and its administration and to create a more homogeneous society.[5]

The works of Moshe Rosman and Gershon Hundert have shown clearly that Jewish self-government during the period prior to the partitions had many variants and that it is hard to construct a single model of its structure and its functioning.[6] They emphasize that Jewish autonomy did not merely establish Jewish administrative independence from the system and structures of non-Jewish authority, but can also be seen a form of corporatism. Some years ago this sparked a discussion on whether talk of a fifth estate in the commonwealth made sense. Certainly, in the pre-partition era the institutions created and run by Jews to govern their community possessed an inner coherence and authority. Their members were elected by the community and exercised power on its behalf, although there were cases where the local landowner interfered. They represented the community to the outside world and co-operated with many political actors, among them the king and his officials and the owners of the estates on which Jews lived. Recent work by Anna Michałowska-Mycielska on the history of the Council of Lithuania has indicated how frequent were the contacts with non-Jewish authorities and the political and economic relationships between Jewish and non-Jewish political institutions.[7]

My goal is to evaluate not so much the changes in the way Jewish self-government and its institutions were perceived in the nineteenth century but rather their activities and the institutional and jurisdictional changes at the local level which reflect their functioning. I will first outline the debate on this topic during the first years of the Congress Kingdom, since this had an important impact on the decision to abolish the *kahal* and establish synagogue supervisory boards. I hope in this way to elucidate the extent to which these boards can be seen as a form of Jewish self-government.

The Relations between the State and the Jewish Authorities

In the Kingdom of Poland, established in 1815, the *kahal* was the sole legal administrative structure of the Jewish community with legal recognition. There can be no dispute about the *kahal*'s autonomous character, although already the qualitative difference between its situation in the pre-partition era and in the nineteenth century could be seen.[8] The Enlightenment state model reflected in the Congress Kingdom's liberal constitution required officials to interfere more actively in the social lives of its subjects. Successive steps by the authorities were aimed more at subordinating various areas of social life to central government than at developing grassroots power structures.[9] Limited to the *kahal* and the *ḥevrot*, Jewish self-government, even in the truncated form in which it existed from the end of the eighteenth century, was clearly at odds with the accepted and ever more effectively introduced models of government.

The situation was even more problematic because, apart from the *kahal* as it functioned in the kingdom between 1815 and 1821, it was only in 1861, with Aleksander Wielopolski's reforms, that structures of urban self-government allowing for participation by all inhabitants of the state irrespective of religion were established.[10] These aroused considerable interest in the Jewish community and provided it with partial involvement in decisions beyond issues affecting just its own social group. Out of 615 elected members of urban councils, 27 (4.4 per cent) were Jewish. In Artur Eisenbach's view, both active and passive participation in elections was one of the elements of Jewish political and social emancipation in the Kingdom of Poland.[11] It is worth pointing out that urban councils, were, apart from synagogue supervisory boards, the only institutions in which Jews could have an official and legal influence on decisions taken at government level. The institutions of rural self-government and local assemblies, which could be seen as forms of self-government in the Congress Kingdom, remained completely beyond the reach of representatives of the Jewish community.

The government of the kingdom was eager to establish close supervision over the *kahals*. This traditional element of Jewish autonomy, with its centuries of history, aroused interest as an institution from 1815 not only in the realm of ideas but also in terms of the mechanics of government. In 1816 the central government carried out an assessment of the state of the *kahals*, paying particular attention to their fiscal responsibilities and to the rabbinate, clearly seen as a form of not only spiritual but also secular leadership.[12] Attempts were made to understand the legal basis for rabbis working in the *kahals*. The authorities were also interested in the way they functioned, especially how they raised income, and in the responsibilities of rabbis and the *kahal* elders in the area of finance. The data collected in tabular form are eloquent. At the beginning of the nineteenth century the principal declared source of income for the *kahal*s was the *krupka*, a tax on kosher meat. The rabbi's duties were limited to the area of religion and the spiritual supervision of the congregation, while the elders were responsible for the assessment and collection of taxes.[13] The accuracy of these reports can be questioned. The debt-laden *kahal*s, run on oligarchic lines, had no reason to reveal possible shortcomings in their operation, or to indicate their broad range of income sources based on the by now traditional income tax as well as an array of other ad hoc payments.[14] Jewish officials adopted a wait-and-see attitude towards the new political system and this attempt by central government to supervise Jewish self-government for the first time in its history.

The assessment of 1816 was followed by several state decrees undermining the autonomous character of the *kahal*. Attempts were made to supervise a number of areas. In 1818 the provincial authorities proposed a new electoral law for offices and positions in the *kahal*. The dates of elections were regulated from above, as were officials' terms of office. The indirect system, described for Poznań and Swarzędz by Anna Michałowska-Mycielska, was, however, retained and legalized by the local authorities.[15] They also defined the role of the *kahal* elders:

> The *kahal* elders are the Jewish local community's representatives in the *kahal*'s area of responsibility. They do not have any real weight when dealing with the country's authorities, but are rather the individuals from whom the government has the right to demand explanations and to impose requirements for the Jewish local community, supervisors of whatever matters central government assigns them. They are in touch with the local municipal council, with whose requests they must comply in all matters affecting the community, and whose orders they are obliged to carry out in the prescribed manner.[16]

This definition is an excellent reflection of the way the government of an enlightened state intended to extend its control over its Jewish citizens and the institutions established by them. By the second half of the nineteenth century the problems of elections and the workings of the supervisory boards slipped into the background. The central government became involved in ancillary matters such as, for instance, the acceptance of Jews into trade guilds[17] or the procedures for electing rabbis.[18]

The *kahal* was thus an institution that collided with the concepts of government which prevailed after 1815 in the Kingdom of Poland. Independent centres of power were not seen as desirable, while those that, under their own momentum, had been inherited from the previous era lost their political significance.[19] Clear centralizing tendencies and Enlightenment state intervention in society are visible in the actions of central government in relation to the *kahal*s. Between 1815 and 1821 these bodies increasingly came under the control of the authorities—provincial committees and religious and fiscal authorities. The goal of controlling the *kahal*s was strengthened by complaints from Jews about pressure from the *kahal* authorities, whose undemocratic practices had been increasingly apparent from the eighteenth century.[20] *Kahal* officials were accused of financial wrongdoing and of putting pressure on the local Jewish communities' poorest members. Irregularities in the distribution of community funds were highlighted, as was the burden of fees collected and used for the community by *kahal* elders in the local communities. In extreme cases it was even predicted that the *kahal* authorities would destroy the communities and their organizations.[21]

Another serious problem was the lack of representation of the Jewish community at the national level after the dissolution of the Council of Four Lands and the Council of Lithuania at the end of the eighteenth century.[22] Their modest equivalent remained the office of advocate (*shtadlan*), known from early modern times but in the nineteenth century taking on a somewhat different function and area of action.[23] Commentators and Christian politicians, such as Julian Ursyn Niemcewicz, and maskilim, such as Stanisław (Ezekiel) Hoge, proposed the organization of various bodies representing all the local Jewish communities, espousing at the same time an integrationist approach to Jewish issues and the primacy of the state's apparatus over the self-governing *kahal*.[24]

The synagogue supervisory boards, established in 1821, worked closely with central government. Administrative, and above all financial, decisions required counter-signatures from different administrative levels: the city or town, the Polish (later Russian) province, and the appropriate government ministry. Central government officials confirmed election dates and ballots and worked with elected board members and rabbis.[25] They also controlled the use of traditional tools for maintaining order by the local Jewish community and its responsibility for ritual, an example of which is the investigation into the use of excommunication (*ḥerem*) in Lublin.[26] Over time, the secular authorities became the court of appeal for injustices in the operation of the boards and the election of their officials, and also adjudicated on tax matters.[27] This picture of dependence is supplemented by the oaths taken by rabbis and members of synagogue supervisory boards, in which the key element is a declaration of loyalty to the tsar, which clearly echoes the oaths taken by Russian civil servants.[28] Similarly, the ceremony marking the transfer of power to newly elected members of supervisory boards by the outgoing team took place in the town hall under the eye of local officials.[29]

After 1815 the authorities of the kingdom sought, as had earlier policies, to extend their influence over the *kahals* as elements of Jewish self-government.[30] The influence consisted of an examination of their condition—above all of the *kahals'* finances and the geographical extent of their jurisdictions. After the dissolution of the *kahals* in 1822 the supervisory boards, with their exclusively Jewish membership, were also subject to central government priorities. Control over them was based on the fact that their authority was derived from the central government, and although their members were elected by the Jewish community it was the central government that conferred legitimacy on their work. Unlike the *kahals*, whose established place in the legal system dated from ancient privileges (including the 1264 Statute of Kalisz) and traditional and historically deep-rooted legal arrangements, the establishment of the supervisory boards was clearly an element in the development of a new adminis-trative structure. It not only severed the historical continuity of the alliance between 'throne and altar' and, in the case of the *kahal*, a system normalized by 'national' law as well as religious regulations, but also sought to fulfil its mission of creating 'civil Christians', as described by Marcin Wodziński.[31] This change in the lineage of an institution administering the Jewish community is clearly an important element in the process of transforming that community's legal and social status in the kingdom.

The Debate and Its Consequences

In 1818 the time was approaching to make key decisions on the place and role of Jews in the Congress Kingdom. The ten-year suspension of their civil rights imposed in the Duchy of Warsaw in 1809 was ending and a decision needed to be taken concerning their status.[32] Amongst other important elements of this debate, which took place in the public sphere and was carried out through pamphlets and leaflets produced by various, above all Christian, groups, one was the issue of Jewish self-government.[33] It was not, however, a new element in public discourse. This problem, with similar overtones, had appeared earlier in the pre-partition era in the writings of Stanisław Staszic, who had called for the abolition of the *kahal* and suggested that the Jewish community be placed under the control of town or city managers and administrators. Staszic saw in the *kahal* one of the reasons for the Jews' backwardness and isolation from the rest of society. He suggested leaving only a rabbi with limited religious responsibility and a schoolmaster to take care of the religious infrastructure. Thus, in practice, his demands were in line with the centralizing trends of the Enlightenment and had as their goal the dissolution of the organized Jewish community.[34]

There were, however, many other participants in the discussion between 1817 and 1822. For the most part, their views were very critical of the traditional form of Jewish self-government. Christian writers emphasized that the *kahal*, with its oligarchical power structure, oppressed the Jewish community and constituted an obstacle to making the Jews 'productive' and 'civilized'. The immediate dissolution of the *kahal* was called for, along with a special financial investigation into the activities of the *kahal* elders. Attention was drawn to the enormous financial demands made on the Jewish population by the traditional structures of self-government:

We have been able to uncover only some of the oppressions suffered by the Jewish community. Many complaints on this subject have already been made in the past and have had no effect, for the sole reason that the [*kahal*] elders with their usual evasions were able to suppress and deflect them, squandering in this way the sums squeezed out with tears from the poor. All this gives the Jewish people just cause to think that the intention of the nation supposedly taking care of them is not to improve their lot and turn them into useful people but rather to leave them to their own devices until they destroy themselves, which doubtless, given the elders' pressure, will shortly come to pass if these are not speedily halted.[35]

The *kahal* oligarchy was criticized for its remoteness and lack of interest in the welfare of the community, which had very destructive consequences for Jews, especially the more impoverished:

This council is developing into an oligarchy with the authority to impose its power on this nation. Being the repository of laws and the interpreter of holy judgements, this tribunal has succeeded in elevating itself above both. It is called the *kahal*. All the areas of the political, civil, economic, and spiritual life are subject to its unlimited authority which unites all kinds of despotism and is always subject to the will and whim of their ruler . . . [The *kahal* elders] have the authority to impose all kinds of levies, not being required to justify themselves to the people as to their reasons, nor on the use of public money. The Jews become reconciled to all kinds of tyranny that oppress them to such an extent that the people burdened in this way appear neither to feel nor to perceive the enormous illegalities which ought to incense the whole nation. The elders use their authority without any real care apart from that forced upon them by the need to hold on to blindly obtained funds, as well as out of fear that the local communities might suddenly spring into life and in their righteous fervour eventually turn on them in a surge of anger and revenge.[36]

The proposed plans for change were often quite far-reaching and were linked to recent attempts to deal with Jewish issues, as with Włodzimierz Gadon's allusions to Napoleonic France:

I think, however, that long-established pernicious habits, originally derived from religion but which are today an impediment [to progress], can be changed and corrected only by a religious high council made up of serious and truly learned people of the faith, who either want to repeat Napoleon's idea of summoning a sanhedrin[37] or to choose another, more effective, great Israelite council at which new rules will be established and harmful old ones corrected; with this step they will render an invaluable service to all Israelites, especially those living in Poland.[38]

Representatives of the Jewish community, for the most part maskilim, expressed various opinions. Some accepted the abolition of the *kahals* as a necessary step on the road to the reform of the Jewish community. Others claimed it would not have beneficial effects.[39] However, in the debates, no realistic policies emerged which could deal with the actual problems of the Jewish community. The overwhelming majority of proposals were utopian and simply reflected the emotion the issue aroused. In many cases the problems were accurately analysed, but the solutions proposed were impossible to realize for a variety of reasons. At the same time, it should be stressed that the discussion was part of the attempt of the central authorities to carry out a reform of Jewish self-government in the Kingdom of Poland.

Apart from the more dubious functions that attacks on traditional Jewish self-government played in public discourse, such criticism did reflect the growing opposition to the *kahal* within the Jewish community. Conflicts over financial and personal issues were emerging with increasing frequency, as in 1818 in the Warsaw *kahal*[40] or in the small towns located around Łódź.[41] This forced the central authorities to adopt an active posture and to tackle the problem in accordance with Enlightenment principles.

From a historical perspective, the uselessness and harmfulness of the *kahal* returned as a topic of discussion among the Jewish intelligentsia in the second half of the nineteenth century. At this time the issue of their political character was not discussed. The integrationist milieus at that time were preoccupied with other issues in Jewish life. Hilary Nussbaum, making his historical comments on the Jewish local community in Warsaw, did not fail, however, to treat critically both the *kahals* and the *ḥevrot*, which he saw as the embodiments of Jewish self-government up to the 1820s.[42]

The Reforms of 1821–1822: *Ḥevrot, Kahals,* Synagogue Supervisory Boards

The reform of Jewish self-government took place in three stages. On 20 March 1821 synagogue supervisory boards were established by a decree issued by General Józef Zajączek, the viceroy of the Kingdom of Poland.[43] Their origin was linked to public criticism of the policies of the *kahal* authorities in social and financial areas and incompetence in their fiscal dealings with central government. The boards were meant to play the role of supervisory institutions, above all from an organizational and fiscal perspective. Surviving sources indicate, however, that right up to the dissolution of the *kahals*, the new institution existed only on paper. This testifies to the Jewish community's very strong attachment to traditional forms of activity and their justified fear of limitations on their freedoms and rights.

On 1 January 1822 the *kahals* were dissolved in the Kingdom of Poland by a decree issued by Alexander I. It was justified by the desire 'to avoid constant Jewish complaints from all sides about the current *kahals*' pressure and impositions on the poor and taking into account depositions by government commissions on the need to abolish these *kahals* after establishing synagogue boards'.[44] In a document issued on 2 January the abolition was justified on the grounds that the government had now established supervisory boards and needed to respond to complaints from within the Jewish community on the functioning of the *kahals*.

At the same time a number of administrative procedures were set up to make dealing with issues affecting the Jewish community more efficient. The *kahals*' former responsibilities were divided between the local branches of central government (taxation) and the supervisory boards (infrastructure and ritual). Special care was taken to ensure the financial transparency of the actions of the newly elected Jewish authorities and the secular authorities and the accurate transfer of materials, money, and debts.[45] In practice, very few documents were handed over by the *kahals*, and a great many injustices and violations of the law were committed. The Jewish response to the creation of the boards as replacements for the existing system of self-government was initially very negative. People wishing to serve as board members were hard to find, and when it came to terminology even lower-level officials continued to use the words *kahal* and *kahal* elders instead of board and board members. The old and the new structures somehow intermingled. Individuals serving as *kahal* elders often became board members, and all that changed was their title and their area of responsibility.[46]

On 28 March 1822 the State Committee for Religious Denominations and Public Enlightenment implemented the third step in the reform, the abolition of the *ḥevrot*.

Their responsibilities had included taking care of the Jewish community's various needs, such as funerals and maintaining schools,[47] which were partly assigned to the supervisory boards (funerals and religious matters) and partly to the appropriate government departments (education).[48] The boards acquired the right to levy at least four types of fees related to funerals, which from the perspective of the kingdom's authorities was perhaps meant to encourage board members and rabbis to ensure the dissolution of the *hevrot*. Among the various arguments produced to justify their dissolution, including that of the *hevrah kadisha* (burial society), was the allegedly unnecessary duplication of responsibilities, the conflicts between the *hevrot* and the local Jewish communities, and their extortionate financial demands. The significance of burial and Jewish attitudes to death had meant that the *hevrah kadisha* enjoyed great prestige. As a result the central government's dissolution of the *hevrot* did not prove effective.[49] From time to time the activities of underground structures can be noted both in the documents created by local officials and in those of the Jewish community.[50] Despite the fact that they operated underground, encountering hostility from the authorities and criticism from progressive groups in the Jewish community, the *hevrot kadisha* continued to operate. They were also able to collect fees from the community. An interesting example is a threat received by an inhabitant of Warsaw in 1873, which he turned over to the Russian police:

Mr Usher Liber son of Aryeh Ber! You must immediately provide two s[ilver] r[oubles] to the [burial] society and set up an account, since the poor deceased need them urgently—do not refuse for you will regret it later and you will be amongst those who shout and complain while no one listens to them.[51]

This threat indicates the unprecedented situation in which the dissolution of an institution of traditional Jewish self-government not only turned out to be ineffective but also did not prevent its members from continuing to make threats to collect fees. However, such materials demonstrate that the central government and the Jewish community were not really interested in the dissolution of the *hevrot*. It might be surmised, although little research has been done in this area, that the specific duties, especially those of the *hevrah kadisha*, including care of the cemetery and the organization of funerals, which imparted ritual impurity, meant that neither central government nor the Jews themselves wanted to get rid of organizations that took care of important elements of social life. According to Marcin Wodziński, the issue of relations between Jews, synagogue supervisory boards, and central government and illegal *hevrot* is even more complicated and depends on the specific reaction of political groups. In his view, the tradition of the *hevrah kadisha* was so strong that the cemetery commissions mandated to operate alongside the boards simply became funeral societies with a different name.

The same was happening to the *kahals* themselves. Initial distrust of the supervisory boards within the Jewish community, and the perception of them as government agencies and a means of exerting fiscal control, strengthened a tendency to retain illegal *kahals* operating independently of the central government. There is almost no research on this issue, but some surviving denunciations to central government and the *pinkasim* (ledgers) of the *kahals* provide evidence of this phenomenon.[52]

The reform also formalized the location of local Jewish communities and their relation to each other. The assigning of Jewish communities in small towns and the countryside to specific synagogue supervisory boards was now settled. The whole process of setting up religious districts, 'Jewish parishes', often continued until the second half of the 1820s, when their territorial area and extent was finalized.[53]

Synagogue Supervisory Boards and Their Duties

The authority of synagogue boards was far narrower than that of the *kahal*. The boards were not responsible for a number of duties in the areas of law and education.[54] They retained a secondary role in taxation, and a number of responsibilities dealing with the upkeep of religious and ritual infrastructure. According to Marcin Wodziński, this constituted a fundamental change in the way the local Jewish community operated. From an institution having the features of a local government body, it became a government agency running a religious community.[55] This had important implications. The structures of self-government were abolished and replaced by a state institution guaranteeing basic religious needs and fulfilling the (originally sole) function of representing the Jews to the central secular authorities. Elements of self-government were put in place by an electoral law that assumed that Jews would elect Jews to be members of supervisory boards. The strong dependence of the supervisory board on the central government made it an element of the central government, yet its officials and officers, elected only from members of the Jewish local community, retained a great deal of freedom. The supervisory boards as executive bodies were not autonomous, and their activities depended on continuous control and inspection at the local level (town halls), regional level (Polish and later Russian provincial commissions), and national level (government commissions). A change was taking place here in the model of self-government, in terms both of organization and of how it was understood. However, board members were selected for a specific term of office and were not initially, in the first half of the nineteenth century, treated as state employees. This changed in the second half of the century.

A synagogue supervisory board consisted of three members chosen for a three-year term. The active and passive electoral laws favoured married Jews permanently residing in a local community's catchment area and paying the liquor tax (from 1830 those who paid the local community tax).[56] Social divisions based on financial criteria were precisely defined, as were the burdens imposed on members of specific groups. The last, fifth, category was those people with no or next to no income, surviving with the assistance of public aid provided through the local Jewish community. They were not granted voting rights on the grounds that, since they contributed nothing in a financial sense, they should not influence expenditure. It was also claimed they could be easily bribed.

The authorities (often local) established specific rules for elections, which were theoretically meant to be secret. In practice, especially in the first half of the nineteenth century when paper was by no means cheap or easy for small town halls to obtain, all manner of abuses occurred (for instance, a member of the commission would write down a vote whispered in his ear by a voter).[57] During elections there were a great many irregularities partly caused by a lack of interest from members of the local communities, who saw them as marked by collusion and fixed in advance. As late as 1898, when the synagogue supervisory boards had already become a place where politics was successfully practised, in Lublin voters were pulled in off the street and forced to vote without regard to their legal eligibility.[58]

Elected board members were confirmed by the urban and provincial authorities, and over time, like civil servants, had to take an appropriate oath, swearing allegiance to the Russian tsar.[59] For the most part the candidates were prominent and wealthy members of the community, experienced at wielding power, although sometimes unsuitable candidates emerged: for example, letters to the city authorities after the elections to the Warsaw synagogue supervisory board in 1851 described candidates as 'superstitious', 'uncouth', 'stupid', and 'crafty'.[60] Such opinions are testimony, above all, to the emotions that could grip voters and candidates. As in Lublin, the battle for places and access to power could be fierce.

In addition to board members who had fixed duties, boards employed a number of people for various religious and social functions. The number and salary range of those hired on a more or less permanent basis depended on the size of the board and its economic situation. The rabbi and his assistant were always among them. They were paid for by the board and worked with its members in taking key decisions for the Jewish community. This was the reason the central authorities exercised strong control over the whole process of elections and the confirmation of rabbis.[61] Boards also hired cantors, synagogue caretakers, an official responsible for the hospital (really a workhouse), teachers and clerks able to handle paperwork in Polish, and sometimes even bookkeepers (initially the town or city bookkeepers carried out these duties).[62]

In general, the work of the synagogue supervisory board consisted of maintaining the community infrastructure (synagogues, prayer houses, and ritual baths), providing alms for the poor,[63] and the organization of items connected with religious ritual, such as the purchase of *etrogim* (citron fruits) for Sukkot. The duties of the *ḥevrot kadisha* were also officially transferred to the supervisory boards, although, as mentioned, it is hard to tell just how far this went. The extensive activities of *ḥevrot kadisha* as late as the end of the nineteenth century confirm their continued importance. It is hard to assess the effects of the reform. It might have led to a situation in which people had to pay twice for a burial: the board for the funeral, the plot, and the erection of the gravestone, and the *ḥevrah kadisha* which continued to levy the traditional fees. Marcin Wodziński argues that in practice the two groups worked together. It is difficult, however, given the present stage of research, to provide a definitive judgement.

The boards had significant financial responsibilities. Their principal source of income was the tax (the 'classification fee'), paid by heads of household[64] who were in the top four of the five taxation bands.[65] The levying of this tax was often converted by the boards into a lease whose aim was to ensure a steady income and to facilitate collection, since they lacked their own means of collection. The boards also benefited from fees for religious services, such as circumcisions and weddings, and from leases, such as of ritual baths.[66] Administration of these was frequently leased out to ensure the boards had a steady income and to ease the work of officials, as the obligations to take care of their upkeep and ensure accessibility to members of the community were imposed on the leaseholder.

Funds were required to support the local infrastructure, salaries, and matters connected with religious ritual (the purchase of *etrogim* for Sukkot and flour for Passover *matsah* for the poor). The boards ran two sets of accounts, one official, the other for their own use. The official budget was often an administrative fiction bearing no relationship to real operations and financial problems.[67] Surviving archival material can serve only to provide information about the supervisory board's evolution as an executive institution,[68] and it is hard to attach much significance to the budgetary figures found there.[69] No systematic historical and economic research has been conducted into the boards' activities, but the surviving material mostly claims that budgetary plans were followed accurately and there was hardly ever a surplus or a deficit. This is hard to believe, since it would have been difficult to have produced enough income from ritual slaughter, funerals, and weddings to allow even a small community to balance its budget.

Also included in the financial obligations of synagogue supervisory boards was the maintenance of assets. This area was strictly controlled by the central government, irrespective of whether it was a large community administering an extensive infrastructure (liquid and fixed assets) or a small one with a single synagogue and a ritual bath.[70]

The boards operated in accordance with the guidelines set down for state institutions. Run hierarchically and dependent on the central government (for instance, they were required to lodge documents with the local town hall archives), they also made attempts to adapt to the demands of the time. The Warsaw synagogue supervisory board, for example, paid pensions to the widows of deceased members and employees.[71] The process of transferring power to new board members from their predecessors was also very bureaucratic, occurring under the tight supervision of local officials, who read out documents confirming the new members' authority after the members had accepted the board's papers and assets.[72]

In addition to fiscal matters, proof of the board members' control over the activities of the local community can be seen in the procedure for granting permission for prayers to be said outside the synagogue or house of prayer in special circumstances, such as when someone was incapacitated or elderly.[73]

The abolition of specific elements of traditional Jewish self-government placed Jewish craftsmen in a new position. They had been deprived not only of the supervision of the *kahal* but also of the structures and organizational framework protecting their rights that craft guilds had represented. In effect, the abolition of the former institutions of self-government left Jewish craftsmen in an organizational vacuum.[74] The problem did not appear to be too serious, since Christian craft guilds were beginning to accept Jews more often.[75] It acquired resonance in the context of the interpretation of the emancipation decree of 1862 and the resultant changes to Jews' legal and social standing.

The activities of the supervisory boards did not, however, escape criticism, as had been the case with the *kahals*. The sources contain denunciations and complaints about their management of assets, financial pressure, conflicts of interest, or simply about the inactivity of board members. Some of these documents indicate fierce political disputes as early as the middle of the nineteenth century.[76]

Synagogue Supervisory Boards as Scenes of Political Conflict

Despite initial difficulties in recruiting members, supervisory boards soon became the scene of political conflict.[77] These conflicts initially resembled those of the pre-partition era, that is to say they were overwhelmingly local and for the most part involved only Jewish communities. Political activity arising from disputes between the Jews in different patron–client relations or from economic rivalry were already evident in the elections of rabbis in the first half of the nineteenth century.[78] Even earlier, the hasidim began to undertake political activity on the boards. Wodziński argues that the hasidim were clearly defensive until the 1820s, when they began to take the opposite tack.[79] The iconic figure here is Izaak of Warka, who at one time was serving as rabbi on a number of boards.[80] Similarly, hasidim were in control of some supervisory boards as early as the 1840s.[81] Over time, when the demands for emancipation and changes in the Jews' legal status grew and acquired a political dimension, the boards became the place for the advancement of political aspirations not only intra-communally but also nationally. In this situation the role of the board as an institution representing a religious union dealing with the secular authorities grew.

In Warsaw, as early as the community elections of 1851, attempts were made to lobby and discredit candidates in a conflict between supporters and opponents of the Haskalah.[82] A similar conflict occurred at the same time in provincial Suwałki.[83] After the uprising of 1863, when polarized attitudes towards integration and acculturation appeared within the Jewish community, the supervisory boards became the battleground for supporters of traditionally understood Jewish distinctiveness and those supporting integration, the 'assimilators'.[84] This was the case in Lublin and Warsaw, where conflicts continued into the 1870s.[85] Over time discussions about the significance of the local supervisory board and its functions also occurred in the public sphere, which became a permanent platform for considering community matters.[86]

The Jewish political parties emerging at the beginning of the twentieth century played only a small role in the functioning of synagogue supervisory boards. Their weakness and limited social support meant that they lacked the ability to engage actively in the struggle for power in the local Jewish communities. They were also operating illegally, so their followers could not openly carry out political activities, including electioneering. That era would arrive only with the rebirth of the Polish state in 1918. During the 1905 revolution the attention of the divided Jewish political scene was focused on the elections to the national duma rather than on the local dimensions of the community board.[87]

Shtadlanut, the Jewish community's informal lobbying of the non-Jewish political world, survived, although in a different form. Despite the progressive and rational nature of the supervisory boards, this form of lobbying remained an element of the Jews' political activities. It was largely independent of the structures of self-government and was a function of these structures' weakness and narrow area of competence, regardless of their nature or the period during which they operated.[88]

Was the Synagogue Supervisory Board a Form of Self-Government?

Scholars have expressed varying views on whether Jewish self-government operated effectively in the Congress Kingdom after 1822 and just what the nature of the synagogue supervisory boards was. Antony Polonsky, author of the latest general history of the Jews in Poland and Russia, claims that for Polish Jews the abolition of the *kahals* was not significant since the traditional and illegally operating *kahal* structures and the *ḥevrot* retained their power.[89] A similar view was expressed over a hundred years ago by Ignacy Schiper, who saw in the boards a change in name but not in activities.[90] Jacek Walicki denies the new institution's claim to be a form of self-government, emphasizing the state's extensive control over it.[91] Israel Bartal points out that the supervisory boards were deprived of the attributes of corporate governance that the earlier *kahals* undoubtedly had, and this point of view corresponds with that of Marcin Wodziński.[92]

The *kahal*, until its abolition in 1822, functioned under many different administrative structures. If it operated in a noble-owned town, the owner of the town had influence over the elections of the officers and officials of the *kahal* and the right to confirm them. It was also not unusual for Jewish communities in royal towns to be subject to the control of the authorities in relation to elections and finance.[93] This control was much less far-reaching than the strict and multi-layered supervision of synagogue supervisory boards, but the authorities operated very differently in the Polish–Lithuanian Commonwealth than in the Kingdom of Poland. If, in the nineteenth century, the supervisory board became the only element in the organizational structure in which Jews had extensive autonomy and was subject to multi-level (mainly financial) control by the authorities, then in the pre-partition era not only the *kahal* but even the Council of Four Lands had been subject to such control.[94]

Within the very limited role allowed them in the Duchy of Warsaw and subsequently the Kingdom of Poland, the *kahals* and the synagogue boards remained among the most important institutions of Jewish self-government.[95] Supervisory boards were certainly dependent on the administrative structures of the Congress Kingdom. This conformed to the French model of local government, which assumed tight links between such agencies and those of central government, including financial control,[96] and was in contrast to the German model, which assumed considerable autonomy from central government. In extreme examples, self-government became a fourth branch of Montesquieu's separation of powers into executive, legislative, and judicial functions.

Isaak Levitats has described the classic *kahal* and its operations in the tsarist empire, and his analysis, despite dealing with Russia, also describes Jewish self-government in the Kingdom of Poland between 1815 and 1822 with all its pathologies and problems.[97] The *kahal's* political role was diminishing in the period before its abolition, while the political role of the synagogue supervisory boards expanded from its originally limited base, especially from the mid-nineteenth century. While the great majority of Jews and central government were happy to see the end of the *kahal*, whose legitimacy had been undermined by oligarchy and nepotism, the supervisory board that replaced it took a long time to build its own political standing. In addition, in the course of the nineteenth century various competing institutions developed, from hasidic courts to local wealthy individuals, which attempted to replace the weak local community and take the place of traditional Jewish self-government.

By the time they were abolished the *kahals* had lost most of their authority, and their fate and real responsibilities had hung in the balance for nearly thirty years. Their situation at the time could be compared to that of the supervisory boards, which were caught between two functions: being an element of central government and being an element of Jewish self-government. Certainly, Jewish self-government never really achieved full independence and sovereignty in the fiscal, political, and legal areas.

Until the middle of the nineteenth century, when the synagogue supervisory boards became the scene of power struggles and, as a result of effective interventions by board members, a means for exercising power, it is hard to speak of Jewish self-government having a political role. Initially, in terms of the model accepted in the Kingdom of Poland, the boards were meant to be an official element in the system of self-government. However, from the middle of the century they took on the characteristics of a more politically and organizationally independent institution running Jewish communities.

One argument in favour of seeing the synagogue supervisory board as a form of Jewish self-government is the fact that it was independent of the collegial bodies that had been established to supervise Jewish affairs. Thus the boards did not report to the Jewish Affairs Committee.[98] They dealt effectively with issues of everyday life and ensured the Jewish community's basic needs were met. They derived their authority from elections, and their financial and structural dependence on central government was a reflection of self-government as defined not only in the nineteenth century but also in the period preceding the partitions. As a result of the dissolution of earlier structures of self-government, the supervisory board, seen as the substitute for the *kahal*, the only surviving part of the system, went through a genuine transformation. However, in the nineteenth century the situation of the *ḥevrot* (officially dissolved but operating illegally) and the position of the rabbi also changed. In the latter case the activities of the maskilim and the leaders of hasidic groups and Lithuanian yeshivas played a key role, as did, in the second half of the century, the followers of Reform Judaism and its leaders, such as Marcus Jastrow.[99]

Translated from the Polish by Jarosław Garliński

Notes

The present chapter is a greatly expanded version of a piece that is to appear in English as the introduction to a selection of documents devoted to the history of Jewish self-government in Polish lands from the Middle Ages to the present (*Sources on Jewish Self-Government in Poland from Its Inception to the Present: A Critical and Annotated Source Reader*, ed F. Guesnet and J. Tomaszewski (Boston, Mass., forthcoming)). The basic research was done under the auspices of a grant provided by the Gerda Henkel Stiftung. I should like to thank Professor Marcin Wodziński and the book's reviewers for their remarks and comments on this version.

1 R. Żebrowski, *Żydowska Gmina Wyznaniowa w Warszawie 1918–1939: W kręgu polityki* (Warsaw, 2012), 10. The Board of the Jewish Community of Warsaw was the name given to the Warsaw synagogue supervisory board in 1871 in a ruling on electoral law. This indicates the greater significance of the Warsaw community in comparison to the other Jewish communities in the Kingdom of Poland and the more political character of the institution. This change has been inadequately studied and requires a deeper analysis of the sources. It is unclear whether it signified an ideological shift in the understanding of the board's function and character and thus that the board should be seen as an agency running its own autonomous community, like the pre-partition *kahal*; or whether it was a sign of its nationalization (in the ideological sense); or whether it was simply a cosmetic change with no ideological or practical meaning. In 1905 the local Jewish community in Łódź also used the name Board of the Jewish Community of Łódź (see Archiwum Państwowe Łódź, 228 Łódzka Gmina Wyznaniowa Żydowska, 10, fo. 13).

2 Grzegosz Smyk argued that 'self-government is thus widely seen as corporations of citizens carrying out the functions of public administration, quite independently from government administrative entities' (G. Smyk, *Administracja publiczna Królestwa Polskiego w latach 1864–1915* (Lublin, 2011), 122).

3 On Enlightenment plans to reform the Jews, see M. Wodziński, 'Reforma i wykluczenie: Wizje reformy społeczności żydowskiej u schyłku polskiego oświecenia', *Pamiętnik Literacki*, 2010, no. 4, pp. 5–21.

4 A. Eisenbach, *Emancypacja Żydów na ziemiach polskich 1785–1870 na tle europejskim* (Warsaw, 1988).

5 Marcin Wodziński and Glenn Dynner discuss the totality of academic work on political, legal, and social issues (G. Dynner and M. Wodziński, 'The Kingdom of Poland and Her Jews: An Introduction', *Polin*, 27 (2015), 6–17).

6 M. Rosman, *Żydzi pańscy: Stosunki magnacko-żydowskie w Rzeczypospolitej XVIII wieku*

(Warsaw, 2005), 59–60; Eng. trans.: *The Lords' Jews: Magnate–Jewish Relations in the Polish–Lithuanian Commonwealth during the 18th Century* (Cambridge, 1990); G. D. Hundert, *The Jews in a Polish Private Town: The Case of Opatów in the Eighteenth Century* (Baltimore, 1992), 108–15.

7 A. Michałowska-Mycielska, *Sejm Żydów litewskich (1623–1764)* (Warsaw, 2014), 248–64.

8 D. Kandel, 'Żydzi w dobie utworzenia Królestwa Kongresowego', *Kwartalnik Poświęcony Badaniu Przeszłości Żydów w Polsce*, 1 (1912), 95–113: 97.

9 A good example of this are Jewish conversions and national policies towards them (see A. Markowski, 'State Policies Concerning Jewish Conversions in the Kingdom of Poland during the First Half of the Nineteenth Century', *Gal-ed*, 25 (2017), 15–40).

10 W. Witkowski, *Historia administracji w Polsce 1764–1989* (Warsaw, 2007), 150.

11 See Eisenbach, *Emancypacja Żydów*, 486–7.

12 Doubtless in connection with a planned reform project (see S. Dubnow, *Noveishaya istoriya evreiskogo naroda: Epokha pervoi reaktsii (1815–1848) i vtoroi emansipatsii (1848–1880)* (Moscow, 2002), 178–9; Archiwum Główne Akt Dawnych, Warsaw (hereafter AGAD), Centralne Władze Wyznaniowe Królestwa Polskiego (hereafter CWWKP), 1429, fos. 14–15).

13 AGAD, CWWKP, 1429, fos. 14–15.

14 For more on *kahal* finances, see A. Michałowska, *Między demokracją a oligarchią: Władze gmin żydowskich w Poznaniu i Swarzędzu* (Warsaw, 2000), 207–40.

15 Archiwum Państwowe w Płocku (hereafter APP), Akta Miasta Płocka (hereafter AMP), 30, fos. 103–4; Michałowska, *Między demokracją a oligarchią*, 84–116.

16 APP, AMP, 30, fo. 230.

17 Archiwum Państwowe w Kaliszu (hereafter APK), Kaliski Zarząd Powiatowy (hereafter KZP), 335, fos. 22–5.

18 Archiwum Państwowe w Lublinie (hereafter APL), Rząd Gubernialny Lubelski (hereafter RzGL), 1909:69, fo. 64.

19 A good example are the local assemblies (see M. Mycielski, *Rząd Królestwa Polskiego wobec sejmików i zgromadzeń gminnych 1815–1830* (Warsaw, 2010)).

20 See Michałowska, *Między demokracją a oligarchią*, 84–117.

21 APP, AMP, 199, fos. 98–9.

22 See A. Leszczyński, *Sejm Żydów Korony 1623–1764* (Warsaw, 1994); Michałowska-Mycielska, *Sejm Żydów litewskich*.

23 For the *shtadlan's* activities, see M. Wodziński, *Władze Królestwa Polskiego wobec chasydyzmu: Z dziejów stosunków politycznych* (Wrocław 2008), 78–220.

24 AGAD, CWWKP, 1429, fos. 79–88.

25 APL, Akta Miasta Lublina (hereafter AML), 2420, fos. 18–19; RzGL, 1909:9, fo. 59; 1898:89, fo. 222.

26 APL, RzGL, 312, fos. 12–14.

27 APL, AML, 540, fo. 34.

28 APL, RzGL, 1909:69, fo. 117; APL, AML, 540, fo. 4.

29 APK, KZP, 298, fo. 3.

30 On such trends during the Duchy of Warsaw based on contacts between the authorities and the local Jewish community, see A. Oniszczuk, 'Władze Księstwa Warszawskiego wobec Żydów: debata, ustawodawstwo, praktyka', Ph.D. thesis (University of Wrocław, 2016), 67–77.

31 M. Wodziński, "'Cywilni chrześcijanie": Spory o reformę Żydów w Polsce 1789–1830', in G. Borkowska and M. Rudkowska (eds.), *Kwestia żydowska w XIX wieku: Spory o tożsamość Polaków* (Warsaw, 2004), 9–42: 20–4.

32 On the nuances of the Jews' legal status in the Duchy of Warsaw, see A. Oniszczuk, 'The Jews in the Duchy of Warsaw: The Question of Equal Rights in Administrative Theory and Practice', *Polin*, 27 (2014), 63–88.

33 For the debate on the situation of the Jews, see L. Jerkiewicz, '"Kwestia żydowska" w Królestwie Polskim w latach 1815–1830', Ph.D. thesis (University of Wrocław, 2014); Wodziński, '"Cywilni chrześcijanie"'; for criticism of the *kahals*, see D. Szterenkac, 'Zniesienie kahałów i utworzenie dozorów bóżniczych (w pierwszych latach Królestwa Polskiego)', MA thesis (University of Warsaw, 1932), 17–25.

34 On Staszic's attitude to Jewish self-government with excerpts from his writings, see J. Kruszyński, *Stanisław Staszic a kwestia żydowska* (Krzeszowice, 2003), 36–7.

35 *Prośba czyli usprawiedliwienie się Ludu Wyznania Starego Testamentu w Królestwie Polskiem zamieszkałego* (Warsaw, 1820), 6–7.

36 [J. A. Radomiński], *Co wstrzymuie reformę Żydów w kraiu naszym i co iąprzyspieszyć powinno* (Warsaw, 1820), 20–5.

37 Artur Eisenbach probably discussed these ideas in his doctoral thesis, which was lost during the Second World War. Presumably some of the material from it appeared in an article and source edition he published before the war (see A. Eisenbach, 'Dokumentn tsu der geshikhte fun departament va'adim un geplante tsentrale va'ad in varshaver firshtentum', *Bleter far geshikhte*, 1938, no. 2, pp. 127–9; id., 'Tsentral represents-organen fun di yidn in varshaver firshtentum', *Bleter far geshikhte*, 1938, no. 2, pp. 33–88).

38 W. Gadon, *Zbiór ustaw i obrzędów wymagających najrychlejszej reformy Izraelitów osiadłych w prowincjach do Polski należących* (Warsaw, 1835), 13.

39 Jerkiewicz, '"Kwestia żydowska" w Królestwie Polskim', 147–8.

40 R. Kempner, 'Agonia kahału', *Kwartalnik Poświęcony Badaniu Przeszłości Żydów w Polsce*, 1 (1912), 71–2; J. Szacki, *Geshikhte fun yidn in varshe*, 3 vols. (New York, 1947–53), i. 264–81.

41 F. Friedman, *Dzieje Żydów w Łodzi od początków osadnictwa do roku 1863* (Łódź, 1935), 16, 21; on intra-*kahal* conflict in the nineteenth century, see Szterenkac, 'Zniesienie kahałów i utworzenie dozorów bóżniczych', 34–46.

42 H. Nussbaum, *Szkice historyczne z życia Żydów w Warszawie od pierwszychśladów pobytu ich w tem mieście do chwili obecnej* (Warsaw, 1881), 51–4.

43 See J. Walicki, 'Dozory bóżnicze w teorii i działaniu: Polska środkowa 1821–1866', in S. Pytlas and J. Kita (eds.), *Historia, społeczeństwo, gospodarka: Profesorowi Wiesławowi Pusiowi w czterdziestolecie pracy naukowej* (Łódź, 2006), 110; W. Gliński, 'Reforma samorządu gminy żydowskiej w początkach Królestwa Polskiego: Ustanowienie dozorów bóżniczych', *Studia z Historii Społeczno-Gospodarczej XIX i XX wieku*, 2 (2004), 51–67.

44 AGAD, CWWKP, 1432, fo. 32.

45 Ibid., fos. 32–4.

46 Friedman, *Dzieje Żydów w Łodzi*, 22.

47 M. Kośka, 'Obyczaje żydowskie w świetle prawa obowiązującego w XIX wieku w Królstwie Polskim', *Żydowskie gminy wyznaniowe*, ed. J. Worończak (Wrocław, 1995), 35–45: 37.

48 APK, KZP, 298, fo. 13.

49 François Guesnet writes extensively about this problem and about the issue of the social reception of illegal ḥevrot (see F. Guesnet, *Polnische Juden im 19. Jahrhundert: Lebensbedingungen, Rechtsnormen und Organisation im Wandel* (Cologne, 1998), 357–86; id., 'Chevrot i achdes: Zmiana w żydowskiej organizacji wewnętrznej w Królestwie Polskim przed 1900

r. oraz powstanie Bundu', in F. Tych and J. Hensel (eds.), *Bund 100 lat historii 1897–1997* (Warsaw, 2000), 71–89; Eng. trans.: 'Khevres and Akhdes: The Change in Jewish Self-Organization in the Kingdom of Poland before 1900 and the Bund', in J. Jacobs (ed.), *Jewish Politics in Eastern Europe: The Bund at 100* (Basingstoke, Hants., 2001), 3–13).

50 APK, KZP, 298, fos. 51–2; Archiwum Państwowe Miasta Stołecznego Warszawy, Kancelaria Gubernatora Warszawskiego, 149, fo. 1.

51 The original scrap of paper with Hebrew text was turned over to the police, who ordered a notarized translation into Polish (Archiwum Państwowe Miasta Stołecznego Warszawy, Kancelaria Gubernatora Warszawskiego, 232, fo. 4).

52 Dubnow, *Noveishaya istoriya evreiskogo naroda*, 183.

53 *Atlas historii Żydów polskich* (Warsaw, 2010), 179 (map); AGAD, CWWKP, 1440, fos. 5–8; Archiwum Państwowe w Suwałkach, Akta Miasta Suwałk, 419, fos. 2–3; A. Markowski, *Między Wschodem a Zachodem: Rodzina i gospodarstwo domowe Żydów suwalskich w pierwszej połowie XIX wieku* (Warsaw, 2008), 40.

54 Jews had to pay a tax to support primary schools (see A. Penkalla, 'Żydzi szydłowieccy w latach 1815–1914', in J. Wijaczka (ed.), *Żydzi szydłowieccy. Materiały sesji popularnonaukowej 22 lutego 1997 r* (Szydłowiec, 1997), 58).

55 M. Wodziński, 'Zniesienie kahałów', in *Atlas historii Żydów polskich*, 162.

56 AGAD, CWWKP, 1429, fos. 6–9; J. Kirszrot, *Prawa Żydów w Królestwie Polskiem: Zarys historyczny* (Warsaw, 1917), 47–8.

57 Walicki, 'Dozory bóżnicze w teorii i działaniu', 112.

58 APL, RzGL, 1898:89, fo. 222.

59 APL, AML, 540, fo. 4.

60 AGAD, CWWKP, 1727, fos. 944–6.

61 APL, AML, 540, fo. 12.

62 Information on this can be found in the three-year budgets of specific boards, which are a frequent treasure trove of archival material from both central and local administrative levels (e.g. Archiwum Państwowe w Częstochowie, Akta Miasta Częstochowy, 247, fos. 1–15; APP, AMP, 33, fos. 175–9; APL, AML, 38, no fo.).

63 On alms-giving in Warsaw, see Szacki, *Geshikhte fun yidn in varshe*, ii. 148.

64 'Heads of households' meant married men, who represented social and, to a certain extent, economic stability.

65 AGAD, CWWKP, 1429, fos. 6–9. For a later period, see K. Horowicz and R. Kempner, 'Podatek gminny w Warszawie 1903–1912', *Kwartalnik Poświęcony Badaniu Przeszłości Żydów w Polsce*, 3 (1913), 160–5.

66 Archiwum Państwowe w Częstochowie, Akta Miasta Częstochowy, 448, fos. 271–2, 433, 435–7.

67 Markowski, *Między Wschodem a Zachodem*, 44–7.

68 Ibid. 46–7.

69 See J. Janicka, *Żydzi Zamojszczyzny 1864–1915* (Lublin, 2007), 79–85; A. Jarota, 'Ustanowienie i funkcjonowanie dozorów bożniczych w latach 1821–1830', *Saeculum Christianum*, 19/2 (2012), 72.

70 Walicki, 'Dozory bóżnicze w teorii i działaniu', 117.

71 AGAD, CWWKP, 1728, fos. 7–9.

72 APK, KZP, 298, fo. 3.

73 APP, AMP, 33, fo. 387.

74 APK, KZP, 335, fos. 22–5.

75 See Guesnet, 'Chevrot i achdes', 71–5; M. Horn, *Żydowskie bractwa rzemieślnicze na ziemiach polskich, litewskich, białoruskich i ukraińskich w latach 1613–1850* (Warsaw, 1998), 87–90.

76 APL, AML, 540, fo. 34; RzGL, 1898:89, fo. 222; 312, fos. 12–14; 1909:69, fo. 100.

77 APP, APM, 31, fo. 18.

78 A good example are the events in Częstochowa (see J. Spyra, 'Miejsce rabina w gminie żydowskiej w Królestwie Polskim w I połowie XIX wieku: Spór o Zachariasza Weingotta w Częstochowie', *Studia Judaica* (Kraków), 19 (2016), 157–86).

79 Wodziński, *Władze Królestwa Polskiego wobec chasydyzmu*, 176.

80 Ibid. 195.

81 Ibid. 209. The influence of hasidic issues on the boards' and the rabbinate's political activities are often discernible in the background of the sources (see e.g. *Źródła do dziejów chasydyzmu w Królestwie Polskim, 1815–1867, w zasobach polskich archiwów państwowych*, ed. M. Wodziński (Kraków, 2011), §§13, 19, 20, 25, 28, 30, 32, 35, 42).

82 Guesnet, *Polnische Juden*, 404–5.

83 AGAD, CWWKP, 1727, fos. 944–6; 1818, fos. 219–21.

84 R. Kuwałek, 'Pomiędzy tradycją a asymilacją: Walka o wpływ i władzę w lubelskiej gminie żydowskiej między ortodoksami i asymilatorami w latach 1862–1915', in K. Pilarczyk (ed.), *Żydzi i judaizm we współczesnych badaniach polskich: Materiały z konferencji Kraków 21–23 XI 1995* (Kraków, 1997), 227–48; APL, RzGL, 1909:69, fo. 100.

85 R. Żebrowski, *Żydowska Gmina Wyznaniowa w Warszawie*.

86 See articles from *Izraelita* ('*Izraelita*' 1866–1915: *Wybór źródeł*, ed. M. Wodziński and A. Jagodzińska (Kraków, 2015), 440–55). Wodziński points to obvious political sympathies and the uneven treatment of Jewish communities (including arrogance and a 'colonial' approach to the provinces) (M. Wodziński, 'Sprawy gminne', in '*Izraelita*' 1866–1915, 438–9).

87 S. Ury, *Barricades and Banners: The Revolution of 1905 and the Transformation of Warsaw Jewry* (Stanford, Calif., 2012), 172–213; F. Guesnet, 'Revolutionary Hinterland: Transformations of Jewish Associational Life in the Kingdom of Poland, 1904–06', in F. Fischer et al. (eds.), *The Russian Revolution of 1905 in Transcultural Perspective: Identities, Peripheries, and the Flow of Ideas* (Bloomington, Ind., 2013), 105–20.

88 Wodziński, *Władze Królestwa Polskiego wobec chasydyzmu*, 240–3.

89 A. Polonsky, *The Jews in Poland and Russia*, 3 vols. (Oxford, 2010–12), i. 292.

90 I. Schiper, 'Samorząd żydowski w Polsce na przełomie wieku 18 i 19-go (1764–1831)', *Miesięcznik Żydowski*, 1931, no. 6, pp. 513–29: 523.

91 Walicki, 'Dozory bóżnicze w teorii i działaniu', 121.

92 I. Bartal, 'From Corporation to Nation: Jewish Autonomy in Eastern Europe, 1772–1881', *Jahrbuch des Simon-Dubnow-Instituts*, 5 (2006), 21; Wodziński, 'Zniesienie kahałów', 162.

93 Michałowska, *Między demokracją a oligarchią*, 251.

94 Michałowska-Mycielska, *Sejm Żydów litewskich*, 249–64. For a property owner's actual legal control over the *kahal*, see Rosman, *Żydzi pańscy*, 91–2; A. Markowski, 'Materiały do dziejów kahału zabłudowskiego z połowy XVIII w.', *Biuletyn Historii Pogranicza*, 9 (2008), 65–73. The academic literature on Jewish local communities in the modern era provides many examples of such control and proof of its variety.

95 On self-government in the Duchy of Warsaw, see P. Cichoń, *Rozwój myśli administracyjnej w Księstwie Warszawskim 1807–1815* (Kraków, 2006), 51–5.

96 See Smyk, *Administracja publiczna Królestwa Polskiego*, 122–34.

97 I. Levitats, *Evreiskaya obshchina v Rossii (1772–1917)* (Moscow, 2013); see also J. D. Klier, 'The *Kahal* in the Russian Empire: Life, Death and Afterlife of a Jewish Institution, 1772–1882', *Jahrbuch des Simon-Dubnow-Instituts*, 5 (2006), 33–50.

98 D. Kandel, 'Komitet starozakonnych', *Kwartalnik Poświęcony Badaniu Przeszłości Żydów w Polsce*, 2 (1912), 85–103.

99 On the rabbinate, see S. Stampfer, 'Inheritance of the Rabbinate in Eastern Europe in the Modern Period: Causes, Factors and Development over Time', *Jewish History*, 13 (1999), 35–7; on Marcus Jastrow, see M. Galas, *Rabin Markus Jastrow i jego wizja reformy judaizmu* (Kraków, 2007); Eng. trans.: *Rabbi Marcus Jastrow and His Vision for the Reform of Judaism: A Study in the History of Judaism in the Nineteenth Century*, trans. A. Tilles (Boston, 2013); Spyra, 'Miejsce rabina w gminie żydowskiej w Królestwie Polskim'.

'Masters of their own offerings no more'

Jewish Perceptions of the Transformation of Jewish Self-Government in the Kingdom of Poland

FRANÇOIS GUESNET

IN CONTRAST to Russia, where the abolition of the *kahal* in 1844 was intended to end any form of institutional representation for local Jewish communities, the central authorities in the Kingdom of Poland created, somewhat earlier, a new body, the synagogue supervisory board (*dozór bóżniczy*), to control and administer such communities. Both central and local authorities considered this as the sole legitimate representative of these communities. The aim of the government to clarify the relationship between Jews and the state administration emerges very clearly from the way this body was established in late 1821, along with the decision, a few weeks later, to abolish the *kahal*, the body traditionally responsible for administering a local Jewish community, together with the traditional Jewish voluntary associations (*ḥevrot*), of which the most important was the burial society (*ḥevrah kadisha*).[1] As had been the case with these bodies, the right to vote for the board was limited to those in the community who paid the most tax. It was made up of three prominent members of the community, three deputies, and the local rabbi, and reported to the local authorities. By 1856, 346 such boards had been established in the Kingdom of Poland.

This reform of Jewish self-government was part of a broader, European-wide process by which governments, inspired by the principles of the Enlightenment, attempted to reduce the power of intermediate authorities such as guilds, estates, parliaments, and free cities in order to establish centralized state administrations. It should also be seen as one element in the attempt of the partitioning powers to streamline the administration of the territories they had acquired. In this attempt, the need to regulate the legal status of the Jews constituted one of the more complex and intricate issues. Both in the history of the Polish lands and that of the Jews, the abolition of the *kahal* as the core institution of Jewish self-government constitutes a significant turning point. It not only reflects the attempt by the partitioning powers to take control of the social and political institutions which had characterized the Polish–Lithuanian Commonwealth but was also a continuation of the process of curtailing Jewish self-government, which had begun in the Polish lands with the abolition in 1764 of the Council of Four Lands. This was a process to which local and provincial Polish administrators made considerable input.

This chapter seeks to investigate the impact of the abolition of the *kahal* in the Kingdom of Poland from the point of view of Jewish perceptions of how Jewish communities should function within the wider administrative and societal fabric of the state and who should run them after the abolition of the traditional institutions of community government. The general mood among members of the Jewish establishment was well expressed by the leaders of the *ḥevrah kadisha* in Zamość, recorded in their *pinkas* (ledger) in 1825, just a few years after the abolition of the *kahal*:

> In the context of the humiliation in their dignity as community leaders which the members of the *kahal* suffered when they came to be described as synagogue supervisors, many of these individuals assume that they have now lost all power and authority. We, however, state and resolve that they continue to have the same power as the former *kahal*.[2]

This statement very clearly demonstrates that, in the eyes of the leading members of the community, the abolition of the *kahal* and the introduction of the synagogue supervisory board constituted a serious undermining of the formerly honourable role of community leader. It also shows that there was considerable reluctance to abandon the traditional institutional form of community organization—the resolution has clearly to be seen as a somewhat contrived attempt to maintain that things had not changed.

All the evidence points to attempts by the major Jewish communities in the Kingdom of Poland to comply with the basic administrative requirements of introducing synagogue supervisory boards, not least in order to make it possible for traditional *ḥevrot* to continue their activities with as little hindrance as possible. This was the situation from the inception of a supervisory board in Warsaw and was also the case in Lublin, where the members of the supervisory board co-operated with the *ḥevrah kadisha*.[3] In Łódź, in the early years after the emergence of this new centre of the Polish textile industry—which was also the period after the abolition of the *kahal*—the wealthiest members of the Jewish community were to play the leading roles in both the community and the burial society.[4]

Dora Szterenkac, author of the first comprehensive analysis of the abolition of the *kahal*, emphasized that this 'was not perceived as a major turning point in the lives of the Jews in Congress Poland and their self-government. The synagogue supervisory board was rather the continuation of the *kahal*, with more restricted prerogatives.'[5] In contrast to the autonomous *kahal* and the outlawed burial societies, however, the responsibilities, accountability, and modus operandi of the board were defined by the law of the state under the formal oversight of both local and provincial administrations.

If the synagogue supervisory boards gained in importance and acquired new functions in the course of the nineteenth century, this was, above all, because, in many communities, individuals with integrationist or reformist agendas saw them as a tool to gain leverage in situations where they were greatly outnumbered by the observant majority, as was the case in practically all Jewish communities in the Kingdom of Poland. Where such individuals managed to obtain one or more seats on the board, they acquired the opportunity to determine community policies, although their ability to implement their integrationist policies was more limited. Frequently, integrationists belonged to the wealthier families in such communities, and, as active electoral rights were dependent on one's status as taxpayer, they constituted a disproportionate number of the members of supervisory boards. Because of this increased leverage through public office, quite a number of dedicated integrationists invested considerable effort in being elected. Those who had a track record in charitable involvement were more likely to be successful in such endeavours. As will be shown below, municipal and provincial administrators often assisted such individuals to be elected.

Despite such support, until the end of the nineteenth century an integrationist majority on a synagogue supervisory board remained an extremely rare occurrence in the Kingdom of Poland. A comprehensive review of archival records as well as reports and letters to the integrationist weekly *Izraelita* show that this occurred first in Lublin in 1878[6] and then in Łódź in 1885.[7] In both cases, the new integrationist majority initiated its activities by introducing half-hearted measures to improve the decorum of Jewish funerals[8]—the limited changes proposed reflected the difficulties of attacking the burial societies, the stronghold of informal community authority—and by denouncing to the authorities unregistered Jewish places of worship. These actions, along with the manipulation of the electoral process which had allowed these majorities to emerge in communities with an overwhelmingly observant majority, led to considerable and long-lasting acrimony. In both Lublin and Łódź, the newly elected supervisory boards compiled comprehensive lists of all privately owned places of Jewish worship, identifying both the place in the land registry and the name of the owner.[9] A will executed in Lublin in 1885 illustrates the impact of these measures. In it, Isaac Rubinstein, a well-to-do homeowner, left the income of his property to contribute to the maintenance of the Besmedrish de Parnes, one of the most prestigious prayer and study houses in the town, on the condition 'that the synagogue supervisory board will in no way be involved in the administration of these funds'.[10]

The desire of the integrationists on supervisory boards to co-operate with the state authorities clearly did not endear them to the observant majority in their communities. The suspect measures they took to achieve their majority further undermined their authority. In December 1884 in Łódź, only massive fraud had allowed Izrael Poznański, then the leading Jewish textile entrepreneur there, to become head of the synagogue supervisory board. Previously, elections to the board had followed a uniform pattern with both the observant and integrationist factions nominating candidates who were then selected at a gathering of around one hundred representatives of the more prosperous Jewish families of the city.[11] This procedure had a rather plebiscitary character and ensured the representation of different religious and cultural groupings, maintaining a balance between these orientations for several decades. As only a small fraction of the Jewish community attended this assembly, it would be misleading to consider it a democratic body. It rather perpetuated traditional practices from the pre-partition period which limited community leadership to those who were well off and paid significant amounts of tax.[12] For both the local authorities and the central government, the balance on the synagogue supervisory board between the small number of better-off integrationists and the observant majority suited their aim of maintaining peace in the Jewish communities, as the mayor of Lublin explained to an assembly of around 200 prominent community members in 1866.[13] A further factor explaining the official desire to ensure Jewish communities tilted neither to the 'obscurantist' nor to the 'progressive' side was the January uprising of 1863–4, which had been a serious military challenge to Russian hegemony over the Kingdom of Poland and in which the Jewish populace had played a significant role, if only because of its demographic weight.[14] Under these circumstances, there was a desire not only to support the integrationist minority but also to count on the conservatism of the majority.

In 1884, for the first time, the elections to the synagogue supervisory board in Łódź took place not in the main synagogue but in the private synagogue of a wealthy member of the community and outside the Jewish quarter. Furthermore, as a prominent member of the observant community complained in a letter to the mayor, they were held on a major market day, preventing a considerable number of potential participants from attending.[15]

It was not until the 1890s that synagogue supervisory boards more frequently came under the control of an integrationist majority. This was the case in Często-chowa in 1895, in Zawiercie in 1897, and in Radom in 1899.[16] In a few instances, such majorities were overturned after only one term. As an *Izraelita* correspondent reported in 1900 from Płock, where the integrationists lost their majority at the next election to the supervisory board: 'The fact that the ignorant masses constitute the large majority is a curse for all of our provincial communities. Because of this, in-dividuals are elected to these honorary positions who have no qualifications what-soever and whose motive in standing for such representative roles is solely personal ambition.'[17]

I. D. Meisner, a prominent progressive member of the Kalisz Jewish community, experienced in 1901 a similar rebuff from the traditionalists. As reported in *Izraelita*, he had campaigned on the promise

to organize appropriately the burial society and to subordinate its activities to a system of regulation with the intention of eradicating certain abuses and especially the exploitation [of members of the community] by the society. But as is frequently the case in our com-munities, Mr Meisner's efforts were met with forceful and tenacious resistance from the trustees of the society.[18]

Meisner resigned his office after one term.

For the vast majority of Jews in the Kingdom of Poland, the burial society emerged as the institution which could best represent the ideals of their community. Even Hilary Nussbaum, a leading representative of the project to integrate the Jews of Poland as Poles of the Jewish faith into the wider fabric of society, did not deny them this historic role.[19] As the cited examples from around 1900 show, they continued to perform this function throughout the nineteenth century. This led to a parallel and somewhat paradoxical structure of Jewish representation, with one representative body highly regarded by most Jews, but illegal (the burial society), and a second, the synagogue supervisory board, considered as a necessary evil which was unfortunately invested with state authority. Despite the esteem in which they were held, the burial societies could not speak on behalf of the Jews to the non-Jewish world, while the supervisory boards were effective only in the restricted sphere of state-sponsored functions in community administration. Exceptions only confirm this overall situation. Thus, as I have shown elsewhere, the Board of the Jewish Community of Warsaw, the representative body introduced for the Jews of Warsaw (on which more below), was able to introduce and develop administrative innovations under the long-lasting leadership of Ludwik Natanson (1821–96).[20] In Łódź, the synagogue supervisory board under Izrael Poznański established a charitable school with vocational training for young Jews which proved quite successful.[21] In communities without such prominent leaders, the supervisory board clearly lacked credibility on the Jewish street and could not undertake such ambitious projects.

The non-acceptance of integrationists by the community is well illustrated by a serious conflict which arose in 1892 over the Jewish cemetery in Hrubieszów. The incident took place at the height of a cholera epidemic, which might have contributed to the tense atmosphere.[22] Founded by the Jagiellonians in the thirteenth century, Hrubieszów, the second largest town in the Lublin gubernia, had, from its earliest days, a major Jewish community. In 1900, of the town's 10,000 inhabitants around half were Jewish.[23] On the basis of a report in the *Varshavskii dnevnik*, the mouthpiece of the higher echelons of the Russian administration in the Kingdom of Poland, *Izraelita* describes how, in the summer of 1892, a wall was erected around the cemetery without formal approval, and the ensuing complications:

It is unknown who commissioned the construction of this wall and who paid for it and the authorities learned about it only after its completion. It is said that it was paid for by the illegal Jewish burial society. The district head rightly saw this as a high-handed course of action by the local Jews and ordered the local magistrate to tear down the wall. On the morning of 22 July, when workers started to do so, the Jews attacked them in great numbers and chased them away throwing stones. However, this was not the end of the matter: by midday, a crowd of around a hundred Jews protested in front of the district administration, shouting and crying, lamenting that their cemetery was being demolished and the graves of their forefathers and children defiled. Jewish agitators roamed the streets and forced more moderate Jews to close their shops and join them, the crowd quickly growing to 1,500 to 2,000. The members of the synagogue board, who do not enjoy the support of the populace, not only were unable to calm down the mob but hid in their houses out of fear of being beaten . . . This occurrence proves once more that the uneducated Jewish masses prefer to follow rabble-rousers rather than the synagogue board. Its conscientious members, selected from among the well-to-do and respectable local Jews, enjoy neither respect nor standing in Hrubieszów, in contrast to a small coterie of former board members and the burial society. The few dozen people who make up this group are determined and able to act as they wish. They intimidate and incite the crowds on the occasion of the board elections and do not refrain from physical violence. They inspire loyalty among the destitute through small gifts. The illegal leaders of the Jews of Hrubieszów were the instigators of the upheaval described above.[24]

There were many similar cases of obstruction and passive resistance against measures affecting Jews taken by the authorities in the Kingdom of Poland. None, however, reached the degree of open resistance and militancy as occurred in Hrubieszów. These conflicts arose, in the first instance, over burial. This is not surprising, taking into account the centrality of burial in Jewish tradition in general and considering the debates on this issue which had taken place over the decades in all the major communities of the Kingdom of Poland. Most communities had only one cemetery, and the considerable social, political, and religious tensions within the rapidly growing and diversifying Jewish population came to a head over how this should be administered.[25]

Matters of religious tradition, changes in the decorum of burial practices, but also, as the example from Hrubieszów shows, the issue of where authority lay in the community manifested themselves with unique urgency over this issue, which came to the surface in numerous confrontations across the kingdom. One such case was when members of the Jewish social democratic Bund in 1905 insisted on honouring a member killed during the revolution of 1905 by singing their hymn during the burial, which led Elias Hayim Mayzel, then chief rabbi of Łódź, to telephone for the intervention of the gendarmerie.[26] However, almost all cases of conflict revolving around burial reflect rather the radical differences between the approach of the state-sponsored authority of the synagogue supervisory board and that derived from the communal consensus embodied in traditional institutions and associations. While the former struggled throughout the period under consideration here to establish its authority, the latter found strength in the large number of often unlicensed places of worship and the many registered and unregistered charitable organizations.

Equally symptomatic of this state of affairs were the conflicts between the various Jewish factions in Warsaw, the capital of the Kingdom of Poland, over elections to the local synagogue supervisory board. These elections were probably closer than any other to our contemporary understanding of a democratic electoral process to a body of local or provincial political representation in the Russian empire in the nineteenth century. As the Warsaw Jewish community grew in size, this situation became more and more problematic in the view of both the Russian administration and the Jewish integrationists of Warsaw, mostly members of the upper echelons of the community. The latter considered control of the rapidly growing community as crucial to their attempt to impose their integrationist policy and saw as a major concern the continued control by the observant majority, both mitnagdic and hasidic, of all major community institutions, including synagogues and the rabbinate, charitable work and education. Representatives of the observant majority considered the synagogue supervisory board an administrative body which was worthy of respect since it had been introduced by the authorities. However, they never agreed with the authorities' view that the supervisory board had an exclusive right to control or administer the core responsibilities of community leadership and pursued a policy of informally channelling funds, for example from burials to charitable, religious, and educational institutions, as the already cited will of Isaac Rubinstein in Lublin in 1885 illustrates. A clear recognition of this situation and of the importance of community leaders who did not serve as synagogue supervisors is reflected in the fact that in the most prominent communities of the kingdom, income from burials appears only as a token sum in the budgets published by the supervisory boards.

A Short-Lived Third Way: Synagogue Supervisory Board Elections in Warsaw, 1851, 1855

The uneasy relationship between the state-sponsored synagogue supervisory boards and the much more respected, though illegal, burial societies was a common feature of Jewish community politics. The elections for the Warsaw supervisory board in October 1851 and December 1855 illustrate that members of the community would have preferred different arrangements and considered neither the intrusive state-sponsored actions of the supervisory boards nor the usually obstructive behaviour of the burial societies as ideal.

In September 1851 the Department for Domestic and Religious Affairs proposed a new procedure for these elections. While it did not introduce active electoral rights for all (male) members of the community, it proposed that 'the Jews of Warsaw identify [electors] from all the classes of the Jewish population'.[27] It instructed the trustees of all registered Jewish places of worship in the capital—of which there were 111—to notify their members at the end of the Rosh Hashanah service that the new synagogue supervisory board for Warsaw would be elected at the city hall and that each congregation should identify ten electors, 'for example, bankers, home-owners, merchants, shopkeepers, business-owners, artisans, or others'. The resulting list of electors numbered 968, of whom 614 turned up for the elections. This is the only known case of the creation of a community leadership where the term 'elections' is more or less appropriate, since the electorate in all previous and current cases was limited to the highest earners and taxpayers in the community, excluding women, and limiting active and passive voting rights to an elite group of well-to-do community members.

In the first round of voting, each elector was asked to write down fifteen names of his choice, from which a final list of candidates, including nine observant and five integrationist candidates, was selected. The electors were then asked to identify their five preferred individuals. Of the five who were selected in the second round, three (Shahna Rejch, Hillel Dawid Erlich, and Moshe Feinkind) were members of the observant majority, while two (Jakób Tugendhold, official censor of Hebrew publications for the government and a community activist, and Jan Glücksberg) were prominent integrationists. It seems that the electors were intent on ensuring that the supervisory board would indeed reflect the diversity of the emerging Jewish metropolis.[28]

In the aftermath of the elections, the city authorities received letters which complained both about the way they had been conducted and their outcome, which was considered a victory for the observant faction. A letter signed 'Israel Emet' (True Israel) claimed that the government's decision to hold elections in this way created a situation in which 'the city hall [was] filled with illiterate vagabonds, hawkers, beggars, scoundrels, offenders, and hasidim, with those few able to write filling in the ballots for them'.[29] Another letter attacked one of the successful traditionalist candidates. Moshe Feinkind, a prominent mitnaged (non-hasidic observant Jew), as 'completely passive and superstitious [who] only sought his own election in order to earn citizens' rights'. Shahna Rejch, it argued, was an 'ardent hasid and completely uncouth', while Hillel Dawid Erlich was similarly 'a hasid and fraudulent bankrupt'. Izrael Gesundheit, member of one of the most prominent mitnagdic families, was described as 'tavern keeper, a hasid, and stupid'. These prejudiced judgements found their way into the city council's assessment of the elections and resulted in its decision to bar most of the candidates.[30] Disregarding the results of the vote, the authorities appointed Jan Glücksberg, as chair, along with Mathias Kohn, Jakób Tugendhold, and Zymel Epstein (who originated from the Russian empire and was thus among the first 'Litvaks' in Warsaw). The only traditionalist candidate on the supervisory board was Pinkus Borowski, who had received the lowest number of votes in both ballots. His appointment further demonstrated the deliberate disregard of the views of the electorate by the authorities.[31]

The community elections of 1851 had shown that the Jewish population could not be trusted by the government. The next election was to be held in 1855, and how it should be conducted was discussed both by members of the Jewish community and by the authorities in the run-up. The Department for Domestic and Religious Affairs originally favoured a more restricted procedure but agreed, after the intervention of the observant faction, to maintain the principle of choosing electors from prayer houses and synagogues, while reducing their number from ten to three for each place of worship.[32] Activists from the integrationist faction intervened. Rafał Glücksohn and Mathias Kohn, two trustees of the 'German' synagogue,[33] criticized this course of action, which would

only lead to the appointment of supporters of talmudic prejudice who place every possible obstacle in the path of the process of civilizing the Jews. The earlier legislation proposed by the commission of the government in February, to have the trustees of the four Jewish institutions in the city—the hospital, the shelter for the poor, the board of education of the elementary schools, and the synagogue supervisory board—nominate fifteen candidates, from among whom the 100 to 150 electors would elect the three members of the supervisory board and their deputies, would certainly yield an entirely different result.[34]

This intervention was clearly intended to prevent the electors nominated in the many dozens of places of Jewish worship across Warsaw from making their voices heard. The four institutions mentioned in the proposal were by no means the only Jewish charities in Warsaw, although they were the only ones recognized by the state administration. In addition, the trustees of all four clearly identified with the integrationists. They included Józef Epstein, who presided over the administrative board of the

Jewish hospital; Meir Behrson, who headed the Dom Schronienia (a shelter for the poor); and Jakób Tugendhold, who was overseer of the Jewish elementary schools (not to be confused with the traditional ḥeders (private primary schools)). The mayor had appointed Jan Glücksberg to preside over the synagogue supervisory board in 1851, against the vast majority of the ballots cast. The proposal was thus an attempt to introduce an electoral system which would have given the integrationists a monopoly of power in the emerging Jewish metropolis of Warsaw.

A number of prominent members of the Jewish observant middle class initiated a counter-attack. Invoking the legislation introducing the synagogue supervisory boards which stipulated that electoral rights should be enjoyed by qualified members of the community rather than 'Jewish institutions', they prevailed. A submission which proved particularly successful was that signed by Izrael Gesundheit,[35] one of the supervisors elected in 1851 and brother of the later Warsaw chief rabbi, Jacob Gesundheit, and twenty-one other individuals who described themselves as 'home-owners'. The signatories claimed that 'the free choice of its representatives should be left to the community. The supervisory board can only preserve its unscathed reputation, trust, and moral dignity if its members can claim the same.' They acknowledged the merit of the four charitable institutions and their presidents, all in one way or another connected to the 'German' synagogue, and continued:

The community, however, has the right to expect that the government in its providential intentions, while considering these merits, does not undermine the dignity and the religious freedom which this nation has held holy for 3,167 years, as well as the supreme providential laws which were introduced to protect this freedom.[36]

The signatories did not reject the validity of 'supreme providential laws' by which they meant the introduction of the supervisory boards in 1821 and their reform in 1830, which in their view were not incompatible with the covenant between God and Moses on Mount Sinai. They should, however, include the right of elected representatives to govern the community. As a result, the authors of this revealing letter stressed the importance of the electoral process involving as many people as possible. They observed that over six thousand Jewish families lived in Warsaw who contributed to the community as a whole, if only through paying the kosher meat tax. All these families had 'the irrefutable right to have their voice heard in free elections to the supervisory board',[37] and accordingly they pleaded for the maintenance of an electoral process based on choosing electors from all prayer houses and synagogues.

In principle, the local authorities complied with this request and the 1855 elections for the Warsaw synagogue supervisory board were held on the basis of a ballot carried out by electors nominated by each of the 110 registered places of Jewish worship in Warsaw with the one modification that the number of electors per place of worship was lowered to three. Of the 297 nominated electors, 216 or 73 per cent took part in the elections in December 1855. The election results were very similar to those in 1851, with the significant difference that the authorities on this occasion did appoint those candidates who had received the highest number of ballots. This led to the establishment of a supervisory board dominated by traditional rabbinical community leaders with a few adherents of hasidism. As in 1851 Tugendhold ranked very high, coming second, despite his strong commitment to integrationist positions. In contrast to the principles of both elections to the *kahal* prior to its abolition and state law, three closely related members of one family, the Gesundheits, were elected, with two of them being actually appointed (Jakub and M. Gesundheit).[38]

The elections to the synagogue supervisory board demonstrated with great clarity the two opposing rationales for community representation and leadership. Members of the observant majority argued in favour of a synagogue board which would reflect and represent the majority of all Jews residing in the capital city, with democratic entitlement defined through a material contribution to the community budget in the form of the kosher meat tax. It is obviously impossible to decide how the authors of the letter discussed above would have defined this entitlement if they had not possessed the majority they had in the mid-nineteenth century. In contrast, members of the integrationist minority argued that community leadership had the duty to contribute to the moral and cultural 'improvement' of their fellow-Jews, the majority of whom they considered lacking in culture and under-educated.

Confrontations on the basis of this configuration occurred frequently throughout the Kingdom of Poland, with the synagogue supervisory board, on the one hand, and the technically illegal burial society on the other, usually constituting the conflicting organizational protagonists. Often, conflict was averted by discreetly avoiding interference in the respective areas of activity of the two bodies or through parallel membership in both the supervisory board and the burial society. In at least one documented case, in Kielce in 1889, members of the supervisory board requested considerable amounts of money (in clear infringement of the official burial fees) not as members of the board but as members of the burial society. On this occasion, their action was successfully challenged in court.[39]

Substructures of Community Representation in an Emerging Jewish Neighbourhood: Bałuty

As I have argued elsewhere, the emergence of very large Jewish communities across eastern Europe challenged both traditional forms of community organization and representation as well as the endeavours of the state to gain control over its Jewish subjects.[40] Pauperization, the deterioration of Jewish–non-Jewish relations with the increase in anti-Jewish violence which resulted, and the emergence of new forms of political mobilization and identification contributed to the loss of relevance of both synagogue supervisory boards and traditional forms of voluntary association.[41] The former suffered not only from a lack of credibility and trust but also from very inadequate structures and resources. Jewish *ḥevrot* still seem to have enjoyed the trust of many Jews in these large communities, but their inability to impose credible sanctions relying on social consent, such as the ban, reduced their overall authority.[42]

Thus, around the turn of the century, inefficient, state-sponsored administrative structures in the Kingdom of Poland competed without much success with conspiratorial forms of consensus-based, traditional self-government and representation. This can be illustrated by an episode from Łódź, the 'new city' par excellence in the Polish lands. As mentioned before, the formal structure of the local Jewish community was dominated by a small number of Jewish industrialists, with Izrael Poznański a key figure. The large and impoverished Jewish population settled in the north of the town in the ill-famed and miserable neighbourhood of Bałuty and created its own economic, social, and religious infrastructure, basically without any interference from outside.

Bałuty, which had drawn to it most of the new inhabitants, did not formally belong to the city of Łódź, but to the northern municipality of Radogoszcz. In 1858, I. Bławat and I. Birentsweyg, two Jewish real-estate investors, purchased a vast stretch of land and started to develop it. Within a generation its population grew: from a few hundred in 1860 to 20,000 in 1890 and 100,000 at the beginning of the First World War.[43] This created a community *ex nihilo*, without local tradition or hierarchies and with a dramatic lack of any form of infrastructure or administrative oversight. A conflict over the use of a plot of land reveals how new structures of Jewish self-government emerged in this neighbourhood without state interference or the knowledge of the synagogue supervisory boards of Radogoszcz and Łódź. The conflict arose in 1897 between the Rapeports, legal heirs of a plot of land in Bałuty, and the owners of a *mikveh* (ritual bath), built and managed on the plot. In a series of submissions to the police, the widow Jeta Rapeport complained about the existence of the *mikveh* and a prayer house on her land, established without the knowledge and approval of the authorities.[44] A Jewish society (described by Rapeport as *evreiskoe obshchestvo* and *obshchestvo bozhnitsy*) and the '*kahal* of the community of Bałuty' were responsible for the management of these institutions, with the local *kahal* also maintaining a community cash office. A certain Ruvin Seyfert was the senior manager of these institutions. Seyfert, Rapeport stated, levied a community tax on the Jewish residents of Bałuty, collected a kosher meat tax on slaughtered poultry, and farmed out the income from the Jewish ritual bath—all roles which traditionally would be the responsibility of a community board, whether the pre-1821 *kahal* or the later synagogue supervisory board.

A special tasks officer delegated by the gubernia administration to investigate the situation could not confirm the accusations. He reported that Seyfert and a few other residents of Bałuty could indeed be seen as synagogue supervisors but only 'because they took responsibility to ensure good order in the local prayer house'. The chief rabbi, Nakhman Maizel of Łódź, testified that there was no synagogue supervisory board in the neighbourhood and added cautiously that the Łódź board had no oversight of any of the institutions which were being investigated. However, more than a dozen residents of Bałuty testified independently that the neighbourhood did indeed have a supervisory board, with Seyfert at its head, and that he also administered the income from the ritual bath, prayer house, and ritual slaughter. In contrast to the usual community board, Seyfert would also take money from the poor but did not support any charitable activities.[45] The authorities concluded their investigation by itemizing deficiencies in the construction of both the ritual bath and the prayer house, but gave permission for them to function after they were repaired.[46]

This episode is a telling example of how community representation and self-government were perceived by poor Jewish city-dwellers at the beginning of the twentieth century. The complainants may well have used the term *kahal* in order to trigger alarm about conspiratorial Jewish structures of government which resonated widely in the public sphere in late tsarist Russia.[47] The fact that a special tasks officer was commissioned with the investigation is an indication of how sensitive the Russian authorities were to intelligence on illegal structures of government, especially in such an unruly context as proletarian Łódź. The testimonies collected in the course of his investigation reflect the assumption that someone had to take care of certain matters, especially those close to the religious needs of an emerging Jewish community. Since the nearby synagogue supervisory board in Łódź was not willing to do so, enterprising individuals stepped in, not without consideration of their own potential profit from providing such services. The fact that the tsarist empire, and especially a centre of rapid demographic development such as Łódź, was insufficiently policed and administered allowed both for the emergence of such informal structures and their surviving a police investigation.

Conclusion: Self-Government, or Being Master of One's Own Offerings

As the episode from Łódź–Bałuty demonstrates, a strong normative framework for the legitimacy and standards of community self-organization of Jews resident in a shared urban space existed until the very end of the nineteenth century. It was strongly informed by a notion of shared rights and mutual obligations and was seen as necessary to ensure the existence of core religious and community institutions. The Jews of Bałuty did not object to a local Jew taking on the task of establishing and managing such institutions and making a livelihood from doing so, given the absence of a formal community. What they objected to was that Seyfert did not redistribute at least some of his profits.

Similar sensitivities had shaped the negative reception of the transformations at the beginning of the nineteenth century reviewed in this chapter. As I have argued, the abolition of the *kahal* was seen as a humiliation and a curtailment of community prerogative, and an infringement of both the Jewish covenant with God and the one between the Polish Jewish communities and the lawful government. Community taxes, charities, and income generated through institutions such as ritual baths, prayer houses, and cemeteries were concrete expressions of such community prerogatives. As a result, the synagogue supervisory boards did not enjoy much respect among the Jewish population of the Kingdom of Poland. Their legal obligations had little to do with its everyday needs, and they were generally considered an undesirable, watered-down, and subservient form of representation towards the state. Despite tax exemptions and the offer of remuneration, prominent community members only rarely agreed to serve as members of these boards.[48] The members of the Jewish Advisory Board to the Komitet Starozakonnych, a body introduced in 1826 to review the legal status of the Jews, explained this reluctance in a memorandum from 1829, in the early period of the synagogue supervisory board's existence.[49] Community members hesitated to become synagogue supervisors (described as 'inspecteurs de synagogues' in the original text) because 'the Jews are no longer masters of their own offerings', as the authors of the memorandum explained in a paragraph that is key to understanding how this new body of representation and administration was perceived.[50]

While the observant majority in the Jewish communities of the Kingdom of Poland deplored the loss of control over their community budgets and the danger of state interference through the synagogue supervisory boards, the expectations of the integrationist minority were equally disappointed. As was illustrated by the small number of supervisory boards where their adherents were actually able to gain access, they were certain to face passive resistance from their observant coreligionists or, as in the case of Warsaw in 1851 and 1855, a wavering attitude from the side of the authorities. The hesitation of the latter only grew after the January uprising of 1863. As the integrationists were considered potential allies of the Polish patriotic faction, local and regional administrators went to great lengths to ensure that neither the observant majority nor the integrationist faction would gain absolute control.[51] As has been shown, this was also true for the few communities where the integrationists gained the majority of seats on the supervisory board. In a few clearly circumscribed cases of paramount significance, such as help for Jewish army recruits or relief measures in the case of epidemics, weather hazards, or anti-Jewish violence, the joint raising and management of funds occurred, but these were the exception.[52] Despite the persistent and widely shared ideal of mutual responsibility among all Jews, the reality of Jewish community affairs was one of confrontation, competition, and growing fragmentation.

Notes

Parts of this chapter have been translated from F. Guesnet, *Polnische Juden im 19. Jahrhundert: Lebensbedingungen, Rechtsnormen und Organisation im Wandel* (Cologne, 1998), Teil VI: 'Jüdische Selbstorganisation im Wandel: Gemeinde und Wohltätigkeit', 333–446, with permission of Böhlau-Verlag.

1 See C. Aust, 'Burying the Dead, Saving the Community: Jewish Burial Societies as Informal Centres of Jewish Self-Government', in this volume.

2 E. Kupfer, 'Pinkas bractwa pogrzebowego i dobroczynnego w Zamościu', *Biuletyn Żydowskiego Instytutu Historycznego*, 2 (1951), 55–80: 69.

3 Guesnet, *Polnische Juden*, 368–9.

4 Among the members of the burial societies were the representatives of the wealthiest

Jewish families of Łódź, Berger, and Orbach, the mitnagdic Saltzman family, and Moshe Pilgrim, a hasid (see A. Alperin, *Żydzi w Łodzi: Początki Gminy Żydowskiej 1780–1822* (Łódź, 1928), 32; Archiwum Państwowe Łódź (hereafter APŁ), Akta Miasta Łodzi (hereafter AMŁ), 1573: mayor of Łódź, letter to the Voivode Commission, 12/24 June 1838).

5 D. Szterenkac, 'Zniesienie kahałów i utworzenie dozorów bóżniczych w pierwszych latach Królestwa Polskiego', MA thesis (University of Warsaw, 1932), 71.

6 Guesnet, *Polnische Juden*, 352.

7 F. Guesnet, '"Die beiden Bekenntnisse leben weit entfernt voneinander, sie kennen und schätzen sich gegenseitig nicht": Das Verhältnis von Juden und Deutschen im Spiegel ihrer Organisationen im Łódź des 19. Jahrhunderts', in J. Hensel (ed.), *Polen, Deutsche und Juden in Łódź 1820–1939: Eine schwierige Nachbarschaft* (Osnabrück, 1999), 139–70: 151.

8 See Guesnet, *Polnische Juden*, 303–25.

9 Archiwum Państwowe Lublin (hereafter APL), Akta Miasta Lublina (hereafter AML) 1874–1915, 537: synagogue board, letter to the local magistrate, 30 Mar. 1881. For Łódź, see APŁ, AMŁ, 7167: Izrael Poznański, head of the synagogue board, letter to the mayor of Łódź, 1 May 1885.

10 APL, AML 1874–1915, 567: copy, 14 Dec. 1910, of Isaac Rubinstein, will, 12 Dec. 1885. According to an online dictionary of Jewish Lublin maintained by the local Grodzka Gate —NN Theatre, this—no longer extant—synagogue was founded by Abraham Heilpern, among the last presidents of the Council of Four Lands in the second half of the eighteenth century, and was located at 2 Szeroka Street ('Synagogi i domy modlitwy w Lublinie', Teatr NN website, visited 1 Nov. 2019).

11 For a description of such an assembly, see APŁ, AMŁ, 1567, Akta tyczące się Dozoru Bóżniczego, ss. 49–54: letter to the head of Łęczyca district, 6/18 June 1866 in reply to request for information from Glavnyi Direktor Vnutrennykh i Dukhovnykh Del, 10/22 Jan. 1866; Guesnet, '"Die beiden Bekenntnisse leben weit entfernt voneinander, sie kennen und schätzen sich gegenseitig nicht"', 11.

12 G. D. Hundert, *Jews in Poland–Lithuania in the Eighteenth Century: A Genealogy of Modernity* (Berkeley, Calif., 2004), 81–2; F. Guesnet, 'The Jews of Poland–Lithuania, 1650–1815', in J. Karp and A. Sutcliffe (eds.), *Cambridge History of Judaism*, 8 vols. (Cambridge, 2018), vii. 805–6.

13 APL, AML 1809–1874, 2419: minutes of meeting between the mayor of Lublin and 'the more prominent and civilized members of the community representing all [religious] parties [in the Jewish community]', 13/25 July 1866.

14 A. Polonsky, *The Jews in Poland and Russia*, 3 vols. (Oxford, 2010–12), i. 309–15. The gendarmerie, local, provincial, and central authorities shared information about potential sympathizers among the Jewish population for the Polish independence and insurrection movement (Guesnet, *Polnische Juden*, 400 n. 211).

15 APŁ, AMŁ 7152: O bozhnichnom dozore i bozhnichnoi kasse, gubernia administration, letter to the mayor of Łódź, 17 Dec. 1884, quoting a letter by Kornvaser and four other community members.

16 Guesnet, *Polnische Juden*, 401.

17 Korespondencja, *Izraelita*, 1900, no. 46, p. 538.

18 Ygred, Korespondencja, *Izraelita*, 1901, no. 30, p. 345; Ignotus, Korespondencja, *Izraelita*, 1904, no. 15, p. 179.

19 H. Nussbaum, *Szkice historyczne z życia Żydów w Warszawie od pierwszych śladów pobytu ich w tem mieście do chwili obecnej* (Warsaw, 1881; repr. 1989), 80–1.

20 F. Guesnet, 'From Community to Metropolis', in G. Dynner and F. Guesnet, *Warsaw: The*

Jewish Metropolis. Essays in Honor of the 75th Birthday of Professor Antony Polonsky (Leiden, 2015), 139–42

21 On a *talmud torah* with vocational training, see Guesnet, *Polnische Juden*, 400 n. 213.

22 K. Kreuder-Sonnen, 'Jewish Bodies and Jewish Doctors during the Cholera Years of the Polish Kingdom', in M. Moskalewicz, U. Caumanns, and F. Dross (eds.), *Jewish Medicine and Healthcare in Central Eastern Europe: Shared Identities, Entangled Histories* (Cham, 2019), 79–95.

23 A number of prominent Poles and Jews grew up in Hrubieszów, most notably Abraham Stern (*c.*1762–1842), among the leading Jewish public intellectuals of the early nineteenth century, and the author Bolesław Prus (1847–1912) (see J. Zętar, 'Hrubieszów: historia miasta', Teatr NN website, visited 1 Oct. 2019).

24 Kronika z miasta i z kraju, *Izraelita*, 1892, no 31, p. 266. So far, the original dispatch in *Varshavskii dnevnik* has not been located.

25 Guesnet, *Polnische Juden*, 303.

26 F. Guesnet, '*Khevres* and *Akhdes*: The Change in Jewish Self-Organization in the Kingdom of Poland before 1900 and the Bund', in J. Jacobs (ed.). *Jewish Politics in Eastern Europe: The Bund at 100* (Basingstoke, Hants., 2001), 3–13: 9.

27 Archiwum Główne Akt Dawnych, Warsaw (hereafter AGAD), Centralne Władze Wyznaniowe Królestwa Polskiego (hereafter CWWKP), 1727, fo. 826: Department for Domestic and Religious Affairs, letter to the mayor of Warsaw, 4/16 Sept. 1851. Jakub Szacki only briefly mentions these elections (J. Szacki, *Geshikhte fun yidn in varshe*, 3 vols. (New York, 1947–53), ii. 54–5).

28 AGAD, CWWKP, 1727, fos. 892–917: Akta Komisyi Rządowej Spraw Wewnętrznych i Duchownych tyczące się Gminy Żydowskiej w Warszawie [1849–1851/2], minutes of the elections to the Warsaw Synagogue Supervisory Board, 19 Sept./2 Oct. 1851 by the mayor of Warsaw, signed by Mayor Teodor Andrault. Among the three deputies there were two observant and one integrationist community members.

29 AGAD, CWWKP, 1727, fos. 945–6: 'Israel Emet', letter to General Wikiński, in Yiddish with Polish translation, 3 Oct 1851.

30 AGAD, CWWKP, 1727, fo. 944: 'Lista Wybranych większością głosów kandydatów na Członków Dozoru Bóżniczego M. Warszawy', n.d.

31 AGAD, CWWKP, 1727, fo. 950: General Wikiński, letter to the mayor of Warsaw, with a list of individuals appointed to the synagogue board, 5/17 Oct. 1851.

32 AGAD, CWWKP, 1727, fos. 393–8, Department for Domestic and Religious Affairs, letter to the mayor of Warsaw, 10/22 Sept. 1855; see also Szacki, *Geshikhte fun yidn in varshe*, ii. 55.

33 This synagogue was founded by the Prussian Jew Isaak Flatau. While it attracted Jews who identified with non-Jewish culture and manners more than the majority of Polish Jews, the synagogue did not introduce reforms to the service (see, most recently, C. Aust, *The Jewish Economic Elite: Making Modern Europe* (Bloomington, Ind., 2018), 101–2).

34 AGAD, CWWKP, 1729, fos. 536–8: Rafał Glücksohn and Mathias Kohn, letter to the head of the Department of Home and Religious Affairs quoted in Administrative Council, letter to the Department for Domestic and Religious Affairs, 17/29 Oct. 1855.

35 On the Gesundheit family, see S. Stampfer, 'An Unhappy Community and an Even Unhappier Rabbi', in Dynner and Guesnet, *Warsaw*, 154–79: 163–4.

36 AGAD, CWWKP, 1729, fos. 365–8: Izrael Gesundheit, letter to General Wikiński, 17/29 June 1855, translated from Hebrew into Polish by Jakób Tugendhold.

37 Ibid.

38 For the election results, see Guesnet, *Polnische Juden*, 408 n. 233.

39   Salezy Majmon, Korespondencja, *Izraelita*, 1889, no. 43, p. 364.

40   G. Dynner and F. Guesnet, 'Introduction', in eid. (eds.), *Warsaw*, 1–16; Guesnet, 'From Community to Metropolis'.

41   Z. Gitelman, 'Introduction', in id. (ed.), *The Emergence of Modern Jewish Politics: Bundism and Zionism in Eastern Europe* (Pittsburgh, Pa., 2003), 12–18; S. Ury, *Barricades and Banners: The Revolution of 1905 and the Transformation of Warsaw Jewry* (Stanford, Calif., 2012), 91–140.

42   Guesnet, *Polnische Juden*, 221–2. Social and religious traditionalism as a hegemonic attitude in the very large Jewish communities of eastern Europe seems to offer yet another example of a challenge to the over-generalizing assumption of early sociology that urban society did 'break the cake of custom' (see R. Park, 'Human Migration and the Marginal Man', *American Journal of Sociology*, 33 (1928), 881–93; repr. in R. Sennett (ed.), *Classic Essays on the Culture of Cities* (Englewood Cliffs, NJ, 1969), 131–42). Rather, it seems that it also was the space of conservative reassertion and reconfiguration. This seems a promising avenue for further investigation. See F. Guesnet, 'Jüdisches Leben in der Teilungszeit zwischen Tradition, Integration, und Nationsbildung', in M. Müller and I. Kąkolewski (eds.), *Polen in der europäischen Geschichte: Ein Handbuch in vier Bänden*, iii: *Die polnisch–litauischen Länder unter der Herrschaft der Teilungsmächte (1772/1795–1914)* (Stuttgart, 2020), 617–47.

43   B. Baranowski and J. Fijałek (eds.), *Łódź: Dzieje miasta (do 1918 r.)* (Warsaw, 1980), 171–2.

44   APŁ, Piotrków Gubernia Government, Administrative Department, 6077, 'Łaźnia żydowska': Jeta Rapeport, letter, 17 Nov. 1897.

45   APŁ, Piotrków Gubernia Government, Administrative Department, 6077, 'Łaźnia żydowska': report by the special tasks officer, 28 Mar. 1898, nos. 1–15, 25.

46   APŁ, Piotrków Gubernia Government, Administrative Department, 6077, 'Łaźnia żydowska': governor of Piotrków gubernia, letters to the chief of police, Łódź, 3 June 1898; chief of police, Łódź, to the gubernia administration, 16 Mar. 1899.

47   J. D. Klier, *Imperial Russia's Jewish Question 1855–1881* (Cambridge, 1995), 263–84.

48   Biblioteka Książąt Czartoryskich, Kraków, MS 3160: 'Memoriał w sprawie żydowskiej' (n.d.); see A. Eisenbach, 'Memoriał o położeniu ludności żydowskiej w dobie konstytucyjnej Królestwa Kongresowego', *Teki Archiwalne*, 21 (1989), 171–217: 182. The memorandum was written in French and addressed to the minister of faith communities and public education, Stanislas (Stanisław) Grabowski. Artur Eisenbach assumes it was drafted by the Advisory Board's secretary, Jan Glücksberg. Some paragraphs of the memorandum were included in *Rzut oka na stan Izraelitów w Polsce, czyli wykrycie błędnego z niemi postępowania na aktach rządowych oparte* (Warsaw, 1831).

49   Polonsky, *The Jews in Poland and Russia*, i. 293–4.

50   Eisenbach, 'Memoriał o położeniu ludności żydowskiej', 182.

51   This was explicitly stated in the central authorities' directives to regional and local authorities shortly after the January uprising (see Guesnet, *Polnische Juden*, 278–9).

52   Ibid. 326–31.

The Synagogue in the System of Jewish Self-Government in Tsarist Russia

VLADIMIR LEVIN

THE PHYSICAL AND SYMBOLIC embodiment of the autonomous Jewish community in the Polish–Lithuanian Commonwealth was the building of a synagogue, which defined and represented the community both in the eyes of its own members and in its relations with the outside world. This chapter will discuss how the symbolic connection between the synagogue and the community underwent significant changes after the annexation of the commonwealth's eastern areas by the Russian empire. Notwithstanding its diminishing centrality, the synagogue was one of the institutions that performed community functions after the abolition of the autonomous *kahal* in Russia, and its role in community government varied in different regions of the empire. Since Russian law recognized the synagogue and its congregation as legal bodies, they could serve as a basis for the construction of a new, modern, and secular Jewish community at the beginning of the twentieth century.

■

For the Jews of the Polish–Lithuanian Commonwealth, the community synagogue, *beit hakeneset* in Hebrew and *di shul* in Yiddish, was the embodiment of the Jewish community, which saw itself as a holy community governed by sacred law. To distinguish the main synagogue of the community from smaller houses of prayer and study, *batei midrash* and *kloyzn*, as well as from private synagogues, I will refer to it as the great synagogue.[1] In almost all the Jewish communities in the Polish–Lithuanian Commonwealth, apart from the largest ones (e.g. Kraków, Poznań, Rzeszów), there was only one great synagogue.[2] To stress its uniqueness, in several places it was called the 'holy synagogue' (*beit hakeneset hakedoshah*): this name was used in the *pinkas* (record book) of Żółkiew (Zhovkva) in 1765 and in the *pinkas* of Dubno in the late eighteenth and early nineteenth centuries, and was mentioned in an epitaph on a tombstone in Satanów (Sataniv) in 1795.[3]

The architecture and decoration of the great synagogue reflected the Jerusalem Temple and stressed submission to God and the Torah.[4] The interior, full of sacred allusions, imbued its worshippers with holiness; their prayers and Torah study were absorbed by the walls and vaults and contributed to the sacredness of the space.[5] A 'holy community' should be governed by people who were endowed with God's sanction. Therefore, the nomination of the officials of the community took place in the synagogue—in sacred space—on the first of the intermediate days of Passover —in sacred time. Although the nomination of community officials was based on rational rules, the first step was usually the selection of electors by drawing lots, a practice that prevented collusion but at the same time allowed for the possibility of divine interference.[6]

Within the system of Jewish self-government in the Polish–Lithuanian Commonwealth, a great synagogue symbolized the independent or semi-independent status of the community vis-à-vis neighbouring Jewish communities. Economic considerations stood behind this arrangement: the community of Zabłudów, for example, was exempted from certain payments to the higher-ranking community of Tykocin in 1621, 'because they have a synagogue, a cantor, and a cemetery'.[7] The existence of a synagogue meant that the members of the dependent community did not use the synagogue of the main community and therefore did not have to pay for its services. However, economic considerations were easily translated into symbolic form: in 1692 the Council of Four Lands decided that villages and small towns that did not have a synagogue should be subordinate to the community of a nearby town and pay all their taxes there.[8]

Every independent or semi-independent community built its own great synagogue. In Lwów (Lviv), where two *kahals* existed from at least the fourteenth century, the community 'inside the walls' and the community in the suburb had separate synagogues.[9] In Ostróg (Ostroh), where the *kahal* had been divided into two in 1731, to fit the division of the city between two owners,[10] a new great synagogue was built in Krasna Góra to serve the newly established community. Like the old great synagogue, it employed a preacher, and all Jews belonging to the new *kahal* had to celebrate their marriages there.[11] The struggle of the Jews of the suburb of Antokol (Antakalnis) for independence from the Vilna community included the erection of two synagogues in the 1760s and 1770s, since the suburb belonged to two owners.[12] Noble landlords of villages sometimes assisted 'their' Jews in getting permission from the local bishop for the erection of a synagogue in order to make them independent of urban communities that burdened them with excessive taxes.[13] The view that the existence of a synagogue meant independence survived into the late nineteenth century. For example, the Jews of Sochocin claimed independence from the community of Płońsk in 1882, because they had built their own synagogue: 'the authority of the community leaders of Płońsk over our community has henceforth ceased because of this synagogue'.[14]

It is possible to say that the autonomous community was identical with the worshippers of the great synagogue. The *kahal* was, in a sense, the governing institution of the congregation of the synagogue, and its rule of the latter could also be seen as self-rule by the synagogue worshippers. Therefore, the *kahal* made great efforts to force all the community members to pray there or in the *batei midrash*, which also belonged to the *kahal*. It also nominated their elders, hired cantors, and licensed preachers.

Ḥevrot, voluntary associations within the Jewish community, tended to organize their own *batei midrash*, sometimes in rooms in the buildings or courtyard of the great synagogue. The *kahal* permitted these *batei midrash* and continued to supervise them, but in general it refrained from interference in their internal affairs. For example, the Hevrat Shivah Keruim in Minsk took the *kahal* to the rabbinical court in 1804 because it extended the contract with the cantor of the community. The *ḥevrah* stated that, since the ownership of the *beit midrash* had been transferred to it, the *kahal* could not appoint a cantor without its consent.[15] This example demonstrates that voluntary associations, both those of an elite character, like Shivah Keruim or the *ḥevrah kadisha*, and the 'plebeian' ones, like the *ḥevrot* of artisans, ran their prayer houses independently of the *kahal*, elected elders, hired cantors, and took responsibility for the buildings and internal order. Membership in a *ḥevrah* was identical with being a worshipper in its *beit midrash*. The same situation characterized private prayer houses: the *kahal* permitted or restricted them, but left their management to their owners.

The great synagogue not only represented the community and provided religious authorization for the community's officials but was also their seat of authority. The *kahal*'s office and prison were situated in its building or courtyard.[16] There were several heads of the *kahal* on a monthly rotation, and during their month in office they were usually obliged to pray in the great synagogue.[17] The great synagogue served also as a place for a general assembly to decide important issues. According to the *pinkas* of Tykocin, in 1704 'the leaders of the *kahal*, may the Rock and Redeemer protect them, and the holy community together with the judges, assembled an assembly for the sake of heaven in the synagogue concerning improvements in the community'.[18] Thus, the building of the great synagogue had at the same time sacral and administrative meanings and these meanings were intertwined: the holy community gathered in the holy synagogue for divine worship and also made decisions on community affairs there. The same is true for the *ḥevrot*: the sacred space of a *beit midrash* strengthened the sacral character of its *ḥevrah* and sanctified its administrative activities.

The partitions of the Polish–Lithuanian Commonwealth and the establishment of Russian rule in its eastern areas slowly brought to an end the predominance of the great synagogue. The first comprehensive Russian law on Jews, the Jewish Statute of 1804, aiming to resolve the struggles between the hasidim and their opponents, stated:

If a division into sects should appear in any place, to such an extent that one sect should not be willing to be with another in the same synagogue, in this case each of them is allowed to build its own synagogue and elect its own rabbi; but in each town there is to be only one *kahal*.[19]

In this way Russian law preserved the unity of the local community in a town. This had clear fiscal benefits, but legalized the existence of several synagogues, thus severing the link between the town's whole community and a particular synagogue.[20]

Nicholas I's far-reaching intervention in the internal workings of Jewish society from the 1820s to the 1850s led to the dissolution of the *kahal* and the conversion of every synagogue and prayer house into a legal body.[21] A decade before the abolition of the *kahal*, the Jewish Statute of 1835 regarded synagogues as similar to churches and mosques and therefore defined them as independent establishments. The statute declared that Jews were entitled to engage in public worship and prayer only in specified buildings—synagogues and prayer houses; it prescribed the procedure for their approval by provincial governors; and it established the number of synagogues and prayer houses permitted in a town according to the number of Jewish households. The statute also defined synagogue worshippers as a legal body 'all Jews who gather regularly in a synagogue or a prayer house for worship and prayer constitute the congregation of that synagogue or prayer house'. Each congregation was obliged to elect a board of three members: a scholar, an elder, and a treasurer, who had to be approved by the provincial authorities and take an official oath. The boards had to supervise the running of the synagogue; manage its finances; hire beadles, cantors, and other functionaries; and keep updated lists of all members and provide the rabbi and the police with copies of them.[22] In this way, the synagogues and prayer houses were exempted from the authority of the *kahal* and became directly subordinate to the state.[23] The text of the oath to be taken by board members was established by a separate law in 1838 and resembled that of the oath for *kahal* elders.[24] It goes without saying that all the worshippers and board members were exclusively men.

The abolition of the *kahal* in 1844 did not imply that Jews became individuals directly subject to the 'general' state institutions. The Russian state continued to define Jews in a given locality as a separate community for the purposes of military conscription, poll tax, and special Jewish taxes: the tax on kosher meat, which had to provide for community activities, including repayment of old debts incurred by the *kahals*, and the tax on sabbath candles, intended for the upkeep of the state-sponsored Jewish schools. All Jews belonged to the *meshchane* (the burgher estate) and were members of the local *meshchanskoe obshchestvo* (burghers' society) but constituted a separate part of that society and had their own elder and tax collector. The distribution of revenues from the kosher meat tax was made by an assembly of 'settled, prosperous and respectful [Jewish] citizens',[25] which the local authorities convened every four years.[26] Thus, the synagogue congregation and its board was only one of a number of Jewish legal bodies recognized and controlled by the state.

The abolition of the *kahal* also led to the updating of the rules for synagogue boards. The law of 15 August 1850 subjected the boards to municipalities and ordered their re-election every three years (as was the case with members of the *kahal* according to the Statute of 1835). It also required the boards to take responsibility for philanthropic institutions, including hospitals and burial societies (previously the responsibility of the *kahals*). Government supervision was increased by obliging the boards to keep accounts of income and expenses and to submit them annually to the magistrates for auditing. The Crown rabbi became *ex officio* a member of the boards of all synagogues and prayer houses in the territory under his jurisdiction.[27] The codification of Russian laws in 1857 included the rules about the synagogues in the Statutes on the Spiritual Affairs of Foreign Faiths under the heading 'On the Spiritual Boards of the Jews'.[28] Consequently, the boards of synagogues and prayer houses became known as 'spiritual boards' (*dukhovnye pravleniia*).[29]

Many of the laws promulgated during the reign of Nicholas I were intended to be in harmony with the norms of Jewish society and the prescriptions of halakhah. However, their provisions were formulated by Christian officials, ignorant of rabbinic Judaism, who relied on information from Jewish 'experts' and were motivated by the desire to introduce 'order' into Jewish affairs.[30] Thus, synagogues and prayer houses were equated with the Christian churches and parishes with which tsarist officials were familiar. The concept of a local community—which united all the Jews in a given locality, had a common rabbi, cemetery, ritual bath, and other institutions, but was divided into several houses of prayer—was alien to them. As a result, Russian law constructed a new entity, the Jewish 'parish', which partly resembled the Christian parish and was partly rooted in the Jewish tradition. Self-government of each synagogue and prayer house according to the Statute of 1835 was a direct continuation of the existing order. The board of three members followed the custom of many communities of having three elders for the synagogue, and the traditional aspect was also stressed by the use of Jewish names for the board members (*gabai* and *ne'eman*).

The recognition of all synagogues and prayer houses as independent institutions in fact legalized the voluntary associations that owned them. It has often been argued that the *ḥevrot*, alongside hasidic courts and Lithuanian supra-community yeshivas, fulfilled many of the functions of the autonomous community structure during its decline and after its abolition.[31] Israel Bartal, for example, has written that the associations 'preserved the traditional way of life by providing it with a social basis [and] served as focal points for socialization'.[32] To a very significant degree, the *ḥevrot* could fulfil the functions of the community authority because they possessed their own bases in the form of independent prayer houses. The state did not recognize the *ḥevrot* but did recognize the congregations of prayer houses. When the membership of a *ḥevrah* and a prayer house coincided, the official status of the latter facilitated the activities of the former. Having a physical seat and an organizational structure was especially important for artisans' associations; conversely, many *ḥevrot* for charity and study functioned in the existing synagogues and did not form separate congregations.

The classical case of a *ḥevrah* that fulfilled various social functions of the community was Hevrat Hatsedakah Hagedolah in Vilna, which was the most important voluntary association in the city from the eighteenth to the early twentieth centuries.[33] However, what is rarely mentioned is that Hatsedakah Hagedolah was directly connected with the Great Synagogue of Vilna. In the late nineteenth century the board of the *ḥevrah* was identical to that of the synagogue and the *ḥevrah* cared for the synagogue's building.[34] In the early twentieth century, the board was elected by the worshippers of the Great Synagogue and the Jewish merchants, university graduates, and representatives on the *meshchanskoe obshchestvo*. The ḥevrah legally owned all the community properties including the cemeteries and the build-ing of the Great Synagogue.[35] It seems that such a prominent role as that played by Vilna's Hevrat Hatsedakah Hagedolah was exceptional in the Russian empire; how-ever, further research on this issue is needed.[36]

The implementation of the 1835 law on spiritual boards and their acceptance by the Jews was a slow process. For example, fifteen years after the promulgation of the law, only 67 per cent of synagogues in Volhynia had officially approved elders, and only 57 per cent had officially approved treasurers. Seventeen years later, in 1867, the governor of Volhynia complained that 'in almost all synagogues and prayer houses, there are no members of synagogue boards approved by the government'.[37] Only in the late nineteenth century did the situation improve when the majority of syna-gogues and prayer houses obtained official registration and began regularly to elect their spiritual boards.

In prohibiting any activities besides prayer and worship in synagogues and prayer houses, the Statute of 1835 undermined the function of the synagogue, especially the great synagogue, as the main public space of the community, even taking into account problems with the implementation of the law in the first decades after its promulgation. Although it seems highly unlikely that the worshippers of a syna-gogue gathered somewhere else for the election of its spiritual board or that tailors refrained from discussion of their problems in the tailors' prayer house, legally such elections and discussions could not be held there.[38] It is possible that activities that were less formal or legal had more chance of being performed in synagogues and prayer houses. For example, Jewish revolutionaries in the early twentieth century and especially during the first Russian revolution of 1905 widely used synagogues for spreading propaganda among worshippers and as places for clandestine meetings. Gatherings before the elections to the state duma in those years were also often held in synagogues.[39]

Azriel Shohat has investigated how Jewish communities functioned after the abolition of the *kahal*, elected their own functionaries and representatives, and even applied the old terminology to those new functionaries.[40] Shohat stressed that the reforms of Alexander II—the ending of the poll tax in 1863 and the introduction of general military service in 1874—reduced the influence of those functionaries and also caused the disappearance of the *kahal* office and the prison where conscripts were held to prevent them running away.[41] Probably at the same time punishment in the *kune*—an iron neck collar at the entrance to the great synagogue—also ceased.[42] By 1865 the former *kahal* office in the Great Synagogue of Kremenets had become a prayer room for tailors,[43] although the *kahal* office in Dubno was still being used for community purposes in the 1880s.[44] At the same time, its counterpart in the Great Synagogue of Vilna served as a classroom for the yeshiva of the butchers' *kloyz*, another room was designated for the heads of yeshivas and teachers, and the *kune* was replaced by a wash-stand.[45] From 1892 the former *kahal* office housed the library that Matityahu Strashun donated to the Jewish community, and after the erection of a special building for the library in 1902, it was converted into an additional women's section of the Great Synagogue.[46]

■

The establishment of spiritual boards for each officially recognized synagogue and prayer house eliminated the difference between these institutions, while the abolition of the *kahal* and the disappearance of its substitutes did away with the special status of the great synagogue. The election of *kahal* officials no longer took place in the synagogue, and there was no institution that could impose the closure of all private synagogues during the holidays.[47] Only loyalty to tradition distinguished the great synagogue from the other prayer houses in a town.

The great synagogue usually had no heating facilities and was therefore uncomfortable during the winter (many were accordingly named *di kalte shul*). Even some *kahal* ordinances from the eighteenth century forbade the use of private homes as prayer halls only in the summer,[48] while in 1803 the Minsk *kahal* nominated five people who were to ensure that there would be 'many worshippers in the great synagogue during the winter'.[49] With the extensive multiplication of prayer houses in the nineteenth century and the absence of a community authority exercising social control, prayer in the great synagogues became more and more problematic. In Lithuania, many great synagogues were used for prayer only on the sabbath during the summer or on the High Holidays. In many Lithuanian towns in the late nineteenth century, if the great synagogue was destroyed by fire, it was not rebuilt, while *batei midrash* usually were.[50] In Volhynia, new great synagogues were built and existing ones renovated in the late nineteenth century, but they were used by the lower and poorer strata of Jewish society.[51] These different developments could be explained by the smaller size and greater poverty of Lithuanian Jewish communities in comparison with the Volhynian ones and by the relative homogeneity of the former.

The only representative function that the great synagogue preserved from the past was the organization of special prayers in the presence of Russian officials on holidays dedicated to the tsar and similar occasions—from the eulogy for Alexander I in the Great Synagogue of Mariampol (Marijampolė) in 1825[52] to the displays of patriotism at the beginning of the First World War in hundreds of Russian synagogues.[53] Thus, great synagogues continued to serve as the main Jewish public space where ceremonial interaction between the Russian authorities and their Jewish subjects took place and the loyalty of Jews to the ruling dynasty and the Russian state was celebrated and confirmed. However, even this function was gradually dispersed among other houses of prayer. For example, the celebrations of the anniversary of the 'miraculous survival' of Alexander III after the Borki train accident of 1888 were held in all the synagogues of Kovno (Kaunas) in 1889 and 1890. In Dinaburg (Daugavpils) in 1889, solemn prayers were organized for this purpose in the community *beit midrash*, while the Torah scroll written for this occasion by Jewish soldiers was festively brought to the Great Synagogue. In Vitebsk in 1890, the state officials attended solemn prayers in the Great Synagogue, but the Great Uzgorsky Beit Midrash also celebrated the event.[54]

Thus, the representative function of the great synagogue was taken over to a significant degree by other prayer houses. These synagogues did remain the symbolic embodiment of the local Jewish community—they were proudly shown to visitors and praised for their beauty and age—but their central role during the existence of the *kahal* now ceased. The main exception to this process was the Great Synagogue of Vilna, which, as described above, was firmly connected with the Hevrat Hatsedakah Hagedolah which became a substitute for the former *kahal*. The name *di shtot shul*, meaning the synagogue of the city, applied to this synagogue in the nineteenth and twentieth centuries, reflected its exceptional status.[55]

The reduced importance of the great synagogue was characteristic of the old communities in the western region of the empire, which had once belonged to the Polish–Lithuanian Commonwealth (Lithuania, Belarus, Right-Bank Ukraine). The division of power among several spiritual boards, representing only segments of the Jewish population and restricted in their responsibility, prevented the creation of a new structure of authority. Physically the great synagogue was still the most prominent edifice, but the majority of other synagogues and prayer houses also occupied separate free-standing buildings.

In contrast, outside the Pale of Settlement, in the Russian 'interior', synagogue boards became substitutes for community authorities and took responsibility for a diverse range of functions. Although Jewish soldiers were sent to the Russian interior from the late 1820s, the appearance of a permanent Jewish population here occurred only in the 1860s when certain categories of Jews received the right to live outside the Pale.[56] The main characteristic of these new Jewish centres was their lack of 'rootedness'—everybody was a newcomer and a tradition of community existence was absent, as is reflected in the title of Yvonne Kleinmann's book, *Neue Orte — neue Menschen* ('New Places, New People').[57]

In St Petersburg, as early as 1863, the wealthy and educated leaders of the community used the board of the prayer house as a form of organized community self-government. Their attempt to obtain official approval for by-laws which would establish a broad community structure similar to those existing in western and central Europe was rejected. Instead the government decided in 1865 that the board should be described as 'economic' (*khozyaistvennoe pravlenie*) to distinguish it from the spiritual boards in the Pale of Settlement, and its function would be restricted to the care of the prayer house (which became the Temporary Choral Synagogue in 1869).[58] In 1868 the government allowed the establishment of prayer houses and economic boards outside the Pale on the pattern of St Petersburg.[59] Despite these restrictions, the leaders of the Choral Synagogue continued to govern all community institutions, and the printed reports of the board included disbursements for the cemetery, the education of poor children, and support for the poor and sick and the orphanage. Although it was clearly associated with the Choral Synagogue, by whose members it was elected, and did not intervene in the affairs of more traditional prayer houses in the capital, the board called itself the Board of the Jewish Community of St Petersburg and did not hide its claim to speak for the whole Jewish population of the city.[60] In 1893 the minister of the interior, Ivan Durnovo, forced the board to change its name in accordance with the law of 1865 to the Economic Board of the St Petersburg Synagogue.[61] Nonetheless, the board of the Choral Synagogue continued to regard itself as responsible for all Jewish community matters in St Petersburg. This remained the case even after the revolution of 1905, when other prayer houses in the capital received official recognition as independent economic boards. The exceptional role of the board was also reflected in the urban fabric: the Choral Synagogue, erected between 1883 and 1894, was the only free-standing Jewish building of worship in the capital.[62] All other prayer houses were situated in rented apartments, thus being invisible to outsiders, and the attempt to erect an additional synagogue in St Petersburg between 1911 and 1912 came to nothing.[63]

A similar situation developed in Moscow, where the Economic Board of the Choral Prayer House, given official approval in 1870, assumed leadership of community affairs. In contrast to St Petersburg, however, the board was elected not only by members of the Choral Prayer House but also by 'honorary members' from other prayer houses. The Choral Synagogue was erected between 1887 and 1888, but the authorities permitted its functioning only in 1906. As in St Petersburg, it was also the only free-standing Jewish building of worship in the city.[64]

Thus, the self-government of the Jewish communities outside the Pale of Settlement was strongly associated with the synagogue. In many aspects, this situation resembled the old *kahal*, where the structure of community self-government and the great synagogue building were inseparable. When several prayer houses existed in the city, as in St Petersburg and Moscow, the influential elite established choral synagogues, whose boards dealt with matters far beyond maintenance of the building and its internal order. In contrast to the Pale of Settlement, where the Jewish *meshchanskie obshchestva* and assemblies of 'settled, prosperous and respectful citizens' existed, the synagogue in the Russian interior constituted the essential core of the Jewish community and its governing body.

The Jewish population in southern Ukraine can be seen as occupying an intermediate position between the old communities of the western regions and the new ones outside the Pale of Settlement. Jews settled in southern Ukraine in the early nineteenth century and migration from the western regions contributed to the constant growth of the relatively affluent Jewish population. In contrast to the Russian interior, the southern communities were governed by *kahals* until 1844 and were collectively responsible for poll tax and conscription until 1863 and 1874 respectively. However, the traditions of self-government were not, as in the west, rooted in the past, which enabled significant diversity in the institutions responsible for community activities in the second half of the nineteenth century.

Mikhail Polishchuk has distinguished three types of community self-government in the south. The first was an assembly of representatives elected by the Jewish population, as in Odessa, where 100 representatives elected rabbis and guardians of philanthropic and educational institutions and decided on other community matters. In 1884 this assembly was replaced by an assembly of 'settled, prosperous and respectful citizens', who were chosen by the municipality to advise it on Jewish affairs.[65] A similar type of community government emerged in Kiev.[66] The second type resembled the system in St Petersburg and Moscow: all philanthropic institutions were controlled by the spiritual board of the main synagogue, in this region usually the choral synagogue. According to Polishchuk, this was the situation in Ekaterinoslav (Dnipro), Melitopol, Feodosiya, Yalta, Simferopol, Mariupol, and Berdyansk. In Ekaterinoslav, the authorities even agreed to recognize ten guardians of philanthropic and educational institutions as 'assistants of the spiritual board'— the title and function alien to the letter and spirit of the law.[67] The third type existed in Kherson and Nikolaev (Mykolayiv), where community matters were dealt with by an assembly made up of the members of all the spiritual boards. An assembly of this type in Kherson was first mentioned in 1884 and in Nikolaev in 1889.[68] Thus, the spiritual boards of the synagogues in the south took upon themselves the functions of community leadership. Probably this worked successfully, since the members of spiritual boards of fifty-three Odessa synagogues and prayer houses were added to the assembly of 'settled, prosperous and respectful citizens' on the eve of the first Russian revolution.[69] During and after the revolution the spiritual boards became an effective substitute for the organized community, as will be described below.

In 1879 Yehiel Mikhel Pines, in his by-laws for the Mogilev community, articulated the idea that synagogues and prayer houses could serve as a basis for community organization:

Worshippers of each synagogue and *beit midrash* in the city elect from themselves two or three representatives, according to the number of worshippers, and empower them in three matters: to choose leaders for the community, to establish new by-laws, and to find new public sources of funding.[70]

It was probably this by-law that led E. Zhukovsky, author of a rather antisemitic description of the Jews of Mogilev province in 1882, to claim that the informal *kahal* still ruling the Jews 'is based in the spiritual boards of prayer houses'.[71]

In 1884 the minister of the interior, Dmitry Tolstoy, in response to a question from Odessa about the election of community officials, stated that the rabbi and his assistants should be elected by all the members of the synagogue congregations, while the guardians of philanthropic institutions should be chosen by the 'settled, prosperous and respectful citizens'.[72] The subsequent rabbinical elections in Odessa in 1886 were organized on this basis, with 6,000 designated voters. The disorderly character of these elections led to their annulment and to the proposal by the city authorities to change the electoral system. Instead of all synagogue members, only representatives of the congregation were entitled to participate in the election of the rabbi in 1888.[73]

The idea that the Crown rabbi should be elected by representatives of the synagogue congregations and not by the *meshchanskoe obshchestvo*, merchants and artisans, spread from Odessa to other cities. For instance, the representatives of the congregations elected the rabbis in Elisavetgrad (Kropyvnytsky) and Riga in 1896[74] and in Zhitomir (Zhytomyr) and Lutsk in 1901.[75] The conduct of elections differed from city to city and the number of representatives from a congregation varied from one to five or six.

The state authorities liked the new system and established the election of rabbis by the representatives of the congregation throughout the whole empire in June 1901. The new law stated that a congregation numbering fewer than 100 members should elect ten representatives, while larger congregations should elect an additional representative for each additional 100 worshippers. The right to vote was restricted to those worshippers who had been members of the congregation for a minimum of two years, were over 25 years old, and did not have a criminal conviction; traders in alcohol were excluded. A special instruction of the minister of the interior in December 1901 described how the elections should be carried out and stressed that they could not be held in synagogues or prayer houses.[76]

The new law on rabbinical elections reflected a change in the perception of the Jews. Whereas previously the rabbi had been elected by 'all the Jews' and thus represented the entire Jewish population, his religious function was now formally connected to the synagogue and his election was placed in the hands of the congregation. 'All the Jews' were still defined by their religion, but the division between the religious and secular spheres of Jewish life became more pronounced.

The new system also put an end to the rule of local oligarchies, at least in the matter of rabbinical elections. While the authorities could arbitrarily decide who belonged to the 'settled, prosperous and respectful citizens', elections by congregations enfranchised thousands of rank-and-file Jews, and hundreds could participate in voting for the rabbi. Thus, in the rabbinical elections of 1903 in Odessa, 524 congregational representatives took part;[77] in Vilna in 1905, 1,008 representatives from ninety-eight synagogues were elected, and 634 of them participated in the vote for the rabbi.[78] The restriction on the age of worshippers did not have a significant influence on the number of voters: of 3,052 worshippers in Zhitomir in 1911, 2,949 were older than 25 (96 per cent).[79] The clause that each congregation numbering 100 members should elect ten representatives gave more power to the small prayer houses, where for the most part poor people prayed, while elite congregations, like those of the choral synagogues, lost their influence. In Kiev in 1903, the elite could not ensure the election of its candidate, and the populist Solomon Lurie was chosen; the only way to get rid of him was to divide the city into two rabbinates.[80] The high number of voters hindered attempts to influence them. Thus, a correspondent from Bobruisk reported that the old Crown rabbi, Vilensky, failed to be re-elected in 1907, because, while he could manipulate voting when each congregation chose only one representative, he could not manage in a situation in which each synagogue had ten.[81] These quasi-democratic features of rabbinical elections by synagogues and prayer houses made them especially popular during the first Russian revolution of 1905 and in the period between the revolution and the First World War.

The question of Jewish community organization emerged on the agenda of Jewish politicians at the beginning of the twentieth century.[82] The ideal solution was seen as the establishment of a legally recognized body which would unite all Jews in a given locality, tax them, and care for their diverse needs. This should be organized along democratic lines with the compulsory membership of all Jews and the election of the community board by general, equal and secret voting (hence the proposed organization was described as a 'democratic community').

During the first Russian revolution Jewish activists believed that the collapse of the 'old regime' would, along with the civil emancipation of Jews, also make possible the establishment of such 'democratic communities'. Until this was achieved substitute forms of community self-government should be used to improve the functioning of Jewish institutions and facilitate the life of poor Jews. Synagogue congregations with their elected spiritual boards could serve as such substitutes.

The tumult of the revolution allowed for semi-legal democratic self-organization at the local level, in which the spiritual boards played the major role. A Council of Spiritual Boards of Synagogues (not including prayer houses) was established in Odessa in 1905 as the institution responsible for community matters.[83] In 1907 a similar council was created in Ekaterinoslav, where previously the board of the Choral Synagogue supervised community institutions.[84] In the same year a Council of Spiritual Boards was established in Vitebsk. It consisted of 180 people and elected an executive described as the *va'ad* (council).[85] An assembly of all members of spiritual boards in Fastov (Fastiv) elected three people to care for the Jewish cemetery and burial affairs,[86] and the representatives of the congregations in Zhitomir discussed the improvement of education in the *talmud torah*.[87] The Representation for Jewish Welfare in Kiev was elected in 1906 by electors from Kiev's synagogues and Jewish community institutions.[88] A council of guardians of all community institutions in Rostov-on-Don was created by the spiritual board of the synagogue and was affiliated with it.[89] In Simferopol, however, an attempt to create a permanent council of sixty representatives of all synagogues failed because of 'reactionaries' who lost 'their places in the community governance'.[90]

Hopes for the reorganization of the community did not disappear after the defeat of the revolution. Many Jewish activists expected that the government of Petr Stolypin, while fiercely hostile to revolutionaries, would look for support among the moderate circles of Jewish society and would be ready to bring more order and logic to Jewish life. While the elimination of anti-Jewish restrictions might be problematic from a political point of view, the reorganization of the community could be considered a purely technical step that made it possible to deal more effectively with the problems of the Jews without changing their discriminated status.[91]

The use of the spiritual boards as a substitute for an organized community until the new laws could be promulgated was recommended by Moyshe Zilberfarb, a leading member of the Jewish Workers' Socialist Party and future minister of Jewish affairs in the Ukrainian People's Republic. Zilberfarb specialized in the policies of community autonomy and held a doctorate on the organization of the Jewish community in Russia from the University of Bern.[92] In a programmatic article published in July 1909 in *Evreiskii mir*, a periodical run jointly by all the non-socialist Jewish political groups in Russia,[93] Zilberfarb stressed that the community administration made up of representatives of spiritual boards 'can be regarded as a form of democratic representation, since they are collegial and elected institutions'.[94]

Zilberfarb's article was a step in a campaign leading to a conference of Jewish activists in Kovno in November 1909,[95] which aimed to discuss the reorganization of the Jewish community. The main presentation at the conference was delivered by Genrikh Sliozberg, a lawyer who specialized in the protection of Jewish interests before the Russian government and in the Russian courts. Sliozberg proposed that the executive of the community be elected by the representatives of the congregations, as was the practice in the election of Crown rabbis. To make possible the participation of those who did not belong to a synagogue—mainly the secular Jewish intelligentsia—Sliozberg recommended that such people register as members of the local great synagogue.[96] His proposal was rejected after most speakers at the conference attacked it as conservative and undemocratic.[97] However, it reflected Sliozberg's personal experience—although non-observant, he was a member of the board of the Choral Synagogue of St Petersburg—as well as his conservatism.[98] The decisions of the conference were intended to be submitted to the government as the basis for a bill on Jewish community organization, and his view was that the indirect form of elections would be more acceptable to the government, which had instituted non-direct elections to the state duma.

As a temporary method of managing community affairs until the passage of the bill, Sliozberg suggested the creation of 'councils of spiritual boards' with the addition of representatives of registered philanthropic institutions, which were usually run by the members of the intelligentsia. However, to administer the kosher meat tax, Sliozberg proposed the election of a body by synagogue members, as was the case with the election of Crown rabbis.[99] This proposal was also attacked and partially rejected. Yehudah Leib Kantor, a prominent maskil and Crown rabbi of Riga, argued that 'representatives of synagogues are only qualified to recite psalms'—they had no education and it was impossible to entrust community affairs to them.[100] In his view, plans to involve the congregations and their spiritual boards in the governing of communities posed a threat to the influence of Jews with a modern education in community affairs. While the election of Crown rabbis through the congregations had eliminated, at least partially, the rule of local oligarchies, placing all community institutions in the hands of representatives of congregations would rule out any influence by the Jewish intelligentsia. Regular synagogue worshippers were more likely to have no secular education and to be associated with Orthodox circles. Kantor's anxiety was well grounded, since the reorganization of the community based on the synagogue congregations was in harmony with the views of the leaders of Jewish Orthodoxy. The Conference of Jews on the Matters of Religious Life in 1910, which was dominated by Orthodox rabbis, resolved that the new community structure should be elected by the synagogue congregations: those who did not pray regularly would vote as members of the great synagogue.[101]

The experience of the revolution and the discussions of 1909 and 1910 demonstrate that the synagogues retained a central place in plans for the recreation of Jewish community structures in Russia. For the Orthodox leaders and the conservatives, they were the best way to represent the Jewish population. However, both the older maskilim and the new left-wing and centrist activists regarded them with suspicion. The congregations of synagogues had both advantages and disadvantages as a tool for the mobilization and organization of Jewish society. Elections by congregations were relatively democratic but did exclude significant sections of the Jewish population: because of their religious character, such bodies usually did not include the secular intelligentsia and the 'progressive-minded' lower classes who had moved away from religion. Since membership in a congregation required donations to the synagogue, the poorest strata of Jewish society were also excluded, as were women, who could not be members of such bodies, though many contemporary projects for the future 'democratic community' included enfranchising women. The plans for the reorganization of the community on a modern basis advanced by the secular intelligentsia would be frustrated by elections through the synagogue congregations, which would place control of the community structures in the hands of conservative and religious people who opposed these plans. As a result, centrist and left-wing activists were ready to use the congregations only as a temporary lesser evil until a modern and 'democratic' Jewish community could be established. The role of the synagogue in this future community structure would be marginal, since its main goal would be to organize Jews as a nationality, not as an ethno-religious group. The communities established in the areas of the Pale of Settlement that were under German occupation in 1915 and in the rest of the Russian empire in 1917 did not have synagogues and prayer houses as their focal points. They became merely part of the large number of institutions supported by these communities.[102]

Synagogues and prayer houses, both as buildings and as institutions, had a long-standing association with the Jewish community structures and their *hevrot*. Membership of the community or of a voluntary association implied being a worshipper in its synagogue or *beit midrash*. The efforts of the Russian state to restrict the role of the *kahal* and its abolition in 1844 placed power in the hands of synagogues and prayer houses, which became legal bodies with elected governing boards. Those bodies inevitably assumed some functions of the former *kahal* and served as an important framework that the Jewish population could use for self-government and the satisfaction of its needs. The connection between the building of a synagogue and its officially recognized congregation made them a convenient basis for the organization of community activities. At the same time, the growing secularization of the Jewish community and its objectives called into question the role of the synagogue congregation in community reconstruction. Given the restrictive nature of the tsarist regime, the proponents of a 'democratic community' were ready to use these congregations as a temporary substitute for a complete reorganization, but envisaged no role for them in the future democratic and secularized community structure. While the Jewish communities in the Polish–Lithuanian Commonwealth had been, in essence, synagogue congregations, the national community of the twentieth century marginalized the synagogue as a vestige of the past.

Notes

1 On different types of Jewish houses of prayer in eastern Europe, see V. Levin, 'Synagogues in Lithuania: A Historical Overview', in A. Cohen-Mushlin et al. (eds.), *Synagogues in Lithuania: A Catalogue*, 2 vols. (Vilnius, 2010), i. 24–8; id., 'The Legal History of Synagogues of Volhynia', in S. Kravtsov and V. Levin, *Synagogues in Ukraine: Volhynia* (Jerusalem, 2017), 21–3.

2 See S. Stampfer, 'What Actually Happened to the Jews of Ukraine in 1648?', *Jewish History*, 17 (2003), 207–27: 211–12.

3 On Żółkiew, see S. Buber, *Kiryah nisgavah hi ha'ir zolkva* (Kraków, 1903), 116; on Dubno, see H. Z. Margoliesh, *Dubno rabati* (Warsaw, 1910), 126–7, 129–30, 136, 142–3, 151, 158–9, 165, 166, 169–71; see also Kravtsov and Levin, *Synagogues in Ukraine*, 199–253; on Satanów, see 'Tombstone of Moshe son of Tzvi Segal (7.11/1)', Bezalel Narkiss Index of Jewish Art website, visited 1 Sept. 2019; see also 'holy courtyard of the synagogue' (*ḥatser hakodesh debeit hakeneset*) in the *pinkas* of Tykocin in the 1680s (*Pinkas kehal tiktin, 1621–1806*, ed. M. Nadav (Jerusalem, 1996), 280).

4 See e.g. S. Kravtsov, 'Synagogue Architecture of Volhynia', in Kravtsov and Levin, *Synagogues in Ukraine*, 59–137 and bibliography; Y. Petrovsky-Shtern, *The Golden Age Shtetl: A New History of Jewish Life in East Europe* (Princeton, NJ, 2014), 275–80.

5 On the sacredness of the old walls of the synagogue, see Kravtsov, 'Synagogue Architecture of Volhynia', 122.

6 On *kahal* elections, see M. Bałaban, 'Ustrój kahalny w Polsce XVI–XVIII wieku', *Kwartalnik Poświęcony Badaniu Przeszłości Żydów w Polsce*, 2 (1912), 17–54: 30–2; id., 'Kagal', in A. I. Braudo et al. (eds.), *Istoriya evreev v Rossii* (Moscow, 1914), 143–5; G. D. Hundert, *Jews in Poland–Lithuania in the Eighteenth Century: A Genealogy of Modernity* (Berkeley, Calif., 2004), 81–82.

7 *Pinkas va'ad arba aratsot: likutei takanot ketavim vereshumot*, ed. I. Halperin (Jerusalem, 1945); 2nd revd. edn., ed. I. Bartal (Jerusalem, 1990), no. 102; *Pinkas kehal tiktin*, 263.

8 *Pinkas va'ad arba aratsot* (ed. Halperin), p. xliii, no. 280.

9 M. Bałaban, *Dzielnica żydowska, jej dzieje i zabytki* (Lwów, 1909), 14–22.

10 A. Kaźmierczyk, 'Podział kahału ostrogskiego w pierwszej połowie XVIII wieku', *Kwartalnik Historii Żydów*, 200 (2001), 545–6.

11 Kravtsov and Levin, *Synagogues in Ukraine*, 504.

12 I. Klausner, *Toledot hakehilah ha'ivrit bevilna* (Vilna, 1938), 153–5; V. Levin, 'Synagogues, Batei Midrash and Kloyzn in Vilnius', in Cohen-Mushlin et al. (eds.), *Synagogues in Lithuania*, ii. 334.

13 J. Kalik, *Scepter of Judah: The Jewish Autonomy in the Eighteenth-Century Crown Poland* (Leiden, 2009), 92–3.

14 D. Shalom, 'Sochocin', *Hatsefirah*, 12 Sept. 1882, p. 271.

15 Y. Brafman, *Kniga kagala*, 2nd edn., 2 vols. (St Petersburg, 1875), ii. 255–6; on the authenticity of the *pinkas* of Minsk translated and published by Brafman, see I. Levitats, 'Lebikoret "sefer hakahal" shel brafman', *Zion*, 3 (1938), 170–8.

16 For Dubno and Kremenets, see Kravtsov and Levin, *Synagogues in Ukraine*, 206, 349; for Zhovkva, see Buber, *Kiryah nisgavah hi ha'ir zolkva*, 2, 116; for Kopyl, see A. I. Paperna, 'Iz nikolaevskoi epokhi', in V. Kelner (ed.), *Evrei v Rossii: XIX vek* (Moscow, 2000), 35; for Kalvarija and Kėdainiai, see Cohen-Mushlin et al. (eds.), *Synagogues in Lithuania*, i. 185, 245; for Vilnius, see Levin, 'Synagogues, Batei Midrash and Kloyzn in Vilnius', 287; for Minsk, see Brafman, *Kniga kagala*, ii. 317–18, 324, 328–9, 333, 360.

17 For Dubno, see Margoliesh, *Dubno rabati*, 104; for Minsk, see Brafman, *Kniga kagala*, ii. 133.

18 *Pinkas kehal tiktin*, 574, see also 668, 684.

19 V. Levanda, *Polnyi khronologicheskii sbornik zakonov i polozhenii, kasayushchikhsya evreev, ot Ulozheniya Tsarya Alekseya Mikhailovicha do nastoyashchego vremeni, 1649–1873* (St Petersburg, 1874), 60. On the 1804 statute, see J. D. Klier, *Russia Gathers Her Jews: The Origins of the 'Jewish Question' in Russia, 1772–1825* (DeKalb, Ill., 1986), ch. 5.

20 See M. Zilberfarb, 'K voprosu o konfessional'nom kharaktere evreiskoi obshchiny', *Evreiskii mir*, 25 Feb. 1910, p. 2.

21 On the Jewish policies of Nicholas I, see M. Stanislawski, *Tsar Nicholas I and the Jews: The Transformation of Jewish Society in Russia, 1825–1855* (Philadelphia, 1983).

22 Levanda, *Polnyi khronologicheskii sbornik zakonov*, 370–1.

23 State control over synagogue boards grew over the years. In 1837 Nicholas I approved special rules on the collection of donations for the erection of new synagogues, which obliged the provincial authorities, upon the approval of a new synagogue, to provide its congregation with a special book for registering donations and to monitor the accuracy of these books (see ibid. 417–18).

24 Ibid. 431–4, 438–9; see Y. Petrovsky-Shtern, 'Russian Legislation and Jewish Self-Governing Institutions: The Case of Kamenets-Podolskii', *Jews in Russia and Eastern Europe*, 56 (2006), 107–130: 111.

25 Levanda, *Polnyi khronologicheskii sbornik zakonov*, 579.

26 On the forms of community governance after the abolition of the *kahal*, see e.g. I. Levitats, *The Jewish Community in Russia, 1844–1917* (Jerusalem, 1981); N. M. Meir, *Kiev, Jewish Metropolis: A History, 1859–1914* (Bloomington, Ind., 2010), 60–5; V. Levin, *Mimahapekhah lemilḥamah: hapolitikah hayehudit berusyah, 1907–1914* (Jerusalem, 2016), 352–60.

27 Levanda, *Polnyi khronologicheskii sbornik zakonov*, 736–8.

28 *Svod zakonov Rossiiskoi imperii izdaniya 1857 goda*, xi: *Ustavy dukhovnykh del inostrannykh ispovedanii* (St Petersburg, 1857), 198.

29 See the decision of the ruling senate of 1910, in its capacity as the court of appeal (Ya. I. Gimpelson, *Zakony o evreyakh: Sistematicheskii obzor deistvuyushchikh zakonopolozhenii o*

evreyakh s raz'yasneniyami Pravitel'stvuyushchego senata i tsentral'nykh pravitel'stvennykh ustanovlenii (St Petersburg, 1914), 724).

30 V. Levin, 'Civil Law and Jewish Halakhah: Problems of Coexistence in the Late Russian Empire', in Y. Kleinmann, S. Stach, and T. Wilson (eds.), *Religion in the Mirror of Law: Eastern European Perspectives from the Early Modern Period till 1939* (Frankfurt am Main, 2016), 237.

31 I. Bartal, 'Ha'otonomyah hayehudit be'et hahadashah: mah nimhak? mah notar? mah nosaf?', in id. (ed.), *Kehal yisra'el: hashilton ha'atsmi hayehudi ledorotav*, iii: *Ha'et hahadashah* (Jerusalem, 2004), 11–12. On *hevrot*, see Levitats, *The Jewish Community in Russia*, 69–84; for the Kingdom of Poland, see F. Guesnet, *Polnische Juden im 19. Jahrhundert: Lebensbedingungen, Rechtsnormen und Organisation im Wandel* (Cologne, 1998), 229–50; for Romanian Moldavia, see E. Feldman, *Ba'alei melakhah yehudiyim bemoldavyah* (Jerusalem, 1982), 125–213; see also C. Aust, 'Burying the Dead, Saving the Community: Jewish Burial Societies as Informal Centres of Jewish Self-Government', in this volume.

32 I. Bartal, *The Jews of Eastern Europe, 1772–1881*, trans. C. Naor (Philadelphia, 2002), 45.

33 See e.g. ibid. On the *hevrah*, see Klausner, *Toledot hakehilah ha'ivrit bevilna*, 97–9; A. Shohat, 'Hahanhagah bikehilot rusyah im bitul "hakahal"', *Zion*, 42 (1977), 175–8; M. Zalkin, '"Hakatsavim depo parku ol": me'afyenim umegamot befe'ilut ma'arekhet harevahah bikehilat vilna bereshit hame'ah hatesha esreh', in D. Assaf et al. (eds.), *Mivilna lirushalayim: mehkarim betoledoteihem uvetarbutam shel yehudei mizrah eiropah mugashim leprofesor shemuel verses* (Jerusalem, 2002), 25–42; id., 'Who Wields the Power? The Kahal and Chevrot in Vilna at the Beginning of the 19th Century', in I. Lempertas (ed.), *The Gaon of Vilnius and the Annals of Jewish Culture* (Vilnius, 1998), 354–60.

34 Adash, 'Vilna', *Hamelits*, 7 July [17 July] 1892, pp. 3–4.

35 B. Borisov [M. Rafes], 'Di yidishe kehile', in *Di naye tsayt: a zamelbukh*, 7 vols. (Vilna, 1908–9), i. 14–26; *Voskhod*, 6 June 1905, pp. 37–8; I. Klausner, *Vilna, yerushalayim delita: dorot aharonim, 1881–1939* (Tel Aviv, 1983), 227–8; Levin, *Mimahapekhah lemilhamah*, 359; Levin, 'Synagogues, Batei Midrash and Kloyzn in Vilnius', 313.

36 Associations under the name *tsedakah gedolah* existed in the beginning of the twentieth century in other cities, but it seems that they borrowed the name from Vilna for umbrella organizations which united many philanthropic institutions and were legally registered as the Societies for Assistance to the Poor (see A. Lindenmeyr, *Poverty is Not a Vice: Charity, Society, and the State in Imperial Russia* (Princeton, NJ, 1996), 198–9). For the list of cities with *tsedakah gedolah* associations, see V. Levin, 'Hapolitikah hayehudit ba'imperyah harusit be'eidan hare'aktsiyah, 1907–1914', Ph.D. thesis (Hebrew University of Jerusalem, 2007), 188 n. 483.

37 Levin, 'The Legal History of Synagogues of Volhynia', 30. For a similar complaint about Mogilev province in 1850, see V. Schedrin, *Jewish Souls, Bureaucratic Minds: Jewish Bureaucracy and Policymaking in Late Imperial Russia, 1850–1917* (Detroit, 2016), 137; for Kherson province in 1854, see O. M. Lerner, *Evrei v Novorossiiskom krae: Istoricheskie ocherki. Po dannym iz arkhiva byvshego Novorossiiskogo general-gubernatora* (Odessa, 1901), 75.

38 There is no systematic information on this issue. A community meeting was held in a synagogue in Mogilev in 1902 (A. Litin (ed.), *Istoriya mogilevskogo evreistva: dokumenty i lyudi*, i (Minsk, 2002), 166). In St Petersburg, in contrast, the elections of the board of the Choral Synagogue in the early twentieth century were held in a specially rented hall. On the choral synagogues, see V. Levin, 'Reform or Consensus? Choral Synagogues in the Russian Empire', *Arts*, 9/72 (2020): 1–49.

39 Levin, 'Synagogues in Lithuania', 36.

40 Shohat, 'Hahanhagah bikehilot rusyah im bitul "hakahal"'.

41 Ibid. 190.

42 Ibid. 214–15.

43 Kravtsov and Levin, *Synagogues in Ukraine*, 349.

44 Ibid. 206.

45 K. Marmor, *Mayn lebens-geshikhte*, 2 vols. (New York, 1959), i. 178. I am grateful to Ekaterina Oleshkevich for this reference.

46 Levin, 'Synagogues, Batei Midrash and Kloyzn in Vilnius', 289.

47 For example, the Minsk *kahal* decided on such closures in 1797 (from the first day of *selihot* until Yom Kippur), 1800 (Rabbi Samuel son of Benjamin was allowed to have a private prayer room, except for Rosh Hashanah and Yom Kippur), and 1806 (from the first day of *selihot* until 1 Heshvan) (see Brafman, *Kniga kagala*, ii. 37, 72, 385). It seems that in the Kingdom of Poland, where community structures were preserved in the form of *dozór bożniczy* (synagogue supervisory boards), the closure of private prayer houses on the High Holidays was still imposed in the late nineteenth century (see e.g. S. Shapira, 'Mariampoli', *Hatsefirah*, 13 [25] Oct. 1876, p. 316).

48 For example in Dubno (Margoliesh, *Dubno rabati*, 104, 142).

49 Brafman, *Kniga kagala*, ii. 236.

50 For example in Vabalninkas in 1883, Seda in 1886, Lygumai in 1887, Čekiškė in 1887, and Žiežmariai in 1918 (Levin, 'Synagogues in Lithuania', 33, 41 n. 99).

51 Berestechko (1827–85; built by the poor), Horodnytsya (1903–13), Klevan (mid-nineteenth century), Kovel (1886–1908), Kremenets (1805–39; built by artisans), Muravytsi (attempted restoration in 1903–13), Novohrad-Volynsky (restored in 1922), Radyvyliv (rebuilt between 1905 and 1912 and again in 1931), Rivne (1840–after 1882), Volodymyr-Volynsky (restored in 1882, 1900, and after the First World War) (Kravtsov and Levin, *Synagogues in Ukraine: Volhynia*, 178, 256, 300–1, 318–19, 339, 466, 570–7, 586, 696–7).

52 A. Haiman Harlap, 'Toledot adat maryampol', in H. Rosenthal and A. M. Radin (eds.), *Yalkut ma'aravi* (New York, 1904), 117–18.

53 See V. Levin, 'Synagogues in Eastern Europe at the Time of War and Revolution', in J. Karlip (ed.), *World War I: Nationalism, and Jewish Culture* (New York, forthcoming).

54 Hatsofeh, 'Dinaburg', *Hamelits*, 22 Oct. [3 Nov.] 1889, p. 2; Ahiezer ben Amishaddai, 'Vitebsk', *Hamelits*, 22 Oct. [3 Nov.] 1890, p. 3. I am grateful to Dror Segev for these references.

55 On the Great Synagogue of Vilna, see Levin, 'Synagogues, Batei Midrash and Kloyzn in Vilnius', 284–93. In 1905 an attempt was made to reduce the importance of the Great Synagogue's board: some members of the spiritual boards of several synagogues in Vilna asked the authorities either to remove all community property from the ownership of the Great Synagogue and to transfer it to a new institution elected by the city's Jews or to allow all Jews to participate in the election of the board of the Great Synagogue (see *Voskhod*, 6 June 1905, pp. 37–8).

56 B. Nathans, *Beyond the Pale: The Jewish Encounter with Late Imperial Russia* (Berkeley, Calif., 2002).

57 Y. Kleinmann, *Neue Orte — neue Menschen: Jüdische Lebensformen in St. Petersburg und Moskau im 19. Jahrhundert* (Göttingen, 2006).

58 Gimpelson, *Zakony o evreyakh*, 1027.

59 Ibid. 1093.

60 On the history of the St Petersburg community, see V. Gessen, *K istorii Sankt-Peterburgskoi*

evreiskoi religioznoi obshchiny, ot pervykh evreev do XX veka (St Petersburg, 2000); Nathans, *Beyond the Pale*, 123–64; Kleinmann, *Neue Orte – neue Menschen*, 176–205.

61 Rossiiskii gosudarstvennyi istoricheskii arkhiv, St Petersburg, f. 821, op. 8, d. 137, fo. 81: minister of the interior, letter to the governor of St Petersburg, 29 Nov. 1893; Tsentral'nyi gosudarstvennyi istoricheskii arkhiv, St Petersburg, f. 422, op. 1, d. 49, fos. 29–34: Economic Board of the St Petersburg Synagogue, report to the minister of the interior, 21 Mar. 1894.

62 On the Choral Synagogue of St Petersburg, see V. Levin, 'The St. Petersburg Jewish Community and the Capital of the Russian Empire: An Architectural Dialogue', in A. Cohen-Mushlin and H. H. Thies (eds.), *Jewish Architecture in Europe* (Petersberg, Hesse, 2010), 197–217.

63 A. Lishnevsky, 'Konkurs na sostavlenie proektov zdaniya Sinagogi i Uchilishcha', *Zodchii*, 16 Dec. 1912, pp. 517–18; 'Otzyv komissii sudei po konkursu proektov zdaniya sinagogi i uchilishcha v Peterburge', *Zodchii*, 19 May 1913, pp. 236–7, tables 28–32.

64 On the history of the community and the Choral Synagogue, see Kleinmann, *Neue Orte — neue Menschen*, 205–19, 335–47.

65 M. Polishchuk, *Evrei Odessy i Novorossii: Sotsial'no-politicheskaya istoriya evreev Odessy i drugikh gorodov Novorossii, 1881–1904* (Jerusalem, 2002), 265–70.

66 Meir, *Kiev, Jewish Metropolis*, 68–85.

67 Polishchuk, *Evrei Odessy i Novorossii*, 270–1.

68 Ibid. 272–3.

69 Ibid. 269.

70 A. L. Mintz, 'She'elat hakahal', *Hamelits*, 23 Jan. [4 Feb.] 1879, p. 69; cited in Shohat, 'Hahanhagah bikehilot rusyah im bitul "hakahal"', 226.

71 E. Zhukovsky, 'Evrei', in A. S. Dembovetsky (ed.), *Opyt opisaniya Mogilevskoi gubernii*, 3 vols. (Mogilev, 1882–4), i. 731 n.

72 Polishchuk, *Evrei Odessy i Novorossii*, 267.

73 Ibid. 274–81.

74 Ibid. 284; M. I. Mysh, *Rukovodstvo k russkim zakonam o evreyakh*, 2nd revd. edn. (St Petersburg, 1898), 78.

75 Derzhavnyi arkhiv Zhytomyrs'koyi oblasti (hereafter DAZhO), f. 62, op. 2, d. 213: 'On the elections of the Crown rabbi of Zhitomir', 1900; Derzhavnyi arkhiv Volyns'koyi oblasti, Lutsk, f. 3, op. 1, d. 531, fos. 3–4: list of representatives of the Lutsk district, 1902. In Zhitomyr, the representatives of congregations also elected the guardians of Talmud Torah in 1899 and 1902 and of the Jewish night shelter in 1902 (DAZhO, f. 62, op. 1, d. 1046: 'On the election of honorary guardians of the *talmud torah*, guardians of the Zhitomir Jewish night shelter and granting an exemption to the family of the late Doctor Cherner [from the kosher meat tax]', 1902–3; f. 62, op. 1, d. 198, fos. 33–9: Invitations to the elections of the guardians of the *talmud torah*, 16 Mar. 1899).

76 I. V. Gessen and V. Fridshtein, *Sbornik zakonov o evreiakh evreyakh s raz'yasneniyami Pravitel'stvuyushchego Senata i tsirkulyaram Ministerstv* (St Petersburg, 1904), 334–7; M. I. Mysh, *Rukovodstvo k russkim zakonam o evreyakh*, 4th revd. edn. (St Petersburg, 1914), 87–90; Gimpelson, *Zakony o evreyakh*, 738–9, 747–9. For example, the election of the congregational representatives in St Petersburg in 1908 took place in the Jewish soup kitchen and in a rented hall (*Rassvet*, 18 Jan. 1908, p. 30; 16 Feb. 1908, p. 30).

77 Polishchuk, *Evrei Odessy i Novorossii*, 293.

78 Lietuvos valstybės istorijos archyvas, Vilnius, f. 938, ap. 5, b. 141, fos. 21–45: Election of the Vilna Crown rabbi and his assistant, 1904–5.

79 DAZhO, f. 318, op. 1, d. 4, fo. 156: 'Data on the number of Jews in the territory under the Pristav of the Third Part of the city of Zhitomir, personally found by the Pristav in the books of synagogues and prayer houses and also from the distribution of the state tax on immovable properties and the local tax', 1911.

80 Meir, *Kiev, Jewish Metropolis*, 272–82.

81 M.L., 'Bobruisk', *Rassvet*, 23 Dec. 1907, pp. 30–1.

82 See D. Fishman, 'Teḥiyat hakehilah: hakehilah bamaḥshavah hale'umit bagolah', in Bartal (ed.), *Kehal yisra'el*, iii. 233–50.

83 S. Gepshtein, 'K voprosu ob obshchine', *Rassvet*, 12 Apr. 1908, p. 3; see also A. Rabinovich, 'Odessa', *Evreiskaya entsiklopediya: Svod znanii o evreistve i ego kul'ture v proshlom i nastoy-ashchem*, 16 vols. (St Petersburg, 1906–13), xii. 62.

84 Gepshtein, 'K voprosu ob obshchine', 3.

85 A. Litovski [I. Efroykin], 'Vitebsker brif', *Folks-shtime*, 12 June 1907, p. 40; Gepshtein, 'K voprosu ob obshchine', 3.

86 Gimpelson, *Zakony o evreyakh*, 725.

87 'Zhitomir', *Hazeman*, 31 May [13 June] 1908, p. 2.

88 Meir, *Kiev, Jewish Metropolis*, 290.

89 I.M., 'Rostov n/D', *Rassvet*, 15 Mar. 1908, p. 27.

90 Gepshtein, 'K voprosu ob obshchine', 3–4; L., 'Simferopol', *Evreiskii mir*, 18 Feb. 1910, pp. 24–5.

91 On Stolypin's religious policy, see A. Ascher, *P. A. Stolypin: The Search for Stability in Late Imperial Russia* (Stanford, Calif., 2001), 295–302. On similar hopes of Jewish Orthodoxy, see V. Levin, 'Orthodox Jewry and the Russian Government: An Attempt at Rapprochement, 1907–1914', *East European Jewish Affairs*, 39 (2009), 187–204.

92 M. Silberfarb [Zilberfarb], *Die Verwaltung der jüdischen Gemeinden in Russland, historisch und dogmatisch dargestellt* (Pressburg, 1911).

93 On *Evreiskii mir*, see Levin, *Mimahapekhah lemilḥamah*, 165, 180; S. Dubnow, *Kniga zhizni*, 3 vols. (Riga and New York, 1934–57), ii. 94; A. Perelman, '"Evreiskii mir" (Glava iz vospominanii)', ed. E. Rabinovich, *Vestnik Evreiskogo universiteta v Moskve*, 2/18 (1998), 228–58.

94 M. Zilberfarb, 'Neotlozhnye zadachi evreiskoi obshchiny', *Evreiskii mir*, July 1909, p. 12.

95 See Levin, *Mimahapekhah lemilḥamah*, 367–82.

96 *Soveshchanie evreiskikh obshchestvennykh deyatelei v g. Kovne 19–22 noyabrya 1909 g.* (St Petersburg, 1910), 42–4.

97 Ibid. 184–5; A. Litvak, 'Der kovner tsuzamenfor', in *Tsayt-fragn*, 5 vols. (1909–11), i. 8.

98 On Sliozberg, see Nathans, *Beyond the Pale*, 325–4; B. Horowitz, *Empire Jews: Jewish Nationalism and Acculturation in 19th- and Early 20th-Century Russia* (Bloomington, Ind., 2009), 139–52; V. Levin, 'Russian Jews and the Russian Right: Why Were There no Jewish Right-Wing Politics in the Late Russian Empire?', in D. Staliūnas and Y. Aoshima (eds.), *The Tsar, the Empire, and the Nation: Dilemmas of Nationalization in Russia's Western Border-lands, 1905–1915* (Budapest, 2021), 368–9.

99 *Soveshchanie evreiskikh obshchestvennykh deyatelei*, 44.

100 Ibid. 75.

101 Rossiiskaya natsional'naya biblioteka, St Petersburg, Otdel rukopisei, f. 183, d. 33, fos. 193, 195: 'Conference of Jews on the Matters of Their Religious Life', protocol of the eighth plenary session, 1910; see Levin, 'Hapolitikah hayehudit ba'imperyah harusit be'eidan

hare'aktsiyah, 1907–1914', 256–72; Levin, *Mimahapekhah lemilḥamah*, 383–7; I. Lurie, *Milḥamot lubavitch: ḥasidut ḥabad berusyah hatsarit* (Jerusalem, 2018), 330–6.

102 On the community of Vilna under German occupation, see T. Shabad (ed.), *Vilner zamlbukh* (Vilna, 1916). For the 'democratic communities' in revolutionary Russia, see Y. Slutsky, 'Yahadut rusyah bishnat hamahapekhah 1917', *He'avar*, 15 (1968), 46–7; M. Altshuler, 'Hakehilah hademokratit berusyah', *Hakongres ha'olami lemada'ei hayahadut*, Section B6 (1973), 229–35; id., 'Kehilat berditshev bitkufat milḥemet ha'ezraḥim (protokolim mishnat 1919)', *He'avar*, 21 (1975), 166–97; A. Gelbard, *Bise'arat hayamim: ha'bund' harusi be'itot mahapekhah* (Tel Aviv, 1987), 224–38; H. Abramson, *A Prayer for the Government: Ukrainian and Jews in Revolutionary Times, 1917–1920* (Cambridge, Mass., 1999), 75–8; A. Zeltser, 'Jews in the Political Life of Vitebsk: Temporary Revival, 1917–1918', *Jews in Eastern Europe*, 34 (1997), 24.

Stewards of the City?

Jews on Kraków City Council in the Second Half of the Nineteenth Century

HANNA KOZIŃSKA-WITT

JEWS SERVED on the councils of 261 cities in Galicia and lacked representation on only forty-five.[1] They constituted 36 per cent of councillors and had an overall majority on twenty-eight councils.[2] In addition, in the second half of the nineteenth century, they served as mayors in ten cities. According to Piotr Wróbel, the ideal of equal rights in the province was most fully realized on city councils, local government being the arena in which constitutional theory came face-to-face with the reality of daily life.[3]

This view is worth examining in more detail, since Jewish activity in local government has not up to now been thoroughly investigated. The pioneering history of the Jews in restored Poland after the First World War, written in the 1930s, does allude to Jewish councillors in Galicia, but devotes much more attention to other topics.[4] Zionist Jewish historians argued that Jewish participation in local government during the liberal period from 1866 to 1914 was limited exclusively to supporting groupings and political parties of other nationalities, so that the Jewish role was restricted to casting votes either for candidates proposed by others or to arrangements proposed by the majority.[5]

Using Kraków as a case study, I shall examine Jewish participation in local government in the second half of the nineteenth century. Jews represented over 30 per cent of the town's inhabitants,[6] and the community was overwhelmingly Orthodox.[7] From the early nineteenth century there began to develop a progressive group, interested in modernizing ritual and acculturation.[8] By the mid-1860s these two forms of Jewish identity were in sharp conflict. In this chapter, I shall first explore the legal basis for municipal self-government and its election procedures. I shall then review Jewish participation in municipal elections and changes in political mobilization and the ideology of the Jews elected to the city council, followed by an analysis of their activities, distinguishing between interventions of general municipal concern and specifically Jewish ones. A point of interest is the presence of municipal officials in the Jewish district of Kazimierz. In the last section, I discuss antisemitism in the municipal arena.

The Electoral Laws in the Provisional Local By-Laws for the City of Kraków, 1866

The Provisional Local By-Laws for the City of Kraków were issued in April 1866[9] and came into effect at the same time as the establishment of the city council, for which the first elections were held on 13 September 1866.[10] Two years later, in November 1868, all religious restrictions in Section II §15 and Section III §46 of the by-laws were abolished as incompatible with the constitution of the Habsburg monarchy adopted in December 1867,[11] and equal rights were finally granted to the Jews of Kraków on 18 January 1868 in accordance with the new constitution.[12]

These by-laws divided the citizens of Kraków into members of the community and outsiders (§§7, 8).[13] Those linked with the community and those owning property and paying taxes qualified as members. Members who held property of a certain value, had a secular education, or paid an appropriate amount of tax were entitled to vote (§22).[14] The by-laws did not restrict voting on religious grounds: the qualifications applied to Jews and non-Jews alike and were intended to create a new elite in accordance with liberal principles.[15]

Voters were divided into three curiae: the first based on education, the second on wealth, and the third on involvement in manufacture and trade (§§32–4).[16] The second and third curiae were further divided into two tiers. Each curia elected twenty councillors.

Few inhabitants of Kraków satisfied the voting requirements. In 1866 only 4.3 per cent of the population was eligible to vote (2,086 individuals and institutions).[17] It is not known how many were Jewish. In 1896 it was estimated that 266 Jewish voters were enrolled in the first curia; 59 in the lower tier of the second curia; 24 in the upper tier of the third curia and 766 in its lower tier.[18] By this date there were thus altogether 1,331 Jewish voters. The provisional by-laws remained in force until 1901 when Franz Josef I approved the Local By-Laws for the Royal Capital of Kraków—the first permanent by-laws conferred on the town. While waiting for these to be adopted, the emperor approved a motion passed by the Galician sejm to extend for one year the term of councillors elected in 1893.[19] This temporary state of affairs lasted until 1902, when elections were held on the basis of the new regulations.

City Council Elections

Since the number of those entitled to vote was severely restricted, it is hardly surprising that initially elections aroused little interest.[20] Thus, in 1866 and 1875 barely half of those eligible to vote did so.[21] Still Jews showed some interest since all religious associations, including the Jewish community board, fell under the control of the local council.[22] All its important decisions had to be approved by the city council, including elections to the board, the collection of taxes, and setting the kosher meat tax. The city council had authority in matters of policing and health and supervised the community board's accounts. It monitored population movements and kept records of births, deaths, and marriages. It could also impose financial levies and acted as an intermediary between the Jewish community board and the provincial government.[23] The interest among Jews in elections to the local council was demonstrated by the fact that Jewish supporters of a particular party sometimes threatened potential opposition voters with raising the religious tax they were obliged to pay or denying them credit.[24]

The press described the local government elections as a battle between the conservative majority and the liberal minority.[25] Jewish councillors were found in both camps. It seems, however, that support for specific candidates often depended not so much on voters' political convictions as on patronage relationships.[26] Voters' behaviour was not determined solely by religion and there were reports of Christians voting for Jews.[27] The prohibition on voting for progressives issued by the Orthodox Kraków rabbi, Szymon Schreiber, also had an influence on breaking down religious barriers; in some cases Schreiber advocated supporting Christian candidates.[28] After Schreiber's death in 1883 the Orthodox and progressives reached an arrangement to run joint compromise Jewish candidates. Non-Jewish politicians seem to have been unaware of this development.[29]

It was agreed that the city's electoral committee should nominate candidates in agreement with the Jewish community board, an arrangement which was criticized by representatives of the progressive minority.[30] However, commentators expressed surprise that some Jewish candidates stood on independent lists 'outside the agreement' and were able to win election to the city council.[31] They took advantage of the pre-election assemblies where any voter could nominate a candidate.[32] In addition to these electoral assemblies, from the late 1860s meetings of Jewish voters also took place.[33] There were also elections in which the alliance of progressives and conservatives failed to work and each group chose candidates from within its own ethno-confessional camp, as happened in 1875.[34] This led to criticism that Jews were not voting on political grounds but were supporting candidates on religious grounds,[35] which was seen as 'separatism'.[36] These commentaries, which did have some basis, were also used to galvanize non-Jewish voters, calling for the closing of 'religious' ranks.[37]

Traditional Divisions along Religious Lines or the Growing Influence of Confession on Elections to the City Council?

Unlike in Lwów (Lviv), in Kraków neither the rabbi nor the preacher at the progressive Tempel Synagogue was elected to the city council.[38] Instead it became traditional to elect the chairman and vice-chairman of the local Jewish community board.[39] The number of Jewish councillors remained constant throughout the second half of the nineteenth century at eleven or twelve, but after 1896 it rose to sixteen (out of a total of sixty).[40]

Initially Jews were elected in the first and third curiae.[41] Over time the first curia became more and more Christian. In 1869 it had three Jewish representatives. In 1884 the city's electoral committee initially nominated two Jewish candidates, but one, Doctor Michał Ichheiser, was dropped without being informed[42] on the grounds that nominating two 'Israelites' would alienate religious voters. Doctor Karol Pieniążek and Father Władysław Chotkowski were nominated to fill the other two places which had been held by Jews in 1869. Chotkowski (1843–1926), a professor of history and chancellor of the Jagiellonian University, was well-known for his stirring funeral eulogies and was very popular in Kraków.[43] He opposed religiously neutral education and wanted to introduce religious schools and his views could be seen as antisemitic.[44] In any event, the first curia, described as 'the curia of the intelligentsia', became over time 'the curia of the non-Jewish intelligentsia'.

The second curia, with its wealth qualifications, was mostly non-Jewish.[45] Its upper tier consisted of traditional conservative landowners and no Jews were elected in it.[46] Its lower tier was made up for the most part of owners of apartment blocks.[47] Jews were sometimes elected in this section.[48] The weak Jewish representation in the second curia can probably be explained by the fact that they were usually owners of medium or small properties and did not fulfil the criteria for inclusion.[49] Many Jewish property owners were able to vote in the third curia, especially in its lower tier where many Jewish merchants and craftsmen were also included.[50] Furious battles were waged over the composition of the electoral list for this curia, resulting in various electoral frauds, such as dead men voting.[51] Over time the custom developed that Jews and a single representative of the Christian merchants and craftsmen should be elected by the lower tier of the third curia.

Non-Jewish circles exaggerated the conflict within the Jewish community between the Orthodox and the progressives, hoping that these disagreements would reduce the number of Jews elected.[52] Certainly, elections seem to have aroused considerably more interest in largely Jewish Kazimierz than in the centre of Kraków.[53] As early as 1893 it was reported that 'Small-scale Christian industrialists and craftsmen have the painful feeling that they have no influence on elections in the third curia'.[54] Reports from the 1880s and 1890s describe the intensity of election campaigns.[55] Interest in elections had risen enormously: in the upper tier of the third curia in 1896 almost everyone eligible to vote did so (73 out of 74); in the lower tier, the figure was 80 per cent (1,058 out of 1,325).[56] In the first curia the turnout was 68 per cent (1,386 out of 2,042).

It is not clear to what extent a 'Catholic rally', organized in Kraków in July 1893 and not free of anti-Jewish overtones, contributed to inflaming the situation.[57] Participants in the rally resolved to create a Polish economic self-defence movement against the Jews.[58] Three months later *Głos Narodu*, a newspaper associated with the Christian Social movement, was established, which claimed to represent the interests of Christian craftsmen and popularized antisemitic slogans.[59]

The press reports suggest that no connection was made between 'removing' Jews from the first curia and their growing presence in the third curia—attention was solely drawn to their strong representation in the latter and its threat to the interests of Christian merchants and craftsmen. In practice, the Jews always won more seats than they were allotted in the agreements with the electoral committees associated with Kraków's dailies, conservative *Czas* and liberal *Nowa Reforma*, because they also stood on independent lists. The disparity between the number of Jews in the official agreements and those elected probably reinforced public convictions of the Jews' political power.

It should be emphasized that the names by which the curiae were known increasingly failed to echo their actual social composition. The changes taking place in the third curia probably reflected the crisis that the crafts were experiencing in the later nineteenth century as a consequence of industrialization and the growth of manufacturing industry.[60] As a result, tradesmen were often unable to meet the voting criteria, while other social groups, above all the professional classes, among whom there were many Jews, were expanding.[61] The fact that the representation of Jewish craftsmen and merchants was simultaneously shrinking was not perceived. Attacking 'Jewish solidarity' at elections and the growing Jewish influence in local government may well have been a way of mobilizing the dissatisfaction caused by these social changes.

The Council's Work: Participation in Committees and Working Groups

The city council's responsibilities were divided into primary and delegated (Section II §§16, 17).[62] Its primary tasks (§17) included granting residence permits, supervising community finances, levying taxes, ensuring the supply of healthy foodstuffs through maintaining sanitary conditions, caring for the poor, safety and public order, and managing the city schools. Its delegated powers included organizing the military draft, for which it received appropriate financing.

The city council had as many committees as the municipality had departments (§80).[63] In 1872 there were five: economic, financial, legal and manufacturing, schools and charitable works, and police and sanitary affairs. From the start in 1866 a Jewish councilman sat on every committee. They also seem to have been represented on ad hoc working parties formed to deal with specific issues.[64] Councillors nominated themselves for specific committees.[65]

According to Łukasz Sroka, Jewish councillors involved themselves in issues which affected all the citizens of Kraków.[66] Anna Jodłowiec-Dziedzic emphasizes their commitment, competence, and selflessness[67] and writes of their dedication and sense of mission.[68] It appears that this type of identification with the city was true of a great many councillors, irrespective of their religion, and formed part of the ideal of citizenship as it was understood in the nineteenth century.

The minutes of the council meetings published by the Kraków City Council from 1880 in *Dziennik Rozporządzeń dla Stoł. Król. Miasta Krakowa*[69] document the Jewish councillors' commitment to all issues raised at council meetings, whether improving salaries for civil servants,[70] tidying up the city archives,[71] or preventing private homes from being built on Wawel Hill.[72] Since the modernization of the city and the improvement of its sanitation were considered important tasks for the council, Jewish activity was also concentrated on these matters, including proposals for the rebuilding of the Sukiennice,[73] for filling in a branch of the Old Vistula,[74] for setting up a fire brigade and regulating its strength,[75] and evaluating a loan that the city sought to contract with an Austrian bank.[76] As doctors, lawyers, and representatives of the local chamber of commerce and crafts, Jewish councillors were marked by high professional standards and were actively involved in drawing up contracts entered into by the city, such as bringing hospitals under state control,[77] regulating the city's health services,[78] bringing the gasworks under city control,[79] drawing up a contract with a tram company,[80] and running a theatrical enterprise.[81] They proposed opening a school of gymnastics and the teaching of gymnastics in every school,[82] opening a senior school for girls[83] and other schools, including one on Biskupi Square,[84] in addition to reorganizing the technical institute and trade schools.[85]

On behalf of the electorate, Jewish councillors proposed motions on licences for trading, leasing, burying the dead,[86] and making and selling alcohol,[87] including upholding the rights of hawkers and stall-holders to sell their goods in their traditional locations.[88] These licences were a very important area of activity for the city council, since the fees involved were a key element of the city's finances.[89]

It is not possible to see a specifically Jewish character in the actions of Jewish councillors—like other councillors they were all simply 'city fathers'.[90] They did not form a united ethno-confessional front when discussing municipal issues but instead belonged either to the liberal 'minority' or the conservative 'majority' political parties, which were defined neither ethnically nor along religious lines.

Situational Ethnicity?

Drawing on the concept of 'situational ethnicity', whereby ethnic identity can be emphasized or downplayed depending upon the situation, Till van Rahden has argued that Jewish municipal councillors in Breslau were, on the one hand, seen as part of a separate group and, on the other, considered as representing the general population.[91] His analysis identified occasions when barriers between various groups were erected and how they affected the process of developing a sense of belonging. This approach seems particularly useful for this present investigation. In accordance with the Provisional Local By-Laws for the City of Kraków, Jewish councillors were explicitly excluded only from dealing with problems declared to be specifically Christian: this referred to Christian schools, institutions, and philanthropy. In the same way, Christian councillors were excluded from dealing with the analogous Jewish areas (§§ 119–23).

Besides their involvement in general city business, Jewish councillors often raised issues affecting the Jewish population and Kazimierz, such as the removal of unsightly huts from Wolnica Square and their replacement with neat stalls,[92] the hiring of teachers of Jewish religion,[93] and the provision of a grant to the Society of Summer Camps to enable sick children from Jewish elementary schools to attend the camps.[94] Some of the motions proposed by Jewish councillors were discussed beforehand at meetings of representatives of the Jewish community board.[95]

An example of the efforts made by Jewish councillors on behalf of the city's Jewish inhabitants was the motion proposed by Józef Oettinger and seventeen other councillors regarding loans for the Jewish community, since difficulties in getting people to pay the rates had made the community insolvent, which had had a catastrophic effect on the Jewish hospital.[96] The number of supporters required for this motion was greater than the number of Jewish councillors, and accordingly it had to be supported by non-Jewish councillors. This was also the case with the collection of funds for fire victims in Brody, which was started by Councilman Salomon Deiches but was led by non-Jewish Councilman Ludwik Helcel.[97] Other examples include the motion proposed by Deiches and eleven colleagues that the finance committee establish a fund from which the Jewish community would be able to borrow 15,000 Austrian zlotys to complete the construction of the Jewish hospital and to repay the loan it had contracted[98] and that by Deiches to pay out already approved grants for 'Jewish orphans of the cholera outbreak'.[99] In the first case the number of supporters of the motion equalled the number of Jewish councillors. All the Jewish councillors joined together in opposing the demolition of houses in Kazimierz, which although indeed in a pitiful state were the only shelter for the poor people living there.[100] The Jewish councillors intervened when the city began building the Helclów Institution, which from the start had been intended only for Christians and was to replace the demolished institute for invalids in the English Garden.[101] They pointed out that the community had an obligation also to take care of poor Jews.

Progressive Jewish councillors became involved in the closing down of ḥeders and the setting up of city schools in Kazimierz.[102] An interesting example of intra-Jewish discussion on the council were the debates on setting up a trade school in Kazimierz in 1889. The councillors supported the idea of religiously neutral education in general,[103] but on this occasion, Jonatan Warschauer attempted to organize a trade school solely for Jews, on the grounds of the harassment of Jewish pupils in the Kraków city schools.[104] Albert Mendelsburg opposed the motion, accusing Warschauer of religious separatism, but Emanuel Mirtenbaum and Józef Oettinger supported it. Mirtenbaum defended the ḥeders, seeing them as 'not harmful', given that the children there were learning only to pray, while they learned other subjects in the state schools.[105] From this comment it emerges that some of the councillors felt that both school systems were beneficial. Oettinger pointed out that the existence of private schools was also beneficial for the city, since it did not have to spend money to set them up, and teachers in private schools were able to support themselves. (Probably it was this last remark that carried the day, for in 1880 the *Dziennik Rozporządzeń* listed thirty-six ḥeders that had been granted licences.[106])

Thus in the case of Kraków the thesis of the situational ethnicity of the Jewish councillors, who saw themselves and were seen as fully fledged representatives of the city but in certain specific circumstances acted also as representatives of a defined ethno-confessional grouping, seems correct.[107] It should, however, be emphasized that 'Jewish matters' were not automatically left to the Jewish councillors and actions were also taken on behalf of the city's Jewish inhabitants by non-Jewish councillors.[108]

Personal Intercession or an Independent Political Line?

The cases discussed reveal that Jewish city councillors were not merely involved in interceding on behalf of the Jewish community, as the *shtadlanim* had been in previous centuries.[109] They also proposed motions and co-operated with non-Jewish councillors to achieve the majorities needed to ensure they were passed by the council. Sometimes these motions were decided upon at earlier meetings of the community board and in this case the councillors acted as representatives of the religious community. Jewish councillors sought to turn paper rights into reality, which seems to confirm Piotr Wróbel's view that equal rights were most fully realized on city councils.[110] They reminded other councillors that Jews were citizens with full rights and should be treated accordingly. Thus their efforts were political actions which succeeding generations could use when formulating more long-term aims. Jewish councillors' actions on behalf of the city's Jewish inhabitants can therefore be seen as the beginnings of modern but still not democratic politics.

Representative Visibility

Representatives of the local Jewish community participated in official celebrations in the city of Kraków,[111] and city councillors undertook some of their duties in the Jewish part of the city. Mayor Mikołaj Zyblikiewicz acted as host when the emperor visited Kazimierz in 1880.[112] The visit highlighted that Franz Josef was the ruler of all his subjects, irrespective of their religion.[113] The programme for the second day saw the emperor visiting the elementary school in Kazimierz (after visiting St Anne's Grammar School).[114] It appears significant that the only place he visited was the school, which was the apple of the council's eye and a tool in 'civilizing' Kazimierz.

When in June 1887 the heir to the throne, Archduke Rudolf, visited Kraków together with his wife,[115] the official programme in the Jewish district was fuller and its highlight was a visit to the Old Synagogue, which henceforth became a fixed point in official visits. An anonymous description of the visit emphasized the quality of the Old Synagogue's architecture and the craftsmanship of the art objects it contained.[116]

Some of the mayors of Kraków, including Ferdynand Weigel and Feliks Szlachtowski, met the community board at the start of their terms, promising to extend 'fatherly' care over the district of Kazimierz and its inhabitants.[117] The establishment of the city council affected the balance of power in the Jewish community, and the progressives celebrated by organizing a religious service in the Tempel Synagogue.[118] The sources do not reveal whether there were similar events in other synagogues.

The mayors of Kraków also made a point of appearing at important events within the Jewish community. Józef Dietl took part in the service in the Tempel Synagogue in 1868 when Szymon Dankowicz was formally installed as preacher.[119] He was also present at a meeting of the community board in 1871 when the community school in Kazimierz was transferred to the control of the city and Polish became the language of instruction,[120] and at the opening of a new school on Dietl Street.[121] A major ceremony accompanied the formal transfer of the Doctor Arnold Rapoport Foundation's shelter for Jewish boys to the Israelite Alliance in Vienna in June 1889.[122] It was attended by members of the city council's Committee for Industry, the chairman and elders of the Jewish religious community, the viceroy's representative, the president of the chamber of commerce, the deputy mayor, and many councillors (the whole of the Kraków City Council had been invited).[123] The mayor and councillors also participated in the end of year ceremony at the Jewish trade school.[124]

In some cases, the city council attended Jewish funerals in Kazimierz. The deaths of Jewish councillors were marked by members rising to their feet, and by appropriate speeches in the council chamber: this honour was accorded to Szymon Samelsohn in June 1881[125] and Salomon Deiches in September 1883.[126] During a council meeting, Mayor Ferdynand Weigel praised Samelsohn's work, calling him a 'Jewish Pole', and invited the council members to attend his funeral. Because of this ceremony the fire brigade postponed a planned excursion.[127] The whole city council, together with Weigel, the rector of the Academy of Sciences, university professors and school teachers, lawyers, citizens, and 'a great number of his co-religionists and the Jewish clergy, attended the funeral'.[128] However, I have been unable to find reports of the council's participation in Salomon Deiches' funeral. He was not considered to have promoted the Polonization of the Jews, was connected with the Orthodox faction, and was aligned with rabbi Szymon Schreiber, unpopular among many Polish Catholic members of the council.[129] To make matters worse, shortly before his death Deiches had been declared bankrupt, which had led to his expulsion from the council. His achievements were merely summed up 'crisply' during the session by the mayor, and councillors honoured the dead man by rising to their feet.[130] However, Weigel, probably as a delegate of the Koło Polskie, the caucus of Polish delegates in the Austrian parliament, did attend the funeral of Rabbi Szymon Schreiber, who had been a member of the Koło Polskie.[131]

A great many Christian and Jewish councillors and city council officials attended the funeral of Jonatan Warschauer, a great advocate of the Polonization of Kraków Jews who died in November 1888.[132] His speeches were described as full of interest and common sense and eschewing any kind of extremism.[133] Henryk Markusfeld's funeral in May 1890 was attended by Deputy Mayor Friedlein, Chamber of Commerce President Baranowski, several professors from the Jagiellonian University, 'and others'.[134] A former mayor, Ferdynand Weigel, spoke at the graveside.[135]

It is clear from these examples that the city council above all honoured those involved in Polonizing the Jews of Kazimierz. Markusfeld, Samelsohn, and Warschauer belonged to the generation that had actively taken part in the revolution of 1848, which meant that they took seriously the granting of equal rights and felt that their extension to 'the masses' should be supervised by an educated elite of which they felt themselves to be members.[136]

The presence of city councillors in the Jewish district usually had a 'non-ceremonial' character and was the fulfilment of an official duty. The city hall sent political commissioners to Kazimierz to supervise elections to each curia.[137] They were obliged to submit detailed reports assessing the atmosphere during the elections. The mayors of Kraków would include Kazimierz in their tours of the city, as Weigel did in 1882.[138] Local officials went to Kazimierz for building inspections[139] or to check that sanitation and hygiene regulations were being followed.[140] Thus, in July 1891 Mayor Szlachtowski, together with the director of public works, Janusz Niedziałkowski, and the fire brigade, carried out an inspection on Szeroka Street considering how best to demolish buildings adjacent to the Old Synagogue that were threatening to collapse.[141]

The mayors of Kraków also went to the Jewish district following accidents and natural disasters: for example, Mikołaj Zyblikiewicz, together with deputy mayors Weigel and Strzelecki, were present when a fire was being put out on Skawińska Street in September 1874;[142] and Weigel toured the city, including Kazimierz, as mayor to assess the damage after the great flood of July 1884.[143] A few days later he devoted his full attention to the district, visiting it together with his district commissioner. Szlachtowski was also present in 1889 when the great fire at Süsser's house was put out.[144]

Royal visits to Kraków were intended to demonstrate that the monarchy cared for all its subjects, irrespective of their faith. For the mayors of Kraków, however, visiting specific districts was part of their formal duties. They visited Kazimierz as often as the other districts outside the city centre. Given this, it is untrue to suggest that the district inhabited by Jews was isolated from the city and its authorities or that non-Jewish councillors never crossed the border between the 'world' and the 'ghetto'.[145] On the contrary, formal visits to Kazimierz were normal for city officials.

Antisemitism

Both Andrzej Żbikowski and Łukasz Sroka maintain that antisemitism was not a major feature of life in Kraków,[146] and I have found little evidence that the city council was affected by antisemitism.[147] Two great 'Jewish debates' took place in the council, the first connected with the dispute aroused by the painter Jan Matejko and the second by the behaviour of Father Władysław Chotkowski.

The Matejko (Gorzkowski)/Eibenschütz Dispute, 1882

Jan Matejko's antisemitic speech during the ceremonies at the beginning of the academic year 1882 at the Academy of Fine Arts has been quoted by a great many scholars.[148] The reason for this speech, in which Matejko accused Jewish students of materialism and a lack of attachment to their country, was alleged cheating by a Jewish student, Samuel Wohl. In his speech, Matejko attributed certain negative characteristics to all Jews, using age-old arguments and crude and stereotypical generalizations. Matejko's secretary, Marian Gorzkowski, an active antisemite, poured oil on the flames in an argument about the speech with Leon Eibenschütz, whom he encountered by chance. Twisting Eibenschütz's words, Gorzkowski accused him of insulting Matejko's good name and saying 'Matejko is a scoundrel'.[149] This led to a lawsuit in which the prosecution was led by Doctor Józef Mochnacki, who was compared to the 'leading antisemite in Galicia', Teofil Merunowicz.[150] The case was then raised in the city council where Councilman Emanuel Mirtenbaum enquired of the mayor whether it was true, as claimed by Mochnacki, 'that allegedly the lawyer, Dr Eibenschütz, explained to you, Sir, Jewish anger at the inaugural speech by the director of the Academy of Fine Arts asking you, Sir, to urge the director to withdraw these words publicly'.[151] The questioner requested that

You, Sir, Mr Mayor, reveal whether Dr Eibenschütz begged you to intercede and whether a deputation of Jews or councillors has approached you, Sir, protesting the naming of a street for Matejko and finally whether you intend to repudiate publicly Dr Mochnacki's tendentious words, and to state that during the voting to name the square of the Academy of Fine Arts nearly all the Jewish councillors were present and that they unanimously voted to name the square for Matejko, despite all these circumstances.[152]

Mayor Ferdynand Weigel replied that there was not a word of truth in Mochnacki's statement. He had summoned Gorzkowski on his own in order to agree on the wording of a certificate granting freedom of the city to Matejko. Gorzkowski asked in passing how the proposal to name a street for Matejko was proceeding. The mayor informed him that the proposal had been submitted to the appropriate committee. Weigel suggested to Gorzkowski that he ask Matejko whether this 'misunderstanding' could be settled and not dragged into the public arena.[153]

In his article examining Matejko's attitude Dymitr Konstantynów points out that Weigel had summoned Gorzkowski on quite another matter, and that the issue of the Matejko/Eibenschütz dispute had 'come up' in passing and had been 'inflated' with the intention of showing Matejko as the victim of a general Jewish plot.[154] Attempts were made to use the alleged 'Jewish attack' in order to raise the painter's standing. Accusing Eibenschütz, Mochnacki was the first to articulate antisemitism in Kraków publicly, aggressively, and demagogically, 'using the language of hatred and violence, calling on the most base instincts and emotions'.[155] In this case, the antisemitism did not arise in the council: it was articulated mostly in the press.

The Case of Father Władysław Chotkowski, 1896

As mentioned above, Władysław Chotkowski entered the council in 1884 in the election which saw Michał Ichheiser stricken from the list of candidates in the first curia. Chotkowski was a member of the Koło Polskie, where he supported the efforts of Prince Alois Liechtenstein to abolish secular schools and introduce religious ones.[156] Chotkowski was a supporter of the complete separation of Christians and Jews in education. On the city council he became known for attacking friendships between individual Jewish and Christian schoolchildren.[157] He also maintained that, because teachers were sometimes absent, school pupils were being forced to attend Jewish religious instruction classes, which he deemed to be scandalous.[158]

At a session of parliament, during a debate on the budget of the Ministry of Religious Denominations and Education, Chotkowski said that 'it has happened in

Kraków that a Jewish teacher substituted and taught Catholic and Jewish children the Bible'.[159] Since no member of the school board nor any school inspector had any information on the subject, it was agreed that this event had not taken place and that Chotkowski's words were untrue. The mayor was obliged to write to the Koło Polskie 'to induce Member of Parliament Chotkowski to amend his statement in parliament'. Members of the Koło Polskie showed the mayor's letter to the priest, who continued to maintain that the event had taken place and that he knew more than the designated officials. He claimed that it had occurred three years earlier and that he had been told about it by Councillor Franciszek Kasparek. Kasparek for his part denied any knowledge of the event. Chotkowski, in addition, claimed that one of the teachers of Jewish religion in a Kraków secondary school had for a long time taught biblical history to Christian and Jewish children. He also maintained that the headmaster of one school had ordered a Catholic teacher to take Christian and Jewish children to a Jewish synagogue on the emperor's name day, but the teacher had disobeyed the order.

Chotkowski claimed that by its resolution the council had harmed his good name and demanded satisfaction. The council ordered the school board to conduct an investigation, which found all of Chotkowski's allegations to be baseless.[160] Therefore, Kasparek moved that Chotkowski be made aware of the school board's findings and be asked to correct his statements. If he was unwilling to do this, then it was suggested that the Koło Polskie might issue the correction. Despite high hopes, Chotkowski refused to acknowledge his error and even claimed that the school board's investigation had confirmed the truth of his allegations.[161] The council, clearly tired and embarrassed by the whole affair, merely noted Chotkowski's statement.

Both these issues were based on the blatant lies of those who advanced an antisemitic agenda. They arose when Galicia, and all of Europe, was experiencing a surge in antisemitism.[162] This also affected Kraków, where, as in other cities, antisemites promoted conspiracy theories and became involved in local political conflicts. The city council was, however, not interested in using antisemitism as a political strategy and did not support these activities.

Support for this comes from another official event in May 1896, when the deputy mayor of Vienna, Karl Lueger, who soon would become the first antisemitic mayor of the city (1897–1910), visited Kraków.[163] He was not welcomed at the station by delegates of the city council, but 'merely' by local 'professional antisemites' with 'the editor of the antisemitic journal' (probably Antysemita[164]) in the lead.[165] Lueger's visit lasted three days. On 26 May he attended the shoemakers' guild jubilee.[166] During the ceremony blessing the guild's new banner he was greeted by a speech from Mayor Józef Friedlein. He then attended a church service and hammered a nail into the pole of the banner. Lueger's role in the ceremonies was rather small, since he spoke only at the end.[167] There are no reports of naked antisemitism in his speeches, but simply his pleasure at finding so much corporate spirit in Kraków and so many Christians in

Galicia. Lueger called for the cultivation of the 'religious spirit'.[168] His visit was not a topic during meetings of the city council, and even his speeches were not mentioned there.

Conclusion

In conclusion it is clear that the Jews of Kraków were relatively well represented on the city council. Because of an extremely limited municipal franchise, only Jews with a secular education and wealth could become councillors. Therefore election to the council reflected high social status. Jewish councillors were highly visible on the council, playing an active part in all aspects of its work. In this regard there was no difference between Jewish and non-Jewish councillors: the Jewish councilmen were respected 'fathers of the whole city'.

In addition, the Jewish councillors brought issues affecting Jewish inhabitants, the Jewish district, and the religious community before the council, and they were very effective in doing so. Thanks to their work, the council was kept informed in some detail about Kraków's Jewish inhabitants and the religious community. Thus Andrzej Żbikowski is correct to assert that 'local government was a key structural element linking the local Jewish microcosm with the outside world' and also the main political forum where issues affecting the Jewish population were raised.[169] In certain cases local government was also the stage for 'official political meetings of the Kraków *kahal* with representatives of the political authorities'.[170]

Translated from the Polish by Jarosław Garliński

Notes

I develop the subject matter of this chapter in greater detail in H. Kozińska-Witt, *Politycy czy klakierzy? Żydzi w krakowskiej radzie miejskiej w XIX wieku* (Kraków, 2019).

1   P. Wróbel, 'Przed odzyskaniem niepodległości', in J. Tomaszewski (ed.), *Najnowsze dzieje Żydów w Polsce w zarysie (do 1950 roku)* (Warsaw, 1993), 78–104: 82; id., 'The Jews of Galicia under Austrian-Polish Rule, 1869–1918', *Austrian History Yearbook*, 25 (1994), 97–138: 103.

2   T. Gąsowski, *Między gettem a światem: Dylematy ideowe Żydów galicyjskich na przełomie XIX i XX wieku* (Kraków, 1997), 51; J. M. Małecki, 'Udział Żydów w organach samorządowych większych miast galicyjskich na początku XX wieku', in K. Ślusarek (ed.), *Polska i Polacy w XIX–XX wieku: Studia ofiarowane Profesorowi Mariuszowi Kulczykowskiemu w 70. rocznicę Jego urodzin* (Kraków, 2002), 61–73.

3   Wróbel, 'Przed odzyskaniem niepodległości', 82; id., 'The Jews of Galicia', 103.

4   F. Friedmann, 'Dzieje Żydów w Galicji (1772–1914)', in I. Schiper, A. Tartakower, and A. Hafftka (eds.), *Żydzi w Polsce Odrodzonej: Działalność społeczna, gospodarcza, oświatowa i kulturalna*, 2 vols. (Warsaw, 1932–3), 377–412: 392; for the research interests of Jewish historians in 1932, see ibid. 575–7; M. Rosman, *How Jewish is Jewish History?* (Oxford, 2007), 83–4.

5   S. R. Landau, *Fort mit den Hausjuden!... Grundlinien jüdischer Volkspolitik* (Vienna, 1907), 4–5.

6   On Jewish history in Kraków, see *Polin*, 23 (2011).

7 R. Manekin, 'Orthodox Jewry in Kraków at the Turn of the Twentieth Century', *Polin*, 23 (2011), 165–98.

8 A. Maślak-Maciejewska, *Modlili się w Templu: Krakowscy Żydzi postępowi w XIX wieku. Studium społeczno-religijne* (Kraków, 2018).

9 *Tymczasowy statut gminny dla miasta Krakowa* (Kraków, 1866). The by-laws were approved by Franz Josef on 1 April 1866 and published and distributed on 13 April 1866 (A. Chmiel, *Ustrój miasta Krakowa w XIX wieku* (Kraków, 1931), 37–8; M. Andrasz-Mrożek, 'Powołanie Rady Miasta Krakowa i mechanizmy jej działania 1866–1869', *Rocznik Krakowski*, 77 (2011), 67–76; M. Śliż, *Żydzi na drodze do równouprawnienia 1848–1914* (Kraków, 2006), 36–7; Ł. T. Sroka, 'Żydzi w Radzie Miasta Krakowa (1866–1939): Zagadnienia prawne i ustrojowe', in Historical Museum of Kraków (ed.), *Budowali nowoczesny Kraków: Żydzi w samorządzie miejskim, gospodarczym i finansowym miasta (1866–1939)* (Kraków, 2015), 62–115: 74).

10 Chmiel, *Ustrój miasta Krakowa*, 26–7.

11 Section 30, which was binding in the Kingdom of Galicia and Lodomeria and the Grand Duchy of Kraków, contained changes to the local by-laws caused by the removal of resolutions limiting the participation of non-Christian members in local government (*Dziennik Ustaw i Rozporządzeń Krajowych dla Królestwa Galicyi i Lodomeryi wraz z Wielkim Księstwem Krakowskiem*, XVI (1868), 107–8).

12 Chmiel, *Ustrój miasta Krakowa*, 27.

13 *Tymczasowy statut gminny dla miasta Krakowa*, 3; A. Jodłowiec-Dziedzic, 'Żydzi w Radzie Miasta Krakowa w latach 1866–1939: Działalność na rzecz miasta', in Historical Museum of Kraków (ed.), *Budowali nowoczesny Kraków*, 233.

14 Gąsowski, *Między gettem a światem*, 51.

15 P. M. Judson, *Imperium Habsburgów: Wspólnota narodów* (Warsaw, 2017), 224.

16 *Tymczasowy statut gminny dla miasta Krakowa*, 32–3.

17 Jodłowiec-Dziedzic, 'Żydzi w Radzie Miasta Krakowa', 236.

18 'Wie die Macht usurpirt hat', *Sprawiedliwość / Die Gerechtigkeit*, 1896, no. 13, p. 1.

19 'Kronika', *Czas*, 8 June 1899, p. 2.

20 'Głos obywatela przed wyborami do rady miejskiej', *Kraj*, 16 June 1872, p. 1.

21 Andrasz-Mrożek, 'Powołanie Rady Miasta Krakowa', 71.

22 A. Żbikowski, *Żydzi krakowscy i ich gmina w latach 1869–1919* (Warsaw, 1995), 139, 148.

23 For instance, when the city supported a proposal by progressives to hire a preacher for their synagogue and then assigned the cost of his salary to the (mainly Orthodox) community board (T. Mahler, *Walka między ortodoksją a postępowcami w Krakowie w latach 1843–1868 (Komitet Starozakonnych a Wydział dla Spraw Żydowskich)*, ed. A. Maślak-Maciejewska (Kraków, 2017), 115–23).

24 'Wybory do Rady miejskiej', *Nowa Reforma*, 11 June 1887, p. 1.

25 'Sprawy miejskie', *Nowa Reforma*, 27 Feb. 1891, p. 2.

26 *Czas*, 23 June 1878, p. 1.

27 Thus in 1872 candidates were chosen jointly (*Dwa życia Ludwika Gumplowicza: Wybór tekstów*, ed. J. Surman and G. Mozetič (Warsaw, 2010), 20; 'Wybory do Rady miejskiej', *Nowa Reforma*, 18 June 1887, p. 2).

28 Manekin, 'Orthodox Jewry in Kraków', 178.

29 An expression of this compromise was seen in the progressives' acceptance of the Orthodox candidate for local rabbi, Hayim Leib Horowitz of Żółkiew (Zhovkva), whom they

had hitherto rejected, in exchange for which the progressive preacher would be granted the right to officiate at weddings ('Korrespondenzen, Krakau', *Österreichische Wochenschrift*, 27 Feb. 1885, p. 5; Maślak-Maciejewska, *Modlili się w Templu*, 95).

30 'Kronika miejska i zagraniczna', *Czas*, 29 June 1875, p. 2.

31 'Sprawy miejskie i powiatowe: Wybory', *Kraj*, 5 July 1872, p. 2; 'Lista nie ogłoszona publicznie', in 'Wybory do Rady miejskiej', *Nowa Reforma*, 21 June 1893, p. 2; 'Tilles przeszedł na własną rękę', in 'Wybory do Rady miejskiej', *Nowa Reforma*, 23 June 1893, p. 2.

32 'Kronika miejska i zagraniczna', *Czas*, 29 June 1875, p. 2.

33 Ibid.; 'Po wyborach do Rady krakowskiej', *Nowa Reforma*, 2 July 1893, p. 1.

34 *Dwa życia Ludwika Gumplowicza*, 39.

35 'Kraków 13 lipca', *Czas*, 14 July 1875, p. 1; Żbikowski, *Żydzi krakowscy i ich gmina*, 72.

36 'Kronika miejscowa i zagraniczna', *Czas*, 24 June 1881, p. 2.

37 'Wybory', *Kraj*, 3 July 1872, p. 2.

38 'Wybór rabina', *Dziennik Polski*, 17 Mar. 1890, p. 1.

39 Żbikowski, *Żydzi krakowscy i ich gmina*, 145. This accounts for the presence on the council of Szymon Samelsohn (chairman; 1870–81), Albert Mendelsburg (1882–93), Leon Horowitz (1893–1905), Samuel Tilles (1906–18), and their Orthodox replacements, Salomon Deiches and Hirsch Landau, as well as the progressives Zygmunt Ehrenpreis and Rafał Landau.

40 Personal calculations made on the basis of data from *Józefa Czecha Kalendarz Krakowski na rok* (Kraków, 1866–1914). For biographical details of some Jewish councillors, see 'Żydowscy radni miejscy Krakowa', Ośrodek Studiów nad Historią i Kulturą Żydów Krakowskich, Uniwersytet Jagielloński website, visited 26 Mar. 2012.

41 Żbikowski, *Żydzi krakowscy i ich gmina*, 71.

42 'Kronika', *Czas*, 1 July 1884, p. 2; *Nowa Reforma*, 29 July 1884, p. 2; 'Wybory miejskie', *Nowa Reforma*, 1 July 1884, p. 2.

43 J. Urban, '"Jawne wyznawanie wiary jest obowiązkiem każdego chrześcijanina": Kazanie ks. prof. Władysława Chotkowskiego wygłoszone w uroczystość św. Stanisława 8 V 1901 r. w katedrze na Wawelu', *Folia Historica Cracoviensia*, 9 (2003), 209–25.

44 'Lex Liechtenstein und Polenclub', *Österreichische Wochenschrift*, 23 Mar. 1888, p. 184. Chotkowski's opponents were gathered around *Nowa Reforma*, which called his philippics in defence of religious schools unpatriotic ('Kronika', *Nowa Reforma*, 11 Dec. 1892, p. 3).

45 'Kronika miejska i zagraniczna', *Czas*, 2 July 1869, p. 2; 'Kraków 8. Lipca', *Czas*, 9 July 1875, p. 1; 'Wybory do Rady miejskiej', *Czas*, 24 June 1887, p. 2.

46 'Wybory do Rady miejskiej', *Nowa Reforma*, 25 June 1893, p. 2.

47 K. Karolczak, *Właściciele domów w Krakowie na przełomie XIX i XX wieku* (Kraków, 1987), 99, 176; Sroka, 'Żydzi w Radzie Miasta Krakowa', 108.

48 Archiwum Narodowe w Krakowie (hereafter ANK), Akta miasta Krakowa (hereafter AMK), Mag II, 325: 'Protokoły obrad Rady Miejskiej I kadencji z lat 1866–1869: Posiedzenia jawne', 417 (1 July 1869);'Wybory do Rady miejskiej', *Nowa Reforma*, 1 July 1893, p. 2; 'Wybory do rady miejskiej', *Czas*, morning edn., 23 June 1896, p. 1; K. Karolczak, 'Ludność żydowska w Krakowie na przełomie XIX i XX wieku', in F. Kiryk (ed.), *Żydzi w Małopolsce: Studia z dziejów osadnictwa i życia społecznego* (Kraków, 1991), 251–71: 252–3; Sroka, 'Żydzi w Radzie Miasta Krakowa', 170–1.

49 Karolczak, *Właściciele domów*, 33.

50 Kazimierz Karolczak notes that towards the end of the nineteenth century one lawyer in three owned an apartment block and so was able to vote in the third curia. Karolczak

quotes the case of Leon Horowitz, who owned several blocks (Karolczak, 'Ludność żydowska w Krakowie', 255; id., *Właściciele domów*, 120).

51 'Sprawy miejskie', *Nowa Reforma*, 12 June 1890, p. 2. For electoral machinations in general, see R. Kułakowska, 'Z badań nad samorządnością miejską na przykładzie krakowskiej Rady miejskiej doby autonomicznej: Problematyka, wybrane źródła', in K. Karolczak (ed.), *Ukryte w źródłach: Z warsztatu historyka XIX wieku* (Kraków, 2009), 110–23: 113.

52 'Wybory do rady miejskiej', *Nowa Reforma*, 17 June 1887, p. 2.

53 'Wybory do rady miejskiej', *Czas*, 11 July 1890, p. 2.

54 'Wybory do rady miejskiej', *Nowa Reforma*, 18 June 1893, p. 2; Żbikowski, *Żydzi krakowscy i ich gmina*, 283.

55 'Sprawy miejskie', *Dziennik Krakowski*, 17 June 1896, p. 4.

56 'Z ruchu wyborczego', *Nowa Reforma*, 17 June 1896, p. 2; 'Z ruchu wyborczego', *Nowa Reforma*, 19 June 1896, p. 1; 'Wybory do rady miejskiej', *Czas*, morning edn., 18 June 1896, p. 1.

57 *Księga pamiątkowa wiecu katolickiego w Krakowie odbytego w dniach 4, 5 i 6 lipca 1893*, ed. [W.] Chotkowski (Kraków, 1893), 257–8; 259–60; 477–8; D. Unowsky, *The Plunder: The 1898 Anti-Jewish Riots in Habsburg Galicia* (Stanford, Calif., 2018), 23.

58 M. Śliwa, 'Obcy czy swoi: Z dyskusji nad kwestią żydowską w Galicji u schyłku XIX wieku', in K. Karolczak and H. W. Żaliński (eds.), *Galicyjskie dylematy* (Kraków, 1994), 18–30: 23.

59 M. Śliwa, 'Obcy czy swoi', 23; G. Krzywiec, 'Katolicyzm polityczny w Galicji: Geneza, rozwój, schyłek (1893–1914); Stan i perspektywa badań', in A. Kawalec et al. (eds.), *Galicja 1772–1918: Problemy metodologiczne, stan i potrzeby badań*, 3 vols. (Rzeszów, 2011), iii. 217–34: 217, 225–6, 230–1, 233.

60 See *Księga pamiątkowa wiecu katolickiego w Krakowie*, 472–3.

61 'Sprawy miejskie', *Nowa Reforma*, 28 May 1896, p. 2.

62 *Tymczasowy statut gminny dla miasta Krakowa*, 4–5; Sroka, 'Żydzi w Radzie Miasta Krakowa', 75.

63 *Tymczasowy statut gminny dla miasta Krakowa*, 23.

64 'Protokoły obrad Rady Miejskiej I', 359–68 (9 Mar. 1869); *Józefa Czecha Kalendarz Krakowski na rok 1879* (Kraków, 1879), 34–5.

65 e.g. Councilman Schönborn (ANK, AMK, Mag II, 326: 'Protokoły obrad Rady Miejskiej II kadencji z lat 1869–1872: Posiedzenia jawne', 5 (28 Sept. 1869)).

66 Ł. T. Sroka, *Żydzi w Krakowie: Studium o elicie miasta 1850–1918* (Kraków, 2008), 128; Jodłowiec-Dziedzic, 'Żydzi w Radzie Miasta Krakowa', 236.

67 Jodłowiec-Dziedzic, *Budowali nowoczesny Kraków*, 24.

68 Jodłowiec-Dziedzic, 'Żydzi w Radzie Miasta Krakowa', 236.

69 Kułakowska, 'Z badań nad samorządnością miejską', 114–16.

70 'Protokoły obrad Rady Miejskiej I', 105 (3 Jan. 1867).

71 'Protokoły obrad Rady Miejskiej I', 226 (2 Jan. 1868).

72 'Kronika', *Nowa Reforma*, 26 Sept. 1891, p. 3.

73 'Protokoły obrad Rady Miejskiej I', 141–3 (13 Apr. 1867).

74 ANK, AMK, Mag II, 327: 'Protokoły obrad Rady Miejskiej III kadencji z lat 1872–1875: Posiedzenia jawne', 668 (7 Dec. 1874).

75 'Protokoły obrad Rady Miejskiej II', 235 (28 Apr. 1873).

76 'Sprawy miejskie (Posiedzenie Rady miejskiej z dn. 18 lutego)', *Nowa Reforma*, 20 Feb. 1892, p. 2.

77 'Protokoły obrad Rady Miejskiej I', 169 (5 July 1867).

78 'Protokoły obrad Rady Miejskiej II', 79–81 (5 Jan. 1869).

79 Jodłowiec-Dziedzic, 'Żydzi w Radzie Miasta Krakowa', 243–4.

80 *Dziennik Rozporządzeń*, 1897, no. 13; Jodłowiec-Dziedzic, 'Żydzi w Radzie Miasta Krakowa', 243–4.

81 'Sprawy miejskie (Posiedzenie Rady miejskiej z dn. 14 czerwca)', *Nowa Reforma*, 16 June 1892, pp. 2–3.

82 'Protokoły obrad Rady Miejskiej III', 489 (5 Feb. 1874).

83 'Protokoły obrad Rady Miejskiej I', 23 (19 Sept. 1872).

84 'Protokoły obrad Rady Miejskiej III', 127 (9 Jan. 1873).

85 'Protokoły obrad Rady Miejskiej I', 340 (7 Jan. 1879).

86 'Protokoły obrad Rady Miejskiej II', 328–30 (3 Dec. 1868).

87 'Protokoły obrad Rady Miejskiej I', 364 (11 Mar. 1869).

88 'Protokoły obrad Rady Miejskiej III', 832 (1 July 1875).

89 E. Strasburger, *Gospodarka naszych wielkich miast: Warszawa, Łódź, Kraków, Lwów, Poznań* (Kraków, 1913), 423. Strasburger was critical of the fact that the city's finances were based on the tax on vodka (ibid. 431).

90 Jodłowiec-Dziedzic, *Budowali nowoczesny Kraków*, 24–5.

91 T. van Rahden, *Juden und andere Breslauer: Die Beziehungen zwischen Juden, Protestanten und Katholiken in einer deutschen Großstadt von 1860 bis 1925* (Göttingen, 2000), 19.

92 'Protokoły obrad Rady Miejskiej I', 349–50 (4 Mar. 1869).

93 'Sprawy miejskie', *Nowa Reforma*, 1 Jan. 1891, p. 3.

94 'Kronika', *Nowa Reforma*, 9 July 1892, p. 2.

95 Archiwum Żydowskiego Instytutu Historycznego, sygn. 107, 558/1: Minutes of full meeting of Jewish representatives, 12 Jan. 1876.

96 'Protokoły obrad Rady Miejskiej I', 357–8 (9 Mar. 1869); Jodłowiec-Dziedzic, 'Żydzi w Radzie Miasta Krakowa', 238.

97 'Protokoły obrad Rady Miejskiej I', 140, 145 (6 June 1867); Sroka, 'Żydzi w Radzie Miasta Krakowa', 123; Jodłowiec-Dziedzic, 'Żydzi w Radzie Miasta Krakowa', 238.

98 'Protokoły obrad Rady Miejskiej III', 178 (6 Mar. 1873).

99 'Protokoły obrad Rady Miejskiej III', 393 (20 Nov. 1873).

100 'Protokoły obrad Rady Miejskiej II', 306 (10 July 1873); 353 (18 Sept. 1873).

101 *Dziennik Rozporządzeń*, 1886, no. 29.

102 'Protokoły obrad Rady Miejskiej III', 635 (24 Sept. 1874). Throughout the whole kingdom, liberals typically favoured expanding education (see Judson, *Imperium Habsburgów*, 277–8).

103 ANK, AMK, Mag II, 332: 'Protokoły obrad Rady Miejskiej VIII kadencji z lat 1887–1890: Posiedzenia jawne', 584 (15 Jan. 1884); *Dziennik Rozporządzeń*, 1889, no. 4; 'Kronika', *Nowa Reforma*, 20 Apr. 1890, p. 2.

104 'Sprawy miejskie', *Nowa Reforma*, 10 Oct. 1883, p. 2; 'Sprawy miejskie', *Nowa Reforma*, 24 Feb. 1884, p. 3; 92. ANK, AMK, Mag II, 330: 'Protokoły obrad Rady Miejskiej VI kadencji z lat 1881–1884: Posiedzenia jawne', 638 (21 Feb. 1884). On the efforts of Warschauer and Oettinger, see Jodłowiec-Dziedzic, 'Żydzi w Radzie Miasta Krakowa', 242.

105 'Protokoły obrad Rady Miejskiej VIII', 177–8 (19 Jan. 1888).

106 'Sprawy wyznań religijnych', *Dziennik Rozporządzeń*, 1880, no. 2. On 11 June 1889, the viceroy's office issued a circular, L. 28682: 'O udzielaniu pozwoleń na otwarcie względnie

przeniesienie chajderów', *Dziennik Rozporządzeń*, 1889, no. 10.

107 Sroka, 'Żydzi w Radzie Miasta Krakowa', 122, 128.

108 'Protokoły obrad Rady Miejskiej III', 343 (11 Sept. 1873); '66. Posiedzenie z dn. 3 października 1889', *Dziennik Rozporządzeń*, 1889, no. 11.

109 S. Ury, 'Shtadlan', in G. D. Hundert (ed.), *YIVO Encyclopedia of Jews in Eastern Europe* (New Haven, Conn., 2008).

110 Wróbel, 'Przed odzyskaniem niepodległości', 82; id., 'The Jews of Galicia', 103.

111 'Podróż Najj: Pana', *Czas*, 31 Aug. 1880, p. 1; H. Kozińska-Witt, *Krakau in Warschaus langem Schatten: Konkurrenzkämpfe in der polnischen Städtelandschaft 1900–1939* (Stuttgart, 2008), 126–31: 128; D. L. Unowsky, *The Pomp and Politics of Patriotism: Imperial Celebrations in Habsburg Austria, 1848–1916* (West Lafayette, Ind., 2005), 60–4. For an account of the visit from the perspective of the Viennese press, see H.-C. Maner, *Galizien: Eine Grenzregion im Kalkül der Donaumonarchie im 18. und 19. Jahrhundert* (Munich, 2007), 212–16.

112 He had toured the Jewish district previously during his visit to Kraków in 1851 (Judson, *Imperium Habsburgów*, 235).

113 Ibid. 103, 235.

114 G. Lichończak, 'Das autonome Krakau', in *Krakau zur Zeit der galizischen Autonomie (1866–1914): Ausstellungskatalog* (Graz, 1989), 98–104; Kozińska-Witt, *Krakau in Warschaus langem Schatten*, 127–31.

115 'Następca tronu z Małżonką w Krakowie', *Czas*, 29 June 1887, pp. 1–3.

116 'Przyjęcie w Synagodze', *Czas*, 1 July 1887, p. 3; 'Pobyt arcyksięcia Rudolfa z małżonką Stefanią w Krakowie', *Nowa Reforma*, 1 July 1887, p. 3.

117 Żbikowski, *Żydzi krakowscy i ich gmina*, 145–6.

118 Andrasz-Mrożek, 'Powołanie Rady Miasta Krakowa', 72. For the patriotic events in the Tempel Synagogue, see A. Maślak-Maciejewska, 'Wydarzenia patriotyczne organizowane w synagodze Tempel w Krakowie', in M. Galas (ed.), *Synagoga Tempel i środowisko krakowskich Żydów postępowych* (Kraków, 2012), 103–28.

119 A. Maślak-Maciejewska, *Rabin Szymon Dankowicz (1834–1910): Życie i działalność* (Kraków, 2013), 56.

120 Żbikowski, *Żydzi krakowscy i ich gmina*, 145.

121 'Kronika', *Nowa Reforma*, 7 Sept. 1892, p. 2.

122 See K. Rędziński, *Fundacyjne szkolnictwo żydowskie w Galicji w latach 1881–1918* (Częstochowa, 1997), 50–1, 60–1, 65, 74, 100, 102.

123 'Kronika', *Nowa Reforma*, 29 May 1889, p. 3; 'Kronika', *Nowa Reforma*, 16 June 1889, pp. 2–3.

124 'Kronika', *Nowa Reforma*, 15 Aug. 1891, p. 2.

125 'Sprawy miejskie', *Czas*, 9 June 1881, p. 1; ANK, AMK, Mag II, 329: 'Protokoły obrad Rady Miejskiej V kadencji z lat 1878–1881: Posiedzenia jawne', 662 (9 June 1881); '81. Posiedzenie nadzwyczajne z dn. 9 czerwca 1881', *Dziennik Rozporządzeń*, 1881, no. 7.

126 'Protokoły obrad Rady Miejskiej VI', 338 (6 Sept. 1883); '74. Posiedzenie z dn. 6 września 1883', *Dziennik Rozporządzeń*, 1883, no. 10; 'Kronika miejska i zagraniczna', *Czas*, 31 July 1883, p. 2; 'Kronika miejska i zagraniczna', *Czas*, 8 Sept. 1883, p. 2.

127 'Kronika miejska i zagraniczna', *Czas*, 12 June 1881, p. 2.

128 'Kronika miejska i zagraniczna', *Czas*, 14 June 1881, p. 2.

129 'Kronika', *Nowa Reforma*, 14 Jan. 1884, p. 3.

130 'Protokoły obrad Rady Miejskiej VI', 338 (6 Sept. 1883)

131 'Kronika', *Nowa Reforma*, 29 Mar. 1883, pp. 2–3.

132 'Protokoły obrad Rady Miejskiej VIII', 492 (6 Dec. 1888); 527–9 (13 Dec. 1888); *Dziennik Rozporządzeń*, 1888, no. 14.

133 'Kronika', *Nowa Reforma*, 13 Nov. 1888, p. 2; Jodłowiec-Dziedzic, 'Żydzi w Radzie Miasta Krakowa', 247–8.

134 'Kronika miejska i zagraniczna', *Czas,* 10 May 1890, p. 2.

135 An obituary in *Czas,* 6 May 1890, p. 2; 'Kronika', *Nowa Reforma,* 10 May 1890, p. 3; 'Protokoły obrad Rady Miejskiej VIII', 1048 (24 Apr. 1890).

136 Judson, *Imperium Habsburgów,* 225.

137 On political commissioners, see *Statut dla zboru izraelickiego* (Kraków, 1870), §26.

138 'Kronika', *Nowa Reforma,* 19 Apr. 1882, p. 2.

139 ANK, AMK, Mag II, 532: 'Pozwolenia na prowadzenie wyszynków, opłaty od psów, fiakrów, czynsze z domów, itp.'.

140 'Protokoły obrad Rady Miejskiej I', 182 (28 Aug. 1867); 227 (2 Jan. 1868).

141 'Kronika', *Nowa Reforma,* 30 July 1891, p. 3.

142 'Kronika miejska i zagraniczna', *Czas,* 4 Sept. 1874, p. 2.

143 'Kronika', *Nowa Reforma,* 19 July 1884, p. 2; 'Kronika', *Nowa Reforma,* 1 July 1884, p. 3.

144 'Kronika', *Nowa Reforma,* 2 July 1889, p. 3.

145 On the perceived separation between Kraków and Kazimierz, see H. Kozińska-Witt, 'Zasypanie Starej Wisły i powstanie Plant Dietlowskich w Krakowie`, in A. Kos-Zabłocka and A. Łupienko (eds.), *Architektura w mieście, architektura dla miasta: Przestrzeń publiczna w miastach ziem polskich w 'długim' XIX wieku* (Warsaw, 2019), 239–56.

146 Żbikowski, *Żydzi krakowscy i ich gmina,* 295; Sroka, *Żydzi w Krakowie,* 173.

147 'Protokoły obrad Rady Miejskiej I', 217 (5 Dec. 1867); Sroka, *Żydzi w Krakowie,* 122; 'Protokoły obrad Rady Miejskiej I', 259 (5 Mar. 1868); 'Protokoły obrad Rady Miejskiej II', 74–5 (17 Nov. 1872); Maślak-Maciejewska, *Modlili się w Templu,* 167–8. For protests by Councillors Warschauer, Blatteis, and Nathan Steinberg, see 'Protokoły obrad Rady Miejskiej I', 398 (26 Apr. 1869).

148 F. Golczewski, 'Anti-Semitic Literature in Poland before the First World War', *Polin,* 4 (1989), 91; E. Mendelsohn, *Painting the People: Maurycy Gottlieb and Jewish Art* (Hanover, 2002), 204–5; Żbikowski, *Żydzi krakowscy,* 280–1; D. Konstantynów, '"Mistrz nasz Matejko" i antysemici', *Kwartalnik Historii Żydów,* 222 (2007), 164–98: 165–8.

149 'Obraza honoru mistrza Matejki', *Nowa Reforma,* 5 Dec. 1882, p. 3.

150 J. Żyndul, *Kłamstwo krwi: Legenda mordu rytualnego na ziemiach polskich w XIX i XX wieku* (Warsaw, 2011), 154.

151 '49. Posiedzenie z dn. 7 grudnia 1882', *Dziennik Rozporządzeń,* 1882, no. 8; 'Sprawy miejskie', *Czas,* 10 Dec. 1882, p. 2.

152 'Sprawy miejskie', *Czas,* 10 Dec. 1882, p. 2.

153 'Protokoły obrad Rady Miejskiej VI', 329 (7 Dec. 1882); *Dziennik Rozporządzeń,* 1882, no. 8.

154 Konstantynów, '"Mistrz nasz Matejko"', 168.

155 Ibid. 186.

156 [W.] Chotkowski, 'V. Kazanie: O szkołach i chrześcijańskiem wychowaniu dzieci', in id., *Sześć kazań o kwestyi socyalnej z uwzględnieniem encykliki ojca św. Leona XIII* (Poznań, 1880), 105.

157 Żbikowski, *Żydzi krakowscy i ich gmina,* 283 n. 42.

158 '71. Posiedzenie zwyczajne z dn. 5 marca 1896', *Dziennik Rozporządzeń,* 1896, no. 5; '82. Posiedzenie nadzwyczajne z dn. 10 czerwca 1896', *Dziennik Rozporządzeń,* 1896, no. 8.

159 '82. Posiedzenie nadzwyczajne z dn. 10 czerwca 1896', *Dziennik Rozporządzeń*, 1896, no. 8; [W.] Chotkowski, *O potrzebie religijnego wychowania dzieci w naszych szkołach* (Kraków, 1896), 17.

160 '81. Posiedzenie z dn. 3 czerwca 1896', *Dziennik Rozporządzeń*, 1896, no. 8; 'Sprawy miejskie', *Nowa Reforma*, 6 June 1896, p. 2.

161 'Sprawy miejskie', *Nowa Reforma*, 12 June 1896, p. 2.

162 G. Krzywiec, 'The Lueger Effect in *fin-de-siècle* Catholic Poland: The Imaginary Jew, the Viennese Christian Socials, and the Rise of Catholic Anti-Semitism in Eastern Europe', in M. König and O. Schulz (eds.), *Antisemitismus im 19. Jahrhundert aus internationaler Perspektive/Nineteenth-Century Anti-Semitism in International Perspective* (Göttingen, 2019), 227–44.

163 T. Buchen, '"Learning from Vienna Means Learning to Win": The Cracovian Christian Socials and "the Antisemitic Turn of 1896"', *Quest: Issues in Contemporary Jewish History*, 3 (July 2012), Fondazione Centro di Documentazione Ebraica Contemporanea website, visited 26 Mar. 2020.

164 M. Śliwa, '"Grzmot" i "Antysemita": Czasopisma antyżydowskie w Krakowie w latach 1896–1898', *Kwartalnik Historii Prasy Polskiej*, 32/3 (1993), 41–2.

165 '"Kochajmy się"', *Sprawiedliwość / Die Gerechtigkeit*, 1896, no. 11, p. 3.

166 'Kronika', *Nowa Reforma*, 27 May 1896, p. 2; 'Kronika', *Dziennik Krakowski*, 27 May 1896, p. 5.

167 In its notice of the ceremony *Czas* did not mention Lueger ('Kronika miejska i zagraniczna', *Czas*, 27 June 1896, p. 2), while *Głos Narodu* did not mention the ceremony at all.

168 'Kronika', *Nowa Reforma*, 27 May 1896, p. 2; 'Kronika', *Dziennik Krakowski*, 27 May 1896, p. 5.

169 Żbikowski, *Żydzi krakowscy i ich gmina*, 130, 90.

170 Ibid. 139, 145.

Polish–Jewish Relations in Lwów City Council during the Period of Galician Autonomy, 1870–1914

ŁUKASZ TOMASZ SROKA

THE RESTORATION of local government was a key element in the constitutional and liberalizing reforms carried out in the Habsburg empire in the late nineteenth century. It more or less coincided with the emancipation of the Jewish population, which came into force in 1867 with the introduction of the December constitution.[1] However, the changes, to which the overwhelming majority of the people had been looking forward, were accompanied by numerous national, ethnic, and religious conflicts. The resulting controversies were particularly acute in Galicia, the Austrian-occupied zone of pre-partition Poland, and its provincial capital, Lwów (Lviv), the population of which was made up of just over a half Roman Catholics, just under a third Jews, one-sixth Byzantine Rite Greek Catholics, and a smattering of Protestants and other religions.[2] Lwów, along with Czerniowce (Chernivtsy) and Kraków, had the highest proportion of Jewish inhabitants of the cities of the Habsburg empire.[3] This is not at all surprising, especially as it was the provincial capital of Galicia, the Jewish 'heartland' within the Habsburg monarchy.[4]

Many of the Polish inhabitants of Galicia opposed Jewish emancipation, claiming it was premature. The fact that they had no influence on the changes only confirmed them in the opinion that the changes were 'contrary to Polish interests'. It is certainly true that an opportunity for public debate in Galicia on this reform might have delayed or even prevented its introduction.[5]

One of the first institutions to address the question of the legal status of the Jews at the beginning of Galician autonomy was the provincial parliament. During its first term Jews were represented by four deputies, Szymon Samelsohn of Kraków, Marek Dubs of Lwów, Majer Kallier of Brody, and Łazarz Dubs of Kołomyja (Kolomyya), who put forward a motion calling for Jewish emancipation. This did not gain the support of the Polish deputies.[6]

The matter was raised again during a debate prompted by the promulgation of the Act of 5 March 1862 for the introduction of municipal statutes in the whole of the Habsburg empire, especially its provincial capitals. This included restrictions related to religion. The demand that the rights of Jewish voters and candidates standing for election be limited was put forward by Polish politicians. The Ukrainian deputies held the same position. One of the arguments given for keeping Jews out of city councils was that they had their own community councils, the *kahals*, to deal with their affairs; hence representation on city councils would have meant them dealing with the same problem for a second time, or with problems which they could handle in their own communities. Moreover, if they were elected or won a majority on a city council they would be taking decisions on matters concerning Christians. This last objection led to the amendment of the Local Government Act of 14 March 1867, which laid down that, in the event of Christian councillors failing to make up at least half of a city council, the Christian voters were to vote a second time in compliance with the election regulations to return enough Christian councillors to make up the 'Christian half of the council'.[7]

The ethno-national and religious conflict which flared up in Lwów in connection with the adoption of the municipal statute caused its introduction to be delayed for several years. The contentious issue was the city council's draft of the statute, in which the councillors proposed a maximum of fifteen seats for Jews in a council of 100 members.[8] Municipal property—real estate in and around the city and public precincts—and the rights which appertained to it—to run bath houses; to distil, brew, and sell alcoholic beverages; and to possess interest-bearing capital—were to be held exclusively by Christians.[9] A group of deputies led by Tomasz Rajski, including Marceli Madejski, Robert Hefern, Florian Ziemiałkowski, Laurenty Ostrowski, Marek Dubs, Oswald Hönigsmann, and Juliusz Kolischer, opposed this, arguing that it was against the law of the Habsburg empire.[10] They gained the support of some deputies, and inspired another group to work out alternative solutions. Agenor Gołuchowski put forward a proposal that thirty-three seats in the council should be reserved for Jewish councillors, since the Jewish inhabitants accounted for one-third of the city's population.[11] As regards the property issue, the Jewish councillors put forward a compromise solution. While Marek Dubs proposed that the situation should be left as it was, Juliusz Kolischer tabled an amendment to the following effect:

The assets of the city of Lwów are the property of the municipality. On the first return of a new city council a commission consisting of the mayor and ten councillors, five Christians and five Jews, shall be elected and appointed to examine and declare what part of the said assets is to be set aside and reserved, as hitherto, for Christian foundations and institutes, for Christian religious, scholarly, and charitable purposes, out of the total of the municipality's property, and designated as the exclusive property of the Christian community.[12]

However, the provincial parliament rejected these compromise solutions. The property issue turned out to be the most controversial. Throughout the debate, Michał Gnoiński, presenting the draft proposed by the Statute Commission, defended the position that only Christians had the right to control municipal assets which had been acquired at a time when the Jews did not enjoy municipal rights. Another objection against the Jewish claim was that the Jews wanted to 'encroach on the rights of ownership and enjoyment of the assets of a municipality which had always been Christian, yet at the same time retain the assets of the Jewish "religious" community'.[13] A motion lodged by Doctor Maksymilian Landesberger to refrain from ruling on this point was also rejected. In his opinion the matter should have been referred to the appropriate court. Another motion tabled by Jewish deputies, calling for the city's division into electoral wards, was thrown out as well. Parliamentary Deputy Teofil Merunowicz saw this as an attempt at gerrymandering: 'to control those districts of the city in which they already have, or may have, a numerical majority'.[14] In the circumstances, Z. Rodakowski, Marek Dubs, and Szymon Samelsohn decided to publish *A Minority Report on the Statute for the City of Lwów*, in which they made a number of critical observations, in particular reminding the people of Lwów that 'the principle of equal rights for all the religious groups was one of the foundations of the modern social order'.[15]

On 26 March 1866 the Galician *sejmik* accepted the proposals approved by a majority of the Statute Commission. However, the draft was rejected by the authorities in Vienna, which apart from the inappropriate treatment of the Jewish population also raised the following objections:

The erroneous and inadequate definition of the city's own scope of activities; the assigning of supervision over associations to the municipality; the attribution of jurisdiction over secondary schools to the provincial authorities instead of the general state authorities; failure to take individual interests into consideration; higher taxation imposed on taxpayers under the same electoral regulations; granting to the city council the unconditional right to appoint head teachers and teachers in the city's schools and other institutions of education; permission for the city council to regulate the manner of licensing and selling of alcoholic beverages; granting to the city council of the right to administer surcharges on general royal taxation without restricting such surcharges to fixed and consumer taxes only; failure to consider the provisions of the Industrial Act pertaining to changes in the price of foodstuffs, and of the Municipal Incorporation Act pertaining to the arbitrary imposition of charges for incorporation in the municipality.[16]

The draft was returned to the city's councillors for review and amendment. A decision was taken by majority vote to accept some of the changes but to maintain the original proposals on the Jewish question and the opposition to the introduction of different electoral curia for different categories of taxpayer. They put forward an elaborate argument in support of their position only on the issue of electoral curiae:

The creation of electoral curiae would not be in accord with local conditions. If electoral curiae were to be introduced the impact as well as the social status of the small number of taxpayers charged the highest rates and assigned to the first electoral curiae would be reduced or even completely eclipsed by other, untaxed members of the municipality. Furthermore, for the past eighteen years the city of Lwów has been electing its councillors without the use of electoral curiae and feels no need for change in this respect, especially as there have been no calls even from taxpayers liable to the highest rates of taxation that their municipal electoral rights are not being sufficiently protected.[17]

On 24 December 1866 the new draft of the statute was submitted to the Galician *sejmik*. Given the delay caused by the disputes over its content, the Statute Commission decided to deal with it without delay. Five days later it was ready to be presented for discussion in the house and voting. It was adopted on the day before the end of the provincial parliament's first term in office and sent to Vienna. In February

1867, at the beginning of the new term, the authorities in Lwów embarked on measures to speed up the acceptance of the statute. Franciszek Smolka, deputy to the provincial parliament and imperial counsel, was asked to gain parliamentary support in Vienna, while another deputy, Professor Maurycy Kabat, undertook to petition the state commissioner.[18] The state authorities in Vienna once again rejected the draft, providing a list of objections. This time, alongside the Jewish question and the electoral issue, they noted other problems. The draft did not stipulate that within its area of jurisdiction the municipality was to handle all matters pertaining to the activities of the political authority for its district and maintain the institutions and equipment necessary for this. In addition, the same grounds should apply for the dismissal of the municipality's permanent staff as were in force for the dismissal of state administrative staff.[19]

However, these objections did not generate the same level of excitement as the ethno-national and religious issues, and an agreement was soon reached on them. The state authorities conceded to Lwów that there should be only one electoral curia. They appear to have accepted the argument put forward by the Lwów councillors that Article XI of the Act of 5 March 1862 did not explicitly require the creation of electoral curiae but only laid down that the interests of voters who paid the higher tax rate should be protected in elections to the local authority, while the higher tax rate in itself was a more effective and much better guarantee of their interests than division into electoral classes.[20] Furthermore, the city councillors pointed out, the 1867 Constitution granted the provincial parliament the right to legislate in matters concerning local authorities, including the provisions for municipal elections.[21]

The discussion of the draft statute dragged on through 1869 and 1870, prompting a growing list of provincial deputies to take action, as Kazimierz Karolczak has observed.[22] The position of the Lwów aldermen was not lost on the local authorities of other cities in Galicia. On 30 December 1866 Klemens Rutowski put forward a resolution on behalf of the city council of Tarnów that its statute guarantee four-fifths of the seats and the office of mayor and deputy mayor to Christians.[23]

A public figure who came out in strong opposition to the curtailing of the rights of the Jewish population was the historian, political journalist, and literary critic Count Stanisław Tarnowski, leader of the Kraków conservatives. In 1866 he published a forthright article on the draft statute for Lwów arguing that to debar a person from the enjoyment of any secular rights whatsoever or to deny him the right to participate in secular affairs solely on the grounds of his religion was intolerance or, indeed, persecution, admittedly without bloodshed, but nonetheless persecution as it involved discrimination.[24]

The breakthrough came in 1870. On 26 August the new Statute of the City of Lwów was adopted. In view of its more conciliatory formulation, it stood a better chance of being accepted by all the interested parties. On 14 October 1870 it was finally ratified by the emperor and promulgated as a statutory act. According to its provisions, Christians were guaranteed eighty seats in the hundred-strong city council. Paragraph 24 of the local electoral regulations for the city of Lwów provided as follows:

In the event of fewer than eighty Christian councillors being returned in a municipal election, the mayor of the city shall without delay call a new round of elections to be held for the Christian voters listed on the voters' register used for the previous municipal election, for the election of the number of Christian councillors required to fill the vacant seats on the city council. The councillors elected in this manner and the Christian councillors returned in the first round shall then comprise the Christian part of the administrative council.[25]

The statute was, in effect, a municipal constitution and guaranteed the city's relative independence. It established a clear-cut line of demarcation between the city council's rights and duties, both with respect to the superior authorities as well as to the city's inhabitants. It remained in force in its essence until the restoration of Polish independence. A further act of 11 April 1896 extended the council's term of office from three to six years, but after three years, fifty of the councillors, selected by lot, stepped down and new councillors were elected to take their places. The mayor's and deputy mayor's terms of office were prolonged in the same manner, while the delegates' term of office was increased to three years. Under an Act of 25 May 1909 the council would henceforward select three deputy mayors.

The statistics presented at the beginning of this study justify the conclusion that the political predominance of Lwów's Polish inhabitants was grounded on the proportions of the respective ethno-religious groups. Nonetheless, if the percentage of the population was to be treated as the criterion for the distribution of power in municipal affairs, the Polish community should have ceded a considerable portion of this power to the Jews and Ukrainians, of whom the latter were mostly Byzantine Rite Greek Catholics. However, they were loath to do so. This is the context in which the Polish endeavours to secure a privileged position by means of various legal measures should be interpreted. The debate between the Poles and the Jews of Lwów over the municipal statute is the best illustration of this. Soon, however, the Ukrainian population also began to press for more and more far-reaching political rights. Expanding on the subtitle of Józef Buszko's book,[26] Galicia was not only the Polish Piedmont but also a Piedmont for the Ukrainians.[27] Lwów was the hub of political activities for these ethno-national groups, and by virtue of this fact all the conflicts came to a sharp focus in this city. Here they took a more radical form, for a secure foothold in Lwów meant a more prestigious status and greater potential for activities in the whole of Galicia.

The religious and ethno-national antagonisms meant that the work of the Lwów city council took place in adverse conditions, despite the fact that once the newly returned council began its work the statute controversy subsided. Mayor Michał Gnoiński, who now abandoned the anti-Jewish stance he had held during the conflict over the statute, was perhaps a symbolic ray of hope. But the antipathies that the representatives of the diverse religious and ethno-national communities harboured against each other proved enduring. They had not been triggered by the dispute over the statute, and, accordingly, its adoption could not have been expected to bring a substantial change. To make matters worse, the partially resolved Polish–Jewish conflict was now accompanied by growing tension between Poles and Ukrainians.

The Christian predominance on Lwów city council was not a natural outcome of the figures but the result of the Christians' privileged status, endorsed by the municipal statute. The statutes of Galicia's two main cities, Lwów and Kraków, were drafted in entirely different ways, and this was reflected in the composition of their respective city councils. Both statutes guaranteed Roman Catholics a clear majority at the expense of the Jews. In 1874 Jews made up about a third of the populations of both Lwów and Kraków; however, in Kraków they held 19 per cent of the seats on the city council, but in Lwów a mere 5 per cent.[28]

Naturally, the religious breakdown of the local governments in Galicia was subject to rapid change. In 1902 there were fifty-three Christian and nineteen Jewish councillors in the Kraków city council, while by 1914 the figures had changed to sixty-seven Christians and twenty Jews.[29] The figures for Greek Catholics on the Lwów city council show that they were another underprivileged group. They always had fewer seats in proportion to the percentage of Ukrainians in the city's population. On the other hand Protestants were over-represented (their group accounted for only a small percentage of the population). The real 'winners' were the Roman Catholics: at times the proportion of seats held by Roman Catholics was as much as 30 per cent higher than their proportion of the city's inhabitants.

Lwów's ethno-national and religious minorities could rely only on their councillors for help in important matters. This is how many of the councillors representing minorities perceived their mission and how they were remembered. Michał Winiarski made use of rather vitriolic similes in an anonymous pamphlet to describe Councillor Natan Mayer: 'he is as wary as a cat, as suspicious as a tiger, and whenever he sniffs out an encroachment on Jewish matters, he is there on the spot in no time, defending the interests of his own, to the very edge of blind fury'.[30] However, regardless of minority councillors' real sensitivity on matters relating to the rights of the groups they represented, the example of Lwów city council shows that they were ineffective. Their activities tended to take the form of interventions, as was the case in other city councils in Kraków, Stanisławów (Ivano-Frankivsk), and Tarnów.[31] Of course the value of every individual or collective intervention or protest should not be underrated. Nonetheless the lack of a coherent and well-planned policy on ethno-national and religious affairs is all too patent. Such a policy could not have been agreed upon without the existence of mutual goodwill among the parties, but of course the greatest responsibility for this failure was that of the Polish councillors, since they made up the overwhelming majority. There was another factor which undermined the effectiveness of the Jewish and Ukrainian councillors. A large part of the business handled by the city council was later passed to the municipal administration or other institutions where the Polish ascendancy was even greater.[32] An insight into how far an administrative authority could go is provided by the alleged 'ritual murders committed by Jews'—a story revived on the very threshold of the twentieth century by a municipal official, Aleksander Czołowski—a deeply embarrassing blot on the reputation of that enterprising enthusiast of Lwów's local history and director of its municipal archives.[33] The complaint brought by Rabbi (and Councillor) Jecheskiel Caro, calling the incident 'an expression of hostility to the Jews, made in order to incite', and what was more, 'by a municipal administrative officer paid out of taxpayers', including Jewish taxpayers', money', only infuriated Czołowski even more.[34] He took the matter further, this time in a printed brochure, resorting to insinuation and declaring he would publish a more detailed study: 'I can assure Dr Caro that the printed and archival sources on the history of ritual murder in Poland are more abundant than he believes and contain details to a large extent hitherto unknown, which notwithstanding all the protests, imprecations, and objections deserve serious consideration.'[35]

The issue that precipitated most conflict within the city council was the distribution of subsidies for social and cultural organizations. Councillors protested whenever an organization associated with adherents of another religion was allocated funding that they considered too generous. The same occurred whenever their co-religionists could not claim the subsidies: this could occur for various reasons, such as missing deadlines. A review of the minutes of the city council shows that a group subjected to particularly acute scrutiny, not only by the councillors but also by members of the public in the gallery, was Jewish businessmen. During the session of 15 May 1884 Councillor Heppe addressed a question to Mayor Dąbrowski demanding to know whether it had been the municipal administration or the council that had leased the Zubrze estate and the shingles factory at Brzuchowice to Jews, even though Christian entrepreneurs had tendered a better offer. The mayor replied that the council had leased out the Zubrze property to Baum, the previous leaseholder, who had tendered the best offer. Only one applicant had lodged a tender for the Brzuchowice factory and a contract was entered into with him. Only once the contract had been signed did Christians submit an offer, which was indeed more favourable, but breach of contract would have been liable to legal proceedings.[36] During the session of 4 July 1900 there was uproar when the information came out that the painting of the new theatre had been entrusted to 'Fleck the Jew', whose tender had been higher than others. Mayor Godzimir Małachowski tried to explain that Fleck 'had given the best guarantee that the work would be completed', and in addition he had offered a reduction in his price. His arguments did not pacify the house. Neither was the threat to clear the gallery effective. There were shouts of 'Shame!' and an allegation of bribery, but not addressed to any particular individual.[37] In the same year Councillor Maksymilian Thullie, who had a reputation for piety, asked Deputy Mayor Michał Michalski whether he was aware that a Jew was doing the painting of the Church of Our Lady of the Snows. This question did not evoke a battle of words. Michalski merely answered the concerned councillor objectively, that the work had been entrusted to a Catholic contractor, but it was not the council's duty to control whom he sent to do the job.[38]

The dispute over Sunday rest, which affected the entire Habsburg empire, was also an issue for the Lwów city council. Christian clergymen and politicians wanted the law to protect Sunday as a day of rest. The problem was that they wanted this to apply to Jews as well, arguing that only then would their Christian employees be guaranteed the right to their Sunday rest. The Jews protested, pointing out that such a regulation would be detrimental to them because their religion required them to close their shops and workshops for the whole of Saturday. If the Sunday rest rule were imposed on them they could only work for five days a week, which would mean a fall in profits and make it harder to compete with Christian businessmen, who closed for only one day a week. They backed their argument with a declaration that they did not compel anyone to work on Sundays, as most of their businesses employed few people, usually members of the family. Secondly, they would not hinder Christian employees from enjoying Sunday as a day of rest. These arguments did not make much difference, as the Christian clergy and representatives did not hide the fact that there was more at stake than just the guarantee of Sunday rest for all hired employees. They wanted to stop Catholics from shopping instead of attending Sunday Mass.

Disputes over Sunday rest revived every time attempts were made to regulate the matter by law. The problem was addressed in clause 75 of the Industrial Act of 1859, a comprehensive regulation of economic matters. The Act of 16 January 1895, which provided for rest from work in industrial establishments on Sundays and holy days, repealed clause 75 of the Industrial Act of 1859 and its amendment of 8 March 1885. The new regulation envisaged the possibility of a limited scope of modifications in consideration of local conditions.[39] The matter then passed to the viceroy's office, which issued an official notification on 30 April 1895 permitting a limited amount of work on Sundays. This generated protests from both parties, and the viceroy requested the council's opinion. The matter was related in the council by Stanisław Głąbiński, who made the following recommendations for Sunday labour in compliance with the Act: bakery shops: 8 a.m. to 8 p.m.; butchers: 7 a.m. to 11 a.m.; sausage and cold meats shops: 8 a.m. to 11 a.m. and 7 p.m. to 8 p.m.; hairdressers: 7 a.m. to 4 p.m. (and all day at carnival time); retail traders: 7 a.m. to 11 a.m.; cake shops, dairy shops, and florists: all day; and restaurants, taverns, cafes, and hotels: all day.[40] The viceroy's office welcomed this compromise solution, as can be seen from its official notification of 22 April 1897, which published the amendments to the provisions concerning Sunday rest laid down in its official notification of 30 April 1895 for Lwów. The first paragraph of the regulation defines Sunday working hours for specific professions:

1. Bakers making bread: until 10 a.m. and from 10 p.m.; those selling bread: all day.

2. Confectioners producing goods which must be made fresh for consumption: until 10 a.m.; those selling cakes: all day.

3. Butchers and venison traders: production and sale permitted to 11 a.m.

4. Sausage-makers: until 10 a.m.; those selling sausages and cold meats: until 10 a.m. and from 6 p.m. to 9 p.m.

5. Hairdressers, barbers, and wig-makers may work until 2 p.m., and all day during carnival time.

6. Dairy shops [probably the legislator wanted to permit the sale of dairy products all day].

7. Floristry and the sale of natural flowers: permitted Sunday working hours, all day.[41]

The viceroy's official notification established detailed regulations, but it did not resolve the Sunday rest problem, which remained a disputed issue until the outbreak of the Second World War.

Some Polish nationalists tried to involve the city council in a dispute they had started concerning the election on 21 January 1911 of Tobiasz Aszkenaze to the office of president of the Lwów Chamber of Legal Representatives. According to them, Aszkenaze had won thanks to an alliance of Jews, Ukrainians, and progressive Poles. Angered by the victory of 'forces inimical to Polishness', the newspaper *Rzeczpospolita* observed that Aszkenaze was one of the deputy mayors of the city of Lwów, who not so long ago had put on the golden chain, pledged a solemn vow to the city and to the country, and had been 'conciliatory and reassuring'.[42] The editors expected 'the city council of Lwów, which is now the main area of Mr Aszkenaze's public activities, to find the occasion and manner to express the lack of confidence the entire serious-minded Polish community feels with respect to him'.[43] Although Aszkenaze's position seemed firm and his work with Polish councillors was satisfactory, he was not re-elected for the next term. He became deputy mayor again after a lapse of three years.

The question of the ethno-national minorities' practice and manner of emphasizing their separate identity is more complex. One of the outward signs of this phenomenon was the separate electoral committees set up by Jews and Ukrainians, which Poles would refer to as 'separatist', turning a blind eye to the fact that they, too, had committees based on ethno-national and religious criteria.

The main problem was seen as Jewish 'separatism'. Jews who assimilated faced severe criticism from Polish nationalists, who considered them particularly devious enemies, able to conceal their true intentions. Jews who did not assimilate (or at least not fully) but stood up for their rights were disparaged by these Poles, who expected absolute loyalty and virtually unconditional co-operation from them. An example of such attitudes is furnished by an editorial in *Gazeta Mieszczańska* on the second election of Tobiasz Aszkenaze to the city council:

Indeed, probably no other person has done as much damage to the public affairs of the city of Lwów as he has; no one has contributed so much disintegrating unrest, caused so many wrangles; there is probably no other individual who has so vehemently and systematically challenged the national interest, the interest of Polish Lwów.[44]

However, despite the conflicts, there was also an area of Polish–Jewish dialogue and consensus. Jews were involved in all projects, not just those which concerned them directly. On an everyday basis the councillors worked together conscientiously on behalf of their city. Where key undertakings came into play all quarrels were put aside. There are examples of the Jewish community's co-operation with the agencies of the local authority for the implementation of statutory and administrative duties.

The Jewish community worked with the municipal administration, for instance, in confirming the trustworthiness of Jewish applicants for Austrian citizenship.[45]

Naturally both Jews and Ukrainians participated in supra-ethnic organizations, primarily in the bodies advocating democracy and reform. Nonetheless the ethno-national committees claimed the right to represent their respective communities. The situation was similar with the Polish community: the Catholic national group based its activities on the assumption that it was the best at expressing the needs of the Polish population. Roman Dmowski (1864–1939), a politician from the Congress Kingdom of Poland but very influential in Galicia, especially Lwów, became a mentor for the National Democrats. In a speech he accused Jews of separatism and failing to understand Polish 'national interests': 'Jews, not having the feeling that their existence and prosperity depend on Polish society, and its well-being is good for their interests, as such, do not have sufficient reason to associate with this society and to break their backs in defending the national interest.'[46]

The attitudes and events I have presented lead to the inevitable conclusion that ethno-national and religious questions were of paramount importance for the city councillors. These were the issues that aroused the most excitement and for which councillors were prepared to sacrifice much. But there is no reason to generalize. For many councillors, concepts like *naród* (literally 'nation', but perhaps 'national ethnicity' would be a better equivalent) and religion were not critical. They were guided by rational thinking, and endeavoured to find a compromise in every situation. The available sources do not allow for a full retrieval of the state of mind and self-identity of all the councillors, but without doubt a councillor's Jewish or Ukrainian background often meant more to others—usually his political opponents—than it did to himself.

The situation is quite clear with ministers of religion. The high degree to which the rabbis identified with their religion and the Jewish people is self-evident. This is confirmed by other evidence apart from their office. Jecheskiel Caro, the rabbi of the progressive synagogue, was not only a defender of his people's reputation but also interested in its history. He published a study entitled *The History of the Jews in Lwów from the Earliest Times to the Division of Poland in 1792 from Chronicles and Archival Sources*.[47] He was one of the pioneers of the library of the Jewish community in Lwów, which opened officially on 6 January 1901, and, after the death of Salomon Buber in December 1906, he was appointed its curator.[48]

Councillor Rabbi Emil Byk presents an interesting case. According to Stanisław Głąbiński, Byk told him 'quite clearly that he was not a Pole but a Jew, but that he was not at liberty to isolate himself from the Polish society in which he lived'.[49] In other words, Byk was committed to his Jewish identity but declared his allegiance to the Polish idea. However, Teofil Merunowicz accused him of entering into an alliance with the Ruthenian (Ukrainian) opposition and the Germans against the Poles during the elections to the Reichsrat of 1873.[50] The words 'against the Poles' are clearly exaggerated, for Byk's subsequent change of political allegiance is unquestionable and became permanent. His life and activities verified his assertion of solidarity with the Poles. He made a conscientious contribution to the work of the city council without focusing on Jewish problems and concerns. The main area of his efforts was the economic development of Lwów. When he was elected to the Austrian parliament in 1891 he joined the Koło Polskie (Polish caucus). His self-identity is another, perhaps more complex, problem. Evidently he viewed his Jewishness from the religious vantage point and was in favour of Jewish assimilation and against Zionism.[51]

The attitude of another Jewish councillor, Natan Löwenstein, was similar to that of Byk. He was in favour of assimilation, and promoted Polish culture among his fellow Jews. He established a college to train prospective secondary-school teachers of Jewish religion and progressive rabbis.[52] However, there was a line beyond which he never ventured—the repudiation of his religion. He turned down the offer of a ministerial post, since the condition attached to it was conversion to Christianity.[53] He enjoyed a reputation as an outstanding orator, often standing up in defence of Jews. The well-known parliamentarian Władysław Leopold Jaworski described Löwenstein as:

A daunting polemicist. Stories circulated about his hits, and those assaulted by them fell into despair: after all, in a duel with rapiers, they could hardly use a battle-axe. Loewenstein's debate with Father Stojałowski could serve as the model of the old practice. Loewenstein rattled off all of his adversary's errors without resorting to language which alas today is tolerated, and maybe the only terminology that can be understood.[54]

Extending the metaphor, Löwenstein just as often drew his rapier in the interest of Poles, and did so with the same dedication as when he was fighting on behalf of his co-religionists. In 1895 he defended a group of Polish grammar-school boys in Tarnopol charged with organizing an anti-Austrian conspiracy. Together with Lieberman, Kwieciński, and Ostrowski he defended a group of Polish soldiers interned at Máramarossziget (Sighetu Marmaţiei) in Hungary. His involvement got him into a conflict with General Schilling, who was presiding over the case. Nevertheless, just before the fall of the monarchy the Emperor Karl received him during an audience.[55]

The lawyer and businessman Filip Zucker was another Polonophile. Ezra Mendelsohn described him as 'the first Polish Jewish patriot'.[56] Zucker paid for his part in the January uprising of 1863 with a heavy prison sentence but managed to regain his freedom. Bernard Goldman was also involved in undercover activities with the Polish national liberation movement. When he was a student he took part in the 1861 demonstrations, for which he was imprisoned and sent to Siberia. He managed to escape, and joined the insurgents of 1863. Arrested a second time, he escaped and fled to Germany, where he graduated in law and established working contacts with Polish émigré activists. Thanks to the assistance of Agenor Gołuchowski he became an Austrian citizen and settled in Lwów, where his main activity was education for Jews.[57]

Leonard Stahl is another interesting personality. Jewish by birth, he became an influential member of the Lwów branch of the Polish National Democratic Party, and served as vice president of its municipal committee. He belonged to a group of nationalists who advocated a hard line against the Ukrainians. His political career progressed rapidly, and he was promoted to membership of the party's central and executive committees. At the same time he continued to work with assimilated Jews in the local authorities of Lwów.[58]

The processes and trends that developed in Galicia and the whole of the Habsburg empire found their reflection in the persons and activities of Lwów's councillors with Jewish roots. But there were also phenomena which were the outcome of the specific features of the city's Jews. The attempt to involve the Jews of Lwów in a Germanization campaign in the city proved a dismal failure, even though a few decades earlier the Habsburgs would have had genuine grounds to expect their commitment to this cause. The historian Majer Bałaban observed their earlier attitude:

The difference was manifest as soon as local communities started sending their delegates and memoranda to Vienna. The Jews of Lwów and East Galicia sent their own delegations and engaged in direct negotiations with Bach, Gołuchowski, and Szmerling, while the Jews of Kraków entrusted their fate to the Polish delegation, electing three men out of their midst who were to present the postulates of the Kraków Jewish community to the Polish delegates in Vienna.[59]

Several factors contributed to the debacle of the Habsburg project, one of the main ones being its inherent lack of logic. The Jews could not be promoters of German culture within Polish society unless they had assimilated into that society, at least to a certain extent. Those Jews who decided to assimilate faced another dilemma: whether to adopt German or Polish culture. Most of the Jews assimilating from the 1840s until the early 1880s chose German culture.[60] However, such a move precluded the development of closer relations with Poles, who perceived such Jews as adherents of the monarchy. By the 1880s, when Jews began to adopt Polish culture, there could no longer be a question of them disseminating German culture. The key to understanding these transformations was the relaxation of the Germanizing campaign to which both Jews and Poles had been subjected earlier. German culture and language lost their attractiveness when Polish was reinstated as the official language in the local offices, public institutions, and the University of Lwów. 'Germanized Lemberg was transformed into the Polish Lwów.'[61]

Apart from this, pro-Polish Jews accomplished a great deal. Their activities were particularly intense in the second half of the nineteenth century, and apparent in the emergence of a large number of social and educational institutions. In 1868 the Society of Israelites for the Promotion of Education and Citizenship among Galician Jews was founded. Of its seven founding members, five—Herman Frenkel, Józef Kolischer, Juliusz Kolischer, Bernard Löwenstein, and Filip Zucker—later had seats on the city council. The other two were Marek Dubs and Maurycy Kolischer.[62] In 1877 an organization called Harbinger of Reconciliation was founded, its aim being to disseminate civic attitudes among Jews and to protect their rights.[63] Another society which strove to instruct Galician Jews in civic virtues was the Society for the

Transformation of the Jews of Galicia into Citizens: The Covenant of Brothers, founded in 1882. Its leaders were Bernard Goldman and Jakub Piepes, and its members numbered many Poles, including the poet Adam Asnyk, the novelist Eliza Orzeszkowa, who was an honorary member, councillors Gustaw Roszkowski and Henryk Rewakowicz, and Mayor Wacław Dąbrowski.[64]

The process of assimilation began to run into difficulties in the 1890s. The ground for the Zionists, who were growing in strength, was prepared by Polish nationalists, who organized a boycott of Jewish shops, came out in oppositions to Jews in political, cultural, and academic affairs, and finally descended to physical assaults. Even more disturbing news was coming from Vienna, Berlin, and Rome.

The Jews of Lwów realized that the arduously constructed 'Polish–Jewish friendship' was not advancing beyond the sphere of declarations. When it came to carrying out the enterprises that were important for them, they tended to come up against a lack of understanding. An example is the series of disappointments attending the opening of the rabbinical college which was to educate 'progressive but also God-fearing' rabbis. On 16 March 1890 the Covenant of Brothers issued a questionnaire to which Stanisław Badeni, Emil Byk, Filip Frochtman, Zdzisław Marchwicki, Jan Franke, Ludomił German, Natan Löwenstein, Tadeusz Romanowicz, and Józef Wereszczyński responded. The question they were asked was how to reform Galician Jewry, and in particular how to enhance their level of education and improve their economic relations and the value of their work. The answers which were submitted were used as the basis for the following resolution:

The questionnaire has revealed general agreement that we should increase the attendance rate of Jewish children at state schools:

(*a*) strict adherence to the law on compulsory school attendance;

(*b*) by making it easier for Jewish children in primary schools to observe the sabbath and Jewish holy days;

(*c*) by the appropriate conducting of religious instruction for the Jewish religion in the primary schools;

(*d*) by measures to educate qualified teachers for religious instruction; and hence

1. The questionnaire shows there is an urgent need to found a teacher training establishment in the province for the Jewish religious instruction.

2. The questionnaire shows there is an urgent need to establish a rabbinical college in the province.[65]

Encouraged by this result, the *kahal* devised a statute and a plan. But they were soon disappointed. The potential benefactors, both Jewish and Polish, turned a deaf ear. In this disagreeable situation, Szymon Schaff, president of the Jewish community, suggested the Jewish girls' primary school be closed down and the funds (about 6,000 Austro-Hungarian gulden) used to establish the rabbinical college.[66] On 5 December 1891 the idea was adopted by the religious council and passed on to the government for approval. The government sent the matter to the city council. But—to put it in the words of Majer Bałaban—'in its short-sightedness, at a session in late November, on Father Mazurak's motion and unwilling to tax the municipal budget by taking the 280 girls into municipal schools, the council brushed the matter aside'.[67] Thus the discussion on the project for a rabbinical college, which had been undertaken for the third time (the previous occasions were in 1828 and 1860), continued to be a vexed topic well into the twentieth century.[68]

The Zionists only established their position on the city council very slowly. Until the outbreak of the Second World War they never managed to secure a substantial number of seats. There were at least two reasons for this. At the time when the Zionists started expanding, the assimilationist and the Orthodox factions already enjoyed established positions in the council. After the restoration of Poland's independence, most of those who held seats on the council had been elected in 1913 or were appointed by the Polish administrative authorities. The first democratic elections in the two decades between the world wars were not held until 1934.[69]

However, many of the assimilationists later became disenchanted and abandoned the cause, and even turned to Zionism. Wiktor Chajes, who was an ardent advocate of assimilation for several decades, noted in his diary for 29 August 1929 that, as a programme, assimilation was a thing of the past.[70] The best-known of the 'converts' from assimilation was Theodor Herzl himself, founder of the Zionist movement. In 1882 the Lwów organization Agudas Achim wound up its activities.[71] In 1893 the first Galician branch of the Zion Alliance of Austrian Societies for the Colonization of Palestine and Syria was founded in Lwów.[72] Despite the adversities, the assimilationists persisted in their activities, focusing on education and politics. In 1903 Bernard Goldman's lending library was founded, directed for many years by Natan Löwenstein. In 1907 students associated with the library set up an organization called Union. In 1912 the same milieu gave rise to another new organization called the Berek Joselewicz Polish Young People's Union. The aim of these organizations was to teach Jews about Polish culture.[73]

Feuds often flared up between assimilationists and Zionists, but they were not conducted within the city council—a wise move by Jewish councillors, who knew that the amount of sympathy they could count on from the other ethno-national groups was very limited. Any arbitration by Poles or Ukrainians would have been of questionable value. Conflicts arising between Jewish politicians were conducted within the community, in the press, or by means of pamphlets and posters. In addition there was still the contention between progressive and Orthodox groups, but its character was religious rather than secular. Representatives of the religious minorities tended not to engage local authorities in the internal affairs of their communities. But there were exceptions. The documents of the Lwów Jewish community contain a complaint brought by Berl Goldstern to the municipal administration, alleging that the community was unlawfully preventing him from seeing his financial reports.[74]

In conclusion it must be said that councillors with minority roots often intervened to protect the good name and specific interests of their co-religionists and ethnic compatriots. The leaders in this practice were the Jews, who fought against anti-semitism and strove to make equal rights more than just the letter of the law. However, they did not stop at that. They were patently involved in all the city's main affairs. A review of their activities shows that Jewish councillors had a preference for the free market, limits to the powers of administrative institutions, and the reduction of all charges and taxes. In the period of Galician autonomy and subsequently in the two decades of Poland's independence prior to the Second World War, the Lwów city council was the scene of co-operation and rivalry between the Jews and the Poles and Ukrainians, as Wacław Wierzbieniec has shown.[75] The councillors did not manage to reconcile their respective communities with one another—it is doubtful whether that could have been achieved at all, although that is beyond the scope of this chapter. It was not reconciliation of the ethno-national and religious communities that was the main business of the city council but the development of the city and the well-being and prosperity of its people. Squabbles caused by religious and ethno-national differences did not facilitate its work, but they never caused it to grind to a halt. The councillors' main achievement is that for the principal modernization projects and in matters serving the welfare of the city's inhabitants they managed to rise above their prejudices and conflicts. If they had not, the beneficial growth and progress of the city of Lwów which took place in the years of Galician autonomy could not have occurred.

Notes

1 J. Buszko, 'The Consequences of Galician Autonomy after 1867', *Polin*, 12 (1999), 86–99; M. Śliż, *Galicyjscy Żydzi na drodze do równouprawnienia 1848–1914* (Kraków, 2006).

2 *Österreichische Statistik*, 1/1–2 (1882); 32/1 (1892); 63/1–2 (1902–3); NS 1/1 (1912); S. Pazyra, 'Ludność Lwowa w pierwszej ćwierci XX wieku', in A. Walawender et al. (eds.), *Studja z historji społecznej i gospodarczej poświęcone prof. dr. Franciszkowi Bujakowi* (Lwów, 1931), 415–46; E. Tomaszewski, 'Pochodzenie ludności m. Lwowa', *Wiadomości statystyczne o mieście Lwowie*, xvii (Lwów, 1939).

3 *Wiadomości statystyczne o mieście Lwowie*, viii/2: *Wyniki spisu ludności z 31. grudnia 1900*, ed. K. Ostaszewski-Barański (Lwów, 1904), 33.

4 Mariusz Kulczykowski claims that the origins of Jewish population distribution go back to the Jews' migration from western Europe in the sixteenth century, when they headed for Red Ruthenia, with the support of the Polish aristocracy. By the seventeenth century they had established positions in the local towns. By the end of the eighteenth century Jewish settlement had developed its specific features, which proved impervious to the profound changes occurring in the nineteenth century (M. Kulczykowski, 'Ze studiów nad rozmieszczeniem ludności żydowskiej w Galicji na przełomie XVIII i XIX wieku', in K. Broński, J. Purchla, and J. Szpak (eds.), *Kraków – Małopolska w Europie środka: Studia ku czci profesora Jana M. Małeckiego w siedemdziesiątą rocznicę urodzin* (Kraków, 1996), 175–88; see also F. Kiryk and F. Leśniak, 'Skupiska żydowskie w miastach małopolskich do końca XVI wieku', in F. Kiryk (ed.), *Żydzi w Małopolsce: Studia z dziejów osadnictwa i życia społecznego* (Przemyśl, 1991), 13–36).

5 E. Horn, 'Kwestia żydowska w obradach Galicyjskiego Sejmu Krajowego pierwszej

kadencji (1861–1866)', in Kiryk (ed.), *Żydzi w Małopolsce*, 171–9; id., 'Udział posłów żydowskich w obradach Galicyjskiego Sejmu Krajowego drugiej kadencji, I: Pierwsza sesja', *Biuletyn Żydowskiego Instytutu Historyczneg*, 160 (1991), 3–14; K. Karolczak, 'Sprawy narodowościowe w Galicyjskim Sejmie Krajowym w latach 1861–1873', in K. Karolczak and H. W. Żaliński (eds.), *Galicyjskie dylematy: Zbiór rozpraw* (Kraków, 1994), 31–49; M. Śliwa, 'Obcy czy swoi: Z dyskusji nad kwestią żydowską w Galicji u schyłku XIX wieku', in Karolczak and Żaliński (eds.), *Galicyjskie dylematy*, 18–30.

6 Horn, 'Kwestia żydowska w obradach Galicyjskiego Sejmu Krajowego', 172.

7 J. Buszko, 'Walka o kształt polityczno-ustrojowy samorządu terytorialnego w autonomicznej Galicji', in J. Malec and W. Uruszczak (eds.), *Ustrój i prawo w przeszłości dalszej i bliższej: Studia historyczne o prawie dedykowane Prof. Stanisławowi Grodziskiemu w pięćdziesiątą rocznicę pracy naukowej* (Kraków, 2001), 197–210: 207.

8 Archiwum Narodowe, Kraków, Akta miasta Krakowa, 6805.

9 Ibid.

10 Ibid.

11 Karolczak, 'Sprawy narodowościowe w Galicyjskim Sejmie Krajowym', 47.

12 Archiwum Narodowe, Kraków, Akta miasta Krakowa, 6805.

13 T. Merunowicz, *Wyniki samorządu w Galicyi. Z powodu 50-lecia istnienia urządzeń autonomicznych w Galicyi* (Lwów, 1916), 38.

14 Ibid.

15 L'vivs'ka natsional'na naukova biblioteka Ukrayiny imeni V. Stefanyka, NAN Ukrayiny, Dział Rękopisów, f. 63, Archiwum Krzeczunowicza, spr. 37/1.

16 Ibid.

17 Ibid.

18 Karolczak, 'Sprawy narodowościowe w Galicyjskim Sejmie Krajowym', 47.

19 Archiwum Narodowe, Akta miasta Krakowa, 6805.

20 Ibid.

21 Buszko, 'Walka o kształt polityczno-ustrojowy samorządu terytorialnego w autonomicznej Galicji', 205.

22 Karolczak, 'Sprawy narodowościowe w Galicyjskim Sejmie Krajowym', 47.

23 Ibid.

24 S. Tarnowski, 'O sesyi sejmowej z roku 1865–66', *Przegląd Polski*, 1 (1866), 190–1.

25 'Statut królewskiego stołecznego miasta Lwowa', in *Zbiór ustaw i rozporządzeń administracyjnych*, ed. J. Piwocki, 5 vols. (Lwów, 1899), i. 513–14.

26 J. Buszko, *Galicja 1859–1914: Polski Piemont?* (Warsaw, 1989).

27 R. A. Mark, 'Polnische Bastion und ukrainisches Piemont, Lemberg 1772–1921', in P. Fäßler, T. Held, and D. Sawitzki (eds.), *Lemberg–Lwów–Lviv: Eine Stadt im Schnittpunkt europäischer Kulturen* (Cologne, 1993), 46–74; J. P. Himka, 'Dimensions of a Triangle: Polish–Ukrainian–Jewish relations in Austrian Galicia', *Polin*, 12 (1999), 25–48.

28 T. Pilat, 'Skład reprezentacji miejskich w Galicji w r. 1874', *Wiadomości Statystyczne o Stosunkach Krajowych*, 2 (1875), 1–34; Karolczak, 'Sprawy narodowościowe w Galicyjskim Sejmie Krajowym'.

29 I. Homola-Skąpska, 'Kuria inteligencji w krakowskiej Radzie Miejskiej (1866–1914)', in I. Homola-Skąpska and G. Nieć, *Z dziejów Krakowa, Galicji i Śląska Cieszyńskiego: Wybór pism historycznych* (Kraków, 2007), 41–87: 77.

30 M. Winiarski, *Sylwetki nowych radnych* (Lwów, 1899).

31 According to Leszek Hońdo the fact that the Jewish community was often compelled to send petitions defending its rights to Vienna is evidence of its ineffectiveness (L. Hońdo, 'Stosunki polsko–żydowskie na przykładzie rady miasta Tarnowa 1867–1914', in B. Breysach et al. (eds.), *Ze sobą, obok siebie, przeciwko sobie: Polacy, Żydzi, Austriacy i Niemcy w XIX i na początku XX wieku* (Kraków, 1995), 151–66: 158). Sometimes local government was passive even when there was outright aggression against Jews: for example, in Tarnów after an anti-Jewish riot on 15 August 1870, when one person was killed, thirty-two were injured, and Jewish properties were looted.

32 In the interwar period the Jewish councillors tried unsuccessfully to change this situation, which got even worse for Jews in the late 1930s. They lost their jobs on trumped-up charges of not having the required professional qualifications (see W. Wierzbieniec, 'Żydzi w samorządach miejskich Lwowa, Przemyśla i Rzeszowa w latach 1918–1939: Wybrane aspekty', *Studia Judaica* (Kraków), 14 (2011), 1–21: 12).

33 Łucja Charewiczowa considered Czołowski a distinguished person, embodying love of Lwów and its heritage, well-informed, indefatigable in his activities and untiring in the initiatives he undertook (Ł. Charewiczowa, *Historiografia i miłośnictwo Lwowa* (Lwów, 1938); see also W. Bieńkowski, 'Aleksander Czołowski: Miłośnik Lwowa i historyk regionalny', in P. Franaszek (ed.), *Celem nauki jest człowiek… : Studia z historii społecznej i gospodarczej ofiarowane Helenie Madurowicz-Urbańskiej* (Kraków, 2000), 47–54).

34 A. Czołowski, *Odpowiedź rabinowi lwowskiemu dr. Jecheskielowi Caro w sprawie 'Mordu rytualnego'* (Lwów, 1899), 4.

35 Ibid. 21–2.

36 *Gazeta Lwowska*, 1884, no. 114.

37 *Gazeta Lwowska*, 1900, no. 152.

38 *Gazeta Lwowska*, 1900, no. 166.

39 'Ustawa przemysłowa i odnoszące się do niej ustawy i przepisy', in J. Piwocki (ed.), *Lwów* (Lwów, 1902), 189.

40 *Gazeta Lwowska*, 1896, no. 262.

41 'Permitted Sunday working hours in retail shops from 7 a.m. to 12 noon and additionally in grocery shops from 7 p.m. to 8 p.m.' ('Ustawa przemysłowa i odnoszące się do niej ustawy i przepisy', §4).

42 *Rzeczpospolita*, 1911, no. 47.

43 Ibid.

44 *Gazeta Mieszczańska*, 1913, no. 126.

45 Tsentral'nyi derzhavnyi istorychnyi arkhiv Ukrayiny, Lviv, f. 701, op. 2, spr. 618.

46 R. Dmowski, *Kwestya Żydowska*, vol. i: *Separatyzm żydów i jego źródła* (Warsaw, 1909), 15.

47 J. Caro, *Geschichte der Juden in Lemberg von den ältesten Zeiten bis zur Theilung Polens im Jahre 1792 aus Chroniken und archivalischen Quellen* (Kraków, 1894). Gąsiorowski criticized Caro for using the printed chronicles on the history of Lwów by Zimorowic, Józefowicz, Zubrzycki, and Chodyniecki, and Salomon Buber's list of bio-biographical materials, but failing to refer to the city's extensive archives. Caro did not cite the literature of the subject and made numerous errors, even in the title (S. Gąsiorowski, 'Stan badań nad dziejami gmin żydowskich na ziemi lwowskiej w XVII i XVIII wieku', in K. Pilarczyk (ed.). *Żydzi i judaizm we współczesnych badaniach polskich: Materiały z konferencji, Kraków 21–23 XI 1995* (Kraków, 1997), 191–212: 200).

48 I. Smolsky, 'Caro Jecheskiel', in A. Kozytsky (ed.), *Entsyklopediya L'vova*, 4 vols. to date (Lviv, 2007–), iii. 124.

49 S. Głąbiński, *Wspomnienia polityczne* (Pelplin, 1939), 124.

50 Merunowicz, *Wyniki samorządu w Galicyi*, 6.

51 I. Smolsky, 'Byk Emil', in Kozytsky (ed.), *Entsyklopediya L'vova*, i. 237–8.

52 *Almanach żydowski*, ed. H. Stachel (Lwów, 1937), 224.

53 O. Kofler, *Żydowskie dwory: Wspomnienia z Galicji Wschodniej od początku XIX wieku do wybuchu I wojny światowej*, ed. E. Koźmińska-Frejlak (Warsaw, 1999), 251.

54 *Almanach żydowski*, 223.

55 Ibid.

56 E. Mendelsohn, 'Jewish Assimilation in Lvov: The Case of Wilhelm Feldman', *Slavic Review*, 28 (1969), 557–90: 580.

57 Ibid.; S. Grodziski, *Wzdłuż Wisły, Dniestru i Zbrucza: Wędrówki po Galicji dyliżansem, koleją, samochodem* (Kraków, 1998), 293.

58 A. Tyszkiewicz, 'Leonard i Zdzisław Stahlowie w polityce i życiu społecznym Lwowa', in K. Karolczak (ed.), *Ludzie Lwowa: Studia z dziejów Lwowa* (Kraków, 2005), 232–44: 233; Wierzbieniec, 'Żydzi w samorządach miejskich Lwowa, Przemyśla i Rzeszowa', 5.

59 M. Bałaban, *Historia Żydów w Krakowie i na Kazimierzu*, 2 vols. (Kraków, 1931–6), ii. 702.

60 I adopt Kopff-Muszyńska's division into time periods (K. Kopff-Muszyńska, '"Ob Deutsch oder Polnisch": Przyczynek do badań nad asymilacją Żydów we Lwowie w latach 1840–1892', in A. K. Paluch (ed.), *The Jews in Poland*, 2 vols. (Kraków, 1992), i. 187–203: 187).

61 E. Mendelsohn, 'From Assimilation to Zionism in Lvov: The Case of Alfred Nossig', *Slavonic and East European Review*, 49 (1971), 521–34: 523. Mendelsohn continued: 'One result being that Jewish dignitaries were obliged to communicate with Polish nationalists rather than with German-speaking Austrian officials. The old German orientation of the Jewish elite was severely challenged, and the Guardian of Israel was eventually obliged to make its peace with the Polish revival' (ibid.; cf. Ł. T. Sroka, 'Der Einfluss Wiens auf die polnisch–jüdischen Beziehungen in Galizien im 19. Jahrhundert, speziell in Lemberg und Krakau', in R. Wichard (ed.), *Kreuzwege: Kulturbegegnung im öffentlichen Raum* (Frankfurt am Main, 2010), 89–101).

62 Kopff-Muszyńska, '"Ob Deutsch oder Polnisch"', 194.

63 Ł. Kapralska, 'Drogi z getta: Uwagi o procesach asymilacyjnych w społeczności Żydów galicyjskich', in K. Zieliński and M. Adamczyk-Garbowska (ed.), *Ortodoksja, emancypacja, asymilacja: Studia z dziejów ludności żydowskiej na ziemiach polskich w okresie rozbiorów* (Lublin, 2003), 97–118: 109.

64 Kopff-Muszyńska, '"Ob Deutsch oder Polnisch"', 199.

65 M. Bałaban, *Historya projektu szkoły rabinów i nauki religii mojż. na ziemiach polskich* (Lwów, 1907), 37–8.

66 The Jewish community had the government's consent to charge a fee for the ritual slaughter of animals and was obliged to maintain two primary schools from the revenue.

67 Bałaban, *Historya projektu szkoły rabinów*, 41.

68 Ibid. 45.

69 W. Wierzbieniec, 'Uwagi nad udziałem Żydów w samorządzie Lwowa w okresie II Rzeczypospolitej', in M. Stolarczyk, A. Kawalec, and J. Kuzicki (eds.), *Historia i dziedzict-wo regionów w Europie Środkowo–Wschodniej w XIX i XX w.* (Rzeszów, 2011), 183–96: 187.

70 W. Chajes, *Semper fidelis: Pamiętnik Polaka wyznania mojżeszowego z lat 1926–1939* (Kraków, 1997).

71 Kopff-Muszyńska, '"Ob Deutsch oder Polnisch"', 201.

72 V. Melamed, *Evrei vo L'vove (XIII – pervaya polovina XX veka): Sobytiya, obshchestvo, lyudi* (Lviv, 1994), 132.

73 W. Wierzbieniec, 'The Processes of Jewish Emancipation and Assimilation in the Multi-ethnic City of Lviv during the Nineteenth and Twentieth Centuries', in J. Czaplicka (ed.), *Lviv: A City in the Crosscurrents of Culture* (Cambridge, Mass., 2000), 223–50: 236–7; id., '"Vom Orient die Fantasie, und in der Brust der Slawen Feuer …": Jüdisches Leben und Akkulturation im Lemberg des 19. und 20. Jahrhunderts', in Fäßler, Held, and Sawitzki (eds.), *Lemberg–Lwów–Lviv*, 75–91; id., 'Enlightenment, Assimilation, and Modern Identity: The Jewish Élite in Galicia', *Polin*, 12 (1999), 79–85.

74 Derzhavnyi arkhiv L'vivs'koyi oblasti, f. 3, op. 1, spr. 4864.

75 Wierzbieniec, 'The Processes of Jewish Emancipation and Assimilation', 191.

3. FROM 1914 TO THE SECOND WORLD WAR

'One of Them' as 'One of Us'

Jewish Demands for National Autonomy as a Means to Achieve Civic Equality during the First World War

MARCOS SILBER

'WE ARE NO WORSE THAN THEM. If you want Jews like these, treat them as
these countries do!'[1] asserted Noyekh Prilutski (1882–1941), the leader of the
Folkist Party in the Warsaw city council in 1916, when asked why German Jews were
satisfied with civil rights and did not also demand national rights. Prilutski's assertion
is noteworthy for several reasons. First and foremost, because a local city council
whose main task was the management of the city was discussing national rights. What
are the links between mundane municipal tasks and minority rights? Certainly Prilutski himself linked the idea of civil equality in Poland with the rights of Polish Jewry
as a minority group.

The revival of the discourse on Jewish autonomy and the demands for national
autonomy at the end of the nineteenth century have usually been discussed in the
context of nationalism—a necessary and fruitful framework to understand this
phenomenon. However, this has frequently led to the neglect of the civil aspects of
the issue. Developing this line of argument, this chapter examines the connection
between Polish views on civil rights and equality for Jews during the First World
War and the increasingly vociferous Jewish demands for national rights. It argues
that this connection is crucial to understanding the increasing popularity of autonomist ideas and demands amongst Polish Jews during the First World War and subsequently.

The chapter is divided into three sections. The first focuses on the dynamics of
viewing the Jews in the Polish lands simultaneously as 'one of us', and therefore
entitled to representation, and as 'one of them', aligned with 'foreign' interests and
therefore requiring that their participation in shaping the 'common good' be limited.
The second section describes the way this dynamic was reflected in the behaviour of
the elected institutions of the emerging Polish state. The key concept in these two sections is Foucault's notion of 'governmentality',[2] which refers to the exercise of organized political power by a state over its subjects. It emphasizes the governing of
people's conduct through 'positive' means rather than a disciplinarian form of power.
In this regard, governmentality is generally associated with the active consent and

willingness of individuals to participate in their own governance resulting from the policy of the authorities. The third section focuses on how autonomist demands attempted to transform 'one of them' into 'one of us' or, in other words, how the autonomist discourse of nationality tried to find an appropriate place for Jews in the new Polish state.

The Simultaneous Construction of 'the Jew' as 'One of Us' and 'One of Them'

The ethnic tensions in Poland on the eve of the First World War are well known. Much has been written about the effects of the elections to the Russian Fourth Duma in 1912, the first case where Jewish voters had a potential majority. In these elections, nobody in the pro-autonomy Jewish parties demanded special rights for the Jews or any kind of autonomy beyond equal rights.[3] Most Jews understood that they were not acknowledged as legitimate partners entitled to elect representatives from among their number. The aim of most Jewish political groups was not to elect a Jewish representative but 'a Christian Pole who supports the principle of equal rights'.[4]

Neither of the two leading candidates proposed by the Poles met this criterion. Not only did Roman Dmowski, the antisemitic candidate of the National Democratic Party (Endecja), lose the battle for a seat in the duma because of Jewish votes but so too did his main rival, Jan Kucharzewski, who supported an 'economic struggle' against Jews.[5] However, the electors' boldness in deciding to elect a secondary figure instead of one of these two candidates was widely attacked and provoked a vicious boycott campaign. The elections were a critical phase in the deterioration of ethnic relations in Warsaw. The Polish right found more support in public life for its anti-Jewish discourse, which envisaged the Jews as a separate element of Polish society. It propagated the image of the Jews as advancing their own interests which were incompatible with those of the Poles. The process of 'Othering' the Jews deepened and broadened and simultaneously weakened the liberal camp in Polish politics.[6]

After the outbreak of the war, the anti-Jewish atmosphere in Congress Poland, still under Russian rule, worsened further. Boycotts, violence, allegations of co-operation with the enemy, or simply accusations of anti-Polonism provoked by the growing xenophobia caused a further deterioration in Polish–Jewish relations.[7] As the country took its first steps towards sovereignty in the wake of the creation of the Kingdom of Poland as a German puppet state in November 1916, one of the questions it faced was whether Jews should be included within the political structure of the new state. In seeking to determine the status of Polish Jewry, the Polish state-in-formation oscillated between two conflicting positions. On the one hand, it adhered to the logic of ethno-nationalism that excluded Jews from the national community, seeing them as 'one of them'. On the other, it attempted to adhere to a logic of inclusion on the lines of Foucault's concept of governmentality. This sought to subject all citizens, including Jews, to the authority of the state. The government thus pursued a set of principles designed to create citizens who granted legitimacy to the state and were subject to its supervision: their acceptance of the state legitimized its authority and practices, transforming Jews into equal citizens, 'one of us'.

The activity of local authorities and city councils as well as the policy of the authorities of the state-in-formation reflect the combination of these two logics, the ethno-national and the state-oriented, which created a dynamic that strengthened Jewish autonomist claims. The issue of elections to city councils was raised in 1915 when the German occupation authorities attempted to set up city councils in Congress Poland both for practical purposes—placing the administration of mundane issues in local hands, freeing German manpower for other tasks—and for propagandistic advantage—gaining the support of the local population and sympathy in neutral countries. The elections were modelled on the Prussian three-class franchise and divided a city's inhabitants into six curiae according to their socio-economic and professional status. Each curia in Warsaw was allocated fifteen representatives on the city council.

Thus, on the eve of the municipal elections in 1916 in Warsaw, Polish political parties negotiated with Jewish representatives on the question of Jewish representation. The general understanding among the Polish parties was that a considerable Jewish presence in the council should be prevented in order to ensure the strong presentation of demands for a Polish state (whatever the concept 'state' meant under the German occupation). Yet some opposed a far-reaching limitation on the number of Jewish councillors, above all because of the negative impact this would have on Poland's foreign image.[8] Konrad Zieliński is largely correct in asserting that without the German occupation, the Jewish representation on the city council would have been even smaller.[9] A thorough examination of the electoral regulations shows that the division of the electorate into curiae was indeed intended to prevent the number of Jews on the city council corresponding to their percentage of the city's population.[10] Although the architects of these electoral regulations sought to prevent the appropriate representation of Jews, they did not deny Jews the franchise: they merely sought ways to curtail their representation. This debate reveals the beginnings of a dialectical process: it allowed representation of the Jews as part of the body of inhabitants, as 'one of us', but their potential political weight was reduced because they were perceived as 'one of them'.[11]

After the announcement of the election regulations, the main political groups prepared for the elections. Although the curiae system was based on socio-economic criteria, Warsaw's population (especially the non-proletarian part) was also divided politically according to ethno-national criteria between Poles and Jews. The Poles were organized in two committees. One, the Central Electoral Committee, was linked with the Endecja. The anti-Jewish attitudes of its leaders, their harsh rhetoric, and their general political orientation are well known, so no description of them is required here.[12] The other committee, the Central Democratic Electoral Committee, consisted of an alliance of conservatives, populists, and progressives and declared that it did not distinguish Catholic Poles from non-Catholic Poles. This was sufficient for Warsaw's Jewish integrationist elite to declare its support for them.[13] However, this committee also included groups which held antisemitic opinions, such as Zjednoczenie, an organization of small retailers and manufacturers, which wished to expel the Jews from their position in Warsaw's economy and society.[14] Moreover, attacks on potential Jewish candidates of the integrationist camp made their incorporation into this committee more difficult.[15] The deep and intense ethnicization of the political leadership prevented any possibility of establishing an alternative committee, uniting Jews and non-Jews in a single electoral list and overcoming the ethnoreligious divide.[16] Most Jewish political groups stressed the need for significant and trustworthy representation on the future council. To that end, after much discussion and negotiation, the leading Orthodox leaders (who were later to establish the Orthodox political group the Agudat Yisrael), together with the main Zionists and the moderate assimilationists, established the United Jewish Electoral Committee.[17] According to their platform, 'the Jews strive for the equal rights that they undoubtedly deserve'.[18] The committee, which included the Zionist organization, did not demand autonomy but inclusion as equals, not as a result of a paternalistic discourse of 'tolerance, since this expresses superiority'.[19]

Simultaneously, a comprehensive debate emerged within Polish political circles on the political significance of these elections. The non-proletarian parties saw the Warsaw city council as a smaller version of the future state parliament for three reasons: the symbolic place of Warsaw in Polish patriotic discourse, the size of the city's population, and the fact that this was the first elected council while others were not envisaged in the near future.[20] Beyond the council's regular municipal functions, they wished to raise the concerns of the Polish national movement, particularly Poland's independence. The feeling was growing in political circles that competition in the municipal elections should be avoided; instead, all groups that wished to be represented on the council should divide the places amongst themselves without consulting the electorate. In this way the United Electoral Committee of All-Polish Parties was established. It proposed that no elections be held in four of the six curiae; instead, the seats should be divided according to a compromise among all the parties which made up the committee.[21] The 'activist' circles, who favoured working with the German occupying authorities, saw this as a means to show the Germans that the population was united in its main demand: Poland's freedom from the yoke of occupation.[22]

The electoral law allowed Jewish residents of Warsaw to vote, so the Polish political parties had to negotiate with the Jewish representatives to persuade them to accept the Polish consensus. Without their co-operation, the elections would have to be conducted according to the electoral regulations established by the German occupiers.[23] In the course of these negotiations the Polish political leadership in Warsaw informed the Jewish representatives that, since the city council represented 'Polish' interests, the number of Jewish representatives on the electoral list could not reflect the true proportion of Jews in the city (about 40 per cent at that time[24]) but rather their proportion of the country's total population (about 14 per cent). It was agreed that in four of the six curiae fifteen Jewish representatives would be included on the list of sixty representatives: this would mean that the Jews would be represented by a proportion much lower than their percentage of the population.

The inclusion of Jewish representatives as 'one of us' in a common list, where Jews were obliged to compromise on their share of the seats on the council, was an acceptable arrangement for all non-Jewish political groups. The Endecja and its supporters anticipated that, without the concession, they would constitute a minority in the city council. With the concession, they hoped to prevent a repeat of their humiliation in the elections to the Fourth Duma in 1912, when they were defeated in Warsaw.[25] Liberal circles also hoped to win some of the seats the Jewish committee would have to forgo.

As for the Jews, most members of the Jewish committee accepted the compromise. Their reasons were manifold. Some accepted it because they believed that it represented an expression of solidarity between Poles and Jews which would improve relations between them without completely abandoning the notion of representation. Others claimed that such representation, though limited, would facilitate defence against discrimination and rising antisemitism.[26] Such attitudes resulted from a genuine identification with the national Polish struggle and the fear that a militant attitude would heighten ethnic tension, as had occurred in the elections to the Fourth Duma.[27] The compromise was even interpreted as recognition of the Jews as 'one of us', as legitimate political partners, entitled to representation and to defend their own interests as they understood them.[28] In the eyes of its Jewish supporters, such a compromise signalled that Jewish interests were being taken into consideration and that the need to halt anti-Jewish sentiments was being acknowledged.[29]

Newspaper articles supporting the compromise assigned no great importance to the reduced number of Jewish representatives given the anticipated benefit: the acknowledgement of the Jews as legitimate partners in local affairs. Furthermore, insisting on realizing their electoral potential might not produce the desired political fruits in due time. According to *Haynt* on 12 July 1916:

Well, let us assume that the Jews get twenty seats. On the council there will be ninety representatives and the Jews will still remain a minority. They will not be able to do anything independently. In the debate over one or two more seats, unification with the Poles would be prevented; and the Jews would join the council as opponents, as an enemy. Any proposition for the benefit of our interests would face the harshest opposition by the majority of the Polish representatives. That way, we would not be able to pass [any resolution]. Is it not better for the sake of our interests to give up on some seats but enter the city council as partners, as friends, in unity and the flag of peace, when one side wants to go towards the other in order to maintain peace also in the future?[30]

Whereas the dominant Polish political leadership considered inclusion as a control mechanism, the Jewish political leadership saw it as creating an opportunity to oppose discrimination and to improve their status. These two frames of inclusion operated simultaneously, constantly competing with each other. Despite their mutual exclusionary relationship they coexisted, leading to distorted political realities.

Not all Jews accepted this rationale. The Bund was very critical of the compromise: 'The slave cannot cast off his shackles', wrote the Bund's weekly, *Lebensfragen*.[31] Critics were also to be found among the Zionists.[32] They joined a group organized around Noyekh Prilutski that saw the compromise as excessive.[33] The core of this group was the Folkist Party, the exponents of an uncompromising autonomist programme. However, they did not seek to destroy the compromise or present their own lists in the curiae, thus forcing elections to be held there. They presented their candidates only in the sixth curia where it had been agreed elections were to be held and achieved a remarkable success, reflecting the Jewish electorate's approval of Prilutski's militant stance.[34]

The result was that of the ninety representatives of the Warsaw municipal council, nineteen (21 per cent) were Jewish. From the point of view of Warsaw Jews they had made a major concession. They had given up half of their representation rights in this key local political institution.[35] For its part, the non-proletarian Polish political leadership considered this percentage a significant concession on its part, since it exceeded the proportion of the Jewish population in Poland as a whole by 7 per cent. Naturally, there was a gain for both sides: the Polish leadership's demand for political independence in the name of the entire population was legitimized by the inclusion of the Jews, while the Jewish political leadership was legitimized as a genuine political partner. In contrast with the bitter memory of the elections to the Fourth Duma three years earlier, this was a hopeful development. This hope was strengthened by the chorus of voices from Warsaw calling for the recognition of the national rights of the Polish nation on Polish soil and the inclusion in this demand of the Jews as 'one of us'. However, in exchange for their inclusion as 'one of us', Jews were forced to accept limited representation since they were also 'one of them'.[36] In short, the Jewish leaders traded their right to fair representation for their right to any representation. This pattern, with its advantages and disadvantages, set a precedent for the future.

The German occupying authorities were satisfied with the deal.[37] Wolfgang von Kries, the head of the civil administration, reported to his superiors that the composition of the Warsaw city council conformed to his expectations. In addition, the result of the elections to the sixth curia were very satisfactory, since he had feared the number of representatives of 'socialist parties and radical [nationalist] Jews' would be higher. He reported with evident satisfaction that the majority of the elected members belonged to the Christian Democrats and the minority comprised 'Social Democrats' and 'Jewish National Radicals [Folkists]'.[38]

The result of the political give and take was the creation of a pattern: in return for inclusion, the Jews were forced to restrict their representation in local government to less than half of their proportion of the city's population, accepting a subaltern position that granted them access to benefits and rights contingent on their ability to conform to and accept Polish hegemony. More than merely belonging to a minority group, Jews were reinscribed as belonging to society as marginalized subjects within the framework of a dominant national discourse that defined their demand for equal inclusion and access to power as transgressive and justifiably subject to social stigma, disregard, and restraint.[39] In many other elections to city councils in Congress Poland during 1916 there were similar patterns.[40] This move was designed to maintain Polish hegemony within the cities, since the Jews in this context were clearly regarded as 'one of them', being against Polish national interests. The same dynamic was evident later on the national level. In the debates of November 1917 aimed at creating institutions of self-government which would make possible the re-establishment of the Polish state, the two main political camps in Congress Poland, 'activists' (who favoured co-operation with the occupying authorities) and 'passivists' (who opposed it), with their diverse parties and factions, agreed on what they considered 'reasonable' Jewish representation on the Council of State: a maximum of five Jewish representatives out of a total of 100 members (much less than their percentage of the total population). They even expressed the view that these Jewish representatives should preferably be affiliated with the integrationist camp.[41] Thus, the electoral law, under the guise of democracy and equality, discriminated against Jewish representation both quantitatively (by limiting the number of representatives) and qualitatively (by disapproving of representatives with a Jewish national consciousness). This consensus naturally triggered much discontent in the Jewish street, as reflected in the contemporary Jewish press, especially in the popular Yiddish press.[42]

The Jewish press demanded proportional (in contrast to majoritarian), nationwide elections, encompassing the whole territory rather than electoral districts. Only an electoral system of this sort, it claimed, would guarantee the fair representation of the Jews dispersed throughout the whole country. Division of the country into electoral districts would result in Jewish lists not reaching the minimum threshold and reduce the number of Jewish representatives.[43]

The electoral law was agreed by the Polish authorities in co-operation with the occupying authorities and adopted on 4 February 1918.[44] According to it, half the council's 110 representatives were to be appointed and half elected.[45] Thus, fifty-five representatives would be elected indirectly by local or regional councils from their own members. The Warsaw city council selected six of its own members as deputies to the Council of State, Łódź selected three city councillors, and the remainder came from the other city and district councils.[46] The extremely complex electoral system was hardly democratic even by the standards of the time. In practice, only Jewish members of the Warsaw or Łódź councils could be elected to the Council of State[47] and then only with great difficulty, as Jewish representation was far below their proportion of the cities' populations. Thus, the complexity of the election process was yet another obstacle to the fair representation of Jews at the national level. The architects of the election law assumed that the number of representatives with autonomist demands would be negligible.

No wonder then that in the wake of this profoundly undemocratic law, dissatisfaction developed not only among Jews but also among Polish democratic and progressive factions.[48] As a consequence the socialists and some members of the passivist faction with democratic tendencies boycotted the elections.[49]

The result was partially expected and partially unexpected. While Jews sat on the

Council of State of the Kingdom of Poland established in 1918—the first legislative institution created in the newly emerging Poland—they held only eight of the 110 seats,[50] half of their proportion of the whole population. Of those eight, three were elected and five appointed.

The five appointees were selected from the assimilationists and the Orthodox, Jewish political groups acceptable to the mainline Polish parties.[51] But their number, five out of fifty-five, did not reflect the Jewish proportion of the population, which required seven or eight representatives. Among their number were Józef Natanson (1855–1929), a banker, scion of the prominent Natanson family, and Bolesław Eiger (1868–1929), also a wealthy member of the radical assimilated elite. Three more were members of the Orthodox faction: Joel Wegmeister (1837–1919), an important figure in the Agudah party, was appointed by the German authorities; Moyshe Pfeffer (1855–1919), an Orthodox leader from Kielce, was appointed by the Austrian authorities; and Rabbi Avraham Perlmutter (1843–1930) was appointed *ex officio* as the senior member of the Warsaw rabbinate. He was highly appreciated by the Polish nationalists because of his firm support for Polish independence and his opposition to any questioning of the political hegemony of Polish ethno-nationalism.[52]

The elected members were Adolf Weissblat (*c*.1855–1942?), a moderate assimilationist from Warsaw; Jerzy (Uriah) Rosenblatt (1872–1938), a Zionist, elected by the Jewish members of the Łódź city council;[53] and Noyekh Prilutski, leader of the strongly autonomist Folkist Party. While no one was surprised by the election of the first two, Prilutski's election was a shock, to say the least. It was possible only on account of realignments following the electoral boycott of the Warsaw city council by democratic parties.[54] The Polish political leadership in Warsaw reported the results to Berlin, stating that 'elections to the Council of State were held with anticipated results, except for the surprising election of a nationalist Jew [*ein nationalistischer Jude*] in Warsaw'.[55] Presumably, the Polish authorities had never intended a fair representation of nationalist Jews and sought ways to limit it. The election of Rosenblatt, a Zionist from Łódź, was not unexpected and was anticipated in light of the composition of the Łódź city council.[56]

Again, as in Warsaw, the Jews won the right of representation as 'one of us' in exchange for limitations on the number of representatives and their political orientation. Theoretically, as members of the council, they had an equal voice with all other members; they had, however, to compromise on deciding its agenda. For instance, to present a bill or to submit parliamentary questions or motions the signature of at least ten council members was required: the Jews numbered eight and were politically fragmented.[57] They were also marginalized within the various committees: only four of the ninety-two members in the nine committees were Jewish, none with an autonomist agenda.[58] Their marginality was especially evident in the general committee of the Council of State. Among its twenty members there was only one Jew: Bolesław Eiger.[59] This was the committee that nominated the ninety-two members of the nine other committees. In the first list suggested by the general committee, only one Jew was proposed: Adolf Weissblat. On the one hand, he was marginalized in the

committee with its twenty-two members;[60] on the other, this was an important committee whose task was to formulate electoral law. Noyekh Prilutski, using his legal
knowledge, protested against this exclusionary practice, but his right to present his
protest was denied. A vital concern, stated again and again, especially by Prilutski,
Rosenblatt, and others in the Jewish press, was that the universalist discourse of equal
rights that disregarded ethno-national differences was being exploited to make possible the exclusion of the Jewish minority.[61]

As a result of the protests, an additional list was presented a week later which
included a few more Jews: Bolesław Eiger was chosen for the treasury and economics
committee,[62] Joel Wegmeister for the education committee, and Józef Natanson for
the budget committee.[63] This development, although on a small scale, points to the
dialectic between inclusion as 'one of us' and exclusion as 'one of them'. The very
limited representation of Jews did enable them to present their demands insistently
and with some success. However, the dual dynamic was still present: the Jews were
discriminated against since the proportion of Jewish members on the committees
was half their proportion on the Council of State, where they were already under-
represented. They were further subject to discrimination, since the appointed members were mainly from the assimilationist camp, one was a representative of the
Orthodox camp, and the nationalist camp was not represented at all.[64] These dynamics reinscribed Jews' potential citizenship within dominant ethnic and cultural
norms. Those who fell outside the boundaries of the ideal dominant image of the
citizen of Poland were regarded as outcast, 'Other', subject to restraint and even exclusion.[65] Jews were condemned to a subaltern position and politically marginalized.
The committees were the primary arenas in which political agendas were promoted
and implemented, and where laws, regulations, queries, and interpellations were
discussed in detail.[66] Although as members of city councils and later of legislative
bodies the Jewish representatives could—and did—attack the discriminatory policies these institutions adopted, their limited representation meant that they were
reduced to verbal protests. Frequently, the only response they received was a dis-
paraging dismissal.[67]

In presenting their views in the council, Jewish delegates had the same rights as
others. However, real possibilities for action on their part were minimal. Sometimes
Jewish representatives protesting against discriminatory policies were suspended
from council sessions on procedural grounds.[68] Their proposals were blocked on
technical grounds;[69] queries were never answered or were buried in the committees.[70]
This created a situation in which Jews were included in the legislative bodies, as
being entitled to representation as citizens, but were excluded from effective political action and from executive functions according to the ethno-national logic that
divided society into ethnic groups, with a clear hierarchy of those with the legitimate
power to decide on the common good and access to state resources.

In this way the Polish majority attempted to reconcile their particular ethno-
national demands with promises of universality, their demands for an ethnic hierarchy, which strengthened the relations of subordination and domination, with claims

for equality. The Jews were simultaneously incorporated into the political body (as formal citizens and as subjects of state power) and excluded from it as 'alien' to the community of belonging. Thus, the emerging Polish state placed the Jews in a 'grey area' between complete equality as 'one of us' and total discrimination as 'one of them'. During the years 1916 to 1918 the ostensibly liberal discourse of representation, rights, inclusion, equality, and citizenship was reconciled with policies of exclusion and discrimination through the logic described here. Rights and benefits were linked to ethnic belonging that was tied to notions of ethno-national identity and increasingly conflated with religious affiliation. Domination was reconciled with the rights usually associated with citizenship. Cultural identity, frequently conflated with religious belonging and the principle of descent and blood ties, became central to the constitution of inclusive citizenship. In this way this Polish project made possible the production and reproduction of the 'Other', first and foremost the omnipresent 'Jew'.

Implementing Being Simultaneously 'One of Them' and 'One of Us'

Municipal and national practice illustrates the tension between the contradictory logics of citizenship and ethno-nationalism. When included because of their citizenship, Jews were clearly entitled to financial support when they met the requirements. However, the ethno-national principle deprived them of equal access to resources. Thus, following an August 1916 resolution by the Russian authorities, municipal institutions refused to pay pensions to the wives of Jewish soldiers serving in the retreating Russian army who could not provide civil marriage documents. Ostensibly a legalistic approach, neutral regarding ethno-national differences, explained the refusal. However, its real motive was the hope that these women would follow their husbands. Such decisions further compounded Jewish alienation and social inferiority.

In most of Congress Poland, city councils subsidized soup kitchens for the needy. According to the principle of inclusivity, Jews were entitled to use them. However, the help available for Jews was less than that available for Christians. This policy was based on data collected in a way that was ostensibly neutral regarding ethno-national differences. However, when the Jewish representatives proved that an unbiased examination of the data demonstrated the pauperization of the Jewish population during the war and a dramatic rise in Jewish child mortality, the policy did not change. Similarly, members of the Jewish community paid a special fee for admission to a general hospital—to whose upkeep they already contributed via the tax paid by all the city's residents. This was justified on the grounds that a tsarist regulation imposed a financial responsibility for public services on the Jewish community. The legislative bodies refused to change this rule even after the March revolution abolished all discriminatory laws. That created the absurd situation that tsarist discriminatory legislation continued to remain in force even in independent Poland, creating one more layer of disadvantage.

Increasingly Warsaw city authorities denied Jewish street traders permits to trade on upper-class 'Catholic streets' in order to cleanse 'Christian districts' of Jews. However, the paternalistic justification argued that this prohibition was to limit excessive competition. Permits, however, were given readily for the streets in the 'Jewish' north-western district.

Jews were discriminated against in seeking jobs in the public service. After vociferous protests in the Warsaw city council at the beginning of 1917 the number of Jews employed in the public sector rose, but only to around 5 per cent. The justification reflected ostensibly liberal attitudes: a six-day week was in operation—Jews who wanted to keep the sabbath thus risked dismissal or a lower salary. Municipal clerkships were only open to those fluent in Polish. Here too the justification was phrased in liberal terms, although many of the people such clerks dealt with did not have a good command of Polish.

In addition to unequal financial support, access to education and culture was also restricted. When compulsory education was introduced, Catholic children were accepted without restriction, but a quota was placed on the Jewish community: in Warsaw 101 schools were open to Jews or in Jewish neighbourhoods. They made up of only 11 per cent of the 881 in the town, far fewer than the Jewish proportion of 40 per cent of the town's inhabitants. The Jewish schools not only constituted a small percentage of the total but were also more crowded. At the same time the government refused to subsidize the modern Jewish educational system which had developed dramatically under the German occupation. As Noyekh Prilutski pointed out, from their early childhood Jews were thus relegated to a secondary place in the social hierarchy. Similarly, theatres paid a tax of 15 per cent. Polish theatres were entitled to a deduction of 8 per cent and subsequently to a subsidy of 7 per cent. Yiddish theatres received no deduction or subsidy.

When in October 1916 Jews built *sukkot* on their balconies in the better-off neighbourhoods of Warsaw, police broke into their homes, fined and even arrested some of them, and destroyed the *sukkot* on the grounds that no construction fee had been paid for them. Similarly, Jews in hasidic dress were denied entry to Łazienki Park because their clothing did not conform to European standards.

In all of these cases—and many others—Jews were discriminated against collectively under the mask of the principles of equality, meritocracy, and effective government, ostensibly without reference to their ethno-national affiliation. In fact, the relationship between the state and its population was highly differentiated, with different categories of citizenship for the two different ethno-national groups. On the one hand, the principle of citizenship included the Jews, granting them—at least formally—a degree of representation and participation in the civic community. On the other, the assignment of socio-cultural and economic privileges gave Christians the upper hand. They had rights beyond those accorded to Jews, and they had greater opportunities to participate in society and governance. This institutionalized the Jews as 'with us' but not 'of us', and intensified the ethnification processes that resulted in the increasing exclusion of the omnipresent 'Other'. The logic of citizenship made possible the inclusion of Jews in the legislature as legitimate representatives, while the logic of ethno-national state building excluded them simultaneously from influencing policy as legitimate partners. This dual process was accompanied by a universalistic rhetoric of tolerance and equality that merely camouflaged the ethno-national logic which led to an ethno-national hierarchy and institutionalized a system that promoted a quasi-ontological division of humanity into clear-cut ethnic groups.

Transforming 'One of Them' into 'One of Us'

The elected institutions constituted spaces for manoeuvre granted to the Jewish political leadership by the new state, and Jewish representatives made use of them as best they could. The inclusive logic of citizenship provided Jewish representatives with a forum to expose the inequality of the system being created. Often, representatives of the Polish Socialist Party-Left and the Social Democracy of the Kingdom of Poland and Lithuania supported them in their demands for the removal of discriminatory rules and policies. Sometimes liberals also joined them. As Robert Blobaum pointed out, in Warsaw, Jewish representatives supported by liberals sometimes succeeded in overturning discriminatory measures. For example, in March 1917 the Warsaw city council voted to restore municipal assistance to the Jewish women whose husbands were serving in the Russian army.[71] Efforts to pass legislation banning all commerce in Warsaw on Sundays were defeated.[72] After long and bitter debate, Warsaw city council finally voted to remove the ban on Jews in gaberdines entering Łazienki Park.[73]

However, declarative inclusive decisions were not always implemented. The restrictions on Jewish access to Łazienki were maintained in practice on the grounds that the gaberdines destroyed the flowers.[74] The proportion of Jews in the public sector did not increase. Public schooling for Jewish children did not improve. Jewish cultural institutions did not receive the same state support as Polish ones.

With the rise of exclusionary politics, many of those who, at the beginning of the war, supported autonomism but had also advocated a conciliatory policy moved towards unconditional demands for separate rights and institutionalized tools to defend equality. Thus on the eve of the Warsaw city council elections, the leader of the Mizrachi party in Poland, Heschel Farbstein, firmly supported a compromise with the Polish national movement as had been advocated by the United Jewish Electoral Committee. By late October 1916, however, at a full session of the Warsaw city council, his disillusionment with this approach was clearly evident:

We came here full of hope, full of good will [and ready] for hard work, shoulder to shoulder, for the good of the state capital and the state. [Now] after three months, we are filled with despair. Until now, we were certain that it was Russian politics which was responsible for the poor relations between Jews and Poles. We believed that once the Polish people took over the reins of power, the relationship would change. And indeed it has changed, but unfortunately, not for the better.[75]

The leaders of the Jewish liberal camp feared that exclusionary politics would bring about the collapse of the integrationist project and the rise of Jewish nationalism as a response to rising Polish ethno-nationalism. Samuel Goldflam, a leading figure in the integrationist camp, emphasized in a speech at Warsaw city council that 'the best way to combat Zionism is complete equality'.[76] Edward Natanson, another well-known integrationist, argued in the same session that there was a connection between Jewish autonomism and the absence of equal rights. In his view discrimination 'would open the gates for a nationalist struggle that would further deepen the antagonisms in the country'.[77]

They were right in their appreciation of this socio-political reality and were aware of the public mood. For instance, inconspicuously, behind the scenes, in November 1916 the leaders of the Zionist and Folkists met in Warsaw to co-ordinate their tactics and goals. On the one hand, this co-ordination reveals a split in the United Jewish Electoral Committee and its partial radicalization. However, on the other, behind closed doors, there were still those who favoured compromise. In the discussion Shloyme Zaidman, a Zionist representative on the Warsaw city council, claimed: 'First and foremost there is a need to conduct negotiations with the Poles, that is, with certain Polish parties. Jews are confronting a great danger and naturally the negotiations must take the form of demands, but these demands must be realistic'.[78]

His speech thus reflected a predisposition to compromise in search of concrete and practical results which was opposed to the uncompromising stance of the Folkists. The more intransigent tone in which he expressed his views was a result of frustration at the inability to make real gains. More and more Jewish councillors and deputies were forced into protest, as their aspirations were confronted by reality, rather than concentrating on working on mundane affairs in committees. This served as a catalyst for intensified ethno-national confrontation.

As fully fledged members of a city council or the legislature, Jews could protest against discriminatory policies and did so vehemently. But given the failure to establish the equality they demanded, Jewish delegates were pushed into the only option open to them—increasingly vociferous, provocative, and harsh speeches.[79] They tried to show that inclusion in the common good was framed differently in accordance with the ethnic distribution of power in society and was used by Polish political groups to support the dominant power structure which could only exacerbate 'the Jewish question'.[80] They received in exchange insults and interruptions.[81] Jewish representatives could certainly speak but they were not listened to.

While internal Jewish divisions were used by their non-Jewish opponents to attack the concept of autonomism, its supporters claimed (without real justification) that there existed a unified, stabilized Jewish identity. They made use of 'strategic essentialism'[82] to mobilize the Jewish masses on the basis of a shared identity to advance an anti-hierarchical position. They called for Jewish equality in a large range of areas, linking this claim for equality with the demand for recognition of Jewish group identity. The use of this discursive strategy, which objected to the creation of a civic hierarchy based on essentialized ethnic criteria, is explicit in their demands.

The observation of Israel Lichtenstein, the Bund representative on the Łódź city council, is apposite: 'Poland will be fortunate only when all inhabitants of this land will be true citizens. General prosperity can be built on complete equality for all citizens, regardless of nationality and language.'[83]

In spite of the disparate character of the Jewish community, the Jewish leadership increasingly demanded the creation of a country-wide Jewish representative body recognized by the state.[84] Jewish nationalists, the Orthodox, and the liberals were united in making this claim, arguing that such a body would defend the equal status of the Jews.[85] Jewish leaders supporting the autonomist agenda introduced legislative proposals for the recognition of the Jewish community board as a national institution, or sought to create regulations for the community board which would give to an institution defined in religious terms an autonomous national character.[86] They also began to demand the recognition of Jewish marriage law in response to the denial of pensions by the authorities in the absence of civil documentation for a marriage.[87] In response to calls for Jewish merchants to observe Sunday as a day of rest, they now demanded the formal recognition of the Jewish sabbath as a day of rest among Jews.[88]

As the distribution of resources for schools between Jews and non-Jews became increasingly unequal, demands grew for state recognition of the developing Jewish schools and for granting them municipal allocations.[89] Jerzy Rosenblatt in Łódź and Noyekh Prilutski in Warsaw demanded autonomy in the educational field and the creation of autonomous municipal educational committees for national minorities. Each population group, they argued, was entitled to schools which used its mother tongue.[90] In Łódź, Israel Lichtenstein demanded the recognition of Yiddish and the institutionalization of Yiddish schools in order to achieve complete equality for Jews. The failure to grant such recognition was a limitation of equal rights: 'Above all it is about being a citizen.' In order to enjoy fundamental rights 'no form of behaviour, no specific demand should be required from any citizen.'[91] He stressed the connection between equal citizenship and the recognition of minority languages in the public sphere, including the city council, the school system and the official channels of communication with the inhabitants of the country.[92] For making this connection, he was strongly attacked.[93]

The description of Yiddish theatre as 'lowbrow' provoked an increasing demand for the recognition of the central role of Yiddish culture in Jewish life and that it be granted support from the state such as that enjoyed by Polish culture. Most Jewish political parties and social movements began to stress the need for a structural transformation in the system of allocation if equality were to be achieved.[94] In this way, they accentuated the interdependence of the politics of distribution and ethno-national identity.

The persistence of discrimination and the delegitimization of demands for equal inclusion radicalized the autonomist discourse. Slowly in 1917 and 1918 Zionists adopted a militant rhetoric similar to that of the Folkists.[95] As exclusionist politics became more established, the willingness of Jewish political leaders, intellectuals, and the general electorate to use the language of autonomy or collective rights increased. In closed circles, there were explicit expressions of radicalization. Thus, in February 1918 the Zionist leader Joshua Gottlieb affirmed in a closed party meeting in Warsaw that 'we demand national rights. But if it appears that the Polish side is willing to compromise, we can forgo some of our demands.'[96] Rather than foster compromise and negotiation, however, the increasing effort to exclude the Jews on the basis of liberal rhetoric had precisely the opposite effect. The results of the elections to city councils in the second part of 1917 and in 1918 demonstrated increasing support for those who claimed that there could be no equality between Poles and Jews as long as the state saw citizenship in ethno-national Polish terms.[97]

In late 1918 the Zionist movement was taken over by a more militant leader, Isaac Grünbaum, returning from revolutionary Petrograd, and began to rival Prilutski's Folkist Party. At the end of the year even Joshua Gottlieb had abandoned a policy of conciliation and had joined those demanding uncompromising national and cultural autonomy.[98]

The denial of state resources, symbolic and real, in the spheres of culture and jobs, language and public services was expressed in liberal and universalistic principles which led autonomists to claim that this rhetoric was merely a cloak for Polish ethno-nationalism. They thus asserted that it should be countered by a similar model—that of the ethno-nationalist Jew. Confronted by an essentialist conception of 'Polishness' and 'Poles', essentialist formulations of Jewish identity as a means of resisting ethno-national domination and oppression gradually became more and more accepted in Jewish circles.

Autonomist leaders and intellectuals claimed that there was an inherent inter-dependence between the equal allocation of resources and the recognition of ethno-national differences.[99] In this way, they sought to sever the issue of equal citizenship from ethno-national affiliation and to ensure that the Polish state's claim to serve all Polish citizens equally could only be implemented in practice by adopting the ethno-national principle as the basis of what was a multi-national state. They held this to be the only effective way of ending the ethno-national hierarchy within the confines of the nation-state.

The statements of autonomist leaders reflected this logic. For instance, on several occasions Noyekh Prilutski stated: 'politically we are Poles, but from a national perspective, we are Jews'.[100] In the same vein, in June 1917 he declared during a session of the Provisional Council of State: 'In this Poland we demand that the Jewish population be recognized as a national minority group and granted full civil rights and national and personal autonomy. This is the only guarantee that we will achieve equal civil rights.'[101] Similarly in October 1917 the Zionist Jerzy Rosenblatt defined the situation in the Łódź city council:

The population of Poland is not homogeneous. Alongside the Polish are other nationalities, which constitute thirty per cent of all inhabitants . . . The Jewish nation wants to live in harmony with the Poles. *Politically* we are Polish; our internal life is *Jewish* . . . We demand national and cultural autonomy, that is to say, the right to self-determination in all internal matters . . . We seek not separatism but mutual understanding, working for the common good and prosperity.[102]

Only on the basis of such a platform could equality of rights and access to public resources be achieved together with the recognition of the sabbath as a day of rest and the acceptance of Yiddish and Hebrew and modern Jewish culture. With this, each minority group would be granted the possibility of full participation in all spheres of activity through a differentiated sense of belonging. This autonomist discourse was invoked to counter exclusionary hegemonic practices and, alongside its call for autonomy, was marked also by the desire for full citizenship and to be a legitimate part of the political structures.

From late 1916 to 1918 more and more Jewish political leaders, like Farbstein, chose to abandon accommodationist politics derived from liberal political paradigms and adopted an escalating, radicalizing, and confrontational attitude towards the policy of the emerging state. The appeal of autonomism to the Jewish masses was a response to the dominant ethno-national discourse within the Polish political elite and the contradictory policies of inclusion and exclusion. Autonomism therefore was neither a Jewish version of east European nationalism nor a chimeric attempt to recreate the former autonomy enjoyed by the Jewish community in Poland–Lithuania. Rather it was a critical act of interlocution in which east European nationalism and the imagined Jewish past were not the sources of a modernized version of Jewish autonomy but the language used in the new arena of contest created by the emergence of a Polish state organized on ethno-nationalist principles.

Conclusion

The interpretation of the demand for national and personal autonomy in the context of nationalism—a necessary and fruitful framework within which to understand the phenomenon—has led to a neglect of the civil aspects of the issue. In this chapter, I have tried to demonstrate that the issue of civil rights was central to understanding the growing popularity of autonomy amongst Polish Jews during the First World War and subsequently. The increasing support for autonomy within the Jewish community in the Polish state-in-formation should be viewed as an attempt to formulate an alternative model of citizenship in a situation in which ethno-nationalism was increasingly dominant. This explains both the many-sided character of the autonomous project and its ultimate failure.

The approach to citizenship adopted by the Polish leadership was based on the ethno-national principle that had crystallized in occupied Poland prior to Polish independence. This marginalized and excluded Jews as 'one of them'. The process of 'Othering' affirmed ethno-national borders and legitimized exclusionist practices and the biased allocation of resources based on an ethno-national hierarchy of belonging. At the same time, the logic of citizenship required accepting the subordinated Jews as 'one of us', granting them—at least formally—a degree of equality. This provided the Jewish leadership with a way to demand their rights and press for an alternative model of citizenship by exposing the inequalities of the emerging system. Between 1916 and 1918 parties which advocated different forms of autonomy—Bundists, Zionists, and Folkists—took over the leadership of the Jewish community. They highlighted the disparity between the ethno-national principle, which perpetuated their second-class status, and the principle of citizenship, which gave them the right to participate as equals. Appealing to the latter, they sought to undermine the former, demanding equality and rights for each group on the basis of its ethno-national identity in a way that reflected the adoption of the ethno-national paradigm. This new leadership used the logic of citizenship as a tool to undermine hierarchical ethno-nationalism as a constitutive principle of state-building, proposing instead an alternative ethno-national principle, that of the multi-national state which would grant equal access to state resources, symbolic or real, to all its citizens.

The autonomist discourse of ethno-national difference, which maintained existing state borders, was thus a means of overcoming exclusion. It was the growing impact of the double process of inclusion and exclusion that caused the growing popularity of autonomism during the First World War as a way to attain equal inclusion. The autonomists ascribed a positive and transformative value to the process of contesting domination and this attitude became a habit of mind among those who had been excluded or marginalized on the basis of their ethno-religious, cultural, or linguistic identity by the use of liberal discourse. The autonomist discourse was an attempt to change the language of the discussion and to substitute a process of ethno-national accommodation for the prevailing system of ethno-national hegemony. It opened up different, innovative, 'other' grounds for belonging, presenting an alternative to the concept of civic equality within the Polish state-building project that changed the very way the concept of this state and its institutionalization should be understood.

In this sense, those involved in the construction of Jewish citizenship in Poland during the First World War faced the same quandary as those attempting to establish a Polish state. On the one hand, they accepted the ethno-national paradigm as determining that the Jews in the Polish lands were members of a distinct ethno-national group. On the other, they made use of the logic of the principle of citizenship which meant that Jews were citizens of the state and had the same rights as other citizens. They accepted nationality as the defining criterion, but their political goal was to replace the principle of ethno-nationalism as the basis of an ethno-hierarchical state with ethno-nationalism as the basis for full and complete equality institutionalized through organs of personal or cultural national autonomy. The partial civil equality Jews gained during the First World War served as a tool with which to fight against the partial civil discrimination under which they suffered in the Polish state-in-formation and was a means of transforming them from outsiders to insiders.

The goal of the leaders of the autonomist faction was the recognition of the Jews as a minority group equal to others in the Polish state, in contradistinction to a situation in which the ethno-national ethos became the constitutive principle of Polish state-building. This inevitably led to a conflict over who was 'one of us' at the state level. Paradoxically, the Jewish struggle to become recognized as 'one of us' reinforced their status as 'one of them'. The fight for inclusion thus tragically led to increased exclusion.

Notes

1 'Di groyse yidishe zitsung in shtot rat', *Der moment*, 5 Nov. 1916, p. 2; see also C. Gilinski-Meller, 'Mifleget hafolkisitim (folks-partei) bepolin, 1915–1939', Ph.D. thesis (Bar-Ilan University, 2004), 105.

2 M. Foucault, 'Governmentality', *Ideology and Consciousness*, 6 (1979), 5–21; repr. in G. Burchell, C. Gordon, and P. Miller (eds), *The Foucault Effect: Studies in Governmentality* (Chicago, 1991), 87–104; id., 'Technologies of the Self', in L. H. Martin, H. Gutman, and P. H. Hutton (eds.), *Technologies of the Self: A Seminar with Michel Foucault* (Amherst, Mass., 1988), 16–49: 19; C. Gordon, 'Governmental Rationality: An Introduction', in Burchell, Gordon, and Miller (eds), *The Foucault Effect*, 1–52; see also B. Curtis, 'The Impossible Discovery', *Canadian Journal of Sociology*, 27 (2002), 505–33.

3 S. D. Corrsin, 'The Jews, the Left, and the State Duma Elections in Warsaw in 1912: Selected Sources', *Polin*, 9 (1996), 45–54: 52–3.

4 Ibid. 53–4.

5 Kucharzewski supported a non-violent 'economic crusade' against Jews using 'honest and cultural means'. This exclusionary position aroused Jewish opposition to his candidacy (K. Zieliński, 'Impact of the Elections to the Russian State Duma in 1912 on the Polish–Jewish Relations in the Kingdom of Poland', *Annales Universitatis Mariae Curie-Skłodowska*, Sectio K: *Politologia*, 20 (2013), 171–84).

6 On the growing antisemitism of this period, see G. Krzywiec, 'The Enemy Within: The Anti-Jewish Boycott and Polish Right-Wing Politics in the Early Twentieth Century', in D. Feldman (ed.), *Boycotts Past and Present* (London, 2019), 53–71. Important earlier studies include S. D. Corrsin, 'Polish–Jewish Relations before the First World War: The Case of the State Duma Elections in Warsaw', *Gal-ed*, 11 (1989), 31–54; id. 'The Jews, the Left, and the State Duma Elections in Warsaw; T. R. Weeks, 'Nationality and Municipality: Reforming City Government in the Kingdom of Poland, 1904–1915', *Russian History*, 21 (1994), 23–47; R. Blobaum, 'The Politics of Antisemitism in Fin-de-Siècle Warsaw', *Journal of Modern History*, 73 (2001), 275–306.

7 K. Zieliński, *Stosunki polsko-żydowskie na ziemiach Królestwa Polskiego w czasie pierwszej wojny światowej* (Lublin, 2005), 154–68.

8 K. Zieliński, 'Stosunki polsko-żydowskie w Królestwie Polskim w czasie I wojny światowej', *Kwartalnik Historii Żydów*, 206 (2003), 164–94: 169–71; id., *Stosunki polsko-żydowskie na ziemiach Królestwa Polskiego*, 265–6.

9 Zieliński, *Stosunki polsko-żydowskie na ziemiach Królestwa Polskiego*, 290.

10 Ibid. 261.

11 Wolfgang von Kries, president of the civil administration in the German-occupied area, described the duality behind the regulation: 'In the electoral regulations, influence to all the political and economic forces of the city was promised . . . Simultaneously just representation of the Jewish population was given . . . although without harming the Polish character of the representatives of the capital city' (Archiwum Główne Akt Dawnych,

Warsaw (hereafter AGAD), Szef administracji przy generalnym gubernatorze warszaw-skim, 6: 'Vierteljahresbericht der Zivilverwaltung für Russisch-Polen für die Zeit vom 1. April 1916 bis zum 30. Juni 1916'). Without discussing the real justice or injustice of such a step, the phrase 'just representation' signified the preservation of the 'Polish character' of the city by reducing the Jewish representation on the elected forum. A few months later, von Kries reported to his superiors that 'the most problematic issue in connection with the election regulations was the Jewish question, since the Jews constitute an absolute majority in the small and medium-sized towns'. He added: 'A Jewish majority on the muni-cipal councils is undesirable' (AGAD, Szef administracji przy generalnym gubernatorze warszawskim, 9: 'Halbjahresbericht der Zivilverwaltung für Russisch-Polen für die Zeit vom 1. Oktober 1916 bis zum 31. März 1917').

12   For instance, it declared in the middle of June that 'the municipal council should be Polish not only according to its name or language but first of all in its spirit, its aspirations, its natural national instinct' ('Varsha: inyenei beḥirot', *Hatsefirah*, 14 June 1916, p. 3). On the pamphlets and articles published by the Endecja, see 'Varsha: inyenei beḥirot', *Hatsefirah*, 18 June 1916, p. 3; 'Varsha: inyenei beḥirot', *Hatsefirah*, 20 June 1916, p. 3; 'Varsha: inyenei beḥirot', *Hatsefirah*, 26 June 1916, p. 3.

13   A.N.F [A. N. Frenk], 'Hava'ad hayehudi', *Hatsefirah*, 18 June 1916, pp. 1–2; see the commit-tee's declaration: 'Varsha: inyenei beḥirot', *Hatsefirah*, 15 June 1916, p. 3.

14   A.N.F [A. N. Frenk], 'Habeḥirot el mo'etset ha'ir', *Hatsefirah*, 11 June 1916, p. 1.

15   'Bay di asimilatorn', *Varshaver togblat*, 22 June 1916, p. 3; see also F. Golczewski, *Polnisch-jüdische Beziehungen 1881–1922: Eine Studie zur Geschichte des Antisemitismus in Osteuropa* (Wiesbaden, 1981), 158–60.

16   'Bay di asimilatorn'.

17   Gilinski-Meller, 'Mifleget hafolkistim', 76–8; K. Weiser, *Jewish People, Yiddish Nation: Noah Prylucki and the Folkists in Poland* (Toronto, 2011), 141; Zieliński, *Stosunki polsko-żydowskie na ziemiach Królestwa Polskiego*, 267.

18   'Varsha: inyenei beḥirot', *Hatsefirah*, 20 June 1916.

19   'Varsha, inyenei habeḥirot kol kore me'et hava'ad hame'uḥad hayehudi', *Hatsefirah*, 26 June 1916, p. 3; see also Central Zionist Archive, Jerusalem (hereafter CZA), A15/VIII/9c: 'Zu den städtischen Wahlen in Warschau' [June 1916].

20   S. Kutrzeba, 'La Question polonaise pendant la guerre mondiale', in M. Handelsman (ed.), *La Pologne: Sa vie économique et sociale pendant la guerre* (Paris, 1933), 3–132: 85–6; M. Han-delsman, 'Les Efforts de la Pologne pour la reconstruction d'un état indépendant', in id. (ed.), *La Pologne*, 133–274: 150–1; P. Roth, *Die politische Entwicklung in Kongreßpolen während der deutschen Okkupation* (Leipzig, 1919), 35–8.

21   The committee was composed of the four curiae of the wealthier population. It was agreed that in two curiae the elections would take place: in the curia of the intelligentsia, where the elections were especially complicated, and in the general curia, that of all the remaining inhabitants of the city with the right to vote. The latter was the largest of the curiae. The number of votes a representative needed to be elected differed in each curia: in the first curia it was only 350 votes, in the second less than 100, in the fourth around 1,000, and in the sixth more than 2,200. See 'Vifl shtimen darf a ratman', *Varshaver togblat*, 2 July 1916, p. 3; 'Ofitsiele protokol fun di valn', *Varshaver togblat*, 17 July 1916, p. 3.

22   J. Pajewski, *Odbudowa państwa polskiego 1914–1918* (Warsaw, 1985), 107.

23   Roth, *Die politische Entwicklung in Kongreßpolen während der deutschen Okkupation*, 36; C. Kozłowski, *Działalność polityczna Koła Międzypartyjnego w latach 1915–1918* (Warsaw, 1967), 99–102; 'Varsha: inyenei beḥirot', *Hatsefirah*, 28 June 1916, p. 3.

24 According to the census of January 1917, Jews made up 41 per cent of the city's population (B. M. Bulska, 'Statystyczny obraz miasta stołecznego Warszawy w początkach Niepodległości', in M. M. Drozdowski and H. Szwankowska (eds.), *Warszawa w pierwszych latach Niepodległości* (Warsaw, 1998), 173–92: 183).

25 See 'Moskva vegn shtot rat', *Varshaver togblat*, 14 Aug. 1916, p. 3.

26 'Be'itonut hapolanim, hitaḥdut haboḥarim', *Hatsefirah*, 3 July 1916, p. 1.

27 M. Sobczak, *Stosunek Narodowej Demokracji do kwestii żydowskiej w latach 1914–1919* (Wrocław, 2008), 79.

28 'El yehudei varsha!', *Hatsefirah*, 4 July 1916, p. 1.

29 A.N.F [A. N. Frenk], 'Hamafridim', *Hatsefirah*, 4 July 1916, pp. 1–2; 'Di poylishe prese vegn der vahl kampanie', *Haynt*, 2 July 1916, p. 2.

30 'Vifl mandatn far yidn?', *Haynt*, 12 July 1916, p. 3. *Hatesfirah* reported high hopes of equal inclusion: 'Do we Jews have to reject a compromise, even if we were given only fifteen seats? Isn't the profit of the general union much greater than the loss of the seats?' (A.N.F [A. N. Frenk], 'Le'aḥar haḥatimah', *Hatsefirah*, 6 July 1916, p. 1).

31 'Der veler darf blaybn in der heym', *Lebensfragen*, 7 July 1916, pp. 2–4.

32 The famous Zionist writer Ben Avigdor opposed the compromise vehemently, and, along with other Zionists, he joined Prilutski (see Weiser, *Jewish People, Yiddish Nation*, 147; 'Bay di tsionistn', *Varshaver togblat*, 5 July 1916, p. 3; 'Khaveyrim tsionistn!', *Varshaver togblat*, 12 July 1916, p. 3).

33 On criticism of the compromise in the Jewish press, see Gilinski-Meller, 'Mifleget hafolk-istim', 78–9; Weiser, *Jewish People, Yiddish Nation*, 141–7. Critics were to be found among the Zionists too.

34 It was concluded that the agreement between the Jews and the Polish political organizations would be valid only as long as the Jews ran with only one list, the one included in the agreement. Should another Jewish list be submitted, and elections become necessary, the agreement with the Jews would be considered void (see 'El yehudei varsha!'). Since the sixth curia was not included in the agreement, the Jews were able to present additional lists there. Noyekh Prilutski and his circle, who expressed great objection to the compromise, formed a list that participated in the elections for the sixth curia.

35 Various assessments of the Jews' electoral power were made in the Jewish press, and with some logic. The *Varshaver togblat*, which opposed the agreement, reported evidence from the Polish press estimating that the Jews would return about thirty-seven delegates out of seventy-five (this calculation does not account for the third curia, which was closed to Jews). Hence, the compromise accepted by the Jews minimized the Jewish presence in the municipal council and the Jews' ability to defend their own specific interests (see C.Y.-V., 'Soides fun heider', *Varshaver togblat*, 14 July 1916, p. 2, which cites *Głos Narodu*). The estimate seems somewhat exaggerated. After all, the Jews constituted approximately 40 per cent of the entire population; thirty-seven seats was about 49 per cent of the seventy-five delegates. The *Varshaver togblat* itself estimated the potential of the Jews in the four curiae for which the agreement was reached as about twenty-seven seats (see C.Y.-V., 'A klorer ḥeshven', *Varshaver togblat*, 6 July 1916, p. 3). The Jewish population was apparently more fully registered on the electoral roll than the non-Jewish population, despite the authorities' wish to minimize the number of Jewish voters. Analysis of voters' numbers and nationality as submitted to the Yiddish daily *Haynt*, which supported the agreement and acted to minimize the proportion of Jewish voters so as to blur the compromise, indicates that the compromise was too big. According to *Haynt*, the Jews could have had twenty-five to twenty-nine delegates in the four curiae in question.

36 The need to include the Jews in municipal institutions arose in other cities of Congress Poland, as did Jews being acknowledged as deserving representation in return for limited representation (Zieliński, 'Stosunki polsko-żydowskie w Królestwie Polskim', 173–7; Sobczak, *Stosunek Narodowej Demokracji do kwestii żydowskiej*, 86–7). As Konrad Zieliński points out, the Jews won better representation in places where the elections were carried out without an electoral compromise (K. Zieliński, 'Żydzi kieleccy w wyborach do samorządu miejskiego w 1916 roku', in U. Oettingen (ed.), *Z dziejów Kielc w latach 1914–1918* (Kielce, 2004), 83–97: 91; id., 'Żydzi pod okupacją austro-węgierską w wyborach do samorządu miejskiego 1916 roku', *Kwartalnik Historyczny*, 109 (2002), 61–78: 74). This emphasizes the importance ascribed by Jewish political circles to the agreement reached with their Polish partners and testifies to the acceptance of the principle of the limitation of representation in return for recognition of the right to be represented.

37 'Halbjahresbericht der Zivilverwaltung für Russisch-Polen für die Zeit vom 1. Oktober 1916 bis zum 31. März 1917'.

38 J. C. Kauffman, 'Sovereignty and the Search for Order in German-Occupied Poland, 1915–1918', Ph.D. thesis (Stanford University, 2008), 96.

39 The term 'subaltern' is used by Antonio Gramsci to refer to those social groups subjected to the hegemony of the ruling classes (A. Gramsci, *Quaderni del carcere*, iii: *Quaderni 12–29 (1932–1935)* (Turin, 1975); Eng. trans.: 'Notes on Italian History', in *Selections from the Prison Notebooks*, ed. and trans. Q. Hoare and G. Nowell Smith (New York, 1971), 44–120). In using the term 'subaltern', I borrow from the insights of postcolonial theory and subaltern studies, which have highlighted the fact that certain voices have been excluded from the dominant narratives and telling of history. Subaltern studies regards hegemonic history as part of modernity's power/knowledge complex, which, in the context of colonialism, was deeply implicated in the 'general epistemic violence of imperialism' (G. C. Spivak, 'Three Women's Texts and a Critique of Imperialism', *Critical Inquiry*, 12 (1985), 243–51: 251; see also R. Guha, 'The Small Voice of History', *Subaltern Studies*, 9 (1997), 1–12; D. Chakrabarty, 'A Small History of Subaltern Studies', in id., (ed.), *Habitations of Modernity: Essays in the Wake of Subaltern Studies* (Chicago, 2002), 3–19: 3–4). In the context of law, subaltern studies challenges the assumptions about universality, neutrality, and objectivity on which legal concepts are based, exposing such concepts to be products of the ruptures produced in and through the colonial encounter (see e.g. D. Otto, 'Subalternity and International Law: The Problems of Global Community and the Incommensurability of Difference', *Social and Legal Studies*, 337 (1996), 337–64).

40 See e.g. Zieliński, *Stosunki polsko-żydowskie na ziemiach Królestwa Polskiego*, 258–77.

41 'Di frage vegn melukhe rat', *Haynt*, 22 Nov. 1917, p. 3.

42 N. Shvalbe, 'Di yidishe politik in poyln (tsu di entshteung fun der poylisher regirung)', *Haynt*, 7 Dec. 1917, p. 2; Y. Kabatski, 'Proportsyonale valn un natsyonale kuryes', *Dos folk*, 8 Mar. 1918, p. 6.

43 See e.g. Shvalbe, 'Di yidishe politik in poyln'; Kabatski, 'Proportsyonale valn un natsyonale kuryes'.

44 According to the daily press, the law was almost complete by December 1917. A few changes were made in the text in January and the first days of February (see 'Der melukhe rat', *Haynt*, 17 Dec. 1917, p. 3; 'A proyekt fun melukhe rat', *Haynt*, 16 Jan. 1918, p. 3; 'Der melukhe rat', *Haynt*, 27 Jan. 1918, p. 3; 'Der val gezets farn poylishn sejm', *Haynt*, 28 Jan. 1918, p. 3).

45 The fifty-five nominated representatives were divided into two categories: twelve were intellectual and spiritual personalities (six Catholic bishops, two evangelical representa-

tives, the chief rabbi of Warsaw, the rectors of the university and polytechnic, and the president of the Supreme Court); the remaining forty-three were to be nominated by the regents' council.

46 The General Government of Warsaw (the region occupied by the Germans) was divided into eight districts, each of which was to choose three delegates, which resulted in a total of twenty-four delegates. The General Government of Lublin (the region occupied by the Austrians) was divided into six districts, each of which was to choose three delegates, which resulted in a total of eighteen delegates (S. Filasiewicz, *La Question polonaise pendant la guerre mondiale: Recueil des actes diplomatiques, traités et documents concernant la Pologne* (Paris, 1920), 342–6).

47 See the estimates sent from Warsaw to Berlin, for instance, in the Central Zionist Archive in Jerusalem (CZA, Z3/172: 'J.C.', letter to the Zionist Bureau, Berlin, 26 Mar. 1918; see also 'Tsu di gmine valn', *Haynt*, 10 Apr. 1918, p. 3).

48 Zieliński, *Stosunki polsko-żydowskie na ziemiach Królestwa Polskiego*, 322.

49 H. Jabłoński, *Polityka Polskiej Partii Socjalistycznej w czasie wojny 1914–1918 r.* (Warsaw, 1958), 447–9; Kozłowski, *Działalność polityczna Koła Międzypartyjnego*, 225–7.

50 On the number of Jewish members of the Council of State, see I. Lewin, *The Political History of Polish Jewry, 1918–1919*, in *A History of Polish Jewry during the Revival of Poland* (New York, 1990), 1–220: 17–20.

51 Zieliński, *Stosunki polsko-żydowskie na ziemiach Królestwa Polskiego*, 322; F. M. Schuster, *Zwischen allen Fronten: Osteuropäische Juden während des Ersten Weltkrieges (1914–1918)* (Cologne, 2004), 408–9.

52 'Di forshteher fun folks partei in melukhe rat', *Dos folk*, 12 Apr. 1918, p. 1; 'Vifl yidn veln zayn in melukhe rat', *Der moment*, 1 Feb. 1918, p. 6; S. Hirszhorn, 'Dzieje Żydów w Królestwie Polskiem od 1864 do 1918 r.', in I. Schiper, A. Tartakower, and A. Hafftka (eds.), *Żydzi w Polsce Odrodzonej: Działalność społeczna, gospodarcza, oświatowa i kulturalna*, 2 vols. (Warsaw, 1932–3), i. 485–503: 502; see also Lewin, *The Political History of Polish Jewry*, 17–26.

53 A controversy arose among the Zionists over which of them should represent the party on the council. Warsaw's Zionists proposed Heschel Farbstein. In the end, he was chosen as Rosenblatt's deputy (see CZA, L6/108: 'Staatsratwahlen', [July 1918?]; CZA, Z3/163: J. Berger, letter to A. Hantke, 8 July 1918).

54 'Judische Chronik: Polen', *Neue Jüdische Monatshefte*, 25 July – 25 Aug. 1918, p. 525.

55 Politisches Archiv des Auswärtiges Amtes, Berlin, Wk 20c, B 23: Aufzeichnung, 17 Apr. 1918.

56 On the circumstances that made the election of Rosenblatt possible and on the singularity of the Łódź case, see M. Silber, 'Ruling Practices and Multiple Cultures: Jews, Poles, and Germans in Łódź during WWI', *Jahrbuch des Simon-Dubnow-Instituts*, 5 (2006), 189–208.

57 'Der regulamen fun di melukhe rat un di yidn', *Haynt*, 24 June 1918, p. 3.

58 'Di ferte zitsung fun melukhe rat', *Haynt*, 5 July 1918. p. 6; 'Di finfte zitsung fun melukhe rat', *Haynt*, 10 July 1918, p. 3.

59 'Di efenung fun melukhe rat', *Haynt*, 23 June 1918, p. 6.

60 'Di ferte zitsung fun melukhe rat'; 'Di finfte zitsung fun melukhe rat'; 'Polin', *Hatsefirah*, 11 July 1918, pp. 10–11; Kozłowski, *Działalność polityczna Koła Międzypartyjnego*, 237.

61 'Di ferte zitsung fun melukhe rat'.

62 Ibid.; 'Di finfte zitsung fun melukhe rat'.

63 Ibid; see also Lewin, *The Political History of Polish Jewry*, 27.

64 'Di ferte zitsung fun melukhe rat'; 'Di finfte zitsung fun melukhe rat'; 'Polin'; Kozłowski, *Działalność polityczna Koła Międzypartyjnego*, 237.

65 The classic account of citizenship is T. H. Marshall's 'Citizenship and Social Class', which examines the emergence of citizenship in the last 250 years in Britain and defines citizenship as 'a status bestowed on those who are full members of a community. All who possess the status are equal with respect to the rights and duties with which the status is endowed' (T. H. Marshall, 'Citizenship and Social Class', in id., *Citizenship and Social Class and Other Essays* (London, 1950), 1–85: 28–9). There has been a proliferation of scholarship that develops this account of citizenship, including its embeddedness in claims to territoriality (see e.g. W. Kymlicka and W. Norman, 'Return of the Citizen: A Survey of Recent Works on Citizenship Theory', *Ethics*, 352 (1994), 352–81; S. Hall and D. Held, 'Citizens and Citizenship', in S. Hall and M. Jacques (eds.), *New Times: The Changing Face of Politics in the 1990s* (London, 1989), 173–88; G. Andrews (ed.), *Citizenship* (London, 1991); D. Heater, *Citizenship: The Civic Idea in World History, Politics and Education* (Manchester, 2004); G. Shafir (ed.), *The Citizenship Debates: A Reader* (Minneapolis, 1998); G. Shafir and Y. Peled, 'Citizenship and Stratification in an Ethnic Democracy', *Ethnic and Racial Studies*, 21 (1998), 408–27; J. L. Cohen, 'Changing Paradigms of Citizenship and the Exclusiveness of the Demos', *International Sociology*, 14 (1999), 245–68.

66 Gilinski-Meller, 'Mifleget hafolkistim', 99.

67 See e.g. *Sprawozdanie stenograficzne z 9 posiedzenia Rady Stanu Królestwa Polskiego z dnia 26 lipca 1918 r.* (Warsaw, 1918), 197.

68 'Z rady miejskiej', *Nowa Gazeta*, morning edn., 29 Dec. 1916, p. 2; 'Z rady miejskiej', *Nowa Gazeta*, morning edn., 23 Mar. 1917, p. l; 'Z rady miejskiej', *Kurjer Warszawski*, morning edn., 23 Mar. 1917, pp. 1–2.

69 N. Prilutski, *Redes in varshever shtotrat* (Warsaw, 1922), 47.

70 Ibid. 8, 55, 57.

71 R. Blobaum, *A Minor Apocalypse: Warsaw during the First World War* (Ithaca, NY, 2017), 165.

72 Ibid. 165–6.

73 Ibid. 166.

74 Ibid.

75 M. Silber, '"Shepolin haḥadashah tihyeh em tovah lekol yeladeha": yehudim upolanim bepolin 1916', *Zemanim*, 65 (1998–9), 83.

76 'Z rady miejskiej', *Nowa Gazeta*, 2 Nov. 1916, p. 1.

77 Ibid. 1–2.

78 YIVO Archives, New York, RG 29 Vilna collection, folder 335: 'Protokol fun der ershter zitsung fun der komisye', 25 Nov. 1916.

79 Prilutski, *Redes in varshever shtotrat*, 9–13, 53–7.

80 'Di groyse yidn debate in shtot rat', *Haynt*, 3 Nov. 1916, pp. 3–4.

81 For instance, ibid.; A.N., 'Nokh der groyser zitsung', *Haynt*, 3 Nov. 1917, p. 3; 'Di groyse yudishe zitsung in shtodt-rat', *Der moment*, 3 Nov. 1916, p. 3.

82 A concept developed by Gayatri Chakravorty Spivak (see G. C. Spivak, 'Subaltern Studies: Deconstructing Historiography', in *The Spivak Reader: Selected Works of Gayati Chakravorty Spivak*, ed. D. Landry and G. MacLean (New York, 1996), 203–36: 214).

83 YIVO Archives, RG 1400, Bund, MG2, Box 15, folder 145: 'Protokół posiedzenia 62-go Rady Miejskiej z dnia 23 stycznia 1918 r.'.

84 M. Silber, 'The German "Ordinance Regarding the Organization of the Religious Jewish Community" (November 1916–1918)', *Studia Judaica* (Kraków), 18 (2015), 35–55.

85 Ibid. 37–42.

86 Ibid. 38, 40–2, 53–5

87 A. Guterman, *Kehilat varsha bein shetei milḥemot ha'olam: otonomyah leumit bekivlei haḥok vehametsiyut 1917–1939* (Tel Aviv, 1997), 69–75, 174–5; National Library of Israel, Jerusalem, Department of Manuscripts, Główna Rada Gmin Żydowskich, 4°1180 file 29: Samuel Poznanski Archive [Jan. 1918?].

88 Gilinski-Meller, 'Mifleget hafolkistim', 115, 126; Prilutski, *Redes in varshever shtotrat*, 17–21.

89 Gilinski-Meller, 'Mifleget hafolkistim', 111–12, 126, 134–40.

90 M. Hertz, *Łódź w czasie wielkiej wojny* (Łódź, 1933), 168.

91 Protokół posiedzenia 62-go Rady Miejskiej z dnia 23 stycznia 1918 r.

92 Ibid.

93 Ibid.

94 Gilinski-Meller, 'Mifleget hafolkistim', 109.

95 M. Silber, *Le'umiyut shonah, ezraḥut shavah! hama'avak lehasagat otonomyah liyehudei polin bemilḥemet ha'olam harishonah* (Tel Aviv, 2014), 203–33; Zieliński, *Stosunki polsko-żydowskie na ziemiach Królestwa Polskiego*, 268–76.

96 CZA, F33/1: Central Committee of Zionists in Poland, minutes of meeting, 10 Feb. 1918.

97 Silber, *Le'umiyut shonah, ezraḥut shavah!*, 203–33; Zieliński, *Stosunki polsko-żydowskie na ziemiach Królestwa Polskiego*, 268–76.

98 'Di forkonferents fun di yidn in poyln', *Haynt*, 29 Dec. 1918, p. 2; Y. Gottlieb 'Derishoteinu mikongres hashalom' *Hatsefira*, 9 Jan. 1919, pp. 14–16.

99 'Di groyse yidn debate in shtot rat'; 'Nokh der groyser zitsung', *Haynt*, 3 Nov. 1916, p. 3; 'Di groyse yudishe zitsung in shtodt-rat'.

100 Gilinski-Meller, 'Mifleget hafolkistim', 111.

101 Lewin, *The Political History of Polish Jewry*, 24.

102 'Mowa d-ra Rozenblata, prezesa frakcji żydowskiej w Łódzkiej Radzie miejskiej', *Głos Żydowski*, 1 Nov. 1917, pp. 6–8: 7–8 (emphasis in the original).

The Struggle in the Polish Parliament for Jewish Autonomy and the Nature of Jewish Self-Government

SZYMON RUDNICKI

FOR THE POLES, the re-establishment of independence was the realization of a dream: 'reborn Poland did not quite reflect the Poland which had been dreamed of, yet it did exist'.[1] The achievement of national sovereignty and the immediate necessity of establishing the state's frontiers exacerbated the tendency to view Poland as a national project in which only Poles were fully fledged citizens, and the participation of other nationalities was rejected. Ethnic minorities obviously took a different view. As newly independent Poland was taking shape, Ukrainians began an armed struggle for their own state; Germans fought to remain within the Reich; and Belarusians also began to manifest aspirations for independence. Refusing to take into account the aims of these groups led to a state of permanent ferment in the country.[2] Such yearnings were also found within the large Jewish minority. The Zionists, the Jewish People's Party (Folkists), and the Bundists saw the Jews as a nation and put forward a programme of national and cultural autonomy, defined by Andrzej Żbikowski as 'a form of self-government for an ethnic minority in a multi-ethnic state, which would allow for the free development of national culture'.[3] In this chapter, I will discuss how the calls for national and cultural autonomy played out in the interwar years in Poland.[4]

The larger history of Polish–Jewish relations and of Jewish attitudes to Poland's independence are beyond the scope of this chapter.[5] The closer Poland came to independence, the greater was the role played by current events, pushing into the background stances adopted in the past. What was important was the extent of the co-operation between Poles and Jews. When discussing Jewish attitudes, the views of political groupings and parties and sometimes those of their leaders dominate the historiography. The degree of engagement of the masses is frequently neglected.

The demand for autonomy featured from their inception in the programmes of the Zionists, the Folkists, and the Bundists. They proposed to base this on ethnic communities, united in a Jewish national council which would be the capstone of the system.[6] This would be recognized as part of the state apparatus. The scope of the autonomy sought would include religion, culture, education at all levels, social welfare, and the organizations of economic life.[7]

On 21 and 22 October 1918 the World Zionist Organization held a conference in Warsaw where the delegates 'as Zionists and citizens' strongly welcomed the unification of the Polish lands and the creation of an independent state. They appealed to

Jews to convene a Jewish national conference. Until delegates could be selected and the conference assembled, a Provisional Jewish National Council (Tymczasowa Żydowska Rada Narodowa) was created to represent all Polish Jews.[8] The conference appealed to all parties 'supporting the national platform' to convene such a body. This proposal was boycotted by all non-Zionist Jewish parties, so that on 2 December the Zionists were compelled to organize the Provisional Jewish National Council on their own.[9] The council was given the impossible task of convening a Jewish congress by March 1919 in order to select a Jewish representative body. Until then, the council was to direct the Jewish national struggle, represent the Jews at the Paris Peace Conference, and conduct an election campaign for the Polish sejm. Attempts to broaden the membership of the council failed, and it remained solely composed of Zionists.

Following his return to Warsaw from internment in Germany in November 1918, Józef Piłsudski received delegates from the different political parties. Isaac Grünbaum, representing the Zionists, set out his concept of Jewish autonomy and its institutions—local community boards (*kehilot*) would establish a Jewish national council to represent the Jews vis-à-vis the state, and Jewish matters would be dealt with by a secretary of state for Jewish national affairs. Piłsudski did not support the proposal.[10] His faction viewed the Jews as a religious group: 'Treating Jews as a religious community, Piłsudski's followers saw Jewish community boards as religious bodies which should not be endowed with powers that would make them the key element in a system of national self-government.'[11]

The Jews were aware that only in a democratic Poland would they achieve full citizenship. They thus participated in elections to the sejm. The balance of forces and the hostile attitude of the National Democrats forced the Jewish caucus (Koło Żydowskie) to vote with the socialists and the radical peasant party, Wyzwolenie. This co-operation was not always harmonious: contrary to what the National Democrats believed, most Jewish deputies did not feel comfortable with socialist ideology, while the groups they supported were not particularly keen to engage with Jewish matters.

In accordance with their own terminology, the Zionists repeatedly stressed that the Poles were the 'ruling nation', but that this did not preclude national minorities from enjoying their rights. They were aware that the situation of the Jews differed from that of territorial minorities. Most Jewish deputies were, however, committed to the principle of national and cultural autonomy. In order to achieve this, they needed to win support for the view that Jews were indeed a nation and hence a national minority in Poland. This most Polish parliamentary parties refused to concede.

The most important task of the First Polish Sejm was to establish a constitution. When its Constitutional Committee was convened on 14 February 1919, Isaac Grünbaum represented the Jewish caucus, with Salomon Weinzieher as his deputy. In the course of the debates on different constitutional proposals, the Jewish parties submitted almost identical demands. According to the Folkist Samuel Hirszhorn:

The constitution should guarantee to all national minorities, including Jews, self-govern-ment in the fields of culture, vernacular education, social welfare, and charity, in other words, national and personal autonomy. This should take a form of a public association, a legal entity with local and national community bodies whose boundaries should follow existing administrative–political divisions. This will be headed by a supreme national coun-cil elected by all members of these bodies by universal, equal, secret, direct, and pro-portional suffrage without sex discrimination . . . In those communities where national minorities amount to no less than 25 per cent of the population, they should enjoy the right to use their vernacular language in all offices of state and local government, which will guarantee them free and clear expression of their needs.[12]

Grünbaum returned to the issue of autonomy during a debate on the principles of Poland's foreign policy. He suggested an amendment to the government's acceptance of 'national and cultural self-government in nationally mixed territories' which would establish the right to institute such self-government 'on the whole territory of the republic' and thus to make this applicable to Jews.[13] This adoption of the principle of public legal associations for minorities seemed to imply the transformation of Poland into a multinational state and raised fears over its territorial integrity. As a result, Grünbaum's proposal was rejected. Even the socialists refused to contemplate such a possibility in relation to Jews.

Jolanta Żyndul has pointed out that in the two-year debate over the constitution, discussion of the rights of national minorities did not occupy much time, either in the Constitutional Committee or in plenary debates.[14] For their part, Jewish deputies paid most attention to those articles of the draft which set out the rights and obliga-tions of citizens and specifically the civil liberties of minorities, including religious freedom. They were above all concerned with the principle of equality for all citi-zens.[15] Starting with the draft of the preamble, they proposed to supplement the clause on equality with a guarantee of 'freedom of development for religions and nationalities'.[16] The rejection of this amendment prompted Ignacy Schiper to claim that the constitution failed to safeguard the rights of ethnic and religious minorities sufficiently.[17] Such fears were justified: only at the final stage of the constitutional debate was the principle of the equality of religious denominations introduced and then with some important limitations.

The Jewish caucus proposed an amendment to article 100 of the draft (article 96 in the finally adopted constitution), which stated that 'all citizens are equal before law', adding a sentence stating that 'ethnicity or religion shall never become obstacles to the enjoyment of citizen's rights and specifically to the holding of public or state offices'.[18] Grünbaum justified this amendment by citing numerous examples of discrimination against Jews.[19]

On the second reading of the draft constitution, the question of whether Jews constituted a nation resurfaced. Grünbaum explained the rejection of the Jewish caucus's amendments as

the result of a single cardinal sin, the refusal to recognize Jewish nationality. It is the effect of the present system, which, on the one hand, does not allow the assimilation of the Jewry, because it fears such assimilation, but, on the other, refuses to recognize Jewish nationality and endow it with appropriate community rights. And I say that until this happens, until the Jewish nation is recognized and receives the community rights due to a nationality, there can be no equality for Jews in Poland, no straightforward equality.[20]

In fact, the problem was not so much solely the position of the Jews as the shape of the state, whether it should be based on the principle of nationality or of citizenship. The National Democrats and centrist parties favoured a national Polish state. The nation was treated as an ethnic not a political entity. The left and the ethnic minorities supported a civic state. Article 1 of the Polish Socialist Party's (Polska Partia Socjalistyczna; PPS) draft for a constitution read: 'All power in the Polish republic is derived from all its citizens.' This draft envisaged special administrative units in ethnically mixed areas.[21]

Attempts to introduce amendments to articles of the constitution to prevent discrimination against minorities failed. In the case of article 113, which stated that 'separate legislation will ensure the full and free development of [the minorities'] national character in the Polish state, by means of autonomous minority associations with the character of public and legal entities within the framework of general self-government',[22] the Jewish caucus proposed to introduce regulations which would facilitate setting up autonomous provinces for those minorities which formed a majority in a given area of the state and allowing ethnic and religious minorities to create autonomous associations, regulated by separate acts of the sejm. Their sphere of activity would include religion, schooling, culture, philanthropy, care for migrants, and registers of population. They would also have the right to tax their members and receive guaranteed state subsidies for their community budgets equal to the cost to the treasury should the state itself undertake the same administrative functions.[23] The call for the right to tax and for government support were in addition to what had previously been demanded in the quest for Jewish self-government.

Mieczysław Niedziałkowski described articles 112 and 113 on autonomous minority associations as 'decisive for the character of our future statehood'. In his speech, he discussed the amendments put forward by the Jewish caucus. He announced that the PPS parliamentary group, which argued for the separation of church and state, would vote against the proposed regulations relating to religious associations. It would support territorial autonomy but not national and cultural autonomy, because 'we thoroughly reject all those conceptions in which the Polish state is seen as the common property of Poles and Jews, in the sense in which Belgium is the common property of the Walloons and the Flemish'.[24] This amounted to a rejection of all the Jewish amendments. Characteristically, when talking of the cultural creativity of minorities, Niedziałkowski failed to mention the Jews.

Rabbi Ojasz Thon described article 113 as 'elastic' and attacked it for talking 'about everything and nothing'. In his view, the statement that separate legislation would ensure 'full and free development' of national minorities raised the question of whether the constitution indeed safeguarded such freedoms or was only a political declaration.[25] Schiper argued against the view that the Jews could not aspire to autonomy because they did not have one language and that one of their languages—Yiddish—was merely a dialect and also because they did not constitute a territorial minority. He defended the concept of autonomy, maintaining that it encompassed those areas of cultural life which were neutral from the perspective of the state and called for it to be established on a non-religious basis.[26] Samuel Hirszhorn claimed that 'whether [the community] is to be a religious body or an ethnic one is irrelevant: as long as it is democratic, it will become national by default and the Yiddish language will play a very large role in it'.[27]

Article 115 of the constitution stated that 'the churches of the religious minorities and other legally organized religious communities govern themselves by their own laws, which the state may not refuse to recognize unless they contain rules contrary to law'.[28] An attempt by the Jewish caucus to amend this so that no one could be forced to violate their religious holidays unless this was necessary for military or state service failed.[29] Szyja Farbstein of the Mizrachi group described the mandatory prohibition of work on Sundays as an 'unprecedented violation of the freedom of conscience' and of the Treaty of Versailles. In support of the proposed amendment, he claimed that its acceptance would protect the Jews, at least in part, from a requirement to violate the precepts of their religion.[30]

All Jews, both believers and non-believers, regarded the issue of religion as essential, bearing in mind its role in Jewish life and its legal status in the state, which considered Judaism a fundamental feature distinguishing Jews from other citizens. This is why, following the adoption at the second reading of draft article 117, which established the leading position of the Roman Catholic confession, Grünbaum proposed at the Constitutional Commission that the words 'among equal religions' be added. His amendment was rejected with, among others, the votes of the socialists, who consistently sought to introduce into the constitution a clause on the separation of religion from the state. As Grünbaum saw it, this meant there would be no equality of religion.[31] However, it proved possible to introduce the amendment at the third reading, and the first sentence of article 114 of the constitution read: 'The Roman Catholic religion, being the religion of the preponderant majority of the nation, occupies in the state the chief position among recognized religions.' Article 115 of the constitution, as mentioned above, regulated the status of the legally recognized denominations other than Catholic, giving them the right to govern themselves. Appropriate legislation was to be adopted by the sejm after considering the opinions of their representatives. The Jewish deputies proposed to supplement the clause 'after considering the opinions of their representatives' with 'constituted under the rules governing a given creed or in an election carried out under the accepted procedures'. This was an attempt to introduce the right of the Jews to national representation.[32] Samuel Hirszhorn stated that the regulation, as it stood, was 'a very clear attack on the religious and national rights of the Jewish minority' and stressed that the Jews did not have a religious hierarchy, so could be represented only through an autonomous national structure.[33] Article 109 of the constitution clearly stated that 'every citizen has the right to preserve his/her nationality and develop his/her mother tongue and national characteristics'.[34] It failed, however, to determine whether Jews constituted a nation, and this problem would return in all the future debates concerning them. Despite the adoption of the constitution, many regulations from the period of the partitions remained in force because they had not been specifically repealed. This state of affairs only came to a formal end in 1931.

In the final debate on the constitution, Samuel Hirszhorn stated that 'the articles which are the most reactionary are those which deal directly with minorities or which overlook minority rights where such rights ought to be safeguarded'.[35] He also made an accurate assessment of the goals pursued by the Jewish caucus in these discussions: 'In writing a constitution, principles should be adopted which safeguard people against the worst possible conditions. Constitutions are written with the worst eventualities in mind, so that a bureaucracy or a reactionary majority in power could not oppress minorities.'[36] After the constitution had been passed, Grünbaum moved at a meeting of the Constitutional Committee that a ministry for national minorities be created. This met with resistance from the delegate of the government, who argued that it would amount to granting privileges to one section of the population. Only the PPS delegates supported the move. The government deemed it sufficient to transfer the Office for Jewish Affairs from the Ministry of Religious Denominations and Public Enlightenment (Ministerstwo Wyznań Religijnych i Oświecenia Publicznego; MWRiOP) to the Ministry of Internal Affairs (Ministerstwo Spraw Wewnętrznych; MSW), where a department of Jewish affairs was to be created.[37] However, the organizational structure of the MSW shows that such a department never existed and Jewish affairs were placed, as Rafał Żebrowski has pointed out, 'in the hands of relatively low-level officials, rather than creating a separate, dedicated department to manage them.'[38]

The adoption of the constitution ended the formative phase of the state's system of government. The Jewish deputies had failed to introduce into it the principle of cultural autonomy. It is possible that they supported this above all because it was part of the programme which they wished to publicize, while anticipating that their demands would be rejected. Their amendments to particular articles were voted down, but, in some instances, solutions were eventually adopted which were close to their proposals. A number of clauses in the constitution were indeed worded in such a way that they lent themselves to different interpretations which resulted in subsequent disputes. All ethnically Polish parliamentary parties were opposed to autonomy. The Polish republic remained a nation-state.[39] The fundamental reason for the rejection of autonomy was the adoption of a national model of the state supported by the National Democrats. This proved relatively easy to achieve because, had autonomy been given to the Jews, other territorial minorities would have demanded the same, which could have threatened the unity of the state.

■

From the dawn of the Zionist movement, its adherents had had no doubts that one of the fundamental elements of Jewish autonomy was the establishment in each country of a Jewish national organization. The issue had been raised repeatedly at successive Zionist congresses and conferences.[40] As early as 1899 Zionists participated in the elections to the Board of the Jewish Community of Warsaw. They continued to do so in later elections in order to gain influence.[41] At the dawn of Polish independence, Apolinary Hartglas described the organizational principles of national self-government: 'The basic cell organizing Polish Jewry ought to be the community ... In Poland this has always had a national and not only religious character, perhaps because of a specific nature of our religion and the close link among us between Jewish national identity and membership of the synagogue.' He also recalled that before the partitions of Poland, the Jewish community board had an added political function.[42] The community board attracted a lot of attention, as attested by an issue of *Materiały w sprawie żydowskiej w Polsce* which analysed its legal status in different parts of Poland.[43] Hence, it is not surprising that the issue was raised in the sejm as an element of a national and cultural autonomy.

From the moment the case for Jewish national autonomy was rejected in the discussions of the constitution, the reform of the system of local Jewish self-government became a central issue for supporters of Jewish autonomy. The community board (in Polish *gmina*, often referred to as the *kehila*) remained the fundamental institution of Jewish society, bringing together all Jews living in a given area, and it had not only religious but also social functions.[44] But whereas, for the Orthodox, the board was to be primarily responsible for the religious aspects of community affairs, for the Zionists it was something else. According to Ozjasz Thon: 'When it was necessary, our nationality limited itself only to religion, but now that our religion is transcending the framework of the synagogue, it is stepping outside that framework and is becoming truly a fully blown nationality, for the time being without a territory.'[45] The issue of autonomy was important for those political parties which considered Jews to be a nation, rather than a religious denomination. According to Rabbi Markus Braude in the senate: 'We Jews look at our Jewish community board not only as a religious body dealing exclusively with Jewish religious matters but as the basic unit in the national organization of a national Jewish society.'[46]

On 7 February 1919 Józef Piłsudski, the head of state, issued a decree, On the Changes in the Organization of Denominational Jewish Community Bodies in the Former Congress Kingdom.[47] On the basis of this decree, the MWRiOP issued an order on 1 May 1919 relating to the Jewish community boards. The decree confirmed their religious character, stating that 'the Jewish community board ought to ensure that members of the community are able to fulfil their religious needs'.[48] Thus the statute of the Kraków community board, typical for former Austrian Galicia, stated: 'The aim of the community board is to meet the religious needs of its members.'[49] The decree was to remain in force until the sejm passed a general law on community boards. It confirmed previously elected community hierarchies with their competences limited mostly to religious tasks. It also retained the Jewish Religious Union, a corporate body created by General Hans von Beseler, governor of the General

Government of Warsaw during the First World War, with compulsory membership extending to all Jews in a given locality. The 1919 decree broadened the scope of state intervention in the functioning of community boards. Budgeting, contribution levels, and other community fees all required the consent of the relevant state administrative organs. The minister for religious denominations and public enlightenment had the right to confirm the election of a rabbi and to appoint six out of the twenty-one members of the Religious Executive, the governing body of the Jewish Religious Union,[50] which, incidentally, was never established. Zionists considered the decree as worsening rather than improving the position of Jewish community boards.

Markus Braude said of the decree:

It clearly and decidedly narrows the scope of [the community's] organizational principles. The decree goes beyond the law granted to the Jewish community by the German occupiers . . . and consistently promotes the idea that Jews in Poland are only a religious community and, on this basis, the Jewish community board is intended solely to meet their religious needs.[51]

He also called on Poland to return to her tradition of treating the community board as an 'organizational cell of the national Jewish community'.[52] Rafał Żebrowski, who devoted around a hundred pages to the legal aspects of the work of community boards, arrived at a similar conclusion: that the decree's intent was to deprive community boards of their supra-religious character. The decree led to a situation in which the legally defined sphere of action of Jewish community boards did not reflect their de facto activities.[53]

The decree met the demands of the Orthodox but provoked the opposition of Zionists and Folkists. The Provisional Jewish National Council resolved that the Jewish caucus ought to submit a motion in the sejm to prevent the enforcement of the decree,[54] but in the end this was never done. In practice, the activity of the Jewish community boards extended beyond their religious functions, and the smaller a council was, the more strongly it influenced its members' lives. Hence, even non-religious parties attempted to gain influence on the boards. Meanwhile, the local administration and the organs of the state supported the Orthodox, quite often ignoring the law. Both the Zionists and the Folkists demanded a democratization of community boards, the introduction of universal, equal, secret, direct and proportional elections with votes for women, and the voting age set at 20. They sought a broadening of the responsibilities of community boards.[55] Of all their demands, the only one which the decree met was for universal, equal, secret, direct, and proportional elections, although the vote was not granted to women.

Parliament now became the arena for attempts to obtain Jewish autonomy. The sejm and senate elections of November 1922 were the first in peacetime and they extended to the whole country. The electoral law was slightly modified with the introduction of state lists which favoured the largest parties, giving them additional seats. In addition, for the first time, Belarusians and Ukrainians participated. The minorities, concerned to defend their interests in an increasingly chauvinist atmosphere, fought the elections united in the National Minorities' Bloc (Blok Mniejszości Narodowych). This gave the Jews a chance to win more seats. As a result they had broader representation and greater influence on parliamentary matters than in any other parliament in the interwar period. Overall, there were thirty-five Jewish members of the sejm (8 per cent of the total) and twelve Jewish senators (13 per cent of the upper chamber). Disputes between Zionist deputies from former Austrian Galicia and former Russian Poland weakened their effectiveness in the sejm. Until the May 1926 coup Jewish deputies remained in opposition to the government.

On 23 June 1924 the Zionist deputies submitted an urgent motion on a statute for the Jewish community boards in Poland. Its proposers again criticized Piłsudski's 1919 decree: in their view it 'limited the responsibility of community boards to purely religious matters' and the present legal situation had created 'far-reaching chaos'.[56] For these reasons, they had submitted a draft statute. In their opinion, 'community boards should be recognized as institutions of the state to which it delegates some of its powers, so that they will be capable of fulfilling their function of self-government'.[57] They should have the right to tax members of the community and be provided with 'appropriate funding from the sums which the state now expends on functions which have been taken away from community bodies'.[58] The public and legal character of the community board they proposed 'would oblige everyone born a Jew to be a member of a community'.[59] Apart from religious matters, community boards were to take responsibility for schooling and culture, social welfare and aid, public health, management of the economic situation, co-operatives, and the registration of the Jewish population. The whole system was to be overseen by a special office for Jewish affairs, which should not report to the MWRiOP, since that would have meant limiting the activity of community boards to religious matters, nor to the MSW, which would threaten a return to the tsarist system.[60]

Article 2 of a draft statute, appended to the motion, stated that all Jews resident in a given administrative district made up a Jewish community. Its board was to have broad powers and would be elected by universal, equal, secret, direct, and proportional elections, as would the proposed provincial councils and the Supreme Jewish Council. Article 53 stipulated that the latter would 'represent the Jewish community vis-à-vis the central state authorities'. It would be its responsibility to 'liaise continuously with the undersecretary of state for Jewish affairs'. His responsibilities were set out in Article 65.[61] This motion was intended to establish national and cultural autonomy, although the term was not used. There is no evidence that it was ever debated in the sejm.

In the following year, talks were conducted between the government and the Jewish parliamentary caucus, concluding in the 'settlement' of 5 July 1925. According to the settlement, concessions were made to the Jews on economic questions, the political rights of citizens, organization of Jewish communities, and the problems of culture, religion, and education in return for Jewish politicians undertaking to actively support the integrity of the state and its borders. However, from the start conflicting interpretations of the government's undertakings emerged, which promptly undermined the credibility of both sides.

Gradually the disparate systems of Jewish self-government in the former partitions were unified. On 28 October 1925 an order from the Council of Ministers extended Piłsudski's decree of February 1919 to the north-eastern borderlands, where the old tsarist law was still in force, preventing the establishment of Jewish community boards.[62] An order from the MWRiOP of 25 June 1927 laid down the borders of individual communities. In this fashion, all the Jewish communities across all the former tsarist territories incorporated into independent Poland became legal entities. In eastern Galicia, after the outbreak of the First World War the Austrian authorities placed government commissioners in charge of most Jewish community boards and appointed their advisory bodies, an arrangement which the Polish authorities later kept in place. These organs gradually lost their effectiveness and the confidence of the members of their communities. Accordingly, Leon Reich, the leader of Galician Jewry, tabled an urgent motion on 16 February 1923 calling for elections to the Jewish community boards in the three south-eastern provinces.

In March 1924 the minister for religious denominations and public enlightenment issued an order to hold elections to the governing bodies of Jewish communities in the former Congress Kingdom and Galicia from 1 June.[63] The Zionists harshly criticized the undemocratic electoral law, the five-year delay in holding the elections, and the ruling that community boards should conduct their debates in Polish. Above all they opposed imposing a religious character on the community boards and what they saw as the lack of effective financing. The 1924 state budget initially earmarked 2,000 zlotys for Jewish education in the whole of Poland, which was subsequently raised to 10,000. In protest, Jewish parliamentarians in both the sejm and the senate proposed that it be removed from the budget.[64]

Grünbaum complained that the electoral regulations created so many obstacles that it appeared that the government wished to prevent the broad mass of people from voting. The Folkist deputy Noyekh Prilutski submitted an urgent motion that voting be based on the principles of universal, equal, secret, direct, and proportional suffrage, with women being granted the right to vote and the age of voting set at 25.[65] The motion was not accepted as urgent, and the elections were conducted under the old franchise with educational and property qualifications and no votes for women. The Jewish parties approached the elections as a test of their influence. Grünbaum expected they would strengthen the position of the Jewish caucus in parliament and that the newly elected councils would become a weapon in the struggle for Jewish self-government. However, there was no clear agreement within the Provisional Jewish National Council as to the role Jewish community boards were supposed to play. One of its most prominent members, Yehoshua Heschel Farbstein, a leader of the religious Zionist organization Mizrachi, took the view that they ought to have a religious and national character.[66]

Very few of the new community bodies began to operate even six months after the elections. In Warsaw, the vote did not take place because of bitter conflicts between the various Jewish groups. Elsewhere, the local administration created obstacles. Where the Zionists won, results were not confirmed, as in Lwów (Lviv), where the city council took six months to investigate the legitimacy of the outcome and finally concluded that the government commissioner had not organized the election correctly. In other localities the elections did not even take place, despite the promise of Bolesław Miklaszewski, the minister for religious denominations and public enlightenment, that the authorities would not interfere in the results.[67]

▦

Following the May 1926 coup, which returned Józef Piłsudski to power, the government's attitude to the Jews changed. The Jewish question was classed as 'objectively, the most difficult for the Polish state, but possibly the least dangerous'[68] and ceased to be a priority for the new regime. Piłsudski's supporters did not treat the Jewish minority as an anti-state element and were hostile to antisemitism. Jews were seen as a religious minority which would need to be assimilated. This attitude was reflected in the legislative initiatives relating to the Jews.[69] The problem of minorities was moved from the sphere of parliament to the administration.[70] Piłsudski's supporters had an ambivalent attitude to the Zionists, but they did not prevent their work.[71] Above all, they sought to co-operate with the religious party, Agudat Yisrael.

After the coup, a debate began about changes to the state's voting system. The Folkists argued for a curial system in which all Jews would be grouped in a Jewish curia.[72] Eliasz Kirszbraun, one of the leaders of the Agudah, proposed a separate Jewish curia, on the grounds that only members of parliament elected in this way would be able to work effectively for the rights of the Jewish population.[73] The idea was not new—it had been considered at the Paris Peace Conference, but even then, it was opposed by the Zionists, who thought that it breached the principle of equality.[74] The issue never reached the forum of the sejm.

A presidential decree of 6 March 1928 established the final version of the Regulations Concerning the Organization of Jewish Denominational Communities on the Territory of the Republic, Excluding the Silesian Voivodeship. Article 3 defined the community board's task as meeting the members' religious needs through organizing the rabbinate; funding and maintaining synagogues, prayer houses, ritual baths, and cemeteries; overseeing religious education; ensuring supplies of kosher meat; and managing community property and foundations. Community boards also had the right to support destitute Jews and set up charitable foundations for this task.[75]

Formally, community boards were thus restricted to religious matters and related economic tasks. They also dealt with charity and religious schooling. According to Jerzy Tomaszewski, the new regulations 'greatly enhanced a practical role of communities in the life of Jewish society'.[76] However, as Andrzej Chojnowski notes, they also remained aligned with traditionalist and conservative groups, above all Agudah.[77] Community boards continued to be supervised by a district head (*starosta*), who had the power to confirm rabbis, community bodies, and budgets. At times, the decisions of *starosta*s created tensions. In such instances, the state administration used its authority to appoint a board headed by a commissioner. The presidential decree attempted to satisfy the expectations of the Orthodox. It completely sidelined the demands of the Zionists to democratize the community boards and transform them into a national body. Not only did the new dispensation fail to loosen the corset of administrative supervision but it also reduced government subsidies.

How weighty a problem the community boards posed is attested by the publication by the Jewish caucus of a brochure setting out their legal status. In its foreword, Józef Dawidsohn, a leading Zionist, wrote of a growing interference by state authorities in community life; he stressed the community board's role as an autonomous Jewish institution: 'Community autonomy in the diaspora is a treasure, which needs to be looked after, and it is a civic crime to waste this treasure.'[78] This statement accorded with the Zionist ideology which envisaged community boards as independent Jewish bodies with wide-ranging competence. Another brochure examined the unresolved question of the planned Religious Council of Jewish Communities.[79] Leon Reich expressed his unease that the principle of universal, equal, secret, direct, and proportional suffrage without sex discrimination, employed in electing legislative bodies, was not employed in electing community boards. In addition, the community boards had an increasingly religious character stripped of national responsibilities. He was critical of local administration, too, which frequently resorted to dissolving community boards and appointing commissioners and allowing electoral commissions with idiosyncratic memberships.[80] Reich, of course, was well aware that this law was an attempt to win over the Orthodox, above all the Agudah. In practice, as Grünbaum admitted, there were discrepancies between the letter of the law and real life. The government was unable to prevent community boards from taking up educational and social work.[81]

In April 1928, in eastern Galicia, the local administration dissolved the boards of many communities and appointed commissioners. Thon and Reich took this up with Deputy Prime Minister Bartel.[82] The following summer elections were called for the community boards. Despite a Zionist victory in Lwów, the Agudah and pro-government bloc candidate, Rabbi Ignacy Jaeger, was appointed president of the community board. Where the Zionists won, the authorities refused to approve their boards and attempted to sneak the Orthodox into power through the back door.[83] The following year, the government went even further and nominated Agudah members for community boards.[84] In a parliamentary question to the MWRiOP, Grünbaum protested against local authorities nominating additional members to community boards, requesting that the ministry take appropriate steps. In his next submission, he protested against a specific nomination in Grodzisk Mazowiecki and pointed out that the local *starosta* had acted unlawfully.[85]

An executive order to the presidential decree was published in the *Journal of Laws of the Polish Republic* on 5 November 1930.[86] It set the next election to community boards for the following May. The government did not conceal that its intention was to create such conditions that 'these boards should be genuinely religious, and not shelters for the Zionists and non-religious Bundists'.[87] An Agudah member of the sejm, Jacob Leib Mincberg from Łódź, claimed that the Orthodox population welcomed the regulations, which stressed the religious and charitable tasks of community boards, and saw the restrictive electoral law as a way to eliminate 'community wreckers'.[88] However, other Jewish members of the sejm were very displeased with the executive order. They were critical of the continuing exclusion of women from voting and of the high age requirement for membership of the boards. Members of electoral commissions were to be selected from the most numerous religious groups. Ozjasz Thon accused the government of walking a dangerous path leading to clerical dominance of the communities. He announced that the Jewish caucus would 'use all means to defend [Jews] against anyone assuming a right to censor observance or non-observance of a Jew and pronounce on his right to belong to a Jewish community'.[89] Spoken by a rabbi, such words carried particular weight. Emil Sommerstein, a Zionist from eastern Galicia, also questioned the concept of religious groups and pointed out that this made it possible to eliminate from electoral commissions those parties which the authorities deemed inconvenient. He questioned articles 14 and 20 of the order. The first allowed local authorities to confirm the composition of electoral commissions, and the second allowed electoral commissions to remove people who 'publicly speak against the Mosaic faith' from the electoral rolls. According to Sommerstein, this opened the gates to abuse. Consequently, he demanded the lifting of all restrictions on community self-government and the provision of guarantees for free elections.[90] Thon stated: 'I don't know if there is anywhere in the world such a horrendous nonsense as this article 20 . . . It decrees that a Jew can lose his vote in Jewish community elections if some mafia concludes that he is insufficiently observant.'[91]

On 11 March 1931 the Jewish caucus submitted a motion abolishing these regulations. They called for amendments to the order to introduce a greater measure of democracy in elections and the democratization of the community boards themselves.[92] Both Felicjan Składkowski, minister of internal affairs, and Sławomir Czerwiński, the minister for religious denominations and public enlightenment, responded. Składkowski explained that article 20 of the electoral law reflected 'the government's care for the preservation of the proper, religious character of Jewish communities' and was designed to defend the communities against communists. Similarly, Czerwiński explained that the government wished to prevent political struggles in the communities, particularly with communists. In his view, the regulations did not prevent community work in the spheres of social care, schooling, and other non-religious areas. He did admit that article 20 was not part of the legislation, but only an executive clause, and the government had not consulted with the communities on it because of their divergent positions.[93] The deputies of the Jewish National Council (Żydowska Rada Narodowa; ŻRN) wrote to him subsequently to recapitulate their arguments and to appeal to him to remove article 20, 'which produces severe dangers to the continuing existence and development of the Jewish communities'.[94] Commenting on Składkowski's words, Thon wrote that he saw article

20 as 'consciously, or unconsciously, but without doubt a shameful humiliation of Polish Jewry'.[95] He also ridiculed the argument about the communist threat.

On 25 June the Jewish caucus sent a memorandum on the developments in the campaign to the minister for religious denominations and public enlightenment, and having received no reply, submitted a formal parliamentary question on 9 October.[96] The signatories claimed that electoral commissions in many places had been taken over exclusively by representatives of the Agudah, and, where they did not hold a majority, the *starostas* intervened and refused to endorse electoral commissions or nominated members themselves. The document listed communities where many people were deprived of the vote, in some cases more than half of the electoral roll. In crossing people off the rolls, political criteria were applied, but, for instance, in Łosice all bachelors were deleted. There were cases where the names of previous members of the board were removed, if they did not belong to the Agudah. In some cases, whole lists of candidates were voided, and there were irregularities during the vote itself. The authors of the question claimed that the elections did not reflect the true balance of forces in the communities and 'all of this put together assumes the dimension of some political scandal'.[97] They demanded an investigation and the annulling of the elections in those communities where irregularities influenced the results.

Since the minister replied that complaints about individual irregularities should be initially directed to a lower level, two months later the deputies lodged a fresh parliamentary question related to this issue. They pointed out that they had not been referring to individual cases but to 'a virtual mass of violations of the law at various stages of the electoral process'.[98] They continued to demand investigations and that the electoral results in communities where irregularities had occurred be declared void. Further questions concerned elected chairs of community boards who were not officially confirmed unless they represented the Agudah, as occurred in Włocławek and Będzin.

With growing frequency, the Zionist deputies complained about official interference with the functioning of communities and trespassing on their autonomy. Henryk Rosmaryn, another east Galician Zionist, accused the authorities of overbearing meddling in internal Jewish affairs, while Thon defined the government policy as harassment for harassment's sake.[99] The Jewish National Council Caucus took exception to the government commissioner in Warsaw, who forbade the Warsaw community board from discussing article 20 of the electoral law and a decree regulating community finances.[100] This was a far-reaching interference in the work of a self-governing community which undermined the very essence of self-government.

The elections sparked off debates on the character of the community board. At a session of the Budget Committee, Sommerstein observed:

No one is evoking the tradition of the old commonwealth in relation to the Jewish community, and the remit of its work is being limited to meeting religious needs, while it is the demand of Jewish population that the Jewish community should embrace all its needs: religious, social and cultural, which is in the interest not only of the Jewry but also the state.[101]

The government consistently defended the community boards' restriction to religious matters, and all attempts by the Zionists to endow them with a national character or to democratize them were immediately rejected.

The executive order concerning the financial matters of the Jewish communities, issued by the minister for religious denominations and public enlightenment on 9 September 1931, was also strongly opposed. Among other things, it regulated how community contributions were to be calculated and collected. Complaints concerned unjust tax burdens, limitation of community rights, and the introduction of fines or arrest of members of the boards if they failed in their voluntary work. There were no such penalties envisaged in any other legislation regulating public bodies. *Nasz Przegląd*, the Warsaw Jewish daily, defined these regulations as 'thoroughly hostile to the development and extension of Jewish communities'.[102] It should be noted that the order was issued without any consultation with the Jewish representatives.

Whereas charitable aid lay within the responsibility of the communities, as religion dictated, the general impoverishment of Jewish society significantly swelled the numbers of those requesting assistance. Increasingly, the community boards had to supplement their religious tasks with a much larger amount of welfare. At the same time the problem of financing communities remained unsolved. Their budgets, amounting to over 20 million zlotys, were supplied by the Jews, who already shouldered an excessive burden of central and local taxation. The state budgeted 26 million zlotys for all religions in 1929/30, of which the Jews received 1 per cent, with half of this sum paying for the upkeep of the Warsaw Seminary for Teachers of the Mosaic Faith. As with previous budgets, the Jewish deputies demonstratively rejected the money.[103] The problem of financing community boards was raised during every budget debate but always with negative results.

From 1930 it was clear that the importance of the sejm was diminishing, with an even more rapid decline in the role of Jewish parliamentary representation. In addition, fewer Jewish deputies were returned to each successive parliament. Apolinary Hartglas wrote of the new position of Jewish deputies: 'These days, our task is not to fight and achieve, but to criticize and pillory.'[104] This diminished the role of the Jewish caucus, but it did reflect reality. The Zionists put themselves forward as the foremost spokesmen of the Jewish community, but their right to do so was questioned by members of the Agudah who continued to advocate close co-operation with the government. In fact, only the Zionist members of parliament maintained an independent political stance.

From 1934 members of parliament from the governing group began to manifest antisemitic tendencies and these became commonplace after Piłsudski's death. They did condemn acts of physical violence against Jews, but their programme displayed an ever stronger desire to limit the Jews' economic role without offering them any alternative other than emigration. Meanwhile, from autumn 1931 the National Democrats greatly strengthened their anti-Jewish propaganda.

Ensuring the security of their compatriots became an essential task for the Jewish caucus, numbering in the 1930–5 parliament only four deputies. Anti-Jewish excesses in the country grew rapidly, and anti-Jewish draft laws were proposed in the sejm with increasing frequency. The growing sense of danger forced the Jewish parties to co-operate, the more so as, in contrast to previous parliaments, they had no allies in the sejm. In the senate, Rabbi Mojżesz Schorr pointed to the National Democrats as the instigators of violence and spoke of them 'riding to power on a Jewish pony' and 'through violence against the weak and defenceless Jew reaching for the helm of government'.[105] Sommerstein, too, posed a rhetorical question:

Why has the Jewish question moved to the forefront of all issues in Poland in the past fifteen months? Is it really that all that is wrong in Poland is linked to the Jewish question? Is it really the fact that all shortcomings and ills, from matters of primary importance to the minutiae of everyday life, will be resolved, as if by a magic wand, the moment there are no Jews left in Poland?[106]

A phenomenon appeared, which Zdzisław Stahl, until 1933 head of the youth movement of the right-wing Obóz Wielkiej Polski, defined as 'Judaeocentricity': that is, reducing all problems to the Jewish question.[107] It became a constant feature of parliamentary sessions, being discussed on average at every third sitting of the sejm, a phenomenon which Sommerstein described as 'nulla dies sine littera Judaica [no day without a Jewish debate]'.[108]

In the summer of 1934 the idea of establishing a Jewish national council returned. The tasks which it should fulfil were different from those put forward at the dawn of the Second Polish Republic. It was now argued that it had become necessary to strengthen the role of Jewish representation in parliament and elsewhere in the face of growing antisemitism. This initiative came from the Central Committee of Zionist Organizations in Poland, which represented the former followers of Grünbaum, who had by now emigrated to Palestine. The Agudah was called on to sever its links with Piłsudski's Sanacja regime, which it refused to do.[109] However, an agreement was reached among the different Zionist organizations to establish a nationwide unified leadership which would co-ordinate policies and then create a homogeneous Jewish representation together with non-Zionist groups.[110] In June 1937 a unified representation in the sejm had been achieved, and this was followed by the creation of the Interim Representation of Polish Jewry (Tymczasowa Reprezentacja Żydostwa Polskiego, TRŻP) by Jewish members of parliament. Apolinary Hartglas raised objections to the establishment of this body without a democratic election and to the leading role of the parliamentary caucus, which, he claimed, did not reflect the wishes of the Jewish community or enjoy its confidence. He thought that in order to create such a representative body there should be an agreed minimum platform: the independence of Jewish politics; a democratic system; full equality of citizens with guaranteed cultural, linguistic, and educational rights; a non-religious, national self-government; and co-operation with non-Jewish groups which took a similar position.[111]

Such a maximalist programme would have doomed the initiative to defeat: it stood no chance of succeeding even in the first few years of independence, let alone in 1937. For Arie Tartakower of Hitahdut the TRŻP had nothing to do with a faithful representation of the views prevailing in the Jewish community. His view was seconded by Noyekh Prilutski, who saw no way of reaching a common stance with those who pinned their hopes on the Sanacja. Jechiel Halperin, a member of the Central Committee of Po'alei Tsiyon, thought that the TRŻP did not even represent political parties. All of them considered calling a common representation as both indispensable and urgent, but under the auspices of a congress of Polish Jewry. Conversely, Jakub Trockenheim of the Agudah thought that the interim body, as it stood, was indeed a nucleus of Jewish representation, but even he opted for it to be fully convened at the congress.[112]

The Representation of Polish Jews (Reprezentacja Żydów Polskich; RŻP) was organized with the participation of various branches of the Zionist and Agudist movements, as well as the TRŻP, but the workers' parties, the Folkists, and Al-Hamiszmar refused to join.[113] The secretariat of the TRŻP collected evidence of the situation of the Jewish population in the provinces, and passed it on to the RŻP to intervene. In February 1938 members of the RŻP made an attempt to liaise closely with Jewish economic organizations and a social-economic division was created in early May 1938. Following the passing of a resolution severely limiting Jewish methods of animal slaughter by the parliamentary commission on administration and self-government, the RŻP called a meeting of all Jewish political parties (except the Bund) and economic bodies, chaired by Sommerstein. At this meeting, it was agreed to convene a United Committee for the Defence of Jewish Rights in Poland (Zjednoczony Komitet do Obrony Praw Żydowskich w Polsce).[114]

Initially, the Jewish deputies blamed Polish nationalists for spreading anti-semitism, but they were soon compelled to take a stance vis-à-vis the policy of the governing camp. After Piłsudski's death, his Sanacja bloc rejected the idea of Jewish assimilation by the state. Jews came to be seen as a threat to the homogeneity of the republic and their isolation was attempted by legislative and administrative means.[115] A sizeable proportion of the Sanacja deputies in the sejm voiced the same sentiments as the nationalists. In his inaugural address to the sejm as prime minister on 4 June 1936, Felicjan Sławoj-Składkowski, observed that 'an honest host does not allow anybody to be harmed in his house. But an economic struggle? That's different [Owszem]'. This owszem became popular and was taken as the government's tacit agreement to an economic boycott. From 19 to 21 May 1938, a conference of the Supreme Council of the pro-government Camp of National Unity (Obóz Zjedno-czenia Narodowego) was held in Warsaw which, among other things, was to establish a unified stance in the Jewish question. It was agreed that 'under present conditions, Jews are an element which weakens the development of the national and state power, and stand in the way of the social evolution, which is now taking place in Poland'.[116]

Speaking of the rivalry between the National Democrats and the Sanacja over the monopoly on antisemitism, Schorr said:

One group would deal with us rapidly and meanly, employing, one might say 'mechanical slaughter'. The other one would act more slowly, by stages, and, above all, in a 'cultural manner', shall I say through 'humanitarian slaughter'? Frankly, I do not care much for these subtle differences, for the delicate shades which separate wild extermination from its cultured variety. The latter looks more dangerous to me, since it is calculated, planned, organized, even refined and therefore the more reprehensible and off-putting, because it employs the concept of culture for such a goal. In the end, there is no difference between a system of rapid starvation and one which starves slowly, at least from the perspective of a future victim.[117]

As the number of Jews diminished in city councils and parliament, the community boards gained in importance. Bent on controlling them, the government increasingly took recourse to appointing commissioners or supporting boards dominated by the Agudah.[118] Warsaw was illustrative of the first solution, Łódź of the second. In February 1939 Leib Mincberg, leader of the Agudah in Łódź, expressed both a sense of mission and of foreboding:

The Jewish community board was supposed to be, and should be, an advocate of the whole Jewish nation. However, Jewish community boards have become, against our will, its sole advocate, and who knows if the course of events will, Lord forbid, make it necessary to broaden this basic function of the boards even further.[119]

From 1936 several legislative drafts made an appearance in the sejm, aimed at removing Jews from various spheres of economic activity. The first and best known was a draft submitted by Janina Prystorowa concerning Jewish methods of animal slaughter.[120] Under the pretext of humanitarian concerns, it sought to make these virtually impossible. The ensuing debate in the sejm showed unequivocally that the humanitarian aim was but a ruse and the real aim was to push the Jews out of the meat market.

The battle lines were drawn at the sitting of the sejm on 29 March 1936, when the arguments from both sides were presented. The issue returned to the sejm when successive amendments were discussed. This was the biggest battle fought by the Jewish deputies since the issue of Sunday rest arose during the constitutional debate. The fight was engaged with a clear awareness of its expected negative outcome. The adoption of the law threatened 40,000 people with unemployment and would constitute a painful blow to the finances of Jewish community boards. To most Jews, the fundamental problem was the threat to the basic tenets of their religion. Because of the composition of the sejm, not a single opposition voice was raised by Polish members of parliament. It was clear that the law aimed a blow against religion, in Thon's words, 'our last fortress'.[121] The struggle to save ritual slaughter united the splintered Jewish community.

The Jewish deputies defended the values they held dear in the knowledge that they stood no chance of acceptance by the sejm. Initially, they fought for national and cultural autonomy and a national organization. Later, they fought to extend its area of operation. They demanded democratization and opposed interference by representatives of the state administration. Throughout the period, the most important issue remained the security of the Jewish community, threatened particularly in 1919 and 1920 and in the second half of the 1930s.

Translated from the Polish by Jarosław Garliński

Notes

1   R. Wapiński, *Pokolenia II Rzeczypospolitej* (Wrocław, 1991), 231.
2   A. Chojnowski, *Koncepcje polityki narodowościowej rządów polskich 1919–1939* (Wrocław, 1979), 19.
3   J. Tomaszewski and A. Żbikowski (eds.), *Żydzi w Polsce. Dzieje i kultura: Leksykon* (Warsaw, 2001), 30.
4   For more on the issues discussed in this chapter, see S. Rudnicki, *Żydzi w parlamencie II Rzeczypospolitej*, 2nd edn. (Warsaw, 2014).
5   S. Rudnicki, 'The Attitude of the Jews towards Poland's Independence', *Polin*, 27 (2014), 181–218.
6   *Materiały w sprawie żydowskiej w Polsce*, 6 vols. (Warsaw, 1919–22), ii. 91–2.
7   'Rada partyjna syjonistów galicyjskich', *Nowy Dziennik*, 25 Aug. 1918.
8   Archiwum Akt Nowych, Warsaw (hereafter AAN), Prezydium Rady Ministrów (hereafter PRM), cz. 2, t. 35, k. 14–15: Organizacja Syjonistyczna w Królestwie Polskim, Biuro Prasowe, Communique no. 25, Warsaw (25 Oct. 1918).
9   Sprawozdanie z działalności TŻRN (Warsaw, 1921), 1–15; E. Mendelsohn, *Zionism in Poland: The Formative Years, 1915–1926* (London, 1981), 91–4.
10 L. Halpern, *Polityka żydowska w Sejmie i Senacie Rzeczypospolitej Polskiej 1919–1933* (Warsaw, 1933), 4–5.
11 W. Paruch, *Od konsolidacji państwowej do konsolidacji narodowej: Mniejszości narodowe w myśli politycznej obozu piłsudczykowskiego (1926–1939)* (Lublin, 1997), 235.
12 *Sprawozdania Stenograficzne Sejmu Ustawodawczego*, 13 May 1919, col. 66.
13 *Sprawozdania Stenograficzne Sejmu Ustawodawczego*, 23 May 1919, col. 62.
14 J. Żyndul, *Państwo w państwie? Autonomia narodowo-kulturalna w Europie Środkowowschodniej w XX w.* (Warsaw, 2000), 95.
15 For the Jewish deputies' proposed redactions of articles 112 and 113 of the draft of the constitution, see *Projekt Ustawy Konstytucyjnej opracowany przez Komisję Konstytucyjną Sejmu Ustawodawczego* (Warsaw, 1919), 41–2.
16 For the amendments to the draft of the constitution submitted at the second reading, starting with Art. 85b, see ibid. 39.
17 *Sprawozdania Stenograficzne Sejmu Ustawodawczego*, 5 Oct. 1920, col. 4.
18 *Projekt Ustawy Konstytucyjnej opracowany przez Komisję Konstytucyjną Sejmu Ustawodawczego*, 39.
19 *Sprawozdania Stenograficzne Sejmu Ustawodawczego*, 4 Nov. 1920, col. 47.
20 *Sprawozdania Stenograficzne Sejmu Ustawodawczego*, 29 Oct. 1920, cols. 48–9.
21 *Konstytucja Rzeczypospolitej Polskiej z dn. 17 marca 1921 r. oraz projekt Związku Polskich Posłów Socjalistycznych opracowany przez posła M. Niedziałkowskiego* (Warsaw, n.d.), 74.
22 *Projekt ustawy konstytucyjnej w redakcji przyjętej przez Sejm Ustawodawczy Rzeczypospolitej Polskiej w drugim czytaniu* (Warsaw, 1921), n.p.

23 *Projekt Ustawy Konstytucyjnej opracowany przez Komisję Konstytucyjną Sejmu Ustawodawczego*, 41–2; see ibid. Annex II/2.

24 *Sprawozdania Stenograficzne Sejmu Ustawodawczego*, 16 Nov. 1920, cols. 36–7. Article 112 stated: 'every citizen has the right to cultivate his nationality, language, and national character', while article 113 added: 'separate legislation will ensure that minorities in the Polish State shall enjoy full and free development of their national character through autonomous minority associations bearing the character of public and legal entities and acting within the framework of general self-government' (*Projekt Ustawy Konstytucyjnej opracowany przez Komisję Konstytucyjną Sejmu Ustawodawczego*, 41–2).

25 Ibid., cols. 42–4, 46.

26 *Sprawozdania Stenograficzne Sejmu Ustawodawczego*, 17 Nov. 1920, cols. 10–11.

27 *Sprawozdania Stenograficzne Sejmu Ustawodawczego*, 23 Nov. 1920, col. 14.

28 *Dziennik Ustaw Rzeczypospolitej Polskiej*, 1921, no. 44, item 267.

29 *Sprawozdania Stenograficzne Sejmu Ustawodawczego*, 29 Oct. 1920, col. 47.

30 *Sprawozdania Stenograficzne Sejmu Ustawodawczego*, 17 Nov. 1920, cols. 29, 35.

31 *Sprawozdania Stenograficzne Sejmu Ustawodawczego*, 29 Oct. 1920, cols. 42–4.

32 R. Żebrowski, *Żydowska Gmina Wyznaniowa w Warszawie 1918–1939: W kręgu polityki* (Warsaw, 2012), 47.

33 *Sprawozdania Stenograficzne Sejmu Ustawodawczego*, 23 Nov. 1920, cols. 8–10, 14, 15.

34 According to W. Komarnicki, this was the only instance of the constitution using the term 'national'. Indeed, the same article, point 2 refers to 'nationality', and similarly in art. 110 (W. Komarnicki, *Polskie prawo polityczne (Geneza i system)* (Warsaw, 1922), 116).

35 *Sprawozdanie Stenograficzne Sejmu Ustawodawczego*, 11 Mar. 1921, col. 46.

36 Ibid.

37 'O ministerstwo dla spraw mniejszości narodowych', *Chwila*, 28 Nov. 1921; 'Sprawa ministerstwa dla mniejszości narodowych', *Chwila*, 29 Nov. 1921; 'Nowa faza w porozumieniu polsko-żydowskim', *Chwila*, 12 July 1921.

38 Żebrowski, *Żydowska Gmina Wyznaniowa w Warszawie*, 32.

39 Komarnicki, *Polskie prawo polityczne*, 215.

40 At the Second Zionist Congress in August 1898, Herzl spoke of the necessity of getting the community boards on side (J. Zineman, *Historia sjonizmu* (Warsaw, 1946), 136–7).

41 Żyndul, *Państwo w państwie?*, 106 *et passim*.

42 A. Hartglas, *Zasady naszego programu politycznego w Polsce: Referat odczytany na 3-ej konferencji sjonistycznej w Warszawie w listopadzie roku 1917* (Warsaw, 1918), 27.

43 *Materiały w sprawie żydowskiej w Polsce*, iii. 63.

44 S. Hirszhorn wrote: 'Our community board, which is nominally only a religious one, in reality has far wider tasks' (S.H. [S. Hirszhorn], 'Kryzys w Gminie Żydowskiej', *Nasz Przegląd*, 23 Nov. 1933; see Żebrowski, *Żydowska Gmina Wyznaniowa w Warszawie*, 33).

45 *Sprawozdania Stenograficzne Sejmu Ustawodawczego*, 16 Nov. 1920, col. 43.

46 *Sprawozdania Stenograficzne Senatu*, 28 July 1924, col. 2.

47 *Dziennik Praw Państwa Polskiego*, 8 Feb. 1919, no. 14, item 175.

48 *Dziennik Urzędowy Ministerstwa Wyznań Religijnych i Oświecenia Publicznego*, 1 May 1919, no. 12, item 5.

49 A. Frenkiel, *Sytuacja Żydów w Polsce w chwili obecnej* (Warsaw, 1923), 6

50 *Dziennik Urzędowy Ministerstwa Wyznań Religijnych i Oświecenia Publicznego*, 1 May 1919, no. 12, item 5.

51 *Sprawozdania Stenograficzne Senatu*, 28 July 1924, col. 3.

52 Ibid.

53 Żebrowski, *Żydowska Gmina Wyznaniowa w Warszawie*, 32–3, 69–71.

54 'Tymczasowa Żydowska Rada Narodowa w sprawie dekretu o organizacji gmin', *Kurjer Nowy*, 16 Feb. 1919.

55 Organizacja Syjonistyczna w Królestwie Polskim, Biuro Prasowe, Communique no. 25, pp. 12–13; *Materiały w sprawie żydowskiej w Polsce*, iii. 46–51.

56 Central Zionist Archives, Jerusalem (hereafter CZA), Grünbaum Archive, A127, f. 80, s. 1–5: Urgent motion of deputies Grünbaum, Thon, Farbstein et al. concerning the Statute of the Jewish Community in Poland, 24 June 1924.

57 Ibid.

58 Ibid.

59 Ibid.

60 Ibid.

61 *Sejm I Kadencji*, Druk sejmowy, 1394 (Warsaw, n.d.).

62 *Dziennik Ustaw Rzeczypospolitej Polskiej* 1925, no. 114, item. 807.

63 'Dokonanie wyborów organów zarządzających w gminach wyznaniowych żydowskich na obszarze województw: Krakowskiego, Lwowskiego, Stanisławowskiego', *Monitor Polski*, 7 Mar. 1924, p. 56.

64 *Sprawozdania Stenograficzne Senatu*, 28 July 1924, col. 4. According to Juliusz Wurzel, the Roman Catholic Church received 1,457 times as much, the Orthodox Church 95 times as much, the Reformed Evangelical Church 46 times as much, and the Muslim community 5 times as much (ibid., 17 Dec. 1924, no.78, col. 40).

65 'Wywiad z posłem Grynbaumem', *Nasz Przegląd*, 27 Mar. 1924; *Wniosek nagły w przedmiocie wyborów organów zarządzających w gminach żydowskich*, Druk sejmowy, 1073 (Warsaw, n.d.).

66 'Żydowska Rada Narodowa wobec wyborów do gmin żydowskich', *Nowy Przegląd*, 4 Apr. 1924.

67 *Sprawozdania Stenograficzne Senatu*, 6 Nov. 1924, cols. 35–6.

68 Paruch, *Od konsolidacji państwowej do konsolidacji narodowej*, 231.

69 Ibid. 235, 239, 240; K. Kawalec, *Spadkobiercy niepokornych. Dzieje polskiej myśli politycznej 1918–1939* (Wrocław, 2000), 128.

70 Paruch, *Od konsolidacji państwowej do konsolidacji narodowej*, 129.

71 Minister of Internal Affairs Kazimierz Młodzianowski issued a circular on 27 May 1926 in which he presented a resolution of the Council of Ministers to the effect that 'the government does not place obstacles to Zionist organizational activity within the country, particularly with the view to emigration, collections of funds, professional transformation of Jewish society, and so on' (A. Hafftka, 'Żydowskie ugrupowania polityczne w Polsce', *Sprawy Narodowościowe*, 1930, nos. 3–4, p. 348).

72 'Program Żydowskiej Partii Ludowej', in A. Bełcikowska, *Stronnictwa i związki polityczne w Polsce* (Warsaw, 1925), 517–20.

73 'W sprawie narodowej kurii wyborczej dla Żydów: Wywiad z prezesem frakcji ortodoksyjnej posłem Eliaszem Kirszbraunem', *Nasz Przegląd*, 8 July 1926.

74 T. Schramm, 'Żydzi wobec odradzania się państwowości polskiej', in *Przełomy w historii: Pamiętnik XVI Powszechnego Zjazdu Historyków Polskich*, ii/2 ([Toruń], 2000), 232–4.

75 *Dziennik Ustaw Rzeczypospolitej Polskiej*, 1928, no. 28, item 159; W. Sudnik, *Prawo polityczne Rzeczypospolitej Polskiej, 1918–1939* (Warsaw, 2002), 495.

76 *Najnowsze dzieje Żydów w Polsce: W zarysie (do 1950 roku)*, ed. J. Tomaszewski (Warsaw, 1993), 189.

77 A. Chojnowski, *Koncepcje polityki narodowościowej rządów polskich w latach 1921–1939* (Wrocław, 1979), 51.

78 J. Dawidsohn, *Gminy żydowskie (z tekstami ustaw i rozporządzeń)* (Warsaw, 1931), 7.

79 J. Grynsztejn and I. Kerner, *Przepisy o organizacji gmin wyznaniowych żydowskich, wraz z ustawami, rozporządzeniami, okólnikami i reskryptami związkowymi oraz orzecznictwem sądowym* (Warsaw, 1931). This brochure is the most comprehensive compilation of this type of document in existence.

80 *Sprawozdania Stenograficzne Senatu*, 13 May 1928, cols. 8–9.

81 CZA, Grünbaum Archive, A 127, f. 118, s. 3: report from the session of the Budget Committee, 1 Dec. 1928. Contribution by Deputy Grünbaum.

82 'Poseł dr Thon u wicepremiera Bartla', *Nowy Dziennik*, 28 Apr. 1928.

83 Grünbaum spoke on the subject in the Budget Committeee on 18 Dec. 1928. Senator Schreiber directed a letter to the MWRiOP; see 'Protest przeciwko rozwią zywaniu zarządów gmin żydowskich', *Chwila*, 7 Dec. 1928.

84 Grünbaum stated that: 'no National Democratic government ever used this law, but the present government already has and did it to satisfy Agudah, the dimmest Jewish clerical party' (*Sprawozdania Stenograficzne Senatu*, 5 Dec. 1929, col. 109).

85 I. Grünbaum, 'Do Ministerstwa Wyznań Religijnych i Oświecenia Publicznego' (18 May 1928), *Biuletyn Klubu Posłów i Senatorów Żydowskiej Rady Narodowej*, 1928, nos. 4–6, p. 1; *Biuletyn Klubu Posłów i Senatorów Żydowskiej Rady Narodowej*, 28 Nov. 1928; *Biuletyn Klubu Posłów i Senatorów Żydowskiej Rady Narodowej*, 1929, no. 4, pp. 102–4.

86 *Dziennik Ustaw Rzeczypospolitej Polskiej*, 1930, no. 75, item 592.

87 *Sprawozdania Stenograficzne Senatu*, 9 Feb 1931, col. 65.

88 *Sprawozdania Stenograficzne Senatu*, 10 Feb. 1931, col. 44.

89 *Sprawozdania Stenograficzne Senatu*, 5 Feb. 1931, col. 50. Thon continued from Hartglas' pronouncement in 1917: 'Should there be a Jew who, being Jewish in the national sense, were religiously indifferent, then his religious views, until such time as he defines them by converting to a different religion, are his personal matter, and do not exclude him from the community' (Hartglas, *Zasady naszego programu*, 34).

90 Sprawozdania Stenograficzne Senatu, 10 Feb. 1931, col. 41. Wilhelm Berkelhammer wrote that the directive meant 'a total annihilation or fragmentation of the Jewish community' ('Tragifarsa', *Nowy Dziennik*, 21 Mar. 1931).

91 *Sprawozdania Stenograficzne Senatu*, 3 Nov. 1932, col. 85.

92 'Jedność i całość gminy żydowskiej w największym niebezpieczeństwie! Wniosek Koła Żydowskiego', *Nowy Dziennik*, 21 Mar. 1931.

93 'Minister Składkowski o Żydach w Polsce', *Nowy Dziennik*, 23 Mar. 1931; 'Rząd wobec spraw żydostwa polskiego: Co o tym mówił min. oświaty Czerwiński', *Chwila*, 21 May 1931.

94 'Pismo posłów żydowskich Rady Narodowej do p. Ministra WRiOP w sprawie wyborów do gmin żydowskich', *Warszawska Informacja Prasowa*, 1931, no. 16, pp. 214–16.

95 O. Thon, 'Nasze poniżenie', *Nowy Dziennik*, 26 Mar. 1931.

96 See J. Tomaszewski, 'Walka polityczna wewnątrz gmin żydowskich w latach trzydziestych w świetle interpelacji posłów', *Biuletyn Żydowskiego Instytutu Historycznego*, 85 (1973), 85–110.

97 AAN, PRM, cz. 3A, t. 1, k. 17–25: 'Interpelacja posła Gruenbauma i tow. z Koła Żydowskiego do pana Ministra Wyznań Religijnych i Oświecenia Publicznego w sprawie

nadużyć władzy, popełnionych przy wyborach do gmin wyznaniowych żydowskich na terenie b. Królestwa Polskiego', 31 Oct. 1931.

98 AAN, PRM, cz. 3A, t. 1, k. 364–6: 'Interpelacja posła Gruenbauma i tow. z Koła Żydowskiego do pana Ministra Wyznań Religijnych i Oświecenia Publicznego w sprawie nadużyć władzy, popełnionych przy wyborach do gmin wyznaniowych żydowskich na terenie b. Królestwa Polskiego', 10 Dec. 1931.

99 *Sprawozdania Stenograficzne Senatu*, 1–2 Oct. 1931, cols. 61–2; *Sprawozdania Stenograficzne Senatu*, 3 Dec. 1932, col. 84.

100 'Pismo Klubu Posłów Żydowskich do Komisarza Rządu w sprawach gminnych', *Nasz Przegląd*, 21 Nov. 1931.

101 Cited in Żebrowski, *Żydowska Gmina Wyznaniowa w Warszawie*, 32.

102 S.W., 'Nowe rozporządzenie Ministra WRiOP', *Nasz Przegląd*, 5 Nov. 1931.

103 *Sprawozdania Stenograficzne Senatu*, 5 Mar. 1928, cols. 80–1. Dropping this item of expenditure was proposed by Grünbaum (CZA, Grünbaum Archive, A 175, f. 118, s. 4: Deputy Grünbaum, address on the budget of the MWRiOP, Report of Budget Committee session, 18 Dec. 1928).

104 A. Hartglas, 'Bez złudzeń', *Nowe Słowo*, 29 Sept. 1930.

105 *Sprawozdania Stenograficzne Senatu*, 21 Feb. 1936, col. 60. Andrzej Friszke summed up: 'The growth of aggressive antisemitism on the right was one of the most important aspects defining the atmosphere of the 1930s' (A. Friszke, *O kształt niepodległej* (Warsaw, 1989), 308).

106 *Sprawozdania Stenograficzne Senatu*, 11 Feb. 1937, col. 45.

107 W. Wasiutyński, *Źródła niepodległości* (London, 1977), 20.

108 Cited in A. Landau-Czajka and Z. Landau, 'Posłowie polscy w Sejmie 1935–1939 o kwestii żydowskiej', in J. Żyndul (ed.), *Rozdział wspólnej historii: Studia z dziejów Żydów w Polsce ofiarowane prof. Jerzemu Tomaszewskiemu w siedemdziesiątąrocznicę urodzin* (Warsaw, 2001), 211–24.

109 L. Halpern, 'Wśród zmagań o jedność żydowską', *Nasza Opinia*, 15 Mar. 1936.

110 AAN, MSW, 963, k. 102–3: Sprawozdanie kwartalne z życia mniejszości narodowych, IV kw. 1935.

111 A. Hartglas, 'Reprezentacja', *Nasza Opinia*, 27 June 1937.

112 'Walka o reprezentację: Ankieta "Naszej Opinii"', *Nasza Opinia*, 4 July 1937; 18 July 1937.

113 'Tymczasowa Reprezentacja Żydostwa Polskiego', *Sprawy Narodowościowe*, 1937, no. 3, 304–5.

114 'Żydzi', *Sprawy Narodowościowe*, 1937, nos. 1–2, p. 121.

115 Paruch, *Od konsolidacji państwowej do konsolidacji narodowej*, 256, 288, 315; id., *Myśl polityczna obozu piłsudczykowskiego, 1926–1939* (Lublin, 2005), 422–3.

116 Uchwały Rady Naczelnej OZN (n.p, n.d.), 18.

117 *Sprawozdania Stenograficzne Senatu*, 5 Mar. 1937, col. 60.

118 R. M. Shapiro, 'Autonomia żydowskich gmin wyznaniowych w Polsce. Łódź 1914–1939', *Biuletyn Żydowskiego Instytutu Historycznego*, 153 (1990), 71, 75.

119 Ibid. 76.

120 *Projekt ustawy złożony przez posła Janinę Prystorową o uboju zwierząt gospodarskich w rzeźniach*, Druk sejmowy, 59 (Warsaw, 1936). On the course of the debate, see S. Rudnicki, 'Ritual Slaughter as a Political Issue', *Polin*, 8 (1992), 147–60; see also Żebrowski, *Żydowska Gmina Wyznaniowa w Warszawie*, 609–725.

121 O. Thon, 'Tanie zwycięstwo, które drogo może kosztować', *Nasz Przegląd*, 8 Mar. 1936.

Jewish Involvement in Local *Kehilot,* the Sejm, and Municipalities in Interwar Poland

ANTONY POLONSKY

JEWISH POLITICIANS devoted enormous efforts during the First World War and in the interwar years to the establishment of a system of national self-government. This was always a somewhat utopian project. For the Orthodox, it raised the spectre of diaspora nationalism and challenged their view that the system should have primarily a religious character. For Polish, Ukrainian, and Lithuanian nationalists, it was anathema, because it undermined the national character of the states they were attempting to create. Even more fundamental was the problem that, with its imposition of a compulsory nationalization on very diverse Jewish communities, it was at odds with the concept of individual rights and the liberal state.

Under these circumstances, the actions of local *kehilot* (also described as 'community boards') and Jewish involvement in municipal affairs in the towns where they lived became more fruitful expressions of Jewish self-government. The last decades of the nineteenth century had seen attempts by the parties linked with the 'new Jewish politics', above all the Zionists, to gain influence in the reformed structures of Jewish community self-government. Indeed, from the days of Herzl, one of the principal goals of the Zionists had been to take over these community bodies under the slogan *kibush hakehilot* ('conquest of the *kehilot*').

Polish independence made possible the creation of a single uniform system of Jewish self-government for the nearly nine hundred *kehilot* in the country, whose total budget in the 1920s amounted to around 20 million zlotys, mostly from Jewish sources.[1] The establishment of this unified *kehilah* system, as described by Szymon Rudnicki in this volume, proved to be a protracted process, partly because of the very different views held by the various Jewish political groups on its nature and functions.[2] As he demonstrates, the autonomists, organized in Poland in the Folkist Party, and the Zionists saw the *kehilah* as the core of a system of Jewish self-government in the diaspora. They envisaged a secular institution, elected by all Jews in a given locality, controlling all aspects of Jewish life including education and social welfare and able to levy taxes. In spite of their anti-religious views, the Bund also supported the idea of Jewish community self-government but with its functions restricted to educational and cultural activities. Orthodox religious organizations as well as the assimilationists, with whom they had frequently been in a tactical alliance before 1914, saw the community board as a body with solely religious functions and sought also to exclude non-religious Jews from involvement in its affairs. They were also against women voting in *kehilah* elections. Language was also a matter of dispute. Most Jewish groups favoured Yiddish as the language of *kehilah* business, while some Zionists favoured Hebrew, and the assimilationists Polish.

Very different systems of Jewish self-government had evolved in the different partitions. The most developed and effective was in the Prussian partition from which most Jews emigrated after 1918. Only a residual system remained in the former Pale of Settlement, where the *kahal* had been abolished in 1844. In the Kingdom of Poland a somewhat restrictive system had been introduced in 1822, and in Galicia a system was established which was more far-reaching than that in the Congress Kingdom but not as effective as in Prussian Poland. In November 1916, as part of the programme of self-government which they were introducing into the General Government, the German occupation authorities proposed a system of local and county autonomous Jewish bodies, which would send representatives to a 'Jewish supreme council'. Under the German proposal, which was modelled on the Jewish community structures established in Prussia and Baden, the *kehilot* would be responsible for the control of Jewish religious life and the supervision of all Jewish religious and charitable societies. In addition they would administer Jewish education, both secular and religious, and take care of the Jewish poor. As in Prussia, the *kehilah* would be a public-legal corporation to which all Jews apart from those who declared themselves to have no religious commitment were obliged to belong. It would be responsible for submitting accounts to the authorities and could levy taxes on its members to supplement its income from other sources. A qualified system of voting was created. Half the members of the community board were to be elected by men over 25 who paid the *kehilah* tax. The remainder were elected by those with secondary or higher education or rabbinic ordination or were nominated by the state, whose influence over these bodies, as in Germany, was to be considerable. The day-to-day business of the *kehilah* was to be conducted by an executive, which in smaller communities would be directly elected and in larger communities selected by the *kehilah* council.[3] This legislation was never fully implemented, and the Jewish supreme council never came into being. Elections were held for *kehilot* in 218 communities, although not in Warsaw and Łódź. In the *kehilah* elections in Białystok, where Jews were in the majority and the Jewish system of self-government had very wide powers, in December 1918, when it was still under German rule, the largest number of votes was won by the Bund (socialist) with fifteen of the seventy-one seats, while the Faraynikte Socialist party won ten. The various religious groups won eighteen seats, the Zionists nineteen, and the Folkists (autonomist) two.[4] Similar results emerged from the *kehilah* elections in Vilna which took place at the end of December after the departure of the German forces. The Zionists won twenty-four of the eighty seats, with an additional three for Po'alei Tsiyon (Zionist socialist), the Bund won twenty-three, the Folkists won ten, the artisans group seven, the Democrats five and the remaining groups (the United Socialists, the Orthodox, Tse'irei Yisra'el (Zionist), and the Union of [Jewish] Merchants) eight.[5]

After the establishment of Polish independence, Józef Piłsudski, in his capacity of head of state, modified the German law by decree on 7 February 1919 and extended it to the Austrian-administered zone of the former Congress Kingdom. The new law weakened the power of the *kehilah*, stressing its religious character, eliminating its supervisory role in relation to private Jewish organizations, abolishing its responsibility for secular education, and making its responsibility for social welfare voluntary. The strong state control over community finances and rabbinic elections was retained. The structure it created was thus much more like that in Galicia before 1914 than that in Prussia. It did, however, introduce a voting system in which all men over 25 were enfranchised and voting was direct, secret, and proportional. The supervision of the *kehilot* was the responsibility first of the Jewish Department of the Ministry of Religious Denominations and Public Enlightenment. and then of the Ministry of Internal Affairs (Ministerstwo Spraw Wewnętrznych; MSW), where a department of Jewish affairs was to be created. However, as Rudnicki points out, such a department was never established, and Jewish affairs were placed in the hands of relatively low-level officials who did not constitute a separate group in the ministry.[6]

It was only after the May coup that this legislation was extended to the rest of Poland (apart from Silesia, whose autonomous status was guaranteed by the League of Nations). The governments of the parliamentary period down to May 1926 were not particularly sympathetic to Jewish autonomy, and disputes arose in the 1920s, particularly in Kresy, over the scope and nature of the system. In towns like Vilna and Białystok, where the *kahals* had been abolished under Nicholas I, councils with wide-ranging authority had been established. Thus in Vilna, the Hevrat Hatsedakah Hagedolah, which, as Vladimir Levin describes, had administered the community since the 1840s, was replaced by a community body with control over all aspects of community activity.[7] Local leaders resisted the attempts of the Polish authorities to impose the February 1919 decree in the town, but on 28 October 1925 it was finally introduced over local Jewish protests.

In Białystok, after the collapse of German rule a far-reaching system of Jewish community self-government was established in which all the main Jewish parties participated.[8] This was disbanded by the communist 'Revkom' which took control of the city in August 1920, and after the Bolshevik withdrawal only the General Zionists and the Orthodox took part in the *kehilah*'s work. It had now lost the trust of the American Jewish Joint Distribution Committee, which was providing extensive aid to the Jewish community in the town, and its activity was restricted to religious matters; running the community registry of births, deaths, and marriages; and maintaining the cemetery. The limited functions of the *kehilah* aroused opposition, and from 1925 attempts were made to lobby the government for permission to reorganize it, giving it the right to levy taxes and extend its scope to make it the focus for autonomous religio-cultural rights.[9]

This period was also marked by a bitter conflict in the Warsaw *kehilah* which brought to an end the long-standing alliance between the Orthodox and the assimilationists dating back to the 1870s. This collapsed when the *kehilah* executive, over Orthodox objections, voted in March 1921 to recognize Doctor Samuel Abraham

Poznański, rabbi of the modern synagogue on Tłomackie Street, as an official member of the Warsaw rabbinate who would therefore be funded by the *kehilah*.[10] Poznański, a Zionist and a graduate of a German university and rabbinical seminary, was anathema to the Orthodox. Writing in the Agudah (the main Orthodox party) paper, *Der yid*, a columnist asserted: 'The Orthodox masses oppose Poznański and everything he represents.'[11] With the support of the Gerer Rebbe, Abraham Mordecai Alter, they now mounted a campaign to reverse the decision of the executive, even appealing to the minister, Maciej Rataj, not to ratify the appointment. This was not successful, and the Agudah even considered, on the analogy of the Orthodox in Frankfurt, of withdrawing from the *kehilah*.[12] Poznański held office as a *kehilah* rabbi only briefly: he became ill and died soon after his appointment. He was, however, replaced by his successor as rabbi at the Tłomackie Street synagogue, Doctor Mojżesz Schorr.

The first *kehilah* elections in interwar Poland took place in mid-1924. In the former Kingdom of Poland and Kresy, all *kehilah* taxpayers automatically had the right to vote, while Jews who were not liable to pay tax because of poverty could participate by submitting a declaration to the election commission of their desire to vote.[13] The conflict between the different Jewish parties took a different form there from that in parliamentary and local government elections. Indeed, it may be that Jewish voters cast their ballots differently in *kehilah* elections than in general and local elections and were more willing in the former to vote for religious parties.

The conflict over the control of the *kehilot* was particularly bitter in the former Kingdom of Poland and Kresy. Certainly the Agudah, whose main strength lay in central Poland, saw control of the *kehilot* as vital to its mission. According to one party activist, Abraham Meir Krongrad, in the sejm elections the Agudah 'fights not to be ignored; in the *kehilah*, it fights for hegemony'.[14] One problem the party faced was opposition from within the Orthodox community, above all from the followers of the Aleksandrover Rebbe and from Rabbi Joseph Isaac Schneersohn, leader of the Lubavitcher hasidim. The Zionists, for their part, were determined to challenge the Orthodox and establish a dominant position in the *kehilot*, while the Folkists, whose political influence had waned significantly, still saw the *kehilah* as the core element in the system of non-territorial national autonomy they were attempting to establish.

The *kehilah* elections in Warsaw in June 1924 were a relative victory for the Agudah, which succeeded in obtaining the support of the Aleksandrover hasidim. Together with this group it won twenty of the fifty seats. The Zionists won fourteen, Mizrachi (Orthodox Zionist) five, the Bund five, and Po'alei Tsiyon Left two. The Folkists' diminished influence was reflected in the fact that they won only three seats. In Łódź, the Agudah won thirteen of thirty-five seats, the 'non-partisan religious' (mostly Aleksandrover hasidim) seven, the Zionists nine, the Bund three, the Po'alei Tsiyon two, and the Folkists one.[15]

In Galicia the conflict between the religious elements in Jewish society and both the assimilationists and the Zionists was less bitter. The restricted pre-war curial franchise, with voting weighted in favour of large taxpayers, was still in operation; it also favoured the religious and the assimilationists. In Kraków, the pre-war religious division persisted between the more religiously progressive Jews who continued to worship in the Tempel, and the followers of the different hasidic dynasties, above all the Sanzer and Bobover rebbes. As before the war, the two groups co-operated on the community board, which was led for much of the interwar period by Doctor Rafał Landau. In the 1924 *kehilah* elections the coalition of integrationists and Orthodox retained their dominant position, winning two-thirds of the votes, while the Zionists won only one seat out of twenty-five.[16] In Lviv, too, the coalition of Orthodox and assimilationists retained power. Many Galician *kehilot* were at this stage ruled by appointed commissions.

It was only in February 1926 that the government finally confirmed the *kehilah* election results in Warsaw and authorized the *kehilah* to elect an executive. This proved a difficult task, and, after considerable dispute, the Orthodox minority succeeded in electing its representatives, Eliasz Kirszbraun and Jacob Trockenheim, president and vice president. However, Kirszbraun recognized that the *kehilah* could not function if he were unable to forge a working relationship with the Zionists, and in June 1926 an agreement was reached by which the Agudah was assigned the vice-presidency of the executive and the presidency of the *kehilah*, while the Zionists took the presidency of the executive and vice-presidency of the *kehilah*.[17] This did not end the conflict over a wide range of issues, including education, the control of *sheḥitah* (ritual slaughter), and support for cultural activities, but at least it allowed the *kehilah* to function.

In Łódź, political division, clearly revealed in the election, made it impossible to create a stable *kehilah* administration. The *kehilah* executive was made up of six members of the Agudah, four Zionists, three non-party religious, a Bundist, and a Folkist. Although the Agudah had won the largest number of seats, a coalition of Zionists and non-party religious succeeded in getting Doctor Jerzy Rosenblatt, the Zionist sejm deputy, elected president, so that the Agudah had to settle for the vice-presidency. This was a recipe for conflict, as the different parties were divided over many issues, including the role of the rabbinate, the language of the *kehilah*, and support for secular and religious education. Debates in the *kehilah* were frequently disrupted and the Agudah constantly appealed to the provincial administration, the Supreme Administrative Tribunal, and the ministry to overturn *kehilah* decisions it opposed.

The Piłsudski government, as mentioned above, was eager to improve relations with the Jewish community. Thus shortly after the coup the minister of religious denominations and public enlightenment dealt with a long-standing Jewish grievance by finally authorizing the *kehilot* to hold meetings in Polish, Hebrew, or Yiddish, so long as all official minutes, records, and correspondence with the state were in the 'state language'.[18] The new government saw the establishment of a uniform system of Jewish self-government as a way of winning the support of the Orthodox, particularly the Agudah, who approved of the limited character proposed by the authorities. A law passed on 14 October 1927 and amended on 6 March 1928 established a single legal system for *kehilot* across the whole of Poland. According to this statute, the

Jewish communities were defined as autonomous organizations exercising particular religious and social functions. Their tasks were to provide rabbinical services and to maintain religious institutions, cemeteries, and Jewish religious schools. They were also responsible for ensuring the supply of kosher meat and operating social welfare agencies. The communities were to be governed by elected boards, which were authorized to levy taxes upon all those benefiting from community services. All those who belonged to the 'Mosaic faith' were required to belong to a Jewish community and could only withdraw by conversion or by declaring that they were atheists.

In a further attempt to consolidate its relations with the Agudah, which was supporting the authorities in the national elections scheduled for 4 March 1928, the government in February of that year backed what Robert Shapiro has described as a 'virtual *coup d'état*' in the Łódź *kehilah* by which the Agudah, headed by its redoubtable leader, Jacob Leib Mincberg, an industrialist and devoted follower of the Gerer Rebbe, seized control of the *kehilah* executive.[19] When this was declared illegal in the courts, the government prevented the former executive from returning to power by dissolving both the *kehilah* and the executive and appointing a provisional executive, dominated by the Agudah, whose running of the *kehilah* was given the full support of the local administration.

Mincberg, who also served in the local city council and the sejm, was to remain president of the Łódź *kehilah* until 1939. According to Robert Shapiro, 'he was simultaneously very much the European businessman in a well-cut suit and hat and a hasid who wore traditional garb on Sabbaths and holidays, including a *shtrayml* when on pilgrimages to Ger'.[20] He was a controversial figure. In the local Bundist paper he was attacked as 'the mini-Mussolini of the Łódź Agudah',[21] while the secretary of the *kehilah* was later to describe his administrative style as 'a mosaic of dictatorship and liberalism, of strict piety and the most modern methods of administration'.[22] Certainly, Mincberg was able to provide an impressive array of social services to the impoverished Jews of Łódź while at the same time attempting to advance the Agudah agenda.

In April 1928 the government imposed the *kehilah* law by decree in Vilna, and elections were held on 29 July of that year. They showed how divided politically the Jews of the town were. Of the twenty-five seats, five were won by the Zionists (including one Mizrachi); four by the artisans; three each by the Bund, Akhdes (non-political religious), and the merchants; two each by the Agudah, retail traders, and Folkists; and one by the property-owners. Since no single party was strong enough to take control, the four 'economic' groups combined with the Zionists to elect Doctor Jakub Wygodzki president. It was decided that Polish, Hebrew, and Yiddish should be used in all official transactions. After some dispute with the residual Hevrat Hatsedakah Hagedolah, still controlled by the Agudah, the buildings it administered, which included the Great Synagogue and its adjoining buildings, the Strashun Library, the town's *mikva'ot* and two Jewish cemeteries, and some other properties were handed over to the *kehilah*.

In Vilna, the appointment of a chief rabbi and his deputies caused controversy between the Agudah, who favoured Rabbi Hayim Ozer Grodziński, a well-known talmudic scholar married to the granddaughter of Rabbi Israel Salanter and who had been active in public life as an opponent of the Zionists since the first decade of the century, and those who supported Rabbi Isaac Rubinstein, who had distinguished himself by his courage during the German occupation. This was finally resolved by the appointment of Rubinstein as chief rabbi and the creation of a special post, 'rabbi of the *kehilah*', for Grodziński. Rubinstein handled relations with the authorities, while Grodziński's primary responsibility was religious rulings.

The first nation-wide elections held under the new law were scheduled for mid-1931. This was a time of considerable political conflict in Poland, and the authorities intervened actively to help the Agudah whose support they sought in the confrontation with parliament. They allowed the party to make considerable use of the provision of the *kehilah* law debarring anyone who 'publicly desecrated the Jewish religion' from participation in *kehilah* elections (article 20),[23] which led the Bund to boycott them.

The government intervention and the belief of a part of the Jewish electorate that in a political crisis it was in the Jewish interest to side with the authorities meant that in Warsaw and Łódź these elections were a victory for the Agudah. In Warsaw, the Agudah and its allies won twenty-four of the fifty seats on the *kehilah*, the Zionists and their allies won eighteen, the Folkists won two, Po'alei Tsiyon Left one and the assimilationists two. In Łódź, the Agudah did even better, winning fifteen seats as against four for the Zionists, one for Mizrachi, two for the Aleksandrover hasidim, and two for the Folkists.[24] Eliahu Mazur of the Agudah became president of the Warsaw *kehilah*, while Leib Mincberg was able to consolidate his power in Łódź. Complaints of widespread abuse of the electoral system were disregarded by Janusz Jędrzejewicz, the minister of religious denominations and public enlightenment.

The Agudah was not slow to draw lessons from its triumph. According to one of its representatives on the Warsaw *kehilah*, Isaac Meir Levin:

The fact that the largest part of the Jewish population gave their votes in the last *kehilah* elections to the list of the United Religious Election Committee [the Agudah and its allies] . . . shows clearly that the majority of Warsaw Jewry want to see the development of their *kehilah* on the basis of Torah and faith and carried out by men who uphold and respect these same fundamentals.[25]

Its opponents were not convinced. They saw the Agudah triumph as the result of fraud and government intervention and bitterly attacked the conduct of the Warsaw and Łódź *kehilot*. In particular, they assailed the refusal of the Łódź *kehilah* to provide support for secular Yiddishist schools of the Tsysho or make grants to the Yiddish Scientific Institute (YIVO) and the Jewish National Fund (Keren Kayemet) because of their 'leftist' and 'irreligious' character.[26]

The different pattern of *kehilah* politics which had been established in Galicia persisted after 1926. In the *kehilah* elections in 1929 in Kraków, in which universal male suffrage now operated, the Zionists did increase their seats to nine. This was not sufficient to undermine the control of the former coalition, which won eleven seats, and Rafał Landau remained chairman of the community board until the outbreak of the war. A similar situation prevailed in Lviv.

As the situation of the Jews worsened, the *kehilot* in Warsaw and Łódź began to take a more vigorous stance in their defence. The Warsaw *kehilah* took an active role in the Jewish-organized trade boycott of Nazi Germany and even expelled a member of the executive for failing to observe it. Eliahu Mazur also called a country-wide conference of *kehilah* representatives in order to prevent adverse changes to the *kehilah* tax laws and to oppose the law prohibiting Jewish methods of slaughter, and lobbied the authorities to curb anti-Jewish violence.[27] Similar actions were taken by Mincberg in Łódź. In addition, once the law restricting the sale of kosher meat to non-Jews went into effect, the Łódź *kehilah* took the initiative of training slaughterers who could remove the veins from the hindquarters of animals, rendering these parts kosher and thus available to religious Jews.

These actions did not succeed in allaying the growing discontent with the actions of these *kehilot*. The alliance with the authorities was not only unpopular but seemed to have lost its rationale, as the government introduced restrictions on *sheḥitah*, a key issue for the Orthodox section of society. Consequently, the Agudah was increasingly riven by dissension. The Bund, for its part, after some internal dispute, now abandoned its boycott of *kehilah* elections. These developments created a new situation. On 30 May 1936 the minister of religious denominations and public enlightenment called for elections in all *kehilot* whose four-year term of office had elapsed. Elections were to be held in smaller *kehilot* on 30 August and in larger ones a week later.[28]

The authorities were apprehensive that the *kehilah* elections would lead to a triumph for the Bund. On 22 August 1936 the Ministry of the Interior sent a 'strictly secret' circular letter to provincial authorities, warning that the Bund's participation in the *kehilah* elections raised

grave fears concerning a change in the character of those institutions . . . Entrance of representatives of the Bund into these institutions, and possibly even here and there attainment by them of a majority, would change the character of the *kehilah*, introducing into it many secular elements, and even making it a convenient instrument of political struggle.

If this took place, the government would be forced 'to intervene and even dismiss *kehilah* executives'. This outcome was to be prevented by active intervention, principally by the use of article 20 of the *kehilah* law, preventing the participation of anti-religious elements in *kehilah* elections.[29]

Such intervention proved ineffective, and the Bund achieved a major triumph in the *kehilah* elections in Warsaw, where, running together with Po'alei Tsiyon Left, it won fifteen of the fifty seats, as against twelve for the Agudah, eleven for the Zionists, four for Mizrachi, two for Po'alei Tsiyon Right, and one each for the Revisionists and the Folkists.[30] It proved impossible to create a viable executive, and the government, which had been dismayed by the Bund's victory, dissolved the community board in

January 1937. In its place it appointed a commissar and advisory council, headed by a Zionist, Maurycy Majzel, with a number of Agudah and Zionist representatives. In Vilna, the Zionists won the largest number of seats followed by the Bund, with the religious bloc in third place. This was also the pattern in Białystok, where 32 per cent of the seats were won by the General Zionists, 25 per cent by the Orthodox, and 14 per cent by economic associations. The Bund and Mizrachi won 9 per cent, the Revisionists 6 per cent, and Po'alei Tsiyon 5 per cent.

Given the unrealistic nature of the attempt to establish Jewish national self-government and the limited scope open to action by the *kehilot*, it does seem as if Jewish political groupings had most to gain from participation in local municipalities, where, with the achievement of full equality in Prussian Poland, Galicia, and the Kingdom of Poland and partial equality in the tsarist empire, Jews were now represented. This is not to gainsay the importance of Jewish representatives in the sejm, whose role is discussed by Szymon Rudnicki.[31]

The establishment of a liberal democratic system in Poland meant, at least until the coup of May 1926, the introduction of free parliamentary elections on the basis of a secret ballot and proportional representation. After the May coup, parliamentary elections continued to be held but, especially after 1930, were marked by much greater administrative interference and, after 1935, were conducted under a much more controlled electoral system. Local government, particularly in the larger cities, was also conducted on a democratic basis, although there too the growing authoritarianism of the Piłsudski regime undermined the extent to which these elections were conducted freely. Jews of all political persuasions participated actively in both parliamentary and local government elections, and the results of these elections in the different towns of the country give an interesting picture both of the different Jewish political traditions and of the way the political allegiances of the Jews changed in the period between the emergence of an independent Polish state and the outbreak of the Second World War. One of the striking features of Jewish political life in Poland was the difference between the political traditions of the former Russian and Austrian Poland. In Kraków and Lviv, the clash between religious and secular parties was less bitter, the decline of the assimilationists somewhat slower, and the policies of the local Zionists more moderate.

The first indication of the balance of political forces on the 'Jewish street' came in the elections to the Polish Constituent Assembly held on 26 January 1919. In Warsaw, the sixteen seats assigned to the capital were contested by 77 Jewish candidates (in nine lists) and 165 Polish (in twelve lists). The elections were, however, boycotted by the Bund. Because of the boycott, the result of the Bund's revolutionary posture in these years, and the unwillingness of some Orthodox Jews, particularly women, to vote, the Jewish turnout was quite low (55.7 per cent compared to 75.4 per cent for Poles in Warsaw). The Folkists repeated their victory in the Warsaw municipal election of July 1916, with two of their candidates elected to the Constituent Assembly, along with one Zionist (Isaac Grünbaum). They won 38.1 per cent of the Jewish vote, as against 24.8 per cent for the Zionists, 17.8 per cent for the Agudah, and 5.2 per cent for the assimilationists.[32] In Łódź, the Agudah succeeded in electing Rabbi Mosheh Eliyahu Halpern, while neither the Folkists nor Zionists received sufficient votes for a seat. The Agudah also won a seat in Lublin. In Białystok, Yehoshua Heschel Farbstein, the Mizrachi candidate, won a seat in a subsequent by-election on 15 June 1919 (the town only came under Polish control on 19 February), with the ultimate support of the General Zionists.

In Kraków, in elections to the sejm, there was a strong incentive for Jews to vote for a single candidate in order to ensure representation in parliament.[33] The elections to the Constituent Sejm showed how much the political attitudes of the local Jewish community had changed during the First World War. The two principal Jewish candidates were Adolf Gross, long-standing representative of Kraków in the Austrian Reichsrat, and Rabbi Ozjasz Thon, who headed the list of the Central Committee of the Zionist Organization of Western Galicia and Silesia.[34] Smaller groups such as the Jewish Social Democratic Party, which was shortly to merge with the Bund, and Po'alei Tsiyon (soon to split into right- and left-wing factions) also nominated candidates.

Gross's integrationist views now commanded much less support, and the elections proved a triumph for the Zionists, who won 73.9 per cent of the votes cast for Jewish lists, as against 16.3 per cent for Gross, 6.4 per cent for the Jewish Social Democratic Party, and 3.4 per cent for Po'alei Tsiyon. Because of the continuing military conflict, it was not possible to organize elections in eastern Galicia (including Lviv) and the area was represented by the pre-war deputies to the Austrian Reichsrat. They included five Jewish assimilationists, including Natan Loewenstein from Lviv.

Elections for the 120 seats on the Warsaw city council took place on 23 February 1919. This time the Bund participated, along with the other parties. By now, the influence of the Folkists was on the wane, and the largest number of votes were won by the Agudah and its allies, the Bund, and the Zionists. Of the 120 seats on the council, sixty-one were won by National Democracy (Endecja), twenty-three by the Polish Socialist Party (Polska Partia Socjalistyczna; PPS), and seven by the Democratic Committee for Urban Reform. The Agudah and its allies won eight seats, the Bund, the Zionists and the Folkists five each, and the assimilationists one.

Politics in Łódź was more polarized than in Warsaw, along both class and ethnic lines. In the city council election of 23 February 1919, twenty-nine seats were won by the Endecja and its ally the National Workers' Party and twenty-five by the PPS; the Zionists won seven seats, the Bund five, the Agudah four, and Po'alei Tsiyon three. The Folkists failed to win a seat.

During this period, no city council elections were held in either Kraków or Lviv, where the pre-war city councils continued to operate. In the Vilna city council elections of July 1919, thirty-four Poles and fourteen Jews were elected. The majority of the Poles were supporters of the Endecja. In Białystok, the Jewish representatives had walked out of the Temporary Civic Committee established after the town came under Polish control, when it insisted that all its members should sign a declaration confirming 'command of the Polish language both written and spoken' and because of disputes over the financing of the *kehilah* and the employment of Jews in the city council.[35] As a result the Jews boycotted the elections to the city council on 7 September 1919.

The next parliamentary elections took place in November 1922. The new electoral system made provision for proportional representation in sixty-three multimember constituencies, supplemented by a national list which would elect an additional seventy-two deputies. This system favoured large parties and was felt by minorities, particularly the Jews, to discriminate against them.[36] This was one of the main reasons, as mentioned above, for the establishment, under the aegis of Jewish leaders in the former Russian partition and those of the German minority, of the National Minorities' Bloc (Blok Mniejszości Narodowych), which was supported not only by the Zionists but also by the Agudah (with some reluctance) and by the Union of Merchants as well as the representatives of the Belarusians and Ukrainians. The Folkists, because of a dispute over the number of seats to be assigned to them, refused to participate. In these elections the majority of Warsaw's Jews voted for the bloc, which won two seats in the city, one by a Zionist and one by a supporter of the Agudah. Another seat was won by Noyekh Prilutski. The bloc won 50.2 per cent of the Jewish vote, as against 23.0 per cent for the Folkists and 18.8 per cent for the Bund. A similar result was achieved in Łódź, where a Zionist and an Agudist, Leib Mincberg, were elected. In Vilna, Jakub Wygodzki, standing on the bloc's ticket, did not obtain sufficient votes to win a seat but was elected from Nowogródek, with some Belarusian support.

In Kraków, the local Zionists, with their stronger ties to Polish society, did not join the bloc, but did express sympathy with its objectives and supported its national list. Separate lists were nominated by the Bund, the Jewish Workers' Election Committee (Po'alei Tsiyon Left), the Polish/Jewish Independent Socialist Election Committee, and the United Election Committee of Po'alei Tsiyon Right and Tse'irei Tsiyon. For their part, the integrationists did not run an independent campaign but campaigned together with the remnants of the Kraków conservatives and moderate democrats for the National-State Union.

As in 1919 the election, held on 5 November, proved a triumph for the Zionists. They won 91.5 per cent of the votes cast for Jewish lists (the Bund received 7.4 per cent) and their candidate, Ozjasz Thon, was elected to the sejm. It is impossible to tell how many Jews voted for the list of the National-State Union. In Lviv, where the Ukrainians boycotted the election, the Zionists won two seats, one of them being held by Leon Reich, who had not sat in the previous parliament, since elections had not been held in Lviv.

In the municipal election of 13 May 1923 in Łódź, the Endecja consolidated its position, and the balance of forces within the Jewish community also shifted against the socialists, with the Zionists and the Agudah each winning four seats as against three for the Bund, two for the followers of Aleksandrover hasidim, who refused to ally with the Agudah, and one for the Folkists. This led to the creation of an Endek administration which the Jews felt was strongly hostile to their interests.

Despite the ostensible neutrality of their parliamentary representatives, Jews mostly supported the coup of May 1926 which brought Piłsudski back to power and forestalled the creation of a centre-right and potentially antisemitic government. This was particularly the case with the Agudah, which established close links with the new regime. However, in the Warsaw city council election of 23 May 1927, few Jews voted for the government list and the combined Zionist–Orthodox list won a significant victory, with 53.3 per cent of the Jewish vote and sixteen seats on the council as against 26.4 per cent for the Bund (eight seats) and two seats each for the Orthodox Workers' group allied with the Agudah (7.1 per cent of the Jewish vote) and two seats for Po'alei Tsiyon (10.4 per cent of the Jewish vote).

The May coup severely weakened the position of the Endecja, which lost control of the Łódź city council in the local election of 9 October 1927. The largest grouping on the seventy-five member council was made up of the PPS (twenty-four seats), the German Socialist Labour Party (six seats), the Bund (five seats), and Po'alei Tsiyon (three seats), which was able to establish a viable administration. The Endecja and its allies had twenty-seven seats and the Zionists and the Agudah four each. In Białystok, the Jews abandoned their boycott and participated in the local government elections held on 13 December 1927. The United Jewish National Bloc, principally made up of Zionists, won nine seats, the Bund six, and the Orthodox two.

In the general election of March 1928 the government appealed to Jews to vote for the newly created Non Party Bloc for Co-operation with the Government (Bezpartyjny Blok Współpracy z Rządem; BBWR). In Warsaw many Jews did so, and two, the Agudah politician Eliasz Kirszbraun and Wacław Wiślicki of the Union of Merchants, were elected on the BBWR list. Three Jews were elected on the list of the National Minorities' Bloc, which Grünbaum had succeeded in recreating, although now without the participation of the Agudah. The National Minorities' Bloc obtained 9.3 per cent of the vote in Warsaw (down on its 1922 performance), the Orthodox General Jewish Bloc won 5.1 per cent, and the Bund 3.9 per cent. In these elections the communists won 14.0 per cent of the vote in Warsaw, much of this from Jewish voters. The National Minorities' Bloc was also successful in Łódź, where the long-time Zionist activist Jerzy Rosenblatt was elected. On this occasion Leib Mincberg did not obtain sufficient votes for election. In Vilna, the bloc also succeeded in electing one Jewish deputy, as it did in Białystok, where Belarusian votes contributed to this victory.

In Kraków, the BBWR sought to win Jewish support and strongly opposed the re-formed National Minorities' Bloc. The election to the sejm again resulted in victory for the Zionists, more significant because it was won in conflict with the Orthodox leaders who decided to support the BBWR. The Zionists won 82.3 per cent of the Jewish votes, the Agudah 11.7 per cent, and the Bund 4.6 per cent. Support among Jews for the BBWR proved quite limited.

A similar situation prevailed in Lviv. The largest share of the vote (29.3 per cent) was won by the east Galician Zionists, who had again decided against participating in the National Minorities' Bloc and who worked tacitly with the new government; the BBWR had come in second (25.5 per cent), and the Komitet Katolicko-Narodowy, the National Democratic list, third (14.3 per cent). The PPS was a close fourth (13.4 per cent). The National Minorities' Bloc won 9.9 per cent of the vote, mostly from local Ukrainians, and the Bund 2.3 per cent. The communists won 3.7 per cent. Of the four seats assigned to the city, two went to the Galician Zionists, one taken by Reich himself and the other by Doctor Maurycy Leser.

Political life was now dominated by the clash between Piłsudski and the parliamentary opposition of the centre and left (Centrolew), which was exerting political pressure to force Piłsudski to re-establish a fully parliamentary system. In this conflict the Jews mostly adopted an uneasy neutrality. In November 1930 Piłsudski arrested most of the opposition leaders and held new elections, in which, at least in eastern Poland, considerable administrative pressure was used to obtain a favourable result. The government also attempted to win Jewish support, using Bernard Hausner, from 1927 economic adviser of the Polish government in Palestine, as an intermediary. In these elections, in many constituencies, Jewish committees supporting the BBWR were established and Jews again voted for this group in significant numbers. The Zionists of the former Russian partition now abandoned the idea of a common front with the other national minorities and sought unsuccessfully to establish a single Jewish list including the Galician Zionists and the Agudah. The Agudah for its part fought the elections together with a section of the Folkists, the Union of [Jewish] Small Traders, the Union of [Jewish] Artisans, and the Union of Merchants.

In the big cities voting was relatively free, although opposition newspapers, including *Haynt* and *Nasz Przegląd*, were attacked by 'unknown assailants', presumably at the behest of the authorities. In Warsaw, the BBWR won 40.4 per cent of the vote, up on the 35.9 per cent it had won in 1928, while the Zionists won 7.0 per cent, the Agudah and its allies 7.0 per cent, the Bund 2.8 per cent, and the communists 8.8 per cent. The Endecja won 20.9 per cent. Both the Zionists and the Agudah won seats, while Wacław Wiślicki was elected on the BBWR list. The Zionists also won a seat in Łódź, where Leib Mincberg was elected on the BBWR list. In Białystok, a common list was presented by the Zionists, Mizrachi, and the Agudah but failed to win a seat. The Zionists also lost their seat in Vilna.

In Kraków, the Zionists triumphed again, but at the cost of worsened relations with Orthodox circles, some of whom again voted for the BBWR. The Zionists won 92.5 per cent of votes cast for Jewish lists, as against 5.9 per cent for the Bund, which stood together with a small leftist socialist group. In Lviv, the Zionists won only one seat—the second seat was lost because of the government's probably illegal disqualification of some of the votes cast for the Zionists. Another seat was won by a Jewish assimilationist.

During the period between 1918 and 1933 there had been no local government elections in Kraków, and the pre-war council was kept in being with additional members being co-opted. It was only on 22 March 1933 that parliament passed a bill on the partial reorganization of local government which finally made possible the establishment of an elected city council.[37] The first elections to the new council were set for 10 December 1933.

In these elections, in order to maximize Jewish representation and to counteract what was felt to be the growing threat from the political right with its openly anti-semitic stance, an attempt was made to create a non-partisan bloc comprising all the main Jewish factions, including those supporting the government. Separate lists were put forward by the Po'alei Tsiyon Left and Po'alei Tsiyon Right together with the Zionist socialist party, Hitahdut. The Bund campaigned jointly with the Polish Socialist Party.[38] The elections were a victory for the BBWR, which won thirty-seven of the sixty-four seats, and on the Jewish street for the Jewish non-partisan bloc, which won thirteen seats. No other Jewish grouping gained representation on the council.

With the onset of the Great Depression the Endecja began to display greater dynamism, particularly given the failure of the government to respond effectively to the economic crisis. It thus fought the city council election in Łódź on 27 May 1934 on the promise of getting rid of the 'Judeo-socialist' administration. This strategy proved highly successful. The Endecja and their allies won a clear majority on the council with thirty-nine seats, as against ten each for the United Socialist list, made up of the Polish, German, and Jewish socialist parties; ten for the Agudah; one for Po'alei Tsiyon; and four for the Zionists. This administration, which saw itself as the precursor of a future Endek government in Poland, proceeded to embark on a series of measures directed against the local Jewish population. The atmosphere on the council was quite threatening to Jews. When in March 1935 Leib Mincberg called for the municipality to give the same support for the local Jewish hospital as was being given to the municipal facility, he was greeted with shouts of 'We want to expel you as was done in Egypt and Spain.'[39]

The new parliamentary electoral system adopted in July 1935 after Piłsudski's death made the free selection of candidates virtually impossible and increased enormously the control the government could exercise over an election. In the lower house, proportional representation was abandoned, and the country was divided into 104 two-member constituencies.[40] Candidates had to be nominated by a special assembly in each constituency composed of local officials and representatives of elected local government bodies; economic organizations, such as chambers of commerce, indus-try, and agriculture; organizations of lawyers, doctors, teachers, and university pro-fessors; and other professional associations. In addition any group of 500 persons was entitled to one representative on the assembly. If only four candidates were pre-sented by the assembly, all could stand in the election. If more than four were nom-inated, only those who obtained more than one-quarter of the votes of the assembly in a single ballot (each member having the right to vote for four persons) could stand. As will be obvious, the scope for electoral manipulation by the government was enormous.

In such circumstances, the Polish opposition groups, from the Endecja to the communists, declined to participate and appealed to the people to boycott the elections. Jewish parties were also strongly critical, but their responses varied. While the Bund decided to boycott the elections, the Zionists were more concerned that the new electoral colleges would exclude Jewish candidates.

The first elections under the new system were held on 8 September 1935. All the opposition parties, with the exception of a group from the Polish Peasant Party 'Liberation', observed the boycott. The government did manage to reach arrangements with the Jews and with the other national minorities, so that they could nominate their own candidates. The socialist parties of the national minorities, including the Bund, observed the boycott.

In Warsaw, five Jewish candidates succeeded in winning through to the second round, but only the Zionist candidate, Joshua Gottlieb, was elected. The Agudah, whose candidate Rabbi Aron Lewin did not get through to the second round, boycotted the election. In Łódź, Leib Mincberg was again elected, as was Isaac Rubinstein, the Zionist candidate in Vilna.

In Kraków the government attempted to secure the election of Captain Leopold Spira, a member of the local executive of the BBWR and chairman of the Kraków branch of the Federation of Jewish Participants in the Struggle for Polish Independence, who had the support of the Agudah. Thon, again the Zionist choice, was unable to obtain the support of sufficient electors in the local electoral assembly to be a candidate.[41] As a result, the local Zionists called on Jews to abstain from voting and succeeded in preventing Spira's election. In Lviv the Zionist candidate, Emil Sommerstein, was elected.

The provocative anti-government and antisemitic stance of the Łódź city council led the government to dissolve it, and on 27 September 1936 new elections were held. The socialist groupings in the city were determined to undo their defeat of May 1934. For tactical reasons it was decided that the different socialist groupings should stand separately to avoid the Polish Socialist Party being attacked as the 'lackey of the Jews'. The result was a triumph for the left. The PPS won thirty-four seats and the Bund, in alliance with Po'alei Tsiyon Left six, giving these groupings a clear majority in the seventy-two strong council. The Endecja won twenty-seven seats, the Agudah three, and the Zionists two.

Three years later, when new parliamentary elections were called for 6 and 13 November 1938, the situation was very different. The government was now committed to a much more hostile stance towards Jews. The Bund and the Folkists still maintained their boycott, as did most Polish opposition parties, but all other Jewish groups saw parliamentary representation as an important means of expressing their discontent. In Warsaw, Salomon Seidenmann was elected on the Zionist ticket along with Jakub Trockenheim of the Agudah and, in Łódź, Leib Mincberg was again elected.[42] In Kraków, the difficult situation eroded the differences between the formerly contending Orthodox Jews and Zionists. The Zionists now sponsored an Electoral Committee of the Representation of the United Jewry of the City of Kraków, including all the Orthodox groupings and the most important community and professional organizations, which succeeded in electing Ignacy Schwartzbart to the sejm. In Lviv, Emil Sommerstein was again elected. Isaac Rubinstein was nominated to the senate, along with Zdzisław Żmygrider-Konopka, vice-president of the Federation of Jewish Participants in the Struggle for Polish Independence, an organization which had in 1938 a membership of nearly 7,000. Rubinstein had been two votes short of the number needed to be nominated by the local electoral college, and the local governor had promised the government would propose him for the senate if the Jews supported the local Camp of National Unity (Obóz Zjednoczenia Narodowego; OZON) candidate, General Stanisław Skwarczyński, which they did.

Towards the end of 1938 the government became less interested in a rightist approach, and, in an effort to win the co-operation of the democratic opposition, it allowed free local government elections in a large number of Polish cities and towns. The opposition, like the Jews, was determined to take part in the municipal elections, which it hoped would, as in Spain in 1931, pave the way for a return to parliamentary democracy.

These elections revealed striking changes in the Jewish political scene. Those in Warsaw in December 1938 proved a triumph for the Bund, which won fourteen seats (61.7 per cent of the Jewish vote), as against five seats for the Jewish National Bloc (which included both Zionists and the Agudah) and one for the Democratic Zionists. In Łódź, the government had been unable to work with the socialist city council, and it called for new elections on 18 December 1938. These merely confirmed the earlier result. The PPS won thirty-three of the eighty-four seats, the Endecja eighteen, the Bund eleven (57.4 per cent of the votes cast for Jewish parties), the pro-government OZON also won eleven seats, the various German parties five, the Zionists three (22.2 per cent of the votes cast for Jewish parties), and the Agudah three (20.4 per cent of the votes cast for Jewish parties).

The Vilna city council elections of April 1939 proved another triumph for the Bund which won ten of the seventy-two seats, as against five for the Zionists and two for Po'alei Tsiyon. However, this triumph was a hollow one, as most seats were won by the Endecja (twenty-six) and OZON (nineteen). The PPS won only nine seats. In Białystok, the Bund made up ten of the fifteen councillors representing Jewish parties.

In Kraków, new elections were called for 17 December 1938. The three principal parties contesting the election were OZON, which, partly as a result of the mediation of the archbishop of Kraków, Adam Stefan Sapieha, reached an alliance with the local Party of Labour, the Polish Socialist Party, and the Endecja. As in the parliamentary election of the previous year, the growing antisemitic climate fostered Jewish unity. Six Jewish lists competed in the elections. The dominant role was still held by the Zionist-sponsored Representation of the United Jewry of Kraków. The two factions of Po'alei Tsiyon reached an agreement this time, forming the Jewish Socialist Electoral Bloc. The Bund was unable to reach agreement with the PPS and put up its own list.

Among the Polish parties, the three largest parties were the Socialists (28.8 per cent of the votes), OZON in alliance with the Party of Labour (29.0 per cent), and the Endecja (18.2%). Within the Jewish community, the Representation of the United Jewry of the City of Kraków was a clear victor, with 58.8 per cent of the Jewish vote. The Bund increased its vote to 17.6 per cent, and the combined Po'alei Tsiyon to 6.1 per cent. The increase in the Bund's vote was significant, but on a much smaller scale than elsewhere in Poland. Overall, Jews won thirteen seats, as they had in 1933. Nine of these were members of the Representation of the United Jewry of the City of Kraków, three of the Bund, and one was elected on the Veterans' list.[43] The Zionists did even better in Lviv, where all sixteen Jewish councillors were elected on the Zionist list.

The long history of Jewish autonomous organizations in pre-partition Poland–Lithuania accustomed Jews to working in representative bodies. In the course of the nineteenth century, in response to governmental efforts to transform or even abolish Jewish self-government, new forms of self-government had emerged and established themselves. With the emergence of national concepts of Jewish identity, these were often seen as the basis for a system of Jewish national self-government. Their involvement in government attempts to reform or even to abolish Jewish self-government in the nineteenth century led to the emergence of very different systems in the different partitions, some more and some less effective. This could not be implemented in the aftermath of the First World War. Jews were, however, actively engaged in the reformed *kehilot* established in independent Poland and Lithuania, in local government, and in the parliaments of the two countries. Jewish unity proved elusive and town councils and parliaments proved above all important arenas for the conflicts between the different groups which dominated the Jewish political scene—the Zionists, the Orthodox, the socialists, and the integrationists. How these conflicts would have played out remains unclear because Jewish life there was tragically cut short by the war.

Notes

1 R. Shapiro, 'Jewish Self-Government in Poland: Łódź 1914–1939', Ph.D. thesis (Columbia University, 1987), 266. The term *kehilah* usually refers to the community and *kahal* to the organization that ran it until 1822 in Poland and until 1844 in Russia. However, on some occasions, the term *kehilah* is also used to denote the taxpayers within a Jewish community.

2 S. Rudnicki, 'The Struggle in the Polish Parliament for Jewish Autonomy and the Nature of the Jewish Community', in this volume.

3 M. Ringel, 'Ustawodawstwo Polski Odrodzonej o gminach żydowskich', in I. Schiper, A. Tartakower, and A. Hafftka (eds.), *Żydzi w Polsce Odrodzonej: Działalność społeczna, gospodarcza, oświatowa i kulturalna*, 2 vols. (Warsaw, 1932–3), ii. 244; Z. Szajkowski, 'The German Ordinance of November 1916 on the Organization of Jewish Communities in Poland', *Proceedings of the American Academy for Jewish Research*, 34 (1966), 111–39: 128–9.

4 Ringel, 'Ustawodawstwo Polski Odrodzonej o gminach żydowskich', 270.

5 Š. Liekis, *A State within a State? Jewish Autonomy in Lithuania 1918–1925* (Vilnius, 2003), 63;

see also S. Kassow, 'Jewish Communal Politics in Transition: The Vilna *Kehile*, 1919–1920', *YIVO Annual*, 20 (1991), 61–93.

6 Rudnicki, 'The Struggle in the Polish Parliament for Jewish Autonomy and the Nature of the Jewish Community'; see also R. Żebrowski, *Żydowska Gmina Wyznaniowa w Warszawie 1918–1939: W kręgu polityki* (Warsaw, 2012), 32.

7 V. Levin, 'The Synagogue in the System of Jewish Self-Government in Tsarist Russia', in this volume.

8 A. S. Hershberg, *Pinkas bialystok: grunt-materyaln tsu der geshikte fun di yidn in bialystok biz nokh der ershter velt-milkohme*, 2 vols. (New York, 1949–50), ii. 269–70.

9 Ibid. ii. 282, 287–8.

10 On this incident, see G. Bacon, 'The Poznanski Affair of 1921: Kehillah Politics and the Internal Political Realignment of Polish Jewry', *Studies in Contemporary Jewry*, 4 (1988), 135–43. On Poznański, see D. Flinker, 'Rabanei varsha', in Y. Grünbaum (ed.), *Entsiklopedyah shel galuyot: varsha*, 12 vols. (Jerusalem, 1953–73), vol. i, cols. 301–2; M. Bałaban, 'Dr. Samuel Poznański (1864–1921): Szkic biograficzny', in *Księga pamiątkowa ku czci Dra. Samuela Poznańskiego* (Warsaw, 1927), pp. ix–xxviii.

11 *Der yid*, 30 Mar. 1921.

12 *Der yid*, 4 Apr. 1921; *Der moment*, 4 Apr. 1921.

13 D. Flinker, 'Kehilat varsha', in Grünbaum (ed.), *Entsiklopedyah shel galuyot*, vol. i, col. 289; *Nayer Haynt*, 2 June 1924; Ringel, 'Ustawodawstwo Polski Odrodzonej o gminach żydowskich', 247.

14 *Ortodoksishe yugnt bleter*, 3/19 (May–June 1931).

15 For the results in Warsaw, see *Nayer Haynt*, 17 June 1924; *Der moment*, 17 June 1924; Flinker, 'Kehilat varsha', col. 290; for the results in Łódź, see *Nayer Haynt*, 8 July 1924.

16 On developments on the community board, see K. Samsonowska, 'Zarys funkcjonowania Żydowskiej Gminy Wyznaniowej w Krakowie w latach 1918–1939', MA thesis (Jagiellonian University, 1991); ead., 'Wybory do władz Żydowskiej Gminy Wyznaniowej w Krakowie: Z dziejów nieznanej samorządności Krakowa', *Historia: Pismo Młodych Historyków*, 2 (1994), 47–66; ead., *Wyznaniowe gminy żydowskie i ich społeczności w województwie krakowskim (1918–1939)* (Kraków, 2005).

17 Flinker, 'Kehilat varsha', col. 290; *Der moment*, 4 June 1926.

18 Ministry of Religious Denominations and Public Enlightenment, letter to Warsaw *kehilah*, 22 Jan. 1926, in *Przepisy o organizacji gmin wyznaniowych żydowskich*, ed. J. Grynsztejn et al. (Warsaw, 1931), 100–1.

19 On these developments, see R. M. Shapiro, 'Aspects of Jewish Self-Government in Łódź, 1914–1939', *Polin*, 6 (2005), 144–65; on Mincberg, see H. Seidman, *Ishim shehikarti* (Jerusalem, 1970), 327–34; *Polski Słownik Biograficzny*, 50 vols. to date (Kraków and Wrocław, 1935–), xxi. 281–2; *Ilustrirter poylisher mantshester*, July 1929.

20 Shapiro, 'Aspects of Jewish Self-Government in Łódź', 136.

21 *Lodzher veker*, 8 June 1928.

22 *Yidishe togblat*, 21 June 1938.

23 Ringel, 'Ustawodawstwo Polski Odrodzonej o gminach żydowskich', 247.

24 *Haynt*, 28 May 1931; 29 May 1931; D. Dąbrowska and A. Wein (eds.), *Pinkas hakehilot, polin: entsiklopedyah shel hayishuvim hayehudiyim lemin hivasdam ve'ad le'aḥar sho'at milḥemet ha'olam hasheniyah*, i: *Lodz vehagalil*, ed. D. Dąbrowska and A. Wein (Jerusalem, 1976–2005), 20.

25 *Dos yidishe togblot*, 11 Jan. 1932.

26 G. C. Bacon, *The Politics of Tradition: Agudat Yisrael in Poland, 1916–1939* (Jerusalem, 1996), 215.

27 *Dos yidishe togblot*, 9 May, 10, 18 June 1934; 11 Nov. 1935.

28 M. Galas and A. Polonsky, 'Introduction', *Polin*, 23 (2011), 3–49: 23–6; *Dziennik Urzędowy Ministerstwa Wyznań Religijnych i Oświecenia Publicznego*, 1936, no. 4, item 86.

29 Archiwum Akt Nowych, Warsaw, Ministerstwo Spraw Wewnętrznych, 1064, mf. 25635: Ministry of the Interior, letter to provincial authorities, Warsaw, 22 Aug. 1936; for the text of the letter, see Shapiro, 'Aspects of Jewish Self-Government in Łódź', 198.

30 See E. Melzer, 'Yahadut polin bema'avak medini al kiyumah bishnot 1935–1939', Ph.D. thesis (Tel Aviv University, 1975), 109; R. Sakowska, 'Z dziejów Gminy Żydowskiej w Warszawie 1918–1939', *Studia Warszawskie*, 14/4 (1981), 177–9; *Yidisher arbeter-kias in yor 1936* Łódź, 1937), 224–5.

31 Rudnicki, 'The Struggle in the Polish Parliament for Jewish Autonomy and the Nature of the Jewish Community'.

32 See L. Hass, *Wybory warszawskie 1918–1926* (Warsaw, 1972).

33 See C. Brzoza, 'Cracow's Jews and the Parliamentary Elections 1919–1939', in S. Kapralski (ed.), *The Jews in Poland*, ii (Kraków, 1999), 163–82.

34 Kraków Zionists also put forward candidates in District 37 (Oświęcim): Dr Max Leser (lawyer) and Dr Dawid Bulwa (lawyer). Their candidate in District 39 (Nowy Targ) was Maurycy Freundlich ('Kandydaci żydowscy w Małopolsce Zachodniej', *Gazeta Żydowska*, 19 Jan. 1919).

35 *Dziennik Białostocki*, 11, 17, 18 Apr., 30 June, 23–5 July 1919; *Dos naye lebn*, 7 Oct. 1919.

36 Archiwum Państwowe Kraków, Zespół akt Starostwa Generalnego Krakowa, t. 133, s. 143: 'Sprawozdanie policyjne z 29 V 1922'.

37 *Dziennik Ustaw Rzeczypospolitej Polskiej*, 1933, no. 35, item 294.

38 Archiwum Państwowe Kraków, Urząd Województwa Krakowskiego, t. 279, s. 384: governor of Kraków, situation report, Nov. 1933.

39 *Dos yidishe togblat*, 1 Apr. 1935.

40 *Dziennik Ustaw Rzeczypospolitej Polskiej*, 1935, no. 47, items 795–810.

41 'Centralny Komitet Organizacji Syjonistycznej w Polsce proklamuje wstrzymanie się od wyborów', *Nowy Dziennik*, 12 Aug. 1935.

42 *Sprawy Narodowościowe*, 1938, no. 6, p. 652; *Mały Rocznik Statystyczny Miasta Łodzi 1935r.* (Łódź, 1935), 181.

43 C. Brzoza, *Kraków między wojnami: Kalendarium 28 X 1918–6 IX 1939* (Kraków, 1998), 424–6.

The End of Jewish Self-Government

Jewish National Soviets in Belarus in the Interwar Period

ANDREI ZAMOISKI

T HE OCTOBER REVOLUTION of 1917 initiated a new epoch in the history of the Jews in eastern Europe. They were now granted all civil rights including freedom of conscience and religion; at the same time the Soviet state gradually deprived Jewish communities of many rights they had possessed historically in the Russian empire. The 1918 Soviet Constitution excluded from voting those Jews who had previously been active in the organs of Jewish self-government (merchants, traders, wealthy artisans, and others).[1] The decree On the Separation of Church from State and School from Church, issued on 23 January 1918, undermined the basis of Jewish religious and community activity. This decree and subsequent circulars of the Soviet authorities prohibited religious education which had been so important in the preservation of religion and Jewishness.[2] Jewish religious communities in the Soviet republics were permitted to exist but lost their property, which now became 'public'.[3] Jews even lost control of their cemeteries, which came under the control of the local municipality.[4] The decree On Religious Associations of the All-Russian Central Executive Committee and the Council of People's Commissars of the Russian Soviet Federative Socialist Republic (Rossiyskaya Sovetskaya Federativnaya Sotsialisticheskaya Respublika; RSFSR) of 8 April 1929 and the circular of the People's Commissariat of Internal Affairs (Narodny Komissariat Vnutrennikh Del; NKVD) of 1 October 1929 further restricted the freedom of religious communities.[5] In some cases, Jews worked together to protect their rights as is described below. The local communist authorities considered such activities as politically hostile to the Soviet regime.[6]

In August 1927 *Rabochii*, the official newspaper of the Communist Party of Soviet Belarus, published an article, 'The Great Struggle over a *Mikveh*'.[7] In it, a local Soviet activist from the small town of Kapatkevichy in Polesie, who signed himself A. Veitsok (the usual pseudonym of a staff reporter), provided information on the 'inter-generational clashes' and the divisions which had developed in the local Jewish community.[8] He described the town surrounded by forests as a remote community, where Jews still attempted to follow the traditional tenets of Judaism. The 'old men' of the town concentrated their activities around the newly built synagogue, erected with generous support from America.[9] They had invited to the town a rabbi from Narowlya (Naroulia), a shtetl in the same region that was considered richer and more 'cultural'. There he had 'eked out a miserable existence' but found more support in Kapatkevichy, where all the residents including poor artisans bought kosher meat, believers prayed actively in their synagogue, and *magidim*—itinerant preachers— were frequent visitors. At the same time the younger Jews of the town were actively involved in activities promoted by the Soviet state. Hence, Kapatkevichy was divided into two distinct camps. While the old people attended synagogue on the sabbath, young Jews organized community work days and other secular activities, including meetings, theatrical performances, and public lectures.

This inter-generational conflict came to a head in the 'great struggle over the *mikveh*'. This arose when the Red Cross earmarked 1,000 roubles for the construction of a new bathhouse as part of its programme of sanitary improvements in the town. Since this was insufficient to build a new bathhouse, the younger Jews decided to rebuild the old *mikveh*. The old men then collected 500 roubles, which they seem to have intended to use either as a bribe for the local Jewish soviet or as a contribution to the construction of a new bathhouse in order that the *mikveh* be preserved. The local physician entered the fray, claiming that the old bathhouse was a 'clear source of infection'. His view was supported by a special commission that examined the building and 'found it extremely dirty'. Not surprisingly, the old men, when called upon to confirm the findings of the sanitary examination, refused to yield and demanded a meeting of all the town's residents. To the reporter's surprise, this was the most active meeting ever held in the town. Conflict arose when an attempt was made to expel those without the right to vote, the so-called *lishentsy*, who had been disenfranchised by the Soviet government on political grounds. In his report, Veitsok claimed that the 'fanatics' actively supported the rabbi, a *shoḥet* (ritual slaughterer), and some rich merchants, whom it was proposed should be expelled, shouting 'We will not remain without them—they are our spokesmen.' When the rabbi and the *shoḥet* were forced to leave the hall, they ordered their supporters to follow them. After the physician reported on the sanitary issues, the remaining old people defended the *mikveh*. An old woman claimed that 'she had given birth to fifteen children and fed them while using this *mikveh*' and could not believe there was anything wrong with it. Nevertheless, according to reporter the 'new world won another victory over clericalism . . . the foul-smelling *mikveh* will be converted into a hygienic bathhouse'.

This article is a clear expression of the ideological clichés actively promoted by Soviet propaganda. The years of the New Economic Policy (NEP), adopted by Lenin in 1921, were marked by a revival of Jewish spiritual life after the years of revolutionary upheaval and oppression of religion in the name of the atheistic policy of the Soviet state.[10] The reporter, clearly a representative of the young Jews of Kapatkevichy, aimed to discredit Judaism and its traditions, openly mocking the behaviour of the older generation and its unsuccessful attempt to preserve its traditional way of life.[11] At the same time, this article shows how the former representatives of Jewish self-government in the shtetl were able to defend their views even in such an unpromising political environment.

Kapatkevichy was a town where a Jewish national soviet (*evreiskii natsional'nyi sovet*) had been established to provide Jews with the 'achievements of the revolution' —free elections, the promotion of the participation of women in public life, and support for the economic and cultural development of the town. As the article implies, the local authority ostensibly remained on the sidelines of the conflict but made use of the young people's protest and the need to uphold sanitary norms to advance its reforming agenda. It was clearly responsible for the decision to expropriate property belonging to the Jewish community, while the commission on sanitary control was clearly dependent on it. This case plainly demonstrates how a local authority could use Soviet legislation to advance its agendas and displace the former Jewish elites and mechanisms of Jewish self-government in a remote area of the former western provinces of the Russian empire.

There is a vast literature on the first decades of Bolshevik rule describing the far-reaching changes which occurred within Jewish communities. This has focused on Soviet policy towards the Jews, the establishment of various Soviet Jewish institutions, the attempts by Jewish communists to undermine traditional Jewish life, and the disruption of Jewish community and spiritual life under the impact of a wide range of Soviet reforms.[12] Before the revolution Jewish self-government regulated many aspects of the life of the Jews of the former Polish–Lithuanian Commonwealth, including traditional education, taxation, and the conduct of elections.[13] This chapter seeks to investigate how the new Soviet reality brought about the end of Jewish self-government. It will also discuss the activity of the Jewish soviets which operated in the Soviet republics from 1924 to 1937, seeking to determine whether these bodies can be seen as a form of Jewish self-government and to what degree their activities and duties resembled traditional forms of Jewish self-government. It will also investigate the role of elections and how the Soviet authorities undermined the position of old elites and replaced them with new ones.

The New Soviet Order and the Jewish Communities

The political transformations after 1917 radically altered the system of local power in Jewish settlements. From 1917 soviets were established, and the Bolsheviks sought to win majorities in these bodies. During the period of war communism and the civil war, soviets were replaced by revolutionary committees and poor people's committees. In Belarus revolutionary committees were set up between 1918 and 1920 as the principal administrative bodies in the territory liberated by the Red Army from German and Polish troops. They were later replaced by soviets. Soviet laws revolutionized the structure of urban and rural government. Urban soviets operated in cities. Small-town soviets ruled urban communities in small towns. Some small towns lost their urban status, were transformed into villages, and, as rural settlements, fell under the jurisdiction of rural soviets.[14]

From 1924, in accordance with Soviet nationalities policy, 'national' soviets were established in villages or small towns inhabited by Jews and other ethnic minorities. In Belarus, Polish, Jewish, Russian, Latvian, German, and Lithuanian national soviets

Table 1 National soviets in Belarus (1924–1932)

Year	Jewish	Polish	Russian	Ukrainian	Latvian	German	Lithuanian	Totals
1924	7				2			9
1925	11	2	1		5	1		20
1926	18	13	1		4	2		38
1927	23	19	16	2	4	2		66
1928	23	19	16	2	5	2		67
1929	25	23	15	3	4	2	1	73
1932	24	40	16	6	5	2	1	94

Source: *Prakticheskoe razreshenie natsional'nogo voprosa v Belorusskoi SSR*, 2 vols. (Minsk, 1927–8), ii. 93–4.

were established (see Table 1). In the 1920s the Soviet authorities claimed that Jewish soviets were a form of Jewish national self-government and would enable Jewish residents to use their mother tongue in official bodies (soviets, schools, courts). Under the NEP, such elected bodies were set up in former provincial towns, small towns, and even in larger villages in Ukraine, Belarus, and the western region of Russia.

By the end of 1924 seven Jewish soviets had been established in Soviet Belarus. By 1932 their number had increased to twenty-four.[15] However, they were not established in all shtetls, of which by the mid-1920s fifty-six were officially recognized. Jewish soviets were set up in settlements with a high proportion of Jewish residents, mainly in small towns and in some former shtetls, which had lost their urban status. In Belarus, four Jewish rural soviets were established, others were located in small towns.[16] The establishment of national soviets in the Belarusian SSR took place on a more limited scale than in Ukraine, where dozens of Jewish soviets and even three Jewish oblasts were established by 1941.[17]

Duties and Functions of Jewish National Soviets

The organization of soviets took place according to the ethnic composition of a small town or its districts. Control of a small town could be divided between Jewish and Belarusian town soviets. Usually the centre (the 'historical shtetl' where mainly Jews lived) was administered by a Jewish soviet. A Belarusian soviet would control the outskirts and some neighbouring villages where non-Jews historically were in the majority. The establishment of Yiddish-language soviets encountered many obstacles, including disputes over the extent of the territory involved and opposition from local authorities. Ethnic diversity and the territorial dispersion of households and their farms greatly complicated the organization of Jewish soviets among the Belarusian population. Many Belarusian families were now subordinated to soviets located a long distance from their homes. In some disputed cases nationally 'mixed' soviets would be set up. Thus, in the small town of Turaw in the mid-1920s three soviets were established: ethnically 'pure' Jewish and Belarusian soviets and a mixed Jewish–Belarusian one to control the ethnically mixed area of the town.[18] In some cases, Jews opposed the establishment of Jewish soviets, preferring for financial and ideological reasons to avoid drawing the attention of Jewish communists and local Soviet bodies to themselves.

The functions of Jewish soviets were various and covered many aspects of local life, including the community taxes levied on all residents and the supervision and repair of local buildings, public bathhouses, roads, bridges, pavements, schools, pasture lands, and health care institutions.[19] Moreover, soviets possessed certain social functions such as supervising and fostering the establishment of artisan artels and co-operatives, assisting the families of Red Army soldiers and officers and former Red partisans, and providing the poor with fuel and bread.[20] These tasks were undertaken by several commissions which were made up of local activists, the *aktiv*, which consisted of 'politically educated' workers, members of craftsmen's artels, and teachers in Jewish schools.

Lishentsy as a Specific Group of Jewish Residents

The Evsektsiya (Jewish section of the Communist Party) was forced to recognize that the establishment of Jewish soviets in some places in Minsk and Sluck districts was not possible because a large proportion of the Jews had been deprived of electoral and other civil rights.[21] Up to two thirds of shtetl residents were *lishentsy* (disenfranchised).[22] In the period from 1918 to 1936 they were defined collectively by state bodies as 'social aliens'.[23] According to the constitution of the RSFSR of 1918 the 'bourgeois classes' should not have the right to vote. This restriction covered agents of the tsarist police, private traders, clerics, soldiers and officers of anti-Soviet military units, bandits, and other 'anti-Soviets', who were either real opponents of the Soviet regime or capitalist elements.[24] In the Jewish communities all members of the clergy (rabbis, *melamedim* (teachers in traditional religious schools), and others) were classed as being 'deprived of civic rights'.[25] Representatives of the 'petite bourgeoisie' such as small traders and even unemployed *luftmenshn* were also disfranchised.[26] In the 1920s, as before the revolution, they were engaged in the 'shadow economy': illegal unlicensed trade, smuggling, and similar activities. Their involvement in trade and commerce allowed them to be treated as speculators.

Deprivation of voting rights meant much more than simply 'disenfranchisement'.[27] Besides the expropriation of property, Jewish *lishentsy* were subject to progressive persecution in the late 1920s. They gradually lost other rights, such as free medical care, education, and access to employment.[28] The daughters of Rabbi Menakhem-Mendel Gluskin moved from Parychy to Minsk and were compelled to study at home since the Soviet regime deprived them of all educational opportunities.[29] During Stalin's 'second revolution' after 1929 *lishentsy* did not even have the right to ration cards for essential food items and were blacklisted by local bodies (small-town and village soviets and the NKVD). They were among the first to be arrested in the waves of repression which followed collectivization.

Jewish rabbis, like priests of other congregations, had been arrested even in the more liberal years of the NEP. Thus, in 1922/3 the chief rabbi of Gomel, Raphael Mordechai Barishansky, was arrested and imprisoned by the Soviet authorities.[30] At the end of the decade a new campaign against rabbis started. Fourteen rabbis, preachers, and members of the soviet in Minsk were arrested in March 1930 and accused of counter-revolutionary activity. They were saved because Western countries exerted pressure on the Soviet government.[31] A survey undertaken at the beginning of the 1930s revealed that many rabbis had already left the small towns of Belarus[32] and sought shelter in other places.[33] Those arrested were exiled to Siberia or kept in prisons or camps.

Elections: Who Held Local Power?

Before the revolution, the holding of elections had been an important part not only of the political but also of the social life of Jewish communities. In the 1920s those Jewish residents who had not been disenfranchised elected the chairman and members of the local soviet. The number of those elected varied. For example, the first Jewish soviet elected in Turaw in 1924 was made up of only eleven members, but by the following year it had increased to twenty.[34] Only local Jews had the right to elect the Jewish soviet. Their Belarusian neighbours were subordinated to a Belarusian soviet.[35]

The Soviet authorities considered elections an important means of political mobilization and carefully controlled them. As mentioned above, the right to vote had been taken away from a considerable section of the Jews in small towns. Further disenfranchisement took place on the eve of the elections when, under the slogan of 'class struggle', the Soviet authorities eliminated 'alien elements' from the public sphere, either by excluding them from voting or by stronger measures such as arrests or deportations. The central and local authorities monitored and regulated the social composition of soviets while the Unified State Political Directorate (Ob"edinennoe Gosudarstvennoe Politicheskoe Upravlenie; OGPU) closely followed the results of elections. Secret agents provided information on politically undesirable candidates proposed by locals. Before political parties were banned in the Soviet republics, a wide political spectrum was to be found in Jewish settlements. Bundist, Zionist, and other Jewish all-Russian political parties, groups, and organizations sought to mobilize their supporters, which were to be found in most small towns. The OGPU reported that Jews in the Davydawka rural soviet had reached an agreement to elect a Zionist.[36] His candidature was blocked by the local authorities.

During election campaigns in the NEP period public life in small towns was rather active. The local authorities noted cases of illegal meetings, where shtetl residents actively discussed such problems as the protection of their economic and political interests and the nomination of their own candidates. Different parties proposed candidates for the local bodies. In the small town of Kholmech in Rechytsa district a Soviet officer reported that all candidates for its rural soviet were widely discussed: at the market place and in the streets, in private houses, and at local organizations. The local branch of OGPU observed that 'rich residents' petitioned the local authorities to allow them to hold a meeting and even to nominate their own candidate for the soviet.[37] However, only candidates approved by the local Communist Party cell were allowed to stand for election.

In the elections of 1927 'loyal' groups of workers, employees, peasants, and artisans dominated all Jewish and non-Jewish soviets. The authorities attempted to advance Communist Party and Komsomol members, but at this stage non-communists dominated.[38] By the end of the 1920s the elections had been brought under the strict control of local Communist Party committees and the state apparatus ensured the nomination of loyal delegates. As a rule, the local administration nominated local activists, preferably communists and women. To increase participation, elections were held on Soviet holidays. The freedom of elections was now a fiction as the lists of delegates were subject to approval and results were determined in advance.

New Soviet Elites versus Defeated Old Classes

The Jewish petite bourgeoisie (former merchants, petty traders, and richer artisans) made up the majority of politically active residents in small towns. In order to consolidate their monopoly of power, the Bolsheviks made efforts to weaken the position of such politically disloyal groups. They also tried to undermine social solidarity and to incite one section of the population against another, exacerbating, for instance, the conflict between generations. Campaigns such as that over the *mikveh* in Kapatkevichy were widely publicized in the Soviet press. In Jewish settlements, where, under the impact of modernization, this political polarization was taking place, the Soviet regime attempted to foment division and channel it for ideological gain. The Evsektsiya, with the assistance of some local Jewish activists, was engaged in public activities against the Jewish religion, including the confiscation of synagogues and the discrediting of Jewish tradition.

The Soviet authorities attempted to replace the older elites with a new Soviet one. The 1920s and the 1930s was a period of rapid formation for the Soviet bureaucratic machine and for the establishment of various state-run institutions (schools, hospitals, and co-operatives). Economic and social instability compelled Jews to seek new occupations which encouraged young 'proletarian' Jews to enter the ranks of the Soviet apparatus. *Sluzhashchie* (teachers, clerks, medical personnel, and officials) constituted a group that was trusted by the Soviet authorities. They were recruited from the local politically loyal population or, where the numbers were insufficient, appointed from outside.

Many Jews in this group (as well as Belarusians and Russians) were appointed by the central authorities to supervise the activity of newly established Soviet institutions. In a Jewish soviet in Uzda, visiting employees (without families) made up about 12 per cent of all members in 1928.[39] In the shtetl of Kolyshki in the Vitebsk region, practically all officials, teachers, and other representatives of non-manual working groups had been sent there from other places.[40]

In the interwar period Jewish women were actively involved by the state in public and cultural life. They played important roles in various public organizations and managed their local branches, groups, and cells. For example, in the shtetl of Chareya, a female physician headed a local group which promoted good sanitary practices.[41] Elections to the soviets demonstrated that they were eager to participate in local administration, but their numbers were still low. In 1927 in Soviet Belarus only ninety-five women (12 per cent) were elected to the soviets.[42] Women chaired some soviets (three in 1927), including a Jewish soviet in Kolyshki.[43] The Soviet state promoted and nominated the candidacy of Jewish women, who also needed to have a good command of the Russian and Belarusian languages and to be members of the Communist Party or Komsomol.

Education

Jewish education and the maintenance of Jewish schools was one of the principal areas entrusted to Jewish self-government. The Bolsheviks gradually destroyed or drove underground the traditional system of Jewish education which had existed for many generations. The state actively promoted the establishment of Soviet Yiddish schools, although they faced strong competition from the now underground ḥeders. *Melamedim* were harshly attacked, and they and the Jewish religion were put on trial in staged court cases.[44] Such trials took place in bigger cities (Vitebsk, Gomel, and elsewhere[45]), where the local Communist Party section chose the judges and witnesses.[46] Bolshevik propaganda accused the *melamedim* of self-interest, since they taught children for money while Soviet education was free and accessible even to poor Jewish families.[47] Jewish soviets promoted the establishment of Yiddish schools and in some cases even synagogue buildings were confiscated for this purpose, as occurred in Turaw (an additional justification was that the synagogue did not conform to the sanitary code).[48]

By the 1930s Ukraine and Belarus possessed a network of Soviet Yiddish schools and pedagogical institutions. Many Jewish families were attracted by the new social opportunities provided for their children by the Bolsheviks, especially the possibility of receiving higher education in large Soviet cities (Moscow, Leningrad, Kiev, and Minsk). In the view of the Soviets, education was an important tool for the modernization of small towns in line with Soviet ideology. In many Belarusian cities (Minsk, Mogilev, and elsewhere) some Jewish parents preferred to send their children to Russian-language schools, since they furnished better career opportunities. The Soviet Yiddish schools, like those of other national minorities (German, Polish, Latvian, and others), were closed in 1937.[49] In Belarus they were transformed into

Belarusian and Russian schools. This took place during the Great Purge (1936–8) and the protests of parents were ignored.

Attacks on Jewish Religious Communities and Their Infrastructure

In comparison with the pre-revolutionary period, in the 1920s religious communities increasingly lost their earlier functions. In the Soviet republics, religious practice was no longer supported by the state. According to a Soviet law adopted in 1918, no church or religious society had the right to own property.[50] Formally the Soviet authorities did not prohibit the activities of religious communities, but in practice local authorities interfered in all spheres of Jewish life. In the 1920s the registration of weddings, deaths, and births became more centralized.[51] The task of civil registration fell to local soviets (mostly in rural areas) and to the registry office in cities. The archives of Jewish communities were confiscated by the authorities and handed over to the local administration. Jewish cemeteries were managed by special departments of local soviets.[52] *Hevrot kadisha*, the traditional Jewish burial associations, were not allowed to operate openly, and the local authorities gradually appropriated property belonged to Jewish communities, including synagogues, *mikva'ot* and cemeteries. In Uzda, a building owned by the local *hevrah kadisha* was confiscated. The local municipal authorities ignored the Jewish protests and failed to return the building.[53]

The Soviet press constantly described the 'liberation of the toiling masses from religion'.[54] Believers were attacked by the Soviet administrative machine and faced anti-religious propaganda and repression. This was intended to discredit the Jewish religion and its customs. 'Red Passovers' were celebrated, accompanied by parades and sacrilegious actions.[55] The local authorities persecuted those responsible for the functioning of Jewish religious communities. The regime regarded as 'clericals' not only rabbis, circumcisers, *shohetim*, and *melamedim* but all who followed Jewish traditions. Various calumnies were spread to discredit the norms of *kashrut*. For example, in late 1925 a trial of a group of *shohetim* was held in Minsk.[56]

Soviet propaganda actively mocked rabbis and other religious officials. Their allegedly bogus attempts to adapt to Soviet reality were ridiculed. In a series of articles promoting atheism in the USSR, an election campaign in a Belarusian shtetl was described. Two candidates had stood: one, supported by a rabbi, represented 'bourgeois' groups that claimed to accept the new reality; the other had a 'proletarian' character. Naturally the proletarian candidate managed to win. The author concluded that 'with the help of such deceitful behaviour, clericals seek to keep the influence on the Jewish community in their hands'.[57]

In Soviet Belarus, many synagogues were destroyed during the First World War, the revolutions, and the civil war. Jews applied for permission to build new synagogues or to renovate those which had been damaged, but usually the local Soviet authorities refused consent.[58] The number of synagogues also decreased drastically because of the activities of the Evsektsiya.[59] Jewish communists knew that synagogues were spiritual centres for the Jewish communities, and the campaign for their closure was accordingly conducted under the pretext that the buildings were needed for social purposes or that the community 'did not need' a synagogue.[60] They were transformed into clubs, warehouses, or used for other community purposes.[61] Sometimes Jewish Komsomol members were even more radical than local authorities and demanded the immediate conversion of closed synagogues into workers' clubs.[62]

The Evsektsiya was aware of the provocative nature of such actions. It called on the party committees to be cautious when closing prayer houses, citing an incident in Vitebsk when believers organized resistance and the authorities were compelled to use force.[63] They proposed that the closure of synagogues should be preceded by intensive propaganda among Jewish workers, meetings with resolutions, and staged court cases. In Gomel district, one Soviet official argued that it 'was advisable to close synagogues and churches simultaneously so that accusations of antisemitism could be dispelled'.[64]

Dissolution of Organizations for Charity and Social Welfare

Historically, Jews had a rich tradition of helping the poor in the community and a well-organized system of social welfare. Traditional societies dealt with different aspects of everyday life (supporting orphans, widows, and beggars; care for the sick; burial of the dead). Jewish self-government was deeply involved in public charity through helping the sick, the elderly, and children; the free distribution of bread and fuel to poor families; the organization of soup kitchens; the granting of loans to artisans and traders; and the provision of shelter for travellers.[65] In addition, rabbis and other prominent individuals in the community created organizations to help poor families by providing clothes, food, and traditional education.

Throughout the difficult years between 1914 and 1921 Jewish communities supported charitable societies and associations designed for mutual aid and religious purposes. In the mid-1920s many Jewish families, who had suffered greatly from pogroms and economic upheaval, also appealed to such institutions, whose number grew rapidly in these years.[66] The Evsektsiya reported to the Central Committee that traditional organizations in shtetls continued to work underground: ḥevrot kadisha continued to exist in most shtetls, while such societies as the loan association and the association for visiting and helping the sick operated illegally.[67] They were confronted with an array of political, social, and even psychological problems. During the NEP the number of marginalized people increased sharply, and community help was not able to deal with the new problems. In the 1920s previously prosperous sections of the shtetl population (merchants, craftsmen) found themselves under severe economic pressure and were unable to provide assistance as they had before. Another reason for the reduction of charitable provision in Jewish communities was the Soviet social and anti-religious policy.[68] Despite the persistence of traditional values, the Soviet measures started to have a negative impact on traditional organizations and their members.

Financial aid from foreign organizations and money transferred from America and other countries to families in small towns also played a great role in the 1920s. Some Jewish communities received considerable financial support from American *landsmanshaftn* and relatives who had left before the First World War. The Jews of Parychy alone received 50,000 roubles every year.[69] Some of these funds were channelled through religious leaders, and local communities used them for public needs such as maintaining synagogues, cemeteries, and *mikva'ot*.[70] In Shchadryn, Jews received money from America to build a new *mikveh*.[71] This aid from abroad clearly supported the older system of Jewish self-government.

All non-governmental charity organizations were regarded by the local and the central authorities with suspicion as clerical. They sought to replace them with socialist mutual aid associations, which had been set up throughout the Soviet Union from the mid-1920s. In all soviets, including Jewish ones, mutual aid associations were established as an alternative to traditional charity. These aimed to win over the poor and undermine the traditional charitable associations. In the view of the authorities, the poor of the national minorities were more difficult to control because of the resonance of calls for national unity: Communist Party functionaries admitted that to fight this phenomenon on the economic plane would be difficult.[72] Propaganda was extensively used to discredit traditional forms of charity.[73]

Jewish soviets also attempted to establish mutual aid associations, which sought to win the support of poor artisans by providing loans.[74] During the NEP, they were not very numerous and in 1926 only operated in a few small towns.[75] Soviet charity stressed a class approach, and only jobless workers and employees were assisted, while bankrupt merchants were treated as social aliens. By the 1930s all unofficial Jewish charity bodies (those that still existed in a few cities and small towns) had to operate clandestinely.

Taxation

The Soviet state abolished all religious taxes, and as a result contributions for religious or charitable purposes were now voluntary. Nevertheless, the traditional Jewish system of collecting funds for self-help survived in some Soviet shtetls until the Holocaust. In the 1920s the Evsektsiya became aware that the candle tax and other non-official collections of funds continued to function in Jewish communities and were used to support rabbis and other clerics.[76] Some rabbis managed to ask respectable (not only aged) people to organize the collection of funds for them.[77] Such aid helped rabbis and other members of the former Jewish elite to survive economically. In some cases, Jewish merchants and craftsmen used donations to pay Soviet taxes and to buy back their property impounded because of debts.[78] Before the war, money from the kosher meat tax was allocated to the various needs of the Jewish community, such as providing charity to the poor and sick. However, the number able to contribute in this way declined steadily. For instance, Hayim Shelomoh Kom, the rabbi of Rechytsa, complained in a letter to his son in Palestine that many residents, even in more liberal (pre-revolutionary) times, had not wanted to pay the tax.[79] In the 1920s the tax fulfilled two main functions, supporting underground traditional Jewish schooling and providing an income for rabbis.[80] By the end of the decade, during the new attack on religion, the Soviet authorities attempted to weaken the role of rabbis in Jewish communities by imposing high taxes of thousands of roubles, often described as 'unbearable'. For instance, the rabbi of Staryya Darohi was compelled to pay 5,200 roubles in taxes. This case was mentioned by the OGPU, as such abuses occurred widely.[81]

Urban–Rural Contradictions: The Decrease in Jewish Representation

Historically the shtetl economy was based on crafts and small-scale industry, trade, and leaseholding. The Jewish quarter was usually located in the centre of town while the periphery was usually non-Jewish (Belarusian, Russian, or Polish). The development of small towns as regional centres, and state investment in them, attracted non-Jews from the neighbouring villages. Jews lost their predominance in rural soviets not only because of disfranchisement but also because they were now outnumbered. In many cases the representatives of different communities were convinced that the interests of their community were being ignored, while others enjoyed preference. Rural people were the dominant group in rural soviets. The large percentage of peasants in the local soviets, and specifically in their administrative apparatus, can be explained by the fact that fewer of them were deprived of their rights compared with other social groups. In many cases the shtetls' outskirts and neighbouring villages were automatically included in the administrative area. This was certainly done deliberately in order to reduce the proportion of unwanted voters, especially artisans, petty traders, and *luftmenshn*.

Jews in rural areas faced a number of problems. The administration frequently did not understand its duties and responsibilities. A Communist Party commission revealed that, in the former small town of Skryhalaw, 'the rural soviet's role was limited to issuing permits'.[82] Additionally social and inter-ethnic conflicts became more acute in small towns where rural soviets were established when local peasants gained the chance to rule the urban population at their centre. The Evsektsiya reported that in many cases rural soviets did not pay attention to the needs of Jewish communities, although Jews were a majority in many settlements. For example, the Lapichy rural soviet served several neighbouring villages, but it had only two Jewish members, and the interests of the Jewish community were often ignored. On one occasion local Jews petitioned the government when the soviet closed the old Jewish cemetery. A Belarusian soviet member (a peasant) claimed that this had been done to 'improve sanitary conditions'. As a consequence, the Jews were now obliged to bury their dead at night-time, by giving bribes, or by appealing to the district executive committee for permission to do so.[83]

There were cases when Jews encountered hostile or antisemitic attitudes from local authorities. The Jews in the small town of Syanno complained to the higher party authorities that the head of the rural soviet—a certain Naumenko—persecuted Jews, accusing them of not paying taxes. He claimed that 'just as in tsarist times Jews were unwilling to pay taxes to Nicholas, so now they do not want to pay them to the Soviet power.'[84] It remains unknown how the Communist Party reacted or if any measures were undertaken against Naumenko.[85] The government admitted that some local employees in Soviet Belarus openly treated shtetl Jews as 'speculators'. For instance, in 1924 the authorities in Valyntsy in Polatsk district refused to allow Jews to join local co-operatives, giving the reason, 'Jews are speculators.'[86]

The Dissolution of the Jewish National Soviets

It is clear that the electoral system of the 1930s was a sham intended only for propaganda purposes. People saw no real connection between their participation in elections and their everyday life. In every case the elections were won by the 'Bloc of Communists and Non-Party Members'.[87] Participation in Soviet elections and the promotion of women were treated by citizens as a necessary formality. Such propaganda caused passivity and indifference among a significant proportion of the population.

By the 1930s it was obvious that the Jewish soviets were not fulfilling the role expected of them by the Soviet authorities. In Belarus, only a tenth of the Jewish population fell under their rule.[88] Their role was, however, actively promoted by Soviet Jewish institutions and the Soviet bodies responsible for 'work on nationalities', which essentially meant the sovietization of ethnic minorities. One propagandist work on the achievements of Soviet policy claimed that the Jewish soviets were 'the organs of proletarian dictatorship, working in their native language and familiar with the life and conditions of the shtetl Jewish population.'[89]

With the intensification of Russification and centralization in the 1930s, the Soviet regime no longer had a need for such 'national' institutions. Additionally, the local leadership was often hostile to them for various reasons. The local administration was criticized for the poor leadership of the national soviets and the inadequate implementation of national policies. In the new political conditions, the population often considered the soviets as administrative bodies whose principal task was to support state campaigns and to fulfil the instructions of the party and the central authorities. The soviets of small towns were 'reorganized' in 1937.[90] Though the elimination of the national soviets aroused some discontent, the situation in the 1930s, and especially during the Great Purge, meant that it was dangerous to openly criticize Communist Party policy.[91]

Jewish soviets had nothing in common with earlier forms of Jewish self-government. The old and new Jewish elites did operate on the same 'Jewish street' but in competition. Traditional Jewish self-government did not have any possibility of survival under such unfavourable political conditions. The reasons for its erosion and subsequent disappearance were complex and linked with economic, social, political, cultural, and demographic developments. In larger cities, the cultural and social assimilation of Jews occurred as a result of the close economic and social ties between Jews and their neighbours. Soviet reforms undermined the traditional infrastructure of the Jewish communities and their economic and social basis. The years between 1921 and 1941 saw increased Jewish labour migration, mainly from former Jewish shtetls to the industrial centres of Russia and Ukraine. The Soviet state also organized the resettlement of Jewish families from small towns. Trying to solve a complex set of social and economic problems in these settlements, the Soviet authorities and Soviet Jewish state-run institutions such as the Society for Settling Jewish Workers on the Land and the Commission for the Settlement of Jewish Workers on the Land,[92] with the support of Agro-Joint and the Association for the Promotion of Skilled Trades, promoted various projects for agricultural colonization. These included the relocation of shtetl residents on Jewish collective farms or their resettlement in Crimea and Birobidzhan.[93]

Conclusion

The First World War and the Russian Revolution and civil war dramatically changed the political, social, and economic landscape of eastern Europe. Historically and culturally a part of the Jewish community of the Polish–Lithuanian Commonwealth, Jews in Soviet Belarus now had to adapt themselves to new realities. Practically all Jewish political and public organizations were undermined and destroyed by the Bolsheviks after 1918. Jewish self-government could no longer exist in the Soviet state, where all spheres of life were subordinated to the control of the Communist Party.

The basis of former Jewish self-government was gradually eliminated by the Soviet regime. The Bolsheviks attempted to replace all old Jewish institutions with new ones—the synagogue with a Soviet club, the *ḥeder* with a Soviet Yiddish school, the *mikveh* with a new bathhouse. Jewish community institutions were powerless in the face of Bolshevik reforms. Religious education in the Soviet republics was strictly forbidden, and all representatives of the Jewish religious community were treated as politically 'hostile'. The Evsektsiya and local Soviet authorities fought against the Jewish community, undermining its financial basis and its control of elections, synagogues, slaughtering, and mutual aid associations—elements which were formerly controlled by the institutions of Jewish self-government.

Soviet policy sought to subordinate traditional Jewish communities to the Soviet state-building processes. To facilitate this it favoured the activity of specific groups (the young, women, ethnic minorities). The new regime channelled all public activities into the framework of the socialist model. The role of Jewish soviets in protecting the rights of Jewish residents should not be overexaggerated. The number of these bodies in Soviet Belarus was too small. Like other national soviets, Jewish soviets did contribute to the development of their towns and villages. They discussed the whole gamut of economic, social, and cultural issues, including state taxes and loans, community taxes, the conduct of elections to Soviet and co-operative bodies, the establishment of co-operatives and artels, and the organization of meetings and conferences. At the same time a considerable section of the Jewish population was excluded from Soviet public life and was prohibited from taking part in elections or nominating candidates.

The Jewish soviets as representatives of Soviet power and the remnants of traditional Jewish self-government were clearly at opposite political poles. Local Jews had little choice over which side to join. It was obvious from the second half of the 1920s that the Soviet state would definitely modernize Jewish communities on the Soviet pattern. Jewish soviets took part in this destruction of the traditional Jewish way of life. In the interwar period they confiscated buildings which were previously owned by institutions that had been part of the fabric of Jewish self-government. All such measures were justified on the grounds of the public good (sanitary concerns, repair work, general reconstruction of a settlement, and so on). This practice was not unique to Jews, and targeted all religious communities in all Soviet republics.

For the most part, Jews were unable to protect their rights in Jewish national soviets or even in urban and rural soviets, where Jewish residents were in a minority because of the incorporation of areas where non-Jews were numerically preponderant and because of Jewish disfranchisement. During election campaigns Jews on national soviets did sometimes attempt to promote candidates supporting Jewish interests, but these were often blocked by the authorities. They did seek to defend their economic and religious rights, for example, regarding the status of former community buildings, synagogues, *mikva'ot*, and others, but they had little chance against the candidates promoted by the Soviet administration, mainly from the ranks of the local 'toiling masses'.

Jewish self-government had a long tradition in this part of eastern Europe. As before the war, Jews made use of both formal and informal methods to protect the interests of their communities (above all the protection of cemeteries, *mikva'ot*, and synagogues). The traditions of Jewish self-government on the territories controlled by the Bolsheviks could not disappear overnight. Their legacy revealed itself in the various activities of the 'old Jewish elites', negatively portrayed in Soviet propaganda. During elections to Jewish national soviets and public debates in the interwar period, an echo of the traditions of Jewish self-government can certainly be heard.

Notes

1 *Pervaya sovetskaya konstitutsiya (Konstitutsiya RSFSR 1918 goda)*, ed. A. Vyshinsky (Moscow, 1938), p. xix.

2 A. Zamojski, 'Soviet Schooling as Reforming Force in *Shtetls* of Soviet Belarus in the Interwar Period', *Rozprawy z Dziejów Oświaty*, 48 (2011), 155–71: 159.

3 'Decree Issued by the Council of People's Commissars of the Russian Soviet Federative Socialist Republic' (23 Jan 1918), in N. Orleansky, *Zakon o religioznykh ob'edineniyakh RSFSR i deistvuyushchie zakony, instruktsii, tsirkulyary s otdel'nymi kommentariyami po voprosam, svyazannym s otdeleniem tserkvi ot gosudarstva i shkoly ot tserkvi v Soyuze SSR* (Moscow, 1930), 5–6.

4 'Decree of the SNK of the RSFSR on cemeteries and funerals' (7 Dec. 1918), ibid. 61–2.

5 'Decree Issued by the Council of People's Commissars of the Russian Soviet Federative Socialist Republic' (23 Jan. 1918), 6–26.

6 This case was discussed by the local Communist Party committee (A. Lebedev and V. Pichukov, 'Politika sovetskoi vlasti po otnosheniyu k iudeiskoi religii na Gomel'shchine v 1920–1930-kh gg.', *Tsaitshryft*, 7/2 (2012), 28–35: 31).

7 A. Veitsok, 'Velikaya bor'ba za mikvu (Kopatkevichskii raion, Minskii okrug)', *Rabochii*, 4 Aug. 1927, p. 3.

8 Rossiiskii gosudarstvennyi arkhiv sotsial'no-politicheskoi istorii, Moscow (hereafter RGASPI), f. 445, op. 1, d. 180, s. 68: Materials collected by the Commission of the Central Committee of the Communist Party of Belarus (CP(b)B) on the political situation in Mazyr district, spring 1926. Kapatkevichy was a typical Jewish shtetl with 216 Jewish and only 56 non-Jewish families. Before the Russian revolution the number of Jewish families here reached 400. The decline was caused by several brutal pogroms committed by anti-Soviet rebels and bandits.

9 In the 1920s Soviet Jews and Jewish religious communities received money from their relatives and *landsmanshaftn* (Jewish mutual aid societies for immigrants from the same eastern European region, city, or shtetl).

10 See A. Zeltser, 'The Belorussian Evsektsiia and Jewish Religious Life in 1927: A Change in Policy', *Jews in Eastern Europe*, 35 (1998), 47–71.

11 'Sirotiner', 'Iz zhizni "Vozdukhetresta" (Evreiskoe naselenie mestechka Sirotino)', in V. Tan-Bogaraz (ed.), *Evreiskoe mestechko v revolyutsii: Ocherki* (Moscow, 1926), 89–120.

12 Z. Gitelman, *Jewish Nationality and Soviet Politics: The Jewish Sections of the CPSU, 1917–1930* (Princeton, NJ, 1972); G. Estraikh, 'The Soviet Shtetl in the 1920s', *Polin*, 17 (2004), 197–258; B. Pincus, *The Jews of the Soviet Union: The History of the National Minority* (Cambridge, 1988); A. Zeltser, 'The Shtetl During the Great Watershed of 1929–1931: The Case of Vitebsk Region', *Jews in Eastern Europe*, 46 (2001), 5–33; id., *Evrei sovetskoi provintsii: Vitebsk i mestechki. 1917–1941* (Moscow, 2006); A. Kaganovich, *Rechitsa: Istoriya evreiskogo mestechka Yugo-Vostochnoi Belorussii* (Jerusalem, 2007); A. Zamoiski, *Transformatsiya mestechek Sovetskoi Belorussii, 1918–1939* (Minsk, 2013); E. Bemporad, *Becoming Soviet Jews: The Bolshevik Experiment in Minsk* (Bloomington, Ind., 2013); K. Karpekin, *Iudeiskie obshchiny v Belorusskoi SSR (yanvar' 1919–sentyabr' 1939 g.)* (Vitebsk, 2016); A. Sloin, *The Jewish Revolution in Belorussia: Economy, Race, and Bolshevik Power* (Bloomington, Ind., 2017).

13 A. Zamoiski, 'Imperial Russia's North-Western and South-Western Provinces, 1815–1914', in F. Guesnet and J. Tomaszewski (eds.), *Sources on Jewish Self-Government in the Polish Lands from Its Inception to the Present* (Boston, Mass., forthcoming).

14 S. Elizarov, *Stanovlenie i razvitie sistemy mestnykh Sovetov BSSR v 1919–1929 godakh* (Gomel, 2016), 55–8.

15 *Prakticheskoe razreshenie natsional'nogo voprosa v Belorusskoi SSR*, 2 vols. (Minsk, 1927–8), ii. 93.

16 Natsyyanal'ny arkhiw Respubliki Belarus' (hereafter NARB), f. 701, op.1, d. 92, s. 175: list of

national soviets of the BSSR (Dec. 1928). The former small town of Azarychy became a village, but it had a Jewish rural soviet.

17 Ya. Kantor, *Natsional'noe stroitel'stvo sredi evreev v SSSR* (Moscow, 1934), 25. Three Jewish oblasts were established in the south of Ukraine (Kalinindorf, Stalindorf, and Novozlatopol); in Crimea, part of the RSFSR, two Jewish oblasts, Fraidorf and Larindorf, were created.

18 L. Smilovitsky, 'A Belorussian Border Shtetl in the 1920s and 1930s: The Case of Turov', *Jews in Russia and Eastern Europe*, 50 (2003), 109–37: 115–17.

19 'Instruktsii sovetam', *Sobranie uzakonenii BSSR*, 45 (Minsk, 1927), art. 189.

20 Ibid.

21 NARB, f. 4, op. 10, d. 6, s. 24: Evsektsiya, report (Sept.–Dec. 1924).

22 B. Brutskus, 'Evreiskoe naselenie pod kommunisticheskoi vlast'yu', in O. Budnitsky (ed.), *Evrei i russkaya revolyutsiya: Materialy i issledovaniya* (Moscow, 1999), 293–319: 296.

23 See G. Alexopoulos, *Stalin's Outcasts: Aliens, Citizens, and the Soviet State, 1926–1936* (Ithaca, NY, 2003).

24 'Konstitutsiya RSFSR 1918 g.', in *Istoriya Sovietskoi Konstitutsii (1917–1956)* (Moscow, 1957), 78–89.

25 *Melamedim* were held in lower esteem than rabbis and were usually very poor. They were included among the clergy as they broke the Soviet law prohibiting religious teaching. Girsh Reles recollected that the local authorities warned his father, a former *melamed* in Chashniki, to stop 'religious propaganda' or he would be arrested. See A. Shulman, 'Ostrov Relesa', in G. Reles, *Evreiskie sovetskie pisateli Belorussii: Vospominaniya*, ed. V. Lyaskovsky, trans. M. Ya. Akkerman and S. L. Liokumovich (Minsk, 2006), 221–84: 225.

26 On Jewish *luftmenshn*, see N. Berg, *Luftmenschen: Zur Geschichte einer Metapher* (Göttingen, 2014).

27 See Alexopoulos, *Stalin's Outcasts*.

28 Ibid. 39–50.

29 M. Gluskina, 'Vospominaniya detstva', in *Evrei Belarusi: Istoriya i kul'tura*, ed. I. Gerasimova, 6 vols. in 5 (Minsk, 1997–2001), iii–iv. 235–52: 247.

30 Jewish Telegraphic Agency, 'Homel Rabbis to Face Soviet Justice', *Daily News Bulletin*, 26 Apr. 1923, p. 2.

31 Archiwum Akt Nowych, Warsaw, Ministerstwo Spraw Zagranicznych, k. 10184: 'Sytuacja kościołów: prawosławnego, katolickiego i protestanckiego oraz żydowskich gmin wyznaniowych': report of the Polish embassy in Moscow to the Ministry of Foreign Affairs in Warsaw (Mar. 1930).

32 *Myastechki BSSR u rekanstruktsyiny peryyad: z materyyalaw absledavannya, pravedzenaha Natskamisiyai TsVK BSSR i yawsektaram BAN u sakaviku – krasaviku 1931 h.* (Minsk, 1932), 40.

33 P. Zaichik mentioned that his father, a rabbi from Smilavichy, left his shtetl on the eve of repressions in 1929 (P. Zaichik, 'Smikha ot velikogo cheloveka (Rasskaz o moem dedushke i ottse)', *Vestnik Evreiskogo universiteta v Moskve*, 1993, no. 4, pp. 90–198).

34 L. Smilovitsky, *Evrei v Turove: Istoriya mestechka Mozyrskogo Poles'ya* (Jerusalem, 2008), 369.

35 Ibid.

36 Gosudarstvennyi arkhiv obshchestvennykh ob'edinenii Gomel'skoi oblasti, (hereafter GAOOGO), f. 69, op. 2, d. 87, s. 89: Mazyr GPU, report (1926).

37 GAOOGO, f. 3, op. 1, d. 443, s. 307: Information Department of the Gomel Provincial Committee of the Russian Communist Party, report (2 Jan. 1929).

38 *Dzeinasts' Uradu BSSR za 1926–1927* (Minsk, 1929), 230–2.

39 I. Zalessky, 'Mestechko Uzda', in *Materialy po demografii i ekonomicheskomu polozheniyu evreiskogo naseleniya v SSSR*, 8 (1930), 60–85: 64.

40 Zeltser, *Evrei sovetskoi provintsii*, 230.

41 NARB, f. 34, op. 1, d. 734, s. 72: NKVD, reports on small towns in Belarus (1926).

42 *Dzeinasts' Uradu BSSR*, 232.

43 Ibid. 233.

44 A. Skir, *Evreiskaya dukhovnaya kul'tura v Belarusi* (Minsk, 1995), 59.

45 Ibid.

46 Zeltser, *Evrei sovetskoi provintsii*, 149.

47 Zamojski, 'Soviet Schooling as Reforming Force in *Shtetls*', 160.

48 Smilovitsky, *Evrei v Turove*, 320.

49 See 'The Jewish Intelligentsia and the Liquidation of Yiddish Schools in Belorussia, 1938: Documents Introduced and Annotated by V. Selemenev and A. Zeltser', *Jews in Eastern Europe*, 43 (2000), 78–97.

50 'Decree Issued by the Council of People's Commissars of the Russian Soviet Federative Socialist Republic' (23 Jan. 1918), 5.

51 V. Bingshtok and S. Novoselskii, 'Estestvennoe dvizhenie evreiskogo naseleniya v SSSR za 1924–1926 gg.', in *Evrei v SSSR* (Moscow, 1929), 73.

52 See M. Altshuler, 'Jews' Burial Rites and Cemeteries in the USSR in the Interwar Period', *Jews in Eastern Europe*, 47–8 (2002), 85–104: 87.

53 Gosudarstvennyi arkhiv Minskoi oblasti, f. 29, op. 1, d. 78, s. 35: Religious Jews, petition to Uzda soviet (1925).

54 P. Fedoseev, *O religii i bor'be s nei* (Moscow, 1938), 131.

55 Sirotiner, 'Iz zhizni "Vozdukhetresta"', 94.

56 The Minsk *shoḥetim* were accused of killing a young *shoḥet* from Vitebsk who slaughtered chickens for half the price they demanded. The Evsektsiya fabricated this political trial, which was widely discussed in the Belarusian and Yiddish press (Skir, *Evreiskaya dukhovnaya kul'tura v Belarusi*, 59).

57 M. Persist, 'Iudaizm v tsarskoi Rossii i SSSR', in M. Enisherlov et al. (eds.), *Voinstvuyushchee bezbozhie v SSSR za 15 let. 1917–1932: Sbornik* (Moscow, 1931), 170–3: 173.

58 Karpekin, *Iudeiskie obshchiny v Belorusskoi SSR*, 62–3.

59 See Gitelman, *Jewish Nationality*.

60 Lebedev and Pichukov, 'Politika sovetskoi vlasti', 30; Karpekin, *Iudeiskie obshchiny v Belorusskoi SSR*, 70–1.

61 Zamoiski, *Transformatsiya mestechek Sovetskoi Belorussii*, 245.

62 Jewish Telegraphic Agency, 'Worshippers Resist Confiscation of the Minsk Synagogues', *Jewish Daily Bulletin*, 3 Apr. 1929, p. 1.

63 Zeltser, *Evrei sovetskoi provintsii*, 43.

64 GAOOGO, f. 1, op. 1. d. 1712, s. 15: A. Merezhin, secretary of the Central Bureau of Evsektsia of the Central Committee of the Russian Communist Party, letter to head of Gomel Provincial Committee of the Russian Communist Party, Khataevichy (13 Dec. 1923).

65 See I. Levitats, *The Jewish Community in Russia*, 2 vols. (Jerusalem, 1981), ii. 70–1.

66 Zeltser, 'The Belorussian Evsektsiia and Jewish Religious Life in 1927', 70–71.

67 NARB, f. 4, op. 10, d. 56, s. 48: Evsektsiya, reports on the situation in small towns (1926).

68 Zamoiski, *Transformatsiya mestechek Sovetskoi Belorussii*, 254.

69 I. Kotler, 'Yawreiskiya myastechki w Belarusi w chase NEPa', in *Belarusika*, vol. 4 (Minsk, 1994), 101–6 : 105.

70 'The Belorussian Evsektsia', 48–9.

71 Rossiiskii gosudarstvennyi arkhiv ekonomiki, f. 5244, op. 1, d. 11, s. 39: B. Shik, agronomist, report on Shchadryn (12 Mar. 1929).

72 *Rezolyutsii plenuma TSK CP(b)B i doklad tov. Knorina (Sentyabr' 1927 g.)* (Minsk, 1927), 50.

73 Zeltser, 'The Shtetl During the Great Watershed of 1929–1931', 18–19.

74 NARB, f. 4, op. 10, d. 56, s. 41: Evsektsiya of the CP(b)B, resolution (24 Nov. 1927).

75 Zamoiski, *Transformatsiya mestechek Sovetskoi Belorussii*, 255.

76 NARB, f. 4, op. 10, d. 56, s. 130: Evsektsiya, 'Politicheskoe nastroenie i politicheskaia aktivnost' naseleniya mestechek' (1927).

77 Kaganovich, *Rechitsa*, 266.

78 NARB, f. 701, op. 1, d. 17, s. 124: data collected by the National Commission (Aug. 1927– Sept. 1928).

79 Kaganovich, *Rechitsa*, 266.

80 Bemporad, *Becoming Soviet Jews*, 121.

81 OGPU, report to the Central Committee of the CP(b)B (14 Apr. 1930), in *Na krutym pavarotse: Ideolaga-palitychnaya barats'ba na Belarusi w 1929–1931 gg. Dokumenty, matery-yaly, analiz*, ed. R. Platonaw (Minsk, 1999), 217–22.

82 Materials collected by the Commission of the Central Committee of the CP(b)B on the political situation in Mazyr district, spring 1926.

83 Ibid. 70.

84 NARB, f. 4, op. 1, d. 2412, s. 5: 'The merchant Shik', letter of complaint to the Central Executive Committee of the BSSR (3 Mar. 1925).

85 NARB, f. 4, op. 10, d. 30, s. 24: Jews of Sianno, letter to the Central Committee of the CP(b)B (17 May 1925),

86 NARB, f. 4, op. 10, d. 38, s. 7: Evsektsiya of Polatsk district, report (Nov. 1924).

87 S. Fitzpatrick, *Everyday Stalinism: Ordinary Life in Extraordinary Times: Soviet Russia in the 1930s* (Oxford, 2000), 182.

88 Kantor, *Natsional'noe stroitel'stvo sredi evreev v SSSR*, 28.

89 Ibid. 26.

90 Rossiiskii gosudarstvennyi arkhiv sotsial'no-politicheskoi istorii,, f. 17, op. 163, d. 994, s. 367: Politburo Protokol 56, 'On the Liquidation of National Regions and Rural Soviets' (1 Dec. 1937).

91 See 'Kolyshki: A Shtetl in the Late 1930s: Introduced and annotated by V. Selemenev and A. Zeltser', *Jews in Eastern Europe*, 46 (2001), 48–73: 63.

92 These bodies actively promoted the resettlement of mostly shtetl Jews to rural areas in Belarus, Ukraine, Crimea, and Birobidzhan.

93 See J. Dekel-Chen, *Farming the Red Land: Jewish Agricultural Colonization and Local Soviet Power, 1924–1941* (New Haven, Conn., 2005).

4. FORUM

A Disenchanted Elijah

The First World War, Conspiracy Theories, and Allegory in S. An-sky's *Destruction of Galicia*

MARC CAPLAN

A Symbolist Ethnography

No writer records the cataclysm of the First World War for east European Jews more acutely than S. An-sky in his 1920 chronicle, *The Destruction of Galicia*.[1] *The Destruction of Galicia* stands as one of his most complex publications. While focusing on the physical destruction of Jewish communities and the variety of duplicitous, hostile, or ineffectual responses from non-Jews, its first-person account deploys literary strategies and embedded narratives that trespass the borders separating the conventions of journalism, political propaganda, and fiction. The author's position within the contradictory social networks through which he moves conveys the extent to which his witnessing of violence undermines his ability to locate himself as a political representative, a writer, and a Jew. The narration of his travels and war-relief efforts contrasts with the embedded testimony of Jewish community leaders, anonymous refugees, and a variety of recurring legends and conspiracy theories told from both Jewish and non-Jewish perspectives. In one sense, therefore, the narrative demonstrates the transformation of oral storytelling genres in the context of warfare, new technologies (telegrams, telephones, aeroplanes, chemical weapons, and so on), dislocation, and unprecedented antisemitic violence. In a more dialectical fashion, An-sky also transforms the role of the narrator in this work, simultaneously recording oral stories and consolidating them into a synthetic narrative. *The Destruction of Galicia* thus stands in a constant state of suspension between the singular narrating act and the multiple voices from which the narrative is derived.

On these shifting borders between folklore and literature, An-sky emerges in *The Destruction of Galicia* not just as the foundational ethnographer of east European Jewry in the pre-war era,[2] but also as the culture's most suggestive allegorist. It is appropriate, in this respect, that he is the first of only three individuals in Yiddish literary history to date to have received a scholarly biography in English.[3] The self-dramatization of his life—his willingness to make of his own work and character a symbol for the role of the Jewish intellectual in east European life—contributes to the allegorical significance of his writing as well as the difficulties in interpreting it.

From a traditional upbringing in the tsarist Pale of Settlement, which produced nearly every major Yiddish writer, to an activist among peasants in the Russian interior, to an exiled leader of the Socialist Revolutionary Party (Partiya sotsialistov-revolyutsionerov; PSR), to the pioneering researcher of Jewish folklore in the early twentieth century, to a relief worker for Jews during the First World War, to an exile for the PSR again, at the opposite end of the political spectrum, following the Bolshevik revolution, An-sky's life overshadows all but two of his works, his drama *The Dybbuk*, and *The Destruction of Galicia*, the travelogue documenting his role in the Russian war effort.

These two works—*The Dybbuk*,[4] a play of hothouse symbolism and decadent eroticism, and *The Destruction of Galicia*, a painfully naturalistic account of depredation, depravity, and despair—are at once a study in contrasts and on a structural level united by common ambiguities. *The Dybbuk* is recognizably and intentionally a synthetic work: the layers of hasidic storytelling, local folklore, pseudo-gematria, and Midrash out of which An-sky constructs the plot are meant to be recognized as deriving from a bona fide collective consciousness, even though the motif central to the drama, of a dead lover possessing his living betrothed from beyond the grave, is an original inspiration, at least as far as Jewish folklore is concerned.[5] The drama's inauthenticity as a product of an individual imagination is supposed to assure its authenticity as a synthesis of ethnographic research.[6] *The Destruction of Galicia* is, too, an intricately imagined narrative, disguised as both reportage and memoir. An-sky's fiction is never more persuasive or compelling than when it is disguised as fact, and this masquerade, as well as the decadent pessimism that motivates it, provides the context for An-sky's modernist critique of the didactic naturalism that previously characterized his narrative fiction.

The boundaries in these works are as much temporal as they are physical or territorial. An-sky's travelogue is situated between the shifting borders of wartime Russia and Austria, whereas *The Dybbuk* takes place between no less unstable boundaries separating life from death. In both works, Jewishness, as a literary presence as well as the object of the author's sympathies, is identified unmistakably with death. This association in each work constitutes An-sky's modernism, however sceptical or resistant he had been towards Yiddish symbolism and the Russian avant-garde in his role prior to the war as a leading Russian Jewish editor, translator, and critic. Each work, in turn, comments on a redemptive, quasi-messianic motivation for the author's investment in folklore during the previous decade. As Brian Horowitz has written,

Even when he rejected revolution as the most effective means to achieve Utopia [after the 1905 revolution], An-sky proposed cultural projects that nonetheless encouraged the struggle for change. In fact, although his folklore studies may seem apolitical, in his treatment he did not just describe (as a scholar would) but attempted to give the Jews a new Torah.[7] This new Torah was supposed to bring about a reconciliation of Orthodox and secular Jews and transform Jewish society.[8]

If folklore during the decade prior to 1914 had been a new 'Tree of Life',[9] during the First World War it had become a Tree of Knowledge, bearing wisdom and death.

The paradox that motivates and animates *The Destruction of Galicia* in narrative terms is the role of the author not only in shaping but also in acting in the events he describes. Where *The Dybbuk* had disguised authorial invention as folklore, *The Destruction of Galicia* dissolves the author's role through several strategies An-sky had adapted from folklore. In particular, his understanding of folklore as preserving, through narrative, the pre-rational character of collective myths is now applied politically and historically to the narratives that circulate about Jews in the contested territories between the Austrian and Russian empires. Indeed, the role of history is what distinguishes these narratives from the folklore that An-sky had collected before the war: in pre-modern folklore, the coexistence of contradictory conditions—the human world, the animal world, and the spiritual world or life and death—can be reconciled because the aesthetic rules governing folklore allow for these states of being to interact. By contrast, the narratives accusing Jews, in supernatural terms, of undermining the Russian war effort underscore the contradictory condition of the war and its victims, because the historical circumstances that call these narratives into being can never be evaded or transcended. An-sky's role as author of the narrative is accordingly awkward, insofar as it obligates him simultaneously to participate in the events of the narrative and stand outside the situation in order to explicate it. As a consequence, his role dissolves into the narrative, both through his acting as a character in the incidents he transcribes, even as a character who figures in the legends told by Jews in contrast to the antisemitic legends told about them, and his ceding narrative authority to the other voices whom he records.

The Destruction of Galicia as a narrative is thus as conflicted as *The Dybbuk* and just as conflicted as the circumstances that led to its production. It stands at the fault line between journalism, ethnography, and autobiography as much as it documents the destruction of Jewish communities in the borderlands between the Russian and Austrian empires. At the same time, although the only one of An-sky's major works to have been published exclusively in Yiddish—even *The Dybbuk*, the quintessential work of folkloric modernism in Yiddish literature, began life as a Russian-language draft[10]—*The Destruction of Galicia* is below its monolingual surface a narrative in constant flux among Yiddish, Russian, and German (all of which An-sky spoke), surrounded by Polish, Hungarian, and Romanian (none of which An-sky spoke or understood). On a semantic level, in fact, the tension among languages can be discerned in the narrative through a persistent linguistic clue: though recording dialogue with Galician and Ukrainian Jews, An-sky habitually uses grammatical structures that appear exclusively in his native Lithuanian Yiddish. He renders, for example, 'on the street' as *afn gas*, a Lithuanian usage unknown in other dialects of modern Yiddish, which instead would say *af der gas*. Such usages demonstrate the extent to which his account is not just reconstructed but translated from Russian into Yiddish and, within its ostensible monolingual formulation, between one dialect and another. In common with many postcolonial narratives, the narrative can be viewed as a translated work for which an original version never existed.

The Destruction of Galicia is therefore an example of Gilles Deleuze and Félix Guattari's 'minor literature' in reverse—not a Russian (major language) work subverted through Yiddish[11] but a Yiddish work depleted of its characteristic idioms by the author's dependence on Russian.[12] This choice of language reflects its author's ideological tentativeness, because, by preparing the book in Yiddish, An-sky addresses the one audience that requires least persuasion about the plight of Jews in the Russian–Jewish borderlands.[13] The Destruction of Galicia is primarily an ethnographic work, but one of a radically different nature from An-sky's work before the First World War: no longer dedicated to the life of traditional Jewish communities at the beginning of the twentieth century but recording instead the death of these same communities and the murder of Jews, whether traditional or modern. Where the objective of his earlier expeditions was to record folk tales, what interrupts the reportorial narrative of the travelogue is a new species of legendary discourse, the conspiracy theory. An-sky's decision to publish The Destruction of Galicia originally in Yiddish is not only evidence of his commitment to Jewish autonomy but also a reflection of the failure of his previous political affiliations. By the time An-sky had completed the work, in February 1920, his prominence in the PSR had assured his permanent exile from the Soviet Union, which meant that publication in Russian was no longer a practical or even viable means of reaching a mass readership.

Moreover, with the border wars between Soviet Ukraine and Poland and the civil war between Whites and Reds—neither of whom An-sky could identify with—the antisemitic violence raging in eastern Europe while he was writing the book far exceeded even the previously unprecedented violence and depravity that the book itself records. Even by 1920 the events of 1915 or 1916 belonged as much to a bygone era as the Julian calendar of the tsars to which the events that An-sky documents compelled him to refer. The narrative is caught between conflicting temporalities, territories, and languages, to which it responds with greater formal ambiguities than An-sky would consciously sanction. If his goal in undertaking his organizational role on behalf of the Jews on the border had been to ensure that relief work would be conducted according to 'new, rational, and democratic principles',[14] by 1920 life in these territories was threatened for a third consecutive year, with no end yet in sight, by forces that were neither rational nor democratic, on any side. Unacknowledged within the narrative is the fact that An-sky's account is dedicated as much to the failed democratic revolution to which he had been devoted as to the Jews whom he had been unable to save. This pathos accounts for the extraordinary conflicts within The Destruction of Galicia, which erupt as the inability of the narrator to maintain control of the tone, discourse, or direction of the story he tells. By the time he had finished writing his account, the rational, idealistic intentions motivating the work had given way to legends, conspiracy theories, and horror stories: those values that motivated An-sky to work on the border between the Russian and Austrian empires had been as defeated as the empires themselves.

On Conspiracies and Conspiracy Theories

The contradictions that animate this work become apparent from its first sentence:

Nearly as soon as the World War broke out, right after the brief moment of half-earnest, half-feigned Jewish patriotism, while rabbis embraced Purishkevich[15] and Petersburg Jews stood on bended knee before the memorial of the worst tormentor of the Jews, Alexander III, to sing *Keyl mole rakhamim*—storm clouds were unleashed over the Jews of Poland, Russia, and occupied Galicia, letting loose the most horrifying libels and persecutions.[16]

Although An-sky reiterates familiar themes of resentment towards bourgeois Jews and religious leaders for making common cause with their Russian oppressors, this rhetorical gesture distracts from the evident fact that An-sky himself is also making a strategic alliance with Russian bureaucrats as well as Jewish community and religious leaders to provide relief for the poor and powerless Jews with whom he identifies. An-sky owes his presence in the war effort, and the existence of this narrative, to the institutional support of the groups whom he mocks at the beginning of his account. More fundamentally, An-sky owes the existence of this report to the internal contradictions of his own position: as a political radical and official representative of Russian relief agencies, he technically served as an officer in the government he wished to overthrow, in territories caught in a struggle among four powers—the Austrian and tsarist empires and the emerging Soviet and independent Polish regimes—none of which he identified with.[17]

As much as An-sky simultaneously underscores and evades the contradictions of his position as observer, participant, and reporter of the war-relief effort, he introduces in this first sentence the spectre of rhetorical violence that becomes an instrumental precursor to the physical mob violence that the Russian army both incited and perpetrated against Jews in Galicia and the Pale of Settlement. These libels recycled traditional themes of Jews as betrayers, connivers, and exploiters of the non-Jewish population, but, functioning in the destructively anti-traditional context of the war, these slanders have been transformed into conspiracy theories. To understand the significance of conspiracy theories—a type of narrative—one must first differentiate them from conspiracies—a category of social experience.[18] In spite of the similarity of the vocabularies used to describe them, the two are in fact antinomies: a conspiracy is the action of a small group of people closely co-ordinating their activities to achieve a commonly sought goal—to steal a painting, to defraud an investor, to foil the election plans of a rival politician.[19] Conspiracies refer to specific and concentrated efforts, whereas conspiracy theories invoke vast and limitless, though always hidden, resources.[20] Conspiracy theories are a narrative genre formulated to explain global events through seemingly rational analysis that in fact offers superficial cover for non-rational, indeed mythical thought.

The Destruction of Galicia documents the role of conspiracy theories in fuelling the antisemitic violence of the Russian army during the First World War.[21] To understand the function of these stories within An-sky's larger narrative, it is necessary to consider the characteristics that connect conspiracy theories with folktales on a formal level, yet distinguish each from the other on a temporal level. Both folktales and conspiracy theories serve as explanatory narratives; both function at a border between orality and literacy. The conspiracy theory, however, belongs to an era of new technologies upon which they depend for their circulation but to which they respond with suspicion about symbols of disruption, power, and invisible omniscience.[22] As An-sky writes:

It all began with whispered accusations, secret allegations, and libels, with the purpose of depicting the Jews as betrayers of Russia and accordingly showing the devotion and loyalty of the Poles: it was reported that when the Germans or the Austrians came to town, the Jews curried their favour, catered to their needs, answered all their questions . . . Jews served the enemy as spies, they communicated with him through secret telephones, conveyed the best-kept secrets through light signals or bonfires, sent him millions of roubles in gold, and so on.[23]

These conspiracy theories provide a commentary on the function of technology as an agent of dislocation, control, and unseen ubiquity. *The Destruction of Galicia* offers one of the clearest depictions of how this discourse functions and why Jews as a minority that is potentially 'invisible', capable of blending into the general population, serve as an ideal focus for the anxieties that fuel conspiracy theories.[24]

In this respect, a Russian officer on the train tells An-sky's narrator:

All the misinformation is spread by the *zhides*. They deliberately circulated a rumour that the Germans had taken Kielce. And their insolence! They openly call out, 'Soon our forces will be here!' They mean the Germans. And they talk German to one another. They should all be strangled!'[25]

Jews function in this description as a phantasm, so that even their language—which at the border of Galicia might indeed be unstable between Pale-of-Settlement Yiddish and Austrian German—is a projection of their disloyalty. The Jews in fact possess no force or power or national claim. They have no loyalties in the mind of their accusers, only multiple disloyalties. This is the crisis that the book dramatizes without ever depicting it directly. An-sky devotes the narrative as a whole to the relationship between language and political power, and the linguistic tension in his writing between Russian and Yiddish reflects and refracts the ideological contradiction between his position as a socialist revolutionary for all Russia and his commitment to national autonomy for Jews specifically. Related to these problems of power is a question of temporality, which can be traced in narrative terms through its relationship to folklore and conspiracy theories. Folktales are 'symbolic', in the sense that they are ahistorical, outside the experiences of ordinary life, though embedded in the everyday through their means of distribution, vernacular speech between neighbours and from parents to children. Conspiracy theories by contrast are atavistic and, as such, allegorical. If secularity is the myth that modernity tells itself, claiming exemptions from sacral thought processes that appear irrelevant and irrational, conspiracy theories in this context signify a 'return of the repressed'.

In a sense that becomes more complex with the development of An-sky's account, the problem of interpreting conspiracy theories is inextricable from the phenomena that these tales seek to explain: how does one come to understand new experiences? And how does one differentiate chance occurrences from signifying clues? As An-sky writes: 'While aeroplanes were flying over Łódź, a Jew was standing by himself on a porch, looking above his head, and began to sneeze. The Poles accused him of sending a signal through his sneezes to the aeroplanes (which were flying more than a half-mile high), as to where to throw their bombs, and the Jew was arrested'.[26] In a time of crisis, when is a sneeze just a sneeze? How does war corrupt language and criminalize the human body? An-sky's account demonstrates the ways in which non-Jews over-determined Jewish behaviour to render Jews into agents of Russian defeat and destruction.[27]

Of all the conspiracy theories that An-sky documents, none is more pervasive than 'the Jewish girl in the window'. The story first appears at the beginning of the war when Cossacks invade the Galician border town of Brody:

Even before I came to Brody I had already heard in military circles the official version of the event: when the first Cossack division came to town, a Jewish girl, the daughter of a hotel owner, fired a gun from a window in the hotel and murdered a Cossack officer. The Cossacks immediately murdered the girl, began bombing the city, and burned the entire quarter where the attack had occurred.[28]

Though An-sky quotes the testimony of a Doctor Kalak, who claims that the daughter of a Jewish hotelier in Brody fled the hotel in a panic when she heard the shot that had wounded or killed a Russian soldier,[29] the persistence of the legend depends on the suggestiveness of its premise as much as the putative occurrence of the incident itself. The hotel as a modern meeting place and ostensible safe haven makes the treachery of the girl's supposed violence all the more outrageous. The family of the hotelier stands for the danger that all Jews represent in the antisemitic imagination, in that they pose as welcoming neighbours but conceal murderous betrayal beneath a facade of friendliness. The erotic insinuation of a Jewish girl, at once wanton and virginal, magnifies the sense of danger, destructiveness, and foreignness implicit among Jews as inassimilable strangers indistinguishably embedded in the native landscape of an eternal border.

Nonetheless, what accounts for the destruction in Galicia is not mythical Jewish treachery—the worst traitors, as the narrator insists, are the Poles[30]—but airborne reconnaissance: the ubiquitous omniscience ascribed to traitorous Jews is only a displacement of the technological superiority of the enemy forces. Similarly, as a Russian surgeon, Doctor Kozhenevsky, explains to the narrator, the fact that Jews, unlike many of their persecutors, are literate and familiar with the local landscape is sufficient to arouse suspicion against them.[31] In this context, the Jewish girl serves as a figure for the allure, danger, and treachery of modern technology in its enticing and dangerous aspects. The capriciousness of these associations can be recognized in the conspiracy theories that An-sky reports from within the Russian interior, which focus on members of the royal family or ethnic Germans living in Petrograd or Moscow.

One such legend contends that a German in Petrograd had instructed his maid to flip a switch on a device that would destroy the entire city. As An-sky notes, 'a common feature of all these rumours and fables was that they almost never mentioned Jews'.[32] The rhetoric of these legends displaces the cause of misfortune from material circumstances—technological inequalities, military mismanagement, the ungovernability of both empires at their border—onto an Other that functions outside of political, military, or moral constraints. If An-sky documents the helplessness of Jews in eastern Europe, the conspiracy theories he records cast Jews and other outsiders as wielders of an incalculable tyranny. In this respect An-sky records the parable of an Old Believer that serves as meta-commentary on all conspiracy theories:

Three kings are waging war. The war will last for three years, three months, and three days. One king will die of natural causes, the second will be killed, the third will conquer the entire world, but nothing will come of his victory because there will be three years of famine, and half the human race will perish. Next will come a year with very rich crops, but when they examine the grain, they will see that each kernel consists half of blood and half of sand, and then the other half of the human race will perish.[33]

Each of these scenarios—the Jewish girl in the window, the aristocracy's betrayal of the empire, and the Old Believer's apocalypse—provides a poetics of dislocation that projects the disruptions of war onto an enemy that is both spectrally imagined and physically proximate.

All such stories react to the trauma of history with a narrative response that renders history legendary, but in the incompatibilities between history and legend they illustrate the marginality of the people repeating these stories to the historical processes of which they have become victims. In a corresponding rhetorical gesture, the narrator crafts an image that synthesizes the ethnic diversity of the European battlefield and links this disunity to the violence against Jews that constitutes its most virulent consequence:

These homeless people, by tens and hundreds of thousands, will come into the interior and spread across the endless fields of Greater Russia, Ukraine, and Siberia . . . And all these former antagonists and deadly enemies will come together on those endless fields and work solemnly by the sweat of their brows. They will till the same soil, eat from the same bowl, drink from the same pitcher, express their deep gloom and yearning with the same universal sigh . . . And as they grow even closer and discuss things openly, they will find so many universal interests, universal joys and sorrows. And when they remember their neighbour, the Jew, who fought none of them, killed none of their people, they will nevertheless unanimously agree that the Jew is the one responsible for everybody's misfortune.[34]

This passage parodies the Tolstoyan idealism that had in part inspired An-sky to political activism thirty years earlier. The bitterness of warfare has eaten away at his previous convictions as much as it has destroyed the shaky relationship between Jews and non-Jews and severed the continuity that each group had maintained with its own traditions. Earlier in the narrative An-sky had dramatized the bankruptcy of such antiquated utopianism by describing an exchange with a Russian officer who, under Tolstoy's influence, had become a vegetarian: "'And yet you go to war, and you kill people", I said. The soldier's response, "War is a different matter. This war will renew the world; it will cleanse mankind of its dirt. For such a goal one can make the supreme sacrifice.""[35] As the narrative around this exchange makes clear, the sacrifice of the war is being made not at the officer's expense but at the Jews', and, instead of redeeming mankind, it is destroying a civilization and imperilling the concept of civilization as such.

Nonetheless, at the very end of his narrative, An-sky writes: 'I have often noted that Galician Jews, tormented and ruined by the Russian army, nevertheless enthuse about the Russian character. They always have a story about a soldier or an officer who displayed a poignant idealism and humanity.'[36] If there is a propagandistic motivation for writing this book in Yiddish, it might consist in attempting to rehabilitate the Russian national character, a project to which An-sky had devoted much of his revolutionary fervour, even during his years of exile in western Europe.[37] The populist belief that Russian folk culture could be elevated above the corrupt tsarist system that had called it into being—the evil of which would require no documentation for a Yiddish readership and which An-sky had devoted his life to overthrowing— seems at the end of the narrative as much of a folktale as the libels about Jews secretly telephoning the Kaiser from basement telephones in shtetls without electricity.[38] The testimony of Russian benevolence shares with the stream of conspiracy theories that precede it the quality of a 'secret history' that inverts the reality otherwise observable throughout An-sky's account. An-sky deflates the presentation of this utopian belief in the Russian army's capacity for generosity by reducing it to another embedded testimony, out of place in the chronicle of destruction that surrounds it.

And yet these testimonials also precede accounts of German atrocity, specifically the decision of the German military to prevent a cholera epidemic among its ranks by placing Jewish cholera patients in a barn, which they set on fire. An-sky contrasts the sadism of Cossack troops towards Jews—which is literally sadism because it has no goal other than the apparent pleasure of the torturers—with the methodical barbarism of the Germans, for whom the ends of self-preservation always justify the means, even inhuman ones. As An-sky writes:

I don't know what is crueller: torching a barrack filled with sick people or making people strip naked, ride on pigs, and gunning them down. The barrack fire, no matter how inhumane, at least had a specific goal. With Germans, you knew who you were dealing with . . . But with the Russians you were never sure of your life, of your dignity.[39]

The contrast here is not merely between Germans and Russians[40] but between the deployment of scientific rationalism to an immoral extreme and the caprices of an irrational and anti-modern hatred. Although An-sky suggests that German rationality is defensible,[41] the action he cites undermines his own allegiance to such rationalism. In this juxtaposition, An-sky articulates the peripheral, 'subaltern' predicament in which Jews are caught hopelessly between both systems of power, neither of which protects their rights, even their right to exist.

Inevitably, Jews concocted their own conspiracy theories in response to the violence of their circumstances, and An-sky records these legends as well:

In Zamość, the Poles informed on the Jews for aiding the enemy. Several Jews were arrested ... but a Russian teacher and a civil judge presented themselves to the judges and, falling on bended knee, asked that no verdict be delivered until their testimony was heard ... 'If you want to know who is truly guilty,' they said, 'come with us' ... When they were followed to the cellar of the Countess Zamojska, they found a whole group of Jews in caftans, in yarmulkes, with long sidelocks, speaking on telephones to the Austrians ... The Russian judge shouted: 'Take them in for questioning!' And when the Jews were taken in for questioning, it was revealed that they were all Poles who had ... dressed up in Jewish clothing, so as to cast aspersions on the Jews.[42]

An-sky reports variants of this Zamość tale from Minsk and Lublin. The circulation of these tales—whether condemning or exonerating the Jews—creates a symbolic geography that parallels the larger destructive processes that warfare brings about. Although the immobility of Jews caught among shifting borders and warring armies puts their lives in danger, the circulation of stories about Jews contrasts their physical entrapment, however incommensurately, with a metaphysical hyper-mobility. This strategy of figurative geography is a technique that An-sky's writing shares with the *folkstimlekhe geshikhtn* or 'stories in a folk-like vein' of Y. L. Peretz, who was the primary Yiddish-language influence on An-sky's writing and who plays a role in An-sky's travelogue through Poland.[43] Perhaps coincidentally, Peretz was a native of Zamość, where the conspiracy theory of the Poles disguised as Jews is said to have originated.

More purposefully, the fictive 'marking of territory' achieved by setting legendary stories in actual locations is a device that Peretz had learned from Polish fiction, invested as Peretz's Yiddish writing was in imagining a cultural nationhood for a people lacking political self-determination. In this respect, An-sky has recorded a story of Poles disguised as Jews to invert lessons he had learned from Peretz, a Yiddish writer who had 'masqueraded' as a Pole. An-sky, who shares a grave in Warsaw with Peretz, learned other techniques from the classic Yiddish author as well. In his description, for example, of the rabbi of Nowe Miasto, An-sky incorporates the rabbi's encounter with a Russian military chief, whom he interrogates ostensibly in the manner of a talmudic sage bantering with a Roman consul, while in fact speaking in humane and rational terms on behalf of the beleaguered Jewish population. The passage reads like a neo-hasidic parable in the style of Peretz. Moreover, when An-sky refers to the rabbi's language as 'almost literary, with some Russian words mixed in with the Yiddish,'[44] he characterizes the register of the travelogue in general. Indeed, the rabbi's 'tall, bony' physique, 'bulging eyes', and 'striding, purposeful gait' suggest that he serves as a physical double for An-sky himself. Just as An-sky serves as both witness and mediator between Jewish relief agencies and the Russian government, the rabbi of Nowe Miasto serves two conflicting functions, as *shtot rabiner* (official intermediary between the Jewish community and the Russian authorities) and Orthodox rabbi (a religious leader within the Jewish community). The doubling of the rabbi and the narrator is one of many instances in which the authorial role is incorporated and effaced within the narrative.

Just as Peretz had fabricated hasidic fables in order to convey an ironic and cosmopolitan critique of tradition and modernity simultaneously, An-sky puts the voices whom he quotes to narrative and documentary use: this embedded hasidic parable disintegrates the authorial voice, diffusing it into the collective for which An-sky speaks. Of course, if Peretz's motivation in imitating and reimagining Jewish folklore by situating it in a recognizable Polish landscape—refiguring Poland as *po-lin*[45]—had been to create a Jewish nation, An-sky's figurative geography reflects the dissolution of this imaginary Jewish space. Where Peretz's refashioning of folklore illustrates both a political and aesthetic use-value for symbolic thinking, An-sky's documentation of conspiracy theories demonstrates the breakdown of the symbol's representational power. Motifs such as the Jewish girl in the window in this respect function not as symbols but as metonymy, and what non-Jewish conspiracy theorists construct in the confusion between these representational strategies is allegory. Allegorical images demonstrate the incompatibility of symbolic thought with historical processes—the irresolvable dilemma that generates conspiracy theories as a symbolic, 'hidden' history that can only be deciphered allegorically by initiates still capable of believing in the magic of pre-rational thought.[46]

What is Allegory?

Allegorical discourse can be characterized as a mode of figuration that couples imagistic language with conceptual terms; metaphor, by contrast, as Benjamin Harshav has written, juxtaposes two species of 'concrete universals', such as the evening sky and a patient etherized on a table in T. S. Eliot's 'The Love Song of J. Alfred Prufrock'.[47] Though Harshav recognizes that in a metaphor the juxtaposed sensuous elements 'represent something beyond them', such as the modern hospital and the approach of death beyond Prufrock's twilight contemplation of the heavens, in allegory the traffic between image and concept remains at a standstill, and this stasis allows the contradictions of temporality and ideology motivating the act of representation to be understood. Allegory manifests itself in *The Destruction of Galicia* through the symbolic value accorded to Jews and other scapegoats in the conspiracy theories that intercut the narrative, in the use of territoriality as a means not of locating but dislocating the narrator,[48] and in the status of the human body as object and agent of destruction.

This final aspect of allegorical figuration serves to articulate its significance for *The Destruction of Galicia* as a whole. If other figurative devices such as metaphor or metonymy propose a constructive relationship between or among images, allegory proposes both a destructive juxtaposition and a deconstructive one. For example, An-sky describes a fatally injured officer on a train:

He had a high fever, visibly agitated, and the entire time he spoke, describing to the doctors his impression of the most recent battle. Throughout he would laugh, loudly and drily. It was as if a skeleton were laughing. With this dead laughter he described how next to him his comrade, a second lieutenant, was killed: 'He was torn to bits ... ha-ha-ha! The pieces of meat were flying every which way, ha-ha-ha![49]

The dying officer's 'skeletal' delirium serves as an allegorical figure and a figure for allegory. It emphasizes the relationship between allegory and death in order to illustrate how allegory, distinctively among rhetorical strategies, can represent what is philosophically inconceivable and psychologically inarticulable. This association with death and dysfunction is a signal characteristic of allegory that serves in part to distinguish it from other modes of figurative representation. With equal significance, the fact that a dying man narrates an account of death underscores the impression of a talking corpse and a living death, the temporal impossibilities to which allegory gives singular voice by underscoring the contradictions of the moment out of which it emerges.

An-sky himself articulates these paradoxes by writing: 'I visited our hospital. What dreadful wounds, what inhuman agonies! How do people go on living with half their heads torn off, with their chests ripped out? But worst of all were the gangrenous bodies—people decaying while still alive.'[50] Where, for example, metaphor posits a relationship between figures that both evolves and develops through their juxtaposition, metonymy functions through the seemingly chance encounter between or among objects that suggests a relationship based on the observer's capacity for movement and shifting perspectives.[51] Allegory, by contrast, is situated between these polarities, triangulating them, and it achieves its expressive force by stressing the static, inorganic nature of its conjunctions, through which not only the arbitrary relationship between signifiers and the signified but also the temporal contradictions of their coupling can be seen, examined, and critiqued.

As Walter Benjamin suggests, allegory is a mode of figuration that has outlived its original purpose, a means of representation that over-determines the relationship between figurative depictions and conceptual interpretations—images and words, respectively—to expose the ideological and temporal contradictions that characterize cultural production in times of crisis. Allegory revokes the first law of introductory writing classes, 'show, don't tell'; allegories always try to tell and show at the same time, while exposing the discrepancy between the showing and the telling.[52] This discrepancy constitutes the literary dimension of non-fictional narratives. The ability to illustrate these contradictions, to reveal 'dialectics at a standstill', is the value that Benjamin attributes to allegory, and An-sky's travelogue not only offers resounding evidence to support Benjamin's theoretical investment in allegory but ultimately indicates structural and thematic affinities between the travelogue as a literary form and allegory as a rhetorical strategy: both transform landscape into a text needing to be deciphered,[53] but both dramatize the ways in which the necessary act of interpretation overwhelms the reader, or in An-sky's case the narrator, charged with the task.

Moreover, allegory functions simultaneously as an illustration of displacement as well as a conceptual internalization of this displacement within the discourse of the narrative. Thus the narrator, in one of the most moving episodes of the entire work, records the testimony of a woman from Dębica who had taken refuge in Tarnów. After dispassionately describing the disappearance of her children and grandchildren in the series of bombings and pogroms that befell her home town, she suddenly broke her monotone to bewail the desecration of Torah scrolls and the slaughter of horses during the same sequence of atrocities.[54] Caught between the physical violence of the pogrom and the mechanized violence of the bombing, this refugee equates the fate of her children simultaneously but only implicitly with the slaughter of helpless animals and the destruction of sacred objects. Her ability to bemoan the fate of horses and Torah scrolls instead of her offspring affects the reader not because the loss of these animals or artefacts is commensurate with the murder of her family members, but because it isn't: the inadequacy of representational language that allegory enacts is, paradoxically, the only form of representation that offers a voice to what cannot be said.[55]

The allegorical strategies that An-sky's narrator deploys are perhaps inevitable for travel writing, given its intrinsic disparities of narratorial privilege and knowledge: travel writing typically depicts the spatial difference between the narrator and the objects of his or her descriptions in temporal terms, as a voyage to the past or the future, yet in the context of world war and revolution, past and future become confused and contested temporal categories. An-sky comments on this aspect of his travelogue in a reflection on a ruined monastery he encounters towards the end of his journey:

The idea gave me pause, why centuries-old ruins possess such majesty, such dramatic beauty, whereas at the same time newer ruins seem chastened and lack even a sense of drama? This derives from the fact that a new ruin is situated around the accidental remains of unburned and undestroyed parts that stand out and create a disharmony and disrupt its internal drama. Old ruins, which have survived for hundreds of years, preserve only those parts that are indestructible and can withstand both time and the elements.[56]

Older ruins belong to their time, whereas newer ruins are disconnected from their time because of the destruction that calls them into being and the persistence of remnants that mark the ambiguity of a recent ruin, like the newly dead.

An-sky's reflection specifically on a ruined monastery, moreover, calls attention not just to the status of a ruin but also its style. The landscapes where An-sky travelled were, and are, replete with baroque architecture, particularly in the context of church structures, and thus qualities of splendour and gloom, ornamentation and fragmentation, cultivated an uneasy visual and structural dynamic. In the context of the First

World War, however, An-sky's sole reference to this style is in a context of devastation. A baroque ruin resonates more fully than other architectural remnants because ruination is already an element in its visual language. Or, more simply, eastern Europe shares the levelling effect of destruction with the West insofar as the First World War visited its violence throughout the continent. The parity that had eluded the East— that made the East 'eastern Europe'—arrives belatedly not as the construction of European modernity, but its destruction.

An-sky represents these paradoxes throughout *The Destruction of Galicia*, never so vividly as when he introduces the testimony of a Jewish soldier in the Russian army by writing: 'Motionlessly by the door stands a tall young man with a sparse beard. Speaking quietly, in a monotone, with downcast eyes, he describes his memories. Suddenly he stops and struggles to recall something, looking at me with astonishment, as if to ask if all that had happened was real, or simply a dream.'[57]

In effect, *The Destruction of Galicia* as a whole takes place in the dreamscape between truth and the various types of fantasy—together with ideology, ethnicity, and mutual suspicion—that An-sky's interlocutors inhabit. This juxtaposition of the testimonial aspects of the work and the phantasms within the embedded narratives that constitute it challenges the notion of an objective truth to the struggle between the Allied and the Central powers beyond the physical suffering of the people caught in its crossfire. What emerges through the recurrence of these subjective testimonies is a pattern of correspondence that demonstrates how conspiracy theories, as a mode of allegorical representation, relate to the problem of locating a narrative perspective among so many competing claims to truth. The displacement that conspiracy theories enact, of superimposing mythical thought processes onto contemporary experience, parallels the displacement of a single narrative perspective onto multiple voices. Both are instances of allegorical figuration, and each in a different sense allegorizes the position of the author.

The Traveller Disguised

Despite the reiterated disjunctions in *The Destruction of Galicia* between physical devastation and rhetorical rationale, An-sky is insistent, to an unprecedented degree in Yiddish literature—as was unprecedented for all literatures prior to the First World War—on describing the physical violence that he has witnessed. While on a train bringing residents of a border shtetl in Belarus to the east, the author describes an aerial grenade attack:

Suddenly a new boom, stronger than the earlier ones. Nobody knew where it came from. When the panic subsided, we saw what had happened. Because of the gasses, the first tank, where the fuel had burned up, had flown off the platform . . . Two corpses were lying nearby. One was an elderly man—almost naked because his clothes had burned off. He lay face-down in a pool of blood. Singed intestines were spilling from a broad, gaping injury in his side. One leg and one hand had been severed as if with a knife and flung nearby.[58]

The purpose of these details is not merely to document a devastation that could scarcely be unfamiliar to a Yiddish readership, but to emblematize the dislocation and depravity of war on the bodies of its victims. Though his Yiddish readers would have no hesitation in identifying the bodies that An-sky describes as Jewish bodies, his descriptions nonetheless emphasize a corporeality in which the Jewishness of these victims, however explicit, nevertheless becomes irrelevant. The Otherness of the Jews that had previously incited their persecutors here becomes the Otherness that all dead bodies inhabit equally.

As is necessarily the case in travel writing, setting amplifies the allegorical function of these descriptions, and therefore it is significant that the most graphic description of violence in the narrative takes place on a train. In the decade preceding the war An-sky's contemporary Sholem Aleichem had been able, through a series of fictive travel vignettes collected as the *Railroad Stories*, to transfer the conventions of Yiddish satire from the shtetl to the third-class railway carriage that conveyed Jews, circuitously and aimlessly, through the Pale of Settlement.[59] Where in nineteenth-century Yiddish satire the role of travel had been reserved for exceptional, authorial figures such as Sholem Aleichem or his predecessor Mendele Moykher Sforim, at the beginning of the twentieth century dislocation had become the common fate for everyone in the Yiddish world. Now, in the First World War, An-sky found it necessary to describe how even this 'portable shtetl' was no longer heading towards oblivion but had become consumed in the conflagration, so that both the simulated home of the Jewish exile as well as the modern technologies that had been promised as a deliverance from the dysfunctionality of tradition were dead ends for the Jews consigned to them.

Indeed, more than merely deciphering the inscrutable and shifting borders between the Russian and Austrian empires or the many individuals whom the narrator encounters as further examples of allegorical representation, the narrator himself comes to take on an allegorical signification of the role An-sky had played in reality. In this respect he masquerades as a Christian with Bilczyński, the 'pro-Jewish' head of the civic commission who confesses his actual antipathy towards Jews.[60] At issue in their discussion is the question of setting up a soup kitchen as opposed to dispensing groceries directly to Jews and peasants, a dilemma that reiterates the central political conflict of An-sky's position: to integrate with non-Jews or remain autonomous. This problem of integrating Jews into a larger war-relief effort or protecting their unique interests and preserving their ethnic distinctness informs *The Destruction of Galicia* as a narrative and connects this work to larger challenges that motivated An-sky's career as a whole.[61] In a sense, this irresolvable conflict is the dialectic on which the work is premised.

Just as an ideological reason for publishing the work in Yiddish can be deduced from An-sky's ultimate commitment to Jewish autonomy,[62] and a propagandistic purpose can be sensed from the deliberately belated testimony documenting instances of Russian generosity towards Galician Jews, an additional justification for publishing it in Yiddish—call it, perhaps, the 'instrumental' motivation—can be understood from the narrator's account of a conference between Jewish relief workers and the Central Relief Committee in Kiev. As An-sky writes: 'I was the last person to take the floor. When I used the word Jew, they all glared at me as if I had broken a verbal taboo.'[63] To insist on the Jewishness of Jewish refugees obligates the author to resist the dominant mode of liberalism motivating relief work that, in pursuit of universalist ethics, refuses to acknowledge the imbalance of power and disproportionate threats that distinguish Jews from other groups displaced in the war zone.[64] Through the decision to prepare his account of Jewish war relief in Yiddish, An-sky signals his protest against this defaced, impotent liberalism.

Nonetheless, the narrator's position, in conspicuous contrast to An-sky's authorial strategies of identification with Jewish war victims, vacillates between identification and withdrawal from both groups and all groups, socially, ethnically, linguistically. During the saga of the soup kitchen, the narrator meets the Gerer Rebbe, leader of the largest hasidic community in Poland at the time, who functions as another mirror of the narrator—denounced by non-Jews for a spurious edict prohibiting his hasidim from sharing food with non-Jews, accused like the narrator of being something he was not—but also a figure of how An-sky's social mediation and detachment can be understood in metaphysical terms, between Heaven and Earth.[65] Contrary to the formal logic of the autobiography, in which the 'I' as protagonist functions distinctly from the 'I' as narrator, in An-sky's travelogue the authorial 'I' disappears into the narrative. And though the motivation for the book is admirably political and documentary, its drama is internalized over distinctions between identity and identification; the absence of the first is figured through the mutability of the second.

In this respect An-sky follows the precedent of his prior folkloric research by recasting his narrator in legendary terms. In Radziwiłłów, for example, he is taken for a Christian on three occasions, itself a number with Christological significance.[66] In Sokal, he is taken for a Russian by both Cossacks—whom he disciplines as agents of the state, while they understandably (mis)take him for an army official—as well as by the local (Galician) Jews, whom he astonishes with his charity and generosity.[67] Commenting on his own inscrutable status, the narrator exclaims, 'I was truly astonished at the reckless trust that the head of the investigation unit was showing toward an unknown person',[68] even though his travelogue owes its existence to such trust. Through this process, the narrator becomes another figure of the war's chaos, as well as of the unstable relationship between author and reader and fact and fiction. *The Destruction of Galicia* is thus aesthetically modernist even though it is not conceived as a work of fiction—that is, even though it does not present itself 'merely' as an aesthetic representation, its objective is identical to modernism as an aesthetic strategy: to represent modernity at the moment of its dissolution.

The narrator's mutability and mercurial temperament, as well as his single-minded benevolence towards the powerless Jewish community, come to resonate with another legend from traditional Jewish folklore, the immortally roving figure of Elijah the Prophet, reconfigured in disenchanted and historicized—which is to say, allegorized—form.[69] An-sky writes of the shtetl of Torskin, for example: 'I heard the story of a Jewish officer who was stopping passers-by, questioning them in Yiddish. He would treat them to tea, give candy to the children, and hand out money . . . No one knows who he is.'[70] Though An-sky's narrator cultivates irony consciously in this passage, the native informant whom he quotes wasn't. In his ubiquity and indecipherability, the narrator has become the protagonist of a conspiracy theory, the benign counterpart to the Jewish girl in the window. As such, An-sky gives voice to the collective 'no one' who fails to recognize him, so that, like Odysseus with the blind Cyclops, 'No One' becomes yet another of the author's pseudonyms. This paradox underscores the complexity of serving as author, narrator, and protagonist: not one An-sky, but several. Like An-sky's narrator, Elijah in the folk tradition plays a variety of roles—tester of the faithful; harbinger of redemption; benefactor of the poor, the sick, the aged, and children—both to substitute for the fractured wholeness of the Jewish people in exile and to help mend the tatters of the community fabric.[71] An-sky in *The Destruction of Galicia*, however, serves as a disenchanted Elijah, a modernist Elijah, who can only further chronicle the community's destruction.

At the end of his narrative An-sky returns to another semi-legendary figure, the Ba'al Shem Tov (*c*.1700–60), to summarize the devastation he has witnessed and chronicled. Describing the failure of a hasidic rabbi to salvage two letters signed by the Ba'al Shem Tov in 1753, An-sky states that when the letters were recovered from their hiding place, his signature had been erased from them, whether by the ravages of the east European climate or divine decree. This calls to mind a memory of shattered tablets of the Ten Commandments that he had found in a desecrated synagogue:

These two symbols, 'shattered tablets' and 'flying letters', summed up the life of the Galician Jews. During my first tour of Galicia, I had virtually followed the trail blazed by the combat . . . I found people who were . . . 'shattered tablets', with blood pouring from every 'break' . . . The catastrophe afflicting the ruined, bloody and degraded populace was huge, almost epic. But in its vast scope . . . there was a severe beauty that transformed these human sorrows and sufferings into an epic tragedy. Now, while traveling through the intact towns and townlets, I no longer encountered the earlier sublime and beautiful drama. Tragedy was commonplace. The heroes of the national tragedy had become professional beggars . . . And all these living corpses trudged past me not as shattered tablets but as tablets from which the letters had been erased.[72]

The phrases 'shattered tablets' and 'flying letters', written in Hebrew in the original, allude to Moses' shattering of the tablets at Mount Sinai in response to the Israelites' worship of the Golden Calf (Exod. 32: 19) and Rabbi Haninah ben Tradyon, whom Roman authorities martyred by setting him on fire with a Torah scroll wrapped around his body: at the moment of immolation he declared to his disciples that he could see letters of the Law soaring upwards (*AZ* 17*b*). With these allusions, An-sky associates the destruction of east European Jewish life with the two great cataclysmic events—the rupture between God and the Israelites in the desert and the destruction of the Temple in Jerusalem—that destroyed the mythical unity of the ancient Jewish people, thereby plunging them into the wilderness of history and exile.

Like the letters of the Ba'al Shem Tov, the bodies of Jewish refugees have become effaced texts, allegorical figures for a community whose tradition has been blotted out by the forces of history. Where once An-sky had used folklore to salvage the spoken wisdom of the Jewish folk but also to signify his own renewed identification with the Jewish people, now folkloric motifs figure the dissipation of Jewish people-hood, physically and spiritually. In *The Destruction of Galicia*, An-sky's strategic and dramatic decision to dissipate into his narrative, to merge with the embedded voices he records, signals his commitment not only to identifying with the Jewish people but to suffering their fate with them as well.

Notes

This chapter was first presented at the Narratives of Violence conference in Budapest in June 2014 and in slightly revised form at the Congress of the European Association for Jewish Studies in Paris the following month. An expanded version was delivered at the Institute for Israel and Jewish Studies at Columbia University in March 2015 at the invitation of Jeremy Dauber. The audiences at these venues have my appreciation for their critical engagement with my work in progress. Research on this article was made possible by consecutive fellowships at the Center for Jewish History in New York and the Frankel Institute for Advanced Judaic Studies in Ann Arbor. Both of these institutions, their staff, and my colleagues at each have my thanks for their support and interest in my research. Particular thanks are due to my friends Jessica Dubow and Sara Nadal-Melsió for their constructive reading of this article in draft form.

1   S. An-sky, *Der yidisher khurbn fun poyln galitsye un bukovine fun togbukh*, in id., *Gezamelte shriftn*, 15 vols. (Warsaw, 1923–8), vols. iv–vi; abridged Eng. trans.: *The Enemy at His Pleasure: A Journey Through the Jewish Pale of Settlement During World War I*, trans. J. Neugroschel (New York, 2002).

2   The best study of An-sky's pre-war ethnographic work, both its scope and its motivations, is N. Deutsch, *The Jewish Dark Continent: Life and Death in the Russian Pale of Settlement* (Cambridge, Mass., 2011).

3   G. Safran, *Wandering Soul: The Dybbuk's Creator, S. An-sky* (Cambridge, Mass., 2010). Preceding Safran's book and instigating the contemporary scholarly attention to An-sky's career is D. Roskies, 'S. Ansky and the Paradigm of Return', in J. Wertheimer (ed.), *The Uses of Tradition* (New York, 1992), 243–60. The other two scholarly biographies of Yiddish writers in English to date are M. Krutikov, *From Kabbalah to Class Struggle: Expressionism, Marxism, and Yiddish Literature in the Life and Work of Meir Wiener* (Stanford, Calif., 2011); J. Dauber, *The Worlds of Sholem Aleichem: The Remarkable Life and Afterlife of the Man Who Created Tevye* (New York, 2013). Surpassing them all, however, is E. Gal-Ed, *Niemandssprache: Itzik Manger—ein europäischer Dichter* (Berlin, 2016).

4   S. An-sky, *Tsvishn tsvey veltn: der dibuk*, in id., *Gezamlte shriftn*, ii.; Eng. trans.: 'The Dybbuk or Between Two Worlds (A Dramatic Legend in Four Acts)', in *The Dybbuk and the Yiddish Imagination: A Haunted Reader*, trans. J. Neugroschel (Syracuse, NY, 2000), 3–52.

5   The single best study to date of *The Dybbuk*'s sources, dramatic milieu, performance history, and literary significance is S. Wolitz's 'Inscribing An-sky's *Dybbuk* in Russian and Jewish Letters', in G. Safran and S. J. Zipperstein (eds.), *The Worlds of S. An-sky: A Russian Jewish Intellectual at the Turn of the Century* (Stanford, Calif., 2006), 164–202.

6 As Izaly Zemtsovsky notes, in an article that resonates with Seth Wolitz's conception of *The Dybbuk* as an effort at Jewish *Gesamtkunstwerk*, 'An-sky created a text that might be called *inter-generic* because it has features of both storytelling and the ethnographic presentation of folklore data. This prose is as much documentary as fictional' (I. Zemtsovsky, 'The Musical Strands of An-sky's Texts and Contexts', in Safran and Zipperstein (eds.), *The Worlds of S. An-sky*, 203–231: 219 (emphasis in original)). It might be said of both *The Dybbuk* and *The Destruction of Galicia* that the prose is 'documentary' but the 'poetry' is fictional, and in the tension between these polarities their respective aesthetic complexities can be understood.

7 'Yet on a par with the book, with the great Written Torah [*Toyre shebiksav*] that we have received as an inheritance from hundreds of generations of the chosen—pious sages and great scholars, thinkers and spiritual guides—we possess yet another Torah, an Oral Torah [*Toyre shebalpe*], which the people themselves, and especially the common folk, have ceaselessly created during their long, hard, and tragic history. This Oral Torah, which consists of folktales and legends, parables and aphorisms, songs and melodies, customs, traditions, beliefs, and so on, is also an enormously significant product of the same Jewish spirit that created the Written Torah. It reflects the same beauty and purity of the Jewish soul, the tenderness and nobility of the Jewish heart, and the height and depth of Jewish thought' (S. An-sky, 'The Jewish Ethnographic Program', trans. N. Deutsch, in *The Jewish Dark Continent: Life and Death in the Russian Pale of Settlement* (Cambridge, Mass., 2011), 103–314: 103; see D. Roskies, 'Ansky Lives!', *Jewish Folklore and Ethnology Review*, 14/1–2 (1992), 66–9: 66).

8 B. Horowitz, 'Spiritual and Physical Strength in An-sky's Literary Imagination', in Safran and Zipperstein (eds.), *The Worlds of S. An-sky*, 103–18: 103.

9 See Prov. 3: 18, which refers to 'the Law' as 'a tree of life to them that lay hold upon her: and happy is every one that retaineth her'.

10 For an edition of this Russian-language variant, prepared by Vladislav Ivanov and translated by Craig Cravens, see 'Appendix: *The Dybbuk*', in Safran and Zipperstein (eds.), *The Worlds of S. An-sky*, 361–436.

11 As Deleuze and Guattari famously—notoriously—proclaimed: 'a minor literature doesn't come from a minor language; it is rather that which a minority constructs within a major language' (G. Deleuze and F. Guattari, *Kafka: Pour une littérature mineure* (Paris, 1975), 29; Eng. trans.: *Kafka: Toward a Minor Literature*, trans. D. Polan (Minneapolis, 1986), 16). What this provocation seems to overlook is the fact that every culture contains within it power relations that can play out as 'major' or 'minor' positions. In the case of traditional Yiddish culture, which partly inspires and distorts Deleuze and Guattari's reading of Kafka, the role played by, for example, religious authorities such as rabbis, scholars, or kabbalists would be vastly different from the role played by market women or dairymen, and this difference would not only be figured linguistically but would be portrayed in Yiddish writing, whether belletristic or otherwise. In the modernizing era of linguistic assimilation, which in the Pale of Settlement began during the latter half of the nineteenth century, analogous tensions would be evident between Jews learning Russian or Polish and Jews continuing to speak Yiddish, and these tensions similarly characterize literary depictions of their encounter, as An-sky and his contemporaries demonstrate. Deleuze and Guattari's ideas of the 'minor' and its relationship to the 'major' are therefore not mistaken so much as they are incomplete. My displacement of their 'major–minor' hierarchy in favour of a lateral process of circulation between 'periphery' and 'centre', turning the 'major–minor' axis on its head, is intended to clarify this distinction.

12 Mikhail Krutikov notes that An-sky's Russian-language writing was as stylistically impoverished as his Yiddish was: 'His Russian style hardly developed beyond the semi-documentary descriptive realism of the late-nineteenth-century populist writers he adopted in his youth. His later attempts to find an adequate Russian idiom for Jewish folk style and mystical discourse were interesting but not convincing artistically' (M. Krutikov, 'The Russian Jew as a Modern Hero: Identity Construction in An-sky's Writings', in Safran and Zipperstein (eds.), *The Worlds of S. An-sky*, 119–36: 131–2). This observation underscores the prospect that An-sky counts as a 'minor' writer, in the Deleuzian sense, whether in his Russian or his Yiddish works, because of the interaction and interference of both languages. In stylistic and linguistic terms, as much as in temporal or territorial ones, An-sky is a writer 'between two worlds', but it is in this sense that he can also be seen as a 'minor', hence a 'revolutionary', or at least modernistically significant writer, despite his own programmatic intentions.

13 Marina Shcherbakova suggested, in a presentation to the Tenth Congress of the European Association of Jewish Studies in Paris, that the decision to publish *The Destruction of Galicia* in Yiddish, despite the fact that, like nearly all of An-sky's writing, the work was based on Russian-language notes, was probably made under the influence of the Zionist theorist Vladimir Jabotinsky. However ideologically distant the PSR partisan An-sky and the founder of Revisionist Zionism might appear at first glance, they shared a commitment to Jewish autonomy, which for An-sky was a growing conviction over the course of the First World War. An-sky's death only a few months after the work's publication is the reason why a Russian-language version never appeared—even though, like most of An-sky's previous writings, the Russian draft had preceded the Yiddish version (M. Shcherbakova, 'Insights into S. An-sky's Political Shift, 1915–1917', paper delivered at the Tenth Congress of the European Association of Jewish Studies, Paris, 21 July 2014).

14 S. An-sky, *Der yidisher khurbn*, vi. 184; see id., *The Enemy at His Pleasure*, 307. Despite the significance of *The Destruction of Galicia* to An-sky's career, it has to date attracted surprisingly little critical attention: even Gabriella Safran and Steven Zipperstein pay almost no attention to it (Safran and Zipperstein (eds.), *The Worlds of S. An-sky*). For a salutary exception to this general critical silence, see S. Spinner, 'Saving Lives, Saving Culture: An-sky's Literary Ethnography in the First World War', *Österreichische Zeitschrift für Volkskunde*, 113 (2010), 543–67.

15 Vladimir Mitrofanovich Purishkevich (1870–1920), a notorious right-wing agitator and violent antisemite, who figures in the Jewish imagination of the period as Bull Connor does in the American civil rights movement.

16 S. An-sky, *Der yidisher khurbn*, v. 5; see id., *The Enemy at His Pleasure*, 3.

17 On Jewish relief work during the First World War in the Pale of Settlement and Galicia and how it was constituted among the competing and conflicting forces of government policy, elite Jewish philanthropists within Russia proper, and populist, often radical cultural activists—such as An-sky, whose example is taken as representative—see S. J. Zipperstein, 'The Politics of Relief: The Transformation of Russian Jewish Communal Life during the First World War', in J. Frankel, P. Y. Medding, and E. Mendelssohn (eds.), *The Jews and the European Crisis, 1914–1921*. (Oxford, 1988), 22–40.

18 Another, perhaps more anachronistic, name for the folklore around which An-sky structures *The Destruction of Galicia* is 'urban legend', a category of modern storytelling that disseminates hearsay as received wisdom. The two features that connect this version of contemporary folklore with the stories An-sky documents in his work are their ubiquity and the anonymity of their authority: though appearing in multiple locations and con-

texts, the urban legend asserts its claims to truth around illusory claims to actuality such as 'a friend of a friend told me . . .'. Jan Harold Brunvard popularized the term (J. H. Brunvard, *The Vanishing Hitchhiker* (New York, 1981)). Although what An-sky documents is similar to urban legend, it is necessary to maintain their status as conspiracy theories for both methodological and political reasons. In methodological, perhaps taxonomical, terms, these stories are not 'urban' insofar as they cut across social and geographical lines—and indeed, the flux through which they are transmitted—railways, military advances, displaced persons—renders distinctions among 'rural', 'urban', or 'shtetl' irrelevant. In political terms, moreover, these stories are frequently too much a catalyst or pretext for actual violence—that is, they leave the world of the popular imagination to exert a pernicious impact on real life—to merit the ultimately benign designation 'legends'.

19 To schematize the distinction from within An-sky's narrative: when the Austrian military distributes a flyer 'in an error-ridden and corrupt Russian' alleging to be a proclamation from Tsar Nicholas urging his soldiers to desert the war being conducted against his will (S. An-sky, *Der yidisher khurbn*, iv. 207–8; see id., *The Enemy at His Pleasure*, 102), they are engaging in a—transparently ham-fisted—conspiracy: what would today be called 'fake news'. When, by contrast, a soldier reports that 'General Rennenkampf's brother was a German general and the brothers met secretly every night so that Rennenkampf could pass on everything he knew' (S. An-sky, *Der yidisher khurbn*, iv. 160; see id., *The Enemy at His Pleasure*, 84), he is repeating a conspiracy theory. Later in the narrative An-sky reports that a Russian commandant in Homel (Gomel) had issued an official statement refuting rumours accusing Jews of hoarding coins (S. An-sky, *Der yidisher khurbn*, v. 215; see id., *The Enemy at His Pleasure*, 217). Surprised by this apparent liberalism, the narrator learns that the statement had come about thanks to the 'gifts' of the local Jews. These Jews had undertaken a conspiracy to confound a conspiracy theory!

20 As Richard Hofstadter writes: 'One may object that there are conspiratorial acts in history, and there is nothing paranoid about taking note of them. This is true. All political behaviour requires strategy, many strategic acts depend for their effect on a period of secrecy, and anything that is secret may be described . . . as conspiratorial. The distinguishing thing about the paranoid style is not that its proponents see conspiracies . . . here or there in history, but that they regard a "vast" or "gigantic" conspiracy as *the motive force* in historical events. History *is* a conspiracy, set in motion by demonic forces of almost transcendent power, and what is felt to be needed to defeat it is not the usual methods of political give-and-take, but an all-out crusade' (R. Hofstadter, 'The Paranoid Style in American Politics', in id., *The Paranoid Style in American Politics and Other Essays* (Cambridge, Mass., 1996), 3–40: 29 (emphasis in original)).

21 Eric Lohr offers an effective summary of the violence that dominates An-sky's narrative: 'The majority of pogroms during World War I were concentrated in the period of the great Russian retreat from April to October 1915, with roughly one hundred separate events that could be categorized as pogroms.' He adds of the characteristic circumstances that distinguish these pogroms from previous mass violence, not only in virulence but also in kind: 'In [a] sample of fifty-four cases, pogroms began only three times without soldiers. The army clearly initiated the violence in nearly every case. More specifically, Cossack units appear to have instigated nearly all of the pogroms' (E. Lohr, '1915 and the War Pogrom Paradigm in the Russian Empire', in J. Dekel-Chen et al., *Anti-Jewish Violence: Rethinking the Pogrom in East European History* (Bloomington, Ind., 2011), 41–51: 42).

22 Witness in this respect the recrudescence of conspiracy theories during the early days of the internet and again today over Twitter and other social media.

23 S. An-sky, *Der yidisher khurbn*, iv. 6; see id., *The Enemy at His Pleasure*, 3.

24 Prior to the First World War Galicia had been the site of both antisemitic conspiracy theories and consequently antisemitic pogroms. As Larry Wolff writes, 'Galicia was the scene of a wave of antisemitic pogroms during the summer of 1898, involving the looting and destruction of Jewish shops and taverns by Polish peasants in the villages of Western Galicia. The spreading riots led to the declaration of martial law, with eventually more than three thousand arrests, and a thousand trials of peasant rioters. The rioters . . . were . . . moved by rumors that Crown Prince Rudolf, who committed murder and suicide with his young lover at Mayerling in 1889, was secretly alive and encouraging attacks upon the Jews of Galicia. Alternatively some Galician peasants held the bizarre conviction that the Jews had murdered Rudolf, and that now Emperor Franz Joseph himself was somehow encouraging the pogroms' (L. Wolff, *The Idea of Galicia: History and Fantasy in Habsburg Political Culture* (Stanford, Calif., 2010), 305). Two primary distinctions differentiate these conspiracy theories from what An-sky documents: first, the element of the supernatural —the dead prince come to avenge himself on the Jews—is sublimated during the First World War into the magic of secret gadgets capable of supernatural power through ostensibly man-made means; second, the pogroms of 1898, which were far less murderous than the war-time atrocities, were actively punished by the Austro-Hungarian regime, whereas the pogroms that An-sky describes were largely perpetrated by the Russian army.

25 S. An-sky, *Der yidisher khurbn*, iv. 108; see id., *The Enemy at His Pleasure*, 52.

26 S. An-sky, *Der yidisher khurbn*, iv. 26; see id., *The Enemy at His Pleasure*, 16

27 An additional distinction can be made between conspiracy theories and their folkloric antecedents that further illuminates the substitution of historical causes for previous motivations in anti-Jewish libels and the violence they could provoke. As Eric Lohr explains, 'many of the prewar pogroms were associated with religious processions, rumors of ritual murder, intercommunal ethnic and cultural tensions, and the like. Traditional religious prejudice helps explain the disproportionate amount of violence directed against Jews as compared to other minorities, such as Germans, who were subjected to similar mass deportations and expulsions. But religious events and rumors do not appear to have directly instigated pogroms *during* World War I. Nearly every report indicates instead that the appearance of the military, in particular the Cossacks . . . precipitated the pogrom' (Lohr, '1915 and the War Pogrom Paradigm', 46 (emphasis in original)).

28 S. An-sky, *Der yidisher khurbn*, iv. 132; see id., *The Enemy at His Pleasure*, 68.

29 S. An-sky, *Der yidisher khurbn*, iv. 133; see id., *The Enemy at His Pleasure*, 68–9.

30 S. An-sky, *Der yidisher khurbn*, iv. 207; see id., *The Enemy at His Pleasure*, 101.

31 S. An-sky, *Der yidisher khurbn*, v. 67; see id., *The Enemy at His Pleasure*, 143.

32 S. An-sky, *Der yidisher khurbn*, v. 44; see id., *The Enemy at His Pleasure*, 129. Eric Lohr provides a crucial historical context for interpreting An-sky's juxtaposition of anti-German libels with anti-Jewish ones: in May 1915 a massive pogrom against Germans took place in Moscow. 'It was the only pogrom in one of Russia's two major cities, and the estimated 70 million rubles in damages made it perhaps the most costly pogrom in Russian history to that date' (Lohr, '1915 and the War Pogrom Paradigm', 45).

33 S. An-sky, *Der yidisher khurbn*, v. 44; see id., *The Enemy at His Pleasure*, 129.

34 S. An-sky, *Der yidisher khurbn*, v. 8–9; see id., *The Enemy at His Pleasure*, 115.

35 S. An-sky, *Der yidisher khurbn*, v. 165; see id., *The Enemy at His Pleasure*, 85.

36 S. An-sky, *Der yidisher khurbn*, vi. 108; see id., *The Enemy at His Pleasure*, 270.

37 As Brian Horowitz notes of An-sky's reactions to the pogroms that erupted at the collapse

of the 1905 revolution: 'An-sky viewed the pogroms of October 1905 not as a symbol of the Russian people's complicity, but, just as in 1881–2, as a provocation by the conservative elite to deflect popular discontent' (B. Horowitz, 'Semyon An-sky: Dialogic Writer', *Polin*, 24 (2011), 131–49: 145).

38 With respect to the 'telephone to Austria' conspiracy theory, An-sky notes that two Jews had been accused of communicating with Austrian forces in Czernowitz because telephone equipment had been left on their property during the evacuation of Austrian forces after the Russian army had retaken their shtetl. Despite the lack of any evidence that they had actually used the telephones for espionage, An-sky reports that one of the Jews was left in a Kiev prison and the other was sent to Siberia (S. An-sky, *Der yidisher khurbn*, vi. 128; see id., *The Enemy at His Pleasure*, 278).

39 S. An-sky, *Der yidisher khurbn*, vi. 112; see id., *The Enemy at His Pleasure*, 272–3.

40 The contrast between Russian and German attitudes towards Jews was not just observed by An-sky or felt by Jews on the borderlands but was a conscious distinction in policy and strategy. German troops occupying eastern Europe tried to recruit Jews to their side, and German Jewish soldiers attest to an unexpected affinity they felt with the Yiddish-speaking, often traditional, Jews whom they encountered. For a summary and thorough documentary of these encounters, see G. Estraikh, 'Introduction: Yiddish on the Spree', in G. Estraikh and M. Krutikov (eds.), *Yiddish in Weimar Berlin: At the Crossroads of Diaspora Politics and Culture* (Oxford, 2010), 1–27: 3–4.

41 In fact, according to the reminiscences of the German anarchist Rudolf Rocker (1873–1958), during his Paris sojourn at the end of the nineteenth century An-sky expressed an ambivalence about the German 'national character': '[An-sky] had a sort of secret fear for this [German] thoroughness. According to An-sky, the Germans, in their zeal to fit everything into a set schema, increasingly lost sight of human beings as such. Humanity was irrelevant to their theorizing and speculations . . . and this would inevitably lead to bad results' (cited in Y. Zerubavel, 'S. an-ski: shtrikhn tsu zayn kharakteristik', *Di goldene keyt*, 48 (1964), 3–16: 7).

42 S. An-sky, *Der yidisher khurbn*, iv. 39–40; see id., *The Enemy at His Pleasure*, 21–2.

43 Peretz is also the author of the *Bilder fun a provints-rayze* (1890), which along with *The Destruction of Galicia* is one of the most important Yiddish travelogues. It was clearly a model for An-sky's narrative (I. L. Peretz, *Ale verk*, 11 vols. (New York, 1947–8), ii. 117–209; Eng. trans.: 'Impressions of a Journey through the Tomaszow Region', in *The I. L. Peretz Reader*, ed. R. Wisse (New Haven, Conn., 1990), 20–84).

44 S. An-sky, *Der yidisher khurbn*, iv. 96–7; see id., *The Enemy at His Pleasure*, 51–2.

45 As Dan Miron explains, 'the myth [of the shtetl] assumes one of its most essential forms in the etiological story that contains a folk etymology of the Hebrew–Yiddish name of Poland—Polin or Poyln—as if it consisted of the two Hebrew words *po lin*, meaning "rest here." The folkloric story repeated by both Agnon and Peretz describes the exiles of Jerusalem being told to make Poland their temporary place of rest. In Peretz's version, the one who had made this decision was the *rosh hagolah* (the exilarch). In Agnon's, the two Hebrew words reach the convoy of exiles on a piece of parchment that falls directly from heaven, the decision having been made by God Himself' (D. Miron, 'The Literary Image of the Shtetl', in id., *The Image of the Shtetl and Other Studies of Modern Jewish Literary Imagination* (Syracuse, NY, 2000), 1–48: 41). Peretz's version of this legend first appears in *Bilder fun a provints-raye*; Agnon's variant first appears in a German-language anthology he co-edited with Ahron Eliasberg. For more on this anthology, and the legendary material it shares with Peretz, see S. Jaworski, 'Legends of Authenticity: *Das Buch von den polnischen*

Juden (1916) by S. J. Agnon and Ahron Eliasberg', in A. Kilcher and G. Safran (eds.), *Writing Jewish Culture: Paradoxes in Ethnography* (Bloomington, Ind., 2016), 48–67.

46   Of course, the proponents of conspiracy theories claim to be reading history or their current situation not allegorically, but literally. Nonetheless, the gnostic need to decipher reality is itself intrinsically allegorizing, and the confusion of literal reality with rhetorical figuration is characteristic of allegorical representation.

47   B. Harshav, 'Metaphor and Frames of Reference', in id., *Explorations in Poetics* (Stanford, Calif., 2007), 32–75: 45–6.

48   With respect to the relationship between territoriality and allegory in particular, Walter Benjamin remarks: 'Whereas in the symbol destruction is idealized and the transfigured face of nature is fleetingly revealed in the light of redemption, in allegory the observer is confronted with the *facies hippocratica* of history as a petrified, primordial landscape' (W. Benjamin, *Ursprung des deutschen Trauerspiels*, in id., *Gesammelte Schriften*, 7 vols. (Frankfurt am Main, 1991), i. 203–430: 343; Eng. trans.: *The Origin of German Tragic Drama*, trans. J. Osborne (London, 1998), 166. My thanks to Michael Löwy for reminding me of this observation.

49   S. An-sky, *Der yidisher khurbn*, v. 142; see id., *The Enemy at His Pleasure*, 175.

50   S. An-sky, *Der yidisher khurbn*, v. 143; see id., *The Enemy at His Pleasure*, 175.

51   My understanding of the relationship between metaphor and metonymy is informed by R. Jakobson, 'Two Aspects of Language and Two Types of Aphasic Disturbances', in id., *Language in Literature*, ed. K. Pomorska and S. Rudy (Cambridge, Mass., 1987), 95–119.

52   Benjamin offers another formulation of how the conjunction of conceptual language with imagistic language signifies a temporal rupture when he remarks: 'If images are timeless, theories certainly are not' (W. Benjamin, 'Wider ein Meisterwerk', in id., *Gesammelte Schriften*, iii. 252–9: 258; Eng. trans.: 'Against a Masterpiece', in id., *Selected Writings*, ed. M. W. Jennings et al., 4 vols. (Cambridge, Mass., 2004–6), ii/1, 378–86: 383).

53   As Benjamin himself writes under the heading 'Mixed Cargo: Shipping and Packing': 'In the early morning I drove through Marseilles to the station, and as I passed familiar places on my way, and then new, unfamiliar ones or others that I remembered only vaguely, the city became a book in my hands, into which I hurriedly glanced a few last times before it passed from my sight for who knows how long into a warehouse crate' (W. Benjamin, *Einbahnstraße*, in id., *Gesammelte Schriften*, iv. 83–148: 133; Eng. trans.: *One-Way Street*, in id., *Selected Writings*, i. 444–88: 477).

54   S. An-sky, *Der yidisher khurbn*, iv. 190.

55   For this reason, I believe that Benjamin misses an opportunity to incorporate an explicit discussion of allegory in his famous essay 'The Storyteller'. Specifically, when he recounts a tale from Herodotus of an Egyptian king defeated in a war with Persia, who was unable to weep at his own fate or the fate of his children but mourned the capture of an old, impoverished servant, he offers four explanations for the emotional discrepancy: that the king had been so full of grief that only the smallest increase could compel him to weep (Montaigne); that the king could not weep for royal defeat because he was royal; that the servant served as a spectacle through which the king's mourning for his own fate could be objectified; or that the greatest grief can be released only when its parameters are diminished through distance rather than intensified through closeness. But it seems to me that when pain is experienced in the profound terms that Herodotus describes, it only finds expression in an arbitrary moment incommensurate with the grief felt. The grief lacks an object just as the mourner has lost a place in the world, just as the woman whom An-sky interviews demonstrates, and just as allegory itself represents (W. Benjamin, 'Der Erzähler', in

id., *Gesammelte Schriften*, ii. 438–65: 445–6; Eng. trans.: 'The Storyteller', in id. *Selected Writings*, iii. 143–66: 148, 163–4 n. 8).

56 S. An-sky, *Der yidisher khurbn*, vi. 89.

57 S. An-sky, *Der yidisher khurbn*, iv. 113.

58 S. An-sky, *Der yidisher khurbn*, v. 190; see id., *The Enemy at His Pleasure*, 204.

59 See S. Aleichem, *Ayznban geshikhtes*, 28 vols. (New York, 1937), xxviii; Eng. trans.: 'Railroad Stories', in id., *Tevye the Dairyman and the Railroad Stories*, trans. H. Halkin (New York, 1996), 133–248. For the best critical treatment of these stories, see D. Miron, 'Journey to the Twilight Zone: On Sholem Aleichem's *Railroad Stories*', in id., *The Image of the Shtetl*, 256–334.

60 S. An-sky, *Der yidisher khurbn*, iv. 92–3; see id., *The Enemy at His Pleasure*, 48.

61 As An-sky declared to a gathering convened in St Petersburg to celebrate the twenty-fifth anniversary of his literary debut, in 1910, 'the fate of a writer generally is difficult, but especially if the writer is a Jew. His writing is torn. He lives on two streets [a Jewish street and a non-Jewish one], in three languages [presumably Yiddish, Hebrew, and Russian]. Living at such a "border" is a misfortune, and this burden has proven to be mine to carry' (see Zerubavel, 'S. an-ski', 5). It may be noted, in response to An-sky's melancholic envy of non-Jewish writers happily consigned to a single language on a single street, that the motivating force of his writing is its location among so many cultural, temporal, and linguistic borders. He nonetheless advises his literary well-wishers at this event that, of the twenty-five years they've gathered to celebrate, they should delete the sixteen of them that, presumably, had been spent working in Russian on behalf of non-Jews. As Safran notes, An-sky delivered these remarks in Russian (Safran, *Wandering Soul*, 170–1).

62 See n. 13 above.

63 S. An-sky, *Der yidisher khurbn*, v. 159; see id., *The Enemy at His Pleasure*, 185.

64 The racism of 'universalizing' the Jewishness of the victims in the conflicts An-sky documents can be likened to the reactionary response to the Black Lives Matter movement that 'all lives matter' or to commemorations of International Holocaust Remembrance Day that fail to mention the murder of Jews in the Holocaust.

65 S. An-sky, *Der yidisher khurbn*, iv. 95–6; see id., *The Enemy at His Pleasure*, 50–1.

66 S. An-sky, *Der yidisher khurbn*, iv. 136–7; see id., *The Enemy at His Pleasure*, 70–1.

67 S. An-sky, *Der yidisher khurbn*, v. 109; see id., *The Enemy at His Pleasure*, 160.

68 S. An-sky, *Der yidisher khurbn*, iv. 208; see id., *The Enemy at His Pleasure*, 102.

69 Larry Wolff similarly records legends about Elijah the Prophet from Galicia during the 1890s: these legends, however, involve not the prophet's intervention on behalf of Jews directly, but on behalf of Emperor Franz Joseph (Wolff, *The Idea of Galicia*, 319–22).

70 S. An-sky, *Der yidisher khurbn*, v. 129; see id., *The Enemy at His Pleasure*, 169.

71 As Safran writes: 'Eastern European Jews believed that any traveler may be Elijah in disguise, bringing news or gifts to reward those who treat him well. As Elijah moves from the "true world" to the human world, so An-sky moved between worlds in disguise. Accepted equally among traditional Jews, radicals, and the Russian liberal intelligentsia, Galician Jews and the Russian soldiers whom they feared, he too revealed his identity when he chose . . . With the success of *The Dybbuk*, people began to compare An-sky to the Messenger, a variant of Elijah, and to see him as bringing news and gifts from the "true world" of the past, making visible a vanished way of life' (Safran, *Wandering Soul*, 293).

72 S. An-sky, *Der yidisher khurbn*, vi. 61–2; see id., *The Enemy at His Pleasure*, 250–1.

The 'Patriotic Left' and the 'Jewish Question' at the Dawn of the Second Republic

PAUL BRYKCZYŃSKI

THE AIM of this chapter is to examine the stance of the Polish 'patriotic left' towards the 'Jewish question' in the formative years of the Second Republic. The term 'patriotic left' (*lewica niepodległościowa*, literally 'pro-independence left') is generally used to describe the progressive wing of the Polish national movement.[1] During the period under discussion, the patriotic left was composed of socialist and peasant parties, unaffiliated radicals and progressives, army officers, and former revolutionaries, the vast majority of whom acknowledged the leadership of Marshal Józef Piłsudski. Obviously a single chapter cannot provide a comprehensive treatment of such a diverse and heterogeneous political movement. My primary objective, therefore, is to sketch the rough outlines of Polish progressive thought regarding the place of the Jews in the imagined community of the Polish nation,[2] with special emphasis on the followers of Piłsudski, who would later play the leading role in Polish politics. Secondly, the chapter will examine the implications of these empirical findings for understanding Polish–Jewish relations in the interwar period and the scope and limits of so-called 'civic nationalism', both in Poland and more generally.

Although the field of Polish Jewish studies has been exceptionally productive in the last quarter of a century, there is a very curious gap in our understanding of Polish attitudes towards Jews, especially during the early 1920s. While the antisemitic ideology of the National Democrats (Endecja) has been the subject of numerous studies, the ideas of other Polish political forces, and especially those of the early followers of Piłsudski and other progressives, regarding the place of the Jews in the imagined community of the Polish nation have never, to the best of my knowledge, been analysed in a sustained and systematic manner.

The situation is further obscured by the existence of two powerful but mutually contradictory narratives which are seldom articulated explicitly but which subtly underpin much of the scholarship and popular discourse on Jewish history in the Second Polish Republic. The first of these narratives, which I would call the 'black legend' of interwar Poland, presents Polish nationalism/patriotism, in all its facets, as hateful, xenophobic, and deeply, perhaps inextricably, intertwined with antisemitism.[3] As Shmuel Almog writes, in one of the most extreme renditions of this view, antisemitism in interwar Poland 'tended to be nearly total'.[4] Piłsudski, who led the Polish state for most of the interwar period, is not explicitly accused of being an antisemite, but he is sometimes portrayed as 'opportunistically' acquiescing in the tide of antisemitism sweeping Poland.[5] His followers are either skipped over in silence or presented as a part of the overall dismal picture. And, indeed, there is little doubt that after Piłsudski's death his successors did adopt political antisemitism as part of their programme and rhetoric.[6] In recent years, scholarly portrayals of interwar Poland as the land of unbridled or 'nearly total' antisemitism have become less explicitly essentialist, but, I would argue, this trope continues to emerge in subtle ways in popular discourse and even some academic studies.[7]

The other theme underlying both popular representations and historiography concerns the continued existence of the civic tradition of Polish patriotism in the Second Republic. Partly in opposition to the black legend, in recent years scholars, Polish publicists, and intellectuals have sought to emphasize the civic and 'multicultural' dimensions of the Polish historical heritage.[8] According to this narrative, a powerful alternative to ethnic nationalism and antisemitism, rooted in the tolerant traditions of the early modern Polish–Lithuanian Commonwealth, existed in the interwar period and was represented by the larger-than-life figure of Józef Piłsudski and his followers. In this vein, Eva Plach writes that 'the Piłsudskiites shared an attachment to nineteenth-century Polish romanticism and to the idea of a brotherhood of nations and were steadfastly committed to maintaining the multiethnic heritage of the old Polish–Lithuanian Commonwealth'.[9] Thus in many accounts Piłsudski and his followers emerge as perfect foils to the ethnic nationalists and antisemites, represented by Roman Dmowski and the (notoriously antisemitic) National Democratic movement.[10]

Obviously, these two views are in tension. How could interwar Poland be such an antisemitic place, if its rulers (for all but four years) subscribed to Piłsudski's civic nationalism? This question raises a host of others: Did Piłsudski's followers, and the patriotic left more broadly, ever stand up to the antisemites? Or did they, as Lucy Dawidowicz suggests, tacitly accept antisemitism?[11] And, perhaps most critically, if Piłsudski's followers really were civic patriots who admired the multicultural heritage of the commonwealth, why did they openly embrace antisemitism so quickly after his death in 1935? In this chapter, I would like to begin moving towards providing an answer to these questions by examining the manner in which thinkers and publicists of the patriotic left, grouped around the charismatic leadership of Piłsudski, articulated the place of the Jewish community within the imagined community of the Polish nation. In the process, I also make some observations regarding the sense of nationhood subscribed to by Piłsudski's followers.

Before proceeding, it is important to offer a few definitions and a closer look at the chronology. In the discourse of civic nationalism, as it is traditionally defined, 'the nation constitutes a common political space, defined around a set of institutions, values, and political projects . . . a free-will union based on the adherence to the principles of the social contract'.[12] Civic nationalism is, at least in theory, inclusive and open to all those who wish to join the national community. This is in stark opposition to ethnic nationalism, in which the nation is defined by ethnicity or blood and is exclusive and closed to outsiders. In this chapter I employ the terms 'civic' and 'ethnic' not as descriptors of an empirical reality but as ideal types, in the Weberian sense, used to analyse, deconstruct, and better understand the sense of 'nation' subscribed to by Piłsudski's followers.[13]

Defining the Jewish question (*kwestia żydowska*), or even using that very term, may strike some readers as problematic. However, the phrase was commonly used by contemporaries, both Poles and Jews of various political stripes, as shorthand for the multiple challenges which the existence of a three-million-strong, mostly un-acculturated Jewish community created for the consolidation of the new Polish state and, conversely, the problems which the existence of this new state created for the Jewish community. The Polish term *kwestia* was routinely used to refer to other per-ceived challenges of state-building, such as *kwestia narodowościowa* (the nationalities question) or *kwestia reformy rolnej* (the land-reform question).

Defining the 'Pilsudskiites' (*piłsudczycy*, a notoriously vague and nebulous term) is not as difficult as it may seem, at least for the early 1920s. While the broadly under-stood 'Piłsudski camp' (*obóz Piłsudskiego*), as it is sometimes called, eventually came to include all ideological shades, including some nationalists and conservatives, in the 1920s there was widespread agreement, among both friends and foes, that Piłsud-ski's followers were a left-wing and 'progressive' movement. The conservative, auth-oritarian streak of the Piłsudski movement would only become evident later. In the early twenties Piłsudski had the full support of the socialists and, with the exception of the communists and the Jewish Bund, the Polish left. Many followers of Piłsudski could be found among the mass-based parties of the left, such as the Polish Socialist Party (Polska Partia Socjalistyczna; PPS) and the Polish Peasant Party 'Liberation' (Polskie Stronnictwo Ludowe 'Wyzwolenie'), in the military, and among unaffiliated urban radicals.

There is widespread agreement among scholars that the key theoretical organ of Piłsudski's followers was the weekly journal *Rząd i Wojsko*. At the beginning of 1922 *Rząd i Wojsko* became a monthly and changed its name to *Droga*.[14] It was edited by Adam Skwarczyński, who was the chief Pilsudskiite ideologue in the 1920s. Skwar-czyński also attempted to start a daily newspaper, which appeared in 1919 under the name *Gazeta Polska*. However, despite a period of growth in readership, the paper was forced to close due to financial difficulties in 1920.[15] The second semi-official organ of Piłsudski's followers was the weekly journal *Głos Prawdy*, edited by Wojciech Stpiczyński, who was considered a radical and something of a troublemaker. None-theless, the two publications were seen as being complementary, with *Droga* taking the intellectual high road, discussing ideas and seldom involving itself in practical political questions, and *Głos Prawdy* striking a more popular tone.[16] The analysis of these two publications can be supplemented by referring to a number of daily papers which were close to the Piłsudski movement, even if they did not have the same 'official' status as *Droga* and *Głos Prawdy*.[17]

Finally, a note on the chronological boundaries of this enquiry. The year 1918 and the creation of an independent Polish state marked the opening of a discursive window in which the authors of various 'imaginings' of the political community could attempt to put their ideas into practice. The year 1922, when the country's first complete elections were held and the political system appeared to be moving towards increasing stability, also witnessed the antisemitic riots ushered in by the election of President Gabriel Narutowicz. The latter had a tremendous negative impact on the left's willingness to publicly stand up to antisemitic rhetoric and signalled the beginning of a new darker chapter in Polish–Jewish relations.[18]

■

As the perceptive Henry Morgenthau Sr., head of the 1919 American mission to Poland, observed, antisemitism and the Jewish question were intimately bound up with the 'family feud' taking place within Polish politics and society.[19] Piłsudski's followers' interest in this matter must be understood at least partly in the context of their struggle with the National Democrats for the 'hearts and minds' of the Poles. But while the Piłsudskiite *Rząd i Wojsko* identified the Jewish question as one of the key issues facing the new Polish state, it actually received very little attention from the journal throughout 1919 and 1920. Even those articles explicitly linked to nationality questions barely mentioned the Jews, and focused on the Slavonic minorities.[20]

In fact, prior to the Treaty of Riga (1921), which finally settled the status of Poland's borders, when Piłsudski's followers discussed the issue of Poland's Jewish minority they usually did so in the context of foreign policy. The main impact of the Jewish question on Poland's relations with the Western powers was related to the recurring episodes of violence against the Jews perpetrated by Polish soldiers which were reported, sometimes in exaggerated form, in the Western press.[21] Obviously, these had potentially negative consequences for the new Polish state in public opinion throughout the world. It was largely in response to anti-Jewish violence that the Western powers, supported by Jewish communities in the West and Polish Zionists, demanded that the newly independent Polish state sign the Polish Minorities Treaty, which was supposed to guarantee ethnic and religious minorities freedom from discrimination.[22] While the followers of Piłsudski claimed their country was ready to respect the rights of the minorities, they thoroughly rejected what they saw as the imperious, high-handed, and hypocritical imposition of the treaty on Poland by the Western powers.[23]

These sentiments notwithstanding, unlike the National Democrats, Piłsudski's followers did not believe in the existence of an international Jewish conspiracy aimed at undermining Poland. As a result, they by and large did not see in the Jewish question, or even the vexing Polish Minorities Treaty, fundamental problems facing the Polish state. It is perhaps for this reason that *Rząd i Wojsko*, which dealt with 'big' geopolitical and ideological questions, very rarely mentioned Jews. *Gazeta Polska* occasionally commented on antisemitic 'excesses', as they were called, committed by Polish soldiers or civilians. These were invariably attributed to the National Democrats and their hateful propaganda and discussed in the context of their impact on Poland's image abroad. A typical article of this sort, entitled 'Jewish Beards', began with the ironic reflection that 'until the present day, beards had played no role in world politics, and if even the greatest statesman made the claim that answers to the problems of politics or statehood are to be found in the question of beards, he would rightly be called insane'.[24] Yet for Poland, the author lamented, 'beards had become an important international issue, because some Polish soldiers had taken it upon themselves to humiliate the Jews of some small town by cutting off their beards'. And while the anonymous author denied that any 'pogroms' had taken place, he acknowledged the 'shameful' anti-Jewish 'excesses'.[25]

However, the problem of antisemitism was generally treated as both epiphenomenal and temporary. According to *Gazeta Polska*, the National Democrats had 'for years used slogans of antisemitism and the uncompromising struggle with the Jews . . . in order to win the allegiance of the dark masses and distract them from questions of social justice'. This was both ethically repugnant and damaging to Poland's international standing. 'The entire Polish nation . . . which knows better than anyone else how disgusting persecution based on faith or ethnicity can be, is paying for the political past of Mr Dmowski, for his savage chauvinism and his demagoguery', the author continued, and 'foreigners are saddened to see that the ideal of "For Your Freedom and Ours" is turning out so poorly in practice'.[26] Antisemitism, then, was seen as a recent political phenomenon not deeply ingrained in Polish culture.

But while *Gazeta Polska* was extremely critical of antisemitism and 'shameful excesses' against Jews, it also criticized what it saw as the disloyalty exhibited by some Jewish groups, and especially the Zionists, towards Poland.[27] In fact, the issue of the Polish Minorities Treaty not only provided Piłsudski's followers with a platform from which to criticize the Polish nationalists but also allowed them to level a critique at the Zionists, the largest Jewish political party in the sejm in the 1920s.[28] The 'Jewish nationalists', as the Zionists were often called by Piłsudski's followers, were seen as presenting a mirror image of the National Democrats.[29] They were also charged with going behind the back of the Polish government and lobbying the Western powers directly, thus behaving treacherously and putting into question the 'sovereignty of the Polish state'.[30]

Ironically, the treaty and the Zionists' role in its 'imposition' upon Poland were condemned most forcefully by those political groups, like Piłsudski's followers, socialists, and peasant radicals from the Liberation party, which opposed antisemitism. The openly antisemitic National Democrats, on the other hand, muted their criticism of the treaty because it was supported by France. In the final vote in the sejm, the treaty was ratified with the votes of the National Democrats, minor centrist parties, and national minorities, while the pro-Piłsudski left voted against it.[31] The criticisms of the Polish Minorities Treaty anticipated the official line on the Jewish minority which would be articulated by Piłsudski's followers following the Treaty of Riga. With the end of the Polish–Soviet War and the relative stabilization of Poland's borders, the Jewish question came to be discussed more extensively in the press, largely due to the ever increasing antisemitic campaign of the National Democrats. In fact, analysing their response to the Jewish question is instrumental in understanding Piłsudski's followers' vision of the nation. As a minority that could not, like the Ukrainians or the Belarusians, eventually be given a state of its own, and as the target of ever-increasing attacks by Polish nationalists, the Jews were the ultimate test of the 'inclusiveness' of Piłsudski's followers' imagined community.

Despite frequent criticism of the Zionists, all Pilsudskiite writing about the Jews prior to the 1922 election consistently and unequivocally opposed antisemitism. The most important reasons given were ethical ones, rooted in the individualist philosophy articulated by Stanisław Brzozowski, embraced by high-ranking followers of Piłsudski, such as Skwarczyński, Janusz Jędrzejewicz, Wojciech Stpiczyński, Tadeusz Hołówko, and Marceli Handelsman, and subscribed to by most Pilsudskiite and many socialist writers.[32] One the most forceful declarations of this sort was offered by Tadeusz Hołówko, a close collaborator of Piłsudski:

Our 'sympathy' towards the Jews is simply the result of our spiritual culture and our respect for the rights of man, as such. We will never accept and we will never stop protesting against treading upon the human dignity of Jews. Cutting off Jews' beards, throwing Jews out of railway cars, mistreating them in the army and discriminating against them in state offices are a shame for Poland.[33]

Antisemitism was seen generally seen as 'unethical', and the language of 'shame' was often invoked when discussing antisemitic excesses.[34] Given the high place accorded to human dignity, subjectivity, and liberty and the positive valuation of the tradition of liberty and respect for differences (*tolerancja*) in Polish history on the pages of the 'official' Pilsudskiite journals, *Rząd i Wojsko* and *Droga*, such a stance should not be surprising.[35]

However, antisemitism was also opposed on pragmatic grounds, as being destructive of Polish statehood and, therefore, harmful to the Polish nation. 'I cannot think of a civilized state that would push away its own citizens', wrote Stanisław Bukowiecki, one of the leaders of the Pilsudskiite National–Civic Union (Unia Narodowo-Państwowa; UNP) party.[36] By fomenting disorder and setting citizen against citizen, antisemitism hurt the interests of all the inhabitants of the state—including the Poles.[37] The ethical and pragmatic considerations went hand in hand. To quote Bukowiecki again:

The programme [of economic discrimination against the Jews] would [cause] entire generations to be raised in an atmosphere of hatred and disdain, elevated to the status of national commandments. Such a programme would be ethically destructive, lower the moral level of our society and, at the same time, cause us great political harm. Poland has enough old enemies and does not need new ones.[38]

This point brings me to what is perhaps the most misunderstood dimension of the Pilsudskiite sense of 'nation'—the boundaries of inclusion and exclusion and the subtle but important difference between 'Poles' and 'Polish citizens'. These two terms were emphatically not the same, and, while both categories deserved respect, only the former were included in the imagined community of the nation. Ethnicity and religion did not matter in defining a Pole, but culture was of paramount importance.

Hołówko was the most forceful in making this point while defending the Polish Jewish historian Szymon Askenazy from National Democratic attacks:

We have a great historian . . . who raised entire generations of Polish historians and broadened the intellectual horizons of the Polish intelligentsia, yet in the [National Democratic daily] *Gazeta Warszawska*, a supposedly highbrow newspaper, we can read the resolutions of various . . . butchers, sausage-makers, and shopkeepers, declaring that this historian should not represent Poland in international relations because he has Jewish roots. It doesn't matter to them that this man taught Polish society to truly love Poniatowski, Łukasiński, and Dąbrowski—any illiterate butcher . . . has the right to deny him the right to Polishness.[39]

Askenazy was a professor of history at the University of Lwów and one of the most respected Polish historians. Although he was fully acculturated, he emphasized his Jewish heritage and saw himself as both a Jew and a Pole. Piłsudski appointed him as independent Poland's first ambassador to the League of Nations, which rendered him a lightning rod for right-wing claims that the Jews controlled Poland's foreign policy.

Similarly, Bukowiecki believed that the Poles should 'accept all the Jews who accept Polishness, with all the consequences thereof, into the fold of the Polish nation'.[40] Of course, exactly what this entailed could be debated, but most of all it was an act of will and individual choice, in which actively embracing Polish culture played a critical part. Polishness was a matter of neither ethnicity nor citizenship but of culture and volition, with volition being at least partly contingent on culture. Therefore, not all Jews were deemed to be Poles: the overwhelming majority were not. Even according to Jan Baudouin de Courtenay, one of the most consistent and prolific opponents of antisemitism in interwar Poland, the majority of Jews were more distinct from the Poles than were the Russians, Germans, Ukrainians, or any other minority or neighbouring people.[41] There was little hope of the 'dark Jewish masses' and the 'dark Polish masses' finding a common language or identity in the foreseeable future.[42] While some may be tempted to perceive a tinge of antisemitism in this position, this was not the case. If Bukowiecki did not feel the need to elaborate exactly what it meant to embrace 'Polishness with all its consequences', that was because from the legal and political standpoint it did not matter. According to Piłsudski's followers, all Polish citizens were to be treated equally by the state even, or precisely, if they were members of a national minority.

On the other hand, I found no suggestion in any Piłsudskiite publication that being a Polish citizen rendered one a member of the Polish nation. For example, *Głos Prawdy* forcefully opposed attempts by the National Democrat-dominated parliamentary commission to change the wording in a parliamentary bill outlining the structure of the armed forces. The original bill made it possible for 'any Polish citizen' to become an officer, while the commission wanted to change the wording to 'any Pole'. According to *Głos Prawdy*, the attempt was a shameful 'nationalist excess' which was both unjust and counterproductive. As the anonymous author (most likely the radical Wojciech Stpiczyński) wrote, 'nobody will have the right to expect loyalty from the national minorities, if the state is unjust towards them'.[43] Jews, then, were to be given the full privileges of Polish citizenship as national minorities, not as Poles.

But despite acknowledging that most Jews were not Poles, most of Piłsudski's followers and the Polish left in general did not recognize them as a nation. The Jews were generally defined as an 'ethno-religious' rather than a national group and thus had to be treated differently than the Belarusians and Ukrainians.[44] The logic of this distinction was highly dubious, as Tadeusz Hołówko, who bucked the trend and forcefully argued for the recognition of the Jews as a nation, pointed out, but its intent was clear.[45] Recognizing the Jews as a separate nationality would raise barriers to their acculturation and assimilation, which remained the ultimate long-term goals. The optimum solution from the Pilsudskiite perspective was to combine Jewish religious or social identity with a Polish national one as described by a play on the old adage *gente Judaeus natione Polonus*. Even Hołówko hoped for the eventual acculturation and assimilation of Poland's Jewish community. In fact, his support for Jewish nationalism was partly tactical. Hołówko believed that Jewish nationalism was 'the battering ram that would break down the walls of the ghetto' and make it possible for the Jewish masses to be integrated (and in the course of generations perhaps even assimilated) into Polish society. For now, he preferred a 'modern Jewish society, even if it speaks Yiddish, where the tone is set by modern educated men like [the Zionist leader] Grünbaum or [the Folkist leader] Pryłucki, rather than by the *tsadik* from Góra Kalwaria'.[46]

In sum, the doors to Piłsudski's followers' conception of Polishness were open, though even the most optimistic writers acknowledged that the full integration of Jews into Polish society would take decades. In the short term, then, the goal was to imbue loyalty to the Polish state and spread Polish culture among the Jewish population. In this vein, *Głos Prawdy* supported the right of the Jews to Yiddish education but expressed the hope that Yiddish would eventually be replaced by Polish. However, it unequivocally opposed giving any state support to Hebrew schools, on the grounds that they enlarged the gulf separating Jews from Poles and as such were harmful to Polish–Jewish integration.[47]

Perhaps the most explicit discussions about the nature and definition of the imagined community of Poland took place in the sejm. Yet, paradoxically, even as Piłsudski and his followers controlled Poland's military and foreign policy, they lacked their own representation in the legislature. While many members of the PPS and Liberation saw themselves as ardent followers of Piłsudski, bona fide Pilsudski-ite publications always maintained that a distinction should be made between their own 'line' and that of the two mass parties.[48] Nevertheless, an analysis of the debates surrounding questions of citizenship and nationality in the sejm is necessary in order to complete any analysis of the national community espoused by Piłsudski's followers and the patriotic left.

The vision of imagined community held by the PPS, most clearly put forth by the party's young theoretician Mieczysław Niedziałkowski, was virtually identical with the one outlined in the Pilsudskiite publications discussed above.[49] In his exposition on articles 112 and 113 of the constitution, which defined the scope of self-government for national minorities, Niedziałkowski recognized the legitimate cultural and national aspirations of the Ukrainians, Belarusians, and Lithuanians and, in somewhat couched language, expressed the hope that these peoples would eventually acquire states of their own.[50] In the meantime, he hoped to provide them with the widest possible scope of 'national and cultural' autonomy. However, he made no attempt to push the boundaries of Polishness so as to include these peoples —they were explicitly designated as 'non-Polish'.[51]

The ever-burning Jewish question was also solved in the spirit advocated on the pages of *Rząd i Wojsko*, *Droga*, *Gazeta Polska*, and *Głos Prawdy*. Speaking in the name of the PPS, Niedziałkowski refused to recognize the Jews as a 'national' minority and argued that they were merely a 'religious' one. As such, he continued, the Jews were entitled to the rights accorded to all citizens and should be free to organize their religious and cultural life as they saw fit. But he was against granting the Jewish community any special collective privileges, just as, he claimed, no special rights or public recognition should be given to Catholics or any other religious group.[52]

What may be surprising, however, is Niedziałkowski's emphatic insistence on the idea of Poland as a Polish nation-state which, at least superficially, may seem at odds with Piłsudski's followers' commitment to 'maintaining the multi-ethnic heritage of the Polish–Lithuanian Commonwealth'.[53] In response to Zionist deputies calling for greater national autonomy for the Jewish community, he offered the following argument:

Calmly and with a clear socialist conscience, we thoroughly reject all those conceptions in which the Polish state is seen as the common property of Poles and Jews, in the sense in which Belgium is the common property of the Walloons and the Flemish. We are ready to provide full guarantees for the ethnic minorities scattered throughout the Polish state, but we must maintain the one basic rule, that Poland is a Polish state only.[54]

The last sentence received an ovation from the entire sejm, including the National Democratic right. It may be tempting to see in Niedziałkowski's statement that Poland is 'a Polish state only' a reiteration of the nationalist mantra 'Poland for the Poles' and, hence, an acceptance of 'ethnic' nationalism. But this is not the case. From the context, it is clear that the term 'Polish' was again used in the cultural sense. It is true that it did not include Jews like the Zionists Grünbaum and Hartglass (who in any case did not see themselves as Poles), despite the fact that they were Polish citizens. But on the other hand, it included self-defined Jewish Poles, like Niedział-kowski's PPS colleagues Diamand, Perl, and Lieberman. Like Piłsudski's followers, Niedziałkowski and the PPS imagined a Polish nation in which the most important criteria for inclusion were culture and volition.

The same tension characterized Piłsudski's followers' first attempts at electoral politics. Their electoral vehicle for the 1922 elections, the aforementioned National–Civic Union, was hastily improvised, poorly planned, and faced competition from better organized pro-Piłsudski mass parties such as the PPS and Liberation. Despite

Piłsudski's support, the party failed to get any seats in the elections and was disbanded almost immediately after. Not surprisingly, it has been almost entirely ignored in the historiography.[55] But the party is interesting, because, to a much greater extent than either Liberation or the PPS, it attempted to actively and explicitly put forth an alternative discourse of the nation and counter the National Democrats' attempts to appropriate the latter. The UNP had considerable support among Piłsudski's followers and, more broadly speaking, Poland's liberal elite. It was supported by influential newspapers, such as *Kurjer Polski* and *Kurjer Poranny*, as well as *Droga* and *Głos Prawdy*. Equally interesting is the fact that among the members of the UNP there were a large number of people who, while relatively unknown at the time, 'would go on to constitute the very pinnacle of [Piłsudski's] Sanacja regime' after the *coup d'état* of 1926.[56]

As its name indicated, the National–Civic Union was explicitly dedicated to working for a civic national identity. UNP leaders imagined a Polish nation which was entirely open to those who wished to join it. And these were not simply empty declarations scribbled away in elite journals with limited circulation: UNP activists were willing to take this message 'to the streets'. Speeches delivered at UNP rallies forcefully condemned the politics of divisiveness, 'beastliness', and hatred, which, they claimed, the National Democrats were engaging in.[57] Unlike their PPS or Liberation counterparts, during the 1922 elections UNP politicians openly addressed the dreaded Jewish question at mass rallies and repudiated antisemitism more openly and forcefully than the Polish left ever would again, not only in their programme but 'on the street'.

The most important speeches on national identity and the Jewish question were delivered by the UNP's leading Warsaw candidates, Stanisław Bukowiecki and Jan Kucharzewski, during the fortnight of the election. Kucharzewski argued that under the partitions, the Poles accumulated 'a large reservoir of hatred, mistrust, and bitterness', which had to be immediately 'liquidated' instead of being directed 'against the sons of our nation and the citizens of our own state'.[58] Kucharzewski's language is interesting: like Skwarczyński and other Pilsudskiite writers, he draws a clear distinction between 'the sons of our nation' and the 'citizens of our state'. Even though the 'citizens of our state' admirably deserved the same respect and protection as the 'sons of our nation', Kucharzewski's distinction between these two groups highlights the problematic and unstable nature of liberal or civic conceptions of the nation in Poland.

Bukowiecki addressed the Jewish question explicitly not only in his highbrow publications but also in political speeches in front of thousands of supporters. His argument, made in a speech in front of some 3,000 people at the UNP's final rally in Warsaw, is so interesting that it is worth quoting at length:

The Polish nation must be understood as a civic nation, in the same way in which the Western states understand this term . . . We must pull [the national minorities] into the orbit of national life to make sure that they become a component of Polish life, that they play an active part in it, and that they have the same obligations as Poles. This is fully compatible with respect for their language, culture, and so on, as long as we respect those differences and allow these people to live their life as they understand it . . . The state cannot stand on the foundation of a never-ending internal conflict. This would deplete the strength of our nation, render our entire social life problematic and destroy us morally. This internal battle with the Jews is the gravest of dangers. The Polish nation cannot afford it.[59]

Clearly, even as Bukowiecki argued for the creation of a civic Polish nation, he used a culturally (rather than politically) defined conception of the national community in his speech. Obviously, 'the Polish nation' which could not afford the battle with 'the Jews' did not (or at least not yet) include the latter. According to Bukowiecki, the goal of Polish policy was full assimilation (albeit without any coercion), but until then it was clear that he did not consider the Jews to be Poles.

My intention in pointing out this contradiction is not to disparage or belittle Bukowiecki or Piłsudski's followers. Their situation was not unusual. Zionist politicians, for example, just like Piłsudski's followers, were inconsistent in their rhetoric when it came to questions of nationality and citizenship. On the one hand, they demanded to be included in the Polish nation, but, on the other, they wanted to maintain a separate national Jewish identity based on ethnicity and culture. For example, Zionist leader Isaac Grünbaum claimed that the word 'Polish' should only ever be used in a civic rather than ethnic sense. Therefore, he claimed, all Jews were civic Poles. But this did not stop him from using the word 'Jewish' in an explicitly ethnic sense. Thus, while he thought it was wrong of the Poles to define themselves as an ethnic nation, he actively encouraged the Jews to think of themselves as one.[60] The contradictions inherent in Bukowiecki's and Grünbaum's respective positions are not raised to criticize their political projects but to illustrate the highly unstable nature of civic conceptions of the nation.

Despite these contradictions, there is little doubt that the imagined community of the Polish nation publicly articulated by Piłsudski's followers in the first years of the Second Republic and the place accorded to the Jews in that community do little to support the black legend view of interwar Polish history. Piłsudski's followers were consistent in their public denunciation of antisemitism and their insistence that the civic rights of Jewish citizens of Poland be respected. They openly challenged and condemned the National Democrats' antisemitic discourse not only in elite publications but also in the realm of mass politics. Their vision of the nation was, at least in principle, open to those who wished to join it, regardless of their religion or ethnic background. While this chapter is concerned with the imagination of the national community, rather than political practice, it should also be noted that no antisemitic measures were undertaken by the Polish government headed by Piłsudski during these years. It is easy to understand the complaints of Piłsudski's supporters, who argued that Poland's record on minorities was superior to that of many established Western democracies, which took the high moral ground and criticized the new Polish state. As Jan Baudouin de Courtenay perceptively pointed out, America's 'shameful' treatment of black people, Britain's oppression of colonial peoples, or France's persecution of the Basque and Breton languages had no parallels in Poland and rendered the Western democracies' critiques of the latter morally dubious.[61]

But while the black legend narrative of interwar Poland cannot be sustained in light of these findings, projections of 'multiculturalism' into the Polish past also require a certain corrective. Although Piłsudski's followers were ready to protect the civic rights of Jews, their ultimate goal was always the acculturation and, ultimately, assimilation of Poland's Jewish community. With the notable though somewhat qualified exception of Tadeusz Hołówko, Piłsudski's followers unequivocally rejected the model advocated by Polish Zionists, in which a person could at the same time claim to be of Jewish nationality and Polish civic identity.[62] Nor, contrary to some opinions, did Piłsudski's followers imagine an overarching civic nation made up of various 'constituent ethno-national groups', such as Poles and Jews.[63] The hope was that the Jews would eventually acculturate, fully embrace 'Polishness', and become Polish by nationality as well as by civil identity. Being of Jewish heritage or religion was not an obstacle to becoming Polish, but a sense of belonging to the Jewish nation was. Polish nationality was not simply ethnic, but it could not be reduced to citizenship either.

A closer look at Piłsudski's followers' approach to the 'Jewish question' reveals certain contradictions inherent in their sense of 'nation', which may help problematize our understanding of civic nationalism. Most importantly, Piłsudski's followers used two distinct though partially overlapping conceptions of 'Polishness'. In the first instance, there was the community of Polish citizens, who were to be accorded full civic rights and freedom from discrimination. But not all 'Polish citizens' were included in the second imagined community—the community of 'Poles': that is, the nation properly speaking, united by a common culture, affective bonds, and a sense of shared identity that went beyond mere citizenship. Therefore, while the followers of Piłsudski considered many people whom the National Democrats would have labelled 'Jews' (for example, Szymon Askenazy) to be 'Poles', despite their ethnic background, most Jews were not Poles, despite their Polish citizenship. Perhaps one of the key problems facing Piłsudski's followers and the patriotic left was the lack of a collective noun capable of including all 'Polish citizens' in a community united by a common identity. As Piotr Wandycz notes in a different context, in Britain the distinction between 'English' and 'British' allowed for the creation of an overarching non-ethnically defined political community, while preserving Englishness for the dominant ethnic group within that community.[64] In Poland, there was no equivalent possibility. Citizens who were not defined as Poles had nothing left save for the awkward, dry, and legalistic 'Polish citizen', a term which could hardly inspire a sense of brotherhood or common identity.

The distinction made by Piłsudski's followers between 'Poles' and 'Polish citizens' is of crucial importance for understanding civic nationalism. While some theorists see the latter as uniting citizens in attachment 'to a shared set of political practices and values',[65] the case of Piłsudski's followers shows the overwhelming role played by culture in defining the national community. Even for the socialist Niedziałkowski, who like most followers of Piłsudski, advocated respect for the cultural and civic rights of Jews, Poland was ultimately a state for the Polish nation, which was defined as a community based on culture rather than by membership in the state. This culturally defined community made use of the state for the purposes of self-government.[66] The Jews were invited into that community only insofar as they were willing to embrace its culture. While Piłsudski's followers' approach to the Jewish question illustrates this problem in particularly stark relief, I agree with Bernard Yack who notes that civic imaginings of the nation are always, whether explicitly or not, underpinned at least in part by a cultural community which is defined (or imagined) independently of the state or any political project.[67] This has been aptly illustrated in recent years by the troubles faced by the French, often considered to be the paragon of civic nationalism, in accepting culturally distinct immigrant groups into the national community.

While Piłsudski's followers may not be unique on this score, I would like to suggest that the contradictions evident in their approach to the Jewish question in the formative years of the Second Republic can, at least in part, explain some of Piłsudski's successors' puzzlingly quick about-turn and acceptance of political antisemitism in the late 1930s. This question cannot be explored at length here, but I would like to conclude by suggesting a fruitful line of enquiry for future research. Leaving the Jews out of the imagined community of the Polish nation, even while continuing to advocate for their acculturation and defending their civic rights, had profound consequences for how the national community and its interests were understood. Most importantly, despite the two groups' joint legal membership in the community of 'Polish citizens', Poles and Jews were not imagined to be a part of the same moral community. Thus when Hołówko defended Jews from physical attacks by Poles, he did so on the grounds of 'universal human rights' rather than a sense of obligation to his own compatriots.

In other words, the moral obligations to these two communities could be construed as being of a different order, with affective ties to compatriots ultimately being more powerful than legal obligations to fellow citizens. It was theoretically possible, even while remaining faithful to the Pilsudskiite vision, to imagine the interests of Poles, the community for which the state was created and whom it was supposed to serve, and Jews as being opposed to one another. Therefore, the distinction between Poles and Polish citizens outlined in this chapter left open certain potentialities which would allow the acceptance of antisemitism without the need for a fundamental re-envisioning of the national community and its boundaries of inclusion and exclusion. Certainly, during Piłsudski's lifetime, his followers continued to steer clear of political antisemitism. But perhaps this distinction can help explain why some of them found it so easy to embrace it so quickly after their leader's death.

Notes

1 The term *lewica niepodległościowa* originated during the partitions in order to contrast those socialists who believed in the independence of Poland from internationalists, like communists, who wanted to struggle for socialism within the framework of the Russian empire. In independent Poland, the latter found themselves in the Polish Communist Party and enjoyed minimal support in Polish society. The patriotic left, on the other hand, included popular mass parties such as the Polish Socialist Party and the Polish Peasant Party 'Liberation'. In the early 1920s both parties recognized the indirect leadership of Piłsudski.

2 I use the term 'imagined community' of the nation in the sense in which it was deployed by Benedict Anderson in his seminal *Imagined Communities* (see B. Anderson, *Imagined Communities* (New York, 1983), 5–7).

3 As Ezra Mendelsohn writes, the proponents of this view assume that Poland was 'an extremely, perhaps even uniquely, antisemitic country' (E. Mendelsohn, 'Jewish Historiography on Polish Jewry in the Interwar Period', *Polin*, 8 (1994), 3–14: 6–7). This could also be seen as a specific case of the more general tendency, still common in western Europe and North America, to 'depict Poland as a land of backward peasants' prone to 'violent xenophobia' (B. Porter-Szűcs, *Poland in the Modern World: Beyond Martyrdom* (London, 2014), 3). For an in-depth discussion of orientalist portrayals of eastern Europe, see L. Wolff, *Inventing Eastern Europe: The Map of Civilization on the Mind of the Enlightenment* (Stanford, Calif., 1994).

4 S. Almog, *Nationalism and Antisemitism in Modern Europe, 1815–1945* (Oxford, 1990), 107. For some other notable examples, underpinned by this narrative to a greater or lesser extent, see W. W. Hagen, 'Before the "Final Solution": Toward a Comparative Analysis of Political Anti-Semitism in Interwar Germany and Poland', *Journal of Modern History*, 68 (1996), 351–81; J. Marcus, *Social and Political History of the Jews in Poland, 1919–1939* (Berlin, 1983); J. A. Fishman, *Studies on Polish Jewry, 1919–1939: The Interplay of Social, Economic and Political Factors in the Struggle of a Minority for Its Existence* (New York, 1974); L. S. Dawidowicz, *The War Against the Jews, 1933–1945* (New York, 1986); H. H. Ben-Sasson, *A History of the Jewish People* (Cambridge, Mass., 1985).

5 As Lucy Dawidowicz writes: 'the creation of the Polish republic in 1919 [*sic*] brought political power to the nationalists. The man who headed the Polish state for most of its brief life, Józef Piłsudski, originally a socialist, a federalist, and not an anti-Semite, as he confronted the raw and reckless anti-Semitism of the [National Democrats], concluded opportunistically that anti-Semitism was irresistible, that if he combatted the [National Democrats'] anti-Jewish nationalism he would lose power' (L. S. Dawidowicz, *The Holocaust and the Historians* (Cambridge, Mass., 1983), 91).

6 *Deklaracja ideowo-polityczna Obozu Zjednoczenia Narodowego*, 2nd edn. (n.p., 1946).

7 For example, in a recent and generally nuanced work, Theodore Weeks writes that as early as 1910, National Democratic antisemitism 'reflected an almost universal attitude in Polish society' (T. R. Weeks, *From Assimilation to Antisemitism: The 'Jewish Question' in Poland, 1850–1914* (DeKalb, Ill., 2006), 161; see also Y. Eliach, *There Once Was a World: A 900-Year Chronicle of the Shtetl of Eishyshok* (New York, 1999), esp. 56–8). The pervasiveness of the narrative can also be discerned through silences. For example, it is noteworthy that the excellent and relatively recent book *Anti-Semitism and Its Opponents in Modern Poland* doesn't actually contain a single chapter on the opponents of antisemitism in Poland during the interwar period (see R. Blobaum (ed.), *Antisemitism and Its Opponents in Modern Poland* (Ithaca, NY, 2005)).

8 According to Agnieszka Pasieka, who masterfully analyses this projection of multicultural-ism into the Polish past, 'present-day ethnically homogenous Poland has found a . . . way of participating in the debate on multiculturalism . . . by celebrating its past diversity' (A. Pasieka, 'Neighbors: About the Multiculturalization of the Polish Past', *East European Politics and Societies*, 28 (2013), 225–51: 227). The term 'multiculturalism' is often poorly theorized and used in a deeply problematic manner. For the role played by this heritage in contemporary Polish debates, see G. Zubrzycki, *The Crosses of Auschwitz: Nationalism and Religion in Post-Communist Poland* (Chicago, 2006), esp. 77–97; for the civic tradition of Polish patriotism, see A. Walicki, *The Enlightenment and the Birth of Modern Nationhood: Polish Political Thought from Noble Republicanism to Tadeusz Kosciuszko* (South Bend, Ind., 1989); id., *Philosophy and Romantic Nationalism: The Case of Poland* (Oxford, 1982).

9 E. Plach, *The Clash of Moral Nations: Cultural Politics in Piłsudski's Poland, 1926–1935* (Athens, O., 2006), 2. Similarly, Waldemar Paruch writes that according to Piłsudski's followers, the Polish state 'had to protect its [civic] nation, with all its constituent ethno-national groups [such as Poles, Ukrainians, Jews, etc.], and regulate relations between citizens belonging to different ethnic groups' (W. Paruch, *Myśl polityczna obozu piłsud-czykowskiego, 1926–1939* (Lublin, 2005), 386; see also A. Friszke, *O kształt niepodległej* (Warsaw, 1989); B. Urbankowski, *Filozofia czynu: Światopogląd Józefa Piłsudskiego* (Warsaw, 1988); A. Chojnowski, *Koncepcje polityki narodowościowej rządów polskich w latach 1921–1939* (Wrocław, 1979)). The most representative English-language texts written in this vein are N. Davies, *God's Playground: A History of Poland*, 2 vols. (Oxford, 2005); T. Snyder, *The Reconstruction of Nations: Poland, Ukraine, Lithuania, Belarus, 1569–1999* (New Haven, Conn., 2003).

10 For example, Joanna Michlic writes: 'The Poland of Roman Domowski . . . represented the model of integral nationalism, and the Poland of Józef Piłsudski . . . represented the model of civic nationalism' (J. B. Michlic, *Poland's Threatening Other: The Image of the Jew from 1880 to the Present* (Lincoln, Nebr., 2006), 70). The pervasiveness of this view in popular accounts is best illustrated by the entry on Piłsudski in Wikipedia, which states that he 'believed in a multi-ethnic Poland . . . including indigenous ethnic and religious minori-ties . . . His principal political antagonist, Roman Dmowski . . . by contrast, called for a Poland . . . based mainly on a homogeneous ethnically Polish population and Roman Catholic identity' ('Józef Piłsudski', Wikipedia website, visited 28 Apr. 2020).

11 Dawidowicz, *The Holocaust and the Historians*, 91.

12 G. Zubrzycki, 'The Classical Opposition between Civic and Ethnic Models of Nation-hood: Ideology, Empirical Reality and Social Scientific Analysis', *Polish Sociological Review*, 3 (2002), 275–95: 278.

13 See ibid. 292.

14 Both *Rząd i Wojsko* and *Droga* were elite publications, without a mass readership. Still, the fact that they represented the political thought of the group which came to rule Poland following 1926 is testified to by the fact that *Droga* was recommended reading for all veterans of Piłsudski's Legions and was subscribed to by the local offices of the Polish Legionnaires' Union (see D. Nałęcz, '"Droga" jako platforma kształtowania się ideologii piłsudczyków', *Kwartalnik Historyczny*, 66 (1975), 589–608).

15 It would reappear after the 1926 coup as one Piłsudski's followers' main organs (A. Pacz-kowski, *Prasa Drugiej Rzeczypospolitej, 1918–1939* (Warsaw, 1971), 70).

16 Nałęcz, '"Droga"', 592.

17 For example, the dailies *Kurjer Poranny* and *Kurjer Polski* were also seen as Pilsudskiite by both friends and foes. The former, edited by the famous journalist Kazimierz Ehrenberg,

was close to Stanisław Thugutt, the Liberation party, and the radical Warsaw intelligentsia. It was considered to be the most Pilsudskiite of the daily papers and was the second most popular Warsaw daily after the right-wing *Kurjer Warszawski*. *Kurjer Polski* was a more conservative daily. Both *Kurjer Polski* and *Kurjer Poranny* published articles by prominent followers of Piłsudski. The same was true of the PPS daily, *Robotnik*, which also published many articles by prominent followers of Piłsudski (many of whom were of course also members of the PPS) and was almost universally supportive of Piłsudski. On the role of the press in interwar Poland and the relationship between newspapers and political groups, see Paczkowski, *Prasa Drugiej Rzeczypospolitej*.

18 See P. Brykczyński, *Primed for Violence: Murder, Antisemitism, and Democratic Politics in Interwar Poland* (Madison, Wis., 2016).

19 H. Morgenthau, *All in a Life-Time* (Garden City, NY, 1922), 358.

20 T. Hołówko, *Kwestja narodowościowa w Polsce* (Warsaw, 1922), 40.

21 For Western portrayals of the violence, see P. Wróbel, 'Polacy, Żydzi i odbudowa Polski na stronach The New York Timesa w 1918 r.', in J. Żyndul (ed.), *Rozdział wspólnej historii: Studia z dziejów Żydów w Polsce ofiarowane profesorowi Jerzemu Tomaszewskiemu w siedemdziesiątąrocznicę urodzin* (Warsaw, 2001), 181–98.

22 On the treaty and its international context, see C. Fink, *Defending the Rights of Others: The Great Powers, the Jews, and International Minority Protection, 1878–1938* (New York, 2004).

23 'Ratyfikacja Traktatu', *Gazeta Polska*, 16 July 1919.

24 'Brody żydowskie', *Gazeta Polska*, 2 July 1919.

25 Ibid.

26 Ibid.

27 'Niech przyjeżdża!', *Gazeta Polska*, 18 July 1919.

28 In the 1919 elections, the Zionists won six of the eleven seats held by Jewish parties in the sejm. Of the remaining five, two were won by Orthodox candidates, two by Folkists, and one by a member of Polaei Zion (S. Rudnicki, *Żydzi w parlamencie II Rzeczypospolitej* (Warsaw, 2004), 28).

29 'Traktat gwarancyjny', *Gazeta Polska*, 10 July 1919. The same assertion was made by Henry Morgenthau, who wrote of the Zionist leaders: 'Some were pro-Russian, all were practically non-Polish, and the Zionism of most of them was simply the advocacy of Jewish nationalism within Poland' (Morgenthau, *All in a Life-Time*, 363).

30 'Traktat gwarancyjny'. American Jews were also criticized for their ill-informed, hateful, and counterproductive 'anti-Polish campaign' ('Żydzi amerykańscy i kampania antypolska', *Gazeta Polska*, 25 July 1919). For debates on this issue in the Polish sejm, see Rudnicki, *Żydzi w parlamencie II Rzeczypospolitej*, 59–66.

31 According to *Gazeta Polska*, 'it is not those who spread antisemitic agitation, but precisely those who fight it in the name of the principles of justice, who will oppose this project of creating a new Jewish ghetto in Poland' ('Ratyfikacja traktatów', *Gazeta Polska*, 28 July 1919).

32 See P. Brykczyński 'Reconsidering "Piłsudskiite Nationalism"', *Nationalities Papers*, 42 (July 2014), 771–90: 777.

33 Hołówko, *Kwestja narodowościowa*, 51.

34 'Niech przyjeżdża!', *Gazeta Polska*, 18 July 1919; 'Wybryki endeckie', *Głos Prawdy*, 4 Mar. 1921, pp. 218–19; S. Bukowiecki, *Polityka Polski niepodległej: Szkic programu* (Warsaw, 1922), 171.

35 The English word 'tolerance' does not quite capture the essence of the Polish *tolerancja*.

While the former implies merely a minimum of acceptance, the latter is much more expansive and is better translated as 'respect' (see B. Porter, *Faith and Fatherland: Catholicism, Modernity, and Poland* (New York, 2011), 5).

36   Bukowiecki, *Polityka Polski niepodległej*, 174.

37   'Myśl państwowa', *Głos Prawdy*, 16 Sept. 1922, p. 515.

38   Bukowiecki, *Polityka Polski niepodległej*, 171.

39   Hołówko, *Kwestja narodowościowa*, 52–3.

40   Bukowiecki, *Polityka Polski niepodległej*, 176.

41   'Żydzi a państwowość polska: Część II', *Gazeta Polska*, 26 July 1919. Jan Baudouin de Courtenay was a radical free-thinker. While he was not strictly speaking a follower of Piłsudski, his writings appeared in many early Pilsudkiite publications.

42   'Żydzi a państwowość polska', *Gazeta Polska*, 20 July 1919.

43   'Wybryki endeckie', 218.

44   *Sprawozdania Stenograficzne Sejmu Ustawodawczego*, 16 Nov. 1920, col. 34; Bukowiecki, *Polityka Polski niepodległej*, 173.

45   Hołówko, *Kwestja narodowościowa*, 63.

46   Ibid. 66.

47   'Żargon czy hebrajski', *Głos Prawdy*, 10 Dec. 1921, pp. 27–8.

48   'Pod znakiem wojny domowej', *Gazeta Polska*, 23 July 1919.

49   Niedziałkowski's exposition is much more detailed than the PPS programme of 1920 but entirely consistent with the latter. For the PPS's nationality policy, see A. Uljasz, *Myśl polityczna Feliksa Perla* (Lublin, 2005), 198.

50   *Sprawozdania Stenograficzne Sejmu Ustawodawczego*, 16 Nov. 1920, col. 38.

51   Ibid., col. 37.

52   Ibid., col. 6.

53   See Plach, *The Clash of Moral Nations*, 2.

54   *Sprawozdania Stenograficzne Sejmu Ustawodawczego*, 16 Nov. 1920, col. 38.

55   J. Lewandowski, 'Unia Narodowo-Państwowa', in S. Herbst (ed.), *Z dziejów wojny i polityki: Księga pamiątkowa ku uczczeniu siedemdziesiątej rocznicy urodzin prof. dra Janusza Wolińskiego* (Warsaw, 1964), 39–47: 40.

56   Ibid. 41.

57   'Wiec Unji NP', *Kurjer Polski*, 3 Nov. 1922, p. 5.

58   'Przemówienie Jana Kucharzewskiego na wiecu Unji Narodowo-Państwowej w dniu 2 listopada 1922 r.', *Kurjer Polski*, 5 Nov. 1922, p. 3.

59   'Przemówienie St. Bukowieckiego na wiecu Unji Narodowo-Państwowej w dniu 2 listopada 1922 r.', *Kurjer Polski*, 5 Nov. 1922, p. 4.

60   *Sprawozdania Stenograficzne Sejmu Ustawodawczego*, 2 Dec. 1921, cols. 50–1. Zionist politicians believed in the existence of a Jewish nation and explicitly rejected the claims of self-defined 'Jewish Poles', such as the socialist Diamand or the conservative Steinhaus, to represent the Jews of Poland. For the Zionist leader Issac Grünbaum, neither man represented the Jewish masses, and, indeed, neither had been elected by Jewish voters. Ironically enough, Steinhaus, who questioned Grünbaum's right to speak for the Jews of Poland and offered himself as an example of a Jewish Pole, owed his seat in the sejm to the undemocratic Austrian electoral franchise. He was utterly defeated by the Zionist-led Bloc of National Minorities when fully democratic elections were held in eastern Galicia in 1922. For the fascinating debate between Grünbaum, Steinhaus, and Diamand, see *Sprawozdania Stenograficzne Sejmu Ustawodawczego*, 18 Mar. 1919, cols. 796–817.

61 J. Badouin de Courtenay, *Kwestia żydowska w państwie polskim* (Warsaw, 1923), 15.

62 For an example of the Zionist position, see Rabbi Ozjasz Thon's speech in the sejm (*Sprawozdania Stenograficzne Sejmu Ustawodawczego*, 20 Nov. 1919, cols. 42–8). Hołówko believed that Jewish 'nationalism' was preferable to religious orthodoxy, because becoming 'national' and 'modern' would make it easier for the Jews to become acquainted with Polish culture.

63 Paruch, *Myśl polityczna obozu piłsudczykowskiego*, 386.

64 P. S. Wandycz, *The Price of Freedom: A History of East Central Europe from the Middle Ages to the Present* (New York, 1992), 67.

65 M. Ignatieff, *Blood and Belonging: Journeys into the New Nationalism* (New York, 1993), 6.

66 B. Yack, 'The Myth of the Civic Nation', *Critical Review*, 10 (1996), 193–211: 201.

67 Ibid. 208.

Index

Bold page numbers indicate a table; CFL = the Council of Four Lands